PRINCIPLES
OF
BANK REGULATION
Third Edition

By

Michael P. Malloy, Ph.D.

Distinguished Professor and Scholar
University of the Pacific
McGeorge School of Law

CONCISE HORNBOOK SERIES®

WEST®

A Thomson Reuters business

Mat #40750124

Concise Hornbook Series and Westlaw are trademarks registered in the U.S. Patent and Trademark Office.

© West, a Thomson business, 1999, 2003
© 2011 Thomson Reuters

    610 Opperman Drive
    St. Paul, MN 55123
    1–800–313–9378

Printed in the United States of America

ISBN: 978-0-314-19456-5

This book is dedicated to
my son
Michael Emil Malloy

Preface to the Third Edition

Since the publication of the second edition of this book appeared in 2003, dramatic challenges have loomed up out of the haze of fast-moving commercial activities to confront the financial services sector. The pace of change and expansion seemed to tick up from moment to moment, until disaster overtook us in the Fall of 2008, when the residential mortgage market collapsed. Not only did that collapse manage to take with it iconic financial services firms like Lehman Brothers and Washington Mutual, but also—because "securitization" of mortgage-related products had spread mortgage risk directly into the securities markets—the collapse of the mortgage market led to a meltdown of U.S. capital markets. The meltdown itself reverberated through many major non-U.S. capital markets as well.

And so the project for the past three years—and doubtless for many years to come—has been to devise ways and means to recover from this financial disaster, to extract practical lessons from the experience of the collapse, and to establish new safeguards for the financial services markets. As to this last task, Congress only lately responded by enacting the Dodd–Frank Act, which touches on virtually every aspect of the regulation of depository institutions, the subject of this book. By its own terms, many of the most significant changes initiated by the act will take years to implement fully. This is the result of effective dates of key provisions that stretch out over two years following the enactment of Dodd–Frank, as well as a lengthy and complex process of regulatory implementation of the provisions of the act. As a result, in this book we examine the current rules governing the financial services sector, while we also confront together the likely future direction of regulation in this area. I hope to share with the reader the exciting intellectual challenges of this area of legal study and the daunting practical demands that we face in the years to come.

I remain, as always, thankful for the support and encouragement of my wife, Susie A. Malloy, during my work on this new edition. The success of the work owes much to the groundwork provided by my past student research assistants, especially Mr. Michael P. Battin, of the Fordham University Class of 1996, Mr. Edward Miklautsch, of the Fordham University Class of 1997, and Ms. Suzanne Uzelac, of the McGeorge Law School Class of 1998. I thank them for all of their invaluable assistance in bringing the project to first light, and I also thank the many students who have participated in my banking courses over the past fifteen years and have made my interest in financial services law a source of continuing delight.

M.P.M.

Preface to the Second Edition

The pace of change and development in depository institutions regulation has continued to be fast and furious in the few years that have intervened since the first edition of this book appeared in 1999. In November of that year, the president signed into law the Gramm–Leach–Bliley Act, which worked remarkable changes in the field. The effects of those changes are still being implemented through regulatory amendment and litigation. In September 2001, the tragedy of terrorist attacks upon the United States of America and its citizens prompted, among other things, regulatory, statutory and multilateral responses that are having a significant impact on the provision of financial services—domestically as well as internationally. These events are dramatic, but they represent only the highlights of a constant stream of developments. Indeed, in the twenty years since I began teaching bank and financial services regulation, the field has transformed itself in so many ways that it almost seems to be a different subject altogether. Now more than ever, we all remain students of the subject, no matter how long our experience. The intellectual and practical challenges that confront us students are fascinating, challenging and, at times, frustrating. This second edition continues to follow the objective of the original book—to help law students satisfy their fascination with the subject without the frustration.

Once again I thank my wife, Susie A. Malloy, for her encouragement, critique and inspiration—to say nothing of her patience. I also thank past student research assistants, particularly Mr. Michael P. Battin, of the Fordham University Class of 1996; Mr. Edward Miklautsch, of the Fordham University Class of 1997; and Ms. Suzanne Uzelac, of the McGeorge Law School Class of 1998 for all of their invaluable assistance in bringing this project to first light.

M.P.M.

Preface to the First Edition

Depository institutions regulation is subject to a fast pace of change and development. In the past twenty years alone, for example, federal statutes governing this area have been broadly amended at least seven times. These legislative changes and the increasingly frequent intervention of the Supreme Court have repeatedly rearranged the furniture. In addition, the growing overlap in competition among depository institutions, insurance companies and securities firms has further complicated regulatory policy. As a result, we all remain students of the subject, no matter how long our experience. That may be one of the things that makes the regulation of depository institutions law so fascinating and, at times, so frustrating. This book is intended to help law students satisfy their fascination with the subject without the frustration.

I thank my wife, Susie A. Malloy, for her encouragement, critique and inspiration. I also thank my student research assistants, Mr. Michael P. Battin, of the Fordham University Class of 1996; Mr. Edward Miklautsch, of the Fordham University Class of 1997; and Ms. Suzanne Uzelac, of the McGeorge Law School Class of 1998.

M.P.M.

Acknowledgements

Limited portions of certain chapters of this study have appeared in the form of reports and articles in scholarly publications, as indicated below. The material is used with permission of the following:

ADMINISTRATIVE CONFERENCE OF THE UNITED STATES, CONSULTANT'S REPORT ON ADJUDICATION PRACTICES AND PROCEDURES OF THE FEDERAL BANK REGULATORY AGENCIES (November 1987).

————, CONSULTANT'S REPORT ON ADMINISTRATION OF THE SECURITIES EXCHANGE ACT OF 1934 BY THE FEDERAL BANK REGULATORY AGENCIES (October 1990).

MICHAEL P. MALLOY, ANATOMY OF A MELTDOWN (Aspen Publishers, 2010).

————, BANKING LAW AND REGULATION (3 vols., Aspen Law & Business: 1994 & Cum. Supps.).

————, FUNDAMENTALS OF BANKING REGULATION (Aspen Law & Business: 1998).

Michael P. Malloy, *Balancing Public Confidence and Confidentiality: Adjudication Practices and Procedures of the Federal Bank Regulatory Agencies*, 61 TEMPLE L. REV. 723 (1988), *reprinted in* 4 BANKING L. ANTH. 631 (1988).

————, *Banking in the Twenty–First Century*, 25 J. CORP. L. 787 (2000).

————, *Bumper Cars: Themes of Convergence in International Regulation*, 60 FORDHAM L. REV. S1 (Survey Issue 1992).

————, *Can 10b–5 for the Banks? The Effect of an Antifraud Rule on the Regulation of Banks*, 61 FORDHAM L. REV. S23 (Survey Issue 1993), *reprinted in* 8 BANKING L. ANTH. 257 (1994).

————, *Capital Adequacy and Regulatory Objectives*, 25 SUFFOLK TRANSNAT'L L. REV. 299 (2002).

————, *Capital Regulation and International Banking: A Questionable Strategy, in* GREGORY T. PAPANIKOS (ed.), ESSAYS ON THE ECONOMICS OF LAW AND INDUSTRIAL ORGANIZATION 155 (Athens Institute for Education and Research, 2006).

————, *Depository Institutions Regulators, in* G. J. EDLES & J. NELSON, FEDERAL REGULATORY PROCESS: AGENCY PRACTICES AND PROCEDURES (PRENTICE HALL LAW & BUSINESS, 2D ED., 1989, REVISED).

————, *Double, Double Toil and Trouble: Bank Regulatory Policy at Mid–Decade*, 63 Fordham L. Rev. 2031 (1995), *reprinted in* 9 BANKING L. ANTH. 269 (1995).

————, *The Emerging International Regime of Financial Services Regulation*, 18 TRANSNAT'L LAW. 329 (2005).

————, *Financial Services Regulation after NAFTA in* KEVIN KENNEDY (ed.), THE FIRST DECADE OF NAFTA: THE FUTURE OF FREE TRADE IN NORTH AMERICA (Transnational Publishers, Inc., 2004).

————, *Financial Services Trends in the Twenty–First Century: Report on a Survey of the Membership of the AALS Section on Financial Institutions and Consumer Financial Services*, 21 ANN. REV. BANKING L. 293 (2002).

———, *Foreword: . . . And Backward: Death and Transfiguration among the Savings Associations*, 59 FORDHAM L. REV. S1 (Survey Issue 1991).

———, *Functional Regulation: Premise or Pretext? in* PATRICIA A. McCOY (ED.), FINANCIAL MODERNIZATION AFTER GRAMM-LEACH-BLILEY (LexisNexis 2002).

———, *The International Financial Crisis and Nation–Based "Prudential Regulation", in* DAVID A. FRENKEL & CARSTEN GERNER-BEUERLE (eds.), SELECTED ESSAYS ON CURRENT LEGAL ISSUES—(Athens Institute for Education and Research: forthcoming, 2010).

———, *International Financial Services: An Agenda for the Twenty–First Century*, 15 TRANSNAT'L LAW. 55 (2002).

———, *International Project Finance: Risk Analysis and Regulatory Concerns*, 18 TRANSNAT'L LAW. 89 (2004).

———, *Nonbanks and Nondefinitions: New Challenges in Bank Regulatory Policy*, 10 SETON HALL LEG. J. 1 (1986), *reprinted in* 3 BANKING L. ANTH. 531 (1986–87).

———, *Nothing to Fear but FIRREA Itself: Revising and Reshaping the Enforcement Process of Federal Bank Regulation*, 50 OHIO ST. L.J. 1117 (1989), Copyright (C) 1990 The Ohio State University.

———, *Public Disclosure as a Tool of Federal Bank Regulation*, 9 ANN. REV. BANKING L. 229 (1990).

———, *The Regulation of Bank Brokerage Activities: Was Rule 3b–9 Benign?* 6 ANN. REV. BANKING L. 181 (1987).

———, *Seeing the Light: Savings Associations Conversions and Regulatory Realignment*, 10 ANN. REV. BANKING L. 189 (1991).

———, *The Sound of Two Hands Flapping: Insurance–Related Activities of National Banks*, 41 ST. LOUIS U. L.J. 75 (1997).

———, *State Change-in-Bank–Control Statutes: Does MITE Make Light of Recent Trends?*, 5 ANN. REV. BANKING L. 29 (1986).

———, *The Subprime Mortgage Crisis and Bank Regulation*, 3 BANKING & FIN. SERV. POL'Y REP. 1 (2008).

———, *The Subprime Mortgage Crisis: An International and Regional Threat in Need of a Solution, in* DAVID A. FRENKEL & CARSTEN GERNER-BEUERLE (eds.), CHALLENGES OF THE LAW IN A PERMEABLE WORLD 9 (Athens Institute for Education and Research: 2009).

———, *Towards a National Community: The CRA and the Contemporary Market*, 29 W. NEW ENGLAND L. REV. 25 (2006).

———, *The 12(i)'ed Monster: Administration of the Securities Exchange Act of 1934 by the Federal Bank Regulatory Agencies*, 19 HOFSTRA L. REV. 269 (1990).

———, *U.S. International Banking and the New Capital Adequacy Requirements: New, Old and Unexpected*, 7 ANN. REV. BANKING L. 75 (1988).

———, *U.S. International Banking and Treasury's Foreign Assets Controls: Springing Traps for the Unwary*, 8 ANN. REV. BANKING L. 181 (1989).

———, *U.S. International Banking Policy: Prospects and Problems in a New Millennium*, 15 ANN. REV. BANKING L. 277 (1996).

———, *When You Wish Upon Winstar: Contract Analysis and the Future of Regulatory Action*, 42 ST. LOUIS U. L.J. 409 (1998).

_____, *Written Statement of Views on D'Oench, Duhme* (Testimony before the Subcommittee on Oversight of Government Management of the Senate Committee on Governmental Affairs, January 31, 1995).

Michael P. Malloy & James T. Pitts, *Post–Mortem on Retail Repurchase Agreements: Where were the Regulators?* 3 Ann. Rev. Banking L. 89 (1984).

List of Figures

Summary of Contents

Table of Contents

PRINCIPLES
OF
BANK REGULATION
Third Edition

Chapter 1

THE REGULATED ENVIRONMENT
OF BANKING

Table of Sections

§ 1.1   Introduction

Banking is a regulated industry. This obvious fact creates legal issues that do not exist for other business enterprises. The regulated nature of the banking industry manifests itself in a variety of ways. First, banks and other bank-like entities are limited and controlled in their corporate and business activities by relatively specific statutory provisions. These activities are regulated not only by state law, but also by federal law. In this context, federal law extends far beyond the disclosure-oriented requirements typical of federal securities regulation.[1] It includes substantive provisions of transactional and corporate law, including incorporation under federal law.[2]

Second, the degree of state and federal regulation is pervasive and thorough, extending to such issues as establishment of a corporation intended to enter the industry, expansion into other

---

§ 1.1

1. *See, e.g.,* 15 U.S.C.A. §§ 78*l*–78n, 78p (Securities Exchange Act of 1934 disclosure requirements for publicly traded companies).

2. *See, e.g.,* 12 U.S.C.A. §§ 21–22, 26–27 (authorizing establishment of national banking association).

1

geographic or product markets, merger with or acquisition of existing entities within the industry, recapitalization, or other reorganization of the entity. Each of these actions—and virtually any other activity undertaken by an entity within the industry—is subject to regulatory oversight or express approval of one or more of the regulators. Each step in the corporate and business life of these entities is subject to regulation.

Third, the industry is typified by a confusing array of specialized types of banking entities, and an equally formidable diversity of regulators. This situation is made even more complex by the fact that in any given corporate or business transaction, any one banking entity may find itself simultaneously subject to the regulatory authority of several of these regulators.[3]

Fourth, underlying the present policies applicable to banking and the current policy controversies affecting the industry is a long, often unstated, historical dialogue. This involves both legal and constitutional debate over the utility of banking and the proper role of state and federal regulation of the industry.

§ 1.2   History

Current bank regulatory policy is still rehearsing the historical controversies surrounding the development of banking and bank regulation. Banking has, of course, longstanding European precursors to the American experience,[1] but this book focuses on U.S. models of bank regulation.

§ 1.3   Early Federal Period

For two centuries, the history of U.S. bank regulation has been the tale of push and pull between federal and state authority, played out from one financial crisis to the next. The ascendancy of the first Bank of the United States and, after a brief hiatus, the second Bank of the United States (of *McCulloch v. Maryland*[1] fame) marked the first period of federal control.

The problem of establishing a coherent credit system for the fledgling United States of America was the initial impetus for the regulation of banking today. On 9 August 1790, the first Congress to meet under the Constitution requested that Treasury Secretary Alexander Hamilton study the financial condition of the new nation

---

3. *See, e.g., Report of the Task Group on Regulation of Financial Services* 9 (1984) (discussing regulatory overlap).

Banking (Michie rev. 1893) (discussing European and colonial precursors).

§ 1.2

1. *See generally* 1 J. Gilbart, The History, Principles and Practice of

§ 1.3

1. 17 U.S. (4 Wheat.) 316 (1819).

and make recommendations with a view to establishing public credit. Hamilton's report[2] concluded that a national bank should be chartered to support the credit market. The report, which turned out to be the opening move in a continuing constitutional controversy, focused almost exclusively on the instrumental effects of creating a national bank. The report argued that "public banks" had a clear utility in established commercial countries, and that utility could assist in the economic development of the new nation.

A bill based on Hamilton's proposal made its way through the Congress. It provided a 20–year charter for the Bank of the United States. The Bank was to have capital of $10 million, $2 million of which could be subscribed for by the federal government. There would be 25 directors. While foreign persons were not prohibited from ownership of the stock of the Bank, such persons could not vote their shares by proxy. The Bank would be limited to an interest rate of six percent on loans and discounts. In addition, it was prohibited from buying and selling real estate, except as it was acquired as foreclosed collateral.

The bill met with opposition from agrarian interests, who feared that the bank's operations would draw funds away from agriculture, increase speculation, and drive "specie" (gold and silver) out of the country. A constitutional dimension emerged to clothe these agrarian prejudices with principle. On 2 February 1791, James Madison opposed the bill in the House, claiming that the proposal was unconstitutional.[3]

Nevertheless, the bill passed. President Washington asked his cabinet officers for their views. On 15 February 1791, Secretary of State Thomas Jefferson delivered an opinion in opposition, essentially grounded on the constitutional aspects.[4] In his view, the power to create a bank, a corporate entity, had not been delegated to the federal government by the Constitution. It was not among the enumerated powers (*e.g.*, taxation, borrowing, regulating commerce). Nor was it within either of the general powers (*i.e.*, taxing to provide for the "general welfare," enacting laws "necessary and proper" for executing enumerated powers).

Attorney General Edmund Randolph had already registered opposition to the bill.[5] On 16 February 1791, the President wrote to Hamilton, enclosing the opinions of Jefferson and Randolph and

2. *Treasury Report on a National Bank*, Dec. 13, 1790, 1 American State Papers 67, *reprinted in* Michael P. Malloy, Banking and Financial Services Law 6 (Carolina Academic Press: 2d ed. 2005).

3. 3 Annals of Cong. 1944 (1791).

4. *Reprinted in* 1 H.E. Krooss (ed.), Documentary History of Banking and Currency in the United States 147 (1969 ed.).

5. *Reprinted in* M. St. C. Clarke & D. A. Hall, Legislative and Documentary History of the Bank of the United States 86 (1832).

requesting his views on the bill. In his reply of 23 February 1791, Hamilton for the first time directly addressed the constitutional dimensions of his proposal. His response served as the conceptual structure of the argument endorsed by the Supreme Court some 18 years later in *McCulloch*. Among other things, Hamilton argued:

> [T]his *general principle* is *inherent* in the very *definition* of government, and *essential* to every step of the progress to be made by that of the United States, namely: That every power vested in a government is in its nature *sovereign*, and includes, by *force* of the *term*, a right to employ all the *means* requisite and fairly applicable to the attainment of the *ends* of such power, and which are not precluded by restrictions and exceptions specified in the Constitution, or not immoral, or not contrary to the *essential ends* of political society....
>
> *[N]ecessary* often means no more than *needful, requisite, incidental, useful* or *conducive to*. It is a common mode of expression to say, that it is *necessary* for a government or a person to do this or that thing, when nothing more is intended or understood, than that the interests of the government or person require, or will be promoted by, the doing of this or that thing....
>
> A bank relates to the collection of taxes in two ways— *indirectly*, by increasing the quantity of circulating medium and quickening circulation which facilitates the means of paying[, and directly] by creating a *convenient species* of medium in which they are to be paid....[6]

The President signed the bill. However, by the time its 20–year charter expired in 1811, Jefferson's party was in power, and there was no hope for renewal of the charter. The classic bank regulatory policy question had already been set, dressed up in basic constitutional terms: the extent to which the federal government could or should regulate banking. The terms of this question, which still incites controversy today, were first delineated in the dispute within President Washington's cabinet over the First Bank, but were essentially set in some of the earliest constitutional rulings of the Supreme Court. These concerned the status of the Second Bank of the United States.

Both before and after the demise of the First Bank, the number of state-chartered banks continued to grow through 1811, with no failures until 1809. From 1809 through the War of 1812, state banks—overextended, inexperienced and undercapitalized—frequently failed. The war left U.S. commercial and financial sectors in disarray. Even within Jefferson's party, support emerged for a

6. *Reprinted in* 1 Krooss at 152 (emphasis in original) (1969 ed.).

central bank to stabilize the economy. Congress adopted a plan in 1816 for a Second Bank of the United States, which President Madison signed into law.

The new bank soon encountered hostility. State banks claimed that the Bank expanded the economy by liberal loans to the state banks during times of favorable financial conditions, but then triggered the collapse of these state banks by demands for repayment during the periods of financial difficulty.[7] Several states passed legislation to curb the activities of the Bank.[8] Maryland's law, taxing bank notes issued by the Baltimore branch of the Bank, eventually precipitated the Supreme Court's decision in *McCulloch*. Constitutional law scholars celebrate the case as one of the first significant constitutional decisions of the Court, but of course it should actually be honored as one of the first significant bank regulatory law decisions. Writing for the Court in *McCulloch*, Chief Justice Marshall focused first on the question of whether Congress had power to incorporate a bank. He admitted that the power of establishing a bank or creating a corporation was not among the enumerated powers granted to the federal government under the Constitution.[9] This fact did not, however, exclude the possibility of "incidental or implied powers."[10] He proceeded by a process of inference, based in large part on Hamilton's constitutional argument:

> Although, among the enumerated powers of government, we do not find the word "bank" or "incorporation," we find the great powers to lay and collect taxes; to borrow money; to regulate commerce; to declare and conduct a war; and to raise and support armies and navies.... [I]t may with great reason be contended, that a government, entrusted with such ample powers, on the due execution of which the happiness and prosperity of the nation so vitally depends, must also be entrusted with ample means for their execution. The power being given, it is the interest of the nation to facilitate its execution.... [R]evenue is to be collected and expended, armies are to be marched and supported. The exigencies of the nation may require that the treasure raised in the north should be transported to the south, that raised in the east conveyed to the west, or that this order should be reversed.... [The Constitution] does not profess to enumerate the means by which the powers it confers may be executed; nor does it prohibit the creation of a corporation, if the existence of such a being be

---

7. *See* R. C. H. Catterall, The Second Bank of the United States 27–65 (1902).

8. *See* Warre, The Supreme Court in United States History 505–506 (rev. ed. 1923).

9. 17 U.S. at 406.

10. *Id.*

essential to the beneficial exercise of those powers. It is, then, the subject of fair inquiry, how far such means may be employed....[11]

In buttressing this inferential argument, Marshall also constructed a textual argument for federal power to intervene in economic policy through the incorporation of a bank. The basis of this argument was, of course, the "necessary and proper" clause of Article II. Marshall argued:

> But the constitution of the United States has not left the right of Congress to employ the necessary means for the execution of the powers conferred on the government to general reasoning. To its enumeration of powers is added that of making "all laws which shall be necessary and proper, for carrying into execution the foregoing powers, and all other powers vested by this constitution, in the government of the United States, or in any department thereof."

> ... [The word "necessary"] frequently imports no more than that one thing is convenient, or useful, or essential to another. To employ the means necessary to an end, is generally understood as employing any means calculated to produce the end, and not as being confined to those single means, without which the end would be entirely unattainable....

> ... The subject is the execution of those great powers on which the welfare of a nation essentially depends. It must have been the intention of those who gave these powers, to insure, as far as human prudence could insure, their beneficial execution. This could not be done by confining the choice of means to such narrow limits as not to leave it in the power of Congress to adopt any which might be appropriate and which were conducive to the end....[12]

Essentially, it is for Congress to choose appropriate means for the accomplishment of powers and objectives entrusted to it under the Constitution. That being the case, Congress may decide that a public bank is an appropriate means for the nation's fiscal operations.[13]

Did it make a difference, however, that the bank was controlled by private investors, and hence was not, strictly speaking, a governmental instrumentality? This issue was raised by counsel in *McCulloch*, but skirted by the Court.[14] It was, however, raised squarely in

---

11. *Id*. at 407–409.

12. *Id*. at 411–415.

13. *Id*. at 422.

14. *See* Plous & Baker, *McCulloch v. Maryland: Right Principle, Wrong Case*, 9 Stan. L. Rev. 710 (1957) (discussing issues raised in *McCulloch*).

Osborn v. The Bank,[15] in which Ohio officials had seized assets of the Bank for failure to pay the Ohio tax on in-state branches of banks chartered outside the state. In another opinion by Chief Justice Marshall, the Court finally expressed itself on the question. Marshall conceded that, if the bank were a private corporate entity "having private trade and private profit for its great end and principal object,"[16] it would be subject to individual state taxing power.[17] However, the bank was not such an entity. Marshall asserted that "[i]t has never been supposed that Congress could create such a corporation."[18]

The significance of *McCulloch* and *Osborn* to the development of constitutional theory is beyond dispute, but what do they tell us about the tensions inherent in the development of banking as a regulated industry in the United States? In the early stages of the history of U.S. bank regulation, arguments about the merits of federal bank regulatory policy were often couched in terms of constitutional theory. This was the case, for example, in President Jackson's July 1832 message vetoing the bill to recharter the Second Bank.[19] This was also the case in Chief Justice Chase's opinion in *Veazie Bank v. Fenno*,[20] upholding federal taxation of state banks. However, while the constitutional dimension of bank regulation may seem to have receded, the attitudes that fueled that debate, and seized upon constitutional rhetoric as a means of expression, continue to be felt. The result is a system of bank regulation that is in some respects irrational, redundant and often painfully indirect.

§ 1.4   State Law Primacy

The controversy that surrounded the birth of the Second Bank continued throughout its life.[1] In 1828, Andrew Jackson was elected to the presidency, the result of a coalition of small business people, agrarian interests, laborers, and others of the populist persuasion. In his 1829 message to the Congress, the new President expressed his opposition to the Bank, and indicated that he would oppose any extension of its charter, which was not due to expire until 1836. The Bank's supporters passed a rechartering bill in 1832, and the President vetoed the bill. His veto message to the Congress[2] may seem strange to the modern reader, unless the reader takes into

---

15. 22 U.S. (9 Wheat.) 738 (1824).

16. *Id.* at 859.

17. *Id.* at 859–860.

18. *Id.* at 860.

19. *Reprinted in* 2 H. E. Krooss at 21 (1983 ed.).

20. 75 U.S. (8 Wall.) 533 (1869).

§ 1.4

1. *See* 1 Krooss at 653–655 (1969 ed.) (discussing political controversy surrounding Second Bank of the United States).

2. *Reprinted in* 2 Krooss at 21 (1983 ed.).

account the fluidity of constitutional doctrine at this relatively early stage of U.S. history. Constitutional arguments aside, Jackson's message expressed in clear terms the populist bias against and suspicion of organized aggregations of economic power. The basic contours of that bias can still be recognized in current debate over bank regulatory policy.

Jackson expressed concern over the bank's monopoly of federal government business. He was bothered by the bank's concentration of economic power in the hands of "foreigners and ... a few hundred of our citizens, chiefly of the richest class."[3] He also attacked the constitutionality of the bank, in the following terms:

> It is maintained by the advocates of the bank that its constitutionality in all its features ought to be considered as settled by precedent and by the decision of the Supreme Court. To this conclusion I cannot assent. Mere precedent is a dangerous source of authority, and should not be regarded as deciding questions of constitutional power except where the acquiescence of the people and the States can be considered as well settled.... There is nothing in precedent, therefore, which, if its authority were admitted, ought to weigh in favor of the act before me.[4]

The Congress failed to override the President's veto, and the Treasury Department began withdrawing U.S. Government funds from the Bank and placing them with state banks.[5] Distrusting bank notes, the Administration took steps to bring specie back into circulation. For example, the Administration announced in the July 1836 "Specie Circular" that only gold and silver would be accepted as payment in sales of public land. This naturally lead to the disparagement of all forms of paper money, including notes issued by strong, creditworthy banks.

With the eclipse of the Second Bank, a long period of state primacy in bank regulation set in, with disparate and inconsequential results. The emerging primacy of the state banks brought with it new problems for state governments. How were these institutions to be regulated? One of the first notable attempts at regulation during this period was in fact not governmental but private. Providing some of the protections of a central bank system, the so-called Suffolk system was instituted in Boston during the 1820s by a group of Boston banks. Suffolk Bank of Boston held deposits for outlying "country banks," the notes of which could be redeemed at Boston at their par value. To police this system and avoid instability due to over-issuance of bank notes, the Boston banks would

---

3. *Id.*

4. *Id.*

5. *See* 1 Krooss at 655–657 (1969 ed.) (discussing events following veto of rechartering bill).

accumulate large number of notes from country banks that were not participants in the system. These notes would be presented *en masse* to the nonparticipating country banks for payment. Faced with the possibility of these burdensome calls on their resources, many country banks were persuaded to join the Suffolk system.

The New York legislature established a New York Safety Fund System in 1829 which was, in many respects, like the federal deposit insurance system established in 1933. Under the New York system, banks seeking a charter to do business in New York were required to contribute .5 percent of the value of their capital to the safety fund. The fund was used to aid insolvent banks.

Over-issuance of state bank notes became a major problem. The 1837 depression, for example, was in part due to the over-issuance problem. Nevertheless, in the same year "free banking" statutes began to emerge, allowing for organization of state banks by general legislation, rather than by a special legislative act. In 1837, the legislature of Michigan enacted one of the first free banking acts and in 1838, the New York legislature enacted a free banking act. The free banking acts made it a condition of incorporation that the bank deposit securities with the state that could be used to pay off the bank's depositors in the event of a failure by the bank. Unfortunately, the quality of the securities deposited in fulfillment of this requirement was often questionable, and supervision of banks under the free banking systems was *laissez faire* in the extreme.

As the effects of the 1837 depression continued to be felt, the proliferation of banks created under the free banking statutes continued as well. The result was a wave of bank failures over a five-year period, wiping out hundreds of state banks.

In 1837 Martin Van Buren, close political adviser to Jackson, became president. Shaken in his confidence in the state banking systems, Van Buren backed a legislative proposal for an independent treasury system to hold all government deposits. The Independent Treasury Act was signed into law by Van Buren in 1840. The system of "subtreasuries" continued until subtreasury functions were transferred to the Department of the Treasury and the Federal Reserve Banks after passage of the General Appropriations Act of May 1920. No major attempt at federalizing regulation of banking would occur until the crisis created by the Civil War.

§ 1.5   Civil War Developments

It required the national crisis of the Civil War before the federal government reentered bank regulation. Prosecution of the war required vast amounts of money and credit. State banks were one obvious source of that credit. By 1861, there were approximately 1,600 state-chartered banks,[1] but no central bank system to monitor credit, and no banks directly subject to federal supervision. Difficulties in financing the war were draining the nation's gold supply, and the gold standard was eventually abandoned as a result.[2] In 1861, Treasury Secretary Salmon P. Chase recommended the establishment of a national banking system. Under this system, national banks would be chartered by the federal government as commercial banks and would be authorized to issue bank notes secured by U.S. government bonds.[3] If Chase's plan were put into operation, it would thus ensure a market for federal debt.

Attempts were first made, however, to finance the war directly through the issuance of U.S. notes, without the captive distribution mechanism of a national bank system. By early 1862, Congress had authorized the issuance of $150 million in U.S. notes, the first of several such issuances.[4] These issuances were not adequate for the credit needs of the wartime budget, and by 1864 a national banking system was created on the model proposed by Chase. The emergence of this national bank system, which outlasted the crisis and became one of the central features of the contemporary bank regulatory system, also established the federal-state "dual banking system" that has been a characteristic of U.S. commercial banking ever since.

The National Currency Act was enacted in 1863,[5] and amended and reenacted as the National Bank Act ("NBA") in 1864.[6] The NBA created the position of the Comptroller of the Currency as an office within the Treasury Department.[7] The Comptroller was vested with the authority to issue national bank charters to groups of incorporators of at least five persons.[8] The system was originally intended to foster the captive market for U.S. bonds, since each newly chartered national bank was required to deliver to the Comptroller government bonds in an amount equal to $30,000 or one-third of its capital, whichever was greater. However, long after the need for this captive market had passed,[9] the system of federally chartered national banks persisted and the role of the Comptroller as administrator of national banks therefore continued to be significant.

§ 1.5

1. *See* 2 Krooss at 1261 (1969 ed.).

2. *See Veazie Bank v. Fenno*, 75 U.S. (8 Wall.) 533, 537 (1869) (discussing financial background leading to passage of National Bank Act).

3. *See* 1861 Annual Report of the Department of the Treasury, *reprinted* in Krooss at 1340–45 (1969 ed.).

4. *See Veazie Bank*, 75 U.S. at 537.

5. 12 Stat. 670 (1863).

6. 13 Stat. 111 (1864).

7. 12 U.S.C.A. § 2.

8. 12 U.S.C.A. § 21.

9. The requirement of a deposit of government bonds was revoked in 1913. *See* Act of December 23, 1913, § 17, 38 Stat. 268, *as amended*, Act of June 21, 1917, § 9, 40 Stat. 239.

As part of Chase's plan for financing the war, the legislation passed during the early 1860s imposed taxes on the capital and bank notes of commercial banks, state and national. The tax on state-chartered banks was an attempt on Chase's part to encourage them to convert to national charters. The Chase plan was challenged in *Veazie Bank v. Fenno*,[10] in which Chase, by then Chief Justice, wrote the majority opinion. The Court upheld the constitutionality of the tax,[11] but it did not directly address the constitutionality of the NBA to grant corporate charters to "national banks." This issue was finally addressed *en passant* in *Farmers' & Mechanics' National Bank v. Dearing*,[12] where the Supreme Court stated:

> The constitutionality of the act of 1864 is not questioned. It rests on the same principle as the act creating the second bank of the United States. The reasoning of Secretary Hamilton and of this court in *McCulloch v. Maryland* ... and in *Osborne v. The Bank of the United States* ..., therefore, applies. The national banks organized under the act are instruments designed to be used to aid the government in the administration of an important branch of the public service. They are means appropriate to that end. Of the degree of the necessity which existed for creating them Congress is the sole judge.[13]

Having accepted the constitutionality of the NBA, the Court went on to express the view that the national banks created under the Act's authority were to be accorded a degree of national favor.[14]

§ 1.6   Second Federal Period

The creation of a "national" banking system marked the beginning of the second federal period of U.S. bank regulation. This second distinct federal period would continue after the monetary panic of 1907, with the eventual establishment of the Federal Reserve System. However, federal involvement in bank regulation

---

10. 75 U.S. (8 Wall.) 533 (1869).

11. *Id.* at 549.

12. 91 U.S. (1 Otto) 29 (1875).

13. *Id.* at 33–34. *See Barnett Bank of Marion County, N.A. v. Nelson*, 517 U.S. 25, 42, 116 S.Ct. 1103, 1113 (1996) (*citing McCulloch* and *Dearing* for proposition that National Bank Act is constitutional). Over-extension of the holdings of these two cases—and particularly of *McCulloch*—is a common occurrence. In *Watters v. Wachovia Bank, N.A.*, 550 U.S. 1, 10, 127 S.Ct. 1559, 1566 (2007), for example, Justice Ginsburg's opinion for the Court inflates the *McCulloch* holding, attributing to it the much broader proposition that "federal law [is] supreme over state law with respect to national banking." *Id.* at 10.

14. *Farmers' & Mechanics' Nat'l Bank v. Dearing*, 91 U.S. at 34. States now have explicit statutory authority to tax national banks. 12 U.S.C.A. § 548 ("For the purpose of any tax law enacted under the authority of ... any state, national bank shall be treated as a bank organized and existing under the laws of the State ... within which its principal office is located").

during this period was at first simply a matter of expediency—the need to fund the war.

Thus, in its narrowest sense a national banking system *was* created by the enactment of the NBA, *i.e.*, authority was granted to the executive to charter banking businesses that were subject to federal law in their corporate structure, powers to do business and the like. However, in a broader sense, a "national" banking system surely entails more than the mere participation by the federal government as a competing incorporator of banks, along with the states. A consistent and coherent national policy for the regulation of banking would seem to be implied in the notion of a "national" banking system. The United States has been slow to achieve anything like that.

In the aftermath of the 1907 panic,[1] a National Monetary Commission was created in 1908 to investigate the causes of the panic and recommend remedial legislation.[2] The Commission eventually proposed the creation of a central banking system to monitor the monetary and credit functions of the nation's financial system.[3] As enacted into law, this central bank system, the Board of Governors of the Federal Reserve System ("the Fed"), was also charged with supervision of the banks that became members of the Federal Reserve System.[4]

§ 1.7   Third Federal Period

A third federal period began in the aftermath of the 1929 stock market crash and the growing depression. This period established the complex structure of federal regulation more or less as we know it today.

The stock market crash of 1929, together with the accompanying nationwide series of bank failures through the mid–1930s, provided catastrophic evidence of the need for further improvements in the nation's bank regulatory system.[1] The resultant statutory improvements included, *inter alia*, the amendment of the Federal Reserve Act in June 1933, which established the Federal

---

§ 1.6

1. For a discussion of the panic, see Ron Chernow, The House of Morgan 121–130 (Atlantic Monthly Press: 1990).

2. 35 Stat. 546 (1908).

3. H.R. Rep. No. 1593, 62d Cong., 3d Sess. (1912).

4. *See* Federal Reserve Act, § 11(a), 38 Stat. 261 (Dec. 23, 1913) (currently codified at 12 U.S.C.A. § 248(a)(1)) (providing for examination of member banks). On the regulatory objectives of the Federal Reserve System, see *Texas State Bank v. United States*, 423 F.3d 1370 (Fed. Cir. 2005).

§ 1.7

1. On the congressional investigation of the causes of the market crash and bank failures, see 2 Michael P. Malloy, Banking Law and Regulation 7.16–7.28 (Aspen Law & Business: 1994 & Cum. Supp.).

Deposit Insurance Corporation ("FDIC").[2] As is characteristic in U.S. bank regulation, however, even the catastrophe of the bank failures of the early 1930s did not lead to a comprehensive realignment of bank regulatory systems. Not only did the state banking systems continue along with the national banking system, but there was also no concerted attempt to exercise complete, preemptive federal regulatory authority over the activities of the existing state banks.

In the 1930s, and continuing until 1989, federal regulation of savings and loan associations ("S & Ls") was made the responsibility of the Federal Home Loan Bank Board ("FHLBB"), for federally chartered S & Ls, and the Federal Savings and Loan Insurance Corporation ("FSLIC"), for federally insured, state-chartered S & Ls.[3]

The National Credit Union Administration ("NCUA") is yet another legacy of the financial crisis that beset the country beginning in 1929. Unlike the federal regulatory systems imposed upon the troubled commercial banking and savings associations industries, however, the passage of the Federal Credit Union Act of 1934[4] was, at least on its face, not prompted by any systematic failure of credit unions.[5]

§ 1.8 Contemporary Developments

While the overall structure of U.S. bank regulation has changed remarkably little since the mid–1930s, the statutory interstices of that structure have grown increasingly complex, so much so that at times it seems that a major federal piece of omnibus bank legislation comes along almost every two years. In sections 1.9–1.11 we examine in detail the elements of the regulatory structure. For a general overview of contemporary developments, the reader may wish to review Figure 1–1, *infra*.

---

2. *See* Act of June 16, 1933, ch. 89, § 8, 48 Stat. 168, *as amended*. This provision, originally codified at 12 U.S.C.A. § 264, was subsequently withdrawn from the Federal Reserve Act and recodified as the separate Federal Deposit Insurance Act, 12 U.S.C.A. ch. 16, in 1950. *See* Act of September 21, 1950, ch. 967, § 1, 64 Stat. 873.

3. *See* Act of July 22, 1932, 47 Stat. 725 (enacting Federal Home Loan Bank Act); 12 U.S.C.A. §§ 1724–1730i (authorizing FSLIC), *repealed*, Financial Institutions Re form, Recovery, and Enforcement Act of 1989, § 407, 103 Stat. 183, 363 (1989).

4. 12 U.S.C.A. §§ 1751 *et seq.*

5. *See, e.g., Barany v. Buller*, 670 F.2d 726, 733 & n. 16 (7th Cir.1982).

Figure 1–1
Contemporary Developments in U.S. Bank Regulation

1907 –monetary panic
1908 –Monetary Commission established

1913 –Federal Reserve Act

1919 –Edge Act (international banking corporations authorized)

1927 –McFadden Act (national bank branches authorized)
1929 –Collapse of stock market
1932 –Federal Home Loan Act (FHLBB established)
1933 ....Banking Act of 1933 (deposit insurance;
1934 ....National Housing Act   limits on securities activities of banks)
1935 –Banking Act of 1935   (FSLIC established)   Securities Act of 1933
        Securities Exchange Act of 1934   Home Owner's Loan Act (chartering of
        (SEC established)   federal S & Ls authorized)
        Federal Credit Union Act
        (federal credit union chartering)
1940 ....Investment Company Act of 1940
        Investment Advisers Act of 1940

1956 –Bank Holding Company Act

1960 –Bank Merger Act
1962 –Bank Service Corporation Act (renamed Bank Service Company Act in 1996)
1964 –Securities Acts Amendments (banks & S & Ls to register under 1934 Act)
1966 ....Bank Merger Act Amendment
        Financial Institutions Supervisory Act
1968 –Savings and Loan Holding Company Amendments of 1967   Bank Holding Company Act Amendments
        Bank Interest Rates legislation

1970 –Bank Holding Company Act Amendments

1973 –Payment of Interest legislation
1974 ....Depository Institutions
1975 ....Banking and Interest and Insurance legislation
1976 ....Bank Holding Company   Rates legislation
1977 –Community   Tax Act of 1976
        Reinvestment Act
1978 ....International Banking Act
        Financial Institutions
1980 –S & L crisis begins to emerge   Regulatory and Interest
        Depository Institutions Deregulation and Monetary Control Act   Rate Control Act of 1978
1982 ....Garn–St Germain Depository
        Institutions Act
        international debt crisis emerges

1987 –Competitive Equality Banking Act
1989 –Financial Institutions Reform,
        Recovery, and Enforcement Act
        of 1989
1991 ....FDIC Improvements Act
        RTC Improvements Act
1994 ....Interstate Banking and Branching
        Efficiency Act
1996 –Economic Growth and Regulatory Paperwork Reduction Act   Community Development and
        Regulatory Improvement Act
1998 –Credit Union Membership Access Act
1999 –Gramm–Leach–Bliley Act
2000 –American Homeownership and Economic Opportunity Act
2001 –USA PATRIOT Act

2006 ....Federal Deposit Insurance Reform
        Act of 2005
        Federal Deposit Insurance Reform
        Conforming Amendments Act of
        2005
        Financial Services Regulatory Relief Act of 2006
2008 ...."Great Recession" begins with
        collapse of subprime mortgage
        market
        Housing and Economic Recovery
        Act of 2008
        Emergency Economic Stabilization Act of 2008
2009 ....American Recovery and Reinvestment Act
2010 ....Dodd–Frank Wall Street Reform
        and Consumer Protection Act

§ 1.9   Current Regulatory Environment

The environment in which depository institutions operate is decidedly regulatory in character. It is defined by a complex set of regulators that charter, supervise, examine, and in many cases specifically approve or disapprove the activities in which the institutions engage. The environment became even more complex after 12 November 1999, when the President signed the Gramm–Leach–Bliley Act into law.[1] This financial services reform effort is probably the most significant—and one of the most massive—pieces of federal banking legislation since the Banking Act of 1933. It affects, to some degree, every chapter of this book. The GLBA will be highlighted at appropriate points throughout the book. The GLBA generally endorses the principle of "functional regulation," which posits that similar activities should be regulated by the same regulator.[2] Accordingly, banking activities are regulated by federal and state bank regulators, securities activities by federal and state securities regulators, and insurance activities by state insurance regulators.[3]

In 2008, the subprime mortgage market collapsed, and that event precipitated a devastating financial crisis that eventually spread into the economies of other countries.[4] One consequence of this ongoing crisis has been the enactment of the Dodd–Frank Wall Street Reform and Consumer Protection Act (Dodd–Frank)[5] in July 2010. Dodd–Frank mandates a further revision of the regulatory structure, as well as substantive statutory changes intended to increase the safety and soundness of the financial services industry. Although most of the DFA amendments do not become effective until July 2011,[6] the intended effects of the act will be highlighted throughout this book.

As to banking activities, regulatory functions performed by the state and federal regulators may be divided into three broad categories:

§ 1.9

1. Pub. L. No. 106–102, Nov. 12, 1999, 113 Stat. 1338 (1999) (codified at scattered sections of 12, 15, 16, 18 U.S.C.A.) ("GLBA").

2. *But cf.* Michael P. Malloy, *Functional Regulation: Premise or Pretext? in* PATRICIA A. McCOY (ed.), FINANCIAL MODERNIZATION AFTER GRAMM-LEACH-BLILEY (LexisNexis 2002) (arguing that GLBA does not consistently or completely apply principle of functional regulation).

3. *See, e.g.*, GLBA, §§ 111–112, 115, 301 (codified at 12 U.S.C.A. §§ 1820a, 1831v, 1844(c)(4)(A)–(B), (g), 15 U.S.C.A. § 6711). However, under the GLBA the Board of Governors of the Federal Reserve System retains the role of "umbrella supervisor" of bank hold-

ing companies ("BHCs") and their subsidiaries. GLBA, § 113 (codified at 12 U.S.C.A. § 1848a). Regulation of BHCs will be examined in Chapters 4 and 6, *infra.*

4. On the subprime mortgage collapse and the crisis that followed, see § 8.2, infra.

5. Pub. L. No. 111–203, 124 Stat. 1376 (2010) (codified at scattered sections of 2, 5, 7, 11, 12, 15, 18, 20, 22, 26, 28, 31, 42, 44 U.S.C.) (DFA). The changes effected by the DFA will be discussed at appropriate points throughout this book. For an overview of the DFA, see 1 Michael P. Malloy, Banking Law and Regulation § 1.4.11 (Aspen Law & Business: 1994 & Cum. Supp.).

6. See, e.g., DFA §§ 311(a), 313 (codified at 12 U.S.C. §§ 5411(a), 5413)

(1) *Chartering and the administration of other, secondary entry restrictions.*[7] The chartering function is performed by the Comptroller of the Currency and (until the Fall 2011) the Director of the Office of Thrift Supervision ("OTS")[8] among the federal regulators, and by various state regulators and regulatory bodies in each state. Secondary entry restrictions are administered by a variety of federal and state regulators.

(2) *Supervision.* The supervision of the activities of depository institutions involves not only the promulgation of regulations pursuant to statutory authority, but also the issuance of more or less formal interpretations of the statutory responsibilities imposed on these institutions and the practices that they should follow, through the use of circulars, memoranda, releases, and other publicly available guidance. The supervisory function also includes informal interpretive services provided by the agencies on a day-to-day basis, as well as the use of their statutory enforcement and investigative authority to inquire into cases of possible violations and abuses. Various federal regulators[9] as well as the state regulators exercise this supervisory function.

(3) *Examination.* The examination function is complementary to the supervisory function. On a periodic basis, whether or not violations or interpretive problems exist, depository institutions are subjected to on-site examination by the staffs of the regulators that supervise them.

(concerning transfer of regulatory authority).

7. "Chartering" involves the establishment of an entity, corporate or otherwise, empowered to engage in the business of being a depository institution of a specified type. The "charter" is the certificate or articles of incorporation, or similar constitutive document. Unlike general business incorporation, chartering involves the review and substantive approval of a charter application by the regulatory official or body empowered by law to authorize an entity to operate as a depository institution. Chartering is, therefore a "primary entry restriction," *i.e.*, a restriction on free entry into the industry. "Secondary entry restrictions" limit the ability of a chartered institution to expand into other segments of the market of the industry (geographic or product). One such secondary entry restriction is the limitation on the power of chartered institutions to establish branch offices or operations. *See, e.g.*, 12 U.S.C.A. § 36 (restrictions on branching by national banks). Other secondary entry restrictions limit the ability of institutions to participate in certain collateral features

of the regulatory system itself, such as deposit insurance or membership in the Federal Reserve System. Withholding some of these features, particularly deposit insurance, could have serious adverse effects on the ability of the institution to compete. *See* Scott, *In Quest of Reason: The Licensing Decisions of the Federal Banking Agencies*, 42 U. Chi. L. Rev. 235, 269–70 (1975) (discussing restrictions).

8. Under DFA § 313, the OTS and the position of the DOTS are scheduled to be abolished. DFA §§ 311(a), 313 (codified at 12 U.S.C. §§ 5411(a), 5413). This event is effective 90 days after the "transfer date"—21 July 2011—on which the functions and authority of the DOTS and the OTS are first exercised by the other federal regulators. *See id.* § 312(b) (codified at 12 U.S.C. § 5412(b)) (mandating transfer of functions).

9. Principally, the following federal regulators exercise supervisory authority over depository institutions: the Office of the Comptroller of the Currency ("OCC"), the Board of Governors of the Federal Reserve System ("Fed"), the

A depository institution may be subject to the authority of more than one regulator.[10] Distributing primary responsibility for the supervisory and examination functions as to any type of depository institution is a task that is determined separately for each type of regulated activity. In addition, among the principal federal regulators—the Office of the Comptroller of the Currency ("OCC"), the Fed, the FDIC, and (until the Fall 2011) the OTS—regulatory responsibilities are usually distributed along the general lines of a now traditional statutory formula.[11]

National banks and District of Columbia banks are generally subject to supervision by the OCC.[12] State-chartered member banks of the Federal Reserve System are generally subject to supervision by the Fed[13] (and, of course, by a state regulator). The Fed is also the federal regulator of bank holding companies,[14] which may also be subject to state regulation.[15] State-chartered nonmember banks the deposits of which are insured by the FDIC are generally subject to supervision by the FDIC,[16] and by a state regulator. Federally chartered savings associations are generally supervised by the OTS,[17] but as of the Fall 2011 by the OCC.[18] State-chartered savings associations are generally supervised by the chartering state regulator and by the OTS, but as of the Fall 2011 by the state regulator and the FDIC.[19] Until its abolishment, the OTS is also the federal regulator of savings and loan holding companies,[20] which may also be subject to state regulation. As of the Fall 2011, the Fed will replace the OTS to regulate the savings and loan holding companies.[21]

Other depository institutions that are not insured by the FDIC are supervised by other regulators. Thus, state-chartered commercial banks and savings associations not insured by the FDIC are

Federal Deposit Insurance Corporation ("FDIC"), (until the Fall 2011) the Office of Thrift Supervision ("OTS"), and the National Credit Union Administration ("NCUA"). The extent of their roles in this regard and the types of depository institutions subject to the supervisory authority of each are discussed in § 1.11, *infra*.

10. For example, a state-chartered commercial bank that has FDIC deposit insurance and is a member of the Federal Reserve System is of concern to its state chartering authority, the FDIC, and the Fed. A national bank, which is required to be a member of the Federal Reserve System and to carry FDIC insurance, is of concern to the OCC, the Fed, and the FDIC.

11. *See, e.g.,* 12 U.S.C.A. § 1813(q) (defining "appropriate Federal banking agency" for purposes of Federal Deposit Insurance Act); 12 U.S.C.A. § 1828(c)(2) (defining "responsible agency" for purposes of prior written approval under Bank Merger Act); 12 U.S.C.A. § 1861(b)(1) (Bank Service Company Act; cross-reference to § 1813(q)); 15 U.S.C.A. § 78c(a)(34)(A) (defining "appropriate regulatory agency" for purposes of Securities Exchange Act of 1934, when used with respect to a "municipal securities dealer"). *Cf.* 15 U.S.C.A. § 78*l*(i) (distributing authority under Securities Exchange Act of 1934 with respect to securities issued by insured banks and savings associations).

12. 12 U.S.C.A. § 1813(q)(1).

13. 12 U.S.C.A. § 1813(q)(2).

14. 12 U.S.C.A. § 1844.

15. 12 U.S.C.A. § 1848.

16. 12 U.S.C.A. § 1813(q)(3).

17. 12 U.S.C.A. § 1813(q)(4) (2009).

18. DFA § 312(b)(2)(B)(i)(I).

19. *Id.* § 312(b)(2)(C).

20. 12 U.S.C.A. § 1813(q)(4) (2009).

21. DFA § 312(b)(1).

supervised by their state regulators. Federal credit unions are chartered and supervised by the NCUA. Federally insured, state-chartered credit unions are supervised by the NCUA and their state regulators. Uninsured, state-chartered credit unions are supervised by their state regulators. Figure 1–2, *infra*, illustrates these lines of authority.

Figure 1–2
Regulatory Lines of Authority

Institution	Primary Regulator(s)	Other Regulators
National Banks	OCC	Fed, FDIC, SEC[a]
D.C. Banks	OCC	Fed, FDIC SEC[a]
State–Chartered Member Banks	Fed, State Regulator	FDIC, OCC,[b] SEC[a]
State–Chartered Nonmember Insured Banks	FDIC, State Regulator	OCC,[b] Fed,[c] SEC[a]
Federal Savings Associations	OTS[d]	FDIC, OCC,[b] Fed,[c] SEC[a]
State Savings Associations	OTS,[d] State Regulator	FDIC, OCC,[b] Fed,[c] SEC[a]
Uninsured State–Chartered Banks	State Regulator	OCC,[b] Fed,[c] SEC[a]
Uninsured State–Chartered Savings Associations	State Regulator	OCC,[b] Fed,[c] SEC[a]
Federal Credit Unions	NCUA	OCC,[b] Fed,[c] SEC[a]
Insured State–Chartered Credit Unions	NCUA, State Regulator	OCC,[b] Fed,[c] SEC[a]
Uninsured State–Chartered Credit Unions	State Regulator	OCC,[b] Fed,[c] SEC[a]
Bank Holding Companies	Fed, State Regulator	OCC,[d] SEC,[a] State Insurance Regulator[e]
Financial Holding Companies	Fed, State Regulator	OCC,[e], SEC,[a] State Insurance Regulator[e]
Savings and Loan Holding Companies	OTS,[d] State Regulator	SEC,[a] State Insurance Regulator[f]

    a. As to securities activities/subsidiaries. *See, e.g.,* 12 U.S.C.A. § 1844(c)(4)(A) (concerning functional regulation of securities activities).
    b. As to transactions by the institution involving investment securities. 12 U.S.C.A. §§ 24 (Seventh), 378.
    c. As to deposit reserves only. 12 U.S.C.A. § 461(b)(1)(A).
    d. Until the Fall 2011. See *DFA* § 312(b) (codified at 12 U.S.C.A. § 5412(b)) (mandating transfer of functions).
    e. As to activities of national bank subsidiaries. *See American Ins. Ass'n v. Clarke,* 865 F.2d 278 (D.C.Cir.1988) (discussing role of OCC).
    f. As to insurance activities/subsidiaries. *See, e.g.,* 12 U.S.C.A. § 1844(c)(4)(B) (concerning functional regulation of insurance activities).

There are certain areas of regulation that apply not only to depository institutions but to all participants in commercial and financial activities, such as antitrust and securities regulation. Here, the primary federal regulators of depository institutions have been given specialized responsibilities. In the area of antitrust law, for example, these regulators have been given the statutory responsibility to review certain transactions by depository institutions in advance of any action by the traditional antitrust regulator, the Department of Justice ("DOJ").[22] However, DOJ retains complete authority to review and regulate in the final analysis.[23]

In the area of securities regulation, the primary federal regulators of depository institutions have generally been given exclusive statutory responsibility at the federal level, preempting the usual authority of the Securities and Exchange Commission ("SEC").[24] However, this preemption does not include the enforcement of the antifraud provisions of the securities laws.[25] Nor does it include the regulation of the issuance of or trading in securities by any holding company of a depository institution. Such companies remain subject to the exclusive authority of the SEC at the federal level.

It should be obvious from this brief review that the structure of the regulatory environment is complex. For any one type of depository institution there may be only one regulator to whom the institution must answer, but the typical pattern is in fact usually more convoluted. The complexity of this regulatory structure has raised questions concerning the effectiveness of a regulatory system as fragmented as that governing the activities of depository institutions.[26] In terms of the development and implementation of overall regulatory policy for depository institutions, the structure is a bewildering network of overlapping lines of authority and regulatory interests, as can be seen from Figure 1–3, *infra*. In order to sort out some of these complexities, the next two sections identify the various types of depository institutions authorized by federal and state law and the corresponding federal regulators.

22. 12 U.S.C.A. § 1828(c) (Bank Merger Act).

23. 12 U.S.C.A. § 1828(c)(7).

24. *See, e.g.*, 15 U.S.C.A. § 78*l*(i) (authorizing primary regulators of depository institutions to administer Securities Exchange Act of 1934 with respect to securities of supervised institutions).

25. 15 U.S.C.A. §§ 77q, 78j.

26. *See, e.g.*, *Report of the Task Group on Regulation of Financial Services* 9 (1984) ("Task Group Report"):

Figure 1–3

U.S. Regulatory Structure
[*post-October 2011*]

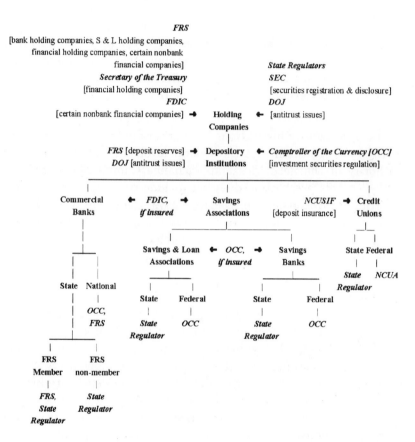

One further complication in understanding—and adequately supervising—banks and other depository institutions lies in the fact that there is a range of other, non-depository firms that engage in "financial intermediation," such as life insurance companies, finance companies, state and local government employee retirement funds, investment companies, non-life insurance companies, money

This fragmentation can impair the effectiveness of the regulatory system in maintaining safety and soundness, especially where ultimate responsibility for a particular program is not clearly identified. Impairment can also occur where the need to coordinate actions among too many different agencies and their field offices delays effective supervisory action.

market mutual funds, securities broker-dealers, and real estate investment trusts and the like. To that extent they are in competition with the depository institutions—all are seeking to attract funds from the investor/consumer to be reinvested in a variety of concerns in need of funds.[27]

The nondepository intermediaries are generally outside the scope of this book. However, we must deal with certain hybrids that potentially blur the distinction between these two sectors of financial intermediaries. First, the "nonbank bank,"[28] and the regulatory problems it raises, can only be fully appreciated in light of the ways in which banks and nonbanks such as securities broker-dealers are respectively regulated. In chapter 4, then, we shall examine the way in which firms chartered as banks, but which do not perform traditional banking services, may still be operated by a regulated bank holding company.[29]

Second, at the enterprise level, a range of financial holding companies[30] exists, with diversified operating subsidiaries—including commercial banks—that make cross-sector competition more complex, because the holding company may control both depository and nondepository intermediaries. Furthermore, since July 2010 federal banking law also recognizes the "nonbank financial company,"[31] which—when determined to be systemically significant—is subject to extensive supervision by the Fed,[32] and which may be administered by the FDIC if it fails.[33]

§ 1.10   Regulated Entities

Until the 1960s, the financial services industry was typified by "distinct kinds of financial institutions, offering distinct financial products, generally in limited geographic areas."[1] Since then, the

27. For a brief summary of the role of financial intermediaries, *see* M. Stigum, The Money Market 11–13 (rev. ed. 1983).

28. *See, e.g., Board of Governors v. Dimension Fin. Corp.*, 474 U.S. 361, 106 S.Ct. 681 (1986) (upholding acquisition of "nonbank bank" by holding company despite contrary Fed regulations).

29. *See* § 4.2, *infra* (discussing bank holding company acquisitions).

30. *See* 12 U.S.C. § 1843(k).

31. *See, e.g., id.* § 5311(a)(4)(B) (defining "U.S. nonbank financial company").

32. *Id.* § 5323(a)(1).

33. *Id.* §§ 5381–5394 (providing "orderly liquidation authority" for FDIC over nobank financial companies under specified circumstances).

§ 1.10

1. Report of the President, Geographic Restrictions on Commercial Banking in the United States 2 (Dep't of the Treasury, Jan. 1981) ("Report of the President").

industry has experienced considerable blurring of the boundaries among the formerly distinct kinds of institutions.[2] There is now a wide range of "financial intermediaries"[3] (*e.g.*, commercial banks, savings associations, credit unions, finance companies, insurance companies, securities firms) in more or less direct competition.

With the increasing expansion beginning in 1980 of the powers of the once highly specialized savings associations (principally savings banks and S & Ls)[4] came a blurring of distinctions between these entities and full-service commercial banks. In this context, the concept of the "depository institution" has become a significant category in regulatory policy. While its factual significance was assured once distinctions based on differences in offered services became blurred, the technical legal significance of the term was not secured until 1980, with the passage of the Depository Institutions Deregulation and Monetary Control Act of 1980.[5] Title I of the Act, the Monetary Control Act of 1980 ("MCA"),[6] marked an important step in deregulation of the products offered by such institutions. Section 103 of the MCA[7] also contained a formal statutory definition of the term as including:

> (1) any commercial bank the deposits of which are federally insured or eligible for federal insurance;

> (2) any mutual savings bank which is federally insured or eligible for insurance;

> (3) any stock savings bank which is federally insured or eligible for insurance;

> (4) any credit union which is insured or eligible for insurance;

> (5) any member of the Federal Home Loan Bank System; and,

---

2. *See id.:*

What was once a financial system consisting of highly segmented *geographic* markets has, for many kinds of banking services, been transformed into a competitive nationwide marketplace. What was once a segmented *product* market has been replaced by head-to-head competition between banks and various non-bank institutions; indeed, there is no longer a single service or product line offered exclusively by commercial banks.

(Emphasis in original.) *See also Marquette Nat'l Bank v. First of Omaha Serv. Corp.*, 439 U.S. 299, 317, 99 S.Ct. 540, 550 (1978) (noting credit market increasingly nationwide in scope). *But see United States v. Connecticut Nat'l Bank*, 418 U.S. 656, 94 S.Ct. 2788 (1974) (maintaining commercial banks and thrift institutions still distinct product markets for antitrust purposes).

3. The Task Group refers to this broad category as "financial service firms." *Task Group Report* at 16.

4. *See* Report of the President at 9–10.

5. Pub. L. No. 96–221, 94 Stat. 132 (March 31, 1980).

6. Pub. L. No. 96–221, tit. I.

7. 12 U.S.C.A. § 461(b)(1)(A).

(6) any savings association (such as an S & L, savings bank, and the like) that is insured or eligible for insurance.

The advantage of this definition, from the point of view of consistent formation of regulatory policy, is that it provides a legally cognizable, generic category to cover a wide range of banking and bank-like institutions. Until the enactment of the Financial Institutions Reform, Recovery, and Enforcement Act of 1989 ("FIR-REA"),[8] as a technical matter this generic concept was directly applicable only to regulatory policy with respect to reserve requirements, which are now fully subject to regulation by the Federal Reserve Board after an eight-year transitional period.[9] Even the technical acknowledgment of this generic concept resulted in at least a heightened awareness of its pertinence as a term of reference for regulatory policy.[10]

Ideally, then, regulatory issues should be resolved in terms of consistency and coherence with respect to the full spectrum of depository institutions taken as a class. For example, the Federal Deposit Insurance Act ("FDIA")[11] now generally refers to "insured depository institutions"[12] rather than "insured banks,"[13] moving federal regulation a step closer to a unified, functional system. Still, the distinct types of depository institutions remain subject to significantly differing regimes.

(a) *Commercial banks.* Commercial banks remain, in terms of percentage of financial assets held and in terms of the range of their products and services, the dominant category of depository institutions. They are to be distinguished from savings associations (savings banks and S & Ls), which—unlike commercial banks—are not empowered to offer the full range of banking services, including demand deposit accounts (*e.g.*, checking accounts) for business and personal use, savings[14] and time deposits, investment and loan

---

8. Pub. L. No. 101–73, 103 Stat. 183 (1989).

9. *See* 12 U.S.C.A. § 461(b)(8).

10. *See, e.g.*, Garn–St Germain Depository Institutions Act of 1982, Pub. L. No. 97–320, 96 Stat. 14 (1982).

11. 12 U.S.C.A. §§ 1811 *et seq.*

12. For purposes of the FDIA, the term "depository institution" is defined to mean any "bank or savings institution." 12 U.S.C.A. § 1813(c). The term "savings association" is defined as a generic concept including federally chartered S & Ls and savings banks, state-chartered building and loan associations, S & Ls, homestead associations, cooperative banks (other than those that are "State banks" under 12 U.S.C.A.

§ 1813(a)(2)) and "any corporation (other than a bank) that the [FDIC] Board of Directors and the Director of the Office of Thrift Supervision jointly determine to be operating in substantially the same manner as a savings association." 12 U.S.C.A. § 1813(b).

13. *See* 12 U.S.C.A. § 1816 (factors to be considered in insurance applications; reference to "depository institution" rather than "bank"); § 1819 (corporate powers of FDIC; same); § 1822 (FDIC as receiver; same).

14. *See Franklin Nat'l Bank v. New York*, 347 U.S. 373, 74 S.Ct. 550 (1954) (commercial banks, though not "savings" institutions, may advertise "savings accounts").

services, and the like.[15] Despite this distinction between commercial and savings banks, the two types of entities (and, indeed, all of the depository institutions) do overlap services. What actually distinguishes them is the regulatory jurisdiction to which they are subject.

In *Franklin National Bank v. New York*,[16] the Supreme Court considered the authority of national banks (federally chartered commercial banks) to engage in "savings" account services offered by state savings banks. Under the New York Banking Law, New York prohibited the use of the word "savings" or its variants by any banks other than its own chartered savings banks and savings and loan associations. On the other hand, the federal government chartered national banks that were authorized to accept savings deposits.[17] Franklin National offered and advertised its savings accounts. The question therefore arose whether such advertisements violated New York law. The Court considered advertising as a permissible power incidental to the acceptance of the accounts.[18] The Court found no indication that Congress intended to make this phase of national banking subject to local restrictions, as it has done by express language in several other instances.[19] Accordingly, the Court held that the New York law was preempted by the NBA on the issue of permissible advertising of "savings" accounts.[20] The approach taken in *Franklin National Bank* and followed in *Barnett Bank*[21] has been utilized to preempt a wide range of state regulatory law that would otherwise be applicable to national banks and their operating subsidiaries. Until it was repudiated in 2009 by the Supreme Court in *Cuomo v. Clearing House Association, L.L.C.*,[22]

---

15. Until recently, savings associations were prohibited from engaging in most of these activities, and were limited mainly to personal savings deposits and personal and home mortgage loans. The range of services that savings associations are permitted to offer has expanded dramatically since 1980. *See, e.g.,* Pub. L. No. 96–221, Title IV, 94 Stat. 151 (1980) (expanding transactional powers of savings associations). *See generally* Roster, *The Modern Role of Thrifts*, 18 Loy.–L.A. L. Rev. 1099 (1985). In practice, however, the traditional distinction between commercial banks and savings associations, based on extent of offered services, is still broadly accurate.

16. 347 U.S. 373, 74 S.Ct. 550 (1954).

17. *Franklin*, 347 U.S. at 376, 74 S.Ct. at 553, *citing* R.S. § 5136, 12 U.S.C.A. § 24 (Seventh) (1952).

18. *Id.* at 377–378.

19. *Id.* at 378. In many situations, the National Bank Act refers a legal question over to the apposite state law rule. *See, e.g.,* 12 U.S.C.A. §§ 24 (Eighth) (contributions to charitable instrumentalities); 36(c) (intrastate branching); 85 (permissible rates of interest on loans).

20. *Franklin, supra.* The preemption analysis utilized in the *Franklin* opinion was explicitly relied upon in the Supreme Court's decision in *Barnett Bank of Marion County, N.A. v. Nelson*, 517 U.S. 25, 116 S.Ct. 1103 (1996) (upholding statutory right of national banks to sell insurance under specified circumstances, despite contrary state law).

21. *Barnett Bank of Marion County, N.A. v. Nelson*, 517 U.S. 25, 42, 116 S.Ct. 1103, 1113 (1996).

22. ___ U.S. ___, 129 S.Ct. 2710 (2009). In *Watters v. Wachovia Bank, N.A.*, 550 U.S. 1, 127 S.Ct. 1559 (2007), the Supreme Court had accepted the

the OCC was engaged in a concerted effort to pursue broad preemption with respect to such state laws.[23]

Franklin National notwithstanding, to what extent are national banks subject to state law? Except for situations in which federal statutes contain a contrary provision, national banks are fully subject to state laws, including those concerning collection of debts, transactions in commercial paper, bank deposits, contracts, and the like.[24]

Commercial banks should also be distinguished from investment banks, financial intermediaries whose business consists primarily of underwriting and distributing securities and acting as brokers and dealers in securities already distributed.[25] Since 1933, federal law has generally required that such activities be carried on by entities other than commercial banks and, from 1933–1999, prohibited most affiliations between commercial and investment banking entities.[26]

Various attempts at an affirmative definition of "commercial bank" or "bank" have been attempted. The traditional definition defines a commercial bank as an institution whose business consists of discounting commercial paper,[27] accepting deposits (particularly demand deposits),[28] and making loans (particularly commercial

OCC's conception of broad preemptive power on the part of the federal regulators, even with respect to the regulation of *nonbanking* subsidiaries of federally chartered banking entities.

23. For example, a February 2003 notice of proposed rulemaking by the OCC proposed revisions to the interpretive provisions of its regulations to strengthen preemption by invoking the exclusive visitorial powers of the federal regulator under 12 U.S.C. § 484. *See Rules, Policies and Procedures for Corporate Activities*, 68 Fed. Reg. 6363 (2003) (to be codified at, *inter alia*, 12 C.F.R. § 7.400(a)(3)(i)–(ii), (b)). For analysis and criticism of the OCC preemption policy, see Fisher, *Toward a Basal Tenth Amendment: A Riposte to National Bank Preemption of State Consumer Protection Laws*, 29 HARV. J.L. & PUB. POL'Y 981 (2006); Arthur E. Wilmarth, Jr., *The OCC's Preemption Rules Exceed the Agency's Authority and Present a Serious Threat to the Dual Banking System and Consumer Protection*, 23 Ann. Rev. Banking & Fin. L. 225 (2004).

24. *See First Nat'l Bank v. Kentucky*, 76 U.S. (9 Wall.) 353, 362 (1870) (noting that national banks "are subject to the laws of the State ... in their daily

course of business"); *Davis v. Elmira Sav. Bank*, 161 U.S. 275, 283, 16 S.Ct. 502, 503–504 (1896); *McClellan v. Chipman*, 164 U.S. 347, 356–357, 17 S.Ct. 85, 87 (1896).

25. For an historical review of the growth of the investment banking business in the United States, see *United States v. Morgan*, 118 F.Supp. 621, 635–55 (S.D.N.Y.1953).

26. 12 U.S.C.A. §§ 24 (Seventh), 78, 377–378. The clarity of this separation of commercial and investment banking has been vigorously litigated. *See, e.g., Securities Indus. Ass'n v. Board of Governors*, 468 U.S. 137, 104 S.Ct. 2979 (1984) (rejecting Fed authorization of certain securities activities by commercial bank); *Securities Indus. Ass'n v. Board of Governors*, 468 U.S. 207, 104 S.Ct. 3003 (1984) (upholding Fed authorization of acquisition of discount broker by bank holding company).

27. *Oulton v. German Sav. & Loan Soc'y*, 84 U.S. (17 Wall.) 109, 118 (1873); *In re Wilkins' Will*, 131 Misc. 188, 226 N.Y.S. 415 (1928).

28. *United States v. Philadelphia Nat'l Bank*, 374 U.S. 321, 326, 83 S.Ct. 1715, 1721 (1963).

loans).[29] More contemporary versions of the definition have stressed the demand deposit and commercial loan aspects only.[30]

(b) *Savings banks.* Savings banks are a relatively early form of the savings association, mainly found in the eastern portion of the United States.[31] They have traditionally been limited by statute to non-commercial deposit and lending activities. In the United States, savings banks have taken two distinct forms: (1) the mutual savings bank, which has no capital stock or stockholders and operates as a mutual association for the benefits of its "members" (*i.e.,* depositors); and, (2) the stock savings bank, of comparatively recent origin, which does operate as a corporate entity with stockholders distinct from depositors.[32] The former has a board of trustees rather than a board of directors, and its net earnings accrue to the mutual benefit of the members. The latter is managed as any other corporate entity. Until recently, both types of savings bank could be chartered only under state law. In 1982, the Garn–St Germain Depository Institutions Act authorized the conversion of state-chartered savings banks insured by the FDIC into federally chartered savings banks, under certain specified conditions.[33]

While their statutory powers have been expanded beyond traditional limits,[34] savings banks remain primarily consumer-oriented

---

29. *Wilshire Oil Co. v. Board of Governors,* 668 F.2d 732 (3d Cir.1981).

30. Statutory provisions have generally been somewhat vague on this issue, often containing no explicit definition of "bank" or "commercial bank" and apparently presupposing the common understanding of the term. *See, e.g.,* 12 U.S.C.A. § 24 (Seventh) (authorizing national banking association to exercise all powers "incidental to the business of banking"). One exception is the provision in the Bank Holding Company Act ("BHC Act") that adopts as one alternative the traditional definition of *bank* as an institution that accepts demand deposits and makes commercial loans. *See* 12 U.S.C.A. § 1841(c)(1)(B). However, this definition is only directly applicable to the BHC Act itself. *Id.*

31. *See Huntington v. National Savings Bank,* 96 U.S. (6 Otto) 388, 395 (1878) (discussing statutory origin of savings banks in England; earliest existence in United States traced to 1834 Massachusetts statute). The savings and loan association (S & L) is the more prevalent type of savings association nationwide.

32. *See Dougherty v. Carver Fed. Sav. Bank,* 112 F.3d 613, 615 (2d Cir.

1997) (discussing distinction between mutual and stock savings banks).

33. *See* 12 U.S.C.A. § 1464(*o*) (1988). Such a conversion is permitted only if it would not be "in contravention of State law." *Id.* § 1464(*o*)(1). *Cf. id.* § 1464(*o*)(2)(F) (providing for FDIC conversion of insured savings bank to prevent closing or to reopen previously closed savings bank, notwithstanding state law). After a year of effectiveness of this new provision, 143 federally chartered savings banks were in operation. *Task Group Report* at 22, n. 10. FIRREA continued authority for chartering of and conversion to the federal stock savings association form (including savings banks). FIRREA § 301, 103 Stat. at 282, 300–301 (codified at 12 U.S.C.A. § 1464(a), (*o*)) (providing chartering and conversion authority, respectively). FIRREA also provides for conversion, notwithstanding any other provision of law, of troubled state-chartered mutual savings banks into federally chartered stock savings banks under certain statutorily specified conditions. *Id.* at 301 (codified at 12 U.S.C.A. § 1464(p)).

34. *See, e.g., Connecticut Nat'l Bank,* 418 U.S. at 665–666, 94 S.Ct. at 2794–2795 (noting expanded role).

depository institutions. Savings banks have traditionally been viewed by the courts as *"quasi* benevolent"[35] or *"quasi* charitable and purely benevolent institutions."[36] The public policy embodied in the original statutes authorizing savings banks was that they were intended to encourage thrift among those of modest means.[37] In contemporary terms, however, savings banks represent one sector of the business of banking, and they operate, within the statutory limits on their powers, like other institutions within that business.

(c) *Savings and loan associations.* Savings and loan associations ("S & Ls"), or building and loan associations as they are called in some states, are the largest category of savings associations. Like savings banks, S & Ls were, until recently, generally limited by statute to the receipt of savings deposits and the making of consumer and mortgage loans. Since 1980, however, their powers have been expanded dramatically.

Since at least the 1930s, S & Ls could be either state or federally chartered. Like savings banks, S & Ls can be either mutual or stock in form. Conversions of mutual S & Ls into stock S & Ls increased through the 1980s as more S & Ls began to seek increased capital through public offerings of stock.[38]

Historically, S & Ls were intended to engage in much the same "thrift" activities that were mentioned with respect to savings banks. These traditional activities were essentially consumer-oriented and local in character.[39] Their "main [statutory] purpose ... is the financing of homes."[40] It was recognized at least by 1951 that S & Ls "do some of the same things which banks do, ... [b]ut they do not do a general banking business."[41] This perception may be less accurate in light of the expanded powers granted to S & Ls in 1980, but in practice S & Ls remain distinct from commercial

---

35. *Huntington v. National Savings Bank,* 96 U.S. (6 Otto) at 394 (emphasis in original).

36. *Hannon v. Williams,* 34 N.J.Eq. 255, 258 (1881) (emphasis in original).

37. The original object of savings banks was said to be:

to receive and safely invest the savings of mechanics, laborers, servants, minors and others, thus affording to such persons the advantages of security and interest for their money, and in this way ameliorating the condition of the poor and laboring classes by engendering habits of industry and frugality.

Id.

38. *Task Group Report* at 22 n.12.

39. *See, e.g.,* 12 U.S.C.A. § 1464(a) (authorizing federally chartered savings associations "for the deposit of funds and for the extension of credit for homes and other goods and services").

40. *State v. Minnesota Fed. Sav. & Loan Ass'n,* 218 Minn. 229, 239, 15 N.W.2d 568, 574 (1944).

41. *North Arlington Nat'l Bank v. Kearny Fed. Sav. & L. Ass'n,* 187 F.2d 564 (3d Cir.1951). *Cf. Connecticut Nat'l Bank,* 418 U.S. at 663–666, 94 S.Ct. at 2793–2795 (1974) (holding thrifts not part of banking market).

banks. They are still charged with their original statutory purpose of fulfilling the community needs for local savings associations.

(d) *Credit unions.* Credit unions[42] may be either state or federally chartered.[43] The first credit union was organized in Germany in the mid–1800s.[44] St. Mary's Bank was the first credit union organized in the United States, chartered by Massachusetts shortly before the enactment of that state's general credit union statute, the first in the United States.[45] By the early 1930s, some 38 states had enacted credit union laws.[46] In 1932, Congress had passed a credit union statute for the District of Columbia,[47] and in 1934 the first federal credit union statute was enacted.[48]

Today credit unions are cooperative associations created to promote thrift among its members. The membership of a credit union is limited to individuals who have a "common bond" of association, occupation or residence in a well defined geographical area.[49] The nature of the common bond is usually identified in the charter of the credit union.

§ 1.11   Regulators

(a) *The Comptroller of the Currency.* The Comptroller of the Currency, the oldest extant federal bank regulator, is the administrator of the national banks chartered by him/her under the National Bank Act ("NBA").[1] The Comptroller and his/her Office ("OCC") constitute a bureau of the Department of the Treasury,[2] and the OCC is responsible for the administration of virtually all federal laws applicable to national banks, including all banks operating in the District of Columbia.[3]

The Comptroller, as the statutory official empowered by the

42. For general discussion of the nature and operations of credit unions, see *State v. Minnesota Fed. Sav. & Loan Ass'n*, 218 Minn. 229, 15 N.W.2d 568 (1944).

43. For definitions of "federal credit union" and "state" or "state-chartered credit union" see 12 U.S.C.A. § 1752(1), (6).

44. *See Barany v. Buller*, 670 F.2d 726, 733 (7th Cir.1982) (discussing history of credit unions).

45. *La Caisse Populaire Ste.–Marie v. United States*, 425 F.Supp. 512, 515 (D.N.H.1976), *aff'd*, 563 F.2d 505 (1st Cir.1977).

46. *See Barany*, 670 F.2d at 733.

47. *See* S. Rep. No. 555, 73d Cong., 2d Sess. 2 (1934) (discussing credit union statutes).

48. Pub. L. No. 73–467, 48 Stat. 1216 (1934).

49. *National Credit Union Admin. v. First Nat'l Bank & Trust Co.*, 522 U.S. 479, 118 S.Ct. 927 (1998). Legislation has expanded the common bond requirement, overriding *First National. See* Credit Union Membership Access Act, Pub. L. No. 105–219, Aug. 7, 1998, 112 Stat. 913 (1998) (codified at scattered sections of 12 U.S.C.A.)

§ 1.11

1. U.S.C.A. §§ 1 *et seq.*

2. 12 U.S.C.A. §§ 1, 2.

3. 12 U.S.C.A. § 1813(q)(1).

NBA,[4] is given personal authority under the Act. In terms of organizational structure, the central office is the Washington, D.C., headquarters of the OCC. The field organization of the OCC consists of six district offices covering the United States and its territories and dependencies.[5] In addition to the district offices, there are some 23 field offices located in major financial centers throughout the districts.[6]

The approval of the Comptroller is required for practically any significant action to be taken by a national bank, including among other things chartering, establishment of branches, changes in corporate control or in the structure of the organization.[7] In addition, the Comptroller has supervisory authority over the day-to-day activities of national banks, including loan and investment policies, trust activities, issuance of securities, and the like. These supervisory responsibilities are carried out, for the most part, through periodic on-site examinations of the banks by national bank examiners. While it is true that the Gramm–Leach–Bliley Act ("GLBA")[8] gives the Board of Governors of the Federal Reserve System the role of "umbrella supervisor" of bank holding companies ("BHCs") and their subsidiaries,[9] the Comptroller is still authorized to adopt "prudential safeguards" governing transactions between a national bank and its BHC or other subsidiaries and affiliates, to avoid, *inter alia*, significant risk to the safety and soundness of the institution.[10]

In addition, under the GLBA, the Comptroller is charged with the responsibility of regulating the financial services activities of subsidiaries of national banks,[11] the privacy of nonpublic personal information of customers of national banks,[12] and consumer protection with respect to insurance sales by national banks,[13] among other things. Effective 20 July 2011,[14] the OCC will succeed to all authority and functions of the Office of Thrift Supervision (OTS),

4. 12 U.S.C.A. §§ 2, 26.

5. 12 C.F.R. § 4.5(a).

6. 12 C.F.R. § 4.5(b).

7. *But cf. American Ins. Ass'n v. Clarke*, 865 F.2d 278 (D.C.Cir.1988) (discussing division of authority between OCC and Fed over certain corporate transactions).

8. Pub. L. No. 106–102, Nov. 12, 1999, 113 Stat. 1338 (1999) (codified at scattered sections of 12, 15, 16, 18 U.S.C.A.) ("GLBA").

9. GLBA, § 113 (codified at 12 U.S.C.A. § 1848a). On the Board's "umbrella supervisor" role, see text and accompanying notes 34–36, *infra*.

10. *Id.*, § 114 (codified at 12 U.S.C.A. § 1828a).

11. GLBA, § 121 (codified at 12 U.S.C. § 24a).

12. GLBA, §§ 501–505, 506(c) 507–509 (codified at 15 U.S.C. §§ 6801–6809).

13. GLBA, § 305 (codified at 12 U.S.C. § 1831x).

14. DFA § 312(b)(2)()(ii) (codified at 12 U.S.C. § 5412(b)(2)(B)(ii)). This effective date is the day before the "transfer date" of OTS powers and functions. DFA §§ 311(a), 312(a) (codified at 12 U.S.C. §§ 5411(a), 5412(a)). The effective date may be extended under certain specified circumstances. 12 U.S.C. § 5411(b). Technical details of the transfer are handled by DFA §§ 302, 312(a)–(b), 317, 319, 322–327.

and its director, with respect to federal savings associations[15] and all rulemaking authority of the OTS and its director with respect to savings associations.[16]

Courts have generally accorded a high degree of deference to the Comptroller's decisions under the NBA and other statutory authority.[17] In *Association of Data Processing Service Organizations v. Camp*,[18] the Supreme Court held that the Comptroller's decisions were subject to judicial review under the Administrative Procedure Act ("APA"). According to *Camp v. Pitts*,[19] the appropriate standard for this review is whether the Comptroller's actions are "arbitrary, capricious, an abuse of discretion, or otherwise not in accordance with law."[20] In applying that standard, the focal point is the extant administrative record, not a *de novo* record made by the reviewing court. However, neither the NBA nor the APA requires the Comptroller to hold a hearing or to make formal findings on the hearing record when passing on applications.[21] Hence, the APA "substantial evidence" test cannot be the appropriate standard of judicial review, since this standard is only appropriate in cases involving the review of findings on a hearing record.[22] Similarly, it is not open to a reviewing court to examine the administrative action *de novo* to decide whether the action was "unwarranted by the facts."[23]

15. DFA § 312(b)(2)(B)(i)(I) (codified at 12 U.S.C. § 5412(b)(2)(B)(i)(I)).

16. DFA § 312(b)(2)(B)(i)(II) (codified at 12 U.S.C, § 5412(b)(2)(B)(i)(II)).

17. *See generally* Scott, *In Quest of Reason: The Licensing Decisions of the Federal Banking Agencies*, 42 U. Chi. L. Rev. 235, 268 (1975) (noting limited judicial review of Comptroller's decisions).

18. 397 U.S. 150, 90 S.Ct. 827 (1970).

19. 411 U.S. 138, 93 S.Ct. 1241 (1973).

20. 5 U.S.C.A. § 706(2)(A); *Camp v. Pitts*, 411 U.S. at 142, 93 S.Ct. at 1244. Cf. *Washington v. Office of Comptroller of Currency*, 856 F.2d 1507, 1511 (11th Cir.1988) (*citing Camp*; reviewing denial of hearing on merger application on "arbitrary, capricious" standard); *American Council of Life Ins. v. Ludwig*, 1 F.Supp.2d 24, 29 (D.D.C.1998), *vac'd and remanded as moot*, 194 F.3d 173 (D.C.Cir.1999) (upholding OCC approval of conversion of state-chartered bank to national bank and allowing converted bank to retain nonconforming insurance subsidiaries as "reasonable"); *McQueen v. Williams*, 177 F.3d 523 (6th Cir.1999)

(reviewing question of law in challenged state-to-federal conversion and relocation of home office *de novo*).

21. *See, e.g.*, 12 U.S.C.A. § 26, which appears to contemplate an *ex parte* investigation by the Comptroller of charter applications. As to the APA, the requirement of a written statement of "findings and conclusions, and the reasons or basis therefor," 5 U.S.C.A. § 557(c)(3)(A), applies only to rulemaking proceedings, *id*. § 553, and to adjudications "required by statute to be determined on the record after opportunity for an agency hearing." *Id*. § 554(a). These APA requirements are not apposite to a charter application under the NBA, since the Act does not require agency hearings in that context. *Camp*, 411 U.S. at 141 n.3, 93 S.Ct. at 1243 n.3.

22. 5 U.S.C.A. § 706(2)(E). *See Camp*, 411 U.S. at 141, 93 S.Ct. at 1243 (discussing review standard).

23. 5 U.S.C.A. § 706(2)(F). *See Camp*, 411 U.S. at 141–142, 93 S.Ct. at 1244 (*citing Citizens to Preserve Overton Park v. Volpe*, 401 U.S. 402, 415, 91 S.Ct. 814 (1971)).

Camp has set the basic approach used in judicial review of all depository institutions regulators. *Camp* has widely been interpreted as severely limiting judicial review of the Comptroller's decisions.[24] Still, the case put to rest the traditional argument that the Comptroller's discretion in charter decisions was subject to no judicial review.[25] *Camp* also suggests that the Comptroller and other OCC officials may be required to submit proof in the form not only of affidavits, but also of testimony subject to cross-examination.[26] The ultimate remedy in such cases is to vacate the agency action and remand to the Comptroller for further consideration.[27] The burden on the party seeking even this limited relief is still particularly difficult to meet.[28]

(b) *The Board of Governors of the Federal Reserve System.* The Federal Reserve Act of 1913[29] created a system of federal reserve banks, each acting in effect as a central bank for its geographical region, and overseen by the Board of Governors of the Federal Reserve System ("the Fed") located in Washington, D.C. This "Federal Reserve System" consists of the Fed and its staff, the twelve Federal Reserve Banks, the Federal Open Market Committee ("FOMC"), the Federal Advisory Council ("FAC"), and the commercial banks which are members of the Federal Reserve System ("member banks"). The Fed, the twelve Reserve Banks and the FOMC have policymaking responsibilities.

The Fed is primarily charged with the responsibility of implementing monetary and credit policy applicable to the financial

24. *See, e.g.*, Scott at 265–268, and cases cited therein.

25. For examples of judicial statements suggesting that the Comptroller's discretionary determinations were beyond judicial review, see *Baltimore & O. R. Co. v. Smith*, 56 F.2d 799 (3d Cir. 1932); *Cooper v. O'Connor*, 99 F.2d 135 (D.C.Cir.1938); *Myers v. Coffey*, 124 F.2d 396 (6th Cir.1941); *United States Nat'l Bank of La Grande v. Pole*, 2 F.Supp. 153 (D.Ore.1932). *Cf.* Stokes, *Public Convenience and Advantage in Applications for New Banks and Branches*, 74 Banking L.J. 921, 930 (1957) ("Well informed opinion is that there is no right of appeal from a decision of the Comptroller of the Currency."); Scott at 258 (noting Comptroller's arguments to this effect as late as mid–1960s). *But see American Council of Life Ins.*, 1 F. Supp.2d at 27–28, 30 (rejecting OCC argument that discretionary approval of conversion of state-chartered bank to national bank was not reviewable, but

upholding approval as not "arbitrary, capricious or an abuse of discretion").

26. *Camp* states:

If ... there was such a failure to explain administrative action as to frustrate effective judicial review, the remedy was not to hold a *de novo* hearing but ... to obtain from the agency, *either through affidavits or testimony, such additional explanation of the reasons for the agency decision as may prove necessary.*

411 U.S. at 142–143, 93 S.Ct. at 1244 (emphasis added).

27. *Camp*, 411 U.S. at 143, 93 S.Ct. at 1244 (*citing Securities and Exch. Comm'n v. Chenery Corp.*, 318 U.S. 80, 63 S.Ct. 454 (1943)).

28. *See, e.g., Klanke v. Camp*, 327 F.Supp. 592, 593–594 (S.D.Tex.1971) (noting difficulties).

29. 38 Stat. 251 (1913) (codified at 12 U.S.C.A. §§ 221 *et seq.*).

system and maintaining monetary and credit growth.[30] The Fed also administers federal laws concerning the reserves required to be held by all depository institutions against their deposits.[31]

The Fed does not perform a chartering function,[32] but it does have supervisory and examination functions with respect to state-chartered member banks. In addition, certain specialized regulatory functions have also been given to it. For example, since 1956, the Fed has had primary responsibility for the administration of federal laws regulating the formation and operation of bank holding companies.[33] Since 1960, it has been charged with the administration of the Bank Merger Act in mergers in which the acquiring, assuming or resulting bank is a state-chartered member bank.[34] In addition, since 1964 the Fed has had responsibility for the administration of the Securities Exchange Act of 1934 ("1934 Act")[35] with respect to securities issued by state-chartered member banks.[36]

In 1999 the GLBA gave the Fed the added role of "umbrella supervisor" of BHCs.[37] The Fed may require any BHC or subsidiary thereof to submit reports regarding its financial condition, systems for monitoring and controlling financial and operating risks, transactions with depository institutions, and compliance with the Bank Holding Company Act (BHCA)[38] or other federal laws that the Fed has specific jurisdiction to enforce. The Fed is authorized to examine each holding company and its subsidiaries, including functionally regulated subsidiaries under limited circumstances.[39] The GLBA also charged the Fed with the responsibility of regulating the privacy of nonpublic personal information of customers of bank holding companies, "financial holding companies" ("FHCs"), diversified holding companies involved in a wide range of financial services activities, and state-chartered banks that are members of the Federal Reserve System,[40] and consumer protection with re-

---

30. *See, e.g.,* 12 U.S.C.A. §§ 225a, 461(b)(4)(A)(i).

31. 12 U.S.C.A. § 461. This authority was expanded to apply fully to the required reserves of all depository institutions by March 1988. 12 U.S.C.A. § 461(b)(8). *See* Pub. L. 96–221, Mar. 31, 1980, § 108, 94 Stat. 132, 141 (effective date provisions).

32. *But see* 12 U.S.C.A. § 611 (Fed chartering of "Edge Act" corporations, specializing in international and foreign banking).

33. 12 U.S.C.A. §§ 1841 *et seq.*

34. 12 U.S.C.A. § 1828(c)(2)(B).

35. 15 U.S.C.A. §§ 78a *et seq.*

36. 15 U.S.C.A. § 78*l*(i).

37. GLBA, § 113 (codified at 12 U.S.C.A. § 1848a). The Comptroller of the Currency has taken the position that the "umbrella supervisor" role of the Fed is a significantly limited one, requiring deference to primary bank regulator to the fullest extent possible. *Comptroller Pokes Holes in Fed's Umbrella,* Am. Banker, July 28, 2000, at 2, col. 2.

38. 12 U.S.C.A. §§ 1841 *et seq.* The BHCA is discussed in detail in Chapters 4 and 6, *infra.*

39. 12 U.S.C.A. § 1848a.

40. GLBA, §§ 501–505, 506(c) 507–509 (codified at 15 U.S.C. §§ 6801–6809).

spect to insurance sales by such entities,[41] among other things. Effective 20 July 2011,[42] the Fed will succeed to all functions of the OTS and its director with respect to the supervision of all savings and loan holding companies and all non-depository subsidiaries of such companies.[43] It also succeeds to all rulemaking authority of the OTS and its director with respect to savings and loan holding companies.[44] In addition, the Fed succeeds to the rulemaking authority of the OTS and its director under the Home Owners Loan Act (HOLA) § 11[45] with respect to affiliate transactions and extensions of credit to insiders, and under HOLA § 5(q)[46] with respect to tying arrangements.[47]

The Fed is a collegial body of seven members, appointed by the President with Senate confirmation.[48] Each member of the Fed is appointed for a term of fourteen years, staggered so that one member's term expires every two years.[49]

The Reserve Banks are separate quasi-governmental corporate entities, the stockholders of which are its member banks. Each Reserve Bank operates within its own geographic district. Each has a board of nine directors, classified according to statutory criteria.[50] Three are bankers elected by the reserve bank's member banks, three are nonbankers, representing the public but elected by the member banks "with due but not exclusive consideration to the interests of agriculture, commerce, industry, services, labor and consumers,"[51] and three are appointed by the Fed.[52] By designation of the Fed Chairman, one of the appointed directors serves as chairman of the Reserve Bank's board of directors, and another as deputy chairman.[53] The nine directors serve three-year terms, staggered so that the terms of three directors, one from each of class, expire each year.[54]

The FOMC consists of the seven Fed board members and five representatives from the Reserve Banks.[55] The legitimacy of the

41. GLBA, § 305 (codified at 12 U.S.C. § 1831x).

42. DFA § 312(b)(1)(B) (codified at 12 U.S.C. § 5412(b)(1)(B)).

43. DFA § 312(b)(1)(A)(i)(I)–(II) (codified at 12 U.S.C. § 5412(b)(1)(A)(i)(I)–(II)).

44. DFA § 312(b)(1)(A)(ii) (codified at 12 U.S.C, § 5412(b)(1)(A)(ii)).

45. 12 U.S.C. § 1468.

46. *Id.* § 1464(q).

47. DFA § 312(b)(2)(A) (codified at 12 U.S.C. § 5412(b)(2)(A)).

48. 12 U.S.C.A. § 241.

49. 12 U.S.C.A. § 242.

50. 12 U.S.C.A. § 302.

51. 12 U.S.C.A. § 304.

52. 12 U.S.C.A. § 305. None of the three appointed directors may be a director, officer or employee of a bank. *Id.* § 303. However, the director designated by the Fed as chairman must "be a person of tested banking experience." *Id.* § 305.

53. *Id.* § 305.

54. *Id.* § 308.

55. *Id.* § 263(a). On the history, structure and operations of the FOMC, see *FOMC v. Merrill*, 443 U.S. 340, 343–347, 99 S.Ct. 2800, 2803–2805 (1979); *Committee for Monetary Reform v.*

FOMC has been subjected to repeated, unsuccessful constitutional attacks, because of the selection of the five reserve bank representatives without appointment by the president and advice and consent of the Senate as provided in the Constitution's appointments clause.[56] One challenge, brought by a member of the U.S. House of Representatives, was held to lack standing to maintain the action either as a legislator or private bondholder.[57] A similar challenge, brought by a senator, was held not necessarily to fail on standing grounds,[58] but was dismissed under the court's equitable discretion to dismiss on the grounds that judicial action would improperly interfere with the legislative process.[59] A third challenge, brought by the Committee for Monetary Reform, a group of private businesses and individuals, was subsequently dismissed on alternative standing grounds.[60]

The last challenge to the FOMC, again instituted by a senator, initially survived the standing question.[61] The district court declined to apply the doctrine of equitable discretion.[62] However, on the merits of the appointments clause challenge, the district court held that the selection of the five reserve bank representatives of the FOMC was constitutional, because open market trading activities could validly be delegated by Congress to private individuals.[63] On appeal, the D.C. Circuit affirmed, but on other grounds. The court rejected the district court's reading of the doctrine of equitable discretion.[64] Instead, the court relied upon the doctrine, in light of its understanding of the "separation-of-powers concerns informing the doctrine of equitable discretion."[65] The district court's opinion was vacated, and its dismissal of the action affirmed on the grounds that "if a legislator could obtain substantial relief from his fellow legislators through the legislative process itself, then it is an abuse of discretion for a court to entertain the legislator's action."[66]

Board of Governors, 766 F.2d 538, 539–540 (D.C.Cir.1985); *Riegle v. FOMC*, 656 F.2d 873, 874–876 (D.C.Cir.), *cert. denied*, 454 U.S. 1082, 102 S.Ct. 636 (1981); *Reuss v. Balles*, 584 F.2d 461, 462–464 (D.C.Cir.), *cert. denied*, 439 U.S. 997, 99 S.Ct. 598 (1978).

56. U.S. Const. art. II, § 2, cl. 2.

57. *Reuss*, 584 F.2d at 469.

58. *See Riegle*, 656 F.2d at 877–879.

59. *Id*. at 881 (finding congressional plaintiff could obtain substantial relief from legislative colleagues).

60. *Committee for Monetary Reform*, 766 F.2d at 542–543 (failure to show economic harm caused by alleged constitutional violation); *id*. at 543–544 (separation-of-powers harm not involved

where plaintiffs not directly subject to authority of challenged agency).

61. *Melcher v. Federal Open Market Committee*, 644 F.Supp. 510, 513–514 (D.D.C.1986), *affirmed on other grounds*, 836 F.2d 561 (D.C.Cir.1987), *cert. denied*, 486 U.S. 1042, 108 S.Ct. 2034 (1988).

62. *Melcher*, 644 F.Supp. at 514–517 (noting post-*Riegle* law of standing substantially changed in light of *Comm. for Monetary Reform*).

63. *Id*. at 522–523.

64. *Melcher*, 836 F.2d at 563–564.

65. *Id*. at 564.

66. *Id*. at 565 (footnote omitted). *See generally* Note, *The Federal Open Market Committee and the Sharing of Gov-*

The FOMC directs the Fed's purchases and sales of U.S. government securities and other obligations in the public securities markets (*i.e.*, the open market).[67] The activities of the FOMC are intended to affect the relative availability of credit in the banking system by direct participation in the market,[68] that is, by competing for liquid assets through sales of securities, or by infusing liquid assets into the system through purchases of securities.

The FAC consists of one representative from each of the twelve Reserve Banks, selected by the boards of the Reserve Banks to serve one-year terms.[69] The FAC advises the Fed on current business conditions and makes recommendations concerning matters of concern to the Federal Reserve System as a whole.[70] These recommendations are advisory, and the FAC is not part of the supervisory apparatus of the System.

The member banks include all national banks in the continental United States,[71] as required by law,[72] and those state-chartered banks and trust companies which have chosen to apply for, and have received, membership.[73]

Much of the day-to-day supervisory and examination responsibilities of the Fed are carried out by the staff of the Fed and the Reserve Banks. The field organization of the Fed consists of the twelve Reserve Banks and the Federal Reserve Agents. Though the Reserve Banks are separate corporate entities, they do operate under the general supervision of the Fed. Thus, in many situations, the Reserve Banks will act as the Fed's field representatives in their respective districts and assist in the implementation, at the field level, of the Fed's regulations and policies.

Decisions by the Fed to grant or deny an application for membership, or to approve any proposed activity subject to its statutory authority, are committed to its discretion, and courts accord a significant degree of deference to the Fed's decisions.[74] Nevertheless, the Fed's decisions are subject, in accordance with

ernmental Power with Private Citizens, 75 Va. L. Rev. 111 (1989) (discussing case law).

67. 12 U.S.C.A. §§ 263(b), 355(2).

68. 12 C.F.R. § 270.3.

69. 12 U.S.C.A. § 261.

70. 12 U.S.C.A. § 262.

71. 12 U.S.C.A. § 221.

72. 12 U.S.C.A. § 222.

73. 12 U.S.C.A. § 321.

74. *See, e.g., Board of Governors v. Investment Co. Inst.*, 450 U.S. 46, 101 S.Ct. 973 (1981) (upholding Fed's authorization of holding company affiliates to act as investment advisers to closed-end investment companies); *Securities Industry Ass'n v. Board of Governors*, 468 U.S. 207, 104 S.Ct. 3003 (1984) (upholding Fed authorization of acquisition of discount brokerage firm by bank holding company); *First Bank & Trust Co. v. Board of Governors*, 605 F.Supp. 555 (E.D.Ky.1984) (upholding Fed's interpretation of application of deposit reserve provisions). *But see Securities Industry Ass'n v. Board of Governors*, 468 U.S. 137, 104 S.Ct. 2979 (1984) (*SIA I*) (rejecting Fed's "post hoc rationalizations" as "entitled to little deference").

Camp to judicial review under the APA, and its actions must be supported by adequate reasoning.[75] The standard of judicial review for the Fed's discretionary decisions is whether the Fed's actions are "arbitrary, capricious, an abuse of discretion, or otherwise not in accordance with law."[76] However, under the BHCA, the Fed's factual findings are reviewed under a "substantial evidence" standard.[77]

(c) *The Federal Deposit Insurance Corporation.* Under the Federal Deposit Insurance Act ("FDIA"), state-chartered member banks[78] as well as national banks and federally chartered savings associations[79] are required to obtain deposit insurance from the FDIC. Federal deposit insurance is optional under the FDIA for state-chartered nonmember banks and savings associations. In fact, however, virtually all state-chartered banks have opted for FDIC insurance.

The primary statutory mandate of the FDIC is to provide deposit insurance to depository institutions qualifying for insurance coverage under the FDIA. The statutory policy behind the act is discussed in *FDIC v. Philadelphia Gear Corp.*[80] *in the following terms:*

> Congress' purpose in creating the FDIC was clear. Faced with virtual panic [after the 1929 stock market collapse], Congress attempted to safeguard the hard earnings of individuals against the possibility that bank failures would deprive them of their savings. Congress passed the 1933 provisions "[i]n order to provide against a repetition of the present painful experience in which a vast sum of *assets and purchasing power* is 'tied up.'" S. Rep. No. 77, 73d Cong., 1st Sess., 12 (1933) (emphasis added). The focus of Congress was therefore upon ensuring that a deposit of "hard earnings" entrusted by individuals to a bank would not lead to a tangible loss in the event of a bank failure.[81]

Until 2006, the FDIC administered a Bank Insurance Fund ("BIF") for deposits of insured banks,[82] and a Savings Association

---

75. *See, e.g., SIA I,* 468 U.S. at 143, 104 S.Ct. at 2982; *Alabama Ass'n of Ins. Agents v. Board of Governors,* 558 F.2d 729 (5th Cir.1977); *Georgia Ass'n of Independent Ins. Agents v. Board of Governors,* 533 F.2d 224 (5th Cir.1976).

76. 5 U.S.C.A. § 706(2)(A). *See Camp,* 411 U.S. at 142, 93 S.Ct. at 1244. *See also Investment Co. Inst. v. Board of Governors,* 551 F.2d 1270 (D.C.Cir. 1977); *Marine Corp. v. Board of Governors,* 325 F.2d 960 (7th Cir.1963).

77. 12 U.S.C.A. § 1848. *See Bank of Boulder v. Board of Governors,* 535 F.2d 1221 (10th Cir.1976); *North Hills Bank v. Board of Governors,* 506 F.2d 623 (8th Cir.1974); *Gravois Bank v. Board of Governors,* 478 F.2d 546 (8th Cir.1973).

78. 12 U.S.C.A. § 329.

79. *See, e.g.,* 12 U.S.C.A. § 222.

80. 476 U.S. 426, 106 S.Ct. 1931 (1986).

81. *Id.* at 432–433, 106 S.Ct. at 1935.

82. 12 U.S.C.A. § 1821(a)(4)–(5) (2005).

Insurance Fund ("SAIF") for deposits of savings associations.[83] As of March 31, 2006, the FDIC merged the BIF and the SAIF into the new Deposit Insurance Fund (DIF), as required by the Federal Deposit Insurance Reform Act of 2005 (FDIRA).[84] Effective 20 July 2011,[85] the FDIC will succeed to all functions and authority of the Office of Thrift Supervision (OTS), and its director, not assigned to the OCC[86] or the Fed[87] with respect to state-chartered savings associations.[88] The FDIC is also given authority to supervise the resolution of any financial crisis—or "orderly liquidation"—with respect to systemically significant financial companies,[89] other than an insured depository institution.[90]

It is the responsibility of the FDIC to pay off depositors of insured institutions that are closed without sufficient assets to satisfy claims of depositors, to the extent of FDIA insurance coverage,[91] and to act as receiver for national banks and federally chartered savings associations in receivership,[92] and for state institutions in receivership where the FDIC has been appointed by the appropriate state regulatory authority.[93] The authority of the FDIC includes not only receivership powers, but also powers to take remedial action to prevent formal closing of an insured bank.[94] In addition, the FDIC is authorized under the GLBA to adopt "prudential safeguards" governing transactions between a depository institution and its BHC or other subsidiaries and affiliates to avoid, *inter alia*, significant risk to the safety and soundness of the institution.[95] This authority is not precluded by the Fed's role as "umbrella supervisor" of BHCs.[96] In addition, the GLBA charged the FDIC with the responsibility of regulating the privacy of nonpublic personal information of customers of state-chartered, FDIC-insured banks that are not members of the Federal Reserve System,[97] and consumer protection with respect to insurance sales

83. 12 U.S.C.A. § 1821(a)(4), (6) (2005).

84. Pub. L. No. 109–171, tit. II, §§ 2101–2109, 120 Stat. 4, 9–21 (Feb. 8, 2006).

85. DFA § 312(b)(1)(B) (codified at 12 U.S.C. §§ 5412(b)(1)(B)).

86. See text and accompanying notes 138–140 (discussing transfer to OCC).

87. See text and accompanying notes 166–171 (discussing transfer to Fed).

88. DFA § 312(b)(1)(A)(i)(I)–(II) (codified at 12 U.S.C. § 5412(b)(1)(A)(i)(I)–(II)).

89. DFA §§ 201–214 (codified at 12 U.S.C. §§ 4403, 5381–5394; 18 U.S.C. § 1032(1)).

90. DFA § 201(a)(8)(B) (codified at 12 U.S.C. § 5381(a)(8)(B)).

91. 12 U.S.C.A. § 1821(f).

92. *Id.* § 1821(c).

93. *Id.* § 1821(e).

94. *See, e.g., id.* § 1823(c).

95. GLBA, § 114 (codified at 12 U.S.C.A. § 1828a).

96. On the "umbrella supervisor" role, see text and accompanying notes 34–36, *supra*.

97. GLBA, §§ 501–505, 506(c) 507–509 (codified at 15 U.S.C. §§ 6801–6809).

by such banks,[98] among other things.

In terms of judicial review, there has been relatively little reported litigation challenging the FDIC's insurance decisions.[99] The FDIC's decisions are committed to the agency's discretion.[100] Nevertheless, the FDIC's administrative discretion is subject to judicial review as to whether or not it had acted in a manner that was arbitrary, capricious, an abuse of discretion or otherwise not in accordance with law.[101]

(d) *The Office of Thrift Supervision.* The Office of Thrift Supervision ("OTS") was the successor to the Federal Home Loan Bank Board ("FHLBB") and the Federal Savings and Loan Insurance Corporation ("FSLIC"), at least with respect to the federal chartering, regulation and supervision of savings associations.[102] The Director of the OTS ("DOTS") became the "appropriate Federal banking agency" with respect to any savings association or any

---

98. GLBA, § 305 (codified at 12 U.S.C. § 1831x).

99. *But cf. Magellsen v. Federal Deposit Insurance Corporation,* 341 F.Supp. 1031 (D.Mont.1972) (involving unsuccessful challenge); *James v. F.D.I.C.,* 231 F.Supp. 475 (W.D.La. 1964); *Freeling v. F.D.I.C.,* 221 F.Supp. 955 (W.D.Okla.1962), *affirmed,* 326 F.2d 971 (10th Cir.1963).

100. *See, e.g., Magellsen, supra.*

101. *Cf. Camp, supra* note 16; *Association of Data Processing Service Organizations, supra* note 9.

102. 12 U.S.C.A. § 1462a(a). For discussion of the FHLBB and the FSLIC, and the transition to the OTS in 1989, see *Olympic Federal Savings and Loan Ass'n v. Director, Office of Thrift Supervision,* 732 F.Supp. 1183 (D.D.C.1990), *appeal rendered moot,* 903 F.2d 837 (D.C.Cir.1990). The FHLBB's functions as a central bank for member savings associations (monitoring members' fiscal soundness and serving as their "lender of last resort") were not transferred to the OTS, but to the new Federal Housing Finance Board, which now administers the Federal Home Loan Bank ("FHLBank") System. 12 U.S.C.A. § 1422a. In 1999, the GLBA reformed the FHLBank System in several important respects. Among other things, mandatory FHLBank membership for federal savings associations was eliminated, in favor of a completely voluntary membership. GLBA, § 603 (codified at 12 U.S.C.A. § 1464(f).) *See* 65 Fed. Reg. 13,866 (2000) (codified at 12 C.F.R. pt. 925) (amending FHFB membership regulations). "Community financial institutions" (FDIC-insured depository institutions with assets less than $500 million) were given expanded access to FHLBank advances. GLBA, § 604(a) (codified at 12 U.S.C.A. §§ 1430(a)(1)–(6).) *See* 65 Fed. Reg. at 13,866 (codified at 12 C.F.R. pt. 950) (amending FHFB advances regulations), *adopted as final rule,* 65 Fed. Reg. 40,979 (2000) (codified at 12 C.F.R. pts. 925, 950); 65 Fed. Reg. 44,414 (2000) (codified at 12 C.F.R. pts. 900, 917, 926, 944, 950, 952, 961, 980) (amending FHFB advances and related regulations). Governance of the FHLBanks was decentralized from the FHFB to the individual FHLBanks. GLBA, § 606 (codified at 12 U.S.C.A. §§ 250, 1422b(a)(5)–(7), 1427(a), (d), (g), (i)(1)–(2), 1429, 1430(c)–(d), 1432(a)–(b), 1436(a); striking 1438(b)(4); repealing 12 U.S.C.A. §§ 1442a, 1447). The GLBA also established a new capital structure for the FHLBanks. GLBA, § 608 (codified at 12 U.S.C.A. § 1426). *See* 65 Fed. Reg. 43,408 (2000) (to be codified at 12 C.F.R. pts. 917, 925, 930–933, 956, 960) (proposing new capital requirements for FHLBanks). For analysis of the new FHFB capital structure mandated by the GLBA, see U.S. General Accounting Office, *Federal Home Loan Bank System: Establishment of a New Capital Structure* (GAO 01–873, July 20, 2001), *available at* 2001 WL 845817.

savings and loan holding company.[103] Under DFA § 313,[104] the OTS and the position of the DOTS are scheduled to be abolished. This dramatic event is effective 90 days after the "transfer date"[105]—21 July 2011—on which the functions and authority of the DOTS and the OTS are first exercised by the other federal regulators.[106]

Until the transition occurs and the abolishment is effected, the DOTS has the authority to charter federal savings associations[107] and is responsible for the examination, safe and sound operation and regulation of such entities.[108] The DOTS has specific enforcement authority with respect to the chartering and permitted activities of federally chartered savings associations,[109] as well as general enforcement authority under the provisions of section 8 of the FDIA.[110] The DOTS has exclusive power and jurisdiction to appoint a conservator or receiver for a federally chartered savings association.[111] The DOTS is also authorized to promulgate regulations for the reorganization, consolidation, liquidation and dissolution of savings associations, for mergers between insured savings associations,[112] and for savings associations in conservatorship or receivership and the conduct thereof.[113] In addition, under statutorily specified grounds, the DOTS has the power and jurisdiction to appoint a conservator or receiver for an insured state-chartered savings association.[114]

Despite significant structural changes introduced in 1989,[115] much of the substance of federal regulation of the thrift industry remains in large part the same.[116] Hence, the prior case law examin-

103. 12 U.S.C.A. § 1813(q)(4).

104. DFA § 313 (codified at 12 U.S.C. § 5413).

105. *Id.* §§ 311(a), 313 (codified at 12 U.S.C. §§ 5411(a), 5413).

106. See *id.* § 312(b) (codified at 12 U.S.C. § 5412(b)) (mandating transfer of functions).

107. 12 U.S.C.A. § 1464(a).

108. 12 U.S.C.A. § 1463(a)(1). On examinations, see 12 U.S.C.A. § 1464(d)(1)(B). As to safety and soundness supervision, the Home Owner's Loan Act specifies that "[a]ll regulations and policies of the [DOTS] governing safe and sound operation of savings associations ... shall be no less stringent than those established by the Comptroller of the Currency for national banks." 12 U.S.C.A. § 1463(c).

109. 12 U.S.C.A. § 1464(d)(1)(A).

110. 12 U.S.C.A. § 1818.

111. 12 U.S.C.A. § 1464(d)(2)(E)(ii).

112. 12 U.S.C.A. § 1828(c)(8).

113. 12 U.S.C.A. § 1464(d)(3)(A). In cases where the FDIC is the conservator or receiver, DOTS regulations must be consistent with regulations prescribed by the FDIC. 12 U.S.C.A. § 1464(d)(3)(B).

114. 12 U.S.C.A. § 1464(d)(2)(C). Written approval of the state official with jurisdiction over the insured association, indicating that one or more of the statutory grounds exists, is generally necessary for the exercise of this authority by the DOTS. 12 U.S.C.A. § 1464(d)(2)(D)(i). *But cf.* 12 U.S.C.A. § 1464(d)(2)(D)(ii) (authority of DOTS to proceed with appointment under certain circumstances).

115. Financial Institutions Reform, Recovery, and Enforcement Act of 1989 ("FIRREA"), Pub. L. No. 101–73, 103 Stat. 183 (1989).

116. *See* FIRREA, §§ 401(f) (savings provisions relating to FSLIC), 401(g) (savings provisions relating to FHLBB), 401(h)–(i) (continuation under DOTS of

ing the authority of the FHLBB continues to be pertinent, at least by analogy, to questions concerning the authority of the DOTS.[117]

(e) *The National Credit Union Administration.* Federal credit unions are granted their charters by the authority of the National Credit Union Administration ("NCUA").[118] The federal credit union system is an integrated system of regulation in which the chartering, insuring, supervisory and "central bank" functions are all the responsibility of the NCUA and its constitutive units.[119]

Insurance of the accounts of credit union members, both state and federally chartered, is provided by the Administrator of the NCUA. Insurance is required for federally chartered credit unions, voluntary in the case of state-chartered credit unions.

Since 1978, the National Credit Union Central Liquidity Facility ("CLF") has assisted credit unions experiencing liquidity problems by granting them loans. Such liquidity assistance is a central bank function. Within the credit union system, it is performed by the CLF, a unit of the NCUA.

The NCUA consists of the NCUA Board, located in Washington, D.C., six regional offices, and the CLF.[120] The NCUA Board is a collegial body of three members.[121] They are appointed by the President with the confirmation of the Senate.[122] The term of each member is six years, staggered so that one member's term expires every two years.[123] One member is designated by the President as Chairman of the NCUA Board, and one as Vice Chairman.[124]

The Credit Union Membership Access Act (CUMAA),[125] enacted in August 1998, added appointment criteria with respect to presidential appointments to the NCUA Board.[126] The president must "give consideration to" individuals with education, training or experience related to financial services, financial services regulation, or financial policy.[127] However, no more than one member of the NCUA Board may be appointed from among individuals who, at

---

orders, resolutions, determinations and regulations of FSLIC and FHLBB), 402(a)–(b) (continuation and coordination of certain regulations).

117. *Cf., e.g., Federal Home Loan Bank Bd. v. Rowe,* 284 F.2d 274 (D.C.Cir.1960) (upholding FHLBB chartering decision).

118. 12 U.S.C.A. § 1753.

119. For the official description of the NCUA and its structure, see 67 Fed. Reg. 30,772 (2002) (codified at 12 C.F.R. §§ 790.2(b)(4), (b)(7)–(9), (b)(11), (b)(13), 792.50(a)–(b), 792.51(a)–(d), 792.54(a), 792.69(a); *removing* 790.2(b)(3), (b)(15); *redesignating*

790.2(b)(4)–(14) as (b)(3)–(13); redesignating 790.2(b)(16) as (b)(14)).

120. 12 C.F.R. § 790.2.

121. 12 U.S.C.A. § 1752a(b).

122. 12 U.S.C.A. § 1752a(b).

123. 12 U.S.C.A. § 1752a(c).

124. 12 U.S.C.A. § 1752a(b).

125. Pub. L. No. 105–219, 112 Stat. 913 (1998).

126. CUMAA, § 204(2), 112 Stat. 913, 922–923 (codified at 12 U.S.C. § 1752a(b)(2)).

127. *Id.,* § 204(2), 112 Stat. at 922–923 (codified at 12 U.S.C. § 1752a(b)(2)(A)).

the time of appointment are or have recently been a committee member, director, officer, employee or institution-affiliated party of an insured credit union.[128]

The members of the NCUA Board also serve as the Board of Directors of the CLF.[129] The Board of Directors is assisted in managing the CLF by the President of the CLF, appointed by the Board, and the NCUA staff.[130] The CLF is also assisted in its operations by "central credit unions,"[131] CLF member credit unions designated as "Agent members."[132] When acting as Agent members, these central credit unions function as rough equivalents of the Federal Reserve Banks, performing "central bank" services on a regional basis for credit unions that do not have direct access to the CLF.[133]

The range of discretionary decisions committed to the NCUA is rather broad. Judicial review of these discretionary decisions is "necessarily limited."[134] The reasoning of *Camp* has been held applicable to these discretionary decisions.[135] Accordingly, the standard of judicial review for such decisions is whether the NCUA's action is "arbitrary, capricious, an abuse of discretion or otherwise not in accordance with law."[136]

(f) *State Regulators.* State regulators of depository institutions play a major role as chartering authorities for commercial banks, savings associations and credit unions within their respective jurisdictions.[137] They also supervise and examine these state-chartered institutions.[138]

128. *Id.*, § 204(2), 112 Stat. at 923 (codified at 12 U.S.C. § 1752a(b)(2)(B)).

129. 12 U.S.C.A. § 1795b.

130. 12 U.S.C.A. § 1795f(a).

131. *See* 12 C.F.R. § 725.2(d) (defining "central credit union" as credit union primarily serving other credit unions).

132. *See* 12 C.F.R. § 790.2(d)(1). Regular and Agent membership in the CLF requires, *inter alia*, subscription to CLF capital stock. 12 C.F.R. §§ 725.3(a)(2), 725.4(a)(2).

133. 12 C.F.R. § 790.2(d)(1).

134. *National Alliance of Postal and Fed. Emp. v. Nickerson*, 424 F.Supp. 323, 325–326 (D.D.C.1976), *citing Rowe*, 284 F.2d at 277–278; *Sterling National Bank of Davie v. Camp*, 431 F.2d 514, 516 (5th Cir.1970). *Cf. Massachusetts Credit Union Share Ins. Corp. v. NCUA*, 693 F.Supp. 1225 (D.D.C.1988) (examining state-chartered credit union insurance cooperative advertisement of "federally insured" accounts).

135. *Nat. Alliance of Postal and Fed. Emp.*, 424 F.Supp. at 326, *citing Camp* and *Overton Park*.

136. 5 U.S.C.A. § 706(2)(A). *See National Alliance of Postal and Fed. Emp.*, 424 F.Supp. at 326–328. *See also Camp*, 411 U.S. at 142, 93 S.Ct. at 1244.

137. Within the District of Columbia, most roles typically performed by state regulatory authorities have been performed by federal regulators. Thus, the Comptroller of the Currency exercises general authority to charter, examine and supervise banks in the District. D.C. Code Ann. §§ 26–101, 26–102, 26–103(b) (1981). The OTS has performed these functions with respect to savings associations in the District. D.C. Code §§ 26–103(c), 26–504(a)–(b), 26–505. *Cf.* D.C. Code §§ 26–601, 26–602 (NCUA approval of credit union conversions).

138. Because of their role in the examination of depository institutions, the view of state regulators is represented within the Federal Financial Institu-

The organizational structures of the state regulators are varied. However, certain general characteristics can be identified. Two basic patterns are evident. A bare majority of the states uses a relatively specialized regulator to supervise all or specified types of depository institutions.[139] The regulator may be an individual "commissioner," "superintendent" or similar official, operating independently or with the advice or general oversight of a board or commission. Alternatively, the regulator may be a collegial body—a "department," "board" or similar body—with an individual official designated as chair or chief executive officer.

A substantial minority of states places regulatory authority for all or specified types of depository institutions in an official or collegial body that is a constituent unit of a larger, less specialized department or division of the state government.[140] The larger department or division may have overall responsibility for corporations, commerce and industry, or the like.

tions Examination Council ("FFIEC"), which coordinates federal examination policies. *See* 12 U.S.C.A. § 3306 (mandating state liaison with FFIEC). In addition, since 1996 state banking views must be represented on the FDIC Board of Directors. 12 U.S.C.A. § 1812(a)(1)(C) (requiring appointment of one FDIC director with "State bank supervisory experience").

139. *See, e.g.,* Ala. Code §§ 5–2A–1 *et seq.* (applying to all institutions); Ariz. Rev. Stat. Ann. §§ 6–110 *et seq.* (finan-

cial institutions); Ark. Stat. Ann. §§ 23–46–205 (financial institutions; banks); Cal. Fin. Code §§ 200, 210–217 (establishing Commissioner of Financial Institutions and Department of Financial Institutions).

140. *See, e.g.,* Alaska Stat. §§ 06.05.005–06.05.075 (financial institutions, subsidiaries and affiliates); La. Rev. Stat. Ann. §§ 6:101–6:103 (financial institutions).

Chapter 2

ENTRY RULES

Table of Sections

§ 2.1   Introduction

In this chapter we examine basic rules that govern initial entry into the depository industry. The typical entry event is the "chartering" or establishment of the entity. In this regard the chapter looks in succession at the rules applicable to the chartering of national and state banks, of federal and state savings associations, and of federal and state credit unions.

We then turn our attention to typical secondary entry restrictions that accompany chartering. The chapter examines deposit insurance, which under federal law is optional for state-chartered depository institutions. However, as a practical matter, deposit insurance is a necessity for almost all depository institutions. The chapter also examines bank membership in the Federal Reserve System, which is optional in the case of state-chartered banks.

Conversions represent another form of "entry." What is involved here is not entry into the industry itself, but rather the

43

transfer from one jurisdictionally distinct sector of the industry (*e.g.*, state-chartered banks) into another jurisdictional sector (*e.g.*, national banks). In this sense, conversions are like reincorporation in the context of general business corporations. These "jurisdictional" conversions should be distinguished from conversions of form, the transfer from one form of organization (*e.g.*, a mutual savings association) to another form of organization (*e.g.*, a stock savings association), a process much like corporate reorganization. The chapter considers both types of conversions, known respectively as charter conversions and conversions of form, as well as "cross-industry" conversions in which one type of depository institution (*e.g.*, a credit union) converts into another type (*e.g.* a mutual savings bank).[1]

§ 2.2   Chartering

In the choice of a charter, the overall goal is to identify a jurisdiction that has sufficiently acceptable (*i.e.*, "permissive") rules with respect to the business objectives, expectations, and proposed activities of the institution that are of particular importance to the organizers. However, unlike general business incorporation, chartering of a depository institution is not "free-floating" with respect to the incorporating jurisdiction. The common corporate practice of incorporating in one state (*e.g.*, Delaware) and operating the business in another state or states is virtually unknown within the depository institutions industry (except for interstate banking, discussed in Chapter 4). The chartering state expects to exercise a significant degree of supervision over institutions seeking charters from it, and it expects them to operate *within* the chartering jurisdiction.

Choice of a charter involves two levels of analysis. First, there is the choice of the type of charter itself, that is, commercial bank, savings association, or credit union.[1] Second, there is a choice of federal or state charter. There are, of course, differences among the powers of the various types of depository institutions. However, within each type of institution, differences in powers between federally and state-chartered institutions have been minimized.[2]

§ 2.1

1. *See, e.g.*, 12 C.F.R. pt. 708a (NCUA rule for cross-industry conversion).

§ 2.2

1. *See* § 1.10, *supra* (identifying and discussing different types of depository institutions).

2. The significance of the differences between state and federally chartered institutions has diminished due to the prevalence of FDIC deposit insurance, which is a virtual necessity for state-chartered banks and savings associations. *See* Helen A. Garten, *Devolution and Deregulation: The Paradox of Financial Reform*, 14 Yale L. & Pol'y Rev. 65, 79 n.72 (1996) ("the potential loss of deposits to insured national banks ... may make federal deposit insurance a less costly option for many banks").

Nevertheless, some significant distinctions remain. One obvious difference is that a national bank is required to be a member of the Federal Reserve System, whereas membership of state-chartered banks is voluntary.[3] Membership in the Federal Reserve System carries with it additional burdens, such as cost of membership. This fact may influence the choice of a national or state charter.[4] Of far greater importance, however, is the fact that membership will also subject the proposed bank to other federal banking statutes expressly applicable to member banks.[5]

§ 2.3   National Banks

Chartering of national banks (or "national banking associations,"[1] as the 1864 statutory language puts it) is within the authority of the Comptroller of the Currency. This authority is derived primarily from the National Bank Act ("NBA") itself,[2] as well as from the Federal Deposit Insurance Act ("FDIA").[3] In

Hence, federal supervision and regulation (at least by the FDIC) will be unavoidable regardless of the choice of chartering authority. *See, e.g.,* Michael P. Malloy, *Seeing the Light: Savings Association Conversions and Federal Regulatory Realignment,* 10 Ann. Rev. Banking L. 189 (1991) (arguing that federal regulation based on FDIC deposit insurance substantially realigned scope of federal jurisdiction). In addition, since there is a relatively high degree of coordination among federal bank regulators on supervisory matters, there should not be radical differences on most issues between the federal regulation of national bank activities and of state-chartered FDIC-insured bank activities. *See, e.g.,* 12 U.S.C.A. § 3301 (mandating uniform principles and standards for federal bank examinations).

3. 12 U.S.C.A. § 222.

4. Such differences may be reduced by the fact that deposit reserve requirements administered by the Fed are now to be applied to all depository institutions, regardless of source of charter. 12 U.S.C.A. § 461, *as amended,* Dodd–Frank Wall Street Reform and Consumer Protection Act, Pub. L. No. 111–203, § 366(2), 124 Stat. 1376, 1556 (2010) (codified at 12 U.S.C.A. § 461(b)).

5. *See, e.g.,* 12 U.S.C.A. §§ 501 (imposing liability on member bank certifying check drawn on account with insufficient funds), 503 (imposing liability on directors and officers of member bank under specified circumstances), 505 (pro-

viding civil money penalties with respect to member banks).

§ 2.3

1. 12 U.S.C.A. § 21.

2. 12 U.S.C.A. §§ 21, 22, 26, 27.

3. *See* 12 U.S.C.A. §§ 1811 *et seq.* It has been persuasively argued by Professor Scott that the standards under which the Comptroller exercises his broad discretion with respect to the decision to grant or deny charter applications are to be found in the FDIA, rather than the NBA, the latter being relatively silent on this question. *See* Kenneth Scott, *In Quest of Reason: The Licensing Decisions of the Federal Banking Agencies,* 42 U. Chi. L. Rev. 235, 238–240 (1975). *But see Sterling Nat'l Bank of Davie v. Camp,* 431 F.2d 514, 516 (5th Cir.1970), *cert. denied,* 401 U.S. 925, 91 S.Ct. 879 (1971) (noting longstanding recognition of "vast discretion" of Comptroller). *See also City Nat'l Bank v. Smith,* 513 F.2d 479 (D.C.Cir.1975); *Warren Bank v. Camp,* 396 F.2d 52 (6th Cir.1968); *Webster Groves Trust Co. v. Saxon,* 370 F.2d 381 (8th Cir.1966) (discussing Comptroller's discretion). *See generally* C. Westbrook Murphy, *What Reason for the Quest?: A Response to Professor Scott,* 42 U. Chi. L. Rev. 299 (1975) (criticizing Scott). Nevertheless, the Comptroller's current regulations explicitly acknowledge the FDIA as one of the statutory sources of his authority

addition, the Office of the Comptroller of the Currency ("OCC") is required by the Community Reinvestment Act ("CRA") to assess a proposed bank's anticipated ability to meet the credit needs of the bank's proposed community, including low- and moderate-income neighborhoods, to the extent consistent with the safe and sound operation of the bank.[4]

In reviewing a charter application, the Comptroller must consider primarily the following statutory factors[5] as reflected in the application's operating plan:

(1) *Future earnings prospects.* The operating plan included in the application must demonstrate that the proposed bank can reasonably expect to achieve and sustain profitability in the market to be served by the proposed bank.[6]

(2) *Character of proposed management.* The NBA requires organization of a national bank by five or more natural persons, who individually enter into the articles of association for the proposed bank.[7] The character of the organizers and executive management of the proposed bank is subject to scrutiny.[8]

(3) *Adequacy of capital structure.* Until 2001, national banks were required to be organized with no less than a statutorily required amount of capital, keyed to the size of the community in which the bank would be located.[9] These requirements were completely impractical in light of current economic conditions,[10] and they have been repealed.[11] Minimum capital requirements for formation are now found only in the OCC regulations.[12]

---

with respect to approving the organization of national banks. *See* 12 C.F.R. § 5.20(a).

4. *See* 12 U.S.C.A. §§ 2901 *et seq., as amended,* Financial Institutions Reform, Recovery, and Enforcement Act of 1989, Pub. L. No. 101–73, §§ 744(q), 1212(a)–(b), 103 Stat. 183 (1989) 103 Stat. 183, 440, 526–527 (codified at 12 U.S.C.A. §§ 2902(1)(D), (2), 2906); Gramm–Leach–Bliley Act of 1999, Pub. L. No. 106–102, §§ 103(b), 712–713, 715, 721, 113 Stat. 1338, 1350, 1469–1470 (Nov. 12, 1999) (codified at 12 U.S.C. §§ 2901 note, 2903(c), 2908); Dodd–Frank Wall Street Reform and Consumer Protection Act (DFA), § 358, Pub. L. No. 111–203, 124 Stat. 1376, 1548 (2010) (codified at 12 U.S.C. §§ 2902(1), 2905; striking § 2902(2)).

5. *See* 12 U.S.C.A. § 1816.

6. 12 C.F.R. § 5.20(f)(2)(i)(D), (h)(2).

7. 12 U.S.C.A. § 21.

8. 12 C.F.R. § 5.20(f)(2)(i)(A)–(B), (g)(2), (h)(3). *See, e.g., Connelly v. Comptroller,* 876 F.2d 1209 (5th Cir.1989) (rejecting proposed president of proposed national bank because of past performance; qualified immunity defense of individual regulators upheld).

9. 12 U.S.C.A. § 51 (2000).

10. For example, under the literal terms of 12 U.S.C.A. § 51 (2000), a national bank could be organized in San Francisco with a minimum required capital of $200,000.

11. *See* American Homeownership and Economic Opportunity Act of 2000, Pub L. No. 106–569, § 1233(c), 114 Stat. 2944 (2000) (repealing 12 U.S.C.A. § 51).

12. *See* 12 C.F.R. § 5.20(f)(2)(i)(C), (h)(4) (regulatory capital). The FDIA requires the Comptroller to consider "the adequacy of [the proposed bank's] capi-

(4) *Convenience and needs of community.* This somewhat elusive standard, at issue in *Camp v. Pitts*,[13] is now discussed in the OCC regulations as "community service."[14] Historically, the lack of an articulated statutory standard in this regard had been a problem,[15] and by the 1920s many states had begun incorporating an explicit "convenience and needs" standard in their banking statutes.[16] Since 1933, the "convenience and needs" standard has been a usual feature of both state and federal law.[17] The standard has sometimes been interpreted to restrict entry into the industry significantly.[18] At other times, it has been interpreted very loosely, in a manner intended to foster competition in the market.[19] This concept is reinforced by the OCC requirement that "the organizing group ... submit a statement that demonstrates its plans to achieve CRA objectives."[20] Under current OCC regulations, the organizing group is required to "evaluate the banking needs of the community, including its consumer, business, nonprofit, and government sectors."[21] The application's operating plan "must demonstrate how the proposed bank [will] respond[ ] to those needs consistent with the safe and sound operation of the bank."[22] In addition, since community support is important to the long-term success of a bank, the OCC regulations require the organizing group to "include plans for attracting and

tal structure." 12 U.S.C.A. § 1816. This determination is clearly committed to the discretion of the regulator. *See generally Magellsen v. Federal Deposit Ins. Corp.*, 341 F.Supp. 1031 (D.Mont.1972) (noting discretion of FDIC). Hence, whatever the implications of the NBA minimum capital standard, the FDIA capital adequacy standard remains a matter for administrative discretion. A national bank applicant thus could be denied a charter in light of the FDIA, even if the NBA were read narrowly to deny discretion to the Comptroller with respect to capital requirements. *Cf. United States v. Shively*, 715 F.2d 260 (7th Cir.1983), *cert. denied*, 465 U.S. 1007, 104 S.Ct. 1001 (involving loss of deposit insurance by national bank). *See generally Edwards v. First Bank of Dundee*, 534 F.2d 1242 (7th Cir.1976) (concerning jurisdiction of district court to review Comptroller's administration of FDIA provisions).

13. 411 U.S. 138, 93 S.Ct. 1241 (1973).

14. 12 C.F.R. § 5.50(h)(5).

15. *See, e.g., Speer v. Dossey*, 177 Ky. 761, 198 S.W. 19 (1917) (discussing convenience and needs problem).

16. *See generally* Note, *Bank Charter, Branching, Holding Company and Merger Laws: Competition Frustrated*, 71 Yale L.J. 502 (1962) (discussing problem).

17. *See* Banking Act of 1933, § 8, 48 Stat. 168 (1933) (codified at 12 U.S.C.A. § 264) (containing "convenience and needs" standard in § 264(g)), *recodified at* 12 U.S.C.A. § 1816, Act of September 21, 1950, ch. 967, 64 Stat. 873 (1950).

18. *Cf., e.g., Hempstead Bank v. Smith*, 540 F.2d 57 (2d Cir.1976) (involving national bank branch application under 12 U.S.C.A. § 36).

19. *Cf., e.g., United States v. Third Nat'l Bank in Nashville*, 390 U.S. 171, 88 S.Ct. 882 (1968) (involving "convenience and needs" defense under Bank Merger Act).

20. 12 C.F.R. § 5.50(h)(5)(ii).

21. 12 C.F.R. § 5.50(h)(5)(i).

22. *Id.*

maintaining community support."[23]

(5) *Financial history and condition of the bank.* In the case of a proposed bank, there is, of course, no available data in this regard. In the case of an application sponsored by a bank holding company, however, or by an organizing group affiliated with an extant institution, the financial history and condition of the holding company or affiliate institution will be subject to analysis and evaluation.[24]

(6) *Compliance with applicable laws.* Approval of the application requires compliance with laws applicable to national banks. For example, the NBA requires that, prior to issuing a certificate of authority to commence business, the Comptroller "shall examine . . . generally whether [the national bank] has complied with all the provisions of this chapter required to entitle it to engage in the business of banking."[25] The application must also meet the requirements of the FDIA, including "whether or not [the bank's] corporate powers are consistent with the purposes" of the FDIA.[26]

Compliance with the NBA itself is, of course, an obvious prerequisite for the national bank in formation to attain its corporate status.[27] As with general business corporations, there is a possibility that preformation activities may be questioned under the corporate law doctrine of *ultra vires* activities. *McCormick v. Market Nat. Bank*[28] illustrates this problem as it existed prior to contemporary OCC regulations. In that case, a national bank in organization had signed a lease for its business premises prior to final approval. The NBA required that "no such association shall transact any business, except such as is incidental and necessarily preliminary to its organization, until it has been authorized by the Comptroller of the Currency to commence the business of banking."[29]

The question facing the Court in *McCormick* was whether the national bank was bound by the lease, according to its provisions. The lessee bank contended that the lease was not incidental and necessarily preliminary to the organization of the corporation, and therefore did not bind the bank. The Court agreed with the bank. Upon filing its articles of association and its organization certificate with the Comptroller, the bank became a corporate entity, but it had not been authorized by the Comptroller to commence the

---

23. 12 C.F.R. § 5.50(h)(5)(iii).

24. *See* 12 C.F.R. § 5.50(g)(5) (discussing sponsor's experience and support).

25. 12 U.S.C.A. § 26.

26. 12 U.S.C.A. § 1816.

27. *See* 12 C.F.R. § 5.50(e)(1) (discussing NBA requirements for organization of national bank).

28. 165 U.S. 538, 17 S.Ct. 433 (1897).

29. Rev. Stat. § 5136.

business of banking. Until it was authorized, the NBA forbade the corporation to "transact any business" whatever, "except such as is incidental and necessarily preliminary" to its organization. The exception would include "electing directors and officers, receiving subscriptions and payments for shares, procuring a corporate seal, and a book for recording its proceedings, temporarily hiring a room, and contracting any small debts incidental to the completion of its organization."[30] It would not include the lease in question.

This restricted approach to the corporate powers of a national bank in organization continued into the 1930s.[31] However, the clause relied upon by *McCormick* in reaching such a decision was omitted from Section 16 of the Banking Act of 1933, as recodified.[32] The Act, popularly known as the Glass–Steagall Act, amended the NBA provision without including in its revised language the language relied upon by the Court in *McCormick*. The House Judiciary Subcommittee on the Revision of the Laws concluded that the effect was to repeal the unnumbered paragraph, and it was excluded from subsequent codified editions of the federal laws.[33]

It would be possible to read post-*McCormick* cases like *Wise v. Citizens National Bank at Brownwood*[34] as endorsing the proposition that the paragraph is still in effect, but the current statute and applicable regulations do not support this reading. The current OCC regulations resolve situations like those in *Wise* and *McCormick* by controlling the process of chartering more closely.[35] The regulations acknowledge the *statutory* procedure for chartering— preparing and filing the incorporating documents—but the *regulatory* procedures for chartering—authorization to commence business—are layered over these statutory requirements.[36]

The regulations also include the separate approval stages of "preliminary approval"[37] and "final approval."[38] Preliminary approval involves a decision by the OCC to permit an organizing group to proceed with the *organization* of the proposed national bank. Typically, preliminary approval is subject to specified conditions that an applicant must satisfy before the OCC will grant final approval.[39] Final approval occurs when the proposed bank has satisfied the conditions and the OCC *issues* a charter certificate and

30. *McCormick*, 165 U.S. at 549, 17 S.Ct. at 436.

31. *See, e.g.*, *Wise v. Citizens Nat'l Bank at Brownwood*, 107 S.W.2d 715 (Tex.Civ.App.1937) (finding employment of executive for national bank in organization to be *ultra vires*).

32. 12 U.S.C.A. § 24 (Seventh).

33. *See* 12 U.S.C.A. § 24 note.

34. 107 S.W.2d 715 (Tex.Civ.App. 1937).

35. 12 C.F.R. § 5.20(e), (i).

36. *See* 12 C.F.R. § 5.20(i) (setting forth regulatory procedures).

37. 12 C.F.R. § 5.20(d)(7).

38. 12 C.F.R. § 5.20(d)(3).

39. 12 C.F.R. § 5.20(d)(7), (i)(5)(i).

authorizes a national bank to open for business.[40] As a practical matter, therefore, it is unlikely that a bank in organization would proceed into transactions such as those involved in *McCormick* or *Wise* at a time when those activities would have been *ultra vires*. However, there is no explicit statutory basis in the NBA for the two stages of "approval" established by the regulations.[41]

The financial crisis precipitated by the failure of the subprime mortgage market[42] has resulted in one important change in the OCC chartering procedure. The normal procedure presupposes a proposed bank whose identity and characteristics are readily known, since the business plan is the construct of the organizers/sponsors of the new national bank. However, the OCC now anticipates situations in which an investor group might seek to purchase a failing financial institution at auction by the FDIC and recapitalize and transform it into a viable new national bank. Hence, in November 2008, the OCC created a new procedure for chartering—a "shelf charter"—that allows a well capitalized investor group to pre-qualify for a national bank charter, so that it may actively compete in an FDIC auction, with the group's preliminary approval for a national charter already in place.[43] If the FDIC accepts the investor group bid, the OCC would almost invariably grant a final approval of a charter. If the bid is not accepted, the preliminary approval of the charter remains "on the shelf" to be used for other bids for up to 18 months.[44]

§ 2.4   State Banks

Commercial banking under state authority requires the granting of a charter from an appropriate state official or agency in accordance with the terms and conditions of the pertinent state statute.[1] The specifics of the chartering process vary broadly from state to state, in keeping with the variety of regulatory structures employed by the states. The chartering decision may be committed to the judgment of a single official, a collegial body, or some combination of the two. In practice, state chartering procedures for

40.   12 C.F.R. § 5.20(d)(3), (i)(5)(iii).

41.   *But cf.* 12 U.S.C.A. §§ 24 (satisfaction of NBA formal filing requirements creates corporate entity); 27 (certificate of authority to commence banking).

42.   For background on the subprime mortgage crisis, see 1 MICHAEL P. MALLOY, BANKING LAW AND REGULATION § 1.4 (1994 & Cum. Supps.).

43.   Mike Ferullo, OCC Move to Create 'Shelf Charter' For Investors Welcomed by Banking Industry, BNA Banking Daily (Nov. 26, 2008), available at http://www.bna.

44.   Id.

§ 2.4

1.   *See, e.g., Oliphant v. Carthage Bank*, 224 Miss. 386, 80 So.2d 63 (1955) (discussing chartering).

the formation of a commercial bank bear obvious similarities to the federal procedures.[2]

§ 2.5 Federal Savings Associations

The procedures available for the formation of savings associations[1] are similar to those available for commercial banks. There are, however, some important differences. For example, savings associations may be formed as mutual or stock entities.

Until July 2011,[2] federal chartering of savings associations is within the authority of the Office of Thrift Supervision ("OTS"). Chartering is approved under OTS regulations, "giving primary consideration [to] the best practices of thrift institutions in the United States."[3] A charter may be granted only upon the satisfaction of the following statutory conditions:

(1) the persons to whom the charter is to be issued are of good character and responsibility;

(2) in the judgment of the Director of the OTS, necessity exists for such an institution in the community to be served;

(3) there is a reasonable probability of the association's usefulness and success; and

(4) the institution can be established without undue injury to properly conducted existing local thrift and home financing institutions.[4]

On receiving its charter, a federal savings association may become a member of the Federal Home Loan Bank System,[5] if they

---

2. *See* Michael P. Malloy, Banking Law & Regulation 2.38–2.39, Figure 2–1 (Aspen Law & Business: 1994 & Cum. Supp.) (providing finding aid for state bank chartering procedures).

§ 2.5

1. Under the Financial Institutions Reform, Recovery, and Enforcement Act of 1989 ("FIRREA"), Pub. L. No. 101–73, 103 Stat. 183 (1989), the term "savings association" is now used as the generic concept including, *inter alia*, federally chartered savings and loan associations and savings banks, state-chartered savings and loan associations, building and loan associations, and similar institutions. *See* FIRREA § 204(b), 103 Stat. at 190–191 (codified at 12 U.S.C.A. § 1813(b)) (definition of "savings association" for purposes of FDIA).

2. 12 U.S.C.A. § 5411(a). The effective date of this transition may be

extended under certain specified circumstances. 12 U.S.C.A. § 5411(b). Technical details of the transfer are handled by Dodd–Frank Wall Street Reform and Consumer Protection Act, Pub. L. No. 111–203, §§ 302, 312(a)–(b), 317, 319, 322–327, 124 Stat. 1376, 1520–1522, 1526, 1528–1538 (2010) (codified at 12 U.S.C.A. §§ 5402, 5412, 5415–5416, 5432–5437).

3. 12 U.S.C.A. § 1464(a). The OTS has promulgated regulations governing the chartering of savings associations. *See* 12 C.F.R. pts. 543, 552 (setting forth OTS chartering regulations).

4. 12 U.S.C.A. § 1464(e)(1)–(4).

5. *Id.* § 1464(f), *as amended*, Gramm–Leach–Bliley Act of 1999, Pub. L. No. 106–102, Nov. 12, 1999, § 603, 113 Stat. 1338, 1450–1451 (1999) (codified at 12 U.S.C. § 1464(f)) (eliminating required membership).

qualify for membership as provided by the Federal Home Loan Bank Act.[6]

The Dodd–Frank Wall Street Reform and Consumer Protection Act[7] transfers the chartering functions and responsibilities of the OTS as of 21 July 2011 to the Office of the Comptroller of the Currency.[8] The OTS and the position of the DOTS are to be abolished 90 days after that effective date.[9]

§ 2.6   State Savings Associations

State chartering procedures for savings associations bear obvious similarities to the federal procedures, with many individual variations among the state statutory provisions.[1] For example, California law presents a unified model of regulation of "savings associations."[2] In contrast, New York law presents a typical example of the traditional approach, separating savings and loan association chartering[3] from savings bank chartering.[4] The statutory trend, manifested in the California statute, is towards a unitary system regulating the formation of any and all institutions that are generically referred to as "associations" or "savings associations."

§ 2.7   Federal Credit Unions

This section examines briefly the federal procedures available for the formation of a credit union.[1] Under the Federal Credit Union Act ("FCUA"),[2] any seven or more individuals may form a federal credit union in accordance with the provisions of the FCUA.[3] The organizers must present an organization certificate, in duplicate, to the Board of the National Credit Union Administration ("NCUA").[4] Among other things, the certificate is required to

---

6. 12 U.S.C. §§ 1421 *et seq.*

7. *Supra* note 51. For an overview of the DFA, see 1 MICHAEL P. MALLOY, BANKING LAW AND REGULATION § 1.4.11 (1994 & Cum. Supp.).

8. DFA §§ 312(b)(2)(B), 314 (codified at 12 U.S.C.A. §§ 1, 4a, 11 5412(b)(2)(B)).

9. DFA § 313 (codified at 12 U.S.C.A. § 5413).

§ 2.6

1. For analysis of the different state statutory provisions for chartering of savings associations, see MICHAEL P. MALLOY, BANKING LAW & REGULATION 2.68–2.69, 2.71, FIGURES 2–3, 2–4 (1994 & CUM. SUPP).

2. *See* Cal. Fin. Code §§ 5000 *et seq.*

3. N.Y. Banking Law §§ 375 *et seq.*

4. N.Y. Banking Law §§ 230 *et seq.*

§ 2.7

1. On federal policies and procedures with respect to credit union chartering, see 63 Fed. Reg. 71,998 (1998) (codified at 12 C.F.R. § 701.1) (federal credit union chartering, field of membership modifications, and conversion rules; incorporating by reference NCUA Interpretive Ruling and Policy Statement 99–1) (here after "IRPS 99–1"), as amended by IRPS 00–1, 65 Fed. Reg. 64,512 (2000), IRPS 02–2, 67 Fed. Reg. 20,013 (2002).

2. 12 U.S.C.A. §§ 1751 *et seq.*

3. 12 U.S.C.A. § 1753.

4. 12 U.S.C.A. § 1754. The Board of the NCUA is also responsible for the insurance of member accounts of federally chartered credit unions (mandatory

include information concerning the proposed field of membership of the credit union, specified in detail.[5]

Membership in a federal credit union is "limited to groups having a common bond of occupation or association, or to groups within a well-defined neighborhood, community, or rural district."[6] The NCUA interpretation of this "common bond" requirement[7] allowed multiple groups—each of which independently shares a common bond—to join together to form a credit union, if all occupational groups "are located within a well defined area." This interpretation was rejected by the Supreme Court as inconsistent with statutory language.[8] Legislation has overridden *First National* and now explicitly allows chartering of a "multiple common-bond credit union."[9]

The decision in *First National* potentially affected the operations of approximately 3,600 multiple group federal credit unions

insurance) and state-chartered credit unions (optional insurance), on a pattern similar in all material respects to that administered by the FDIC. 12 U.S.C.A. §§ 1781–1783. *Cf. Massachusetts Credit Union Share Ins. Corp. v. National Credit Union Admin.*, 693 F.Supp. 1225 (D.D.C.1988) (holding state-chartered credit union insurance cooperative lacked standing to challenge NCUA regulation concerning advertisement of "federally insured" accounts). In addition, through its Central Liquidity Facility ("CLF"), it performs such "central bank" functions as acting as lender of last resort to CLF member credit unions experiencing liquidity problems. 12 U.S.C.A. §§ 1795b–1795c, 1795e–1795f. State courts apply similar concepts of standing to judicial review of challenges to state chartering and other administrative decisions. One pertinent example in this regard is provided by *Pennsylvania Bankers Ass'n v. Pennsylvania Dept. of Banking*, 598 Pa. 313, 956 A.2d 956 (2008), in which competing banks appealed a decision of the Pennsylvania Secretary of Banking dismissing the banks as intervenors in administrative actions in which state-chartered, "group-based" credit unions gave formal notice to the Department of Banking of their intent to expand their fields of membership to "geography-based" community credit unions. The trial court affirmed the dismissal for lack of standing. On appeal, the state supreme court reversed and remanded, holding that dismissal of the banks as intervenors on the ground that they failed to show a

"direct interest" in the administrative proceeding offended due process.

5. 12 U.S.C.A. § 1753(5).

6. 12 U.S.C.A. § 1759. On the common bond requirement, see generally *La Caisse Populaire Ste.–Marie v. United States*, 425 F.Supp. 512 (D.N.H.), *aff'd*, 563 F.2d 505 (1st Cir.1977); *Board of Directors and Officers, Forbes Federal Credit Union v. National Credit Union Admin.*, 477 F.2d 777 (10th Cir.1973), *cert. denied*, 414 U.S. 924, 94 S.Ct. 233; *National Alliance of Postal and Fed. Employees v. Nickerson*, 424 F.Supp. 323 (D.D.C.1976).

7. NCUA Interpretive Ruling and Policy Statement 82–1, 47 Fed. Reg. 16,-775 (1982).

8. *National Credit Union Admin. v. First Nat'l Bank & Trust Co.*, 522 U.S. 479, 118 S.Ct. 927 (1998).

9. Credit Union Membership Access Act, Pub. L. No. 105–219, § 101, Aug. 7, 1998, 112 Stat. 913, 914–916 (1998) (codified at 12 U.S.C.A. § 1759(a)–(e)) (CUMAA). The NCUA has implemented the provisions of the CUMAA. *See e.g.,* 63 Fed. Reg. 65,532 (1998) (codified at 12 C.F.R. Pt. 708a) (conversion of insured credit unions to mutual savings banks effective 27 November 1998); 63 Fed. Reg. 71,998 (1998) (codified at 12 C.F.R. Pt. 701) (federal credit union chartering, field of membership modifications, and conversion rules, incorporating IRPS 99–1 by reference, effective 1 January 1999).

serving approximately 158,000 groups.[10] The CUMAA reinstated NCUA multiple group policy, with some modifications.[11] This was the first time since 1934 that Congress had updated the statutory common bond rules.[12]

The CUMAA authorizes three types of credit union charters. These charter types include a single occupational or associational common bond,[13] a multiple common bond,[14] or a local community, neighborhood, or rural district serving a well defined area.[15]

The CUMAA also embodies some policy trade-offs; in addition to reestablishing the NCUA multiple common-bond credit union policy, the act also imposes some significant regulatory requirements on the credit union industry. Among other things, the CUMAA includes the following provisions:

> (1) *New financial statement requirements*. These include the application of uniform, generally accepted accounting principles (GAAP), with limited exceptions.[16]

10. 63 Fed. Reg. 49,164, 49,164 (1998).

11. CUMAA, § 101(2), 112 Stat. at 914–917 (codified at 12 U.S.C. § 1759(b)(2), (c)–(e)). *See also id.* § 102, 112 Stat. at 917 (codified at 12 U.S.C. 1759(f)) (providing criteria for approval of expansion of membership of multiple common-bond credit unions). *See generally American Bankers Ass'n v. National Credit Union Admin.*, 271 F.3d 262 (D.C.Cir.2001) (upholding NCUA decision not to include family and household members when determining whether group has fewer than 3,000 members, thus eligible to join multiple common-bond credit union *per* CUMAA).

12. 63 Fed. Reg. at 49,164.

13. CUMAA, § 101(2), 112 Stat. at 914 (codified at 12 U.S.C. § 1759(b)(1)). For interpretive guidance with respect to the single occupational common bond, see IRPS 99–1, Chapter 2, § II.A, as amended by IRPS 00–1, 65 Fed. Reg. at 64,521. For interpretive guidance with respect to the single associational common bond, see IRPS 99–1, Chapter 2, § III.A.1, as amended by IRPS 00–1, 65 Fed. Reg. at 64,521–64,522.

14. CUMAA, § 101(2), 112 Stat. at 914–917 (codified at 12 U.S.C. § 1759(b)(2), (c)–(e)). *See also id.* § 102, 112 Stat. at 917 (codified at 12 U.S.C. § 1759(f)) (providing criteria for approval of expansion of membership of multiple common-bond credit unions).

15. *Id.* § 101(2), 112 Stat. at 915 (codified at 12 U.S.C. § 1759(b)(3)). *See also id.* § 103, 112 Stat. at 917–918 (codified at 12 U.S.C. § 1759(g)) (providing geographical guidelines for community credit unions). On the requirement of a well-defined local community, neighborhood or rural district, see IRPS 02–2, 67 Fed. Reg. 20,013 (2002) (incorporated by reference in 12 C.F.R. § 701.1). For interpretive guidance with respect to the community common bond, see IRPS 99–1, Chapter 2, Section V.A.2, as amended by IRPS 00–1, 65 Fed. Reg. at 64,526. In December 2001, the NCUA eased the regulatory requirements for community charters, eliminating the requirement that a community credit union document in writing its plans to serve the entire community. 66 Fed. Reg. 65,625 (2001) (codified at 12 C.F.R. § 701.1) (interim final rule amending chartering and field of membership manual).

16. CUMAA, § 201(a), 112 Stat. at 918 (codified at 12 U.S.C. § 1782(a)(6)(C)). This requirement does not apply to an insured credit union with total assets less than $10 million. 12 U.S.C. § 1782(a)(6)(C)(iii). In addition, where the NCUA determines that application of a specific generally accepted accounting principle is not appropriate, it may prescribe an alternative principle "no less stringent than [GAAP]." *Id.* § 1782(a)(6)(C)(ii). *See* IRPS 02–3, *supra* note 27.15 (imposing GAAP requirements with respect to allowances

(2) *New audit requirements.* An insured credit union with total assets of $500 million or more is required to have an annual independent audit of financial statements performed in accordance with GAAP by an independent certified or licensed public accountant.[17]

(3) *New rules with respect to conversion of an insured credit union to a mutual savings association.*[18] The NCUA was required to promulgate final rules regarding charter conversions within six months of the enactment of the CUMAA (*i.e.*, 7 August 1998) that are consistent with the charter conversion rules promulgated by other financial regulators.[19] These rules must be no more or less restrictive than rules applicable to charter conversions of other financial institutions.[20] In November 1998, the NCUA issued interim rules governing the conversion of insured credit unions to mutual savings associations.[21]

(4) *New limits on member business loans.* The CUMAA imposes a new aggregate limit on an insured credit union's outstanding member business loans.[22] In September 1998, the NCUA issued an interim rule implementing this statutory limitation, as well as updating, clarifying and streamlining its existing rules concerning member business loans and appraisals for federally insured credit unions.[23]

(5) *NCUA Board membership.* The CUMAA adds appointment criteria with respect to presidential appointments to the NCUA Board.[24]

(6) *Prompt corrective action.* The CUMAA requires the NCUA to adopt, by regulation, a system of "prompt corrective action" indexed to each of five capital categories that the new provision establishes for federally insured credit unions.[25]

---

for loan and lease losses for federally-insured credit unions).

17. CUMAA, § 201(a), 112 Stat. at 918–919 (codified at 12 U.S.C. § 1782(a)(6)(D)(i)). In addition, if a federal credit union with total assets between $10 million and $500 million conducts an audit for any purpose, the audit must be performed "consistent with the accountancy laws of the appropriate State or jurisdiction, including licensing requirements." 12 U.S.C. § 1782(a)(6)(D)(ii).

18. CUMAA, § 202(3), 112 Stat. at 919–920 (codified at 12 U.S.C. § 1785(b)(2)).

19. 12 U.S.C. § 1785(b)(2)(G)(i).

20. *Id.* The NCUA has indicated that it does not interpret the CUMAA as precluding state regulatory authorities from imposing more restrictive charter conversion rules on federally insured state-chartered credit unions. 63 Fed. Reg. 65,532, 65,533 (1998).

21. 63 Fed. Reg. 65,532 (1998) (codified at 12 C.F.R. pt. 708a).

22. CUMAA, § 203, 112 Stat. at 920–922 (codified at 12 U.S.C. § 1757 note, 1757a).

23. 63 Fed. Reg. 51,793 (1998) (codified at 12 C.F.R. pts. 701, 722–723, 741).

24. CUMAA, § 204(2), 112 Stat. at 922–923 (codified at 12 U.S.C. § 1752a(b)(2)).

25. *Id.*, § 301(a), 112 Stat. at 923–929 (codified at 12 U.S.C. § 1790d).

(7) Amended conservatorship and liquidation provisions. The CUMAA amended the conservatorship[26] and liquidation provisions[27] of the FCUA to facilitate prompt corrective action.

The NCUA Board is required to undertake an appropriate investigation to determine if the proposed credit union meets the following approval factors: (1) conformity of the organization certificate with the provisions of the FCUA;[28] (2) general character and fitness of the subscribers;[29] and, (3) economic advisability of establishing the proposed credit union.[30]

§ 2.8   State Credit Unions

State chartering procedures for the formation of credit unions are similar to the federal procedures. However, there are many individual variations.[1] For example, New York law[2] follows the traditional approach to credit union chartering, similar to the Federal Credit Union Act. By contrast, California law provides for an incorporation procedure, similar to general business incorporation.[3]

§ 2.9   Secondary Entry Restrictions

In the following sections we examine two important forms of secondary entry restriction. These restrictions limit the ability of depository institutions to participate in certain features of the regulatory system itself. One such restriction is eligibility for federal deposit insurance. Withholding deposit insurance could have serious adverse effects on the ability of the institution to compete in the deposit market.[1]

The second restriction is eligibility for membership in the Federal Reserve System. As a practical matter, this concerns only commercial banks.[2] Compared to the virtual necessity of deposit

---

26. *Id.*, § 301(b)(1), 112 Stat. at 930 (codified at 12 U.S.C. § 1786(h)(1)(D)–(G), (2)(A), (C)).

27. *Id.*, § 301(b)(2), 112 Stat. at 930 (codified at 12 U.S.C. § 1787(a)(1)(A), (3)).

28. 12 U.S.C.A. § 1754(1).

29. 12 U.S.C.A. § 1754(2).

30. 12 U.S.C.A. § 1754(3). *See generally National Alliance of Postal and Fed. Employees v. Nickerson*, 424 F.Supp. 323 (D.D.C.1976) (discussing requirements).

§ 2.8

1. *See* MICHAEL P. MALLOY, BANKING LAW AND REGULATION §§ 2.83–2.84, FIGURE 2–5 (1994 & CUM. SUPP.) (identifying state statutory provisions for credit union chartering).

2. N.Y. Banking Law §§ 450 *et seq.*

3. Cal. Corp. Code §§ 7110 *et seq.*; Cal. Fin. Code § 14100.

§ 2.9

1. *See generally* Kenneth Scott, *In Quest of Reason: The Licensing Decisions of the Federal Banking Agencies,* 42 U. Chi. L. Rev. 235, 269–70 (1975) (discussing restrictions).

2. Savings associations may be eligible for membership in the Federal Home Loan Bank System. *See* 12 U.S.C.A. § 1424(a) (providing for FHLBS membership).

insurance, this is not a critical concern for banks, but it is nonetheless a requirement for most national banks.[3] Thus, eligibility and maintenance of Fed membership is a necessary precondition to their operation.

§ 2.10   Deposit Insurance

As a matter of federal law, deposit insurance is generally not required for commercial banks that are not members of the Federal Reserve System.[1] As a matter of fact, however, federal deposit insurance is virtually a necessity for all depository institutions.[2] Even for those banks that are required to be FDIC-insured (national banks and state member banks), prior to 1991 there was usually no separate approval process undertaken by the FDIC itself. The Federal Deposit Insurance Corporation Improvement Act of 1991 ("FDICIA")[3] provides that a specific application to, and approval by, the FDIC is required for FDIC insurance of the deposits of all depository institutions.[4]

Every national member bank[5] that receives or will receive non-trust fund deposits is required to obtain FDIC deposit insurance.[6] The situation of state-chartered banks is more complicated. If a state-chartered nonmember bank opts to obtain FDIC insurance— as virtually all such banks do[7]—it must obtain the approval of the Board of Directors of the FDIC.[8] If a state-chartered bank opts to become a member of the Federal Reserve System, FDIC insurance requirements are automatically imposed.[9] If a state-chartered bank is converted into a national member bank, the requirement of FDIC insurance is automatically imposed, in the same way in which FDIC insurance is required for *de novo* national member banks.[10]

---

3. *See* 12 U.S.C.A. § 282 (requiring Fed membership for national banks).

§ 2.10

1. 12 U.S.C.A. § 1815(a). However, state-chartered banks that are subsidiaries of bank holding companies, and banks that are themselves holding companies of other banks, are generally required by the Bank Holding Company Act to be FDIC-insured. 12 U.S.C.A. § 1842(e).

2. *See* Helen A. Garten, *Devolution and Deregulation: The Paradox of Financial Reform*, 14 Yale L. & Pol'y Rev. 65, 79 n.72 (1996) ("the potential loss of deposits to insured national banks ... may make federal deposit insurance a less costly option for many banks").

3. FDICIA, Pub. L. No. 102–242, 105 Stat. 2236 (Dec. 19, 1991).

4. 12 U.S.C.A. § 1815(a).

5. National banks located in U.S. territories are not required to become members of the Federal Reserve System. 12 U.S.C.A. §§ 282, 1813(d)–(e), 1815(a). However, a national nonmember bank that receives or will receive non-trust fund deposits, and that subsequently opts to become a member bank, is required to be FDIC insured. *Id.* § 1814(b).

6. *Id.* § 1814(b).

7. *See* Report of the Task Group on Regulation of Financial Services 18 n. 6 (1984).

8. 12 U.S.C.A. § 1815(a).

9. *Id.* § 1814(b).

10. *Id.* § 1814(b).

In each of the situations described above, an application to and examination by the FDIC is required, with approval of the application by the FDIC Board of Directors.[11] However, if a state-chartered insured bank subsequently becomes a member of the Federal Reserve System, it is not required to reapply for FDIC insurance; its status as an FDIC-insured bank continues despite subsequent acceptance of Fed membership.[12] Similarly, if a state-chartered, FDIC-insured bank subsequently converts to a national charter, its insurance continues without a new application.[13]

The deposit insurance system for savings associations has been subjected to a number of significant changes in recent years. Throughout the 1970s and 1980s, the deposit system of the Federal Savings and Loan Insurance Corporation ("FSLIC") was becoming increasingly burdened, not only by crises precipitated by savings associations failures, but also, ironically, by the rapid growth of the savings industry in certain states.[14] Thus, in 1985 the now defunct Federal Home Loan Bank Board announced that it had stopped granting deposit insurance for *de novo* state-chartered S & L's in such states as California, Florida, and Texas, which were the sites of dramatic industry expansion.[15]

The situation was exacerbated by the fact that the now defunct FSLIC insurance fund itself was in the midst of a major financial crisis, reflecting the critical condition of the savings industry generally. Despite a $10.8 billion dollar recapitalization of the FSLIC in August 1987 in response to the savings industry crisis, by March 1988 it was apparent that another significant capital infusion might be required.[16]

The Financial Institutions Reform, Recovery, and Enforcement Act of 1989 ("FIRREA") mandated the immediate abolition of the FSLIC,[17] and gave the FDIC responsibility for insurance of deposits of savings associations.[18] The FDIC now administers a Bank Insur-

---

11. *Id.* § 1815(a).

12. *Id.* § 1814(b).

13. *Id.* The same is true for a state-chartered, FDIC-insured bank that results from a merger or consolidation between FDIC-insured banks or between an FDIC-insured bank and an uninsured bank. *Id.*

14. *See, e.g.,* Wynter, *Bank Board Stops Granting Insurance For S & Ls in California, Florida, Texas,* Wall St. J., June 17, 1985, at 7, col. 1 (describing problems of FSLIC system).

15. *Id.*

16. *See, e.g.,* Nash, *F.S.L.I.C.'s 2d Bailout Is Studied,* N.Y. Times, March 7, 1988, at D1, col. 1 (noting insufficiency of $10.8 billion fund over next three years, in light of continuing losses at insolvent S & Ls).

17. FIRREA, § 401(a)(1), 103 Stat. at 354.

18. FIRREA § 205(1), 103 Stat. at 194 (codified at 12 U.S.C.A. § 1814(a)). The FDIC amended its deposit insurance provisions, pursuant to Section 402(c)(3) of FIRREA, to provide for uniform deposit insurance regulations for deposits in all federally insured depository institutions, including savings associations formerly insured by the now defunct FSLIC. *See* 55 Fed. Reg. 20,111 (1990) (codified at 12 C.F.R. Pt. 330;

ance Fund ("BIF"), formerly the Permanent Insurance Fund, with respect to deposits of insured banks,[19] and a Savings Association Insurance Fund ("SAIF"), replacing the functions of the FSLIC.[20] FIRREA also established an FSLIC Resolution Fund, to wind up the affairs of the FSLIC.[21]

Further changes in the federal deposit insurance system were mandated by FDICIA. The principal features of the legislation in this regard are as follows. First, the FDICIA created the requirement for specific application and approval of deposit insurance, even in the case of a national bank or a state member bank.[22]

Second, new rules were imposed on depository institutions that were not insured by the FDIC.[23] Private deposit insurers are now required to obtain an annual audit from an independent auditor, using generally accepted auditing standards.[24] The private insurer is required to provide copies of the annual audit report to depository institutions insured by it.[25] The insurer must also provide copies to the appropriate state supervisors of the insured depository institutions.[26]

The depository institutions must provide copies of the annual audit report upon request to any current or prospective customer.[27] In addition, every depository institution that is not insured by the FDIC is required to include a conspicuous notice on specified documentation[28] stating that it "is not federally insured, and that if the institution fails, the Federal Government does not guarantee that depositors will get back their money."[29] The institution must display a notice to the effect that it is not federally insured in all its advertising and at each place where it receives deposits.[30] Depositors of such institutions must sign a written statement acknowledging that "the institution is not federally insured, and that if the institution fails, the Federal Government does not guarantee that depositors will get back their money."[31]

removing 12 C.F.R. Pt. 331, §§ 386.1(a)–(c), 386.2–386.13, Appendix).

19. FIRREA § 211(3), 103 Stat. at 218–219 (codified at 12 U.S.C.A. § 1821(a)(4)B(5)).

20. FIRREA, § 211(3), 103 Stat. at 218–220 (codified at 12 U.S.C.A. § 1821(a)(4), (6)).

21. FIRREA, § 215, 103 Stat. at 252–254 (codified at 12 U.S.C.A. § 1821a).

22. FDICIA, § 115(a) (codified at 12 U.S.C.A. § 1815(a)).

23. FDICIA, § 151(a)(1), (b) (codified at 12 U.S.C.A. § 1831t).

24. 12 U.S.C.A. § 1831t(a)(1).

25. *Id.* § 1831t(a)(2)(A)(i). The copies must be provided not later than 14 days after completion of the audit. *Id.*

26. *Id.* § 1831t(a)(2)(A)(ii). The copies must be provided not later than seven days after completion of the audit. *Id.*

27. *Id.* § 1831t(a)(2)(B).

28. The statement must appear on all periodic account statements, signature cards, passbook, certificate of deposit, or similar instrument evidencing a deposit. *Id.* § 1831t(b)(1).

29. *Id.*

30. *Id.* § 1831t(b)(2).

31. *Id.* § 1831t(b)(3).

A depository institution that is not a bank and that lacks federal deposit insurance (*e.g.*, an uninsured savings association or uninsured credit union[32]) is prohibited from using the mails or any instrumentality of interstate commerce to receive or facilitate receiving deposits, with certain exceptions.[33] First, an institution whose state chartering authority has determined that it meets all the eligibility requirements for federal deposit insurance is excepted from the prohibitions.[34] Second, the Federal Trade Commission, in consultation with the FDIC, is authorized to except the institution from the prohibition.[35]

Third, the FDICIA required the establishment of a risk-based assessment system for federal deposit insurance.[36] The FDIC has promulgated regulations implementing the risk-based system.[37]

In September 1996, the president signed into law the Economic Growth and Regulatory Paperwork Reduction Act ("EGRPR Act").[38] The Act makes a number of significant changes to the structure of regulation of depository institutions, and also refines or reduces the regulatory requirements applicable to such institutions in a wide variety of statutory provisions. Of particular note in the present context are the EGRPR Act's amendments to the deposit insurance system.

The EGRPR Act imposes a special assessment on insured depository institutions holding SAIF-insured deposits in order to recapitalize the ailing SAIF.[39] It also provided for the merger of the BIF and SAIF into a new Deposit Insurance Fund ("DIF"), if there were no more savings associations by 1 January 1999,[40] which did not happen.

§ 2.11 Federal Reserve Membership

For national banks, membership in the Federal Reserve System is generally mandatory.[1] For state-chartered banks,[2] membership is

---

32. *Id.* § 1831t(f)(3).

33. *Id.* § 1831t(e)(1).

34. *Id.* The state chartering authority's determination that the institution is eligible for federal deposit insurance does not bind or otherwise affect the authority of the FDIC or the NCUA in making such a determination. *Id.* § 1831t(e)(2).

35. *Id.* § 1831t(e)(1).

36. *Id.* § 1817(b).

37. *See* 57 Fed. Reg. 45,263 (1992) (codified at 12 C.F.R. Pt. 327) (promulgating transitional risk-based assessment system); 58 Fed. Reg. 34,357 (1993) (codified at 12 C.F.R. Pt. 327) (establishing new risk-based assessment

system; limited changes to transitional system).

38. Pub. L. No. 104–208, title II, 110 Stat. 3009 (1996) (codified at scattered sections of 5, 12, 15, 26, 42 U.S.C.A.).

39. EGRPR Act, § 2702 (*to be codified at* 12 U.S.C.A. § 1817 note).

40. EGRPR Act, § 2704.

§ 2.11

1. 12 U.S.C.A. § 282. *See generally United States v. Davenport*, 266 Fed. 425 (W.D.Tex.1920) (discussing Fed membership). *But cf.* 12 U.S.C.A. §§ 1813(e), 1814(b) (concerning national nonmember banks).

2. *See* 12 C.F.R. § 208.1(a) (defining "State bank"). Fed membership is also

optional,[3] subject to approval of an application for membership by the Fed.[4] Similarly, if a national bank converts into a state-chartered bank, Fed membership of the converted institution is optional.[5]

In the case of a merger or consolidation of a national bank with a state-chartered nonmember bank in which the state-chartered bank survives or results, Fed membership of the surviving or resulting institution is optional.[6] If the state-chartered bank participating in the merger or consolidation had been a member bank, then its Fed membership will continue in the surviving or resulting bank.[7]

The Fed has asserted the authority to condition approval of an application for membership, as public interest requires, in its judgment.[8] Fed decisions on membership are rarely challenged, and are unlikely to be successful, given the typical judicial deference given such decisions. One such challenge did reach the Supreme Court in *Eccles v. Peoples Bank of Lakewood Village,*[9] but was disposed of without reaching the merits. The bank had sought Fed membership, but its application was rejected.[10] On a request for reconsideration, the Fed stated that favorable action depended on a showing that the Transamerica Corporation, a bank holding company, did not have, and was not intended to have, any interest in the bank.[11] The condition having been satisfied, the Fed granted membership, subject to certain specified conditions, including the following:

> If, without prior written approval of the Board of Governors of the Federal Reserve System, Transamerica Corporation, or any

available to mutual savings banks. 12 U.S.C.A. § 333. *See also Hiatt v. United States,* 4 F.2d 374 (7th Cir.1924), *cert. denied,* 268 U.S. 704, 45 S.Ct. 638 (1925) (concerning trust company Fed membership); *Louisville Bridge Comm'n v. Louisville Trust Co.,* 258 Ky. 846, 81 S.W.2d 894 (1935).

3. *Fidelity–Philadelphia Trust Co. v. Hines,* 337 Pa. 48, 10 A.2d 553 (1940).

4. 12 U.S.C.A. § 321. On the constitutionality of the statutory provision for membership of state-chartered banks in the Federal Reserve System, see *Hiatt,* 4 F.2d 374. The Fed has promulgated detailed regulations governing applications for, and conditions of, Fed membership of state-chartered banks. 12 C.F.R. Pt. 208. On the validity of these regulations and of conditions of membership imposed thereunder, see *Continental Bank & Trust Co. of Salt Lake City, Utah v.*

Woodall, 239 F.2d 707 (10th Cir.1957), *cert. denied,* 353 U.S. 909, 77 S.Ct. 663; *Eccles v. Peoples Bank of Lakewood Village, Cal.,* 333 U.S. 426, 68 S.Ct. 641 (1948), *reh'g denied,* 333 U.S. 877, 68 S.Ct. 900.

5. 12 U.S.C.A. § 321.

6. *Id.* § 321.

7. *Id.*

8. *See, e.g., Eccles, supra* (conditioning approval of membership on restriction of control by holding company); *Continental Bank and Trust Co., supra* (noting longstanding Fed rules relating to conditions of membership of state banking institutions).

9. 333 U.S. 426, 68 S.Ct. 641 (1948), *reh'g denied,* 333 U.S. 877, 68 S.Ct. 900.

10. *Eccles,* 333 U.S. at 427, 68 S.Ct. at 642.

11. *Id.*

unit of the Transamerica group, including Bank of America National Trust and Savings Association, or any holding company affiliate or any subsidiary thereof, acquires, directly or indirectly, through the mechanism of extension of loans for the purpose of acquiring bank stock, or in any other manner, any interest in such bank, other than such as may arise out of the usual correspondent bank relationships, such bank, within 60 days after written notice from the Board of Governors of the Federal Reserve System, shall withdraw from membership in the Federal Reserve System.[12]

Some time thereafter, Transamerica acquired just over 10 percent of the outstanding stock of the bank, without its prior knowledge. The bank advised the Fed of this fact, but requested that it be relieved of the condition quoted above.[13] The Fed refused to do so, though it was not clear that the Fed intended to enforce the condition in the absence of the exercise of control by Transamerica.[14]

When the Fed's position was challenged, the D.C. District Court in an unreported opinion held that the bank was bound by the condition on which it had accepted membership.[15] The D.C. Circuit reversed, characterizing the condition as "only as a statement that, if the Board of Governors should determine, after hearing, that Transamerica's ownership of the bank's shares has resulted in a change for the worse in the character of the bank's personnel, in its banking policies, in the safety of its deposits, or in any other substantial way, it may require the bank to withdraw from the Federal Reserve System."[16]

Since this was a declaratory judgment action, the Supreme Court was of the view that, "[e]specially where governmental action is involved, courts should not intervene unless the need for equitable relief is clear, not remote or speculative."[17] The Court noted that the Fed, "having imposed the condition to safeguard [the bank's] independence, disavows any action to terminate the Bank's membership, so long as the Bank maintains the independence on which it insists."[18] In light of the existing uncertainty regarding any future enforcement of the condition, the Court held that injunctive relief would be inappropriate.[19]

Despite the ambiguity of the result in *Eccles*, currently it is not unusual to find that a regulator has attached conditions to its

---

12. *Id.* at 427–428, 68 S.Ct. at 642.
13. *Id.* at 428. 68 S.Ct. at 643.
14. *Id.*
15. *Id.* at 428–429, 68 S.Ct. at 643.
16. *Id.* at 429, 68 S.Ct. at 643.
17. *Id.* at 431, 68 S.Ct. at 644.
18. *Id.* at 432, 68 S.Ct. at 644.
19. *Id.* at 435, 68 S.Ct. at 645.

approval of an application. Unlike the situation at the time *Eccles* was decided, violation of such a condition is now explicitly identified as one of the grounds for an administrative cease and desist order under the FDIA.[20] The use of general approval conditions has been particularly important in, for example, capital adequacy supervision.[21] Although the regulators' authority to enforce strict capital adequacy standards has occasionally been challenged,[22] it is now a significant, legislatively confirmed feature of contemporary depository institution regulation.

While the field of Fed membership may be limited to national and state-chartered banks (including savings banks), this does not affect the scope of the Fed's jurisdiction over deposit reserves. The Fed directly supervises the deposit reserve requirements for all depository institutions, not just member banks.[23]

§ 2.12   Conversions

In this section, we examine depository institution "conversions," quasi-entry transactions in which a formal change occurs in the nature of the charter that leaves the type of depository institution essentially unaffected. There are two major, traditional kinds of conversion. The first, a "conversion of charter," is similar to a change in the state of incorporation in general corporate law.[1] In the depository institutions context, however, the *situs* of the institution remains the same; what changes is the statutory source of the charter. Reincorporation and charter conversion are contrasted in Figure 2–1, *infra*.

20. *See* 12 U.S.C.A. § 1818(b)(1) (providing for initiation of cease and desist proceedings for violation of "any condition imposed in writing by the agency in connection with the granting of any application or other request by the depository institution").

21. *See, e.g., Board of Governors v. First Lincolnwood Corp.*, 439 U.S. 234, 99 S.Ct. 505 (1978) (conditioning approval of bank holding company formation on adequacy of capital); *Kaneb Servs., Inc. v. Federal Sav. & Loan Ins. Corp.*, 650 F.2d 78 (5th Cir.1981) (upholding condition on savings and loan holding company approval).

22. *See, e.g., MCorp Fin., Inc. v. Board of Governors*, 900 F.2d 852 (5th Cir.1990) (challenging, *inter alia*, Fed authority to impose capital conditions on holding company; distinguishing *First Lincolnwood*), *aff'd in part and rev'd in part on other grounds*, 502 U.S. 32, 112 S.Ct. 459 (1991); *First Nat'l Bank of Bellaire v. Comptroller of the Currency*, 697 F.2d 674 (5th Cir.1983) (challenging OCC authority to enforce capital adequacy requirements; subsequently reversed by legislative amendment, 12 U.S.C.A. § 3907). *But cf. Kaneb Servs., Inc.*, 650 F.2d 78 (upholding FSLIC authority to impose capital conditions on holding company).

23. 12 U.S.C.A. § 461(b).

§ 2.12

1. *See* FRANKLIN A. GEVURTZ, CORPORATION LAW 41 n. 16 (2000) (discussing reincorporation).

Figure 2–1

Reincorporation v. Charter Conversion

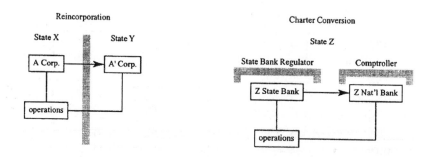

Because of the dual regulatory system under which depository institutions operate, a bank might convert from a national to a state charter, or from a state to a national charter, but the geographical *situs* of the institution—and that of its operations—remains unchanged. The type of institution also remains essentially unchanged (*e.g.*, a commercial bank), but the primary regulator having jurisdiction over the institution would change (*e.g.*, from the Comptroller to a state banking official).[2]

The second type of conversion, a "conversion of form," is similar to a corporate reorganization or recapitalization in the general corporate law context.[3] However, in the depository institutions context, the conversion involves a change from a mutual form of organization and ownership to a stock form.[4] The conversion does not change the primary regulator of the institution, unless the conversion of form is accompanied by a charter conversion. Recapitalization and conversion of form are contrasted in Figure 2–2, *infra*.

---

2. Accordingly, this type of conversion may be described as a "jurisdictional conversion." *See, e.g.*, Wisc. Stat. Ann. § 215.57 (concerning "jurisdictional conversion," state to federal charter).

3. *See* GEVURTZ at 743–746 (discussing recapitalization in general business corporation context).

4. This type of conversion may be described as an "organizational conversion." *See, e.g.*, Wisc. Stat. Ann. § 215.58 (concerning "organizational conversion," mutual to stock).

Figure 2–2
Recapitalization v. Conversion of Form

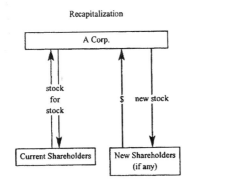

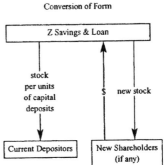

§ 2.13   Conversion of Charter

The requirements for conversion of charter from federal to state or state to federal differ. Conversions of charter should be distinguished from the related process of merger between state- and federally chartered depository institutions.[1]

A fundamental question of jurisdiction is at issue in a conversion of charter. The result of the process is the relinquishment of jurisdiction over the depository institution by one chartering authority and the acquisition of such authority by another. Hence, the interrelationship between the interested federal and state chartering authorities involved in this process is particularly important.[2] The authority of one regulator to approve the conversion over the objections of the chartering regulator of the converting institution has raised serious questions of competing federal and state authority.[3]

The courts have reacted in varying ways to this issue in cases under the NBA[4] and the Home Owners' Loan Act ("HOLA").[5] It has long been established, for example, that the NBA could authorize the Comptroller to approve the conversion of a state-chartered bank to a national bank charter, even in the absence of approval by the state chartering authority.[6]

§ 2.13

1. *See, e.g., Federal Home Loan Bank Bd. v. Elliott,* 386 F.2d 42 (9th Cir.1967), *cert. denied,* 390 U.S. 1011, 88 S.Ct. 1260 (1968) (noting conversion requirements and procedures exclusive of requirements and procedures applicable to mergers); *Opdyke v. Security Sav. & Loan Co.,* 99 N.E.2d 84 (Ohio App. 1951), *aff'd,* 157 Ohio St. 121, 105 N.E.2d 9 (1952).

2. *See, e.g., Hopkins Fed. Sav. & Loan Ass'n v. Cleary,* 296 U.S. 315, 56 S.Ct. 235 (1935) (involving state to federal conversion); *Federal Home Loan Bank Bd. v. Greater Del. Valley Federal Sav. and Loan Ass'n,* 277 F.2d 437 (3d Cir.1960) (federal to state conversion).

3. *Hopkins Fed. Savings, supra.*

4. 12 U.S.C.A. §§ 1 *et seq.*

5. *Id.* §§ 1461 *et seq.*

6. *Casey v. Galli,* 94 U.S. (4 Otto) 673 (1876).

In a similar situation, involving a state-chartered savings and loan association seeking approval from the Federal Home Loan Bank Board of a conversion to a federal charter, the Supreme Court held, in *Hopkins Fed. Savings & Loan Association v. Cleary*,[7] that to the extent that HOLA, as amended in 1934, permitted conversion of state-chartered associations in contravention of state law, it was "an unconstitutional encroachment upon the reserved powers of the states" under the Tenth Amendment of the U.S. Constitution.[8] Justice Cardozo's opinion has never been overruled.

The Court distinguished the situation in *Hopkins Fed. Savings* from its earlier decision in *Casey v. Galli*[9] on several grounds. Among other things, the constitutional question at issue in *Hopkins Fed. Savings* had not been raised in *Casey*. This distinction does not seem very satisfying. As the *Hopkins Fed. Savings* Court characterized it, the precise issue raised in *Casey* was whether "the change from one form of association to another was to be condemned as *ultra vires*."[10] Is it to be assumed that a serious issue of constitutionality under the Tenth Amendment would not have affected the *Casey* Court's analysis of the *ultra vires* question, or that the Court would not have raised the issue *sua sponte*? In some question-begging *dicta*, the *Hopkins Fed. Savings* Court suggested that distinctions might "conceivably exist between the power of Congress in respect of [commercial] banks ... and its power in respect of [savings] associations...."[11] It is difficult to imagine what those distinctions might be.[12] In any event, under current federal statutes, the general rule is that a conversion of a state-chartered depository institution to a federal charter must be in conformity with state law.[13]

The apparent disparity in the treatment of state-to-federal conversions under the NBA (in light of *Casey*) and under HOLA (in light of *Hopkins Fed. Savings*) is no longer a practical consideration, since the NBA had already been amended, prior to *Hopkins Fed. Savings*, to require that such state-to-national bank conversions "not be in contravention of the State law."[14] That condition is currently contained in the NBA.[15] A similar condition is imposed on

---

7. 296 U.S. 315, 56 S.Ct. 235 (1935).

8. 296 U.S. at 335, 56 S.Ct. at 240.

9. 94 U.S. (4 Otto) 673 (1876).

10. *Hopkins Fed. Savings*, 296 U.S. at 342–343, 56 S.Ct. at 243.

11. 296 U.S. at 343, 56 S.Ct. at 243–244.

12. *Cf. Veazie Bank v. Fenno*, 75 U.S. (8 Wall.) 533, 549–555 (1869) (Nelson, J., dissenting) (arguing that federal government lacked power to deprive states of power to issue commercial banking franchises, citing Tenth Amendment).

13. *See, e.g.*, 12 U.S.C.A. § 35 (NBA provision); *id*. § 1464(i) (HOLA provision). *But cf. id*. § 1464(p) (providing for emergency savings and loan association conversions notwithstanding contrary law).

14. Act of December 23, 1913, § 8, 38 Stat. 258 (1913) (codified at 12 U.S.C.A. § 35).

15. *See* 12 U.S.C.A. § 35 (governing state-to-federal conversions of commercial banks).

conversion of a national-to-state bank charter.[16] OTS regulations also generally require compliance with applicable state law as a condition of approval of a conversion of a state-chartered savings association to a federal charter.[17]

FIRREA generally subjects conversions of savings associations to regulations prescribed by the OTS.[18] Despite *Hopkins Fed. Savings*, however, the OTS is authorized by FIRREA, *notwithstanding any other provision of law*, to approve conversion of a mutual savings association into a federal stock savings association or federal stock savings bank if the OTS determines that severe financial conditions exist that threaten the stability of the association to be converted, and that the conversion is likely to improve the financial condition of the association.[19] Such action by the OTS is also authorized where the FDIC has contracted to provide financial assistance to the association.[20] These conversions are also authorized if intended to assist an institution in receivership.[21] The question naturally arises whether this authority is consistent with *Hopkins Fed. Savings*. In fact, the Tenth Amendment, relied upon so heavily by *Hopkins Fed. Savings*, may have since been virtually overwhelmed by the Commerce Clause authority of Congress to make laws, in which case decisions limiting federal regulatory power based upon the amendment may simply be *hors de combat*.[22] One is tempted to think of *Hopkins Fed. Savings* as having fallen into desuetude.[23]

§ 2.14   Changes of Charter from Federal to State

Conversion of a national bank to a state charter in the state in which the bank is located requires an affirmative vote representing at least two-thirds of each class of its capital stock.[1] Shareholders of the converting bank are entitled to dissenters' appraisal rights.[2] Shareholders wishing to exercise these rights must vote against the

16. *See* 12 U.S.C.A. § 214c. *Cf. Ellis v. State Nat'l Bank of Ala.*, 434 F.2d 1182 (5th Cir.1970), *cert. denied*, 402 U.S. 973, 91 S.Ct. 1661 (1971) (concerning state law limitations on bank merger).

17. *See,   e.g.,*   12   C.F.R. §§ 543.9(c)(2), 552.2–6.

18. 12 U.S.C.A. § 1464(i)(1).

19. *Id.* § 1464(p)(2)(A).

20. *Id.* § 1464(p)(2)(B).

21. *Id.* § 1464(p)(2)(C).

22. *See* Van Alstyne, *The Second Death of Federalism*, 83 Mich. L. Rev. 1709 (1985) (discussing Tenth Amendment jurisprudence); Field, *Garcia v.* *San Antonio Metropolitan Transit Authority: The Demise of a Misguided Doctrine*, 99 Harv. L. Rev. 84 (1985) (same).

23. *See, e.g., Watters v. Wachovia Bank, N.A.*, 550 U.S. 1, 22, 127 S.Ct. 1559, 1573 (2007) (rejecting Tenth Amendment argument by Michigan that amendment protected state regulation of mortgage finance subsidiary of national bank from federal preemption). *But cf. Garcia v. San Antonio Metro. Transit Auth.*, 469 U.S. 528, 586, 105 S.Ct. 1005, 1036 (1985) (O'Connor, J., dissenting) (citing *Hopkins* with approval).

§ 2.14

1. 12 U.S.C.A. § 214a.

2. *Id.* § 214a(b).

conversion, or give notice of dissent in writing to the bank at or prior to the shareholders' meeting called to approve the conversion.[3] Shareholders who qualify for dissenters' appraisal rights are entitled to receive the value of their shares in cash, if and when the conversion is consummated, upon written request to the resulting state-chartered bank. This written request must be made within 30 days of the conversion, and it must be accompanied by the surrender of stock certificates.

Upon conversion, the resulting state-chartered bank may be admitted to membership in the Federal Reserve System by the Fed.[4] If the resulting bank does not obtain Fed membership, the stock of the Federal Reserve Bank owned by the converted national bank must be canceled and repaid.[5] If the resulting bank is an FDIC-insured, nonmember bank, and it will have less capital stock or surplus than the converting bank, an FDIC application may be required for consent to convert.[6]

A federal savings association may convert into a state savings association or savings bank,[7] organized under the laws of the state in which the principal office of the association is located, if the following conditions are met: (1) The state must permit conversions of state savings associations or savings banks into federal savings associations;[8] (2) The conversion is approved on the requisite vote, in person or by proxy, of members or stockholders of the association in accordance with state law, but in no event by less than 51 percent of the votes cast at the members' or stockholders' meeting.[9] The approval must comply with any other requirements reciprocally equivalent to the requirements of state law for conversion of a state chartered institution into a federal savings association;[10] (3) The requisite notice of the meeting must be given;[11] (4) If the converted institution is mutual in form, in any dissolution after the conversion the members or shareholders must share on a mutual basis in the assets of the association in exact proportion to their relative share or account credits;[12] and, (5) If the converted institution is stock in form, in any dissolution after the conversion the stockholders must share on an equitable basis in the assets of the

---

3. *Id.*

4. *Id.* § 321.

5. *Id.* §§ 287, 321.

6. 12 C.F.R. § 303.3(c).

7. *See generally Federal Home Loan Bank Bd. v. Greater Del. Valley Fed. Sav. & Loan Ass'n,* 277 F.2d 437 (3d Cir.1960) (concerning FHLBB challenge to statutory conversion of federal savings and loan association to state charter as legally ineffective, per prior statutory language).

8. 12 U.S.C.A. § 1464(i)(3)(A)(i).

9. *Id.* § 1464(i)(3)(A)(ii)(I)–(II).

10. *Id. See Federal Home Loan Bank Bd. v. Greater Del. Valley Fed. Sav. & Loan Ass'n,* 277 F.2d 437 (3d Cir.1960) (interpreting prior statutory language).

11. *See* 12 U.S.C.A. § 1464(i)(3)(A)(iii) (notice requirements under HOLA).

12. *Id.* § 1464(i)(3)(A)(iv).

association.[13] The conversion is effective on the date that all provisions of the HOLA have been fully complied with, and the state in which the savings association is located has issued the new charter.[14]

A converted savings association remains subject to the authority of the OTS.[15] Insurance of the converted savings association's accounts may be terminated in connection with the conversion, so long as the termination is effected consistent with applicable law and regulations.[16]

Conversion of a federal credit union to a state charter is subject to the following conditions specified in the FCUA. (1) A majority of the directors of the converting federal credit union must first approve the conversion and set a date for a vote by the members on the conversion.[17] (2) The conversion must be approved by a majority vote of the members voting on the proposal.[18] (3) A verified statement of the results of that vote must be filed with the NCUA within 10 days of the vote.[19] (4) Within 90 days of the vote, the converting credit union must take all necessary action under applicable state law to become a state-chartered credit union.[20] (5) Finally, within 10 days of receipt of the state charter, the converted credit union must file a copy thereof with the NCUA.[21] At that point, the converted credit union is no longer subject to any of the provisions of the FCUA.[22]

As discussed later in this chapter,[23] a new type of conversion—a "cross-industry" conversion—representing a hybrid of the conversion of charter and conversion of form is now authorized under federal law. The Credit Union Membership Access Act allows an insured credit union, under specified circumstances, to convert to a mutual savings association charter.[24] Such a conversion does not require the prior approval of the NCUA.[25] A proposal for the conversion must be approved by a majority of the directors of the insured credit union and by a majority of the members of the credit

---

13. *Id.* § 1464(i)(3)(A)(v).

14. *Id.* § 1464(i)(3)(A)(vi).

15. *Id.* § 1464(i)(3)(B)(i)–(ii).

16. *Id.* § 1464(i)(3)(B)(iii).

17. *Id.* § 1771(a)(1).

18. *Id.*

19. *Id.* § 1771(a)(2).

20. *Id.* § 1771(a)(3).

21. *Id.*

22. *Id.* § 1771(a)(4).

23. *See* § 2.17, *infra* (discussing cross-industry conversions).

24. Pub. L. No. 105–219, § 202(3), Aug. 7, 1998, 112 Stat. 913 (1998) (codified at 12 U.S.C.A. § 1785(2)).

25. 12 U.S.C.A. § 1785(2)(A). However, notice to the NCUA Board is required. *Id.* § 1785(2)(D). The NCUA is also required to "administer" the required vote of the members of the insured credit union seeking to convert. *Id.* § 1785(2)(G)(ii). The vote must be verified by the federal or state agency that would have jurisdiction over the converted institution. *Id.*

union.[26]

State regulatory policy has an interest in the conversion of federally chartered depository institutions into state-chartered institutions. Approaches to state regulation of such conversions varies. For example, New York law permits conversion of a national bank to a state charter provided that the conversion complies with federal law and the state statutory requirements governing conversions.[27] Similarly, a federal savings association with its place of business in New York is authorized to convert to a state charter.[28] These conversions require approval at a duly noticed shareholders meeting by an affirmative vote representing two-thirds of the book value of all outstanding shares or three-fourths of the outstanding shares represented at the meeting.[29] Similar provisions apply to the conversion of a federal credit union to a state charter.[30]

In contrast, California law presents a relatively more progressive model. California permits conversion of national banks to state charters with the approval of the Commissioner of Financial Institutions (formerly the Superintendent of Banks).[31] In granting approval, the Commissioner must be satisfied that the converting bank has complied with disclosure requirements, and has met general requirements applicable to conversion.[32] Upon conversion, the resulting bank is deemed to be the successor corporate entity of the converting national bank for all purposes.[33]

Conversions of federally chartered savings associations to state charters have been regulated under California's Unitary Savings Association Law.[34] Federal associations are permitted to convert into state-chartered savings associations in accordance with the requirements and procedures set forth in the Law.[35]

California also provides for cross-industry conversions, *i.e.,* conversions from one type of depository institution (*e.g.,* a commercial bank) to another type of depository institution (*e.g.,* a savings

---

26. *Id.* § 1785(2)(B). If the NCUA or the federal or state agency that would have jurisdiction over the converted institution does not approve of the methods by which the member vote is taken, the member vote must be taken again, "as directed by the [NCUA] or the agency." *Id.* § 1785(2)(G)(ii).

27. N.Y. Banking Law § 136(1).

28. N.Y. Banking Law § 136(2).

29. *Id.*

30. N.Y. Banking Law § 480–a.

31. Cal. Fin. Code § 4941(a). An amendment to the California law, effec-

tive 1 July 1997, abolished the office of the Superintendent of Banks and the State Banking Department and the office of the Commissioner and the Department of Savings and Loan, transferring their powers to the Commissioner of Financial Institutions and the Department of Financial Institutions. Cal. Stats. 1996, ch. 1064, §§ 28.5, 29.5 (codified at Cal. Fin. Code §§ 200, 210–217).

32. Cal. Fin. Code §§ 4942–4945.

33. Cal. Fin. Code § 4950.

34. Cal. Fin. Code §§ 5000 *et seq.*

35. Cal. Fin. Code § 5709.

association), under its Depository Corporation Sale, Merger, and Conversion Law.[36]

California law also provides for conversion of federal credit unions to state charters.[37] A federal credit union can convert under California law, upon the recommendation of its board of directors, by complying with the requirements of the FCUA and obtaining a certificate of authorization to act as a credit union under California law.[38]

§ 2.15   Change of Charter from State to Federal

The National Bank Act ("NBA") authorizes the Comptroller to approve conversions of state banks to national charters on the following conditions.[1] The converting bank must have sufficient unimpaired capital to have allowed its chartering as a national bank.[2] The conversion must be approved by an affirmative vote of shareholders representing not less than 51 percent of the capital stock of the converting bank. The NBA requires that the name of the resulting national bank contain the word "national." The NBA also expressly requires that the conversion "not be in contravention of the State law."[3]

Under certain circumstances, it appears that a converting state bank may have relatively greater powers than a newly organized

---

36. Cal. Fin. Code §§ 4800 *et seq.* On the effect of other savings association and banking laws on the Depository Corporation Sale, Merger, and Conversion Law, see Cal. Fin. Code § 4827. These cross-industry conversion provisions create a third category of conversions, in addition to conversions from state to federal or federal to state charter and conversions from mutual to stock organization. The third category is cross-industry conversion from one type of state-chartered depository institution to another type of state-chartered depository institution. *See* Cal. Fin. Code §§ 4920 *et seq.* (concerning cross-industry conversions of state depository corporations). However, certain cross-industry conversions have been prohibited under the Law. Conversions of state-chartered banks to mutual savings associations, federally or state-chartered, are not permitted. Cal. Fin. Code § 4825(a). Likewise, conversions of state-chartered mutual savings associations to state commercial banks are prohibited, Cal. Fin. Code § 4825(b), as are conversions of federal or state mutual savings associations to state-chartered commercial banks and *vice versa.* Cal. Fin. Code

§ 4825(c)–(d). In addition, a savings association has been prohibited from converting into a commercial bank, if the ownership of the converting savings association, as ownership of the resulting bank, would be prohibited by the restrictions on interstate bank holding companies under the Douglas Amendment to the Bank Holding Company Act of 1956 (BHCA). Cal. Fin. Code § 4826. *See* 12 U.S.C.A. § 1842(d) (1992) (setting forth former interstate holding company restrictions). The BHCA interstate restrictions were removed in September 1994.

37. Cal. Fin. Code §§ 15350 *et seq.*

38. Cal. Fin. Code § 15350. *See* Cal. Fin. Code §§ 14100 *et seq.* (formation of state-chartered credit union).

§ 2.15

1. 12 U.S.C.A. § 35.

2. *Id.*

3. *Id. See generally Marion Nat'l Bank v. Saxon,* 261 F.Supp. 373 (N.D.Ind.1966); *Traverse City State Bank v. Empire Nat'l Bank,* 228 F.Supp. 984 (W.D.Mich.1964).

national bank. In *American Council of Life Ins. v. Ludwig,*[4] the
D.C. District Court explored the interplay of section 35 with section
92, permitting operation of an insurance business by a national
bank if the business is located in a community of less than 5,000
inhabitants. The court upheld OCC approval of a conversion of
state-chartered bank with two insurance subsidiaries that in fact
did not conform to the requirements of section 92.[5] In allowing the
converted bank to retain the nonconforming subsidiaries, the OCC
relied on language in section 35 that gives the Comptroller the
discretion to permit a converting state bank to "retain and carry"
certain nonconforming assets.[6] The court found that the "retain
and carry" language was plain in meaning and did not suggest that
ultimate divesture of nonconforming assets was required under
section 35.[7] In addition, the legislative history appeared to show
that the purpose of the section was to remove impediments from
state banks seeking to convert to national bank status by allowing
them to retain such nonconforming assets.[8] Accordingly, the court
found that the Comptroller had express authority to permit a
converting bank to retain its nonconforming assets "subject to such
conditions as he may prescribe," including the permanent retention
of the nonconforming assets.[9] It held that the Comptroller's decision to allow the converting bank to retain its nonconforming
assets was not arbitrary, capricious or an abuse of discretion.

There are apparently some limits to the Comptroller's authority to create variances in connection with a conversion. An attempt
by the Comptroller to authorize a state bank converting to a
national charter to "inchworm" the location of its home office
successively through three states—in an effort to create a post-
conversion tri-state network of branches—was invalidated as a
sham unauthorized in substance by the NBA[10] and relevant state
laws.[11] The Sixth Circuit took the position that selection of an
existing branch office of the converting bank as its new "main" or
"principal" office was properly treated as a "relocation," rather
than a new charter "designation," notwithstanding similarities
between conversion and *de novo* chartering, since, under relevant
state law, the post-conversion bank was deemed to be a continua-

4. 1 F.Supp.2d 24 (D.D.C.1998),
vac'd and remanded as moot, 194 F.3d
173 (D.C.Cir.1999).

5. The insurance subsidiaries operated in part in offices situated in communities with populations that exceeded
5,000. *American Council of Life Ins.,* 1
F.Supp.2d at 26.

6. 12 U.S.C. § 35.

7. *American Council of Life Ins.,* 1
F.Supp.2d at 28

8. *Id.*

9. *Id.* at 29. In *dicta,* the court also
suggested that, even if the language of
section 35 were not clear on its face, it
"would still find the Comptroller's interpretation to be proper insofar as it was
reasonable." *Id.*

10. 12 U.S.C. §§ 30(b), 36(c).

11. *McQueen v. Williams,* 177 F.3d
523 (6th Cir.1999).

tion of the pre-conversion bank.[12] "Relocation" during the conversion process was impermissible, because state agency approval required for pre-conversion relocation under Michigan law had not been obtained,[13] and post-conversion relocation was barred by federal limitations on a national bank's relocation of its "main office" to a location within thirty miles of its original location.[14] Furthermore, even if a branch office of a state bank could be designated as its "main office" during its conversion to a national bank charter, designation of the Michigan branch office as the "main office" was, in the court's view, a sham and hence improper, since the post-conversion bank never intended to establish its "main office" at the designated branch office.[15] In fact, the facility was selected because it was within 30 miles of the *next* intended "main office" in Indiana, to facilitate a subsequent merger with another bank, as part of its holding company's attempt to combine its affiliate banks in Michigan, Indiana, and Ohio while retaining a tri-state network of branches, thus circumventing laws that would otherwise have prevented this multistate branching scheme.[16]

Conversion of any state savings association that is, or is eligible to become, a member of a federal home loan bank into a federal savings association, and any accompanying conversion from mutual to stock or stock to mutual form,[17] is subject to regulations prescribed by the OTS.[18] Further, any federal savings association may change its designation from a federal savings association to a federal savings bank, or *vice versa*.[19]

Conversion of a state savings bank that is a member of the BIF into a federal savings bank is permitted, subject to the provisions of the amended Home Owners' Loan Act ("HOLA")[20] and pursuant to regulations promulgated by the OTS.[21] The OTS is authorized to provide for the organization, incorporation, operation, examination, and regulation of such converted savings banks.[22] The converted savings bank continues to be a BIF member until such time as it changes its status to membership in the SAIF.[23]

Section 125 of the Federal Credit Union Act ("FCUA")[24] provides for the conversion of a state-chartered credit union to a

---

12. *Id.*

13. M.C.L.A. § 487.457.

14. 12 U.S.C. § 30(b).

15. *McQueen, supra.*

16. *Id.*

17. Conversion of any savings association from mutual to stock or stock to mutual form is prohibited except in accordance with regulations promulgated by the OTS. 12 U.S.C.A. § 1464(i)(2)(A).

18. *Id.* § 1464(i)(1).

19. *Id.* § 1464(i)(2)(C).

20. *Id.* § 1464(o)(2)(B)–(E).

21. *Id.* § 1464(o)(1).

22. *Id.*

23. *Id.* § 1464(o)(2)(A).

24. *Id.* § 1771.

federal charter.[25] Such conversions require approval of the NCUA.[26] They are treated by the NCUA like an initial application for a federal charter, "including mandatory on-site examination by NCUA."[27] Approval is conditioned on the following factors. (1) There must be compliance with all applicable state law requirements.[28] (2) The institution must file with the NCUA satisfactory proof of such compliance.[29] (3) The institution must file with the NCUA an organization certificate, as required under the FCUA.[30]

State practice varies. For example, New York law freely permits conversions of state-chartered banks to national bank charters.[31] These conversions do not require the approval of any state authority.[32] The proposed conversion must be approved by a vote of stockholders representing at least two-thirds of the stock of the converting bank and must be effected in the manner provided by federal law.

State-chartered savings associations are also permitted to convert to a federal charter, subject to procedures imposed by the New York statute.[33] The conversion must be approved at a duly noticed meeting of shareholders,[34] by an affirmative vote representing at least two-thirds of the book value of all outstanding shares,[35] or at least three-fourths of the book value of the outstanding shares represented at the meeting.[36] Similar state law provisions apply to conversions of state-chartered credit unions to federal charters.[37]

A more progressive model is provided by California law, which freely permits state-chartered banks to convert to national bank charters, so long as the converting bank complies with all conversion requirements of federal law.[38] The resulting national bank is deemed to be the successor corporate entity of the converting state-chartered bank.[39] The resulting bank may be required to file a report with the Commissioner of Financial Institutions detailing the conversion.[40] The converting bank must surrender its certificate of authority to do a banking business to the Commissioner for cancellation.[41]

---

25. 12 U.S.C.A. § 1771(b). For interpretive guidance with respect to such conversions, see IRPS 99–1, as amended by IRPS 00–1, 65 Fed. Reg. 64,512 (2000).

26. *Id.* § 1771(b)(2).

27. 54 Fed. Reg. at 31,179.

28. *Id.* § 1771(b)(1)(A).

29. *Id.* § 1771(b)(1)(B).

30. *Id.* § 1771(b)(1)(C). *See id.* § 1753 (setting forth organization certificate requirement).

31. N.Y. Banking Law § 137.

32. N.Y. Banking Law § 137(1).

33. N.Y. Banking Law § 409.

34. *See* N.Y. Banking Law § 409 (notice requirements).

35. N.Y. Banking Law § 409(a).

36. N.Y. Banking Law § 409(b).

37. *See* N.Y. Banking Law § 487 (credit union conversions).

38. Cal. Fin. Code § 4961(a).

39. Cal. Fin. Code § 4940, 4963.

40. Cal. Fin. Code § 4964(b).

41. Cal. Fin. Code § 4964(a).

Conversions of state-chartered savings associations to federal charters are regulated under California's unitary Savings Association Law.[42] State-chartered savings associations have been permitted to convert into federally chartered savings associations in accordance with the requirements and procedures set forth in the Law.[43]

California also provides for cross-industry conversions, *i.e.,* conversions from one type of depository institution (*e.g.,* a commercial bank) to another type of depository institution (*e.g.,* a savings association), under its Depository Corporation Sale, Merger, and Conversion Law.[44]

In cross-industry state-to-federal conversions, California law also permits conversion of a state-chartered bank to a federally chartered savings association.[45] Conversion of a state-chartered savings association to a national bank is also permitted.[46]

California law provides for conversion of a state-chartered credit union to a federal charter.[47] A state-chartered credit union can convert under California law, on the recommendation of its board of directors, by an affirmative vote of a majority of the members of the credit union.[48] Within ten days of the vote, the credit union is required to file with the Commissioner a verified certificate containing a copy of the minutes of the members' meeting or a copy of the written ballot and results of the vote, together with a statement that the proposed conversion has been approved.[49] A copy of the certificate must be filed with the Secretary of State.[50]

§ 2.16 Conversion of Form

This section examines the other major type of depository institution conversion, the conversion from one organization form, the mutual institution, to another, the stock institution. The main focus is upon savings associations, such as savings and loan associations and savings banks, which may be organized in mutual form. Accordingly, particular attention is given to the applicable provisions of Home Owners' Loan Act ("HOLA").[1]

---

42. Cal. Fin. Code §§ 5000 *et seq.*

43. Cal. Fin. Code § 5700.

44. Cal. Fin. Code §§ 4800 *et seq.* On the effect of other savings association and banking laws on the Depository Corporation Sale, Merger, and Conversion Law, see Cal. Fin. Code § 4827. *See also supra* § 2.14, note 36 (discussing California cross-industry conversion provisions).

45. Cal. Fin. Code § 4961(b).

46. *Id.*

47. Cal. Fin. Code §§ 15300 *et seq.*

48. Cal. Fin. Code § 15301.

49. Cal. Fin. Code § 15302. *See also* Cal. Fin. Code § 15303 (certificate as presumptive evidence).

50. Cal. Fin. Code § 15302.

§ 2.16

1. 12 U.S.C.A. § 1464(i). *See generally York v. Federal Home Loan Bank Bd.,* 624 F.2d 495 (4th Cir.1980), *cert. denied,* 449 U.S. 1043, 101 S.Ct. 621 (concerning

For various reasons, conversions of form have become increasingly prevalent in recent years. One reason is that conversion to the stock form of ownership may offer the institution an opportunity to attract new capital from the investing public, rather than from mutual depositors. Also, the conversion may facilitate reorganization into a holding company pattern of ownership.[2] Finally, during the 1980s, the organizational conversion played an important role in the rehabilitation of savings associations in danger of default.[3] Conversion from mutual to stock form of organization may be the first step in a reorganization or private sale of a mutual savings association which, as it begins to return to profitability, has particular needs for a capital infusion.[4]

HOLA provides general authority for the conversion from mutual to stock form of any savings association converting to a federal charter.[5] In addition, consistent with the purposes of the HOLA, the OTS has been authorized, notwithstanding any other provision of law, (1) to approve or (in the case of a federal savings association) require conversion of a mutual savings association or an FDIC-insured federal mutual savings bank into a federal stock savings association or federal stock savings bank; (2) to charter a federal stock savings association or federal stock savings bank to acquire the assets of such a mutual institution; or (3) to charter a federal stock savings association or federal stock savings bank to merge with such a mutual institution.[6]

Such a conversion is authorized only if any one of the three following conditions is met: (1) The conversion can be authorized or required if the OTS determines that severe financial conditions exist that threaten the stability of the association to be converted, and that the conversion is likely to improve the financial condition

conversion from federal mutual to federal stock savings association). In August 2002 the Office of Thrift Supervision (OTS) extensively revised its regulations concerning mutual-to-stock conversions. 67 Fed. Reg. 52,010, 52,020–52,035 (2002) (codified at 12 C.F.R. pt. 563b).

2. However, since 1987, authority has existed in federal law for the establishment of a mutual holding company as well. See 12 U.S.C.A. § 1730a(s) (1988) (providing for mutual holding companies). Section 1730a was repealed in 1989. See Financial Institutions Reform, Recovery, and Enforcement Act of 1989, Pub. L. No. 101–73, § 407, 103 Stat. 183, 363 (1989) ("FIRREA") (repealing § 1730a). Mutual holding companies are now governed by Section 10 of HOLA, as amended by FIRREA. 12

U.S.C.A. § 1467a(o), *as amended*, FIRREA § 301, 103 Stat. at 336–338. For the OTS regulations governing mutual holding companies, see 12 C.F.R. pt. 575.

3. *See, e.g.,* Berg, *State Savings Banks Thriving,* N.Y. Times, Feb. 7, 1987, at 33, col. 3 (discussing role of conversions).

4. This factor has been an underlying motive of the sudden rise of the federal stock savings bank authorized since 1982. See Pub. L. No. 97–320, § 121, 96 Stat. 1479–1480 (1982) (codified at 12 U.S.C.A. § 1464(p)), *as amended,* FIRREA § 301, 103 Stat. at 301.

5. 12 U.S.C.A. § 1464(i)(1).

6. 12 U.S.C.A. § 1464(p)(1).

of the association.[7] (2) The conversion can be authorized or required if the FDIC has contracted to provide assistance to the association under Section 13 of the FDIA.[8] (3) The conversion can be authorized or required if it is intended to assist an institution in receivership.[9]

A federal savings bank chartered under these provisions would have the same authority and be subject to the same restrictions that would apply if it had been chartered as a federal savings bank under any other provision of HOLA.[10] Furthermore, it can engage in any investment, activity, or operation that the converting institution was engaged in, if the latter was a federal savings bank, or would have been authorized to engage in if the latter had converted to a federal charter.[11]

§ 2.17   Cross–Industry Conversions

The Gramm–Leach–Bliley Act ("GLBA")[1] permits cross-industry conversions, a type of conversion that is like a hybrid of the traditional conversions of charter and form. The GLBA permits a federal savings association chartered prior to the date of the GLBA enactment (12 November 1999) to convert into one or more national or state banks, subject to the approval of the Comptroller or the appropriate state bank supervisor, with each converted bank encompassing one or more of the branches of the federal savings association in one or more states.[2] Each resulting national or state bank must meet all applicable financial, management, and capital requirements that would otherwise apply to a *de novo* charter applicant.[3] Any federal savings association that converts its charter to a national or state bank charter after the enactment of the GLBA is permitted to retain the term "Federal" in its name, if it remains an insured depository institution.[4]

---

7. *Id.* § 1464(p)(2)(A).

8. *Id.* § 1464(p)(2)(B). *See id.* § 1823 (FDIA Section 13, providing for financial assistance to institutions in default or in danger of default under specified circumstances).

9. *Id.* § 1464(p)(2)(C). The authority of the OTS to force a conversion of a state-chartered mutual savings association to a federal stock savings association, notwithstanding contrary state law, was upheld in *Smallwood v. Office of Thrift Supervision*, 925 F.2d 894 (6th Cir.1991). The court expressed the view that "FIRREA and its legislative history demonstrates [*sic*] an unmistakable purpose to insure that Federal authority is paramount regarding the maintenance of the solvency of the Federal deposit insurance system, and therefore that § 5(p) [of HOLA, 12 U.S.C.A. § 1464(p)] impliedly preempts state laws that could impede the authority of the [OTS] to approve or deny conversions." *Smallwood*, 925 F.2d at 898.

10. 12 U.S.C.A. § 1464(p)(3).

11. *Id.*

§ 2.17

1. Pub. L. No. 106–102, Nov. 12, 1999, 113 Stat. 1338 (1999) (codified at scattered sections of 12, 15, 16, 18 U.S.C.A.).

2. GLBA, § 739 (codified at 12 U.S.C.A. § 1464(i)(5)).

3. 12 U.S.C.A. § 1464(i)(5)(A).

4. GLBA, § 723 (codified at 12 U.S.C.A. § 30(d)(1)).

Chapter 3

BRANCHING

Table of Sections

§ 3.1 Introduction

Establishment of a branch[1] is one means by which a depository institution can enter another geographic segment of the industry market. This is subject to an approval process similar to the one that applies to chartering. Branches are normally considered to be geographically distinct outlets of one institutional entity. Functionally, however, other institutional structures or arrangements may operate as "branches" of a single enterprise. For example, in "chain banking," separately operating banks may be interrelated through common stock control,[2] interlocking directorates,[3] or other similar control devices. The members of the chain functionally act like branches, but to the extent that they are independently struc-

---

§ 3.1

1. On the meaning of the term "branch," *see, e.g.,* 12 U.S.C.A. § 36(j) (defining the term for purposes of National Bank Act ("NBA")). *See also First Nat'l Bank in Plant City v. Dickinson,* 396 U.S. 122, 90 S.Ct. 337 (1969); *Independent Bankers Ass'n of Am. v. Smith,* 534 F.2d 921 (D.C.Cir.), *cert. denied,* 429 U.S. 862, 97 S.Ct. 166 (1976) (interpreting and applying NBA definition).

2. There are statutory limitations on common control through stock ownership of depository institutions. *See* 12 U.S.C.A. § 1817(j) (Change in Bank Control Act). *Cf.* 12 U.S.C.A. § 1467a (regulating holding companies of savings associations); §§ 1841 *et seq.* (regulating holding companies of banks).

3. There are statutory limitations on management interlocks between otherwise unaffiliated depository institutions. *See* 12 U.S.C.A. §§ 3201 *et seq.*

tured and operated, they are not subject to the legal principles applicable to branches.[4] To the extent that the independence of the chain members is open to question, however, these principles may be applied to them by their regulator.[5]

Common control exerted by a holding company enterprise over constituent operating subsidiaries is often referred to as "group banking." Group banking differs from chain banking in the formality of the control relationship. However, group banking is as vulnerable in principle as chain banking to the possibility that the regulator may consider it to be an impermissible evasion of branch banking regulation.[6] Before the enactment of federal law in 1994 permitting interstate branch banking,[7] this concern over group banking was an important issue for state regulators.[8]

This chapter focuses on restrictions on traditional branch banking. As a general rule, within any state, both state-chartered and federally chartered depository institutions have the power to branch. Where a state statute prohibits or restricts state banks from intrastate branching, national banks located in that state are subject to the same branching rules.[9]

This chapter first considers the regulatory principles that apply to *intrastate* branching by national banks. It then provides a brief survey of state law restrictions on intrastate branching. Thereafter, the chapter considers savings association branching and credit union branching, and concludes with analysis of the 1994 federal legislation authorizing *interstate* branching.

§ 3.2   National Bank Branching

A key provision of the National Bank Act ("NBA") authorizes the establishment of intrastate branches of national banks, with the approval of the Comptroller, to the extent that "such establishment and operation are at the time expressly authorized to State banks by the law of the State in question...."[1] In addition, the branch is permitted to be established outside the city in which the principal office of the national bank is located only if state statutory law permits such branching by state banks "affirmatively and not

---

4. *See National State Bank, Elizabeth, N.J. v. Howell,* 49 N.J. 330, 230 A.2d 377 (1967).

5. *See Bank of N. Am. v. State Banking Bd.,* 468 S.W.2d 529 (Tex.Civ.App. 1971).

6. *See, e.g., Commercial Nat'l Bank of Little Rock v. Board of Governors,* 451 F.2d 86 (8th Cir.1971); *Whitney Natl. Bank in Jefferson Parish v. James,* 189 So.2d 430 (La.App.1966).

7. Pub. L. No. 103–328, 108 Stat. 2338 (1994) (codified at scattered sections of 12 U.S.C.).

8. *See, e.g., Commercial Nat'l Bank of Little Rock v. Board of Governors,* 451 F.2d 86 (8th Cir.1971); *Whitney Nat'l Bank in Jefferson Parish v. James,* 189 So.2d 430 (La.App.1966).

9. 12 U.S.C.A. § 36(c).

§ 3.2

1. 12 U.S.C.A. § 36(c)(1).

merely by implication or recognition."[2] Establishment of the branch is also subject to capital requirements that would apply to a state bank application for a branch.[3] In addition, until 1996, the aggregate capital of the bank and its branches was required to be at least equal to the aggregate minimum required capital for the establishment of the bank and each of its branches as separate national banks.[4]

§ 3.3   Policy of Competitive Equality

The NBA provision concerning branching was enacted in 1927 as part of the McFadden Act.[1] According to its chief sponsor, Representative McFadden, the provision was intended "to restore as nearly as possible the equilibrium between state and national banks within the Federal Reserve System."[2] Prior to this enactment, several states allowed branch banking for state chartered institutions; national banks could not compete effectively in those jurisdictions without converting from federal to state charters. The McFadden Act authorized the Comptroller of the Currency to allow national banks to establish branch offices in any state that permitted branching for state chartered institutions, but only under the same terms and conditions.[3]

In *First National Bank of Logan v. Walker Bank & Trust Co.*,[4] the Supreme Court considered how specifically this requirement was to be interpreted and applied in assessing the legality of the Comptroller's decisions approving branching applications of two Utah-based national banks. *Walker Bank* viewed the NBA branching provision as fundamentally controlled by a policy of "competitive equality" between state and national banks with respect to branching.

The Utah branching statute prohibited Utah banks, with certain exceptions, from branching except through the acquisition of an existing bank that had been in operation for not less than five years.[5] The two applicant national banks had sought to establish *de*

---

2. *Id.* § 36(c)(2).

3. *See First–Citizens Bank & Trust Co. v. Camp*, 409 F.2d 1086 (4th Cir. 1969) (applying "solvency" of the branch" test under state law).

4. *Id.* § 36(h), *repealed*, Pub. L. No. 104–208, § 2204, 110 Stat. 3009 (Sept. 30, 1996).

§ 3.3

1. For discussion of the legislative history of the McFadden Act with respect to its branching provisions, see *Clarke v. Securities Indus. Ass'n*, 479

U.S. 388, 404–408, 107 S.Ct. 750, 759–762 (1987); *First Nat'l Bank of Logan v. Walker Bank & Trust Co.*, 385 U.S. 252, 256–260, 87 S.Ct. 492, 495–497 (1966); *Cheshire Nat'l Bank v. Smith*, 427 F.Supp. 277, 279–280 (D.N.H.1977).

2. 68 Cong. Rec. 1296 (1924) (remarks of Cong. McFadden).

3. 12 U.S.C.A. § 36(c).

4. 385 U.S. 252, 87 S.Ct. 492 (1966).

5. Utah Code Ann., tit. 7, ch. 3, § 6 (1965 Supp.).

novo branches.[6] In upholding the Comptroller's approval of these applications over competitor challenge,[7] one district court had found "express authority" for state bank branching in general, and would not apply the specific conditions that would have attached to a branch application of a state bank.[8] In other words, the court interpreted Section 36 as "referencing over" to state law on *whether* a national bank could branch, and possibly *where*, but not as to *how* it might branch. The Court of Appeals reversed, holding that Section 36(c) created a policy of "competitive equality" between state and national banks, which required "reference over" to all pertinent provisions of state branching law.[9] In the other application, another district court "imposed all of the restrictions of . . . Utah law on the establishment of national banks and the Court of Appeals for the District of Columbia Circuit affirmed."[10]

On *certiorari*, the Supreme Court endorsed this broad policy of competitive equality, arguing:

> It appears clear from . . . the legislative history of § 36(c)(1) and (2) that Congress intended to place national and state banks on a basis of "competitive equality" insofar as branch banking was concerned. Both sponsors of the applicable banking Acts, Representative McFadden and Senator Glass, so characterized the legislation. It is not for us to so construe the Acts as to frustrate this clearcut purpose so forcefully expressed by both friend and foe of the legislation at the time of its adoption. To us it appears beyond question that the Congress was continuing its policy of equalization [of state and national banks] first adopted in the National Bank Act of 1864. . . .[11]

In response, the Comptroller tried to parse the NBA provision narrowly, as mandating reference over to state law "only as to 'whether' and 'where' branches may be located and not the 'method' by which this is effected."[12] The Court refused to read the section and its legislative history so narrowly. It explained:

6. *Walker Bank*, 385 U.S. at 254, 87 S.Ct. at 493.

7. Competing banks in the area where a proposed national bank branch is to be established have standing to object to the branch application, but there is no indication that the Comptroller need give notice to competing banks. *See Community Bank of Washtenaw v. Smith*, 378 F.Supp. 235 (E.D.Mich.1974) (holding failure to notify not denial of due process).

8. *Walker Bank*, 385 U.S. at 255, 87 S.Ct. at 494.

9. *Id.* But see *First Nat'l Bank of Smithfield v. Saxon*, 352 F.2d 267 (4th Cir.1965) (holding *contra*).

10. *Walker Bank*, 385 U.S. at 256, 87 S.Ct. at 495.

11. 385 U.S. at 261, 87 S.Ct. at 497.

12. *Id.* Ironically, the Comptroller successfully made essentially the same argument as to U.S. branching by foreign banks in *Conference of State Bank Supervisors v. Conover*, 715 F.2d 604 (D.C.Cir.1983), *cert. denied*, 466 U.S. 927, 104 S.Ct. 1708 (1984). The D.C. Circuit rejected application of Section

We believe that where a State allows branching only by taking over an existing bank, it expresses as much "whether" and "where" a branch may be located as does a prohibition or a limitation to the home office municipality. As to the restriction being a "method," we have concluded that since it is part and parcel of Utah's policy, it was absorbed by the provisions of §§ 36(c)(1) and (2), regardless of the tag placed upon it.[13]

Hence, whether, where, and how national banks may branch intrastate are all questions subject to reference over to applicable state law embodied in Section 36(c). This policy of "competitive equality" has been extended to such issues as whether the needs of the community in which a proposed national bank branch would operate were sufficiently served by existing branches.[14] Failure to follow explicitly such a state law requirement would render the Comptroller's decision in contravention of law.[15] This analysis descends to a minute level of detail, including such issues as whether or not the Comptroller's approval properly determined, for example, that the proposed site of a branch was a "town" within the meaning of applicable state law.[16]

Some modest limitations on the "reference over" analysis under Section 36(c) have been recognized by the courts. A state statutory requirement that prohibits a branch in any city or town in which its principal place of business is located, except by acquiring an existing bank, apparently does not prevent the Comptroller from authorizing a national bank to acquire existing *branches* of another national bank in exchange for its existing branches.[17] The congressional policy of competitive equality can be read to authorize exchange of branches under the NBA if state banks are able to exchange branches under state banking law.[18] In addition, if a

36–like limitations to the Comptroller's decision to license federal branches of foreign banks without "reference over" to state law restrictions on state licensing of such branches. Unlike the legislative policy that informed *Walker Bank*, *Conference* was guided in its decision by the policy of "national treatment" of foreign banks that informed the International Banking Act of 1978, 12 U.S.C.A. §§ 3101 *et seq.*

13. *Walker Bank*, 385 U.S. at 262, 87 S.Ct. at 497.

14. *Hempstead Bank v. Smith*, 540 F.2d 57 (2d Cir.1976).

15. *Id.*

16. *First Union Bank & Trust Co. v. Heimann*, 600 F.2d 91 (7th Cir.1979) (applying Indiana branch banking requirement, Ind. Code § 28–1–17). *See*

also American Bank & Trust Co. v. Saxon, 373 F.2d 283 (6th Cir.1967); *Peoples Bank of Trenton v. Saxon*, 373 F.2d 185 (6th Cir.1967); *Security Bank v. Saxon*, 298 F.Supp. 991 (E.D.Mich.1968); *Marion Nat'l Bank v. Van Buren Bank*, 418 F.2d 121, 124 (7th Cir.1969); *First Nat'l Bank of Crown Point v. Camp*, 463 F.2d 595 (7th Cir.1972); *Albion Nat. Bank v. Department of Fin. Insts.*, 171 Ind.App. 211, 355 N.E.2d 873 (1976).

17. *State ex rel. Edwards v. Heimann*, 633 F.2d 886, 889–890 (9th Cir. 1980) (noting Section 36(c) reference to establishment and operation of "new branches").

18. *Id.* (*citing Seattle Trust & Sav. Bank v. Bank of Cal.*, 492 F.2d 48, 52 (9th Cir.), *cert. denied*, 419 U.S. 844, 95 S.Ct. 77 (1974); *Dakota Nat'l Bank &*

particular state has no explicit statutory provisions for branching of state-chartered banks, but does have such provisions for other depository institutions, such as state savings associations, then the Comptroller may authorize branching by national banks in the state.[19]

Alternatively, where a state restricts branching into the "home office" location of another bank, the Comptroller may still authorize a national bank branch in a home office location, if the national bank relocates *its* home office to the site of the proposed branch.[20] However, an attempt by the Comptroller to authorize a state bank converting to a national charter to "inchworm" the location of its home office successively through three states—in an effort to create a post-conversion tri-state network—was invalidated as a sham unauthorized in substance by the NBA[21] and relevant state laws.[22]

On the other hand, the Southern District of New York held that the Comptroller of the Currency did not act arbitrarily or capriciously when he determined that the area in which a national bank sought to establish a branch office was not an "unincorporated village" under New York law, and that as a result New York's home office rule-barring the establishment of a bank branch within an unincorporated village containing the home office of another banking institution-did not apply.[23] The fact that the state banking commissioner had already determined that the area *was* a village did not make a difference to the outcome.

§ 3.4 Meaning of "Branch"

One issue that has been the source of considerable controversy is the meaning of "branch" for purposes of the NBA. The federal statutory definition provides in part that a branch is "any branch bank, branch office, branch agency, additional office, or any branch place of business located in any State or Territory of the United States or in the District of Columbia at which deposits are received, or checks paid, or money lent."[1] Despite the fact that the NBA provides its own definition for this concept, in *First National Bank in Plant City v. Dickinson*[2] the Supreme Court interpreted the term

---

Trust v. First Nat'l Bank, 554 F.2d 345, 355 (8th Cir.), *cert. denied*, 434 U.S. 877, 98 S.Ct. 229 (1977)).

19. *Department of Banking v. Clarke*, 809 F.2d 266 (5th Cir.), *cert. denied*, 483 U.S. 1010, 107 S.Ct. 3240 (1987).

20. *Ramapo Bank v. Camp*, 425 F.2d 333 (3d Cir.1970), *cert. denied*, 400 U.S. 828, 91 S.Ct. 57 (applying 12 U.S.C.A. §§ 30, 36).

21. 12 U.S.C.A. §§ 30(b), 36(c).

22. *McQueen v. Williams*, 177 F.3d 523 (6th Cir.1999).

23. *Community Bank of Sullivan County v. First Nat. Bank of Jeffersonville*, 125 F.Supp.2d 659 (S.D.N.Y.2000).

§ 3.4

1. 12 U.S.C.A. § 36(j).

2. 396 U.S. 122, 90 S.Ct. 337 (1969).

in light of the policy of "competitive equality" that it had previously held to be the basic principle embodied in the NBA branching provision.[3] The end result, counterintuitive as it may seem, was that armored cars and deposit drop boxes were interpreted to be branches.

The situs of the national bank in *Plant City* was Florida, which prohibited all branch banking by state chartered banks, and hence by all national banks as well.[4] The Comptroller permitted the bank to operate an armored car messenger service and an off-premises receptacle for the receipt of packages containing cash or checks for deposit.[5] The Comptroller's letters authorizing the services contained explicit requirements that deposits received through these services not become bank liabilities until actually in the hands of the bank teller at the office of the bank, and that checks cashed for customers be deemed paid at the bank when the cash was handed to the messenger, not when delivered to the customer by the armored car teller.[6] The Florida Bank Comptroller challenged the services, arguing that Florida unequivocally prohibited off-premises banking of any kind.[7] Thus, the question was whether the services constituted the establishment and operation of a "branch." In the Court's view, this question was governed by federal law.[8] Nevertheless, the Court invoked the policy of competitive equality in resolving the issue. The Court explained:

> The policy of competitive equality is ... firmly embedded in the statutes governing the national banking system. The mechanism of referring to state law is simply one designed to implement that congressional intent and build into the federal statute a self-executing provision to accommodate to changes in state regulation. . . .
>
> Although the definition [of branch] may not be a model of precision, in part due to its circular aspect, it defines the minimum content of the term "branch"; by use of the word "include" the definition suggests a calculated indefiniteness with respect to the other limits of the term. However, the term "branch bank" at the very least includes any place for receiving deposits or paying checks or lending money apart from the chartered premises; it may include more. It should be emphasized that, since § 36(f) [currently codified as § 36(j)] is phrased in the disjunctive, the offering of any one of the three

---

3. *First Nat'l Bank of Logan v. Walker Bank & Trust Co.*, 385 U.S. 252, 87 S.Ct. 492 (1966).

4. *Plant City*, 396 U.S. at 124–125, 90 S.Ct. at 339.

5. 396 U.S. at 125–126, 90 S.Ct. at 339.

6. 396 U.S. at 126, 90 S.Ct. at 339.

7. 396 U.S. at 130–131, 90 S.Ct. at 342.

8. 396 U.S. at 133–134, 90 S.Ct. at 343.

services mentioned in that definition will provide the basis for finding that "branch" banking is taking place. Thus not only the taking of deposits but also the paying of checks or the lending of money could equally well provide the basis for such a finding. . . .

Because the purpose of the statute is to maintain competitive equality, it is relevant in construing "branch" to consider, not merely the contractual rights and liabilities created by the transaction, but all those aspects of the transaction that might give the bank an advantage in its competition for customers. Unquestionably, a competitive advantage accrues to a bank that provides the service of receiving money for deposit at a place away from its main office; the convenience to the customer is unrelated to whether the relationship of debtor and creditor is established at the moment of receipt or somewhat later. . . .

Since the putative deposits are in fact "received" by a bank facility apart from its chartered place of business, we are compelled, in construing § 36(f), to view the place of delivery of the customer's cash and checks accompanied by a deposit slip as an "additional office, or * * * branch place of business * * * at which deposits are received." . . .[9]

The broad sweep of *Plant City*'s approach to the meaning of the term "branch" caused its own complications. Rather than the simple dichotomy of things that were "branches" and things that were not, *Plant City* created a banking world in which there was a middle category of things that *might* be "branches" in some rarified sense. In this realm, "common sense" was no longer the guide.[10]

---

9. 396 U.S. at 133, 135–137, 90 S.Ct. at 343–345.

10. Justice Douglas in dissent in *Plant City* invoked common sense as a guide to his decision:

It will come as a shock, where common sense is the guide, to learn that an armored car picking up merchants' cash boxes and checks is a branch bank. Conceivably a bank could use an armored car as a place of business by stationing it at designated places during designated hours for opening accounts, receiving, deposits, making loans, and the like. But no armored car was so used in these cases.

. . . The opinion of the Court leaves the impression that the McFadden Act created "competitive equality" between national and state banks across the board. But as we stated in the *Walker Bank* case, that Act "intended to place national and state banks on a basis of 'competitive equality' *insofar as branch banking was concerned.*" *Id.*, at 261. (Italics added.) There was no other or additional overriding principle of "competitive equality" that limited off-premises services of national banks to those that state banks could provide.

Among those off-premises activities of national banks was the furnishing of armored car messenger services, which, we are advised by the Comptroller of the Currency, antedated by many years the 1927 McFadden Act. One can read the legislative history of the Act without finding any hint that Congress was providing "competitive

§ 3.5 *Plant City* and the Emergence of New Technologies

One major difficulty that arose in the wake of *Plant City* concerned the newly emerging technology of customer-bank communication terminals, or ATMs ("automated teller machines"), as they are now generally known.[1] In the face of *Plant City*, the Comptroller approved the use of ATMs, relying upon precisely the sort of rationale that was rejected by the Supreme Court in the case of armored cars and drop boxes.

Following *Plant City*, many federal courts had occasion to reaffirm the preeminence of "reference over" to state law with respect to branching. In *First National Bank v. Camp*,[2] the District of Columbia Circuit held that, in considering a branch application, the Comptroller was not bound by an opinion of a state administrative officer interpreting state law. However, the court also emphasized that the Comptroller was bound by the statute law of the state. In *Driscoll v. Northwestern National Bank*,[3] the Eighth Circuit expressed concern over the Comptroller's determination that a national bank could maintain a group of walk-up television tellers, where a state bank would be limited to one, and remanded the case to the Comptroller for further consideration.

Several district courts were confronted with the question whether ATMs of various types were "branches" within the meaning of Section 36. In *Independent Bankers v. Camp*,[4] the District of Oregon held that, in the absence of a specific state statute authorizing state banks to install and operate ATMs, Section 36(c) prohibited their establishment by national banks. In *Colorado ex rel. State Banking Board v. First National Bank*,[5] the District of Colorado held that an electronic facility was a "branch" within the meaning of Section 36, because it received deposits, not because it paid checks or lent money. In *Illinois ex rel. Lignoul v. Continental Illinois National Bank & Trust Co.*,[6] the Northern District of Illinois held that "the functions performed by [ATMs], both un-

---

equality" as respects armored car messenger services. . . .

. . . Certainly the Comptroller, who is the supervisory agent for policing § 36, has some authority to define "deposits" as used in § 36(f) [currently codified as § 36(j)], and this case affords no excuse for disparaging him. 396 U.S. at 138–140, 90 S.Ct. at 345–346.

§ 3.5

1. Despite considerable litigation, discussed *infra*, this question was not definitively resolved by the Congress until 1996, with the amendment of Section 36(j) (formerly 36(f)) by Pub. L. No. 104–208, § 2205(a), 110 Stat. 3009 (Sept. 30, 1996) (codified at 12 U.S.C.A. § 36(j)).

2.   465 F.2d 586 (D.C.Cir.1972).

3.   484 F.2d 173 (8th Cir.1973).

4.   357 F.Supp. 1352 (D.Or.1973).

5.   394 F.Supp. 979 (D.Colo.1975).

6.   409 F.Supp. 1167 (N.D.Ill.1975).

manned and manned, constitute making a deposit or lending money within the meaning of 12 U.S.C.A. § 36(f) [now codified at § 36(j)] . . . [but that] cash withdrawals as presently effectuated by ATMs do not constitute cashing checks."[7] Other district courts in the meantime came up with conflicting answers on the question of whether ATMs were branches.[8]

The definitive challenge to the Comptroller's authorization of national bank ATMs came in *Independent Bankers Association of America v. Smith* (*"Independent Bankers"*).[9] There the D.C. Circuit held that ATMs were "branches" within the meaning of Section 36 of the National Bank Act, because all ATMs—whether on-line directly to the bank or independent—perform at least one of the three specified branch services ("deposits . . . received, checks paid, or money lent"). In so holding, the court relied explicitly on *Plant City* and its application of the "competitive equality" policy to the federal definition of "branch."[10] Several circuits quickly followed the reasoning in *Independent Bankers* and held that similar electronic devices established by national banks were "branches," and thus subject to federal and state restrictions on branch banking.[11]

Following the decision in *Independent Bankers*, the Comptroller abandoned its previous position.[12] Thereafter, it seemed clear "that when a national bank makes use of [an ATM], it is engaging in 'branch banking,' at least where the [ATM] is located away from the bank's main business premises."[13]

However, in *State Bank of Fargo v. Merchants' National Bank & Trust*,[14] the Eighth Circuit confronted a curious conceptual problem that arose out of the uneasy fit between Section 36(c) and the actions that several states had taken in response to the Comptroller's original position on ATMs. In North Dakota, public policy with respect to branch banking had been restrictive, and North Dakota banks were generally not permitted to engage in off-

---

7. *Id.* at 1181. In September 1994, § 36(f) was redesignated as "36(j)." *See* Pub. L. No. 103–328, § 102(b) (1)(A), 108 Stat. 2349, 2352 (Sept. 29, 1994) (redesignating former § 36(f) as 36(j)), *as amended*, Pub. L. No. 104–208, § 2205(a), 110 Stat. 3009 (Sept. 30, 1996) (codified at 12 U.S.C.A. § 36(j)).

8. *Missouri ex rel. Kostman v. First Nat'l Bank*, 405 F.Supp. 733 (E.D.Mo. 1975) (holding ATMs to be branches); *Oklahoma ex rel. State Banking Bd. v. Utica Nat'l Bank & Trust Co.*, 409 F.Supp. 71 (N.D.Okla.1975) (*contra*).

9. 534 F.2d 921 (D.C.Cir.), *cert. denied*, 429 U.S. 862, 97 S.Ct. 166 (1976).

10. *Id.* at 928–930.

11. *Illinois ex rel. Lignoul v. Continental Ill. Nat'l Bank and Trust Co.*, 536 F.2d 176 (7th Cir.), *cert. denied*, 429 U.S. 871, 97 S.Ct. 184 (1976); *Missouri ex rel. Kostman v. First Nat'l Bank in St. Louis*, 538 F.2d 219 (8th Cir.), *cert. denied*, 429 U.S. 941, 97 S.Ct. 357 (1976); *Colorado ex rel. State Banking Bd. v. First Nat'l Bank of Fort Collins*, 540 F.2d 497 (10th Cir.1976), *cert. denied*, 429 U.S. 1091, 97 S.Ct. 1102 (1977).

12. 41 Fed. Reg. 48,333 (1976).

13. *State Bank of Fargo v. Merchants Nat'l Bank & Trust*, 593 F.2d 341, 344 (8th Cir.1979).

14. *Id.*

premises operations. As of 1975, the powers of state banks in North Dakota law did not include the operation of ATMs. The Comptroller's original position on ATMs caused understandable concern among state banks, which feared competition with national banks using ATMs. In response, the North Dakota Legislature adopted legislation in 1975 that permitted state banks to provide electronic services to its customers "to the same extent that other financial institutions chartered and regulated by any agency of the federal government are permitted to provide such services within this state."[15] However, the legislation explicitly provided that an ATM was not considered a "branch."[16]

Consider the position of competing state and national banks in North Dakota following the 1976 decision in *Independent Bankers*. A national bank ATM could only be authorized if it complied with Section 36(c), that is, if state law "expressly authorized to State banks"[17] or authorized "affirmatively and not merely by implication or recognition"[18] such *branches*. But under state law, ATMs, though authorized, were not "branches."

Did this mean, in light of *Independent Bankers*, that ATMs could not be authorized for national banks operating in North Dakota?[19] At the time that the State Bank of Fargo challenged the Comptroller's authorization of ATMs to Merchants National Bank & Trust in 1977, federal savings and loan associations and federal credit unions were being permitted to operate ATMs, known as remote service units ("RSUs").[20] Apparently, this situation would be enough to authorize state banks to operate ATMs, but not as "branches" under North Dakota law. What, then, of national banks in the state? The Eighth Circuit construed the interplay of federal law and the North Dakota statute to permit the Comptroller under Section 36(c) to authorize Merchants National Bank & Trust to maintain and operate its Fargo ATMs as "branches."[21]

This case may represent vengeance upon Judge Wilkey's hypothetical in *Independent Bankers*. Law professors endure all sorts of abuse about the unrealistic nature of their hypotheticals, no matter

---

15. N.D. Cent. Code § 6–03–02(8).

16. This was a prevalent problem among a large number of states that authorized state bank ATMs but explicitly did not define them as "branches." See *Independent Bankers Ass'n of N.Y. v. Marine Midland Bank*, 757 F.2d 453, 461 n. 4 (2d Cir.1985) (noting that many states did not classify ATMs as "branches").

17. 12 U.S.C.A. § 36(c)(1).

18. *Id.* § 36(c)(2).

19. Fighting the hypothetical, the D.C. Circuit in *Independent Bankers* had simply denied that this situation would present a practical problem. *Independent Bankers*, 534 F.2d at 948 n. 104.

20. *State Bank of Fargo v. Merchants Nat'l Bank & Trust Co. of Fargo*, 451 F.Supp. 775, 784 n. 14 (D.N.D. 1978). Furthermore, at the time of the district court's decision in 1978, federal credit unions were still being permitted to use RSUs. *Id.* at 790 nn.32–33.

21. *State Bank of Fargo*, 593 F.2d at 344–346.

how elegant they (always) are. Yet consider Judge Wilkey's famous hypothetical from *Independent Bankers*:

> Suppose, for example, that the national bank in *Plant City* is now receiving deposits, paying checks, and lending money through the agency of several [ATMs], rather than an armored car and a shopping center receptacle. Florida prohibits all branch banking by state chartered banks, and we will assume that since *Plant City* there has been only the following change in Florida banking law: According to a recent state administrative opinion or ruling interpreting state law, [ATMs] are not considered "branches" for purposes of state law. Because under these assumed facts Florida statute law does not specifically and affirmatively grant to state banks the authority to establish and operate [ATMs] without complying with the state's anti-branching statute, narrow interpretation of section 36(c) could prevent the Comptroller from approving national bank [ATMs] in Florida. We reject this narrow construction of section 36(c) for two reasons. First, as Judge MacKinnon recognized in *First Nat'l Bank v. Camp*, 465 F.2d at 597, the Comptroller can consider and follow the Florida administrative opinion or ruling interpreting the state's branching laws so long as that opinion does not violate the anti-branching standard imposed by the statute law of the state. Second, this narrow reading of section 36(c) would resurrect the precise form of competitive inequality which the McFadden Act was designed to cure.... By manipulating their banking statutes and administrative rulings, the states would again be able to secure a competitive advantage for state banks in the field of branching, *i.e.*, under this narrow reading of section 36(c) national bank [ATMs] would be subject to the state's anti-branching statute while state bank [ATMs] would be exempt under a permissive opinion or ruling issued by the state's banking commissioner. We refuse to frustrate legislative intent by adopting this narrow reading of section 36(c)'s language.[22]

What Judge Wilkey failed to realize, of course, was that: (1) the problem was not hypothetical, but reflected the emerging practice of many states with respect to ATMs;[23] and (2) the dilemma presented by his hypothetical problem arose not because of a "narrow reading" the language of the federal statute, but because of the broad sweep of his interpretation of that language.

22. *Independent Bankers*, 534 F.2d at 948 n. 104.

23. *See Independent Bankers Ass'n of New York*, 757 F.2d at 461 n. 4 (noting that many states did not classify ATMs as "branches").

In *Independent Bankers Association of New York v. Marine Midland Bank*,[24] the Second Circuit confronted yet another interpretive problem left over in the fallout of *Independent Bankers*. If a third party (whether another bank or, in *Marine Midland*, a nonbank) installs an ATM, and makes it available to depositors of a national bank, must that national bank first comply with Section 36(c)? In the typical situation, the ATM is controlled and maintained by the third party, and as to participating banks, it is a shared ATM. However, while it may be clear under *Independent Bankers* that the shared ATM is a "branch" for purposes of Section 36, is it Marine Midland's branch?

The Comptroller took the position that an ATM is not a "branch" of a national bank unless it owns or rents the ATM.[25] Thus, the narrow legal question presented by *Marine Midland* was what the language of Section 36 meant by the phrase "establish and operate" a "branch." The *Independent Bankers* opinion appeared to focus on the relation between "establishing" and "owning or renting."[26] Ultimately, the *Marine Midland* court deferred to the Comptroller's interpretation of Section 36 as a "reasonable construction."[27]

In 1996 Congress brushed up against the implications of the *Plant City* interpretation of "branch" without going to the heart of the matter. The definition of "branch" was amended to read as follows:

> The term "branch" as used in this section shall be held to include any branch bank, branch office, branch agency, additional office, or any branch place of business located in any State or Territory of the United States or in the District of Columbia at which deposits are received, or checks paid, or money lent. *The term "branch", as used in this section, does not include an automated teller machine or a remote service unit.*[28]

Despite this resolution of the question posed by *Independent Bankers* concerning the status of ATMs, the consequences of the decisions in *Plant City* and *Independent Bankers*—creating the middle category of things that might or might not be "branches"—remain untouched by the 1996 amendment of Section 36. When some other new technology or technique emerges[29] that intuitively

---

24. *Id.*

25. 12 C.F.R. § 5.31(b) (1985).

26. *See Independent Bankers*, 534 F.2d at 941, 946 n. 98, 951.

27. *Marine Midland Bank*, 757 F.2d at 462.

28. 12 U.S.C.A. § 36(j) (emphasis added).

29. *See, e.g.,* Guenther, *Citicorp Skips Computer In New Home–Banking Plan*, Wall St. J., Feb. 28, 1990, at B1, col. 5 (discussing banking at home by means of telephone-like device provided by bank).

is not a "branch" if "common sense is the guide,"[30] the broad and counterintuitive interpretation of *Plant City* is still the definitive guidance on the subject.

Another problem connected with ATMs also went unaddressed by the Congress in 1996. It was becoming common to find a bank imposing a fee on nondepositors who wished to access their accounts at some other depository institution through its ATMs.[31] Some states and local governments responded to this practice by prohibiting the imposition of nondepositor ATM fees. Litigation involving challenges to such prohibitions usually claimed federal preemption of the prohibition, for example based on provisions of the National Bank Act ("NBA") authorizing incidental powers,[32] or the applicability of the federal regulatory scheme imposed by the Electronic Funds Transfer Act ("EFTA").[33]

Congress finally reentered the ATM controversy in 1999, with the passage of the Gramm–Leach–Bliley Act ("GLBA").[34] The GLBA requires ATM operators who impose a noncustomer ATM fee to post a notice on the machine and on the screen that a fee will be charged and the amount of the fee.[35] ATM operators are exempt from liability if properly placed notices on the machines are subse-

30. *Plant City*, 396 U.S. at 138, 90 S.Ct. at 345 (Douglas, J., dissenting).

31. *See, e.g., Bank of America v. City & County of San Francisco*, 309 F.3d 551, 559 (9th Cir. 2002) (preempting San Francisco and Santa Monica ordinances prohibiting banks from charging ATM fees); *Fleet Bank v. Burke*, 23 F.Supp.2d 196 (D.Conn.1998) (holding that Connecticut statute did not prohibit surcharge fees for ATM use by nondepositors), *vacated*, 160 F.3d 883 (2d Cir.1998) (holding district court lacked subject matter jurisdiction), *cert. denied*, 527 U.S. 1004, 119 S.Ct. 2340 (1999); *Metrobank, N.A. v. Foster*, 193 F.Supp.2d 1156 (S.D.Iowa 2002) (holding NBA preemption of state regulation of ATM nondepositor fees); *Wells Fargo Bank Texas, N.A. v. James*, 184 F.Supp.2d 588 (W.D.Tex.2001) (holding NBA preemption of state prohibition against nondepositor fees for cashing checks); *First Union Nat. Bank v. Burke*, 48 F.Supp.2d 132 (D.Conn.1999) (granting preliminary injunction against enforcement of state administrative cease and desist orders on nondepositor ATM surcharge fee; holding orders interfered with OCC exclusive enforcement authority over national banks); *Burke v. Fleet Nat. Bank*, 252 Conn. 1, 742 A.2d 293 (1999) (holding ATM nondepositor fees permissible under Connecticut law).

32. 12 U.S.C. § 24(Seventh). *Cf. Franklin Nat. Bank v. New York*, 347 U.S. 373, 74 S.Ct. 550 (1954) (preempting state law governing advertisement of accounts in light of national bank powers under 12 U.S.C.A. § 24).

33. 15 U.S.C.A. §§ 1693–1693r. For a representative case raising these preemption issues, see *Bank One, Utah v. Guttau*, 190 F.3d 844 (8th Cir.1999), *cert. denied sub nom. Foster v. Bank One, Utah*, 529 U.S. 1087, 120 S.Ct. 1718 (2000).

34. Pub. L. No. 106–102, Nov. 12, 1999, 113 Stat. 1338 (1999) (codified at scattered sections of 12, 15, 16, 18 U.S.C.A.).

35. GLBA, § 702 (codified at 15 U.S.C.A. § 1693b(d)(3)). The GLBA grants a temporary exemption from the screen notice requirement (through 31 December 2004) for older machines that are unable to provide such a notice. 15 U.S.C.A. § 1693(d)(3)(B)(ii). For a case considering the scope of the notice requirement, see *Morrissey v. Webster Bank, N.A.*, 417 F.Supp.2d 183 (D.Mass. 2006) (rejecting plaintiff's interpretation of statute).

quently removed, damaged, or altered by anyone other than the ATM operator.[36] When ATM cards are issued, the GLBA also requires a notice that surcharges may be imposed by other parties when transactions are initiated from ATMs not operated by the card issuer.[37] If these provisions are construed as expressing a federal policy that the noncustomer fee problem should be addressed *only* by the imposition of disclosure requirements, then federal law may directly preempt state and local government attempts to prohibit such fees.[38]

This legislative solution does not mean that the problem has disappeared. A March 2001 survey released by the Public Interest Research Group indicates that the average cost to the consumer for using another bank's ATM has risen from $1.01 nationally in 1996, when the ATM networks first allowed member banks to impose fees, to $2.86 in 2001.[39] Nevertheless, Iowa is currently the only state in the nation that prohibits ATM operators from charging nonaccountholders for ATM use.[40] In April 2001, five national banks with branches in Iowa brought suit against Iowa bank regulators claiming that federal law preempts a state ban on nondepositor ATM fees.[41]

New technologies continue to emerge. Electronic technologies such as automation, the Internet, wireless communication, and the like have already had a substantial impact on the way in which financial products and services are delivered, and also on the substantive characteristics of many products and services.[42] In May 2002, the OCC amended its regulations to facilitate the conduct of

36. GLBA, § 705 (codified at 15 U.S.C.A. § 1693h(d)).

37. GLBA, § 703 (codified at 15 U.S.C.A. § 1693c(a)(10)).

38. *Cf. Crosby v. National Foreign Trade Council*, 530 U.S. 363, 120 S.Ct. 2288 (2000) (holding state law restricting authority of state agencies to purchase goods or services from companies doing business with Burma preempted because of possible frustration of federal statutory objectives).

39. Joyce E. Cutler & Richard Cowden, *U.S. PIRG Survey Finds Rising Costs for Non–Customers Using Banks' ATMs*, BNA Banking Daily, Apr. 2, 2001, at d4. For more information online, see http://www.pirg.org. Analysis from the Federal Reserve System ("Fed") does not agree with these findings. The Fed's Annual Report to Congress on Retail Fees and Services of Depository Institutions (*available online at* www.federalreserve.gov/boarddocs/rpt

congress/2001fees) indicated that average ATM access fee remained $1.25 in 2000, unchanged since 1999. Adam Wasch, *Bank Fees Rise Significantly; ATM Fees Remain Mostly Flat*, BNA Banking Daily, Aug. 2, 2001, at d2.

40. R. Christian Bruce, *National Banks Sue Iowa Bank Regulators, Saying Ban on ATM Usage Fees Preempted*, BNA Banking Daily, May 2, 2001, at d5.

41. *Metrobank N.A. v. Foster*, 193 F.Supp.2d 1156 (S.D.Iowa 2002). *See* Bruce, *National Banks Sue, supra* at d5 (discussing litigation).

42. *See, e.g.*, Veronica Agosta, *Nation's Small Banks Have Big Plans for the Internet*, Am. Banker, Mar. 9, 2001, at 5; Steve Marlin, *B2B: Swirling E–Marketplace Pulls in Banks*, Bank Systems & Technology, June 2000, at 32; *Online Finance Survey: Paying Respects*, The Economist, May 20, 2000, at 24; Carol Power, *Banks Start to Click into Wireless Banking*, Am. Banker, June 7, 2000, at 16.

the business of national banks using electronic technologies,[43] consistent with safety and soundness.[44] This amendment grouped together new and revised regulations addressing a series of basic concerns about e-banking: (i) exercise of federally authorized powers through electronic means;[45] (ii) the location, for purposes of federal banking laws, of a national bank that engages in electronic activities;[46] and, (iii) disclosure requirements for national banks that provide customers with access to other service providers through hyperlinks in bank websites or other shared electronic space.[47]

Another issue that is emerging is the *"location"* of *a national e-bank* for regulatory purposes. Traditional legal analysis of the location of a national bank is not particularly helpful. The NBA indicates that a national bank is deemed to be a citizen of the State in which it is located. But where is a national e-bank "located"?[48] Presumably, the organization certificate of a national e-bank will tell us the listed state, but where is the "principal place of business" of an e-bank?

A conflict in the circuits emerged on this issue.[49] In *Wachovia*

---

43. 67 Fed. Reg. 34,992 (2002) (codified at 12 C.F.R. §§ 7.1002, 7.500–7.5010; removing *id*. § 7.1019). For the proposed version of these amendments, see 66 Fed. Reg. 34,855 (2001).

44. *See, e.g.*, Technology Risk Management—Guidance for Bankers and Examiners, OCC Bulletin 98–3 (February 4, 1998) (discussing safety and soundness issues). *See also* 66 Fed. Reg. 8616 (2001) (providing jointly issued information security guidelines implementing GLBA requirements). *See generally* GLBA § 501(b), codified at 15 U.S.C. § 6801 (concerning information security).

45. *See, e.g.*, 12 C.F.R. §§ 7.1002 (acting as finder); 7.5001 (concerning e-banking activities part of, or incidental to, business of banking); 7.5002 (furnishing of products and services by electronic means and facilities); 7.5003 (concerning composite authority to engage in e-banking activities); 7.5004 (concerning excess electronic capacity); 7.5005 (acting as digital certification authority); 7.5006 (concerning data processing); 7.5007 (concerning correspondent banking). *See generally* Comptroller's Handbook, Other Income Producing Activities: Internet Banking (Oct. 1999) (discussing business and technical issues). For information concerning electronic banking activities,

including a list of pertinent opinion letters, approval letters, supervisory guidance, and other issuances, with links to the documents, see www.occ.treas.gov/netbank/netbank.htm.

46. *See, e.g.*, 12 C.F.R. §§ 7.5008 (concerning location of national bank conducting e-banking activities); 7.5009 (concerning location of Internet-only bank under 12 U.S.C. § 85).

47. *See, e.g., id*. §§ 7.1002(d) (acting as finder); 7.5010 (concerning shared electronic space).

48. *See, e.g., Firstar Bank, N.A. v. Faul*, 253 F.3d 982 (7th Cir. 2001) (holding that national bank is citizen of state of its principal place of business *and* state listed in organization certificate).

49. *Compare Horton v. Bank One, N. A.*, 387 F.3d 426, 429, 431 (5th Cir. 2004) (holding that, for diversity purposes, "a national bank is not 'located' in, and thus [is] not a citizen of, every state in which it has a branch"), *and Firstar Bank, N.A., supra* (looking to principal place of business and state listed in organization certificate) *with Wachovia Bank v. Schmidt*, 388 F.3d 414, 432 (4th Cir. 2005) (considering national bank to be citizen of both state of main office and every state with branch operations), *and World Trade Center Proper-*

Bank v. Schmidt,[50] the Supreme Court resolved the conflict, indicating that in answering the question of where a national bank is located—at least for purposes of determining diversity jurisdiction—the determining factor is the state designated in its articles of association as locus of its main office, *not* the states where it has branch offices. The Court did not address the issue of where a national bank's "principal place of business" is.

§ 3.6 Possible Relaxed Approach to the *Plant City* Analysis

The Supreme Court did not reconsider the implications of *Plant City* until 1987, when it decided *Clarke v. Securities Industry Association*,[1] which concerned the legality of the Comptroller's approval of national bank establishment or purchase of discount brokerage subsidiaries. While the case principally affected the scope of Glass–Steagall Act restrictions on securities activities of banks,[2] one argument raised by the Securities Industry Association was that offices of a discount brokerage operation of a national bank would constitute "branches" under the broad concept laid out in *Plant City*. The Comptroller had concluded that the discount brokerage offices would not constitute "branches" because, among other things, no defined branching functions would be performed there.[3] The brokerage operation would provide margin lending, but loan approval would take place at the bank's chartered offices. The brokerage operation would maintain interest-bearing customer balances, but the Comptroller believed "that these accounts differ sufficiently in nature from ordinary bank accounts that Discount Brokerage would not be engaged in receiving deposits."[4]

In one respect, the Court's response in *Clarke* was consistent with *Plant City*. Both cases essentially swept aside or ignored the technical issues presented and disposed of the question before it with a dose of legislative history. After twisting and turning through legislative history arguments on both sides of the question, the Court concluded that Congress did not intend to subject a bank's conduct of a securities business to the branching restrictions.[5] How, then, can this decision be squared with the rather

---

ties, *LLC v. Hartford Fire Ins. Co.*, 345 F.3d 154, 161 (2d Cir. 2003) (dictum) (same).

50. 546 U.S. 303, 126 S.Ct. 941 (2006).

§ 3.6

1. 479 U.S. 388, 107 S.Ct. 750 (1987).

2. 12 U.S.C.A. §§ 24 (Seventh), 377–378 (1982).

3. *Clarke*, 479 U.S. at 391, 107 S.Ct. at 753.

4. 479 U.S. at 391–392, 107 S.Ct. at 753 (footnote omitted).

5. 479 U.S. at 409, 107 S.Ct. at 762. It should be noted that pre–1927 activities thereafter caught by the federal definition of "branch" were well recognized by Congress in passing the McFadden Act. Prior to the passage of the McFad-

broad reading given to the definition of "branch" in *Plant City*? Basically, by ignoring the implications of that decision. To accomplish this, the Court introduced a new interpretive gloss on the federal definition of "branch." The Court's opinion explained:

> The Comptroller reasonably interprets the statute as requiring "competitive equality" *only in core banking functions*, and not in all incidental services in which national banks are authorized to engage. We are not faced today with the need to decide whether there are core banking functions beyond those explicitly enumerated in § 36(f); it suffices, to decide this case, to hold that the operation of a discount brokerage service is not a core banking function.[6]

This conclusion embodies a very odd reading of the scope of *Plant City* and an even odder characterization of the issue presented in *Clarke*. The Court in *Plant City* does not make use of the "core banking functions" terminology; the Court simply applies the NBA definition of "branch" for purposes of Section 36. Nor is there any sense in characterizing the issue before the Court in *Clarke* as a question of whether "operation of a discount brokerage service is ... a core banking function."[7] The question should be whether a discount brokerage's margin lending and holding of free credit balances (*i.e.*, deposits) caused it to be considered a "branch." The Court's reconstruction of the issues before it is particularly apparent in a footnote in which the Court suggests, hypothetically:

> If the "competitive equality" principle were carried to its logical extreme, the ability of a national bank to carry on an incidental activity such as the safe-deposit business would be limited to the same extent as a state bank's ability to do so under state law. However, as we have noted, the legislative history of the McFadden Act rather clearly indicates that Congress intended national banks to be able to carry on a safe-deposit business without locational restrictions.[8]

Only if the safe deposit business involved "deposits ... received, or checks paid, or money lent"[9] would this issue be raised. Under *Plant City*, the fact that the issue would involve a "safe-deposit business"—or a brokerage business—should be as irrele-

---

den Act, for example, national banks operated "agencies" and other "offices," limited to such activities as deposit taking or certain check transactions. On the pre–1927 operations of such offices, *see Cheshire Natl. Bank v. Smith*, 427 F.Supp. 277 (D.N.H.1977). These operations, captured by the broad definition of "branch" contained in former Section 36(f), were grandfathered by Section 36(a).

6. *Clarke*, 479 U.S. at 409, 107 S.Ct. at 762 (emphasis added; footnote omitted).

7. *Id.*

8. 479 U.S. at 409 n. 23, 107 S.Ct. at 762 n. 23.

9. 12 U.S.C.A. §§ 36(j).

vant as the fact that an armored car or a dropbox was being used. That this fact is not irrelevant may suggest that the Court is no longer comfortable with the competitive equality principle, which had already been "carried to its logical extreme" in *Plant City* itself. We may expect to see some continued relaxation in judicial approaches to the application of the *Plant City* rationale, as the courts struggle to make sense of the broad implications of that case.

§ 3.7 State Bank Branching

As discussed in § 3.3, *supra,* national banks are, to a significant extent, subject to the same restrictions on branching that apply to state banks in the same state of operation, through the "reference over" provisions of the NBA.[1] However, certain state banks will also be subject to conditions and restrictions on branching under federal statutory law.

This indirect effect occurs through the jurisdiction of the Federal Reserve Board over state member banks and the jurisdiction of the FDIC over state nonmember insured banks. Section 9 of the Federal Reserve Act[2] provides for branching by state member banks to the same extent permissible to national banks. Similarly, the Federal Deposit Insurance Act subjects state nonmember insured banks to prior approval by the FDIC before a branch bank can be established.[3] The FDIC's determination in this regard will be based upon the same factors that the FDIC considers in deciding whether or not to insure a principal office.[4]

Nevertheless, for the most part, the substantive restrictions on state bank branching are a matter of state law, and they can vary considerably from state to state. The latest trend in state branching policy has been to link state bank powers (including, in some cases, the ability to branch) to permissible national bank powers.[5] A majority of states now appear to have adopted such a "wild card" approach to the scope of state bank powers.

§ 3.8 Savings Association Branching

Savings association branching is not subject to the strictures applicable to national banks under Section 36(c).[1] However, savings

§ 3.7

1. 12 U.S.C.A. § 36(c).

2. *Id.* § 321.

3. *Id.* § 1828(d).

4. *See id.* § 1816, 1828(d).

5. *See, e.g., State Bank of Fargo v. Merchants Nat'l Bank & Trust,* 593 F.2d 341 (8th Cir.1979) (discussing N.D. Cent. Code § 6–03–02(8)). *See also* Henry N. Butler, *The Competitive Equality Doctrine and the Demise of Intrastate Bank Branching Restrictions,* 55 Tenn. L. Rev. 703 (1988) (discussing "wild card" state banking statutes).

§ 3.8

1. *State Bank of Fargo v. Merchants Nat'l Bank & Trust,* 593 F.2d 341 (8th Cir.1979).

associations are required to obtain approval from their regulator before establishing and operating branches.[2] For example, in the case of federally chartered savings associations, Section 5 of HOLA[3] makes no reference to branching. From the beginning, the Federal Home Loan Bank Board ("FHLBB") and its successor, the OTS, have taken the position that the agency has statutory power to authorize branches,[4] and this position has been upheld.[5] HOLA is still largely silent on the subject,[6] except for interstate branching rules applicable to savings associations.[7]

§ 3.9 Credit Union Branching

In an interpretive ruling and policy statement published in July 1989,[1] the NCUA took a markedly different approach to branching from that expressed in *Independent Bankers Association*

2. *See generally* Kenneth E. Scott, *In Quest of Reason: The Licensing Decisions of the Federal Banking Agencies*, 42 U. Chi. L. Rev. 235, 239–242 (1975) (contrasting branch approval processes of Comptroller and FHLBB, predecessor to Office of Thrift Supervision).

3. 12 U.S.C.A. § 1464.

4. 12 C.F.R. § 545.92 (authorizing branch offices). Establishment of a drive-in or pedestrian office opened in conjunction with an approved branch or home office requires no additional approval from the OTS. *Id.* § 545.92(g).

5. *See, e.g., Independent Bankers Ass'n v. Federal Home Loan Bank Bd.*, 557 F.Supp. 23 (D.D.C.1982) (upholding FHLBB policy statements allowing federally regulated savings and loan associations to acquire or open branch offices in states other than association's home state as exempt from APA notice and comment requirements under 5 U.S.C.A. § 553).

6. *But see* 12 U.S.C.A. § 1464(m)(1), which provides:

(m) Branching

(1) In general

(A) No savings association incorporated under the laws of the District of Columbia or organized in the District or doing business in the District shall establish any branch or move its principal office or any branch without the Director's prior written approval.

(B) No savings association shall establish any branch in the District of Columbia or move its principal office

or any branch in the District without the Director's prior written approval.

For purposes of Section 1464(m)(1), "branch" is defined to mean:

any office, place of business, or facility, other than the principal office as defined by the Director [of the Office of Thrift Supervision], of a savings association at which accounts are opened or payments are received or withdrawals are made, or any other office, place of business, or facility of a savings association *defined by the Director as a branch within the meaning of such sentence.*

12 U.S.C.A. § 1464(m)(2) (emphasis added). Thus, unlike NBA, HOLA specifically allows the OTS to define the scope of the term "branch" for these purposes. *Compare* 12 U.S.C.A. § 36(j) (NBA definition of "branch"), *with* 12 U.S.C.A. § 1464(m)(2) (HOLA definition).

7. 12 U.S.C.A. § 1464(r). *See* 12 C.F.R. § 556.5 (interstate branching by federal savings associations generally permitted). Interstate branching is subject to prior approval by the OTS. 12 C.F.R. §§ 545.92, 556.5(c).

§ 3.9

1. 54 Fed. Reg. 31,165 (1989). The NCUA has retained this policy with respect to ATMs in the revised version of its rules. *See* 63 Fed. Reg. 71,998, 72,002 (1998) (codified at 12 C.F.R. Pt. 701) (discussing IRPS 99–1, replacing previous IRPS 89–1 but retaining ATM policy).

v. Smith.[2] In discussing its policy with respect to chartering of a federal credit union to serve a combination of distinct occupational and associational groups (a "multiple-group charter"),[3] the NCUA has stated that, "[f]or chartering purposes, 'branch office' means any office of a Federal credit union where an employee accepts payment on shares and disburses loans. *An ATM or similar cash disbursing machine does not qualify as a 'branch office.'* "[4]

§ 3.10   Interstate Branching

The Riegle–Neal Interstate Banking and Branching Efficiency Act of 1994 ("IBBEA")[1] has authorized interstate geographic expansion by banks, without regard to artificial barriers to interstate expansion heretofore imposed by the branching provisions of state law and the NBA.[2] IBBEA permits interstate branching directly, through the establishment of *de novo* interstate branches.[3]

The Comptroller of the Currency is authorized by the IBBEA to approve the establishment and operation of *de novo* interstate national bank branches.[4] This authority is available only if the law of the state in which the branch is or will be located would permit the establishment of the branch if the national bank were a state bank chartered by that state.[5] Branching is subject to stated condi-

---

2. 534 F.2d 921 (D.C.Cir.), *cert. denied*, 429 U.S. 862, 97 S.Ct. 166 (1976).

3. Multigroup charters were invalidated as unauthorized under the Federal Credit Union Act in *National Credit Union Admin. v. First Nat'l Bank & Trust Co.*, 522 U.S. 479, 118 S.Ct. 927 (1998). Subsequent legislation has overridden *First National*. Credit Union Membership Access Act, Pub. L. No. 105–219, § 101(2), Aug. 7, 1998, 112 Stat. 913, 914–917 (1998) (codified at 12 U.S.C.A. § 1759(b)–(e)).

4. 54 Fed. Reg. at 31,170 (emphasis added). The status of bank ATMs has been made consistent with the NCUA approach by statute. The Economic Growth and Regulatory Paperwork Reduction Act, Pub. L. No. 104–208, § 2204 (a), 110 Stat. 3009 (1996) (codified at 12 U.S.C.A. § 36(j)), eliminated ATMs from the federal definition of "branch" for purposes of the National Bank Act.

§ 3.10

1. Pub. L. No. 103–328, 108 Stat. 2338 (Sept. 29, 1994) ("IBBEA").

2. *See, e.g.,* 12 U.S.C.A. § 36(c) (limiting branching by national banks). Cf. *First Nat'l Bank of Logan v. Walker*

Bank & Trust Co., 385 U.S. 252, 87 S.Ct. 492 (1966) (construing § 36(c)); *First Nat'l Bank in Plant City v. Dickinson*, 396 U.S. 122, 90 S.Ct. 337 (1969), (considering meaning of "branch" for purposes of § 36(c)).

3. IBBEA § 103, 108 Stat. at 2352 (codified at 12 U.S.C.A. §§ 36(g), 1828(d)(4)).

4. For these purposes, *"de novo* branch" is defined to mean a national bank branch that

(i) is originally established by the national bank as a branch; and

(ii) does not become a branch of such bank as a result of—

(I) the acquisition by the bank of an insured depository institution or a branch of an insured depository institution; or

(II) the conversion, merger, or consolidation of any such institution or branch.

12 U.S.C.A. § 36(g)(3)(A)(i)–(ii).

5. 12 U.S.C.A. § 36(g)(1)(A), as amended, Dodd–Frank Wall Street Reform and Consumer Protection Act (DFA), § 613(a), Pub. L. No. 111–203,

tions in the IBBEA as well.[6]

Approval of a *de novo* interstate national bank branch is subject to the same requirements and conditions applicable to interstate merger transactions concerning state filing requirements,[7] community reinvestment,[8] and adequacy of capital and management.[9] In addition, each *de novo* interstate national bank branch is subject to state and federal antitrust laws[10] and to limitations on the operation of additional branches,[11] to the same extent that such laws and limitations would apply to a branch resulting from an interstate merger transaction.[12]

The FDIC is authorized by the IBBEA to approve *de novo* interstate branches of insured state nonmember banks, if the law of the state in which the branch is or will be located would permit the establishment of the branch if the bank were a bank chartered by the receiving state.[13] Such branching is subject to stated conditions in the IBBEA as well.[14] These rules corresponding to those applicable to interstate national bank branches; that is, approval of interstate branches of insured state nonmember banks requires state legislation expressly permitting such branches.[15] FDIC approval is also subject to compliance of the interstate branch with state filing requirements, community reinvestment, and adequacy of capital and management applicable to interstate merger transactions.[16] Finally, state and federal antitrust laws and limitations on the operation of additional branches also apply to these interstate

---

124 Stat. 1376, 1614 (2010) (codified at.12 U.S.C.A. § 36(g)(1)(A)). Prior to the DFA amendment, IBBEA authorized an interstate branch of a national bank if there was in effect in the host state a law that applied equally to all banks and expressly permitted all out-of-state banks to establish de novo branches in the state. 12 U.S.C.A. § 36(g)(1)(A)(i)–(ii) (2009).

6. 12 U.S.C.A. § 36(g)(1)(B).

7. *See* 12 U.S.C.A. § 1831u(b)(1).

8. *See id.* § 1831u(b)(3).

9. *Id.* § 36(g)(2)(A). *See id.* § 1831u(b)(4) (setting forth capital and management adequacy requirement); *as amended* Dodd–Frank Wall Street Reform and Consumer Protection Act, Pub. L. No. 111–203, § 607(b),124 Stat. 1376, 1608 (2010) (codified at 12 U.S.C.A. § 1831u(b)(4)) (requiring bank to continue to be "well capitalized and well managed").

10. *Id.* § 1831u(c).

11. *Id.* § 1831u(d)(2).

12. *Id.* § 36(g)(2)(B).

13. 12 U.S.C.A. § 1828(d)(4)(A)(i), as amended, Dodd–Frank Wall Street Reform and Consumer Protection Act (DFA), § 613(b), Pub. L. No. 111–203, 124 Stat. 1376, 1614 (2010) (codified at.12 U.S.C.A. § 1828(d)(4)(A)(i)). Prior to the DFA amendment, IBBEA authorized an interstate branch of an insured state nonmember bank if there was in effect in the host state a law that applied equally to all banks and expressly permitted all out-of-state banks to establish de novo branches in the state. 12 U.S.C.A. § 1828(d)(4)(A)(i)(I)–(II) (2009).

14. 12 U.S.C.A. § 1828(d)(4)(A)(ii).

15. *Compare id.* § 36(g)(1)(A) (NBA provision), *with id.* § 1828(d)(4)(A)(i) (corresponding FDIA provision).

16. *Compare id.* § 36(g)(1)(B), (2)(A) (NBA provision), *with id.* § 1828(d)(4)(A)(ii), (B)(i) (corresponding FDIA provision).

branches.[17]

The federally authorized possibility of interstate banking raises two policy problems that Congress has directly addressed. The first problem, the adverse effect of interstate banking on access to banking services by low- and moderate-income customers, is treated in IBBEA itself. The second, inconsistent application of regulatory restrictions on interest rates charged on loans, was not addressed by the Congress until the passage of the Gramm–Leach–Bliley Act ("GLBA") in 1999.[18]

a. Interstate banking and low- and moderate-income customers. Following the creation of an interstate branching operation under the IBBEA, a bank might consider consolidating its operations to eliminate unnecessary or unprofitable branches. The effect on a low-or moderate-income areas[19] served by such a branch could be seriously adverse. The IBBEA requires interstate banks to comply with branch closure notice requirements of the Federal Deposit Insurance Act.[20] If a person from an affected area submits a written request to the appropriate federal banking agency (including a statement of specific reasons for the request and a discussion of the adverse effect of the closing on the availability of banking services in the area)[21] and the agency concludes that the request is not frivolous,[22] the agency is required to consult and meet with community leaders and other appropriate parties

> to explore the feasibility of obtaining adequate alternative facilities and services for the affected area, including the establishment of a new branch by another depository institution, or the establishment of a community development credit union, following the closing of the branch.[23]

However, no action by the agency in this regard affects the authority of the bank to close the branch, so long as it meets the

---

17. *Compare id.* § 36(g)(2)(B) (NBA provision), *with id.* § 1828(d)(4)(B)(ii) (corresponding FDIA provision).

18. Pub. L. No. 106–102, Nov. 12, 1999, 113 Stat. 1338 (1999) (codified at scattered sections of 12, 15, 16, 18 U.S.C.A.).

19. For these purposes, the term "low-or moderate-income area" is defined to mean

> a census tract for which the median family income is—
>
> (i) less than 80 percent of the median family income for the metropolitan statistical area (as designated by the Director of the Office of Management and Budget) in which the census tract is located; or

(ii) in the case of a census tract which is not located in a metropolitan statistical area, less than 80 percent of the median family income for the State in which the census tract is located, as determined without taking into account family income in metropolitan statistical areas in such State.

Id. § 1831r–1(d)(4)(B)(i)–(ii).

20. *Id.* § 1831r–1(d)(1) (subjecting interstate banks to notice requirement of § 1831r–1(b)(2)).

21. *Id.* § 1831r–1(d)(2)(A)(i)–(ii).

22. *Id.* § 1831r–1(d)(2)(B).

23. *Id.* § 1831r–1(d)(2).

generally applicable provisions with respect to branch closure notice.[24] The bank still controls the timing of the branch closing.[25]

The IBBEA requires the banking agencies to promulgate implementing regulations that include guidelines ensuring that interstate branches of an out-of-state bank reasonably help to meet the credit needs of the communities within the host state where the branches are located.[26] The regulations must also require that, not later than one year after establishment or acquisition of an interstate branch in a host state, the branch must be appreciably serving the credit needs of its local community.[27] If the appropriate agency determines that the bank's level of lending in the host state is less than half the average of total loans in the host state relative to total deposits for all banks for which the interstate bank's host state is the home state, the agency must then review the loan portfolio of the bank to determine if it is reasonably helping to meet the credit needs of the communities served in the host state.[28]

If the agency determines that the bank is not meeting this responsibility, it may order the interstate branch to be closed, unless the bank provides reasonable assurances, to the agency's satisfaction, that it has an acceptable plan reasonably designed to help the credit needs of the local community.[29] In addition, the bank is prohibited from opening any new interstate branch in the host state, unless it provides such reasonable assurances.[30]

Of course, the traditional approach to ensuring local community involvement by banks has been to condition approval of bank regulatory applications on adequate performance by the applicant under the Community Reinvestment Act of 1977 ("CRA").[31] The IBBEA amended the CRA to provide specific rules for CRA evaluation of banks with interstate branches.[32] A bank with domestic branches in two or more states must be evaluated by its federal regulator under the CRA not only on its entire record of performance,[33] but also on a state-by-state basis,[34] and on a separate basis, for each multistate metropolitan area served by branches in different states within the area.[35]

---

24. *Id.* § 1831r–1(d)(3).

25. *Id.*

26. *Id.* § 1835a note.

27. IBBEA, § 109(c)(1).

28. IBBEA, § 109(c)(1)(A).

29. IBBEA, § 109(c)(1)(B)(i). *See* IBBEA, § 109(c)(3) (procedures applicable to branch closing).

30. IBBEA, § 109(c)(1)(B)(ii).

31. 12 U.S.C.A. §§ 2901 *et seq.*

32. *Id.* § 2906(d)–(e).

33. *See id.* § 2906(a)–(c), (d)(1)(A).

34. *Id.* § 2906(d)(1)(B). On the required content of these state-by-state evaluations, see *id.* § 2906(d)(3).

35. *Id.* § 2906(d)(2). *Cf.* *id.* § 2906(b)(1)(B) (requiring separate presentations for each metropolitan area in which a regulated depository institution maintains a domestic branch).

b. Interstate banking and allowable interest rates. As we shall see later,[36] the interest rate that a bank may charge on a loan is generally governed by the applicable law of its home state (and, in the case of a national bank, by federal law, which may reference over to home state law).[37] If Bank *A* is operating from *its* home state and reaching interstate customers through the mails, the home state *of the customers* may be preempted from regulating the interest charged.[38] Thus, Bank *A* may have a competitive advantage over local Bank *B* if *B* is subject to an artificially low rate set by local regulation that makes the loan business marginal or unprofitable for it. However, if Bank *A* is operating *within* the customers' home state-through the use of an interstate branch authorized under IBBEA-the competitive advantage over Bank *B* may seem particularly unfair.

It was not until the passage of the GLBA in 1999 that this problem was resolved. The GLBA provides that, if an interstate bank can charge a particular interest rate, then a local bank in the state into which the interstate bank has branched may charge a comparable rate.[39] The legislative history of the act indicates that this amendment was intended to "provide[ ] loan pricing parity among interstate banks."[40] At least one court has found that the provision reflects an explicit congressional intention to preempt contrary state law.[41]

36. *See* § 5.3, *infra* (discussing federal regulation of interest rates charged on loans).

37. *See, e.g., Marquette Nat'l Bank of Minneapolis v. First of Omaha Serv. Corp.*, 439 U.S. 299, 99 S.Ct. 540 (1978) (so holding).

38. *Id.* (involving nationwide credit card business of national bank).

39. GLBA, § 731 (codified at 12 U.S.C.A. § 1831u(f)).

40. *Conference Report on S. 900, reprinted in* 145 Cong. Rec. H11255–01, 11302 (1999) (discussing congressional intent concerning GLBA section 731).

41. *Johnson v. Bank of Bentonville*, 122 F. Supp.2d 994 (W.D.Ark.2000), *affirmed*, 269 F.3d 894 (8th Cir.2001).

Chapter 4

CONTROL TRANSACTIONS

Table of Sections

§ 4.1   Introduction

Regulatory concerns over the exercise of control have steadily increased since the 1950s, and the area is now one primarily governed by statutory solutions. This chapter considers federal statutory and regulatory efforts specifically intended to supervise acquisitions and other changes in control of depository institutions.

It may be useful, as a preliminary matter, to consider the meaning of the concept of "control." This term has a diverse range of general and technical meanings. Regulatory concepts of "control" reflect the notion, first advanced by Berle and Means,[1] that

§ 4.1

1. *See* A. A. BERLE & G. MEANS, THE MODERN CORPORATION AND PRIVATE PROPERTY 69–70 (1932) (establishing concept).

corporate control is exercised by the individual or group having actual power, directly or indirectly, to select the directors, or otherwise to dictate, directly or indirectly, the management and policies of the corporation. The obvious problem is, of course, how to identify situations involving "indirect" dictation of management and policies.

The federal change-in-control statute, examined later in this chapter, deals with this problem by defining the concept of "control" as "the power, directly or indirectly, to direct the management or policies ... or to vote 25 per centum of any class of voting securities."[2] The Bank Holding Company Act ("BHCA")[3] contains a similar, but more elaborate, version of this definition of "control."[4] It defines the concept primarily in terms of (1) direct or indirect ownership of at least 25 percent of any class of voting securities;[5] or (2) control "in any manner" of the election of a majority of the directors or trustees.[6] In addition, the BHCA adds an explicit statutory device for an administrative determination that a company "directly or indirectly exercises a controlling influence over the management or policies of [a] bank."[7]

The federal securities laws provide other, more specialized concepts of "control."[8] The concept is used more as a trigger for the

---

2. 12 U.S.C.A. § 1817(j)(8)(B). On the concept of "control" under Section 1817(j), see *Federal Deposit Ins. Corp. v. D'Annunzio*, 524 F.Supp. 694 (N.D.W.Va.1981).

3. 12 U.S.C.A. §§ 1841 *et seq.*, *as amended*, Economic Growth and Regulatory Paperwork Reduction Act, Pub. L. No. 104–208, title II, 110 Stat. 3009 (1996), §§ 2202(d) 2206, 2207(a)–(b), 2214, 2304(a)–(b), 2610, 2612, 2704(d)(17) (codified at 12 U.S.C.A. §§ 1841(b), (c)(2)(F), (g), (j)(2), (o), 1843(c)(2), (c)(8), (f)(3)(B), (i)–(j)) (qualified family partnerships under BHCA; limited-purpose bank provisions; elimination of approval requirement for divestitures; stream-lining procedures for certain nonbanking acquisitions; elimination of duplicative requirements; technical and conforming amendments in light of prospective merger of BIF and SAIF into DIF); Gramm–Leach Bliley Act of 1999 (GLBA), Pub. L. No. 106–102, §§ 102(a), 103(a), (c)–(d), 105, 107, 111, 112(a), 113, 116, 118–119, 122, 131, 724, 734, 113 Stat. 1338, 1341–1351, 1359–1369, 1372–1373, 1381–1382, 1471, 1478 (Nov. 12, 1999) (codified at 12 U.S.C.A. §§ 1841 note, 1841(a)(5)(E)(i),

(c)(2)(H), (n)–(q), 1842(g)(2), 1843 note, 1843(c)(8), (f)(2)–(4), (f)(14), (j)(1)(A), (E), (j)(3), (k)–(o), 1844(a), (c), (e)(1), (g), 1848a, 1849(b)(1); repealing 1842(f)); Dodd–Frank Wall Street Reform and Consumer Protection Act (DFA), §§ 354(1)–(3), 355, 604(a)–(b), (c)(1)–(2), (d), (e)(1)–(2), 606(a), 607(a), 616(a), 618–619, 622, 623(b)(1)(A)–(B), (b)(2), 628, Pub. L. No. 111–203, 124 Stat. 1376, 1546–1547 1599–1602, 1607, 1615–1635 1640–1641 (2010) (codified at 12 U.S.C.A. §§ 1841(c)(2)(F)(v), 1841(j)(3), 1841(o)(4), 1842(c)(7), 1842(d)(1)(A), 1843(i)(8), 1843(j)(2)(A), 1843(k)(6)(B), 1843(l)(1), 1844(b), 1844(c)(1)–(2), 1844(c)(5)(B), 1850a, 1851, 1852, 1872(1); repealing 12 U.S.C. § 1848a).

4. The federal savings and loan holding company ("SLHC") provisions, 12 U.S.C.A. § 1467a, contain a definition of "control" that is in all material respects identical to that contained in the BHCA.

5. 12 U.S.C.A. § 1841(a)(2)(A).

6. *Id.* § 1841(a)(2)(B).

7. *Id.* § 1841(a)(2)(C). On the meaning of "control" for purposes of the BHCA, see *Huston v. Board of Governors*, 758 F.2d 275 (8th Cir.1985).

imposition of disclosure duties[9] or secondary liability[10] than as the basis for direct, substantive regulation of the control relationship itself,[11] as is the case under bank regulatory law.

§ 4.2 Holding Company Acquisitions

Holding company acquisition of a depository institution may involve the establishment of a new holding company enterprise or the expansion of an existing one. The use of the holding company structure is a dominant trend in the corporate law and practice of depository institutions. The creation of such a structure typically occurs in one of three circumstances, as illustrated in Figure 4–1, *infra*. In many cases, a depository institution may "spin up" a holding company of its own. The formation of the holding company amounts to a reorganization of the corporate structure of a preexisting enterprise.[1]

---

8. For discussion of "control" with respect to securities regulation, see *Chromalloy Am. Corp. v. Sun Chem. Corp.*, 611 F.2d 240 (8th Cir.1979) (discussing influence as element of "control"); *FMC Corp. v. Boesky*, 727 F.Supp. 1182 (N.D.Ill.1989), *aff'd sub nom. In re Ivan F. Boesky Sec. Litig.*, 36 F.3d 255 (2d Cir.1994) (finding recapitalization not involving change in control of corporation). *Graphic Sciences, Inc. v. International Mogul Mines Ltd.*, 397 F.Supp. 112 (D.D.C.1974) (discussing realities of commerce as determinative of control).

9. *See, e.g.*, 15 U.S.C.A. § 78p(a) (requiring disclosure of insider securities purchases).

10. *See, e.g.*, 12 U.S.C.A. § 78t(a) (concerning secondary liability of "controlling person").

11. *But cf.* 15 U.S.C.A. § 78c(a)(18) (including "person directly or indirectly controlling, controlled by, or under common control with such broker or dealer" within meaning of term "person associ-

ated with a broker or dealer"); *Id.* § 78c(a)(21) (including "person directly or indirectly controlling, controlled by, or under common control with such member" within term "person associated with a member"); *Id.* § 78c(a)(32) (including "person directly or indirectly controlling [municipal securities dealer's] activities or controlled by the municipal securities dealer in connection with such activities" within term "person associated with a municipal securities dealer"); *Id.* § 78c(a)(45) (including "person directly or indirectly controlling, controlled by, or under common control with ... government securities broker or government securities dealer" within term "person associated with a government securities broker or government securities dealer").

§ 4.2

1. E.g., *Board of Governors v. First Lincolnwood Corp.*, 439 U.S. 234, 99 S.Ct. 505 (1978) (providing example of spin up establishment of bank holding company).

Figure 4-1
Creating the Holding Company Structure

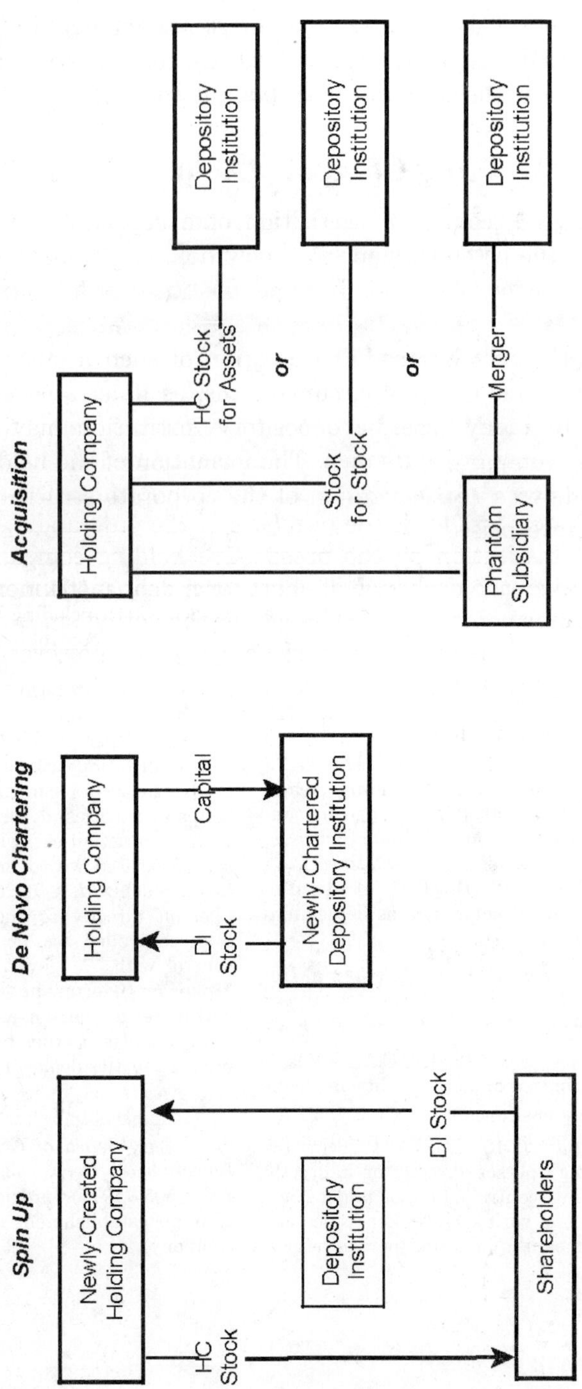

Acquisition

Holding Company

Depository Institution — HC Stock for Assets

or

Depository Institution — Stock for Stock

or

Depository Institution — Merger — Phantom Subsidiary

De Novo Chartering

Holding Company — Capital → Newly-Chartered Depository Institution

Newly-Chartered Depository Institution — DI Stock → Holding Company

Spin Up

Newly-Created Holding Company

Depository Institution

Shareholders — DI Stock → Newly-Created Holding Company

Newly-Created Holding Company — HC Stock → Shareholders

In other cases, a company may emerge as a holding company of a depository institution through the *de novo* chartering of a depository institution subsidiary.[2] Finally, a holding company enterprise may emerge or expand through the acquisition of a preexisting, independent depository institution.[3] In these last two situations, the process of formation of the holding company enterprise may be viewed as a method of entry into the regulated industry by the holding company. In general, the statutory requirements applicable to the process of formation of a holding company enterprise do not make appreciable distinctions between reorganization- and entry-motivated acquisitions.

Essentially, holding company formation or expansion involves some form of corporate reorganization or acquisition following typical acquisition methods. Tax consequences aside, the most obvious and straightforward method for forming the holding company system would be the purchase of the outstanding stock of the subject institution by the prospective holding company, or in the alternative, the exchange of short-term debt instruments issued by the holding company in exchange for the voting stock of the subject institution. The purchase or exchange would, however, be a taxable event for the institution's former shareholders.

In order to make the transaction more attractive to the institution's shareholders, therefore, the prospective holding company will structure it as a corporate reorganization that is not considered a taxable transaction under the Internal Revenue Code,[4] thus postponing indefinitely the recognition of taxable gain. Three principal alternative methods of reorganization have been frequently utilized in this regard.[5] First, a statutory merger or consolidation may involve the merger of the target bank with a "phantom bank" subsidiary of the holding company. The merger itself would be governed by the Bank Merger Act ("BMA").[6] Typically, the merger

---

2. *See, e.g., Deerbrook State Bank v. Conover,* 568 F.Supp. 696 (N.D.Ill.1983) (involving challenge to chartering of 31 national banks by Dimension Financial Corp.). *See also Board of Governors v. Dimension Fin. Corp.,* 474 U.S. 361, 106 S.Ct. 681 (1986) (upholding acquisitions despite contrary Fed regulations). *Cf. Synovus Fin. Corp. v. Board of Governors,* 952 F.2d 426 (D.C.Cir.1991) (finding no Fed authority over "acquisition" by relocation of subsidiary bank from one state to another); *State of Idaho, Dep't of Fin. v. Clarke,* 994 F.2d 1441 (9th Cir.1993) (declining to follow *Synovus*).

3. *See, e.g., Commercial Nat'l Bank of Little Rock v. Board of Governors,* 451 F.2d 86 (8th Cir.1971) (involving challenge to acquisition of preexisting bank by one-bank holding company); *Centerre Bancorporation v. Kemper,* 682 F.Supp. 459 (E.D.Mo.1988).

4. *See* 26 U.S.C.A. §§ 351 *et seq.*

5. *Id.* § 368(a)(1).

6. 12 U.S.C.A. § 1828(c), *as amended* Dodd–Frank Wall Street Reform and Consumer Protection Act (DFA), §§ 363(7), 604(f), 623(a), Pub. L. No. 111–203, 124 Stat. 1376, 1553–1554, 1602, 1634 (2010) (codified at 12 U.S.C.A. §§ 1828(c)(2)(A), (c)(2)(C), (c)(5), (c)(13)).

itself would require approval of a two-thirds majority of the shareholders of the target. Second, a stock-for-stock exchange between the prospective holding company and the shareholders of the target institution could be used, with the target becoming a subsidiary of the holding company. Third, the acquisition could involve purchase of the assets and assumption of liabilities of the target institution by the prospective holding company. Typically, the consideration paid for the assets of the target institution will then be distributed by the former target to its shareholders, with liquidation of the institution to follow upon that event. Formal shareholder approval of the sale of assets may be required, but dissenters' appraisal rights are usually not available.

§ 4.3 Bank Holding Company Act

The Bank Holding Company Act ("BHCA")[1] is the product of congressional concern that economic concentration could lead to conflicts of interest, self-dealing, involuntary tying arrangements, and generally to a derogation of competition.[2] Bank holding company regulation at the federal level is uniformly administered by the Fed, without regard to the status of a holding company's subsidiary banks, whether they are national, state member, or state nonmember insured banks.[3]

§ 4.3

1. 12 U.S.C.A. §§ 1841 *et seq., as amended*, Economic Growth and Regulatory Paperwork Reduction Act, Pub. L. No. 104–208, title II, 110 Stat. 3009 (1996), §§ 2202(d) 2206, 2207(a)–(b), 2214, 2304(a)–(b), 2610, 2612, 2704(d)(17) (codified at 12 U.S.C.A. §§ 1841(b), (c)(2)(F), (g), (j)(2), (o), 1843(c)(2), (c)(8), (f)(3)(B), (i)–(j)) (qualified family partnerships under BHCA; limited-purpose bank provisions; elimination of approval requirement for divestitures; stream-lining procedures for certain nonbanking acquisitions; elimination of duplicative requirements; technical and conforming amendments in light of prospective merger of BIF and SAIF into DIF); Gramm–Leach Bliley Act of 1999 (GLBA), Pub. L. No. 106–102, §§ 102(a), 103(a), (c)–(d), 105, 107, 111, 112(a), 113, 116, 118–119, 122, 131, 724, 734, 113 Stat. 1338, 1341–1351, 1359–1369, 1372–1373, 1381–1382, 1471, 1478 (Nov. 12, 1999) (codified at 12 U.S.C.A. §§ 1841 note, 1841(a)(5)(E)(i), (c)(2)(H), (n)–(q), 1842(g)(2), 1843 note, 1843(c)(8), (f)(2)–(4), (f)(14), (j)(1)(A), (E), (j)(3), (k)–(o), 1844(a), (c), (e)(1), (g), 1848a, 1849(b)(1); repealing 1842(f));

Dodd–Frank Wall Street Reform and Consumer Protection Act (DFA), §§ 354(1)–(3), 355, 604(a)–(b), (c)(1)–(2), (d), (e)(1)–(2), 606(a), 607(a), 616(a), 618–619, 622, 623(b)(1)(A)–(B), (b)(2), 628, Pub. L. No. 111–203, 124 Stat. 1376, 1546–1547 1599–1602, 1607, 1615–1635 1640–1641 (2010) (codified at 12 U.S.C.A. §§ 1841(c)(2)(F)(v), 1841(j)(3), 1841(o)(4), 1842(c)(7), 1842(d)(1)(A), 1843(i)(8), 1843(j)(2)(A), 1843(k)(6)(B), 1843(l)(1), 1844(b), 1844(c)(1)–(2), 1844(c)(5)(B), 1850a, 1851, 1852, 1872(1); repealing 12 U.S.C. § 1848a).

2. *Cf. Hearings on H.R. 6778 Before the House Comm. on Banking and Currency*, 91st Cong., 1st Sess., pt. 1, at 20–26 (1969) (discussing bank holding company regulation).

3. State bank holding company regulation is not preempted by federal bank holding company regulation. 12 U.S.C.A. § 1846(a). *See Northeast Bancorp, Inc. v. Board of Governors*, 472 U.S. 159, 168–173, 105 S.Ct. 2545, 2550–2553 (1985) (discussing state authority to regulate bank holding companies in light of 12 U.S.C.A. § 1842(d)).

The BHCA pursues three regulatory objectives. First, it provides authority for the Fed to regulate the formation and expansion of bank holding companies.[4] Second, it prohibits, with specified exceptions, diversification of bank holding companies into nonbanking or nonfinancial sectors.[5] Third, the act seeks to contain the tendency of bank holding companies to restrict competition.[6] In this chapter we focus primarily on BHCA restrictions that are concerned with the first and third objectives of the act.

The BHCA does not regulate the formation of the bank holding company as a business entity since the company will be organized and incorporated under state law, typically a general business corporation statute.[7] However, when the company seeks to acquire control over a bank,[8] or over an existing bank holding company, the BHCA intervenes, requiring prior approval by the Fed of the acquisition of control.[9]

The BHCA prohibits, absent prior Fed approval, any action taken that causes any company to become a bank holding company.[10] In addition, bank holding companies are subject to a number of prohibitions with respect to their acquisition of control over any additional bank or any other bank holding company. Thus, bank holding companies are prohibited from taking any of the following actions, absent prior Fed approval: (1) Any action that would cause a bank to become a bank holding company subsidiary.[11] (2) Acquisition of direct or indirect ownership or control of any voting shares of any bank by a bank holding company if, after the acquisition, the company would own or control more than five percent of the voting shares of the bank.[12] (3) Acquisition of all or substantially all of the

---

4. 12 U.S.C.A. § 1842.

5. *Id.* § 1843. Regulation of non-banking activities of bank holding companies will be discussed in Chapter 6, *infra*.

6. *See* 12 U.S.C.A. §§ 1842(c)(1)(A)–(B) (anticompetitive factors in approval of bank holding company acquisition); 1843(c)(8) (competitive factors in "proper incident" test for "closely related" nonbanking activities); 1971–1976 (antitying provisions).

7. Despite this fact, one still sees sloppy terminology in the case law. *See, e.g., Northeast Bancorp v. Board of Governors,* 849 F.2d 1499, 1505 n. 11 (D.C.Cir.1988) (referring to § 1842 applicants as seeking "a bank holding company charter").

8. *See* 12 U.S.C.A. § 1841(c) (defining "bank" for purposes of BHCA). The fact that a "bank" is in formation, and not yet operating, does not deprive the

Fed of authority to act on a simultaneous bank holding company application. *See, e.g., First State Bank of Clute, Tex. v. Board of Governors,* 553 F.2d 950 (5th Cir.1977); *Gravois Bank v. Board of Governors,* 478 F.2d 546 (8th Cir.1973).

9. 12 U.S.C.A. § 1842(a).

10. *Id.* § 1842(a)(1). *See generally Pharaon v. Board of Governors,* 135 F.3d 148 (D.C.Cir.1998), *cert. denied,* 525 U.S. 947, 119 S.Ct. 371; *Marshall & Ilsley Corp. v. Heimann,* 652 F.2d 685 (7th Cir.1981), *cert. denied,* 455 U.S. 981, 102 S.Ct. 1489 (1982); *First Nat'l Bank of Homestead v. Watson,* 363 F.Supp. 466 (D.D.C.1973) (discussing § 1842).

11. 12 U.S.C.A. § 1842(a)(2).

12. *Id.* § 1842(a)(3). *See generally First Nat'l Bank in Billings v. First Bank Stock Corp.,* 306 F.2d 937 (9th Cir.1962) (discussing § 1842).

assets of a bank by the bank holding company or any nonbanking subsidiary of the company.[13] (4) Merger or consolidation with any other bank holding company.[14]

Any company or bank holding company seeking to engage in any of these specified transactions must therefore submit an application[15] to the Fed for its prior approval.[16] Upon receipt of such an application, the Fed is required to give notice to the Comptroller of the Currency (if the target bank is a national bank or a D.C. bank), or to the appropriate state supervisor (if the target bank is state-chartered).[17] The Comptroller or state supervisor is afforded an opportunity thereby to submit "views and recommendations" with respect to the transaction that is the subject of the application, generally within 30 days of the date of notice.[18]

At the conclusion of any hearing on an application, the Fed is required to grant or deny the application, by order, on the basis of the record made at the hearing.[19] If the Fed fails to act on a BHCA application within 91 days of submission of the complete record on the application, the application is deemed to be granted.[20]

---

13. 12 U.S.C.A. § 1842(a)(4). *See generally South Dakota v. National Bank of S.D., Sioux Falls*, 335 F.2d 444 (8th Cir.1964), *cert. denied*, 379 U.S. 970, 85 S.Ct. 667 (1965) (discussing § 1842).

14. 12 U.S.C.A. § 1842(a)(5).

15. *See id.* § 1842(a) (mandating prior approval).

16. *See id.* § 1842(a), (b).

17. *Id.* § 1842(b)(1).

18. *See, e.g., First Lincolnwood Corp. v. Board of Governors*, 560 F.2d 258 (7th Cir.1977), *rev'd*, 439 U.S. 234, 99 S.Ct. 505 (1978); *Whitney Nat'l Bank in Jefferson Parish v. Bank of New Orleans & Trust Co.*, 379 U.S. 411, 85 S.Ct. 551 (1965) (involving views of appropriate supervisor). If the Fed advises the Comptroller or the state supervisor that an emergency exists requiring expeditious action, then the notice period is shortened to 10 days. 12 U.S.C.A. § 1842(b)(1). Furthermore, if the Fed determines that it must act immediately to prevent probable failure of the target bank or bank holding company, it may dispense with the notice requirements, or require that "views and recommendations" be submitted immediately. *Id.* On the effects of comments by the appropriate supervisor, see generally *Farmers and Merchants Bank of Las Cruces v. Board of Governors*, 567 F.2d 1082 (D.C.Cir.1977); *Grandview Bank &*

Trust Co. v. Board of Governors, 550 F.2d 415 (8th Cir.), *cert. denied*, 434 U.S. 821, 98 S.Ct. 64 (1977); *Bank of Boulder v. Board of Governors*, 535 F.2d 1221 (10th Cir.1976); *Commercial Nat'l Bank of Little Rock v. Board of Governors*, 451 F.2d 86 (8th Cir.1971); *Kirsch v. Board of Governors*, 353 F.2d 353 (6th Cir.1965); *First Wisc. Bankshares Corp. v. Board of Governors*, 325 F.2d 946 (7th Cir.1963); *Northwest Bancorporation v. Board of Governors*, 303 F.2d 832 (8th Cir.1962).

19. 12 U.S.C.A. § 1842(b)(1).

20. *Id.* The 91–day period does not begin to run until the Fed has received all final material needed for its decision. *See First Lincolnwood Corp. v. Board of Governors*, 546 F.2d 718 (7th Cir.1976), *reh'g*, 560 F.2d 258 (1977), *rev'd on other grounds*, 439 U.S. 234, 99 S.Ct. 505 (1978); *Tri–State Bancorporation, Inc. v. Board of Governors*, 524 F.2d 562 (7th Cir.1975). A Fed request for further information on a relevant issue with respect to a BHCA application before it may "retrigger" the 91–day period. *See Central Wisc. Bankshares, Inc. v. Board of Governors*, 583 F.2d 294 (7th Cir. 1978). In addition, the 91–day period may not begin to run until at least the close of the public comment period following the Fed's publication of notice in the Federal Register. *See Republic of*

Factors the Fed considers when reviewing a BHCA application are as follows:

(1) *Monopolization.* The application should be disapproved if the proposed transaction would result in a monopoly, or would be in furtherance of a combination or conspiracy to monopolize or to attempt to monopolize the business of banking in any part of the United States.[21]

(2) *Anticompetitiveness.* The application should be disapproved if the effect of the proposed transaction in any section of the country would be substantially to lessen competition, or to tend to create a monopoly, or would be in any other manner in restraint of trade, unless the Fed finds that these anticompetitive effects "are clearly outweighed in the public interest by the probable effect of the transaction in meeting the convenience and needs of the community to be served."[22]

(3) *Traditional Banking Factors.*[23] The Fed must take into consideration the financial[24] and managerial

---

Tex. Corp. v. Board of Governors, 649 F.2d 1026 (5th Cir.1981). Oral argument on facts already in Fed's possession is not part of the "complete record" for the purpose of tolling the 91–day period. *See North Lawndale Economic Dev. Corp. v. Board of Governors*, 553 F.2d 23 (7th Cir.1977). Likewise, Fed staff reports and recommendations are not part of the "complete record" for this purpose. *See Tri–State Bancorporation, Inc., supra.*

21. 12 U.S.C.A. § 1842(c)(1)(A).

22. *Id.* § 1842(c)(1)(B). *See generally Wyoming Bancorporation v. Board of Governors*, 729 F.2d 687 (10th Cir.1984); *Republic of Tex. Corp. v. Board of Governors*, 649 F.2d 1026; *Mercantile Tex. Corp. v. Board of Governors*, 638 F.2d 1255 (5th Cir.1981); *Mid–Nebraska Bancshares, Inc. v. Board of Governors*, 627 F.2d 266 (D.C.Cir.1980); *First State Bank of Clute, Tex. v. Board of Governors*, 553 F.2d 950 (5th Cir.1977); *Orbanco, Inc. v. Security Bank of Oregon*, 371 F.Supp. 125 (D.Or.1974) (concerning anticompetitiveness). On hearing requirements generally, see *Northeast Bancorp v. Board of Governors*, 849 F.2d 1499, 1505 n. 11 (D.C.Cir.1988) (rejecting argument that hearing was required before Fed refusal to allow participation in management by person subject to removal order, *per* 12 U.S.C.A. § 1818(e)(5), (j)).

23. 12 U.S.C.A. § 1842(c)(2). These factors are traditional criteria throughout federal bank regulatory policy. *See Bank of Boulder v. Board of Governors*, 535 F.2d 1221 (10th Cir.1976).

24. *See generally Board of Governors v. First Lincolnwood Corp.*, 439 U.S. 234, 99 S.Ct. 505 (1978); *Northeast Bancorp v. Board of Governors*, 849 F.2d 1499; *Grandview Bank & Trust Co. v. Board of Governors*, 550 F.2d 415 (8th Cir.), *cert. denied*, 434 U.S. 821, 98 S.Ct. 64 (1977); *Western Bancshares, Inc. v. Board of Governors*, 480 F.2d 749 (10th Cir.1973). The Fed's essential view in this regard is that a BHC should act as a "source of strength" for its bank subsidiary. *See First Lincolnwood Corp., supra* (requiring source of strength showing even when BHC results from spin-up from an existing bank).

The source of strength has been challenged as not based upon the BHCA. *See MCorp Financial, Inc. v. Board of Governors*, 900 F.2d 852 (5th Cir.1990), *affirmed in part and reversed in part on other grounds*, 502 U.S. 32, 112 S.Ct. 459 (1991) (rejecting application of doctrine). *See generally* James F. Groth, Comment, *Can Regulators Force Bank Holding Companies to Bail Out Their Failing Subsidiaries?–An Analysis of the Federal Reserve Board's Source-of-Strength Doctrine*, 86 Nw. U.L. Rev. 112 (1991) (discussing doctrine). However, it

resources[25] of the company or companies and bank(s) concerned; the future prospects of the company or companies and bank(s) concerned;[26] and, the convenience and needs of the community to be served.[27]

(4) *Supervisory Factors.* The Fed is required to disapprove an application if the applicant company fails to provide adequate assurances that it will make information available on the operations or activities of the company and its affiliates, as the Fed deems appropriate to determine and enforce compliance with the BHCA; or, in the case of an application involving a foreign bank, if the foreign bank is not subject to comprehensive supervision or regulation on a consolidated basis by the bank's home country authorities.[28] In addition, the Fed must take into consideration in every case the effectiveness of the holding company in combatting money laundering activities, including in its overseas branches.[29]

Any party aggrieved[30] by an order of the Fed[31] under the BHCA is entitled to judicial review of the order in the federal court of

appears that the Gramm–Leach–Bliley Act, Pub. L. No. 106–102, Nov. 12, 1999, 113 Stat. 1338 (1999) (codified at scattered sections of 12, 15, 16, 18 U.S.C.A.) ("GLBA"), may enhance the source of strength doctrine by, in certain circumstances, protecting the federal banking agencies and the deposit insurance funds from claims brought by the bankruptcy trustee of the holding company or other person for the return of capital infusions made by the company to the banking subsidiaries. GLBA, § 730 (codified at 12 U.S.C.A. § 1828(t)). Statutory protection for such capital transfers from parent BHC to subsidiary banks would be consistent with the source-of-strength doctrine.

As to applications for the formation of a one-bank holding company specifically, the Fed is prohibited from applying any policy or practice that would result in the rejection of an one-bank holding company application "solely because the transaction ... involves a bank stock loan which is for a period of not more than twenty-five years." 12 U.S.C.A. § 1842(c)(4). However, other unsatisfactory financial arrangements in connection with such an application may be the basis of Fed rejection of a one-bank holding company application. *Id.* In addition, in considering one-bank holding company applications involving bank stock loans with a maturity of 12 or more years, on a case-by-case basis, the

Fed may not approve such applications if it believes that the safety or soundness of the subject bank would be jeopardized thereby. *Id.*

25. *See generally First Lincolnwood Corp., supra; Northeast Bancorp, supra; Grandview Bank, supra; Western Bancshares, supra.* By statute, consideration of managerial resources must include "consideration of the competence, experience, and integrity of the officers, directors, and principal shareholders of the company or bank." 12 U.S.C.A. § 1842(c)(5).

26. *See generally Grandview Bank, supra.*

27. *See generally County Nat'l Bancorporation v. Board of Governors,* 654 F.2d 1253 (8th Cir.1981); *Northwest Bancorporation, supra.*

28. 12 U.S.C.A. § 1842(c)(3)(A)–(B).

29. *Id.* § 1842(c)(6).

30. A "party aggrieved" generally would be required to have presented an objection to the Fed in the application proceedings. *See, e.g., Bank of Commerce v. Smith,* 513 F.2d 167 (10th Cir.1975); *First Nat'l Bank of St. Charles v. Board of Governors,* 509 F.2d 1004 (8th Cir. 1975); *But cf. Northeast Bancorp,* 849 F.2d at 1504 (questioning whether court could review Fed refusal to allow participation in management by person sub-

appeals in the circuit in which the party has its principal place of business, or before the D.C. Circuit.[32] A petition must be filed before the appropriate circuit court within 30 days of the entry of the Fed order in question.[33] The jurisdiction of the courts of appeals in the first instance is exclusive.[34] Generally, federal district courts have no jurisdiction over matters involving the BHCA.[35]

A copy of the petition is required to be transmitted by the clerk of the court to the Fed.[36] The Fed is then required to file with the court the record made before it.[37] In reviewing the factual findings in the Fed's order, the court is required to apply a substantial evidence standard.[38] As to questions of law, the standard of judicial review is whether the Fed's action was arbitrary, capricious, an abuse of discretion or not otherwise in accordance with law.[39] The

ject to removal order, *per* 12 U.S.C.A. § 1818(e)(5), (j)). A "party aggrieved" would not include a target bank that did not participate in the application proceedings before the Fed. *See, e.g., Blackstone Valley Nat'l Bank v. Board of Governors,* 537 F.2d 1146 (1st Cir.1976). On the meaning of "party aggrieved" for these purposes, see generally *Jones v. Board of Governors,* 79 F.3d 1168 (D.C.Cir.1996); *State of Idaho, Dep't of Finance v. Clarke,* 786 F.Supp. 885 (D.Idaho 1992), *aff'd,* 994 F.2d 1441 (9th Cir.1993); *Synovus Fin. Corp. v. Board of Governors,* 952 F.2d 426 (D.C.Cir. 1991).

31. Only a final order approving (or denying) an application triggers judicial review under the BHCA. *See Executive Nat'l Bank v. Board of Governors,* 889 F.2d 556 (5th Cir.1989); *BankAmerica Corp. v. Board of Governors,* 596 F.2d 1368 (9th Cir.1979). *But cf. Investment Co. Inst. v. Board of Governors,* 551 F.2d 1270 (D.C.Cir.1977); *National Ass'n of Ins. Agents v. Board of Governors,* 489 F.2d 1268 (D.C.Cir.1974). The Comptroller's preliminary action in authorizing the creation of the new target bank is not the final subject of review in this context. *See Whitney Nat'l Bank supra; Bank of Boulder, supra. But see American Ins. Ass'n v. Clarke,* 865 F.2d 278 (D.C.Cir.1988) (discussing *Whitney*).

32. 12 U.S.C.A. § 1848.

33. *Id.*

34. *Id. See, e.g., Association of Data Processing Serv. Orgs., Inc. v. Board of Governors,* 745 F.2d 677 (D.C.Cir.1984); *Wyoming Bancorporation v. Board of Governors,* 729 F.2d 687 (10th Cir.1984); *Nehring v. First DeKalb Bancshares,*

Inc., 692 F.2d 1138 (7th Cir.1982); *BankAmerica Corp. v. Board of Governors,* 596 F.2d 1368 (9th Cir.1979); *Kirsch v. Board of Governors,* 353 F.2d 353 (6th Cir.1965). *Cf. Investment Co. Inst. v. Board of Governors,* 551 F.2d 1270 (D.C.Cir.1977).

35. *See, e.g., Nehring, supra;* Memphis *Trust Co. v. Board of Governors,* 584 F.2d 921 (6th Cir.1978). *Cf. Mid Am. Bancorporation, Inc. v. Board of Governors,* 523 F.Supp. 568 (D.Minn. 1980); *Investment Co. Inst., supra; American Bank of Tulsa v. Smith,* 503 F.2d 784 (10th Cir.1974); *NoDak Bancorporation v. Clarkson,* 471 N.W.2d 140 (N.D.1991) (finding minority shareholder's state law cause of action preempted).

36. 12 U.S.C.A. § 1848.

37. *Id.*

38. *Id. See generally Association of Data Processing Serv. Orgs., Inc. v. Board of Governors,* 745 F.2d 677 (D.C.Cir.1984); *Wyoming Bancorporation v. Board of Governors,* 729 F.2d 687 (10th Cir.1984); *Bank of Boulder, supra; North Hills Bank v. Board of Governors,* 506 F.2d 623 (8th Cir.1974); *Gravois Bank v. Board of Governors,* 478 F.2d 546 (8th Cir.1973).

39. *See, e.g., Association of Data Processing Serv. Orgs., Inc. v. Board of Governors,* 745 F.2d 677 (D.C.Cir.1984); *Wyoming Bancorporation v. Board of Governors,* 729 F.2d 687 (10th Cir.1984); *Investment Co. Inst., supra; Marine Corp. v. Board of Governors,* 325 F.2d 960 (7th Cir.1963). *Cf. First Wisc. Bancshares Corp. v. Board of Governors,* 325 F.2d 946 (7th Cir.1963).

Fed's determinations are usually accorded great weight by reviewing courts.[40]

§ 4.4 Home Owners' Loan Act

Savings and loan holding companies (SLHCs) have grown considerably and now represent an important alternative for expansion of savings association activities and the further concentration of financial and economic power in the savings association sector.[1] The savings and loan holding company provisions[2] of the HOLA broadly parallel the Bank Holding Company Act ("BHCA").[3] This section examines the restrictions and procedures imposed on the formation of savings and loan holding companies.

The language of the savings and loan holding company provisions is quite similar to that of the BHCA,[4] and parallels in judicial treatment of the two acts are therefore understandable. The alternative structures available for formation and expansion of a savings and loan holding company are substantially similar to those available for formation or expansion of a bank holding company.[5] The tax treatment of these alternative structures for formation of a

---

40. *See Association of Data Processing Serv. Orgs., Inc. v. Board of Governors*, 745 F.2d 677 (D.C.Cir.1984); *Wyoming Bancorporation v. Board of Governors*, 729 F.2d 687 (10th Cir. 1984); *First Lincolnwood Corp., supra*; *Grandview Bank, supra*; *Commercial Nat'l Bank of Little Rock v. Board of Governors*, 451 F.2d 86 (8th Cir.1971).

§ 4.4

1. Sen. Rep. No. 810, *reprinted in* 1959 U.S. Code Cong. and Admin. News 2883.

2. 12 U.S.C.A. § 1467a, *as amended* Dodd–Frank Wall Street Reform and Consumer Protection Act (DFA) Pub. L. No. 111–203, §§ 367(2), 604(g), (h)(2), (i), 606(b), 616(b), 623(c), 624, 625, 124 Stat. 1376, 1556, 1564–1565, 1602–1604, 1607, 1615–1616, 1635–1638 (2010) (codified at 12 U.S.C.A. §§ 1467a note, 1467a(a)(1)(D)(ii), 1467a(b)(2), (b)(4), 1467a(c)(2)(H), 1467a(e)(2)(E), 1467a(g)(1), 1467a(m)(3)(A), (m)(3)(B)(i)(III)–(IV), 1467a(o)(11)).

3. 12 U.S.C.A. §§ 1841 *et seq.*

4. A bank holding company acquiring control of a savings association or of a savings and loan holding company may be subject to the BHCA but not the savings and loan holding company provisions. Thus, prior approval under the savings and loan holding company provisions is not required

> in connection with the control of a savings association, ... acquired by a bank holding company that is registered under, and subject to, the Bank Holding Company Act of 1956, or any company controlled by such bank holding company.

Id. § 1467a(e)(1)(B)(iii).

5. One major difference between the two concerns the treatment of "spin ups" resulting in the creation of a holding company for a single depository institution. Such a transaction, if involving control of a bank, is fully subject to prior Fed approval under the BHCA. *Id.* § 1842(a). If involving control of a savings association, however, the result is not parallel under the HOLA. Prior approval is not required

> in connection with the control of a savings association, ... acquired in connection with a reorganization in which a person or group of persons, having had control of a savings association for more than 3 years, vests control of that association in a newly formed holding company subject to the control of the same person or group of persons....

Id. § 1467a(e)(1)(B)(ii).

savings and loan holding company will also be quite similar to that applicable to formation of a bank holding company.[6] Until the mid 1980s, however, special tax treatment was given to acquisitions and reorganizations involving financially troubled thrift institutions.[7] With the enactment of the Tax Reform Act of 1986,[8] this special treatment was repealed, generally effective as to transactions after December 31, 1988.[9]

Until the Fall of 2011, the savings and loan holding company provisions require registration of an SLHC with the Office of Thrift Supervision (OTS),[10] within 90 days of becoming an

6. *See generally* 26 U.S.C.A. §§ 351 *et seq. Cf.* 12 U.S.C.A. § 1730a(e)(4) (1988) (concerning loss of certain tax benefits under prior legislation).

7. *See* 26 U.S.C.A. § 597 (1982) (excluding FSLIC financial assistance from income; basis reduction requirement).

8. Pub. L. No. 99–514, 99th Cong., 2d Sess. (Oct. 22, 1986).

9. *Id.* § 904(b)(1), (c)(2)(A). *See also* 26 U.S.C.A. § 597 (providing early termination of special reorganization rules for financial institutions; treatment of transactions involving federal financial assistance).

10. For these purposes, a savings and loan holding company is defined as "any company which directly or indirectly controls a savings association or controls any other company which is a[n SLHC]." 12 U.S.C.A. § 1467a(a)(1)(D)(i). *But see* DFA § 604(i) (codified at 12 U.S.C.A. § 1467a(a)(1)(D)(ii)) (excluding certain companies from definition of SLHC). On the meaning of "control" for these purposes, see *id.* § 1467a(a)(2). The term "company" is defined for these purposes to include:

> any corporation, partnership, trust, joint-stock company, or similar organization, but does not include the Federal Deposit Insurance Corporation, the Resolution Trust Corporation, any Federal home loan bank, or any company the majority of the shares of which is owned by the United States or any State, or by an instrumentality of the United States or any State.

Id. § 1467a(a)(1)(C). A "savings association," control of which may trigger the application of the savings and loan holding company provisions, is defined to include "a savings bank or cooperative

bank which is deemed by the Director [of the Office of Thrift Supervision] to be a savings association...." *Id.* § 1467a(a)(1)(A). The term "savings and loan holding company" does not include the following:

> (1) a BHC that is registered under, and subject to, the BHCA and any company directly or indirectly controlled by a BHC (other than a savings association);

> (2) a company that controls a savings association that functions solely in a trust or fiduciary capacity as described in BHCA § 2(c)(2)(D) (12 U.S.C.A. 1841(c)(2)(D)); or,

> (3) a company that is an existing unitary SLHC solely by virtue of its control of an "intermediate holding company" established pursuant to HOLA § 10A.

Id. § 1467a(a)(1)(D)(ii)(I)–(III). An "intermediate holding company" can be established under § 626 of the Dodd–Frank Wall Street Reform and Consumer Protection Act (DFA), 124 Stat. 1376, 1638–1640 (2010) (codified at 12 U.S.C.A. § 1467b). This would be triggered if and when a grandfathered unitary SLHC conducts activities other than financial activities, and the Fed requires the company to establish and conduct all or some specified portion of its financial activities in or through an intermediate holding company created for that purpose. 12 U.S.C.A. § 1467b(b)(1)(A). The intermediate company becomes the SLHC, *per id.*, and the parent company is no longer considered an SLHC under *id.* § 1467a(1)(D)(ii)(III). (The Fed's authority over SLHCs does not become effective until 21 July 2011. DFA § 311(a).)

SLHC.[11] Under section 313 of the Dodd–Frank Wall Street Reform and Consumer Protection Act,[12] the OTS and the position of the DOTS are scheduled to be abolished. This dramatic event is effective 90 days after the "transfer date"[13]—21 July 2011—on which date the functions and authority of the DOTS and the OTS over SLHCs are first exercised by the Fed.[14]

Until this transfer of power occurs, the OTS continues to supervise SLHC formation. Absent prior written approval of the OTS, SLHCs are prohibited from engaging, directly or indirectly, in any of the following activities:

> (1) acquisition or retention of control of a savings association or an SLHC in violation of the savings and loan holding company provisions;[15]

> (2) acquisition, by merger, consolidation or purchase of assets, of another savings association or an SLHC, or the acquisition of all or substantially all the assets of any such association or SLHC;[16]

> (3) acquisition or retention of any voting shares of a nonsubsidiary savings association or SLHC[17] or (in the case of a multiple SLHC[18]) acquisition or retention of more than five percent of the voting shares of any nonsubsidiary company engaged in any business activity other than those permitted to a multiple SLHC itself;[19] and

In addition, an SLHC is not deemed to control a savings association or another SLHC solely by reason of purchase of shares in a "qualified stock issuance," if the purchase is approved by the Director, until 21 July 2011, and thereafter by the Fed, unless the acquiring SLHC owns, controls or has the power to vote (or holds proxies representing) in the aggregate, directly and indirectly, more than 15 percent of the voting shares of the association or savings and loan holding company. *Id.* § 1467a(a)(4). On qualified stock issuances (limited to undercapitalized associations and savings and loan holding companies) and their approval, see *id.* § 1467a(q).

11. *Id.* § 1467a(b)(1). The OTS is given authority to extend, upon application, the time within which a savings and loan holding company must register. *See id.*

12. Pub. L. No. 111–203, § 313, 124 Stat. 1376, 1523 (2010) (codified at 12 U.S.C.A. § 5413) (DFA). For discussion of the impact of the DFA, see 1 Michael P. Malloy, Banking Law and Regulation § 1.4.11 (1994 & Cum. Supps.).

13. DFA §§ 311(a), 313 (codified at 12 U.S.C.A. §§ 5411(a), 5413).

14. See *id.* § 312(b) (codified at 12 U.S.C.A. § 5412(b)) (mandating transfer of functions).

15. *Id.* § 1467a(e)(1)(A)(i).

16. *Id.* § 1467a(e)(1)(A)(ii).

17. *See id.* § 1467a(a)(1)(G) (defining "subsidiary" by reference to 12 U.S.C.A. § 1813).

18. For these purposes, a multiple savings and loan holding company is defined as "any savings and loan holding company which directly or indirectly controls 2 or more savings associations." *Id.* § 1467a(a)(1)(E).

19. *Id.* § 1467a(e)(1)(A)(iii). On activities permitted to multiple savings and loan holding companies, see *id.* § 1467a(c)(2), *as amended* DFA § 606(b), 124 Stat. at 1607 (codified at 12 U.S.C.A. § 1467a(c)(2)(H)) (setting conditions for SLHC to operate as financial holding company). On the exceptions to this prohibition, see *id.* § 1467a(e)(1)(A)(iii)(I)–(VIII).

(4) acquisition or retention of control of an uninsured institution.[20]

In addition, the savings and loan holding company provisions prohibit any other company from acquiring direct or indirect control of one or more savings associations without prior written approval of the OTS.[21] Approval by the OTS may not be given if the OTS finds "the financial and managerial resources and future prospects of the company and association ... to be such that the acquisition would be detrimental to the association or the insurance risk of the Deposit Insurance Fund."[22] However, three exceptions exist with respect to this requirement of prior approval. First, approval is not required for control of a savings association acquired by devise under the terms of a will creating a trust that is itself excluded from the Act's definition of "savings and loan holding company."[23] Second, approval is also not required where control of a savings association is acquired in connection with a reorganization in which a holding company is "spinning up" from an association that has been controlled for more than three years by a person or group of persons who will control the holding company upon completion of the reorganization.[24] No such exception is available for bank holding companies that spin up from an existing bank.[25] Third, approval is not required for an acquisition of a savings association by a bank holding company that is registered under, and subject to, the BHCA, or any company controlled by such bank holding company.[26]

As with the BHCA—though stated in a slightly different order—a proposed acquisition of control subject to prior approval under the savings and loan holding company provisions is to be reviewed in light of the following considerations:

(1) *Traditional factors.* The OTS must take into consideration the financial and managerial resources and future prospects of the company and association involved, the effect of the acquisition on the association, the insurance risk to the Deposit

20. *Id.* § 1467a(e)(1)(A)(iv). Retention of control is permitted for one year, and, upon application, the OTS may extend this period of retention for no more than three successive one-year periods. *Id.* The term "uninsured institution" is defined for these purposes to mean "any depository institution the deposits of which are not insured by the Federal Deposit Insurance Corporation." *Id.* § 1467a(a)(1)(B).

21. *Id.* § 1467a(e)(1)(B).

22. *Id.*

23. *Id.* § 1467a(e)(1)(B)(i). On the exclusion of certain trusts from the definition of "savings and loan holding company," see *id.* § 1467a(a)(3)(B).

24. *Id.* § 1467a(e)(1)(B)(ii).

25. *See, e.g., Board of Governors v. First Lincolnwood Corp.,* 439 U.S. 234, 99 S.Ct. 505 (1978) (subjecting spin-up establishment of bank holding company to BHCA).

26. 12 U.S.C.A. § 1467a(e)(1)(B)(iii).

Insurance Fund ("DIF"), and the convenience and needs of the community to be served.[27]

(2) *Monopolization*. The acquisition must be disapproved if it would result in a monopoly or would be in furtherance of a combination or conspiracy to monopolize or to attempt to monopolize the savings association business in any part of the United States.[28]

(3) *Anticompetitiveness*. The acquisition must be disapproved if it *may* have the effect in any section of the country of substantially lessening competition, or of tending to create a monopoly, or would in any other manner be in restraint of trade, "unless [the OTS] finds that the anticompetitive effects of the proposed acquisition are clearly outweighed in the public interest by the probable effect of the acquisition in meeting the convenience and needs of the community to be served."[29]

(4) *Supervisory Factors*. The OTS is required to disapprove an application if the company fails to provide adequate assurances that it will make information available on the operations or activities of the company and its affiliates, as the OTS deems to be appropriate to determine and enforce compliance with the HOLA;[30] or, in the case of an application involving a foreign bank, if the foreign bank is not subject to comprehensive supervision or regulation on a consolidated basis by the bank's home country authorities.[31]

(5) Deposit Concentration. In the case of an interstate acquisition by an SLHC of an insured depository institution, the OTS must disapprove the acquisition if the applicant (including all insured depository institution affiliates of the applicant) controls, or on consummation of the transaction would control, more than 10 percent of the total amount of deposits of insured depository institutions in the United States.[32] This rule does not apply if the acquisition involves an insured depository institution that is in default or in danger of default, or that has received FDIC "open bank" assistance.[33]

Since 1987, the predecessor to the savings and loan holding company provisions provided specifically for the formation of mutu-

27. *Id.* § 1467a(e)(2). In the case of an acquisition of control of a savings association by a company that is not yet an SLHC (*id.* § 1467a(e)(1)(B)), consideration of the managerial resources of a company or savings association explicitly is required to include consideration of the competence, experience, and integrity of the officers, directors, and principal shareholders of the company or association. *Id.* § 1467a(e)(1).

28. *Id.* § 1467a(e)(2)(A).

29. *Id.* § 1467a(e)(2)(B).

30. *Id.* § 1467a(e)(2)(C).

31. *Id.* § 1467(e)(2)(D).

32. *Id.* § 1467a(e)(2)(E)(i)–(ii).

33. *Id.* § 1467a(e)(2)(E)(iii). "Open bank" assistance under 12 U.S.C.A. § 1823 is discussed in § 8.16, *infra*.

al holding companies by the reorganization of a mutual insured institution.[34] An institution could effect such a reorganization by chartering an "interim savings institution," the stock of which would be wholly-owned by the mutual institution,[35] at which time the mutual institution would transfer a substantial part of its assets and liabilities[36] to the interim institution.[37] The plan of reorganization was required to be approved by a majority of the mutual institution's board of directors[38] and, if they exercised voting rights, by a majority of the account holders and obligors of the institution.[39] The permitted activities of such a mutual holding company were rather limited, consisting of little more beyond holding the stock of the subsidiary mutual institution.[40] In 1989, the Financial Institutions Reform, Recovery, and Enforcement Act ("FIRREA") continued to grant the OTS authority to approve reorganization of mutual savings associations into the mutual holding company form.[41]

Unlike chartering provisions, the savings and loan holding company provisions do not regulate the formation of the SLHC as a business entity. However, when such an entity seeks to acquire control over a savings association, or over an SLHC, the savings and loan holding company provisions intervene at that stage of "formation," requiring prior approval until 21 July 2011 by the OTS of the acquisition of control, and thereafter by the Fed.[42] The

---

34. Competitive Equality Banking Act ("CEBA"), Pub. L. No. 100–86, § 107(a), 101 Stat. 552 (1987) (codified at 12 U.S.C.A. § 1730a(s)). *Cf.* CEBA, § 107(b), codified at 12 U.S.C.A. § 1842(g) (providing for reorganization of mutual savings or cooperative bank to form mutual bank holding company). These provisions of the savings and loan holding company were repealed in August 1989. Financial Institutions Reform, Recovery, and Enforcement Act ("FIRREA"), Pub. L. No. 101–73, § 407, 103 Stat. 183, 363 (1989).

35. *See* 12 U.S.C.A. § 1730a(s)(1)(A) (1988).

36. On retention of capital assets at the holding company level, see *id.* § 1730a(s)(3)(D). Transferred liabilities were required to include all insured liabilities. *See id.* § 1730a(s)(1)(B).

37. *Id.* § 1730a(s)(1). Notice of the planned reorganization was required to be given to the FSLIC 60 days prior to the chartering and transfer of assets and liabilities. *Id.* § 1730a(s)(3)(A). FSLIC review was similar to that provided under the Change in Savings and Loan

Control Act, *id.* § 1730(q), with any FSLIC disapproval action required within 60 days (and an extension period of 30 days), on specified statutory grounds. *Id.* § 1730a(s)(3)(C) (1988).

38. *Id.* § 1730a(s)(2)(A).

39. *Id.* § 1730a(s)(2)(B). In any event, persons with ownership rights in the mutual institution had the same ownership rights in the mutual holding company. *See id.* § 1730a(s)(4).

40. *See id.* § 1730a(s)(5), (6).

41. *See* FIRREA, § 301, 103 Stat. at 336–338 (codified at 12 U.S.C.A. § 1467a(*o*)), *as amended* DFA § 625, 124 Stat. at 1636–1638 (codified at 12 U.S.C.A. § 1467a(*o*)(11)) (requiring prior notice to regulators of dividends by savings association subsidiaries of mutual SLHC).

42. 12 U.S.C.A. § 1467a(e), *as amended* DFA § 623(c), 124 Stat. at 1635–1636 (codified at 12 U.S.C.A. § 1467a(e)(2)(E)) (imposing limits on deposit concentration resulting from SLHC acquisition of savings association).

OTS is required to render its decision on any such application within 90 days of submission of the complete record on the application.[43] Before approving an application, the OTS is required to request from the Attorney General a report on the competitive factors involved in the proposed acquisition,[44] and to consider any such report in its evaluation of the application.[45] In contrast to the situation under the BHCA, the role of the Attorney General, and of the federal antitrust laws in general, under the savings and loan holding company provisions is rather limited.[46]

Any party aggrieved[47] by an order of the OTS under the savings and loan holding company provisions is entitled to judicial review of the order in the federal court of appeals in the circuit in which the party has its principal place of business, or before the D.C. Circuit.[48] A petition must be filed before the appropriate circuit court within 30 days of the issuance of the OTS order in question.[49] The jurisdiction of the courts of appeals in the first instance is exclusive.[50] Generally, federal district courts have no jurisdiction over such petitions.[51]

43. *Id.* § 1467a(e)(2). *See, e.g., Fidelity Fin. Corp. v. Federal Sav. & Loan Ins. Corp.*, 359 F.Supp. 324 (N.D.Cal. 1973) (decision under prior statutory provision). *Cf. Nasser v. Federal Home Loan Bank Bd.*, 723 F.2d 1437 (9th Cir. 1984).

44. *Id.* § 1467a(e)(2). On the consideration of anticompetitive effects involved in a proposed acquisition undertaken by the OTS's predecessor agency, see generally *Fort Worth Nat'l Corp. v. Federal Sav. & Loan Ins. Corp.*, 469 F.2d 47 (5th Cir.1972); *Fidelity Fin. Corp., supra.*

45. 12 U.S.C.A. § 1467a(e)(2). Any such report must be rendered within 30 days. *Id.*

46. *See, e.g., id.* 1467a(k)(2), which provides as follows:

Nothing contained in [the savings and loan holding company provisions], other than [an acquisition approved under subsection (e)(2) or the emergency acquisitions provisions of 12 U.S.C.A. § 1823], shall be interpreted or construed as approving any act, action, or conduct which is or has been or may be in violation of existing law, nor shall anything herein contained constitute a defense to any action, suit, or proceeding pending or hereafter instituted on account of any act, action, or

conduct in violation of the antitrust laws.

47. For these purposes, a state may be a "party aggrieved" in cases where the OTS is required to consult with state supervisory officials in "emergency acquisitions." *See Hartigan v. Federal Home Loan Bank Bd.*, 746 F.2d 1300 (7th Cir.1984) (involving predecessor to savings and loan holding company provisions). A frustrated bidder for a financially troubled savings association, but not a trade association of competing commercial banks, may also be a "party aggrieved." *See id.*

48. 12 U.S.C.A. § 1467a(j).

49. *Id.*

50. *Cf., e.g., Fort Worth Nat'l Corp. v. Federal Sav. & Loan Ins. Corp.*, 469 F.2d 47 (5th Cir.1972) (discussing corresponding provision of predecessor to savings and loan holding company provisions).

51. *Cf., e.g., North Am. Sav. Ass'n v. Federal Home Loan Bank Bd.*, 755 F.2d 122 (8th Cir.1985); *Independent Bankers Ass'n v. Federal Home Loan Bank Bd.*, 557 F.Supp. 23 (D.D.C.1982); *Fidelity Fin. Corp. v. Federal Sav. & Loan Ins. Corp.*, 359 F.Supp. 324 (N.D.Cal.1973) (discussing corresponding provision of predecessor to savings and loan holding company provisions).

A copy of the petition is required to be transmitted by the clerk of the court to the OTS.[52] The OTS is then required to file with the court the record made before it.[53] The court's review is subject to the Administrative Procedure Act,[54] by express reference in the savings and loan holding company provisions.[55] Unlike the more explicit and specific language in the BHCA,[56] the savings and loan holding company provisions do not indicate whether, in reviewing any factual findings or assumptions in the OTS order, a court is required to apply a substantial evidence standard.[57] As to nonfactual issues, however, it may be assumed that the standard of judicial review is whether the OTS action was arbitrary, capricious, an abuse of discretion or not otherwise in accordance with law.[58]

§ 4.5   State Holding Company Law

State supervisory officials have an express role to play in the review of bank holding company applications under the BHCA.[1] In addition, state authority to supervise formation or expansion of bank holding companies is expressly preserved from preemption by the BHCA.[2]

The BHCA explicitly reserves to the states the exercise of "such powers and jurisdiction which [they] now ha[ve] or may hereafter have with respect to companies, banks, [bank holding companies], and subsidiaries thereof."[3] This reservation is merely preservative and does not broaden the permissible scope of state

52. 12 U.S.C.A. § 1467a(j).

53. *Id. See also* 28 U.S.C.A. § 2112.

54. *See* 5 U.S.C.A. §§ 701 *et seq.*

55. *See* 12 U.S.C.A. § 1467a(j).

56. *See id.* § 1848 (subjecting factual findings to "substantial evidence" standard of judicial review).

57. *Cf. North Am. Sav. Ass'n, supra.*

58. *Cf. id.*

§ 4.5

1. *See* 12 U.S.C.A. § 1842(b)(1) (providing for notice to and comment from state supervisor). *But cf. North Hills Bank v. Board of Governors,* 506 F.2d 623 (8th Cir.1974) (discussing role of state supervisor).

2. *See* 12 U.S.C.A. § 1846(a) (reservation of rights to states). *See Security Nat'l Bank & Trust Co. v. First W. Va. Bancorp., Inc.,* 166 W.Va. 775, 277 S.E.2d 613 (1981), *appeal dismissed,* 454 U.S. 1131, 102 S.Ct. 986 (1982). *See also Heritage Fin. Servs. Corp. v. Common-*

wealth Bancshares Corp., Pa. Ct. Common Pleas No. 4504 Equity, *reprinted in* [1988–1989 Transfer Binder] Fed. Banking L. Rep. (CCH) & 87,302 (April 22, 1988) (Section 1846 allows state banking department jurisdiction for preapproval of a resident bank holding company acquisition of stock of another bank holding company). However, interstate bank holding company acquisitions are now governed by federal law. 12 U.S.C.A. § 1842(d). On the role preserved to the states, prior to the change in federal law regarding interstate acquisitions, see generally *Whitney Nat'l Bank in Jefferson Parish v. Bank of New Orleans & Trust,* 379 U.S. 411, 85 S.Ct. 551 (1965); *Iowa Indep. Bankers v. Board of Governors,* 511 F.2d 1288 (D.C.Cir.1975), *cert. denied,* 423 U.S. 875, 96 S.Ct. 144. *But cf. Independent Community Bankers Ass'n v. Board of Governors,* 838 F.2d 969 (8th Cir.1988) (finding restrictive South Dakota statute allowing limited entry by out-of-state bank holding companies in violation of Commerce Clause).

3. 12 U.S.C.A. § 1846(a).

regulation beyond the general strictures of, for example, the Commerce Clause of the U.S. Constitution.[4] Thus, it is permissible for a state to prohibit the formation of bank holding companies.[5] State regulation may also reasonably limit the degree of entry permitted to bank holding companies, rather than prohibit them outright,[6] subject to federal law concerning interstate bank holding company acquisitions (discussed in §§ 4.6–4.8, *infra*). State regulation of bank holding companies may affect holding companies seeking to control national as well as state-chartered banks.[7]

Prior to the 1994 passage of federal legislation governing interstate bank holding company acquisitions,[8] a regional interstate model had already emerged as the dominant approach of state regulation. A growing number of states were adopting statutes permitting out-of-state bank holding companies located in states within a specified region to operate a bank within their respective borders. In 1985, the New England regional banking arrangement was upheld by the Supreme Court, in a unanimous decision, in *Northeast Bancorp, Inc. v. Board of Governors*,[9] as against challenges based upon then-applicable BHCA restrictions on interstate acquisitions, known as the Douglas Amendment to the BHCA,[10] as well as, *inter alia*, the Commerce Clause. In this regard, the Court emphasized that the BHCA reflected congressional "policies of community control and local responsiveness of banks."[11] However, the importance of state policy in this regard has been minimized by the emergence of federal rules on interstate acquisitions.

§ 4.6 Interstate Acquisitions

A dramatic development in bank holding company interstate practice occurred in September 1994, with the enactment of the Riegle–Neal Interstate Banking and Branching Efficiency Act of

4. U.S. Const. art. 1, § 8, cl. 3. *See BT Inv. Managers, Inc. v. Lewis*, 461 F.Supp. 1187 (N.D.Fla.1978), *aff'd in part, vacated in part on other grounds*, 447 U.S. 27, 100 S.Ct. 2009 (1980); *Independent Community Bankers Ass'n, supra. But see Northeast Bancorp, Inc. v. Board of Governors*, 849 F.2d 1499 (D.C.Cir.1988) (upholding Connecticut bank holding company statute). *Cf. Sears, Roebuck and Co. v. Brown*, 806 F.2d 399 (2d Cir.1986).

5. *See, e.g., Commercial Nat'l Bank of Little Rock v. Board of Governors*, 451 F.2d 86 (8th Cir.1971).

6. *See Northeast Bancorp, Inc., supra* (permitting regional interstate banking

compacts). *But see Independent Community Bankers Ass'n, supra.*

7. *See Security Nat'l Bank & Trust Co., supra; Braeburn Sec. Corp. v. Smith*, 15 Ill.2d 55, 153 N.E.2d 806 (1958), *appeal dismissed*, 359 U.S. 311, 79 S.Ct. 876 (1959).

8. Riegle–Neal Interstate Banking and Branching Efficiency Act of 1994, Pub. L. No. 103–328, 108 Stat. 2338 (Sept. 29, 1994).

9. 472 U.S. 159, 105 S.Ct. 2545 (1985).

10. 12 U.S.C.A. § 1842(d) (1988).

11. *Northeast Bancorp, Inc.*, 472 U.S. at 169, 105 S.Ct. at 2551.

1994 ("IBBEA").[1] The IBBEA permits geographic expansion by banks without regard to the artificial barriers to interstate expansion heretofore imposed by the Douglas Amendment[2] to the BHCA and by the branching provisions of state law and the National Bank Act ("NBA").[3]

§ 4.7   Bank Holding Company Acquisitions

As of 29 September 1995, the Fed has been authorized to approve BHCA applications for acquisition of control of out-of-state banks "without regard to whether such transaction is prohibited under the law of any State."[1] This authority is limited to acquisitions by BHCs that are well capitalized and well managed.[2] Permitted "acquisitions" include acquisition of a *de novo* bank chartered to establish a presence of the acquiring bank holding company within the target state.[3]

Specified state law restrictions affecting interstate acquisitions continue in effect. First, the Fed is generally not permitted to approve an acquisition that would contravene applicable state statutory law requiring a bank to be in existence for a minimum period of time before acquisition.[4] The Fed may approve such an acquisition if the target bank has been in existence for at least five years, notwithstanding any longer minimum period in the statutory law of the host state.[5]

Second, state law requirements that a portion of the assets of a target bank be held available for call by a state-sponsored housing entity remain applicable to such acquisitions, if four conditions are

---

§ 4.6

1. Pub. L. No. 103–328, 108 Stat. 2338 (Sept. 29, 1994).

2. 12 U.S.C.A. § 1842(d) (1988).

3. *See, e.g.,* 12 U.S.C.A. § 36(c) (NBA provision limiting branching by national banks to branching permitted to state banks in same state). *See generally First Nat'l Bank of Logan v. Walker Bank & Trust Co.,* 385 U.S. 252, 87 S.Ct. 492 (1966) (construing § 36(c)); *First Nat'l Bank in Plant City v. Dickinson,* 396 U.S. 122, 90 S.Ct. 337 (1969) (meaning of "branch" for purposes of § 36(c)).

§ 4.7

1. 12 U.S.C.A. § 1842(d)(1)(A).

2. *Id.* § 1842(d)(1)(A), as amended, Dodd–Frank Wall Street Reform and Consumer Protection Act (DFA) § 607(a), 124 Stat. 1376, 1607 (2010) (raising standards from "adequately

capitalized" and "adequately managed" to "well capitalized" and "well managed"). A BHC is considered "well capitalized" if it "significantly exceeds the required minimum level for each relevant capital measure." 12 U.S.C.A. § 1841(*o*)(1)(B)(ii). On the meaning of "well managed," see *id.* § 1841(*o*)(9). The increase in standards is effective 21 July 2011. DFA § 607(c), 124 Stat. at 1608.

3. *See, e.g., id.* § 1842(d)(1)(A), (C) (acquisitions of "shell banks" included within new rules).

4. *Id.* § 1842(d)(1)(B)(i). For these purposes, a "shell" or "phantom" bank, created to be controlled by the acquiring bank holding company and to receive an existing target bank, is deemed to have been in existence for as long as the target bank has been. *Id.* § 1842(d)(1)(C).

5. *Id.* § 1842(d)(1)(B)(ii).

met: (1) State law must not have the effect of discriminating against out-of-state banks, bank holding companies and their subsidiaries.[6] (2) State law must have been in effect prior to September 29, 1994.[7] (3) The FDIC has not made a determination that compliance with the state law would result in an unacceptable risk to the BIF or SAIF.[8] (4) Finally, the "appropriate Federal banking agency"[9] of the target bank has not made a determination that compliance with the state law would place the bank in an unsafe or unsound condition.[10]

Third, certain nationwide and statewide concentration limits apply to the newly-authorized interstate bank holding company acquisitions:

> (1) The Fed is not permitted to approve an interstate acquisition if the applicant[11] controls, or would control upon consummation of the acquisition, more than 10 percent of the total amount of deposits of insured depository institutions in the United States.[12]

> (2) As to acquisitions other than initial entry into the target state, the Fed is not permitted to approve an acquisition if, immediately before the proposed acquisition, the applicant controls an insured depository institution or any branch of such an institution in the home state of the target bank, or in any host state in which the target bank maintains a branch; and, upon consummation of the proposed acquisition the applicant would control 30 percent or more of the total amount of deposits of insured depository institutions in any such state.[13]

6. *Id.* § 1842(d)(1)(D)(i).

7. *Id.* § 1842(d)(1)(D)(ii).

8. *Id.* § 1842(d)(1)(D)(iii).

9. For these purposes, the term "appropriate Federal banking agency" has the same meaning as in Section 3 of the FDIA, 12 U.S.C.A. § 1813(q). IBBEA, § 101(c), 108 Stat. at 2341 (codified at 12 U.S.C.A. § 1841(n)).

10. 12 U.S.C.A. § 1842(d)(1)(D)(iv).

11. For these purposes, the "applicant" would include all insured depository institutions that are affiliates of the applicant bank holding company. *Id.* § 1842(d)(2)(A).

12. *Id.* "Deposit" has the same meaning as in Section 3(*l*) of the FDIA, 12 U.S.C.A. § 1813(*l*). 12 U.S.C.A. § 1842(d)(2)(E). *See generally FDIC v. Philadelphia Gear Corp.*, 476 U.S. 426, 106 S.Ct. 1931 (1986) (construing the term "deposit" under § 1813(*l*)). For a Fed order illustrating the scope of this limitation, see *Bank of America Corporation Charlotte, North Carolina Order Approving the Acquisition of a Savings Association and an Industrial Loan Company*, (Nov. 26, 2008) available at http://www.federalreserve.gov/newsevents/press/orders/orders20081126a1.pdf. *See also* R. Christian Bruce, *Bank of America Gains Fed Approval For Acquisition of Merrill Lynch & Co.*, BNA Banking Daily (Nov. 28, 2008), *available at* http://www.bna.com (reporting on Merrill acquisition).

13. 12 U.S.C.A. § 1842(d)(2)(B)(i)–(ii). IBBEA provides certain exceptions to the statewide concentration restriction. The acquisition will be permitted if there is state deposit cap limitation that permits a bank or bank holding company (and affiliates thereof) to control a greater percentage of total deposits in the target state. *Id.* § 1842(d)(2)(D)(i). Alternatively, the acquisition will be permitted if it is approved by the appropri-

The nationwide and statewide concentration provisions do not affect the authority of any state to limit, by statute, regulation, or order, the percentage of the total amount of deposits of insured depository institutions in the state held or controlled by a bank, bank holding company, and subsidiaries thereof.[14]

Approval of interstate acquisitions are fully subject to compliance with the Community Reinvestment Act ("CRA").[15] The Fed must also take into account the record of the applicant bank holding company in complying with applicable state community reinvestment laws.[16]

Similarly, approval of interstate acquisitions are fully subject to applicable antitrust laws.[17] The Fed must also take into account the applicability of any similar state anticompetitive laws.[18]

An exception exists for acquisitions of banks in default or in danger of default. Notwithstanding the restrictions discussed above, the Fed may approve an interstate acquisition of one or more banks in default or in danger of default,[19] or an interstate acquisition as to which financial assistance is provided by the FDIC under Section 13(c) of the FDIA.[20]

§ 4.8   Effects on State Authority

Prior to the enactment of the IBBEA, the BHCA generally did not affect the authority of states to regulate banks and bank holding companies subject to their jurisdiction.[1] Aside from preempting state authority to prohibit interstate bank holding company acquisitions, the IBBEA not only confirms state authority over bank holding companies, but also explicitly provides that nothing in the Act is to be construed as affecting the authority of states and their political subdivisions to subject banks, bank holding companies, foreign banks, and affiliates thereof to state taxation.[2]

---

ate state bank supervisor of the host state, and the applicable standard of approval does not have the effect of discriminating against out-of-state banks, bank holding companies and subsidiaries thereof. *Id.* § 1842(d)(2)(D)(ii).

14. *Id.* § 1842(d)(2)(C). These state deposit caps are given effect so long as they do not discriminate against out-of-state banks, bank holding companies and subsidiaries thereof. *Id.*

15. *Id.* § 1842(d)(3)(A). *See id.* §§ 2901 *et seq.* (CRA requirements).

16. *Id.* § 1842(d)(3)(B).

17. *Id.* § 1842(d)(4)(A).

18. *Id.* § 1842(d)(4)(B).

19. *Id.* § 1842(d)(5)(A).

20. *Id.* § 1842(d)(5)(B).

§ 4.8

1. *See* 12 U.S.C.A. § 1846 (1988) (pre-IBBEA BHCA provision; state authority preserved), *redesignated by* IBBEA, § 101(b)(1), 108 Stat. at 2341 (codified at 12 U.S.C.A. § 1846(a)).

2. 12 U.S.C.A. § 1846(b). This state authority is confirmed "to the extent that such tax or tax method is otherwise permissible by or under the Constitution of the United States or other Federal law." *Id. See also* IBBEA, § 111 (codified at 12 U.S.C.A. § 1811 note) (restat-

Pre–IBBEA, questions sometimes arose as a matter of state law over whether or not a depository institution subsidiary of a bank holding company could undertake transactions as an agent for an affiliate institution.[3] The IBBEA resolves these questions, as a natural extension of its authorization of interstate acquisitions by bank holding companies.

A bank subsidiary is generally permitted to "receive deposits, renew time deposits, close loans, service loans, and receive payments on loans and other obligations as an agent for a depository institution affiliate."[4] A bank acting in this capacity "shall not be considered to be a branch of the affiliate."[5] Any such agency relationship must be consistent with safe and sound banking practices, and all applicable regulations of any appropriate federal banking agency.[6]

Similarly, an insured savings association that was an affiliate of a bank on 1 July 1994, is permitted to act as agent for the bank in the same manner as an insured bank affiliate could act.[7] However, the agency activities must be conducted only: (1) in a state in which the bank is not prohibited from operating a branch,[8] and the savings association maintained an office or branch and conducted business as of 1 July 1994;[9] or (2) in a state in which the bank is not expressly prohibited from operating a branch under a state law prohibiting interstate bank mergers,[10] and the savings association maintained a main office and conducted business as of that date.[11] Any such agency relationship must be consistent with safe and sound banking practices, and all applicable regulations of any appropriate federal banking agency.[12]

Certain prohibitions apply to agency activities of depository institutions. The institution may not conduct on an agency basis

ing existing law with respect to state taxation of banking enterprises).

3. The issue might involve, for example, whether the institution was, in effect, acting as a branch of its affiliate rather than simply as an agent. *See, e.g., Commercial Nat'l Bank of Little Rock v. Board of Governors*, 451 F.2d 86 (8th Cir.1971) (discussing use of bank as functional branch of affiliated bank).

4. 12 U.S.C.A. § 1828(r)(1). The question may be raised whether the list of permitted agency activities is intended to be exclusive. According to the IBBEA, the list is not to be construed as limiting the authority of the bank to act in such a capacity "under any other provision of law." *Id.* § 1828(r)(4)(A).

5. *Id.* § 1828(r)(2). However, if the bank acts in an agency capacity under

another provision of law, the IBBEA does not affect the question of whether or not the bank so acting is to be considered a branch of the principal. *See id.* § 1828(r)(4)(B).

6. *Id.* § 1828(r)(5).

7. *Id.* § 1828(r)(6).

8. *Id.* § 1828(r)(6)(A)(i).

9. *Id.* § 1828(r)(6)(A)(ii).

10. *Id.* § 1828(r)(6)(B)(i). *See* IBBEA, § 102(a), 108 Stat. at 2343 (codified at 12 U.S.C.A. § 1831u(a)(2)) (state election to prohibit interstate merger transactions).

11. 12 U.S.C.A. § 1828(r)(6)(B)(ii).

12. *Id.* § 1828(r)(5).

any activity prohibited to it as principal under any applicable federal or state law.[13] Correspondingly, the institution, as principal, may not authorize an agent to conduct any activity on its behalf that it is prohibited from conducting under applicable federal or state law.[14]

§ 4.9   SLHC Acquisitions

The savings and loan holding company provisions[1] of the HOLA restrict the OTS from approving a proposed acquisition that would result in the formation of an interstate multiple savings and loan holding company.[2] Under section 313 of the Dodd–Frank Wall Street Reform and Consumer Protection Act (Dodd–Frank Act),[3] the OTS and the position of its director (DOTS) are scheduled to be abolished. This dramatic event is effective 90 days after the "transfer date"[4]—21 July 2011—on which date the functions and authority of the DOTS and the OTS over SLHCs are first exercised by the Fed.[5]

Until this transfer of power occurs, the OTS continues to supervise SLHC formation. The OTS may approve interstate SLHC acquisitions in any of the following situations:

(1) Pursuant to emergency acquisition provisions,[6] the company or an insured institution subsidiary thereof is authorized to acquire control of an insured institution subsidiary in the additional state or states in question, or is authorized to operate a home or branch office there.[7]

(2) The company controls an insured institution subsidiary that already operated a home or branch office in the additional state or states in question as of 5 March 1987.[8]

(3) The statute laws of the state in which the target insured institution is located "specifically authorize ... by language to that effect and not merely by implication" that an

---

13. *Id.* § 1828(r)(3)(A).

14. *Id.* § 1828(r)(3)(B).

§ 4.9

1. 12 U.S.C.A. § 1467a, *as amended* Dodd–Frank Wall Street Reform and Consumer Protection Act (DFA) Pub. L. No. 111–203, §§ 367(2), 604(g), (h)(2), (i), 606(b), 616(b), 623(c), 624, 625, 124 Stat. 1376, 1556, 1564–1565, 1602–1604, 1607, 1615–1616, 1635–1638 (2010) (codified at 12 U.S.C.A. §§ 1467a note, 1467a(a)(1)(D)(ii), 1467a(b)(2), (b)(4), 1467a(c)(2)(H), 1467a(e)(2)(E), 1467a(g)(1), 1467a(m)(3)(A), (m)(3)(B)(i)(III)–(IV), 1467a(o)(11)).

2. *Id.* § 1467a(e)(3).

3. Pub. L. No. 111–203, § 313, 124 Stat. 1376, 1523 (2010) (codified at 12 U.S.C.A. § 5413) (DFA). For discussion of the impact of the DFA, see 1 MICHAEL P. MALLOY, BANKING LAW AND REGULATION § 1.4.11 (1994 & Cum. Supps.).

4. DFA §§ 311(a), 313 (codified at 12 U.S.C.A. §§ 5411(a), 5413).

5. See *id.* § 312(b) (codified at 12 U.S.C.A. § 5412(b)) (mandating transfer of functions).

6. *See id.* § 1823(k).

7. *Id.* § 1467a(e)(3)(A).

8. *Id.* § 1467a(e)(3)(B).

insured institution chartered by that state can be acquired by an insured institution chartered by the state in which the acquiring insured institution or savings and loan holding company is located, or by a holding company that controls such a state-chartered insured institution.[9]

However, the Dodd–Frank Act requires disapproval of an interstate SLHC acquisition if the applicant (including all of its insured depository institution affiliates) controls, or on consummation of the acquisition would control, more than 10 percent of the total amount of deposits of insured depository institutions in the United States.[10] This restriction does not apply to SLHC acquisitions in which the insured depository institution is in default or in danger of default, or is receiving FDIC "open bank" assistance.[11]

§ 4.10   **Mergers and Consolidations**

Both bank holding company formations and bank mergers involve some form of acquisition activity directed at a target bank. The typical acquisition methods, discussed in the holding company context and illustrated in Figure 4–1, *supra*, are therefore equally pertinent in the present context.

The following sections begin with an examination of the corporate law of mergers and consolidation of commercial banks and then consider the corresponding rules for savings associations. Mergers of depository institutions are also subject to the Bank Merger Act ("BMA").[1] In addition, depository institutions are affected by the 1994 federal statutory amendments authorizing interstate mergers.

Strictly speaking, a "consolidation" involves the business combination of two or more corporate entities into a new, third entity, with the termination of the corporate existence of the two prior entities.[2] The consolidation need not involve all of the assets and liabilities of the parties to the transaction.[3] In contrast, a "merger"

---

9. *Id.* § 1467a(e)(3)(C).

10. *Id.* § 1467a(e)(2)(E)(i)–(ii).

11. *Id.* § 1467a(e)(2)(E)(iii). On "open bank" assistance, see § 8.16, *infra*.

§ 4.10

1. 12 U.S.C.A. § 1828(c), *as amended* Dodd–Frank Wall Street Reform and Consumer Protection Act (DFA), §§ 363(7), 604(f), 623(a), Pub. L. No. 111–203, 124 Stat. 1376, 1553–1554, 1602, 1634 (2010) (codified at 12 U.S.C.A. §§ 1828(c)(2)(A), (c)(2)(C), (c)(5), (c)(13)).

2. *See, e.g., United States v. Philadelphia Nat'l Bank,* 374 U.S. 321, 83 S.Ct. 1715 (1963); *Braak v. Hobbs,* 210 N.C. 379, 186 S.E. 500 (1936); *Collinsville Nat'l Bank v. Esau,* 74 Okla. 45, 176 P. 514 (1918).

3. *Cf. Dauphin Deposit Trust Co. v. Myers,* 388 Pa. 444, 130 A.2d 686 (1957); *Personal Credit Plan v. Kling,* 130 N.J.Eq. 41, 20 A.2d 704 (1941); *Seattle–First Nat'l Bank v. Spokane County,* 196 Wash. 419, 83 P.2d 359 (1938).

continues the corporate existence of one of the parties to the transaction, now possessed of assets and liabilities of the merged party, with the termination of the corporate existence of the latter.[4] Figure 4–2, *infra*, illustrates the basic structures of the typical acquisition transactions, all of which are subject to regulatory oversight.

Figure 4–2
Typical Acquisition Structures
Merger

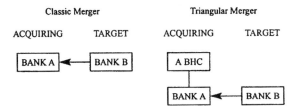

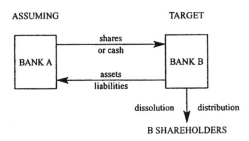

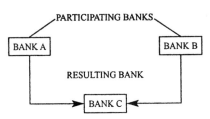

In addition to supervision by depository institution regulators, parties to certain mergers and acquisitions are required by the Hart–Scott–Rodino Act ("HSR") to file reports with the Federal Trade Commission (FTC) and the Assistant Attorney General in

---

4. *See, e.g., Philadelphia Nat'l Bank, supra. Cf. Exchange Bank of Commerce* *v. Meadors,* 199 Okla. 10, 184 P.2d 458 (1947).

charge of the Antitrust Division, and to wait a specified period of time before consummating such transactions.[5] The reporting and waiting period requirements are intended to enable these enforcement agencies to determine whether a proposed merger or acquisition may violate the antitrust laws if consummated and, when appropriate, to seek a preliminary injunction in federal court to prevent consummation.[6] However, the act exempts from premerger notification certain mergers and acquisitions involving banking institutions and thrifts that receive advance antitrust review by federal bank regulatory agencies.[7] The Gramm–Leach–Bliley Act of 1999 (GLBA),[8] has amended the act to make it explicit that in certain circumstances, where a transaction includes portions that receive premerger antitrust review by banking agencies and other portions that do not, the nonbanking parts must go through the premerger notification process, provided size criteria are met and no other exemption applies.[9] In March 2002, the FTC promulgated final rules implementing the GLBA provisions.[10] Under these rules, the portion of a "mixed transaction"[11] that does not require prior BMA review and approval[12] is subject to the HSR and the implementing FTC rules as if it were being acquired in a separate acquisition.[13]

§ 4.11 National Bank Transactions

Merger, consolidation, and purchase/assumption transactions[1] between banks are subject to a range of restrictions. Foremost among these are: (1) the prior approval requirement of the BMA;[2]

5. 15 U.S.C. § 18a.

6. *See* 66 Fed. Reg. 8723, 8723 (2001) (FTC discussion of HSR policy).

7. 15 U.S.C.A. § 18a(c)(7)–(8).

8. Pub. L. No. 106–102, Nov. 12, 1999, 113 Stat. 1338 (1999) (codified at scattered sections of 12, 15, 16, 18 U.S.C.) (GLBA).

9. GLBA, § 133(c), 113 Stat. at 1383 (codified at 15 U.S.C. § 18a(c)(7)–(8)).

10. 67 Fed. Reg. 11,898 (2002) (codified at 16 C.F.R. §§ 801.4(b), 801.14(b), 801.15(a)(2), (b)–(c), 801.90, 802.2(g), 802.6(b), 802.8(a), 802.50–802.52) (providing for premerger notification; reporting and waiting period requirements). For the prior interim final rules and proposed rules, see 66 Fed. Reg. 8679 (2001) and 66 Fed. Reg. 8723 (2001), respectively.

11. For these purposes, the term "mixed transaction" is defined to mean: one that has some portion that is exempt under [15 U.S.C. § 18a](c)(6), (c)(7) or (c)(8) because it requires regulatory agency premerger competitive review and approval, and another portion that does not require such review.

16 C.F.R. § 802.6(b)(1).

12. *See id.* § 802.8(a) (providing HSR exemption for acquisitions subject to prior review by depository institution regulators).

13. *Id.* § 802.6(b)(2).

§ 4.11

1. These three are treated as equivalents for purposes of the BMA. *See* 12 U.S.C.A. § 1828(c)(2) (referring to all three).

2. *Id.* § 1828(c), *as amended* Dodd–Frank Wall Street Reform and Consumer Protection Act (DFA), Pub. L. No. 111–203, §§ 363(7), 604(f), 623(a), 124 Stat. 1376, 1553–1554, 1602,1634 (2010) (codified at 12 U.S.C.A. § 1828(c)(2), (c)(5), (c)(13)).

(2) the application of the general federal antitrust laws to such transactions, regardless of prior BMA approval;[3] and, (3) in the case of transactions involving banks subject to the Securities Exchange Act of 1934,[4] the application of the proxy disclosure rules.[5] In addition, as to transactions involving national banks, certain provisions of the National Bank Act ("NBA")[6] will govern the approval, terms, and conditions of any such transaction.

(a) *Consolidations.* The NBA requires that the consolidation of any national bank with any other national bank or state-chartered bank under a national bank charter be approved by the Comptroller of the Currency.[7] The capital stock of the resulting national bank must be "not less than that required under existing law for the organization of a national bank in the place in which it is located."[8] Capital stock to be issued under the consolidation agreement is not subject to preemptive rights of the shareholders of the predecessor banks.[9] The consolidated bank will be liable for all liabilities of its predecessors.[10]

The consolidation may be effected "on such terms and conditions as may be lawfully agreed upon by a majority of the board of directors of each [national bank] or [state-chartered] bank proposing to consolidate."[11] The agreement must be ratified and confirmed by the affirmative vote of shareholders representing at least two-thirds of the capital stock outstanding of each bank.[12] At least 10 days prior to the meeting, notice must also be sent to each shareholder of record by certified or registered mail.[13]

If the consolidation is approved by the necessary majorities and subsequently approved by the Comptroller, a shareholder of the predecessor banks is entitled to dissenters appraisal rights for all shares held at the time the consolidation is approved by the

---

3. *See id.* § 1828(c)(6)–(8) (applying federal antitrust laws to transactions approved by BMA).

4. 15 U.S.C.A. §§ 78a *et seq. See generally* 2 MICHAEL P. MALLOY, BANKING LAW AND REGULATION § 6.2 (1994 & CUM. SUPP.) (discussing 1934 Act).

5. 15 U.S.C.A. § 78n(a).

6. 12 U.S.C.A. §§ 1 *et seq.*

7. *Id.* § 215(a).

8. *Id.* § 215(b).

9. *Id.* § 215(g).

10. *Id.* § 215(b). *See generally First Nat'l Bank in Oklahoma City v. Harris,* 27 F.2d 117 (8th Cir.1928); *U.S. Fidelity & Guar. Co. v. Citizens' Nat'l Bank,* 13 F.2d 213 (D.N.M.1924) (interpreting prior provision).

11. 12 U.S.C.A. § 215(a).

12. *Id.* In the case of a state-chartered bank involved in such a proposed consolidation, the NBA provides for an affirmative vote "by a greater proportion of such capital stock in the case of such State bank if the laws of the State where it is organized so require." *Id.*

13. *Id.* § 215(a). Shareholder notice need not be sent to shareholders "who specifically waive notice." *Id.* In the case of state-chartered banks involved in such a consolidation, the shareholders thereof must be given "any additional notice ... which may be required by the laws of the State where [the state-chartered bank] is organized." *Id.*

Comptroller.[14] To qualify for these rights, the shareholder must either: (1) have voted against the consolidation at the shareholders' meeting; or (2) have given notice of dissent from the plan of consolidation, in writing, at or prior to the meeting to the presiding officer.[15] In order to exercise these rights, the shareholder must make a written request to the consolidated national bank within 30 days of the date of consummation of the consolidation, accompanied by the surrender of the shareholder's stock certificates.[16]

The value of the shares must be determined as of the effective date of the consolidation.[17] Appraisal of this value is made by a committee of three persons: (1) one person selected by the vote of the dissenting shareholders representing the majority of the stock entitled to payment in cash; (2) one selected by the directors of the consolidated national bank; and (3) one selected by the other two members of the committee.[18] The valuation agreed upon by a majority of the committee governs.[19] A dissenting shareholder dissatisfied with the valuation may appeal to the Comptroller within five days of notice of the appraised value of the shares.[20] The Comptroller has authority to require a reappraisal to be made that is final and binding as to the value of the shares.[21]

If for any reason any member of the appraisal committee has not been selected within 90 days of the date of the consummation of the consolidation, or if the committee fails to determine the value of the shares of dissenting shareholders, the Comptroller is authorized to make a final and binding appraisal, upon the written request of an interested party.[22]

In August 1988, the OCC issued a bulletin explaining the methods of valuation that it used in estimating the value of the

---

14. *Id.* § 215(b).

15. *Id.* Failure to comply with the procedures specified in the NBA may destroy the dissenting appraisal rights. *See, e.g., Hiatt v. Peddy*, 73 F.2d 235 (5th Cir.1934) (interpreting prior provision).

16. 12 U.S.C.A. § 215(b).

17. *Id.* § 215(c). *Cf. Central–Penn. Nat'l Bank of Philadelphia v. Portner*, 201 F.2d 607 (3d Cir.1953), *cert. denied*, 346 U.S. 815, 74 S.Ct. 26 (purchase of shares by "dissenter" after announcement of consolidation agreement).

18. 12 U.S.C.A. § 215(c).

19. *Id.*

20. *Id.*

21. *Id.*

22. *Id.* § 215(d). The NBA requires that the Comptroller's expenses be paid by the consolidated national bank. *See id.* The NBA provides, however, that

> [t]he appraisal of such shares of stock in any State bank shall be determined in the manner prescribed by the law of the State in such cases, rather than as provided in [12 U.S.C.A. § 215], if such provision is made in the State law; and no such consolidation shall be in contravention of the law of the State under which such bank is incorporated.

Id. For a useful analysis of dissenters' appraisals handled by the OCC, see Austin & Nigem, *Dissenters' Appraisals Revisited*, 106 Banking L.J. 246 (1989). *See also Lewis v. Clark* [sic], 911 F.2d 1558, 1561–1564 (11th Cir.1990) (discussing Comptroller's appraisal methods with approval).

shares of a bank involved in a conversion, merger, or consolidation.[23] The objective of the appraisal process is "to arrive at a fair estimate of the value of a bank's shares."[24] In fulfilling this objective, the OCC will select, in light of the particular facts of the case, an appropriate method or combination of methods to determine share value.[25] The OCC methodology essentially applies the traditional Delaware weighted block method.[26]

The primary method consulted is the market value method. If the shares are sufficiently traded, and prices are available from direct quotations from the WALL STREET JOURNAL or a market maker, those price quotations "are considered in determining market value."[27] If either no market value is readily available, or the available market value is "not well established"[28] then other methods of estimating value will be used.[29]

Another method is the investment value method. This requires "an assessment of the value to investors of a share in the future earnings of the target bank."[30] An average price/earnings ratio of peer group banks having similar earnings potential to the target bank is applied to the estimated earnings per share of the target.[31] Difficulty may arise in selecting the peer group, which is generally based on location, size, and earnings patterns. Where the state in which the target is located provides a sufficient number of potential peer group banks, the price/earnings ratio assigned to such banks can be readily applied to the target. However, if there are too few comparable independent banks in a comparable location, then the pool of banks from which a peer group is selected is broadened by including one-bank bank holding companies in a comparable location, or by selecting banks in a less comparable location (including adjacent states) with similar earnings patterns.[32]

---

23. OCC Banking Bulletin 88–22, *reprinted in* [1988–1989 Transfer Binder] Fed. Banking L. Rep. ¶ 70,195 (Sept. 9, 1988). For a discussion of the Comptroller's appraisal methods, see *Lewis*, 911 F.2d at 1561–1564.

24. OCC Banking Bulletin 88–22, at 46,191.

25. *Id.*

26. *See, e.g.,* Note, *Valuation of Dissenters Stock*, 79 Harv. L. Rev. (1966); Note, *Elements in Valuation of Corporate Stock*, 55 Mich. L. Rev. 689 (1957) (discussing valuation methods). *But cf. Weinberger v. UOP, Inc.*, 457 A.2d 701, 712–714 (Del.1983) (rejecting traditional weighted block method as exclusive valuation methodology).

27. OCC Banking Bulletin 88–22, at 46,191.

28. *Id.* Typically, this would occur if the shares are thinly traded, raising questions about the representativeness of the historical quotations available.

29. *Id.*

30. *Id.*

31. *Id.* Though the OCC Bulletin does not expressly so state, the investment value method normally involves application of the price/earnings ratio to an average—typically, a five-year average—of estimated earnings. *See, e.g., In re Olivetti Underwood Corp.*, 246 A.2d 800 (Del.Ch.1968).

32. OCC Banking Bulletin 88–22, at 46,191.

A third method of valuation is the book value method. The OCC, however, has expressed some reservations about the use of this method. Book value "is based on historical acquisition costs of the bank's assets[ ] and does not reflect investors' perceptions of the value of the bank as a going concern."[33] Accordingly, the OCC tends to use a variant, "adjusted book value."[34] The utility of the adjusted book value is impaired to the extent that a sufficient peer group of comparably situated banks are not readily available. However, the OCC expressly rejects the use of unadjusted book value of the target bank as a basis for valuation.[35]

If more than one method of valuation is employed, the resulting values will be weighted to reach the overall valuation of the target bank.[36] The relative weight given to each resulting value will be "based on how accurately the given method is believed to represent market value."[37] The weighting assigned to the various resulting values will reflect the Comptroller's judgment of the credibility of the respective methods employed. For example, where the earnings patterns of the target bank have been irregular, or may reflect in given years certain unusual (and probably nonrecurring) developments in such years, it is likely that the value resulting from application of the investment value method would receive a relatively lower weight than, for example, the value resulting from the market value method. On the other hand, thinness in the trading market of the target bank's shares may lower the weight that might otherwise be assigned to the value resulting from application of the market value method.

Contrary to developments in the general corporate law with respect to valuation,[38] the OCC does not contemplate the use of other, less traditional methods of valuation in arriving at the fair value of the shares of a target bank. While recognizing that purchase premiums do exist in the merger and consolidation context, the OCC will not consider them in arriving at the value of

---

33. *Id*. Similar reservations are often expressed in the case law concerning the cogency of the asset value method. *See, e.g., Swanton v. State Guar. Corp.*, 42 Del.Ch. 477, 215 A.2d 242 (1965).

34. "Adjusted book value" may be described as follows:

Adjusted book value is calculated by multiplying the book value of the target bank's assets per share [by] the average market price to book value ratio of comparable banking organizations. The average market price to book value ratio measures the premium or discount to book value which

investors attribute to shares of similarly situated banking organizations.

OCC Banking Bulletin 88–22, at 46,191.

35. *See id*. ("As a rule, the OCC does not place any weight on 'unadjusted book value' ").

36. *Id*.

37. *Id*.

38. *See, e.g., Weinberger v. UOP, Inc.*, 457 A.2d at 712–714 (Del. 1983) (rejecting traditional weighted block method as exclusive valuation methodology).

shares.[39]

(b) *Mergers.* A merger between a national bank and another national bank or a state-chartered bank under the national bank charter of the surviving bank also requires approval of the OCC under the NBA.[40] The merger agreement must specify, *inter alia*, the amount of capital stock of the surviving national bank and the stock that will be outstanding on completion of the merger,[41] in an amount not less than would be required for the chartering of a national bank in the place where the surviving bank is located.[42] The agreement must also specify the amount of stock to be allocated, if any, and cash to be paid, if any, to the target bank shareholders.[43] The NBA also requires that the merger agreement provide that the surviving bank shall be liable for all liabilities of the target bank.[44]

The merger agreement must be approved in writing by a majority of the board of directors of each national bank or state-chartered bank participating in the merger.[45] The agreement must be ratified and confirmed by the affirmative vote of the shareholders of each participating bank representing at least two-thirds of its capital stock outstanding.[46] Notice of the meeting must be sent to each shareholder of record, at least 10 days prior to the meeting, by certified or registered mail.[47]

If the merger is approved by the necessary majorities and is subsequently approved by the Comptroller, a shareholder of a target bank is entitled to dissenters appraisal rights for all shares held at the time the Comptroller approves the merger.[48] To qualify for these rights, the shareholder must either: (1) have voted against the merger at the shareholders' meeting; or (2) have given notice of

---

39. OCC Banking Bulletin 88–22, at 46,192.

40. 12 U.S.C.A. § 215a(a). *See generally Nehring v. First DeKalb Banc-shares, Inc.,* 692 F.2d 1138 (7th Cir. 1982). For two successful challenges to merger approvals by minority shareholders, see *Lewis,* 911 F.2d at 1560–1561 (invalidating take-out merger; lack of statutory authority cited); *Bloomington Nat'l Bank v. Telfer,* 916 F.2d 1305 (7th Cir.1990) (invalidating reorganization plan involving buy-back of stock at depressed price; lack of statutory authority cited).

41. 12 U.S.C.A. § 215a(a)(3).

42. *Id.*

43. *Id.* Capital stock to be issued under the merger agreement is not subject to preemptive rights of the shareholders of the merging banks. *See id.* § 215a(g).

44. *Id.* § 215a(a)(4).

45. *Id.* § 215a(a)(1).

46. *Id.* § 215a(a)(2). *See generally Rogers v. First Nat'l Bank of St. George,* 297 F.Supp. 641 (D.S.C.1969), *aff'd and remanded,* 410 F.2d 579 (4th Cir.) In the case of a state-chartered bank involved in such a proposed merger, the NBA provides for an affirmative vote "by a greater proportion of such capital stock in the case of a State bank if the laws of the State where it is organized so require." 12 U.S.C.A. § 215a(a)(2).

47. 12 U.S.C.A. § 215a(a)(2). This notice need not be sent to those shareholders who have specifically waived notice. *Id.* In the case of a state-chartered bank involved in such a merger, any additional notice must be given that "may be required by the laws of the State where it is organized." *Id.*

48. *Id.* § 215a(b).

dissent from the plan of merger, in writing, at or prior to the meeting to the presiding officer.[49] To exercise these rights, the shareholder must make a written request to the surviving national bank within 30 days of the date of consummation of the merger, accompanied by the surrender of the shareholder's stock certificates.[50]

The value of the shares is determined as of the effective date of the merger.[51] Appraisal is made by a committee of three persons: (1) one person selected by the vote of the dissenting shareholders representing the majority of the stock entitled to payment in cash; (2) one selected by the directors of the surviving national bank; and (3) one selected by the other two members of the committee.[52] The valuation agreed upon by a majority of the committee governs.[53] Any dissenting shareholder dissatisfied with this valuation may appeal to the Comptroller within five days of notice of the appraised value of the shares.[54] The Comptroller has authority for a reappraisal, which is final and binding as to the value of the shares.[55] If for any reason any one of the members of the appraisal committee has not been selected within 90 days of the date of the consummation of the consolidation, or if the committee fails to determine the value of the shares of dissenting shareholders, the Comptroller is authorized to make a final and binding appraisal, upon the written request of an interested party.[56]

The valuation methods that apply to consolidation apply to mergers as well,[57] and so the OCC valuation procedures in the consolidation context apply directly to the case of mergers as well.

49. *Id.*

50. *Id.*

51. 12 U.S.C.A. § 215a(c).

52. *Id.* § 215a(c)(1)–(3).

53. *Id.* § 215a(c).

54. *Id.*

55. *Id.*

56. 12 U.S.C.A. § 215a(d). The NBA requires that the Comptroller's expenses be paid by the surviving national bank. *Id.* The NBA provides, however, that [t]he appraisal of such shares of stock in any State bank shall be determined in the manner prescribed by the law of the State in such cases, rather than as provided in [12 U.S.C.A. § 215a], if such provision is made in the State law; and no such merger shall be in contravention of the law of the State under which such bank is incorporated.

Id. 215a(d). *See Beerly v. Department of Treasury,* 768 F.2d 942 (7th Cir.1985),

cert. *denied,* 475 U.S. 1010, 106 S.Ct. 1184 (1986) (dissenter's appraisal rights under 12 U.S.C.A. § 215a). *See generally* Austin & Nigem, *Dissenters' Appraisals Revisited,* 106 Banking L.J. 246 (1989) (analysis of dissenters' appraisals handled by the OCC). Despite the apparent finality of the appraisal remedy, two cases have allowed minority shareholders to challenge the approval of mergers on the merits. *See Lewis v. Clark* [sic], 911 F.2d 1558, 1560–1561 (11th Cir. 1990), *reh'g denied,* 972 F.2d 1351 (11th Cir.1991) (invalidating take-out merger); *Bloomington Nat'l Bank,* 916 F.2d at 1308–1310 (invalidating reorganization plan involving buy-back of stock). *But see NoDak Bancorporation v. Clarke,* 998 F.2d 1416 (8th Cir.1993) (finding no inconsistency with NBA in minority shareholders forced to accept only cash in exchange for acquired shares).

57. *See* OCC Banking Bulletin 88–22, at 46,191.

§ 4.12   State Bank Transactions

State law restrictions on mergers and acquisitions involving depository institutions vary considerably from state to state.[1] These restrictions coexist with corresponding federal restrictions, and, in merger transactions involving both federally and state-chartered institutions, compliance with both applicable federal and state law restrictions may be required before such a transaction may be consummated.[2]

§ 4.13   Savings Associations

Prior to the enactment of the Financial Institutions Reform, Recovery, and Enforcement Act ("FIRREA"),[1] mergers and acquisitions involving savings associations were not subject to any specific federal regulatory statute corresponding to the BMA[2] requiring prior regulatory approval of savings association mergers. On the other hand, unlike bank mergers, mergers involving savings associations were subject to the prior notification and filing requirements of the Hart–Scott–Rodino Antitrust Improvements Act.[3] Under section 313 of the Dodd–Frank Wall Street Reform and Consumer Protection Act (Dodd–Frank Act),[4] the OTS and the position of its director (DOTS) are scheduled to be abolished. This dramatic event is effective 90 days after the "transfer date"[5]—21 July 2011—on which date the functions and authority of the DOTS and the OTS over S & L mergers are first exercised by the Fed.[6]

Until this transfer of power occurs, the OTS continues to supervise S & L mergers, which are subject to regulations of the Office of Thrift Supervision (OTS)[7] and to the requirements of the

§ 4.12

1. *See generally* 3 MICHAEL P. MALLOY, BANKING LAW AND REGULATION § 9.5 (1994 & Cum. Supp.) (DISCUSSING STATE LAW RESTRICTIONS ON MERGERS).

2. *But cf.* McKenna, *Federal Preemption of State Anti–Trust Law in Transactions of Federally Chartered Banks*, 58 Conn. B. J. 355 (1984).

§ 4.13

1. Pub. L. No. 101–73, 103 Stat. 183 (1989).

2. *See* 12 U.S.C.A. § 1828(c) (1988) (pre-FIRREA BMA applicable only to banks).

3. *See* 15 U.S.C.A. § 18a, *as amended*, FIRREA, § 1214, 103 Stat. at 529 (codified at 15 U.S.C.A. § 18a(c)(7)–(8)) (exempting from requirements, *inter alia*, holding company acquisitions sub-

ject to approval under 12 U.S.C.A. § 1467a(e) and savings association acquisitions subject to approval under § 1464 or § 1828). *See also supra* § 4.10, text and accompanying notes 5–9 (discussing applicability of Hart–Scott–Rodino to financial services merges and acquisitions).

4. Pub. L. No. 111–203, § 313, 124 Stat. 1376, 1523 (2010) (codified at 12 U.S.C.A. § 5413) (DFA). For discussion of the impact of the DFA, see 1 MICHAEL P. MALLOY, BANKING LAW AND REGULATION § 1.4.11 (1994 & Cum. Supps.).

5. DFA §§ 311(a), 313 (codified at 12 U.S.C.A. §§ 5411(a), 5413).

6. See *id.* § 312(b) (codified at 12 U.S.C.A. § 5412(b)) (mandating transfer of functions).

7. *See, e.g.,* 12 C.F.R. §§ 546.1–546.3, 563.22, 571.5.

BMA.[8] In addition, savings association mergers are generally subject to the Sherman Act[9] and the Clayton Act.[10] Effective 20 July 2011,[11] the Office of the Comptroller of the Currency will succeed to all authority and functions of the OTS,[12] and its director, with respect to federal savings associations[13] and all rulemaking authority of the OTS and its director with respect to savings associations.[14]

§ 4.14   Bank Merger Act

As originally enacted in May 1960,[1] the BMA did not focus on anticompetitiveness with respect to bank mergers and acquisitions. Indeed, it was not clear from the language of the 1960 version what the relationship was, if any, between the BMA and federal antitrust laws generally. In any event, the BMA had had little appreciable effect on the fevered pace of bank mergers. In the meantime, the Justice Department began to challenge bank mergers under the antitrust laws, particularly Section 7 of the Clayton Act,[2] despite the fact that federal banking agencies had approved the mergers under the BMA. In *United States v. Philadelphia National Bank*,[3] the Supreme Court held that Section 7 of the Clayton Act was applicable to bank mergers.[4]

Philadelphia National had argued that the acquisition, structured as a statutory merger, was in fact a purchase of assets, to

8. See 12 U.S.C.A. § 1828(c), *as amended*, FIRREA, §§ 201(a)(1), 221(2)(A)–(D), 103 Stat. 183, 187, 266–267 (1989) (codified at 12 U.S.C.A. § 1828(c)(2)(C)–(D), (c)(3), (c)(4), (c)(6), (c)(7), (c)(9); *repealing* 12 U.S.C.A. § 1828(c)(12)); Dodd–Frank Wall Street Reform and Consumer Protection Act (DFA), Pub. L. No. 111–203, §§ 363(7), 604(f), 623(a), 124 Stat. 1376, 1553–1554, 1602,1634 (2010) (codified at 12 U.S.C.A. § 1828(c)(2), (c)(5), (c)(13)).

9. 15 U.S.C.A. §§ 1 *et seq. See* 12 U.S.C.A. § 1828(c)(7)(B) (applying Sherman Act to, *inter alia*, savings association mergers).

10. 15 U.S.C.A. §§ 12 *et seq. See* 12 U.S.C.A. § 1828(c)(7) (applying federal antitrust laws to, *inter alia*, savings association mergers).

11. Dodd–Frank Wall Street Reform and Consumer Protection Act (DFA), Pub. L. No. 111–203, § 312(b)(2)(B)(ii), 124 Stat. 1376, 1522 (2010) (codified at 12 U.S.C.A. § 5412(b)(2)(B)(ii)). This effective date is the day before the "transfer date" of OTS powers and functions. DFA §§ 311(a), 312(a) (codified at 12 U.S.C.A. §§ 5411(a), 5412(a)). The effective date may be extended under certain

specified circumstances. 12 U.S.C. § 5411(b). Technical details of the transfer are handled by DFA §§ 302, 312(a)–(b), 317, 319, 322–327.

12. DFA § 363(7)(A)(i) (codified at 12 U.S.C.A. § 1828(c)(2)(A)) (transferring responsibility for mergers in which federal savings association survives).

13. DFA § 312(b)(2)(B)(i)(I) (codified at 12 U.S.C.A. § 5412(b)(2)(B)(i)(I)).

14. DFA § 312(b)(2)(B)(i)(II) (codified at 12 U.S.C.A. § 5412(b)(2)(B)(i)(II)).

§ 4.14

1. Pub. L. No. 86–463, 79 Stat. 437 (1960) (codified at 12 U.S.C.A. § 1828(c)).

2. 15 U.S.C.A. § 18.

3. 374 U.S. 321, 83 S.Ct. 1715 (1963).

4. 374 U.S. at 352, 83 S.Ct. at 1736. The Court did not go on to the question of whether the merger in question was also prohibited by the Sherman Act. 374 U.S. at 324, 83 S.Ct. at 1720. On the applicability of the Sherman Act, see *infra* this section.

which the Clayton Act would not apply.[5] In response, the Justice Department argued that the statutory merger was essentially a stock acquisition fully subject to Section 7 of the Clayton Act. In the Court's view,

> [b]oth positions ... have merit; a merger fits neither category neatly. Since the literal terms of § 7 thus do not dispose of our question, we must determine whether a congressional design to embrace bank mergers is revealed in the history of the statute. ...
>
> ... Congress contemplated that ... the entire range of corporate amalgamations, from pure stock acquisitions to pure assets acquisitions, [would be] within the scope of § 7. Thus, the stock-acquisition and assets-acquisition provisions, *read together*, reach mergers, which fit neither category perfectly but lie somewhere between the two ends of the spectrum. ... So construed, the specific exception for acquiring corporations not subject to the FTC's jurisdiction excludes from the coverage of § 7 only assets acquisitions by such corporations when not accomplished by merger. ...[6]

The enactment of the BMA was not intended to displace the general antitrust laws to the extent that they were otherwise applicable.[7] In assessing the lawfulness of the proposed merger under Section 7 of the Clayton Act, the Court refused to accept affirmative justifications of an anticompetitive merger based on, *inter alia*, the benefits that the merger might confer upon the affected banking community.[8]

Similarly, in *United States v. First National Bank & Trust Co. of Lexington*,[9] the Court held that such mergers were also subject to the Sherman Act.[10] In both *Philadelphia National Bank* and *First*

---

5. Section 7 of the Clayton Act only reached assets acquisitions undertaken by a person subject to FTC jurisdiction, but banks were not subject to that jurisdiction. 15 U.S.C.A. § 18.

6. *Philadelphia Nat'l Bank*, 374 U.S. at 337, 342, 83 S.Ct. at 1727, 1730 (emphasis in original).

7. 374 U.S. at 350–355, 83 S.Ct. at 1734–1737.

8. *See* 374 U.S. at 370–372, 83 S.Ct. at 1745–1746. Among other things, Philadelphia National had argued:

> Philadelphia needs a bank larger than it now has in order to bring business to the area and stimulate its economic development. ... [The Court was] clear, however, that a merger the effect of which "may be substantially to

lessen competition" is not saved because, on some ultimate reckoning of social or economic debits and credits, it may be deemed beneficial. A value choice of such magnitude is beyond the ordinary limits of judicial competence, and in any event has been made for us already, by Congress when it enacted the amended § 7.

374 U.S. at 371, 83 U.S. at 1745, *quoting* 15 U.S.C.A. § 18.

9. 376 U.S. 665, 84 S.Ct. 1033 (1964).

10. 376 U.S. at 667, 84 S.Ct. at 1034. However, with the Court's decision in *Philadelphia Nat'l Bank* opening the way to Clayton Act challenges to bank mergers, the government would rarely rely in the future, as it had in *First*

National Bank, the Court went on to apply traditional antitrust analysis, without regard to the "convenience and needs" of the community to be served by the surviving bank.[11]

An amended BMA was enacted in February 1966.[12] As further amended in 1989, the BMA applies to any insured depository institution[13] that intends to: (1) merge or consolidate with an uninsured depository institution;[14] (2) assume liability to pay deposits in, or similar liabilities of, such an institution;[15] or, (3) transfer

Nat'l Bank, solely on Sherman Act arguments. 376 U.S. at 673, 84 S.Ct. at 1038 (Harlan, J., dissenting).

11. *See, e.g., Philadelphia Nat'l Bank*, 374 U.S. at 371, 83 S.Ct. at 1746 (Clayton Act "proscribed anticompetitive mergers, the benign and the malignant alike").

12. Pub. L. No. 89–356, 80 Stat. 7 (1966) (codified at 12 U.S.C.A. § 1828(c)). The FIRREA has amended the BMA in light in the significant changes in the federal regulatory structure. The FDIC is identified as the "responsible agency" for approval with respect to covered mergers and acquisitions "if the acquiring, assuming, or resulting bank is to be a State nonmember insured bank (except a District [of Columbia] bank) or a savings bank supervised by the Director of Thrift Supervision." FIRREA, § 221(2)(A), 103 Stat. at 266–267 (codified at 12 U.S.C.A. § 1828(c)(2)(C)). In addition, insured savings associations were brought under the jurisdiction of the BMA, FIRREA, § 201(a)(1), 103 Stat. at 187 (codified at 12 U.S.C.A. § 1828), and the OTS was identified as the "responsible agency" for approval with respect to covered mergers and acquisitions "if the acquiring, assuming, or resulting institution is to be a savings association." FIRREA, § 221(2)(A), 103 Stat. at 266–267 (codified at 12 U.S.C.A. § 1828(c)(2)(D)). In July 2011, the functions and authority of the DOTS and the OTS over mergers in which the surviving party is a savings association are first exercised by the OCC and the FDIC for federal and state savings associations, respectively. DFA § 363(7)(A)(i), (iii) (codified at 12 U.S.C.A. § 1828(c)(2)(A), (C)) (transferring to OCC and FDIC OTS responsibility for mergers in which federal or state savings association survives).

13. From 1982 to 1989, the BMA did not apply to a merger transaction involving an insured federal savings bank unless the resulting depository institution would have been an insured bank other than a federal savings bank. Pub. L. No. 97–320, § 113(n), 96 Stat. 1474 (1982) (codified at 12 U.S.C.A. § 1828(c)(12)). Section 504(b)(1) of the Competitive Equality Banking Act of 1987, Pub. L. No. 100–86, 101 Stat. 552, 632 (1987), further amended this provision to read as follows:

> The provisions of this subsection shall not apply to any transaction where the acquiring, assuming, or resulting institution is an insured Federal savings bank or an institution insured by the [FSLIC], except that any insured bank involved in the transaction shall notify the [FDIC] in writing at least 30 days prior to consummation of the transaction and, if any approval by the [FHLBB] or the [FSLIC] is required in connection therewith, such approving authority shall provide the [FDIC] with notification of the application for approval, consult with the [FDIC] before disposing of the application, and shall provide notification to the [FDIC] of the determination with respect to said application.

12 U.S.C.A. § 1828(c)(12) (1988). With the inclusion of all insured depository institutions (including savings associations) under the jurisdiction of the BMA, this provision was repealed by the FIRREA. FIRREA, § 221(2)(B), 103 Stat. at 267.

14. 12 U.S.C.A. § 1828(c)(1)(A).

15. *Id.* § 1828(c)(1)(B). A 1978 amendment of this provision expressly included "liabilities which would be 'deposits' except for the proviso in [12 U.S.C.A. §] 1813(*l*)(5)," concerning deposits payable only at off-shore offices of a bank, within the coverage of this subsection of the BMA. Pub. L. No. 95–630,

assets to such an institution in consideration of the assumption of liabilities for any deposits in the insured depository institution.[16] Any such transaction requires the prior written approval of the FDIC under the BMA.[17]

The BMA also applies to any insured depository institution that intends to "merge or consolidate with any other insured depository institution or, either directly or indirectly, acquire the assets of, or assume liability to pay any deposits" in any other insured depository institution.[18] All such transactions require the prior written approval under the BMA of the appropriate banking agency (including, as to savings associations, the OTS).[19]

Section 606 of the Financial Services Regulatory Relief Act (FSRRA)[20] made two changes to the Bank Merger Act with respect to mergers that solely involve an insured depository institution and one or more of its affiliates: (i) For these affiliate mergers, FDIA § 18(c)(4)[21] was amended to eliminate the requirement for the responsible federal banking agency to request competitive factors reports from either the other federal banking agencies or the Attorney General of the United States; and, (ii) FDIA § 18(c)(6)[22] was revised to eliminate the post-approval waiting period for affiliate mergers. In September 2008 the FDIC amended § 303.61(b) of its merger regulations to conform it to the FSRRA by defining the term "corporate reorganization" to mean a merger that involves solely an insured depository institution and one or more of its affiliates.[23]

In July 2010, the Dodd–Frank Wall Street Reform and Consumer Protection Act (DFA)[24] amended the BMA to reflect the transfer of powers and responsibility from the OTS to the OCC[25] and to the FDIC.[26] The DFA also amends the BMA to impose limits on interstate mergers resulting in significant concentrations of

§ 306, 92 Stat. 3677 (1978) (codified at 12 U.S.C.A. § 1828(c)(1)(B)).

16. 12 U.S.C.A. § 1828(c)(1)(C).

17. *Id.* § 1828(c)(1).

18. *Id.* § 1828(c)(2).

19. *Id.* § 1828(c)(2)(A)–(D).

20. Pub. L. No. 109–351, § 606, 120 Stat. 1966, 1981–1982 (2006) (codified at 12 U.S.C.A. § 1828(c)(4), (6)).

21. *Id.* § 1828(c)(4).

22. *Id.* § 1828(c)(6).

23. 73 Fed. Reg. 55,432 (Sept. 25, 2008) (codified at 12 C.F.R. pts. 303, 308–309). Having received no public comments on its interim rule, 73 Fed.

Reg. 2143 (January 14, 2008), the FDIC confirmed the rule as final without change. The amendments were effective September 25, 2008.73 Fed. Reg. at 55,-432.

24. Pub. L. No. 111–203, 124 Stat. 1376 (2010) (DFA).

25. DFA § 363(7)(A)(i) (codified at 12 U.S.C.A. § 1828(c)(2)(A)) (transferring to OCC OTS responsibility for mergers in which federal savings association survives).

26. DFA § 363(7)(A)(iii) (codified at 12 U.S.C.A. § 1828(c)(2)(C)) (transferring to FDIC OTS responsibility for mergers in which state savings association survives).

deposits in the United States.[27]

When a BMA application is filed with the appropriate banking agency,[28] notice of the proposed acquisition generally must be published prior to the approval of the acquisition, in a form approved by the appropriate banking agency,[29] at appropriate intervals during the period of regulatory consideration[30] of the application.[31] The decision whether or not to grant a hearing on the application is within the discretion of the agency.[32]

Before acting on the application, the appropriate banking agency generally must request a report on the competitive factors involved in the proposed acquisition from the Attorney General and must send a copy of the request to the FDIC.[33] The reports generally must be furnished within 30 calendar days of the request.[34]

If upon completion of its review of the application the appropriate agency approves the proposed acquisition, it is required to notify the Attorney General immediately of this decision.[35] Generally, an approved acquisition may not be consummated before 30 calendar days after the date of approval.[36] However, if the approving agency had requested agency reports during its review of the application on an emergency basis within 10 days, rather than 30 days, of its request,[37] then the acquisition may be consummated after the fifth calendar day following the approval.[38] If the approving agency had dispensed with agency reports because of the danger of probable default of one of the depository institutions involved in the acquisition,[39] then the acquisition may be consummated imme-

27. DFA § 623(a) (codified at 12 U.S.C.A. § 1828(c)(13)).

28. *Id.* § 1828(c)(1), (2).

29. *Id.* § 1828(c)(3)(A)–(B).

30. The "period of regulatory consideration" will generally be 30 days, unless an emergency exists, in which case the period is 10 days. 12 U.S.C.A. § 1828(c)(3)(C), (4).

31. *Id.* § 1828(c)(3).

32. *See Washington v. Office of Comptroller of Currency,* 856 F.2d 1507, 1511–1512 (11th Cir.1988), *citing* 12 C.F.R. § 5.10(b)(3).

33. 12 U.S.C.A. § 1828(c)(4), *as amended* Financial Services Regulatory Relief Act of 2006 (FSRRA), § 606(a), Pub. L. No. 109–351, 120 Stat. 1966, 1981 (2006). The responsible agency still has the authority to act immediately on the application if it finds that that is necessary to prevent the probable failure

of an insured depository institution involved in the merger. *Id.* § 1828(c)(4)(C)(i). The FSSRA adds a new exception from requesting reports for cases in which "the merger transaction involves solely an insured depository institution and 1 or more of the affiliates of such depository institution." *Id.* § 1828(c)(4)(C)(ii).

34. *Id.* § 1828(c)(4)(B)(i). This period is shortened to 10 days when the requesting agency advises the Attorney General that an emergency exists that requires expeditious action on the application. *Id.* § 1828(c)(4)(B)(ii).

35. *Id.* § 1828(c)(6).

36. *Id.*

37. *See id.* § 1828(c)(4) (concerning emergency requests).

38. *Id.* § 1828(c)(6).

39. *See id.* § 1828(c)(4) (concerning immediate action to prevent default).

diately upon its approval.[40]

In reviewing the transaction, the appropriate agency must consider the following statutory factors:

(1) *Monopolization.* The agency cannot approve a proposed transaction that would result in a monopoly, or that would be in furtherance of any combination or conspiracy to monopolize or to attempt to monopolize the business of banking in any part of the United States.[41]

(2) *Anticompetitiveness.* The agency cannot approve a proposed transaction the effect of which in any section of the country[42] may be substantially to lessen competition,[43] or to tend to create a monopoly, or that in any other manner would be in restraint of trade.[44] However, in a departure from *Phila-*

---

40. *Id.* § 1828(c)(6).

41. *Id.* § 1828(c)(5)(A).

42. On the delineation of the geographic market, see generally *United States v. Long Island Jewish Med. Ctr.,* 983 F.Supp. 121 (E.D.N.Y.1997) (delineating geographic market for hospital) *Federal Trade Comm'n v. Freeman Hosp.,* 69 F.3d 260 (8th Cir.1995) (same); *United States v. Mercy Health Servs.,* 902 F.Supp. 968 (N.D.Iowa 1995) (same), *vacated as moot,* 107 F.3d 632 (8th Cir.1997); *United States v. Gillette Co.,* 828 F.Supp. 78 (D.D.C.1993) (concerning market for pens); *Ansell Inc. v. Schmid Labs., Inc.,* 757 F.Supp. 467 (D.N.J.1991), *aff'd,* 941 F.2d 1200 (concerning nationwide market for condoms); *United States v. Country Lake Foods, Inc.,* 754 F.Supp. 669 (D.Minn. 1990) (delineating geographic market for milk); *United States v. M. P. M., Inc.,* 397 F.Supp. 78 (D.Colo.1975); *United States v. Phillipsburg Nat'l Bank & Trust Co.,* 399 U.S. 350, 90 S.Ct. 2035 (1970); *Southwest Mississippi Bank v. Federal Deposit Ins. Corp.,* 499 F.Supp. 1 (D.Miss.1979); *Washington Mut. Sav. Bank v. Federal Deposit Ins. Corp.,* 347 F.Supp. 790 (W.D.Wash.1972), *aff'd* 482 F.2d 459 (9th Cir.1973). The burden of proof on the issue of delineation of the geographic market is plaintiff's. *Country Lake Foods, Inc., supra.*

43. On the effects of a proposed transaction on competition, see generally *New York v. Kraft Gen. Foods, Inc.,* 926 F.Supp. 321 (S.D.N.Y.1995); *Mercy Health Servs., supra*; *Bon–Ton Stores, Inc. v. May Dep't Stores Co.,* 881 F.Supp. 860 (W.D.N.Y.1994); *SCFC ILC, Inc. v.*

Visa U.S.A. Inc., 819 F.Supp. 956 (D.Utah 1993), *aff'd in part & rev'd in part,* 36 F.3d 958 (10th Cir.1994), *cert. denied sub nom. MountainWest Fin. Corp. v. Visa U.S.A., Inc.,* 515 U.S. 1152, 115 S.Ct. 2600 (1995); *United States v. Gillette Co.,* 828 F.Supp. 78 (D.D.C. 1993); *Federal Trade Comm'n v. University Health, Inc.,* 938 F.2d 1206 (11th Cir.1991); *United States v. Baker Hughes Inc.,* 908 F.2d 981 (D.C.Cir. 1990); *United States v. Marine Bancorporation, Inc.,* 418 U.S. 602, 94 S.Ct. 2856 (1974); *Washington Mut. Sav. Bank v. Federal Deposit Ins. Corp.,* 482 F.2d 459 (9th Cir.1973). On the burden of proof with respect to anticompetitive effects, see *United States v. United Tote, Inc.,* 768 F.Supp. 1064 (D.Del.1991).

44. 12 U.S.C.A. § 1828(c)(5)(B). On the determination of the "line of commerce" affected by the possible anticompetitive effects of the proposed transaction, see generally *Long Island Jewish Med. Ctr., supra* (concerning hospitals); *Community Publishers, Inc. v. Donrey Corp.,* 892 F.Supp. 1146 (W.D.Ark.1995), *aff'd,* 139 F.3d 1180 (8th Cir.1998) (concerning small town newspapers); *Appraisers Coalition v. Appraisal Inst.,* 845 F.Supp. 592 (N.D.Ill.1994) (concerning appraisal services); *Bon–Ton Stores, Inc., supra* (concerning submarkets); *Federal Trade Comm'n v. Alliant Techsystems Inc.,* 808 F.Supp. 9 (D.D.C.1992) (servicing of 120 millimeter ammunition rounds); *Ansell Inc., supra* (concerning cross-elasticity of demand in condom market); *United States v. Connecticut Nat'l Bank,* 418 U.S. 656, 94 S.Ct. 2788 (1974) (thrift institutions excluded);

delphia National Bank,[45] the BMA permits approval of such a transaction if the agency finds that its anticompetitive effects "are clearly outweighed in the public interest by the probable effect of the transaction in meeting the convenience and needs of the community to be served."[46]

(3) *Traditional Banking Factors.* The agency must take into consideration the financial and managerial resources and the future prospects of the existing and proposed institutions, and the convenience and needs of the community to be served.[47] In addition, the responsible agency must take into consideration in every case the effectiveness of any insured depository institution involved in the proposed merger in combatting money laundering activities, including in overseas branches.[48]

Approval under the BMA does not shield the proposed transaction from attack by the Attorney General as violative of federal antitrust law, but any action brought by the Justice Department under the antitrust laws arising out of an approved acquisition must be commenced prior to the earliest time at which the acquisition could be consummated under the BMA.[49] Commencement of

---

Washington Mut. Sav. Bank, supra (same); *United States v. First Nat'l Bank of Jackson,* 301 F.Supp. 1161 (S.D.Miss. 1969) (*contra*); *United States v. Crocker–Anglo Nat'l Bank,* 277 F.Supp. 133 (N.D.Cal.1967). Complainant bears the burden of proof on the issue of delineation of the product market. *United States v. Engelhard Corp.,* 970 F.Supp. 1463 (M.D.Ga.1997).

45. *See* 374 U.S. at 371, 83 S.Ct. at 1745–1746 (rejecting convenience and needs defense).

46. 12 U.S.C.A. § 1828(c)(5)(B). On the convenience and needs defense, see generally *Marine Bancorporation, supra*; *Phillipsburg Nat'l Bank & Trust Co., supra*; *United States v. Third Nat'l Bank in Nashville,* 390 U.S. 171, 88 S.Ct. 882 (1968); *United States v. First Nat'l Bank of Md.,* 310 F.Supp. 157 (D.Md.1970); *United States v. Provident Nat'l Bank,* 280 F.Supp. 1 (E.D.Pa.1968); *Crocker–Anglo Nat'l Bank, supra.*

47. 12 U.S.C.A. § 1828(c)(5). On the balancing of anticompetitive and banking factors, see generally *Phillipsburg Nat'l Bank, supra*; *Third Nat'l Bank in Nashville, supra*; *United States v. First City Nat'l Bank of Houston,* 386 U.S. 361, 87 S.Ct. 1088 (1967).

48. 12 U.S.C.A. § 1828(c)(11).

49. *See* 12 U.S.C.A. § 1828(c)(7)(A). *See First City Nat'l Bank of Houston, supra* (involving Justice Department challenge despite Comptroller's approval); *United States v. Citizens & Southern Nat'l Bank,* 339 F.Supp. 1143 (N.D.Ga. 1972) (same; FDIC's approval). The BMA does not alter the antitrust rules generally applicable in determining whether a proposed acquisition would be violative of the antitrust laws. *See Third Nat'l Bank in Nashville, supra*; *Philadelphia Nat'l Bank, supra.* There has been some dispute whether the language of the BMA restricts the Justice Department to Sections 1 and 2 of the Sherman Act and Section 7 of the Clayton Act, or whether the DOJ may draw upon the federal antitrust laws generally. *Compare United States v. Provident Nat'l Bank,* 259 F.Supp. 373 (E.D.Pa.1966), *with United States v. Manufacturers Hanover Trust Co.,* 240 F.Supp. 867 (S.D.N.Y.1965); *United States v. First Nat'l Bank & Trust Co. of Lexington,* 208 F.Supp. 457 (E.D.Ky.1962), *rev'd on other grounds,* 376 U.S. 665, 84 S.Ct. 1033 (1964). The better view is that the action is based upon the antitrust laws, not the BMA, but with the additional "convenience and needs" defense provided by the BMA. *See, e.g., First City Nat'l Bank of Houston, supra*; *United*

the action automatically stays the effectiveness of the agency approval of the proposed acquisition,[50] although the court has authority to remove the stay by specific order.[51]

§ 4.15 Interstate Mergers

As of June 1, 1997,[1] under the Riegle–Neal Interstate Banking and Branching Efficiency Act of 1994 ("IBBEA"), the responsible federal agencies[2] are generally permitted to approve interstate merger transactions under the BMA between insured banks with different home states, regardless of state law prohibitions. This authority is subject to election by the home state of a merging bank to enact a law expressly prohibiting merger transactions involving out-of-state banks.[3] Any such state law must be applicable to all out-of-state banks.[4] State election has no effect on merger transactions approved before the effective date of the state law.[5]

The responsible federal agency (OCC, Fed, or OTS) is generally not permitted to approve an interstate merger that would contravene applicable state statutory law requiring a bank to be in existence for a minimum period of time before a merger.[6] However,

States v. County Nat'l Bank of Bennington, 330 F.Supp. 155 (D.Vt.1971).

50. *Id.*

51. *Id.*

§ 4.15

1. Interstate merger approvals by the responsible federal agency were permitted prior to June 1, 1997, if the home state of each bank involved in the transaction had already elected to permit interstate mergers. 12 U.S.C.A. § 1831u(a)(3)(A). The state law had to apply equally to all out-of-state banks, *id.* § 1831u(a)(3)(A)(i), and it had to expressly permit such transactions with all out-of-state banks. *Id.* § 1831u(a)(3)(A)(ii).

In early merger situations, the host state was permitted under the IBBEA to impose certain conditions on instate branches of the resulting bank in an interstate merger transaction. *Id.* § 1831u(a)(3)(B). Such conditions could not have the effect of discriminating against out-of-state banks, bank holding companies, or subsidiaries thereof. *Id.* § 1831u(a)(3)(B)(i). The restriction against discriminatory conditions would not apply to a nationwide reciprocal treatment requirement. *Id.* § 1831u(a)(3)(B)(i). The imposition of the conditions must not otherwise be preempted by federal law. *Id.*

§ 1831u(a)(3)(B)(ii). Finally, any such conditions must lapse after May 31, 1997. *Id.* § 1831u(a)(3)(B)(iii).

2. For these purposes, the "responsible agency" means the Comptroller, if the acquiring bank is a national bank or a District of Columbia bank; the Fed is the "responsible agency" if the bank is a state member bank (other than a District of Columbia bank); the FDIC, if the bank is a state nonmember insured bank (other than a District of Columbia bank or a savings bank supervised by the OTS); and the OTS, if the acquiring institution is a savings association. *Id.* § 1828(c)(2)(A)–(D).

3. *Id.* § 1831u(a)(2)(A)(ii).

4. *Id.* § 1831u(a)(2)(A)(i).

5. *Id.* § 1831u(a)(2)(B).

6. *Id.* § 1831u(a)(5)(A). For these purposes, a "shell" or "phantom" bank, created to be controlled by the acquiring bank holding company and to receive an existing target bank, is deemed to have been in existence for as long as the target bank has been in existence. *Id.* § 1831u(a)(6). *But see TeamBank, N.A. v. McClure*, 279 F.3d 614 (8th Cir.2002) (upholding OCC approval of merger of national bank in Kansas and national bank that had relocated to Missouri three years before; OCC opinion that

the agency may approve such a merger if the target bank has been in existence for at least five years, notwithstanding any longer minimum period specified in the statutory law of the host state.[7]

Under IBBEA, an interstate merger transaction may involve the acquisition of a branch[8] of an insured bank without the acquisition of the entire target bank.[9] Such acquisitions will be permitted only if the law of the state in which the target branch is located permits out-of-state banks to acquire a branch without acquisition of the entire target bank.[10]

Essentially the same rules apply to a consolidation involving a national bank.[11] There is now express authority for a consolidation or merger by a national bank with an out-of-state bank, if the consolidation or merger is approved pursuant to the interstate merger transaction provisions.[12] This authority was not available for any consolidation or merger before June 1, 1997, unless the home state of each bank involved in the transaction had an early interstate merger transaction provision.[13]

Any interstate merger involving insured depository institutions is subject to the application and approval requirements of the BMA.[14] In addition, IBBEA requires compliance with certain state filing requirements.[15] Material failure to comply with these state filing requirements bars approval of the BMA application.[16] A bank that files a BMA application for an interstate merger transaction must comply with filing requirements of any host state of the resulting bank, so long as the requirements do not have the effect of discriminating against out-of-state banks, bank holding companies, or subsidiaries thereof.[17] The filing requirements must also be similar in effect to any requirement imposed by the host state on out-of-state nonbanking corporations engaging in business in the host state.[18] The applicant must submit a copy of the BMA applica-

---

merger did not violate IBBEA entitled to *Chevron* deference).

7. *Id.* § 1831u(a)(5)(B).

8. Where an interstate transaction involves acquisition of a branch of an insured bank, without acquisition of the bank itself, the branch will be treated as an insured bank, the home state of which is the state in which the branch is located. *Id.* § 1831u(a)(4)(B).

9. *Id.* § 1831u(a)(4)(A).

10. *Id.*

11. *See* IBBEA, § 102(b)(4), 108 Stat. at 2351–2352 (codified at 12 U.S.C.A. §§ 215, 215a–1).

12. 12 U.S.C.A. § 215a–1(a).

13. *Id.* § 215a–1(b). *See id.* § 1831u(a)(3) (state early interstate merger transaction provision).

14. *See id.* § 1828(c).

15. *See id.* § 1831u(b)(1).

16. *Id.* § 1831u(b)(1)(B).

17. *Id.* § 1831u(b)(1)(A)(i)(I).

18. *Id.* § 1831u(b)(1)(A)(i)(II). In other words, the filing requirement applicable to the out-of-state bank must essentially be similar to generally applicable corporate law provisions requiring registration of foreign corporations doing business within the state. *See, e.g.,* N.Y. Bus. Corp. Law art. 13 (foreign corporations).

tion to the state bank supervisor of the host state.[19]

In addition, certain nationwide and statewide concentration limits will apply to interstate merger transactions, except for transactions involving only affiliated banks.[20] First, the responsible federal agency is not permitted to approve an interstate merger transaction if the resulting bank[21] would control upon consummation of the transaction more than 10 percent of the total amount of deposits of insured depository institutions in the United States.[22] Second, as to transactions other than initial entry into the host state, the agency is not permitted to approve a transaction if: (1) any bank involved in the transaction has a branch in any state in which any other bank involved in the transaction has a branch;[23] and, (2) upon consummation, the resulting bank would control 30 percent or more of the total amount of deposits of insured depository institutions in any such state.[24] These concentration provisions do not affect state authority to limit the percentage of the total amount of deposits of insured depository institutions in the state held or controlled by any bank, bank holding company, and subsidiaries thereof.[25]

Approval of an interstate merger is subject to the following considerations identified in the IBBEA:

> (1) If the merger would give the resulting bank a branch or bank affiliate in a state in which the acquiring bank had no branch or bank affiliate, the responsible federal agency must

---

19. 12 U.S.C.A. § 1831u(b)(1)(A)(ii).

20. *Id.* § 1831u(b)(2)(E).

21. For these purposes, the "applicant" would include all insured depository institutions that are affiliates of the resulting bank. *Id.* § 1831u(b)(2)(A).

22. *Id.* § 1831u(b)(2)(E). For examples, see *Bank of America Corporation Charlotte, North Carolina: Order Approving the Acquisition of a Savings Association and an Industrial Loan Company,* (Nov. 26, 2008) *available at* http://www.federalreserve.gov/newsevents/press/orders/orders20081126a1.pdf (considering concentration limit with respect to BHC acquisition under 12 U.S.C. § 1842(d)); *Wells Fargo & Company San Francisco, California: Statement by the Board of Governors of the Federal Reserve System Regarding the Application and Notices by Wells Fargo & Company to Acquire Wachovia Corporation and Wachovia's Subsidiary Banks and Nonbanking Companies* at 7 (Oct. 21, 2008), available at http://www.federalreserve.gov/newsevents/press/orders/orders

20081021a1.pdf. (approving Wells Fargo acquisition of Wachovia, on condition that acquirer reduce post-acquisition deposits if necessary to comply with concentration limit).

23. 12 U.S.C.A. § 1831u(b)(2)(E).

24. *Id.* § 1831u(b)(2)(B)(ii). However, the transaction will be permitted if a state deposit cap limitation (*see* text, *infra*; 12 U.S.C.A. § 1831u(b)(2)(C)) permits a bank or bank holding company (and affiliates thereof) to control a greater percentage of total deposits. 12 U.S.C.A. § 1831u(b)(2)(D)(i). The transaction will also be permitted if approved by the appropriate state bank supervisor of the host state under a standard that does not have the effect of discriminating against out-of-state banks, bank holding companies, and subsidiaries thereof. *Id.* § 1831u(b)(2)(D)(ii).

25. 12 U.S.C.A. § 1831u(b)(2)(C). These state deposit caps are given effect so long as they do not discriminate against out-of-state banks, bank holding companies, and subsidiaries thereof. *Id.*

apply the Community Reinvestment Act ("CRA") in its consideration of the application.[26] It must take into account the most recent written CRA evaluation of any bank that would be an affiliate of the resulting bank.[27] The agency must also take into account the record of any applicant bank in complying with applicable state community reinvestment laws.[28]

(2) The responsible federal agency must take into account adequacy of capital and management. The agency is permitted to approve an interstate merger transaction only if each bank involved is adequately capitalized as of the date on which the application is filed.[29] It must also determine that the resulting bank will continue to be well capitalized and well managed upon consummation of the transaction.[30]

(3) Interstate transactions remain fully subject to applicable antitrust laws.[31] The agency must also take into account the applicability of any similar state anticompetitive laws.[32]

A general exception exists for interstate merger transactions involving banks in default or in danger of default. In these situations IBBEA waives the following requirements: (1) state election to prohibit interstate merger transactions; (2) branch acquisition provisions; (3) state law provisions concerning required minimum years of existence prior to merger; (4) compliance with state filing requirements; (5) concentration limits; (6) community reinvestment compliance; and (7) adequacy of capital and management.[33] The responsible federal agency may approve an application for an interstate merger in which one or more banks in default or in danger of default are involved, or as to which financial assistance is provided by the FDIC under Section 13(c) of the Federal Deposit Insurance Act ("FDIA").[34]

If the interstate merger transaction is approved, the charters of all banks involved, except for the resulting bank, must be surrendered, upon request, to the federal or state chartering authority.[35] Subject to the approval of the appropriate federal banking agency,

---

26. *Id.* § 1831u(b)(3)(A).

27. *Id.* § 1831u(b)(3)(B).

28. *Id.* § 1831u(b)(3)(C).

29. *Id.* § 1831u(b)(4)(A).

30. *Id.* § 1831u(b)(4)(B), as amended Dodd–Frank Wall Street Reform and Consumer Protection Act (DFA) § 607(b), 124 Stat. 1376, 1608 (2010) (raising standards from "adequately capitalized" and "adequately managed" to "well capitalized" and "well managed"). A BHC is considered "well capitalized" if it "significantly exceeds the required minimum level for each relevant capital measure." 12 U.S.C.A. § 1841(*o*)(1)(B)(ii). On the meaning of "well managed," see *id.* § 1841(*o*)(9). The increase in standards is effective 21 July 2011. DFA § 607(c), 124 Stat. at 1608.

31. *Id.* § 1831u(c)(2)(A).

32. *Id.* § 1831u(c)(2)(B).

33. *Id.* § 1831u(e).

34. *See id.* § 1823(c) (financial assistance under FDIA).

35. *Id.* § 1831u(b)(5).

the resulting bank may retain and operate, as a main office or branch, any office that any bank involved in the transaction was operating immediately before the merger transaction.[36] In addition, after consummation of the transaction, the resulting bank is permitted to establish, acquire, or operate additional branches at any location where any involved bank could have done so under federal or state law, if it had not been involved in the transaction.[37]

§ 4.16   Effect on Branch Ownership and Control

One effect of the interstate merger transaction provisions will be to create new interstate patterns of branch ownership and control. The IBBEA therefore includes certain conforming amendments to other provisions of federal law concerning branches.

Domestic branching by national banks is governed by the NBA.[1] IBBEA amends the NBA on this point in several respects.[2] A national bank that results from an interstate merger transaction is permitted to maintain and operate a branch in a host state, in accordance with the interstate merger transaction provisions.[3] Effective June 1, 1997, a national bank generally may acquire, establish, or operate a branch in a host state (including a host state in which it already has a branch) only if authorized by the amended NBA, the emergency acquisition provisions of the FDIA,[4] or the new interstate merger transactions provision.[5] If a national bank relocates its main office from one state to another after May 31, 1997,[6] the bank may retain and operate its branches within its former home state only to the extent that the bank would be authorized to acquire, establish, or commence operation of a branch in such a state.[7]

---

36. *Id.* § 1831u(d)(1). However, IBBEA has required the federal banking agencies to promulgate regulations prohibiting any out-of-state bank from using any authority to engage in interstate branching primarily for the purpose of deposit production. *Id.* § 1835a.

37. *Id.* § 1831u(d)(2).

§ 4.16

1. 12 U.S.C.A. § 36.

2. *See id.* § 36(d)–(f), (h)–(*l*).

3. *Id.* § 36(d). However, IBBEA required the federal banking agencies to promulgate regulations prohibiting any out-of-state bank from using any authority to engage in interstate branching primarily for the purpose of deposit production. *Id.* § 1835a.

4. *See id.* § 1823(f), (k).

5. *Id.* § 36(e)(1).

6. *Cf. id.* § 30(c) (coordinating NBA relocation provision with new § 36(e)(2) governing retention of branches).

7. *Id.* § 36(e)(2). In determining whether the national bank would have been authorized "to acquire, establish or commence to operate" such a branch, the provision contemplates a situation in which:

(1) the bank had no branches in the former home state (*i.e.*, where it had previously operated only a main office in the former home state); or,

(2) the branch resulted from either an interstate merger transaction under section 1831u, or a transaction after May 31, 1997, pursuant to which the bank received financial assistance from the FDIC under section 1823(c).

In general, any host state branch of an out-of-state national bank will be subject to host state laws concerning community reinvestment, consumer protection, fair lending, and establishment of intrastate branches to the same extent as a state-chartered bank would be.[8] However, this rule does not apply if federal law preempts the application of any such state law to a national bank.[9] The rule also does not apply if the Comptroller of the Currency determines that application of any such state law would have a discriminatory effect on the national bank branch, as compared to its effect on branches of state-chartered banks.[10] All other laws of the host state, except for the application or administration of any tax or method of taxation, apply to the in-state branches of an out-of-state national bank to the same extent such laws would apply if the in-state branch were itself a national bank with its main office in the host state.[11]

The FDIA has also been amended to apply to branches of state nonmember banks in host states rules that correspond to those applicable to branches of national banks in host states.[12] Thus, such state nonmember banks will be subject to corresponding exclusive rules with respect to the acquisition, establishment, and operation of host state branches,[13] retention of branches upon out-of-state relocation of the main office,[14] and applicability of host state law to the activities of the in-state branch.[15] In addition, the FDIA has been amended to prohibit an in-state branch of an out-of-state state nonmember bank from conducting any activity that is not permissible for a state-chartered bank in the host state.[16]

§ 4.17   State Authority

The interstate merger transaction provisions do not affect the authority of any state or political subdivision thereof to adopt, apply, or administer any tax or method of taxation to any bank,

---

Id. § 36(e)(2)(A)–(B).

8. *Id.* § 36(f)(1)(A). Enforcement of these state laws with respect to national bank branches is the responsibility of the Comptroller of the Currency, not the applicable state authority. *Id.* § 36(f)(1)(B).

9. *Id.* § 36(f)(1)(A)(i). This provision does not affect the generally applicable legal standards with respect to preemption of the application of state law to national banks. *Id.* § 36(f)(3). On notice requirements for federal bank agency decisions preempting state law, see *id.* § 43.

10. *Id.* § 36(f)(1)(A)(ii).

11. *Id.* § 36(f)(2).

12. *Id.* §§ 1828(d)(3), 1831a(j).

13. *Compare id.* § 36(e)(1), *as amended* (NBA provision), *with id.* § 1828(d)(3)(A) (corresponding FDIA provision applicable to state nonmember banks).

14. *Compare id.* § 36(e)(2), *as amended* (NBA provision), *with id.* § 1828(d)(3)(B) (corresponding FDIA provision applicable to state nonmember banks).

15. *Compare id.* § 36(f)(1)(A), *as amended* (NBA provision), *with id.* § 1831a(j)(1) (corresponding FDIA provision applicable to state nonmember banks).

16. *Id.* § 1831a(j)(2).

bank holding company, foreign bank, or any affiliate thereof.[1] However, the tax or tax method must be one that is otherwise permissible under the U.S. Constitution or other federal law.[2] In addition, in the case of an in-state branch of an out-of-state bank resulting from an interstate merger transaction, the value of the bank's shares may be subjected to any bank shares tax of the host state or its political subdivisions, on a proportional basis.[3]

As to supervisory concerns, under IBBEA the states retain the authority to supervise, regulate, and examine their respective state-chartered banks.[4] In addition, IBBEA also does not limit the right of a state to determine the authority of its state-chartered banks to establish and maintain branches.[5] A host state may also impose notification or reporting requirements on branches of out-of-state banks.[6]

Furthermore, the interposition of IBBEA does not necessarily preempt previously imposed conditions on and commitments of out-of-state banks by host states.[7] If, in connection with approval of a pre-IBBEA acquisition of a bank by an out-of-state bank holding company, the home state of the target bank imposed conditions or the company made commitments to the home state, the state may continue to enforce those conditions or commitments.[8] Indeed, the state may enforce the conditions or commitments to the same extent even with respect to an affiliated successor company that controls an in-state bank or branch as a result of an interstate merger transaction.[9]

§ 4.18   Change–in–Control Transactions

In the area of control transactions, the difference between the regulated industry and other sectors is often merely a matter of degree. Mergers and acquisitions are, after all, generally subject to a potentially significant degree of regulation. Similarly, interlocking directorates of depository institutions may be subject to a significant degree of restriction and regulation,[1] and yet there are also

<hr>

§ 4.17

1. 12 U.S.C.A. § 1831u(c)(1)(A).

2. *Id.*

3. *Id.* § 1831u(c)(1)(B).

4. *Id.* § 1831u(c)(3)(B).

5. *Id.* § 1831u(c)(3)(A).

6. *Id.* § 1831u(c)(4). Such requirements must not discriminate against out-of-state banks or bank holding companies. *Id.* § 1831u(c)(4)(A). They may be subject to preemption by federal laws other than the IBBEA on the same subject. *See id.* § 1831u(c)(4)(B) (permitting states to impose notification and report-ing requirements if "not preempted by any Federal law").

7. *See id.* § 1831u(d)(3) (rules governing prior conditions and commitments). On notice requirements for federal bank agency decisions preempting state law, see *id.* § 43.

8. *Id.* § 1831u(d)(3)(A)–(B).

9. *Id.* § 1831u(d)(3).

§ 4.18

1. *See, e.g.,* 12 U.S.C.A. §§ 3201 *et seq.* (Depository Institutions Management Interlocks Act).

restrictions on interlocks under generally applicable federal anti-trust law.[2]

However, acquisitions in the depository institution sector are not only subjected to antitrust review and securities disclosure requirements, but also to substantive review on the merits. The pervasiveness of regulation is particularly marked when we consider acquisitions of control of depository institutions, undertaken by individuals through stock purchases, not involving publicly-traded corporate entities. Such acquisitions would rarely if ever attract antitrust analysis or securities disclosure requirements. Yet they remain subject to a significant degree of substantive review on the merits under change-in-control requirements in depository institutions law.

§ 4.19 Change in Bank Control Act

The Change in Bank Control Act ("CBCA")[1] was enacted in 1978 to provide the "statutory authority ... needed to give financial institution regulators authority over ... transfers"[2] of control by individuals.[3] An acquisition of control by any person of an existing FDIC-insured depository institution or of a holding company[4] is subject to the CBCA's relatively passive disapproval process.[5] The scope of the CBCA was significantly expanded in 1989, with the passage of the Financial Institutions Reform, Recovery, and Enforcement Act ("FIRREA").[6] As amended, the CBCA now applies

---

2. 15 U.S.C.A. § 19. *See generally Bankamerica Corp. v. United States*, 462 U.S. 122, 103 S.Ct. 2266 (1983) (discussing interlock provision of Clayton Act; holding interlock provision inapplicable to bank holding company/insurance company interlock).

§ 4.19

1. 12 U.S.C.A. § 1817(j).

2. H.R. Rep. No. 1383, 95th Cong., 1st Sess. (1978), *reprinted in*, 1978 U.S. Code Cong. & Admin. News 9273, 9292.

3. On changes in control, see generally *Sletteland v. Federal Deposit Ins. Corp.*, 924 F.2d 350 (D.C.Cir.1991); *Citibank Fed. Sav. Bank v. Federal Deposit Ins. Corp.*, 836 F.Supp. 3 (D.D.C.1993). A persuasive case has been made for the proposition that the statute is not intended to grant a private right of action. *See Indiana Nat'l Corp. v. Rich*, 712 F.2d 1180 (7th Cir.1983) (reviewing CBCA legislative history); *Quaker City Nat'l Bank v. Hartley*, 533 F.Supp. 126 (S.D.Ohio 1981) (rejecting *First Alabama, infra*). *But see First Alabama Bancshares, Inc. v. Lowder*, [1981 Trans-fer Binder] Fed. Sec. L. Rep. (CCH) ¶ 98,015 (N.D.Ala.1981) (finding private right of action); *Mid–Continent Bancshares, Inc. v. O'Brien*, [1981 Transfer Binder] Fed. Sec. L. Rep. (CCH) ¶ 98,734 (E.D.Mo.1981) (relying on *First Alabama*); *CityFed Fin. Corp. v. Federal Home Loan Bank Bd.*, 615 F.Supp. 1122 (D.D.C.1985) (interpreting prior statutory language; finding SLHC to be "party aggrieved").

4. By its own terms, the CBCA applied to acquisitions of control of FDIC-insured depository institutions, but it defined "insured depository institution" for these purposes to include "any depository institution holding company" and any other company that controls an insured depository institution. 12 U.S.C.A. § 1817(j)(18)(A)–(B).

5. *See id*. § 1817(j)(1) (affirmative regulatory approval of change in control not required).

6. Pub. L. No. 101–73, 103 Stat. 183 (1989), §§ 201(a)(1), 201(b), 208(8)–(13), 905(c), 907(d), 103 Stat. at 187–188, 213,

to insured depository institutions rather than insured banks.[7] Until July 2011, the OTS is the "appropriate Federal banking agency" for these purposes with respect to savings associations.[8] Thereafter, the OCC and the FDIC are the appropriate federal banking agencies for federal and state savings associations, respectively.[9]

The CBCA prohibits any person,[10] directly or indirectly or through or in concert with one or more other persons, from acquiring "control"[11] of an insured depository institution or holding company through the purchase, assignment, transfer, pledge, or other disposition of the target's voting stock, unless: (1) the person has given prior notice to the "appropriate Federal banking agency;" and, (2) the agency has not disapproved the acquisition within the statutory time period.[12]

460, 468–469 (codified at 12 U.S.C.A. § (j)(2)(A), (j)(2)(D), (j)(7)(F), (j)(15), (j) (16)–(18)).

7. *See* FIRREA, § 201(a)(1), 103 Stat. at 187 (codified at 12 U.S.C.A. § 1817).

8. 12 U.S.C.A. § 1813(q)(4) (2009).

9. 12 U.S.C.A. § 1813(q), *as amended*, Dodd–Frank Wall Street Reform and Consumer Protection Act (DFA) § 312(c)(1), Pub. L. No. 111–203, 124 Stat. 1376, 1522–1523 (2010) (codified at 12 U.S.C.A. § 1813(q)(1)–(3); striking (q)(4)).

10. For these purposes, "person" is defined to mean "an individual or a corporation, partnership, trust, association, joint venture, pool, syndicate, sole proprietorship, unincorporated organization, or any other form of entity not specifically listed herein." *Id.* § 1817(j)(8)(A). *But cf. id.* § 1817(j)(17) (acquisitions subject to 12 U.S.C.A. §§ 1467a, 1828(c), 1842 not subject to CBCA).

11. For these purposes, the term "control" is defined to mean "the power, directly or indirectly, to direct the management or policies of an insured depository institution or to vote 25 per centum or more of any class of voting securities of an insured depository institution." *Id.* § 1817(j)(8)(B) On the meaning of "control" under the CBCA, see *Zinman v. Federal Deposit Ins. Corp.*, 567 F.Supp. 243 (E.D.Pa.1983); *Citizens First Bancorp v. Harreld*, 559 F.Supp. 867 (W.D.Ky.1982); *Southeast Banking Corp. v. Adler*, [1982–1983 Transfer Binder] Fed. Sec. L. Rep.

(CCH) ¶ 99,183 (S.D.Fla.1982); *Riggs Nat'l Bank v. Allbritton*, 516 F.Supp. 164, 179 (D.D.C.1981).

12. 12 U.S.C.A. § 1817(j)(1). For these purposes, until July 2011, the term "appropriate Federal banking agency" is defined to mean:

(1) the Comptroller of the Currency, in the case of any national banking association, any District [of Columbia] bank, or any Federal branch or agency of a foreign bank;

(2) the Board of Governors of the Federal Reserve System, in the case of—

(A) any State member insured bank (except a District bank),

(B) any branch or agency of a foreign bank with respect to any provision of the Federal Reserve Act which is made applicable under the International Banking Act of 1978[, 12 U.S.C.A. §§ 3101 *et seq.*],

(C) any foreign bank which does not operate an insured branch,

(D) any agency or commercial lending company other than a Federal agency,

(E) supervisory or regulatory proceedings arising from the authority given to the Board of Governors under section 7(c)(1) of the International Banking Act of 1978, including such proceedings under the Depository Institutions Supervisory Act, and

(F) any bank holding company and any subsidiary of a bank holding company (other than a bank);

The CBCA requires that, except as otherwise provided by regulation, the CBCA notice filed by the acquiring party must contain the following information:

(A) The identity, personal history, business background and experience of each person by whom or on whose behalf the acquisition is to be made, including his material business activities and affiliations during the past five years, and a description of any material pending legal or administrative proceedings in which he is a party and any criminal indictment or conviction of such person by a State or Federal court.

(B) A statement of the assets and liabilities of each person by whom or on whose behalf the acquisition is to be made, as of the end of the fiscal year for each of the five fiscal years immediately preceding the date of the notice, together with related statements of income and source and application of funds for each of the fiscal years then concluded, all prepared in accordance with generally accepted accounting principles consistently applied, and an interim statement of the assets and liabilities for each such person, together with related statements of income and source and application of funds, as of a date not more than ninety days prior to the date of the filing of the notice.

(C) The terms and conditions of the proposed acquisition and the manner in which the acquisition is to be made.

(3) the Federal Deposit Insurance Corporation in the case of a State nonmember insured bank (except a District bank), or a foreign bank having an insured branch; and

(4) the Director of the Office of Thrift Supervision in the case of any savings association or any savings and loan holding company.

Id. § 1813(q)(1)–(4) (2009). Thereafter, the OCC and the FDIC are the appropriate federal banking agencies for federal and state savings associations, respectively, and the Fed is the appropriate federal banking agency with respect to SLHCs. 12 U.S.C.A. § 1813(q), *as amended*, Dodd–Frank Wall Street Reform and Consumer Protection Act (DFA) § 312(c)(1), Pub. L. No. 111–203, 124 Stat. 1376, 1522–1523 (2010) (codified at 12 U.S.C.A. § 1813(q)(1)–(3); striking (q)(4)). As to the statutory time period for disapproval of changes in control, the appropriate federal banking agency generally has 60 days from the submission of a CBCA notice to decide whether to disapprove the change in control. *Id.* § 1817(j)(1). In the agency's

discretion, this time period may be extended "for an additional 30 days during which such a disapproval may issue." *Id.* The period of disapproval "may be extended not to exceed 2 additional times for not more than 45 days each time," *id.*, but on the explicit condition that

(A) the agency determines that any acquiring party has not furnished all the information [required under 12 U.S.C.A. § 1817(j)(6), discussed *infra*];

(B) in the agency's judgment, any material information submitted is substantially inaccurate;

(C) the agency has been unable to complete the investigation of an acquiring party under paragraph (2)(B) because of any delay caused by, or the inadequate cooperation of, such acquiring party; or

(D) the agency determines that additional time is needed to investigate and determine that no acquiring party has a record of failing to comply with the requirements of [31 U.S.C.A. §§ 5311–5324].

(D) The identity, source and amount of the funds or other consideration used or to be used in making the acquisition, and if any part of these funds or other consideration has been or is to be borrowed or otherwise obtained for the purpose of making the acquisition, a description of the transaction, the names of the parties, and any arrangements, agreements, or understandings with such persons.

(E) Any plans or proposals which any acquiring party making the acquisition may have to liquidate the bank, to sell its assets or merge it with any company or to make any other major change in its business or corporate structure or management.

(F) The identification of any person employed, retained, or to be compensated by the acquiring party, or by any person on his behalf, to make solicitations or recommendations to stockholders for the purpose of assisting in the acquisition, and a brief description of the terms of such employment, retainer, or arrangement for compensation.

(G) Copies of all invitations or tenders or advertisements making a tender offer to stockholders for purchase of their stock to be used in connection with the proposed acquisition.

(H) Any additional relevant information in such form as the appropriate Federal banking agency may require by regulation or by specific request in connection with any particular notice.[13]

Upon receipt of the notice, the appropriate agency must "within a reasonable period of time" publish the name of the target and each proposed acquiring person and solicit public comment, before the agency's final consideration of the notice, on the proposed change in control, particularly from persons in the geographic area in which the target is located.[14] If the target institution is state-chartered, the agency must forward a copy of the notice to the appropriate state supervisory agency.[15] In any event, the agency

---

12 U.S.C.A. § 1817(j)(1)(A)–(D).

13. 12 U.S.C.A. § 1817(j)(6)(A)–(H).

14. *Id.* § 1817(j)(2)(D)(i)–(ii). Each of these requirements is eliminated if the agency makes a written determination that the required disclosure or solicitation would seriously threaten the safety or soundness of the target bank. *Id.* § 1817(j)(2)(D).

15. *Id.* § 1817(j)(2)(A). In such cases, the agency must give the state agency 30 days to submit its views and recommendations with respect to the proposed acquisition. *Id.* However, in situations in which the agency must act immediately to prevent probable failure of the target, the agency may dispense with notice to the state agency, or require that the agency's views and recommendations be submitted immediately. *Id.* The federal agency receiving CBCA notice must also immediately furnish a copy of the notice to the other "appropriate Federal banking agencies." *Id.* § 1817(j)(11).

determination of whether or not to disapprove the acquisition may be based on any of the following statutory factors:

(A) the proposed acquisition of control would result in a monopoly or would be in furtherance of any combination or conspiracy to monopolize or to attempt to monopolize the business of banking in any part of the United States;

(B) the effect of the proposed acquisition of control in any section of the country may be substantially to lessen competition or to tend to create a monopoly or the proposed acquisition of control would in any other manner be in restraint of trade, and the anticompetitive effects of the proposed acquisition of control are not clearly outweighed in the public interest by the probable effect of the transaction in meeting the convenience and needs of the community to be served;[16]

(C) the financial condition of any acquiring person is such as might jeopardize the financial stability of the bank or prejudice the interests of the depositors of the bank;[17]

(D) the competence, experience, or integrity of any acquiring person or of any of the proposed management personnel indicates that it would not be in the interest of the depositors of the bank, or in the interest of the public to permit such person to control the bank;[18]

(E) any acquiring person neglects, fails, or refuses to furnish the appropriate Federal banking agency all the information required by the appropriate Federal banking agency; or

(F) the appropriate Federal banking agency determines that the proposed transaction would result in an adverse effect on the Bank Insurance Fund or the Savings Association Insurance Fund.[19]

If the agency disapproves a proposed transaction, it must notify the acquiring party in writing of the disapproval within three days after the decision to disapprove is made.[20] Within 10 days of receipt of this notification, the acquiring party may request an APA

---

16. On the convenience and needs concept, see *United States v. Central State Bank*, 564 F.Supp. 1478 (W.D.Mich.1983).

17. The CBCA explicitly requires the agency to conduct an investigation of financial ability. 12 U.S.C.A. § 1817 (j)(2)(B)(i). On the agencies' investigative and enforcement authority for these purposes, see *id.* § 1817(j)(15).

18. The CBCA explicitly requires the agency to conduct an investigation of competence, experience, and integrity. *Id.* § 1817(j)(2)(B)(i). On the agencies' investigative and enforcement authority for these purposes, see *id.* § 1817(j)(15).

19. *Id.* § 1817(j)(7)(A)–(F). The CBCA requires the agency to make an independent determination of the accuracy and completeness of information in the submitted notice. *Id.* § 1817(j)(2)(B)(ii).

20. *Id.* § 1817(j)(3).

hearing[21] on the proposed acquisition.[22] At the conclusion of the hearing, the agency is required to approve or disapprove the proposed acquisition by order, on the basis of the hearing record.[23]

If the agency issues an order of disapproval after hearing on the record, the acquiring party may obtain judicial review of the order in the U.S. court of appeals for the circuit in which the home office of the target is located, or in the U.S. Court of Appeals for the District of Columbia.[24] The agency is required to certify and file promptly in the court the record upon which the disapproval was based.[25] However, despite the existence of a certified record on an APA hearing, the specified standard of judicial review is whether the findings of the agency are "arbitrary or capricious or . . . violate procedures established by [the CBCA]."[26]

The agency may issue a written notice of its intention not to disapprove the acquisition prior to the expiration of the notice period.[27] In any event, if the acquisition of control is not disapproved by the agency and a change in control results, the target is required to report promptly to the agency "any changes or replacement of its [CEO] or any director occurring in the next twelve-month period."[28] The report must include a statement of past and current business and professional affiliations of the new CEO or directors.

§ 4.20   State Change–in–Control Provisions

There is a wide divergence in state regulatory approaches to changes in control.[1] However, several distinct trends can be identified among the various approaches taken by states, together with a range of hybrids.[2] A small number of states have tended to require little or no regulatory oversight of such transactions.[3] A few others generally follow a "pure notification" model, requiring formal notification to the supervisory authorities upon a change in control.[4] Beginning in the 1980s, however, the predominant trend among the

---

21. *See* 5 U.S.C.A. § 554.

22. 12 U.S.C.A. § 1817(j)(4). All issues are to be determined on the record, with the length of the hearing determined by the agency. *See id.*

23. *Id.*

24. *Id.* § 1817(j)(5). On judicial review under the savings association predecessor statute to the CBCA, see *Investors Sav. Ass'n v. Federal Sav. & Loan Ins. Corp.*, 583 F.Supp. 974 (S.D.Tex. 1984).

25. 12 U.S.C.A. § 1817(j)(5).

26. *Id.*

27. *Id.* 1817(j)(1)(D).

28. *Id.* § 1817(j)(12).

§ 4.20

1. For extended discussion of state change-in-control provisions, see 1 MICHAEL P. MALLOY, BANKING LAW AND REGULATION §§ 4.5–4.5.3 (1994 & CUM. SUPP.).

2. *See id.* § 4.5.1, Figures 4.1–4.2.

3. *See, e.g.*, Del. Code Ann. tit. 5, §§ 821–826; Me. Rev. Stat. Ann. tit. 9–B, §§ 1011–1019–A; N.M. Stat. Ann. § 58–1–64.

4. *See, e.g.*, Kan. Stat. Ann. § 9–903.

states by a narrow margin was one that followed the prior notice approach of the federal CBCA,[5] prohibiting acquisition of control or consummation of a control transaction in the absence of prior regulatory review.[6]

At the other extreme, the second most prominent model for change-in-control regulation at the state level was one that prohibited, in the absence of approval by the state supervisor, tender offers for, requests or invitations for tenders of, or offers to exchange securities for, any voting securities of a bank.[7] In some cases, these provisions were so restrictive, that they could raise questions of federal preemption because of possible conflicts between state bank regulatory law and, for example, the federal securities law provisions concerning the conduct of tender offers for the securities of registered companies.[8]

5. 12 U.S.C.A. § 1817(j).

6. See, e.g., Ala. Code § 5–5A–44; Ark. Stat. § 23–48–317; N.Y. Banking Law § 583–a; 19 R.I. Stat. Ann. § 19–8–2. For an application of one such statute, see *Alvarez–Stelling v. Siebert*, 98 Misc.2d 1055, 415 N.Y.S.2d 378 (1979) (interpreting prior version of N.Y. Banking L. § 583–a).

7. *See, e.g.*, Cal. Fin. Code § 701(a).

8. *Cf., e.g., Great W. United Corp. v. Kidwell*, 577 F.2d 1256 (5th Cir.1978), *rev'd on venue grounds sub nom. Leroy v. Great W. United Corp.*, 443 U.S. 173, 99 S.Ct. 2710 (1979) (Idaho antitakeover statute); *Edgar v. MITE Corp.*, 457 U.S. 624, 102 S.Ct. 2629 (1982) (Illinois antitakeover statute). *See generally* 1 MALLOY, *supra*, § 4.5.3 (discussing interaction between state change-in-control statutes and federal securities law).

Chapter 5

TRANSACTIONAL RULES

Table of Sections

§ 5.1   Introduction

As a practical matter, state and national banks appear to be
equally and entirely subject to state laws governing collection of
debts, transactions in commercial paper, bank deposits, contracts,

and the like.[1] For national banks, however, there is one important exception to this rule—federal law, primarily that administered by the Office of the Comptroller of the Currency ("OCC"), defines the rights and obligations of national banks as corporate entities.[2] It is this balance of generally applicable state transactional law and fundamental, federal corporate law that defines the framework in which banks operate. Attempts by state authority to intrude into the fundamental governance of federally chartered depository institutions have generally been held to be constitutionally preempted.[3]

Federal law has come to play an increasingly important role in the powers of depository institutions, state and federal, to engage in particular types of transactions. There are a number of reasons for this development. First, and most importantly, despite the dual nature of the depository institutions industry, it has become markedly federalized, primarily due to the fact that virtually all depository institutions are subject to federal supervision through the federal deposit insurance system. Hence, despite occasional suggestions that the dual system should be modified, the fact is that the system has already been significantly modified over time, due to the prevalence of federal deposit insurance.

Second, at a technical level, standards of conduct in transactions are subject to a distinctive federal regime. The authority of state-chartered banks to engage in activities not permitted to national banks has been significantly curtailed by the enactment of the Federal Deposit Insurance Corporation Improvements Act ("FDICIA").[4] With certain specified exceptions, FDICIA generally

§ 5.1

1. It has long been recognized, for example, that national banks

> are subject to the laws of the State, and are governed in their daily course of business far more by the laws of the State than of the Nation.... It is only when the state law incapacitates the banks from discharging their duties to the government that it becomes unconstitutional.

First Nat'l Bank v. Kentucky, 76 U.S. (9 Wall.) 353, 362 (1870). *See also Davis v. Elmira Sav. Bank*, 161 U.S. 275, 283, 16 S.Ct. 502 (1896); *McClellan v. Chipman*, 164 U.S. 347, 356–357, 17 S.Ct. 85 (1896).

2. *See, e.g.,* 12 U.S.C.A. § 24 (concerning powers of national banking associations). *See also Easton v. Iowa*, 188 U.S. 220, 23 S.Ct. 288 (1903) (recognizing sole power of Congress to define powers of national banks); *Bullard v. National Eagle Bank*, 85 U.S. (18 Wall.) 589 (1873); *Coon v. Smith*, 4 F.Supp.

960 (E.D.Ill.1933). Arguably, another exception is provided by the constitutional doctrine of preemption, under which federal law applicable to banks, or to depository institutions more generally, might replace otherwise applicable state transactional law. For discussion of the application of preemption doctrine in the bank regulatory context, see §§ 5.4, 10.10 (*infra*).

3. *See, e.g., Franklin Nat'l Bank v. New York*, 347 U.S. 373, 74 S.Ct. 550 (1954) (preempting state law governing advertisement of accounts in light of national bank powers under 12 U.S.C.A. § 24); *Fidelity Fed. Sav. & Loan Ass'n v. de la Cuesta*, 458 U.S. 141, 102 S.Ct. 3014 (1982) (preempting state law governing due-on-sale clauses applicable to savings associations).

4. Pub. L. No. 102–242, 105 Stat. 2236 (Dec. 19, 1991) (codified at scattered sections of 12 U.S.C.A.).

requires that insured state banks not engage in any type of activity not permissible for national banks.[5] Hence, in the sections that follow, the emphasis will be on regulation at the federal level, focusing primarily on national banks.

In general, when examining the powers of any depository institution to engage in particular types of transactions, one must keep in mind that these institutions remain creatures of their constitutive statutes. This principle has traditionally been interpreted by the courts as defining the limits of the institution's power to engage in transactions.[6] Banks generally have authority only to exercise express statutory powers and powers necessarily incident to such express powers.[7] Typical express powers include the power to adopt a corporate seal;[8] to make contracts;[9] to sue and be sued;[10] to elect and appoint executive management;[11] to adopt bylaws;[12]

5. FDICIA, § 303 (codified at 12 U.S.C.A. § 1831a).

6. *See, e.g., City of Yonkers v. Downey*, 309 U.S. 590, 60 S.Ct. 796 (1940) (using statutory provisions as measure of bank's powers); *Texas & Pac. Ry. v. Pottorff*, 291 U.S. 245, 54 S.Ct. 416 (1934), *amended sub nom. Texas & Pac. Ry. v. First Nat'l Bank of El Paso, Tex.*, 291 U.S. 649, 54 S.Ct. 525, *reh'g denied sub nom. Texas & Pac. Ry. v. Pottorff*, 292 U.S. 600, 54 S.Ct. 627 (using statutory provisions as measure of bank's powers); *First Nat'l Bank of St. Louis v. Missouri*, 263 U.S. 640, 44 S.Ct. 213 (1924) (limiting national banks to express statutory powers and necessary incidental powers); *Easton v. Iowa*, 188 U.S. 220, 23 S.Ct. 288 (1903); *California Nat. Bank v. Kennedy*, 167 U.S. 362, 17 S.Ct. 831 (1897) (limiting banks to express statutory powers and necessary incidental powers); *Logan County Nat'l Bank v. Townsend*, 139 U.S. 67, 11 S.Ct. 496 (1891) (limiting national banks to express statutory powers and necessary incidental powers); *Kimen v. Atlas Exch. Nat'l Bank of Chicago*, 92 F.2d 615 (7th Cir.1937), *cert. denied sub nom. Awotin v. Healy*, 303 U.S. 650, 58 S.Ct. 746 (1938); *Berylwood Inv. Co. v. Graham*, 43 Cal.App.2d 659, 111 P.2d 467 (1941); *Commonwealth Trust Co. v. First–Second Nat'l Bank*, 260 Pa. 223 103 A. 598 (1918), *cert. denied*, 246 U.S. 675, 38 S.Ct. 425.

7. *Williams v. Merchants' Nat'l Bank of St. Cloud*, 42 F.2d 243 (D.Minn. 1930); *Suburban Trust Co. v. Nat'l Bank of Westfield*, 211 F.Supp. 694 (D.N.J. 1962); *Bank of California v. Portland*, 157 Or. 203, 69 P.2d 273 (1937), *cert. denied*, 302 U.S. 765, 58 S.Ct. 476 (1938).

8. 12 U.S.C.A. § 24 (First).

9. 12 U.S.C.A. § 24 (Third). On the power to make contracts, see *G.H. Crawford Co. v. Dixon*, 22 F.Supp. 636 (E.D.S.C.1938). Specific types of contracts may, however, be prohibited by other statutory provisions. *See, e.g., Kimen, supra* (invalidating repurchase agreement as guaranty); *Awotin v. Atlas Exch. Nat'l Bank of Chicago*, 295 U.S. 209, 55 S.Ct. 674 (1935) (same).

10. 12 U.S.C.A. § 24 (Fourth). On the power to sue and be sued, see *Miller v. King*, 223 U.S. 505, 32 S.Ct. 243 (1912); *Casey v. Adams*, 102 U.S. (12 Otto) 66 (1880); *Kennedy v. Gibson*, 75 U.S. (8 Wall.) 498 (1869). This power would preempt any state law requirement of a certificate to sue as "foreign corporation." *Indiana Nat'l Bank v. Roberts*, 326 So.2d 802 (Miss.1976).

11. 12 U.S.C.A. § 24 (Fifth).

12. 12 U.S.C.A. § 24 (Sixth). On the use of this express power, see *Western Nat'l Bank v. Armstrong*, 152 U.S. 346, 14 S.Ct. 572 (1894) (concerning credits and obligations under bylaws); *Rankin v. Tygard*, 198 F. 795 (8th Cir.1912) (considering effect of invalid provision on remainder of bylaws); *McKee & Co. v. First Nat'l Bank*, 265 F.Supp. 1 (S.D.Cal.1967), *aff'd*, 397 F.2d 248 (9th Cir.1968) (discussing general power to adopt bylaws; bylaw specifying residence requirements for directors); *Bath Sav. Inst. v. Sagadahoc Nat'l Bank*, 89 Me.

and, to carry on the business of banking.[13]

Carrying on the business of banking—in effect the theme of this chapter—has become a complicated undertaking. The statutory language that supports it is complex. In the case of national banks, the language begins simply enough, with the mandate that a national bank has the power "[t]o exercise by its board of directors or duly authorized officers or agents, subject to law, all such incidental powers as shall be necessary to carry on the business of banking."[14] This seems inverted; the statute expressly grants the incidental powers before the express powers of which they are incidental are even specified. There follows a disjointed list of five activities that appear to represent "the business of banking,"[15] though the text does not so identify them:

> by discounting and negotiating promissory notes, drafts, bills of exchange, and other evidences of debt; by receiving deposits; by buying and selling exchange, coin, and bullion; by loaning money on personal security; and by obtaining, issuing, and circulating notes....[16]

By a later amendment of the section, we are told that "[t]he business of dealing in securities and stock by the association shall be limited to purchasing and selling such securities and stock without recourse, solely upon the order, and for the account of, customers, and in no case for its own account, and [a national bank] shall not underwrite any issue of securities or stock,"[17] with certain exceptions with respect to eligible "investment securities."

In the wake of the capital markets meltdown that began in 2008,[18] a dramatic attempt at reform of the practices of financial services firms—as yet still in transition until regulatory implementation fully unfolds—was initiated on July 21, 2010, when the President signed into law the Dodd–Frank Wall Street Reform and

---

500, 36 A. 996 (1897) (upholding bylaw imposing lien on bank stock of debtor).

13. 12 U.S.C.A. § 24 (Seventh).

14. *Id.*

15. *See, e.g., First Nat'l Bank v. National Exch. Bank,* 92 U.S. (2 Otto) 122 (1875) (construing language not as limitation on incidental powers, but as description of "banking").

16. 12 U.S.C.A. § 24 (Seventh). On discounting and negotiating, see *National Bank v. Johnson,* 104 U.S. (14 Otto) 271 (1881); *National Bank of the Republic v. Price,* 65 Utah 57, 234 P. 231 (1923). *Cf. Cooper v. National Bank of Savannah,* 21 Ga.App. 356, 94 S.E. 611 (1917), *aff'd sub nom. Evans v. National*

Bank of Savannah, 251 U.S. 108, 40 S.Ct. 58 (1919) (holding power to discount includes power to take interest in advance). On the power to accept deposits, see *Eastern Townships Bank v. Vermont Nat'l Bank,* 22 F. 186 (C.C.D.Vt. 1884). On the power to make loans, see *First Nat'l Bank v. Harris,* 27 F.2d 117 (8th Cir.1928); *Murphy v. Hanna,* 37 N.D. 156 164 N.W. 32 (1917).

17. 12 U.S.C.A. § 24 (Seventh). On the meaning of "without recourse" for these purposes, see *Awotin, supra; Genessee Trustee Corp. v. Smith,* 102 F.2d 125 (6th Cir.1939).

18. For discussion of the crisis, see 1 MICHAEL P. MALLOY, BANKING LAW AND REGULATION § 1.4 (1994 & Cum. Supp.).

Consumer Protection Act ("Dodd–Frank Act").[19] Its basic objectives are to mandate effective supervision and controls over large and "systemically significant" financial institutions on the one hand, and to initiate genuine consumer protection mechanisms at the federal level on the other. Since many of the provisions of the Dodd–Frank Act will not be effective until at least 21 July 2011, and since administrative implementation of the act will likely stretch out over several years, the practical balance between these important objectives remains to be seen. The principal features of the act with respect to the regulation of corporate powers of financial services firms are summarized below.

1. The Dodd–Frank Act establishes a Consumer Financial Protection Bureau within the Fed to promulgate and enforce effective consumer protection principles with respect to financial services.[20] Title X of the Dodd–Frank Act also appears to repudiate the broad preemptive effect of *Watters v. Wachovia Bank, N.A.*,[21] and its progeny.[22]

2. The act imposes new mortgage lending standards.[23]

3. The act restricts "proprietary securities trading" by banks,[24] in which banks deal in securities for their own accounts.

4. For all market participants, it imposes new standards with respect to securitization of pools of financial instruments.[25]

19. Pub. L. No. 111–203, 124 Stat. 1376 (2010) (codified at scattered sections of 2, 5, 7, 11, 12, 15, 18, 20, 22, 26, 28, 31, 42, 44 U.S.C.A.) (DFA).

20. DFA §§ 1001–1067 (codified at 12 U.S.C.A. §§ 25b, 1465, 5481, 5491–5497, 5511–5519, 5531–5536, 5551–5587; 20 U.S.C.A. § 9702(c)(1), (d)). For an excellent survey of the history and current state of consumer protection law and policy in the United States, see Mark E. Budnitz, The Development of Consumer Protection Law, the Institutionalization of Consumerism, and Future Prospects and Perils, 26 Ga. St. U. L. Rev. 1147 (2010) (arguing that consumer protection principles are embedded in U.S. law and policy, both in terms of individual litigation and likely state and federal legislative policy).

21. 550 U.S. 1, 127 S.Ct. 1559 (2007).

22. *See, e.g.*, DFA § 1044 (codified at 12 U.S.C.A. § 25b(b)) (establishing narrow grounds for federal preemption of state consumer protection laws).

23. *Id.* §§ 1401–1484 (codified at 12 U.S.C.A. §§ 1701p–2, 1701x(a)(4),

(c)(5)(A)(ii)(III)–(V), (e), (g)–(i), 1701x–1, 2603(c), 2604(a)–(d), 2605(e)–(f), (g), (k)–(m), 3310, 3332(a)(1), (5)–(6), (b), 3335, 3338(a)–(b), 3339, 3341(b), 3342, 3345(c), (e), 3346, 3347(a), (b)(2), 3348(a)(2), 3350(6), (8), (11), 3351(a)(1), (b), (d), (g)–(i), 3353–3355, 5219a–5219b, 5220b; 15 U.S.C.A. §§ 1602, 1604(h), 1607(a)(7), 1638(a)(16)–(19), (b)(4), (f), 1638a, 1639(e), (j)–(v), 1639a–1639h, 1640(a), (e), (k)–(*l*), 1691(e); 42 U.S.C.A. § 3533(g), 8108; repealing 15 U.S.C.A. § 1639(c)(2)).

24. DFA § 619 (codified at 12 U.S.C.A. § 1851).

25. *Id.* §§ 941–945 (codified at 15 U.S.C.A. §§ 77d(5), 77g(c)–(d), 78c(a)(4)(B)(vii)(I), 78c(a)(77), 78o(d), 78o–11). See also DFA § 621(a) (codified at 15 U.S.C.A. § 77z–2a) (concerning conflicts of interest with respect to securitizations). Cf. DFA § 619(g)(2) (codified at 12 U.S.C.A. § 1851(g)(2)) (protecting otherwise authorized sale or securitization of loans by banking entity or systemically significant nonbank financial company from prohibitions on proprietary trading).

5. It requires hedge and private equity fund advisers to register with the SEC, and it will subject them to SEC inspection and examination.[26]

6. It provides for comprehensive regulation of swaps and security-based swaps by the SEC and the Commodity Futures Trading Commission (CFTC),[27] in consultation with the Fed.[28]

§ 5.2 Lending

Commercial banks generally have the broadest lending powers, both as to types of loans and extensions of credit and as to types of borrowers.[1] Lending is, however, subject to statutory and regulatory limitations with respect to, for example, lending limits, certain specified limitations on loans to insiders, prohibitions on involuntary tying, and traditional usury prohibitions.

Note that the Federal Deposit Insurance Corporation Improvements Act ("FDICIA"),[2] enacted in December 1991, has changed certain selective aspects of the regulation of lending activities. First, FDICIA has had a direct impact on activities of insured state banks. With certain specified exceptions, FDICIA generally requires that insured state banks not engage in any type of activity not permissible for national banks.[3]

Second, FDICIA requires the agencies to adopt uniform regulations restricting real estate lending by prescribing standards for such extensions of credit in accordance with certain general principles specified in the act.[4] FDICIA also recodified the statutory provisions restricting extensions of credit to insiders of depository institutions.[5]

---

26. DFA §§ 401–412, 419 (codified at 15 U.S.C.A. §§ 80b–2(a)(11), (29)–(30), 80b–3(b), (l)–(n), 80b–3a(a), 80b–4, 80b–10(c), 80b–11, 80b–18b). As a general rule, these registration requirements are effective as of 21 July 2011, except that an investment adviser may, in its discretion, register with the SEC under the Investment Advisers Act of 1940 during this one-year transition period, subject to rules to be promulgated by the SEC. 15 U.S.C.A. § 80b–2 note.

27. DFA §§ 711–716, 718 (codified at 7 U.S.C.A. §§ 6d(h), 24(c); 15 U.S.C.A. §§ 78o(c)(3)(C), 8301–8306).

28. *Id.* § 712(a)(8) (codified at 15 U.S.C.A. § 8302(a)(8)).

§ 5.2

1. *See, e.g.,* 12 U.S.C.A. § 24 (Seventh) (authorizing lending by national banks).

2. Pub. L. No. 102–242, 105 Stat. 2236 (Dec. 19, 1991) ("FDICIA") (codified at scattered sections of 12 U.S.C.A.).

3. FDICIA, § 303 (codified at 12 U.S.C.A. § 1831a).

4. FDICIA, § 304(a) (codified at 12 U.S.C.A. § 1828(o)). *See also* FDICIA, § 304(b) (codified at 12 U.S.C.A. § 371(a)) (conforming amendment to Federal Reserve Act).

5. FDICIA, § 306(a) (codified at 12 U.S.C.A. § 375b). Restrictions on transactions with affiliates and insiders apply to insured nonmember insured banks as well as member banks. FDICIA, § 306(k) (codified at 12 U.S.C.A. § 1828(j)). Corresponding rules apply to savings associations. FDICIA § 306(i)–(j) (codified at 12 U.S.C.A. §§ 1468(b)(1), 1972(2)(H)(i)). Existing transactions are

§ 5.3   Federal Lending Limits

Federal lending limits restrict the total amount of loans and extensions of credit[1] by a national bank[2] to any one person[3] at any one time in an amount equal to a statutorily specified percentage of total unimpaired capital and surplus[4] of the bank.[5] This is a common and traditional regulatory device of state and federal law,[6] which is intended to ensure the safety and soundness of banks by preventing excessive concentrations of lending to one person (or to related persons that are financially dependent).[7] This device also has the effect of promoting diversification of loans and equitable access to banking services.[8]

not affected by these new rules. FDICIA § 306(n).

§ 5.3

1. For these purposes, the term "loans and extensions of credit" is defined to include the following:

all direct or indirect advances of funds to a person made on the basis of any obligation of that person to repay the funds or repayable from specific property pledged by or on behalf of the person and, to the extent specified by the Comptroller of the Currency, such term shall also include any liability of a national banking association to advance funds to or on behalf of a person pursuant to a contractual commitment.

12 U.S.C.A. § 84(b)(1). *See, e.g., Anderson v. Akers*, 9 F.Supp. 151 (W.D.Ky.1934) (construing purported "investment" by national bank in rubber company as "obligation" subject to lending limits).

2. On federal lending limits applicable to savings associations, see 12 C.F.R. §§ 560.93, 560.100–560.101.

3. For these purposes, the term "person" is defined to include "an individual, sole proprietorship, partnership, joint venture, association, trust, estate, business trust, corporation, sovereign government or agency, instrumentality, or political subdivision thereof, or any similar entity or organization." 12 U.S.C.A. § 84(b)(2).

4. On calculation of capital and surplus for these purposes, see *Jaynes v. First Nat'l Bank of Ketchikan, Alaska*, 236 F.2d 258 (9th Cir.1956).

5. 12 U.S.C.A. § 84(a).

6. *See Northway Lanes v. Hackley Union Nat'l Bank & Trust Co.*, 334 F.Supp. 723 (W.D.Mich.1971), *aff'd*, 464 F.2d 855 (6th Cir.1972) (contrasting state and federal lending limits).

7. *See Valente v. Dennis*, 437 F.Supp. 783 (E.D.Pa.1977) (discussing purposes of lending limits); *Huff v. Union Nat'l Bank of Oakland*, 173 F. 333 (C.C.N.D.Cal.1909). *See also* 12 C.F.R. § 32.1(b) (discussing purpose of lending limit regulations).

8. *Valente, supra*. While this diversification effect remains at the heart of the public policy underlying federal lending limits, in 2001 the Office of the Comptroller issued a final rule amending its lending limits regulation to give special encouragement to community-oriented lending activities. 66 Fed. Reg. 31,114 (2001) (codified at 12 C.F.R. §§ 32.2(i)–(s), 32.7, 32.3(c)(5)); 66 Fed. Reg. 55,071 (2001) (codified at 12 C.F.R. §§ 32.2(f)(1)(iii)–(iv), (m)(1), 32.3(a), (b)(1)(i), (b)(5)) (correcting six cross-references in existing lending limits regulation to reflect community bank-focused regulation review pilot program). The rule establishes a three-year pilot program that creates new special lending limits for 1–4 family residential real estate loans and loans to small businesses. 12 C.F.R. § 32.7. For these purposes, the term "residential real estate loan" is defined to mean "a loan or extension of credit that is secured by 1–4 family residential real estate." *Id.* § 32.2(p). The term "small business loan" is defined to mean "a loan or extension of credit 'secured by nonfarm nonresidential properties' or 'a commercial or industrial loan'...." *Id.* § 32.2(r). Eligible national banks with main offices located in states that have a lending limit available

The applicable lending limit will vary depending upon whether or not the loan is fully secured by readily marketable collateral. If it is not, the applicable lending limit is fifteen percent.[9] If it is, the applicable limit is ten percent.[10] This ten percent limit is in addition to and separate from the basic fifteen percent limit.[11] Hence, because the second limit is *in addition* to the first limit, working carefully with these two limits a bank may lend a total amount to one person equal to 25 percent of the bank's unimpaired capital and surplus.[12] However, because the second limit is *separate from* the first limit, the two limits are not simply aggregated.[13] A loan that is not fully collateralized by readily marketable collateral cannot benefit from the second limit,[14] even though total lending to the borrower is less than 25 percent of unimpaired capital and surplus. Figure 5–1, *infra*, illustrates the parameters of the federal lending limits.

for residential real estate, small business or unsecured loans that is higher than the current Federal limit may apply to take part in the pilot program. The term "eligible bank" is defined for these purposes to mean a national bank that (*i*) is well capitalized as defined in 12 CFR 6.4(b)(1); and (*ii*) has a composite rating of 1 or 2 under the Uniform Financial Institutions Rating System in connection with the bank's most recent examination or subsequent review, with at least a rating of 2 for asset quality and for management. *Id.* § 32.2(i)(1)–(2). The rule also permanently modifies the lending limit exemption for loans to, or guaranteed by obligations of, state and local governments. *Id.* § 32.3(c)(5). The rule became effective 10 September 2001. 66 Fed. Reg. at 31,114.

9. 12 U.S.C.A. § 84(a)(1). For discussion of the implications of § 84(a)(1) for a national bank and its holding company, see *Marx v. Centran Corp.*, 747 F.2d 1536 (6th Cir.1984), *cert. denied*, 471 U.S. 1125, 105 S.Ct. 2656 (1985).

10. 12 U.S.C.A. § 84(a)(2).

11. *Id.*

12. See 12 C.F.R. § 32.3(a) (providing that national bank's total outstanding loans and extensions of credit to any one borrower "may not exceed 15 percent of the bank's capital and surplus, plus an additional 10 percent of the bank's capital and surplus").

13. *See* 12 C.F.R. § 32.2(a) (providing that amount exceeding 15 percent general limit must be "fully secured by readily marketable collateral").

14. *See* 12 C.F.R. § 32.2(a), which provides in pertinent part:

To qualify for the additional 10 percent limit, the bank must perfect a security interest in the collateral under applicable law and the collateral must have a current market value at all times of at least 100 percent of the amount of the loan or extension of credit that exceeds the bank's 15 percent general limit.

Figure 5–1
Parameters of Federal Lending Limits

National Bank *A*

Total unimpaired capital and surplus = $1,000,000
84(a)(1) Limit = $ 150,000
84(a)(2) Limit = $ 100,000

Case 1:
No Loans to Borrower Fully Collateralized by Readily Marketable Collateral

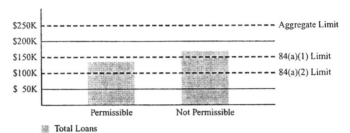

Case 2:
Some Loans to Borrower Fully Collateralized by Readily Marketable Collateral

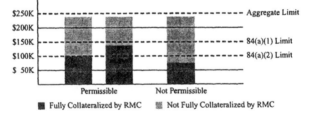

Case 3:
All Loans to Borrower Fully Collateralized by Readily Marketable Collateral

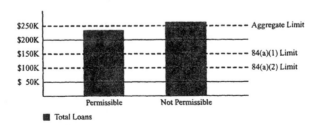

Thus, if National Bank *A* had no loans or extensions of credit outstanding to a particular borrower that qualified for the additional lending limit of ten percent, it would be absolutely limited to $150,000 in total outstanding loans and extensions to that borrower (Figure 5–1, Case 1). However, to the extent that some of the loans and extensions qualified, Bank *A* could utilize the aggregate limit of $250,000 per borrower in virtually any combination of qualifying and nonqualifying loans and extensions, so long as the nonqualifying portion did not exceed the $150,000 limit (Figure 5–1, Case 2). This means, of course, that even if all loans and extensions to the borrower were qualifying, Bank A would still be limited to the $250,000 aggregate amount (Figure 5–1, Case 3).

The lending limits provisions also include a range of specified exceptions.[15] These contain their own special lending limits or other conditions, and are separate from and in addition to the generally applicable limits.

The Office of the Comptroller of the Currency ("OCC") has statutory authority to administer and carry out the purposes of the National Bank Act ("NBA") lending limits through promulgation of rules and regulations,[16] including "rules or regulations to define or further define terms" used in the statutory provisions.[17] The Comptroller has issued extensive rules in this regard.[18] The NBA also gives the Comptroller the authority to establish limits or requirements other than those specified in the lending limit provisions for particular classes or categories of loans or extensions of credit,[19] but the Comptroller generally has not done so.

Finally, the NBA gives the Comptroller the express authority "to determine when a loan putatively made to a person shall for purposes of [NBA lending limits] be attributed to another person."[20] The Comptroller's lending limit regulations contain detailed "combination rules" in this regard.[21] Whether viewed as "attribution" or "combination" of loans and extensions of credit, this is a process that has long been applied by the Comptroller in administering the NBA lending limits.[22]

It is a longstanding rule that directors are directly responsible for supervision of a national bank's compliance with its lending limits.[23] Directors who participate or acquiesce in a violation of the

15. 12 U.S.C.A. § 84(c).

16. 12 U.S.C.A. § 84(d)(1).

17. *Id.*

18. *See* 12 C.F.R. Pt. 32 (setting forth Comptroller's lending limit rules).

19. 12 U.S.C.A. § 84(d)(1).

20. *Id.* § 84(d)(2). For cases construing combination rules prior to the 1982 amendment of the statute to provide more explicit authority, see *Hughes v. Reed*, 46 F.2d 435 (10th Cir.1931); *Keller, supra*. The 1982 amendments and the implementing regulations would have had a significant effect on the analysis in cases like *Keller*. First, and most obviously, the post–1982 general lending limit is fifteen percent, not ten percent as it was at the time *Keller* was decided. Second, the statutorily authorized combination rules of 12 C.F.R. § 32.5 would have applied. (However, as in *Keller*, 12 C.F.R. § 32.5(d)(1) would still have re-

quired parent control of more than 50 percent of the stock of the subsidiary for combination purposes.) Third, the "common enterprise" test of 12 C.F.R. § 32.5(c) would have governed the analysis in the case. Fourth, in any event no more than 50 percent of the national bank's unimpaired capital and surplus could have been lent to any one corporate group under 12 C.F.R. § 32.5(d)(1).

21. 12 C.F.R. § 32.5.

22. *See, e.g., First Nat'l Bank of Barron v. Strimling*, 308 Minn. 207, 241 N.W.2d 478 (1976) (applying lending limits to loan obtained by one borrower on behalf of another).

23. *See, e.g., Atherton v. Anderson*, 99 F.2d 883 (6th Cir.1938); *Anderson v. Gailey*, 33 F.2d 589 (D.Ga.1929) (discussing director responsibility). *See also* 12 U.S.C.A. § 93 (providing for director liability for certain violations).

lending limits are subject to liability for losses to the bank that result from the loans or extensions of credit.[24] This liability may include contribution for another executive officer's violation of the lending limits.[25] Both direct and derivative actions may be available to shareholders of the bank involved[26] or its holding company.[27] However, no such action is available to the borrower,[28] and as between bank and borrower, violation of the lending limits does not render the loan or extension of credit void or unenforceable.[29]

§ 5.4   Mortgage Lending

Banks typically have the power to engage in real estate lending directly or through an operating subsidiary.[1] In the case of national banks, these subsidiaries participate in mortgage lending "subject to the same terms and conditions that govern the national bank itself; [and] that power cannot be significantly impaired or impeded by state law."[2]

Unfortunately, preemption of state laws meant that the localized supervisors were without power to prevent abuses in mortgage lending. In the early 2000s, mortgage loan originators began to make residential mortgage loans based on lower underwriting standards, often referred to as subprime loans.[3] In the first half of the decade, there were no apparent negative repercussions from this increasingly common lending practice, but by mid–2006 home values had leveled off and soon began to decline. This trend led to a

24. *Cockrill v. Cooper*, 86 F. 7 (8th Cir.1898); *Federal Deposit Ins. Corp. v. Mapp's Executor*, 184 Va. 970, 37 S.E.2d 23 (1946).

25. *Cache Nat'l Bank v. Hinman*, 626 F.Supp. 1341 (D.Colo.1986).

26. *See Harmsen v. Smith*, 542 F.2d 496 (9th Cir.1976) (requiring knowing violation by bank directors).

27. *Marx, supra.*

28. *Valente, supra; Municipal Leasing Sys., Inc. v. Northampton Nat'l Bank of Easton*, 382 F.Supp. 968 (E.D.Pa.1974).

29. *Union Gold–Mining Co. of Colo. v. Rocky Mtn. Nat'l Bank of Central City*, 96 U.S. (6 Otto) 640 (1877); *First Am. Nat'l Bank of Iuka v. Alcorn, Inc.*, 361 So.2d 481 (Miss.1978).

§ 5.4

1. *See, e.g., Watters v. Wachovia Bank, N.A.*, 550 U.S. 1, 6, 127 S.Ct. 1559, 1564 (2007).

2. *Id.* (citing 12 U.S.C.A. §§ 24 (Seventh), 24a(g)(3)(A), 371).

3. While there is no standard definition of the term, the "subprime loan" can be described generally as a mortgage loan that does not conform to the underwriting standards required for sale to government-sponsored enterprises ("non-conforming loans") and is made to a mortgagor who: (*i*) has a weakened credit history; (*ii*) has reduced repayment capacity as measured by credit scores, debt-to-income ratios, loan-to-value ratios, or other similar criteria; or, (*iii*) has not provided documentation to verify all or some of the information, particularly financial information, in the loan application; or some combination of these factors. For background on the subprime mortgage crisis, see Federal Housing Finance Board, *Proposal to Establish Affordable Housing Homeownership Set–Aside Programs*, 73 Fed. Reg. 20,552, 20,552–20,553 (2008); Securities and Exchange Commission, *Proposed Rules for Nationally Recognized Statistical Rating Organizations*, 73 Fed. Reg. 36,212 (2008).

gradual increase in delinquencies and defaults in subprime mort-gage loans.[4] This marked increase in subprime loan delinquencies and, ultimately, in defaults has had substantial adverse effects on the markets for, and market values and liquidity of, residential mortgage-backed securities backed by subprime loans and on collat-eralized debt obligations (CDOs) linked to such loans.

The situation was further exacerbated by the adjustable rate feature that was characteristic of the subprime mortgages. Typical examples of the subprime adjustable rate mortgages (ARMs) in-clude "2/28" and "3/27" loans, in which the mortgagor pays an introductory—often a low "teaser"—interest rate, fixed for the first two or three years, after which the rate becomes adjustable, usually on an annual basis. Principal and interest payments increase be-cause they are typically "recast" or "reset" on two common types of nontraditional loans: interest-only loans and option ARMs. For an interest-only loan, the mortgagor pays only interest for a speci-fied period (e.g., five years). Payments are then recast to include the loan's principal, which is amortized over the remaining term of the loan. With an option ARM, the mortgagor has the monthly option of paying less than the fully amortizing principal and inter-est payment, and may pay as little as a minimum payment that includes no principal and less than the full amount of interest. Unpaid interest is added to the loan balance resulting in "negative amortization." In most option ARMs, the lender recasts the pay-ment to re-amortize the increased principal and interest either periodically (e.g., every 5 years), or whenever the negative amorti-zation reaches a specified cap, typically 125% of the original loan amount. Nontraditional loans may have adjustable interest rates, which can compound the increase in the amount of the monthly payments and the amount of negative amortization.

Not surprisingly, the interest rates on subprime ARMs and other nontraditional mortgages increased substantially over time.[5] As these mortgages reset, many of the mortgagors confronted an unaffordable increase in their mortgage payments. Many were not able to sustain homeownership without a reduction in their month-ly mortgage payments, but many could not sell or refinance their homes into more affordable mortgage arrangements because the

4. 73 Fed. Reg. at 36,212, (citing Testimony of John C. Dugan, Comptrol-ler of the Currency, before the U.S. Sen-ate Committee on Banking, Housing, and Urban Affairs (Mar. 4, 2008) at 8–12); Statement of Sheila C. Bair, Chair-man, Federal Deposit Insurance Corpo-ration, before U.S. Senate Committee on Banking, Housing, and Urban Affairs (Mar. 4, 2008) at 5–6.

5. About 1.5 million subprime ARMs were scheduled to reset upward during 2008. 73 Fed. Reg. at 20,553 (citing speech by Ben S. Bernanke, Chairman, Federal Reserve Board, Fostering Sus-tainable Homeownership, at the Nation-al Community Reinvestment Coalition Annual Meeting, Washington DC (Mar. 14, 2008)).

decline in home values had left them without sufficient equity to qualify for new mortgages. The resulting "payment shocks," high housing-cost-to-income ratios, and the inability to refinance led to foreclosures in many cases. More than 20 percent of the roughly 3.6 million subprime ARMs outstanding at the end of 2007 either were in foreclosure or 90 days or more past due.[6] This problem was exacerbated by the fact that subprime and other nontraditional mortgages were often concentrated geographically.[7] Higher than average numbers of foreclosures and unoccupied homes in a community adversely affected the home values and quality of life of other homeowners in the same neighborhood. Beyond the subprime problem, however, as the crisis worsened in the last three quarters of 2008, mortgage foreclosures and delinquencies in lower-risk prime loans more than doubled.[8]

While the subprime mortgage market emerged as a result of aggressive marketing by non-bank lenders such as "lightly regulated" mortgage finance companies (MFCs)[9] to less creditworthy borrowers, larger depository institutions responded to the increased MFC market share by easing credit standards, often through state-chartered MFC subsidiaries. Lenders of all types vigorously sold these loan products to subprime mortgagors, and then packaged the portfolios of mortgages into such securitized products as CDOs that were analyzed and rated by credit rating agencies and marketed to institutional investors by investments banks.

Securitization of these portfolios ameliorated lending risk, and the net proceeds of CDO placements provided lenders with funding to expand the subprime mortgage market itself. The cycle continued to operate, expanding as it drew more investors into the system and encouraged ever-increasing competition for subprime products and programs. When the cycle eventually wobbled—as the inherent counterparty risk manifested itself in the inability of the mortgagors to sustain markedly increasing levels of indebtedness—the system began to break down, and the value of the CDO portfolios dramatically contracted.

The results of this systemic breakdown have been dramatic. CDOs have been the source of significant losses across the U.S. banking sector. In November 2008, for example, Citibank an-

---

6. *Id.*

7. *Id.* (*citing* U.S. Department of Housing and Urban Development, *Subprime Lending and Alternative Financial Service Providers: A Literature Review and Empirical Analysis* (Mar. 2006)).

8. Mike Ferullo, *Regulators Finds* [*sic*] *More Prime Mortgages Under Stress, Problems With Modifications,* BNA Banking Daily (Apr. 3, 2009), available at http://www.bna.com.

9. Thecla Fabian, *Regulatory Lapses Spurred Crisis, Bair Says; Reform Effort Should Restore Common Sense,* BNA BANKING DAILY (Feb. 25, 2008), *available at* http://pubs.bna.com/ip/bna/bbd.nsf/eh/A0B6B5J7X3 (quoting FDIC Chairman Sheila Bair).

nounced losses of $8 billion to $11 billion on its subprime invest-ments.[10] The recent losses have been so striking that the Chair of the Basel Committee on Banking Supervision at the Bank for International Settlements[11] has suggested that the newly revised capital adequacy rules[12] may have to be reevaluated in light of the risk from CDO downgrading.[13] There is serious question "whether the capital charges for these types of exposures are calibrated appropriately in relation to their risks and complexity."[14] Quite simply, the crisis precipitated by the contraction of CDO values was unanticipated. As the Basel Chair observed, "when [CDO portfol-ios] start experiencing losses, these can build very rapidly, produc-ing a real cliff effect.... This explains the unprecedented down-grades we have seen on triple-A super senior tranches, which exceed anything we have seen in traditional corporate bonds."[15]

The subprime mortgage crisis is not just about the personal financial tragedies triggered by improvident mortgage lending. Fu-eling the dramatic expansion of this sector was the "securitization" of these mortgages into CDOs sold to a wide range of institutional investors. The existence of the CDO market had the apparent effect of moderating the risk of mortgage lenders and feeding their liquidity levels, with the result that the subprime mortgage market

---

10. *See, e.g.,* Daniel Pruzin, *Subprime Crisis Signals Need for More Work On Capital Accord Basel Panel Head Says,* BNA BANKING DAILY (Mar. 6, 2008), *available at* http://pubs.bna.com/ip/bna/bbd.nsf/eh/A0B6D7Y0T7 (reporting on Citibank experience).

11. On the role of the Basel Committee, particularly in the establishment of international capital adequacy standards, see § 9.7, *infra.*

12. For the revised rules, see Committee on Banking Supervision, Bank for International Settlements, *International Convergence of Capital Measurement and Capital Standards: A Revised Framework* (June 26, 2004), *available at* http://www.bis.org/publ/bcbs107.htm. In December 2007 the Office of the Comptroller of the Currency, the Federal Reserve, the FDIC, and the Office of Thrift Supervision jointly published final rules implementing the revised Basel rules for the largest, internationally active U.S. banks. 72 Fed. Reg. 69,288 (2007) (codified at 12 C.F.R. pts. 3 (OCC rules), 208, 225 (Fed rules), 325 (FDIC rules), 559–560, 563, 567 (OTS rules)). For simplicity, the final rule uses the term "bank" to include banks, savings associations, and bank holding companies (BHCs). 72 Fed. Reg. at 69,288 n.1. The terms

"bank holding company" and "BHC" do not include savings and loan holding companies regulated by the OTS. *Id.* The final rules were effective April 1, 2008. 72 Fed. Reg. at 69,288. While U.S. banking institutions are expected to begin a preliminary phase of implementation early in 2008, compliance with the revised Basel rules is not required until January 1, 2009, when the new standards will begin to be phased in over a three-year period. R. Christian Bruce, *Fed's Governors, Eyeing Credit Turmoil, Welcome New Capital Rules Under Basel II,* BNA BANKING DAILY (Nov. 5, 2007), *available at* http://pubs.bna.com/ip/bna/bbd.nsf/eh/A0B5H8M7E8. However, the overwhelming majority of U.S. banking institutions will be required either to continue to apply the original 1988 Basel standards, or a new and more risk-sensitive version of the 1988 standards expected to be promulgated by the regulators within the next few months. *Id.*

13. *See, e.g.,* Daniel Pruzin, *Subprime Crisis, supra* (discussing public remarks by Basel Committee Chair Nout Wellink).

14. *Id.*

15. *Id.* (quoting public remarks of Wellink).

experienced growth at significant rates. The poor quality of the underlying mortgage obligations, however, eventually had serious adverse effects on the value of CDO portfolios, to the great distress of many institutional investors.

Regulatory reforms soon followed. Effective July 30, 2008, the Housing and Economic Recovery Act of 2008 (HERA)[16] transferred the supervisory and oversight responsibilities of the Office of Federal Housing Enterprise Oversight (OFHEO) over the Federal National Mortgage Association and the Federal Home Loan Mortgage Corporation (respectively, Fannie Mae and Freddie Mac; hereinafter collectively the enterprises)[17] and the oversight responsibilities of the FHFB over the FHLBanks and the Office of Finance (which acts as the FHLBanks' fiscal agent) to a new independent agency, the Federal Housing Finance Agency (FHFA). The FHFA is responsible for ensuring that the enterprises and the FHLBanks operate in a safe and sound manner, including maintenance of adequate capital and internal controls, that their activities foster liquid,

---

16. Pub. L. 110–289, div. A (Federal Housing Finance Regulatory Reform Act of 2008), §§ 1001–1605, 122 Stat. 2654, 2659–2830 (July 30, 2008) (codified at 5 U.S.C.A. §§ 3132 note, 3132(a)(1)(B), (D)–(F), 5313, app. 3 § 11, 11 U.S.C.A. § 783, 12 U.S.C.A. §§ 250, 1422(11)–(12), 1423–1424, 1426(a)(3)(A), (B), (b)(1), (c)(4)(B), (d)(2), 1426a, 1427(a)–(d), (f), (i)(1), (l), 1428, 1430(a)–(b), (j)(2)(A), (B)–(C), (12)(C)–(D), (k), 1430c, 1431(b)–(b), (f), (l), 1432, 1435, 1436, 1440, 1440a, 1441(b)(5), 1441a–1441b, 1442–1446, 1452 note, 1452(a)(2)(A)–(C), (b)(2), (d)(4), (h)(2), (4), 1454 note, 1454(a)(2), 1455(c)(2), (I), (j)(2), (l), 1456(e)–(f), 1701 note, 1701x note, 1708(e)(5), 1715z–23, 1717 note, 1717(b)(2), 1718(c)(2), 1719(g), 1723 note, 1723(b), 1723a(d)(3)(B), (k)(1), (m)–(n), 1787(c)(10(C)(I), 1813(I), 1820(d)(5)(B), 1821(d)(2)(F), (G), (e)(10)(C)(I), (m)(1), (6), (9), (15)–(16), (18), (n)(1)(A)–(B)(I), (E), (2)(A), (4)(C)–(D), (H), (5)(D), (8)(A)–(B), (11)–(13), (t)(2)(A)(vii), 1822, 1831o(j)(2), 1833(a)(3), (b)–(c), 3413(o), 4501 note, 4502(2), (8)–(11), (13), (19)–(20), (24), (25)–(31), 4511 note, 4511–4513, 4513a, 4513b, 4514, 4514a, 4515(a), (c)–(f), 4516–4521, 4523–4526, 4541–4548, 4561–4569, 4581–4588, 4588(c), 4611, 4612(a)–(f), 4613 note, 4613(a)–(b), 4614 note, 4614(a)–(f), 4615(b)(1)–(2), (c), 4616(a)(2), (b)(5), (7), (c), 4617, 4618, 4619(a)(3), 4622–4623(a)(1), 4624 note, 4624, 4631(a)–(e), 4632(a)–(e), 4633, 4634(a), 4635(a)–(b), 4636(a)–(d), (g), 4636a, 4636b, 4637–4642, 4715(a)(1), (4)–(5), 4716, 5101 note, 5101–5116, 15 U.S.C.A. §§ 78oo, 1639a, 7215(b)(5)(B)(ii)(II), 18 U.S.C.A. §§ 212, 657, 1006, 1014, 1905, 26 U.S.C.A. § 414(l)(2)(G), 42 U.S.C.A. §§ 1437f note, 4012a(f)(3)(A), 44 U.S.C.A. § 3502(5)); redesignating 12 U.S.C.A. § 1422(2)–(9), (12)–(13) as § 1422(1)–(10); redesignating 12 U.S.C.A. § 4502(2)–(7), (8)–(12), (16)–(19) as § 4502(5)–(7), (12), (14)–(18), (21)–(23); redesignating 12 U.S.C.A. § 4614(c)–(d) as § 4614(d), (f); redesignating 12 U.S.C.A. § 4616(b)(5) as § 4616(b)(6); redesignating 12 U.S.C.A. § 4715(a)(1)–(2) as § 4715(a)(2)–(3); repealing 12 U.S.C.A. §§ 1422(1), (9)–(10), 1422a–1422b, 1427(f)(2), 1438(b), 1451 note, 4502(13)–(15), 4520(b), 4541, 4542, 4547–4548, 4562 note, 4589, 4616(b)(6), 4619–4621, 42 U.S.C.A. § 3534(d)).

17. *See, e.g.*, 74 Fed. Reg. 2347 (Jan. 15, 2009) (codified at 12 C.F.R. pt. 1250) (codifying FHFA authority and responsibility to oversee and enforce statutory requirements affecting flood insurance operations of Federal National Mortgage Association and Federal Home Loan Mortgage Corporation under the Flood Disaster Protection Act of 1973 (FDPA); implementing congressionally mandated adjustments to the civil money penalties applicable to violations of FDPA; replacing prior HUD regulations, 12 C.F.R. pt. 1773).

efficient, competitive and resilient national housing finance markets, and that they carry out their public policy missions through authorized activities.[18] The enterprises and the FHLBanks continue to operate under regulations promulgated by OFHEO and the FHFB until the FHFA issues its own regulations.[19]

The FHFA Director is required to adopt regulations specifying the critical capital level for each FHLBBank.[20] In establishing this requirement, HERA provides that the Director shall take due consideration of the critical capital levels established for the enterprises, with such modifications as the Director determines to be appropriate to reflect the difference in operations between the FHLBanks and the enterprises. HERA also requires the Director to issue regulations establishing the critical capital levels for the banks no later than the expiration of the 180 day period from the date that HERA was enacted.[21] In addition, HERA requires the Director, no later than 180 days from its enactment, to establish for the FHLBanks the following four capital classifications and criteria for each classification: adequately capitalized, undercapitalized, significantly undercapitalized, and critically undercapitalized.[22] HERA specifies that the criteria should be based on the amount and types of capital held by an FHLBank and the risk-based, minimum and critical capital levels for the FHLBanks, taking due consideration of the capital classifications established for the enterprises, with such modifications as the Director determines to be appropriate to reflect the difference in operations between the FHLBanks and the enterprises. HERA also provides the FHFA with prompt corrective action (PCA) authority over the FHLBanks and amends the Federal Housing Enterprises Safety and Soundness Act of 1992[23] so that specific mandatory or discretionary supervisory actions and restrictions under that statute would apply to any FHLBank determined to be undercapitalized, significantly undercapitalized or critically undercapitalized.[24] The general purpose of the PCA framework is to

---

18. *See* HERA § 1102, 122 Stat. 2663–64.

19. *See id.* at §§ 1302, 1313, 122 Stat. 2795, 2798.

20. *See id.* at § 1141, 122 Stat. 2730 (codified at 12 U.S.C.A. § 4613(b)).

21. *See* 74 Fed. Reg. 5595 (2009) (codified at 12 C.F.R. §§ 1229.1–1229.12) (establishing interim capital classifications and critical capital levels for FHLBanks; delineating PCA authority over FHLBanks). The interim final rule was effective January 30, 2009. *Id.* at 5595.

22. *See* HERA § 1142, 122 Stat. 2730–32. *See also* 12 C.F.R. §§ 1229.2–

1229.4 (concerning determination of criteria for FHLBank capital classification reclassification by Director). *Cf. id.* § 1229.12 (establishing procedures related to capital classification and other actions).

23. Pub.L. 102–550, Title XIII, Oct. 28, 1992, 106 Stat. 3941 (1992) (codified at 12 U.S.C.A. §§ 4501 *et seq.*).

24. *See* HERA §§ 1143–1145, 122 Stat. 2732–34. *See also* 12 C.F.R. §§ 1229.6–1229.10 (authorizing mandatory and discretionary actions applicable to undercapitalized FHLBanks and applicable to significantly undercapitalized FHLBanks). *Cf. id.* § 1229.11 (concerning capital restoration plans).

supplement the FHFA's other regulatory and supervisory authority and provide for timely and, in some situations, mandatory intervention by the regulator.

§ 5.5   Limitations on Types of Loans

Loans to directors, officers, principal shareholders, and affiliates are subject to special statutory restrictions.[1] On their own terms, these provisions apply only to "member banks," *i.e.*, national and state-chartered member banks. However, provisions of the Federal Deposit Insurance Act[2] and the Home Owners' Loan Act[3] make these provisions applicable to nonmember insured banks and savings associations, respectively. Under the Dodd–Frank Wall Street Reform and Consumer Protection Act,[4] the statutory rules governing these types of loans have been extensively revised,[5] effective 21 July 2012.[6]

§ 5.6   Extensions of Credit to Directors, Executive Officers, and Principal Shareholders

As a general rule, a member bank[1] is prohibited from making an extension of credit[2] to any of its insiders[3] (*i.e.*, its directors,

§ 5.5

1. *Cf.* 12 U.S.C.A. § 376 (prohibiting payment of preferential rate of interest by member bank to director, officer, attorney, or employee); § 1972(2) (prohibiting tying between bank extending credit to insider of another bank and insider's own bank).

2. 12 U.S.C.A. § 1828(j)(1)–(2). *See Fitzpatrick v. Federal Deposit Ins. Corp.*, 765 F.2d 569 (6th Cir.1985) (discussing § 1828(j)(2)).

3. 12 U.S.C.A. § 1468(a)–(b), as amended, Dodd–Frank Wall Street Reform and Consumer Protection Act (DFA) § 369(9), Pub. L. No. 111–203, 124 Stat. 1376, 1565 (2010) (codified at 12 U.S.C.A. § 1468) (conforming amendments; replacing "Director" with "appropriate Federal banking agency").

4. Pub. L. No. 111–203, supra note 57.

5. DFA, §§ 608(a), (b), 609(a), 614(a), 615(b),124 Stat. at 1608–1611, 1614–1615 (2010) (codified at 12 U.S.C.A. §§ 371c, 371c(e), 371c–1(e), 375b(9)(D)(i); revoking 12 U.S.C.A. § 375(d)) (enhancing existing restrictions on bank transactions with affiliates; eliminating exceptions for transactions with financial subsidiaries; applying lending limitations to certain transactions involving derivatives; revoking provision concerning limitations on purchases of assets from insiders).

6. DFA §§ 608(d), 609(c), 124 Stat. at 1611 (setting effective date of revisions of restrictions on affiliate transactions, subsidiary transactions). However, once effective, the revisions as to bank transactions with subsidiaries are to be applied "prospectively" to all transactions "entered into on or after the date of enactment" of the DFA. *Id.* § 609(b) (codified at 12 U.S.C.A. § 371c note).

§ 5.6

1. For these purposes, the term "member bank" includes a subsidiary of a member bank. 12 U.S.C.A. § 375b(9)(E).

2. For these purposes, the term "extension of credit" is defined as follows:

A member bank extends credit by making or renewing any loan, granting a line of credit, or entering into any similar transaction as a result of which a person becomes obligated (directly or indirectly, or by any means whatsoever) to pay money or its equivalent to the bank.

executive officers,[4] and principal shareholders[5]), or to any related interest of an insider,[6] except to the extent specifically permitted by statute.[7] A member bank is permitted to extend credit to its insiders, or to related interests, if the credit is made on substantially the same terms (including interest rates and collateral requirements), as those prevailing at the time for comparable transactions by the bank with persons who are not insiders.[8] Such credits must not involve more than the normal risk of repayment or present other unfavorable features.[9] Furthermore, in making such extensions of credit, the bank must follow credit underwriting procedures that are no less stringent than those applicable to comparable transactions by the bank with persons who are not insiders.[10]

Id. § 375b(9)(D)(i). However, the Fed is authorized by regulation to "make exceptions to clause (i) for transactions that the [Fed] determines pose minimal risk." *Id.* § 375b(9)(D)(ii).

3. *See also id.* § 375b(8) (treating directors, executive officers, and principal shareholders of certain affiliates insiders of member bank for purposes of § 375b).

4. For these purposes, the term "executive officer" is defined to mean a person who "participates or has authority to participate (other than as a director) in major policymaking functions of [a] company or bank." 12 U.S.C.A. § 375b(9)(C). *See generally Bullion v. Federal Deposit Ins. Corp.*, 881 F.2d 1368 (5th Cir.1989) (discussing meaning of term).

5. For these purposes, the term "principal shareholder" is defined to mean:

any person that directly or indirectly, or acting through or in concert with one or more persons, owns, controls, or has the power to vote more than 10 percent of any class of voting securities of a member bank or company.

12 U.S.C.A. § 375b(9)(F)(i). The term does not include a company of which the member bank is a subsidiary. *Id.* § 375b(9)(F)(ii).

6. For these purposes, the term "related interest" of a person is defined to mean:

(i) any company controlled by that person; and

(ii) any political or campaign committee that is controlled by that per-

son or the funds or services of which will benefit that person.

Id. § 375b(9)(G)(i)–(ii).

7. *Id.* § 375b(1). *See generally Fitzpatrick, supra* (discussing private right of action for violations); *Marx, supra*; *Lode v. Leonardo*, 557 F.Supp. 675 (N.D.Ill.1982). While the prohibitions and restrictions in section 375b are generally targeted at the member bank, the section also provides that

No executive officer, director, or principal shareholder shall knowingly receive (or knowingly permit any of that person's related interests to receive) from a member bank, directly or indirectly, any extension of credit not authorized under this section.

12 U.S.C.A. § 375b(7).

8. 12 U.S.C.A. § 375b(2)(A)(i). *But cf. id.* § 375b(2)(B), which provides:

Nothing in this paragraph shall prohibit any extension of credit made pursuant to a benefit or compensation program—

(i) that is widely available to employees of the member bank; and

(ii) that does not give preference to any officer, director, or principal shareholder of the member bank, or to any related interest of such person, over other employees of the member bank.

See generally Bullion, supra (discussing prohibition against preferential terms).

9. 12 U.S.C.A. § 375b(2)(A)(ii). *See generally Bullion, supra* (discussing requirement).

10. 12 U.S.C.A. § 375b(2)(A)(iii).

A member bank also may extend credit to an insider and related interests in an aggregate amount that exceeds amounts prescribed by regulation only if the following two conditions are met: (1) The credit must be approved in advance by a majority vote of the bank's entire board of directors;[11] and, (2) The insider must abstain from participating, directly or indirectly, in the deliberations or voting on the extension of credit.[12]

Moreover, a member bank may extend credit to an insider or a related interest only if the aggregate extensions of credit to the insider would not exceed the NBA lending limits[13] on loans to a single borrower.[14] In addition, as a general rule, a member bank may extend credit to an insider or related interest if aggregate extensions of credit to all insiders and related interests is in an amount that would not exceed the bank's unimpaired capital and unimpaired surplus.[15] The Fed is authorized by statute to prescribe by regulation a more stringent limit.[16] In addition, it may make exceptions for member banks with less than $100 million in deposits if it determines that the exceptions are important to avoid constricting the availability of credit in small communities or to attract directors to such banks.[17]

As a general rule, a member bank is not permitted to allow overdrafts in deposit accounts of its *directors* and *executive officers*.[18] There are, however, two exceptions to this prohibition: (1) The bank may allow overdraft protection, in the form of a written preauthorized, interest-bearing extension of credit specifying a method of repayment;[19] and, (2) The bank may allow sweep arrangements, in the form of a written preauthorized transfer of funds from another account of the director or officer at the bank.[20]

§ 5.7   Loans to Executive Officers

As a general rule, no member bank is permitted to extend credit in any manner to any of its own executive officers.[1] No

---

11. *Id.* § 375b(3)(A).

12. *Id.* § 375b(3)(B).

13. *Id.* § 84.

14. *Id.* § 375b(4). For these purposes, the NBA lending limits apply to a state-chartered member bank as if it were a national bank. *Id.*

15. *Id.* § 375b(5)(A).

16. *Id.* § 375b(5)(B). *See, e.g.,* 12 C.F.R. § 215.1(b)(2) (limiting member bank extension of credit to any insider or affiliate thereof in aggregate amount not exceeding $500,000, except as specifically approved by Fed).

17. 12 U.S.C.A. § 375b(5)(C). The aggregate amount of all outstanding extensions of credit to a bank's insiders and related interests cannot exceed an amount equal to 200 percent of the bank's unimpaired capital and unimpaired surplus. *Id. See* 12 C.F.R. § 215.4(d)(2)(i)–(ii) (providing exceptions for member banks with deposits of less than $100,000,000).

18. 12 U.S.C.A. § 375b(6)(A).

19. *Id.* § 375b(6)(B)(i).

20. *Id.* § 375b(6)(B)(ii).

§ 5.7

1. 12 U.S.C.A. § 375a(1). *See generally First Nat'l Bank of Bellaire v. Comptroller of the Currency,* 697 F.2d

executive officer of any member bank is permitted to become indebted to the bank, except through an extension of credit that the bank is specifically authorized to make by statute.[2] Furthermore, even an authorized extension of credit must be promptly reported to the board of directors of the bank.[3]

Such extensions of credit can be made only if they meet the following requirements: (1) The bank must be authorized to make such an extension of credit to borrowers other than its officers;[4] (2) The credit must be on terms no more favorable than those afforded other borrowers;[5] (3) The borrowing officer must submit a detailed current financial statement;[6] and, (4) The credit must be granted on the condition that it becomes due and payable on demand of the bank at any time when the officer is indebted to any other banks on account of mortgage, educational, or general limit loans in an aggregate amount greater than the amount of credit of the same category that could be extended to the officer by his or her own bank.[7]

A member bank may make a mortgage loan to an executive officer if, at the time the loan is made, the following two conditions are met: (1) The loan must be secured by a first lien on a dwelling that will be used by the officer as his or her residence;[8] and, (2) No other mortgage loan by the bank to the officer can be outstanding.[9] In addition, a member bank may make extensions of credit to any executive officer of the bank to finance the education of the children of the officer.[10]

A member bank may also make "general limit" loans, extensions of credit not otherwise specifically authorized by statute, to any executive officer of the bank in an amount prescribed in a regulation of the member bank's "appropriate Federal banking agency."[11] Aside from these loans, however, a member bank is

---

674 (5th Cir.1983) (interpreting prior version of statute). This provision does not prohibit an executive officer of a member bank from endorsing or guaranteeing, for the protection of the bank, any loan or other asset previously acquired by the bank in good faith, or from incurring any indebtedness to the bank for the purpose of protecting the bank against loss or giving financial assistance to it. 12 U.S.C.A. § 375a(7).

2. 12 U.S.C.A. § 375a(1).

3. *Id.*

4. *Id.* § 375a(1)(A).

5. *Id.* § 375a(1)(B).

6. *Id.* § 375a(1)(C).

7. *Id.* § 375a(1)(D). Whenever an executive officer of a member bank becomes indebted to any other bank for

mortgage, educational or general limit loans in an aggregate amount greater than the aggregate amount of credit of the same category that could lawfully be extended to the executive officer by his or her own bank, the officer is required to make a written report to the board of directors of the bank, stating the date and amount of each such extension of credit, the security therefor, and the purposes for which the proceeds have been or are to be used. *Id.* § 375a(6).

8. *Id.* § 375a(2)(A).

9. *Id.* § 375a(2)(B).

10. *Id.* § 375a(3).

11. *Id.* § 375a(4). For regulations of the appropriate federal regulator with respect to insider and affiliate transactions, see, *e.g.*, 12 C.F.R. §§ 31.1–31.2,

prohibited from extending credit to a partnership in which one or more of its executive officers are partners, having either individually or together a majority interest.[12]

§ 5.8   Affiliate Transactions

Transactions with bank affiliates,[1] including loans and extensions of credit, are subject to restrictions expressed as percentages

Appendices A, B (setting forth OCC regulations applicable to national banks), *id.* Pt. 215 (setting forth Fed regulations applicable to member banks); *id.* §§ 349.1–349.4 (setting forth FDIC regulations applicable to state-chartered, FDIC-insured banks).

12. 12 U.S.C.A. § 375a(5).

§ 5.8

1. For these purposes, an "affiliate" of a member bank is defined to mean the following:

(A) any company that controls the member bank and any other company that is controlled by the company that controls the member bank;

(B) a bank subsidiary of the member bank;

(C) any company—

(i) that is controlled directly or indirectly, by a trust or otherwise, by or for the benefit of shareholders who beneficially or otherwise control, directly or indirectly, by trust or otherwise, the member bank or any company that controls the member bank; or

(ii) in which a majority of its directors or trustees constitute a majority of the persons holding any such office with the member bank or any company that controls the member bank;

(D)(i) any company, including a real estate investment trust, that is sponsored and advised on a contractual basis by the member bank or any subsidiary or affiliate of the member bank; or

(ii) any investment company with respect to which a member bank or any affiliate thereof is an investment advisor as defined in [15 U.S.C.A. § 80a–2(a)(20)]; and

(E) any company that [the Fed] determines by regulation or order to have a relationship with the member bank or any subsidiary or affiliate of

the member bank, such that covered transactions by the member bank or its subsidiary with that company may be affected by the relationship to the detriment of the member bank or its subsidiary....

12 U.S.C.A. § 371c(b)(1). *See, e.g., Northwest Nat'l Bank, Fayetteville, Ark. v. United States Dep't of the Treasury,* 917 F.2d 1111 (8th Cir.1990) (discussing affiliation of banks through direct and indirect ownership of stock by director). On the meaning of "control" for these purposes, see 12 U.S.C.A. § 371c(3)(A). *See also Greenberg v. Board of Governors,* 968 F.2d 164 (2d Cir.1992) (discussing "control"). The statute explicitly identifies certain entities as *not* being considered an "affiliate" for these purposes. These entities are:

(A) any company, other than a bank, that is a subsidiary of a member bank, unless a determination is made under [12 U.S.C.A. § 371c(b)(1)(E), *supra*] not to exclude such subsidiary company from the definition of affiliate;

(B) any company engaged solely in holding the premises of the member bank;

(C) any company engaged solely in conducting a safe deposit business;

(D) any company engaged solely in holding obligations of the United States or its agencies or obligations fully guaranteed by the United States or its agencies as to principal and interest; and

(E) any company where control results from the exercise of rights arising out of a bona fide debt previously contracted, but only for the period of time specifically authorized under applicable State or Federal law or regulation or, in the absence of such law or regulation, for a period of two years from the date of the exercise of such

of capital and surplus.[2] These statutory rules are scheduled for extensive revision effective 21 July 2012.[3] Thus, a member bank and its subsidiaries may engage in a covered transaction[4] with an affiliate[5] only if: (1) the aggregate amount of covered transactions of the member bank and its subsidiaries with any one affiliate does not exceed ten percent of the capital stock and surplus of the member bank;[6] and, (2) the aggregate amount of covered transactions of the member bank and its subsidiaries with all affiliates does not exceed twenty percent of the capital stock and surplus of the member bank.[7] Specified collateral requirements apply to affiliate loans.[8] Required collateral that is subsequently retired or amortized must be replaced by additional eligible collateral, as necessary to keep the percentage of the collateral value, relative to the amount of the outstanding loan or other obligation, equal to the minimum percentage required at the inception of the transaction.[9]

In addition, a member bank and its subsidiaries are prohibited from purchasing a low-quality asset[10] from an affiliate.[11] Finally,

---

rights or the effective date of this Act, whichever date is later, subject, upon application, to authorization by [the Fed] for good cause shown of extensions of time for not more than one year at a time, but such extensions in the aggregate shall not exceed three years.

12 U.S.C.A. § 371c(b)(2).

2. 12 U.S.C.A. § 371c(a).

3. Dodd–Frank Wall Street Reform and Consumer Protection Act (DFA) §§ 608(d), 609(b)–(c), Pub. L. No. 111–203, 124 Stat. 1376, 1611 (2010) (codified at 12 U.S.C.A. § 371c note) (effective date of amendments to § 371c).

4. For these purposes, the term "covered transaction" is defined to mean the following:

(A) a loan or extension of credit to the affiliate;

(B) a purchase of or an investment in securities issued by the affiliate;

(C) a purchase of assets, including assets subject to an agreement to repurchase, from the affiliate, except such purchase of real and personal property as may be specifically exempted by the [Fed] by order or regulation;

(D) the acceptance of securities issued by the affiliate as collateral security for a loan or extension of credit to any person or company; or

(E) the issuance of a guarantee, acceptance, or letter of credit, including an endorsement or standby letter of credit, on behalf of an affiliate.

Id. § 371c(b)(7).

5. For these purposes, a transaction by a member bank with any person is deemed to be a transaction with an affiliate to the extent that the proceeds of the transaction are used for the benefit of, or are transferred to, the affiliate. *Id.* § 371c(a)(2).

6. *Id.* § 371c(a)(1)(A).

7. *Id.* § 371c(a)(1)(B).

8. *See Fitzpatrick v. Federal Deposit Ins. Corp.*, 765 F.2d 569 (6th Cir.1985) (discussing collateral requirements).

9. 12 U.S.C.A. § 371c(c)(2).

10. For these purposes, the term "low-quality asset" is defined to mean an asset that falls into one of the following categories:

(A) an asset classified as "substandard", "doubtful", or "loss" or treated as "other loans especially mentioned" in the most recent report of examination or inspection of an affiliate prepared by either a Federal or State supervisory agency;

(B) an asset in a nonaccrual status;

(C) an asset on which principal or interest payments are more than thirty days past due; or

covered transactions and exempt transactions[12] are required to be on terms and conditions consistent with safe and sound banking practices.[13]

The restrictions on affiliate transactions are subject to a series of exemptions, except for the requirement[14] that transactions be on terms and conditions that are consistent with safe and sound banking practices.[15] These include exemptions for affiliated interbank transactions;[16] deposit transactions involving affiliated banks;[17] credits for uncollected items, such as checks and drafts;[18] certain loans fully secured by U.S. issued or guaranteed obligations;[19] purchasing securities issued by an affiliated service company;[20] purchasing certain readily marketable loans and assets from an affiliate;[21] and, repurchasing certain loans and assets permissibly sold to an affiliate.[22]

There are also statutory restrictions that focus on the substance of affiliate transactions, rather than percentage limitations.[23] A member bank and its subsidiaries may engage in covered transactions[24] and certain other specified transactions[25] with an affiliate[26]

(D) an asset whose terms have been renegotiated or compromised due to the deteriorating financial condition of the obligor.

Id. § 371c(b)(10).

11. *Id.* § 371c(a)(3). The prohibition does not apply if the bank or subsidiary, pursuant to an independent credit evaluation, committed itself to purchase the asset *before* the asset was acquired by the affiliate. *Id.*

12. *I.e.*, transactions exempt under subsection 12 U.S.C.A. § 371c(d). *See* discussion of § 371c(d) *infra.*

13. 12 U.S.C.A. § 371c(a)(4). *See, e.g., Senior Unsecured Creditors' Comm. of First RepublicBank Corp. v. Federal Deposit Ins. Corp.*, 749 F.Supp. 758 (N.D.Tex.1990) (discussing safety and soundness of guaranty issued by subsidiary banks).

14. 12 U.S.C.A. § 371c(a)(4).

15. *Id.* § 371c(d).

16. *Id.* § 371c(d)(1).

17. *Id.* § 371c(d)(2).

18. *Id.* § 371c(d)(3).

19. *Id.* § 371c(d)(4).

20. *Id.* § 371c(d)(5).

21. *Id.* § 371c(d)(6).

22. *Id.* § 371c(d)(7).

23. *See, e.g., id.* § 371c-1 (setting forth restrictions on transactions with affiliates).

24. For these purposes, the term "covered transaction" has the same meaning as in § 371c, not including any transaction exempt under § 371c(d). *Id.* § 371c-1(d)(3). On the meaning of "covered transaction," see *supra* note 3 (setting forth statutory definition).

25. In addition to "covered transactions," these other transactions are specified by statute as follows:

(B) The sale of securities or other assets to an affiliate, including assets subject to an agreement to repurchase.

(C) The payment of money or the furnishing of services to an affiliate under contract, lease, or otherwise.

(D) Any transaction in which an affiliate acts as an agent or broker or receives a fee for its services to the bank or to any other person.

(E) Any transaction or series of transactions with a third party—

(i) if an affiliate has a financial interest in the third party, or

(ii) if an affiliate is a participant in such transaction or series of transactions.

12 U.S.C.A. § 371c-1(a)(2)(B)–(E).

26. For the purposes of this provision, a transaction by a member bank or its subsidiary with any person is deemed

only on terms and under circumstances that are substantially the same, or at least as favorable to such bank or its subsidiary, as those prevailing at the time for comparable transactions with or involving other nonaffiliated companies.[27] Furthermore, in the absence of comparable transactions, such a bank and its subsidiaries are permitted to engage in such transactions on terms and under circumstances that in good faith would be offered to, or would apply to, such transactions with nonaffiliated companies.[28]

Certain types of transactions are prohibited by statute.[29] A member bank and its subsidiaries are prohibited from purchasing as fiduciary any securities or other assets from an affiliate, unless the purchase is permitted (1) under an instrument creating the fiduciary relationship; (2) by a court order; or, (3) by the law of the jurisdiction governing the fiduciary relationship.[30] Furthermore, whether it is acting as a principal or as a fiduciary, a member bank or its subsidiary is prohibited from *knowingly* purchasing or otherwise acquiring, during the existence of any underwriting or selling syndicate, any security if a principal underwriter of the security is an affiliate of the bank.[31]

§ 5.9 Tying Arrangements

Under federal law, certain involuntary tying arrangements involving loans are prohibited.[1] While these prohibitions have their analogs in antitrust law,[2] they are distinct from antitrust insofar as

to be a transaction with an affiliate of the bank if any of the proceeds of the transaction are used for the benefit of or transferred to the affiliate. *Id.* § 371c–1(a)(3).

27. *Id.* § 371c–1(a)(1)(A). These terms and circumstances include similar credit standards. *Id.*

28. *Id.* § 371c–1(a)(1)(B). These terms and conditions include similar credit standards. *Id.*

29. *Id.* § 371c–1(b).

30. *Id.* § 371c–1(b)(1)(A).

31. *Id.* § 371c–1(b)(1)(B). This prohibition does not apply if the purchase or acquisition has been approved, before the securities are initially offered for sale to the public, by a majority of those directors of the bank who are not officers or employees of the bank or of any affiliate thereof. *Id.* § 371c–1(b)(2).

§ 5.9

1. 12 U.S.C.A. § 1972. Despite the title of the section, the substantive provisions of Section 1972 speaks in terms of "conditioning" or "requiring," rather than "tying." Nevertheless, the case law and literature usually characterizes the prohibited activity under the section as "tying." On the meaning and application of the term "tying" for these purposes, see *Doe v. Norwest Bank of Minnesota, N.A.*, 107 F.3d 1297 (8th Cir. 1997); *Kenty v. Bank One, Columbus, N.A.*, 92 F.3d 384 (6th Cir.1996); *Gushi Bros. Co. v. Bank of Guam*, 28 F.3d 1535 (9th Cir.1994); *Sanders v. First Nat'l Bank & Trust Co. in Great Bend*, 936 F.2d 273 (6th Cir.1991); *Graue Mill Dev. Corp. v. Colonial Bank & Trust Co. of Chicago*, 927 F.2d 988 (7th Cir.1991); *McGee v. First Fed. Sav. & Loan Ass'n of Brunswick*, 761 F.2d 647 (11th Cir. 1985), *cert. denied*, 474 U.S. 905, 106 S.Ct. 273.

2. *See, e.g., Kenty, supra* (discussing relation of anti-tying provisions to Sherman Act prohibitions of anticompetitive tying arrangements); *Swerdloff v. Miami Nat'l Bank*, 584 F.2d 54 (5th Cir. 1978) (discussing purposes of anti-tying provisions); *New England Co. v. Bank of Gwinnett County*, 891 F.Supp. 1569

they do not require a showing of adverse effects on competition or other restraint of trade to be actionable.[3] Nor do the anti-tying prohibitions require a showing of the relative degree of control exercised by the bank over the tying, or of a minimum amount of commerce.[4]

A bank[5] is prohibited from extending credit,[6] leasing or selling property of any kind, or furnishing any service,[7] or fixing or varying the consideration for any of these financial services, on the condition that the customer[8] obtain some additional credit, property, or service from the bank, other than a loan, discount, deposit, or trust service.[9] In addition, the bank cannot tie such financial services to a requirement that the customer obtain some additional credit, property, or service from the bank holding company of the bank, or from another subsidiary of its holding company.[10]

Nor can the customer be required to provide additional credit, property, or service to the bank, other than that related to, and usually provided in connection with, a loan, discount, deposit, or

---

(N.D.Ga.1995) (contrasting general antitrust law and anti-tying provisions); *Alpine Elec. Co. v. Union Bank*, 776 F.Supp. 486 (W.D.Mo.1991), *aff'd*, 979 F.2d 133 (8th Cir.1992) (discussing purposes of anti-tying provisions); *Shulman v. Continental Bank*, 513 F.Supp. 979 (E.D.Pa.1981) (same); *Freidco of Wilmington, Delaware, Ltd. v. Farmers Bank*, 499 F.Supp. 995 (D.Del.1980) (same).

3. *Gage v. First Fed. Sav. & Loan Ass'n of Hutchinson, Kan.*, 717 F.Supp. 745 (D.Kan.1989).

4. *Id.*

5. On the meaning of the term "bank" for these purposes, see *Flintridge Station Assocs. v. American Fletcher Mortgage Co.*, 761 F.2d 434 (7th Cir.1985); *Nordic Bank PLC v. Trend Group, Ltd.*, 619 F.Supp. 542 (S.D.N.Y. 1985).

6. On the meaning of "extending credit" for these purposes, see *Amerifirst Props., Inc. v. Federal Deposit Ins. Corp.*, 880 F.2d 821 (5th Cir.1989); *Boulevard Bank Nat. Ass'n v. Adams Newspapers, Inc.*, 787 F.Supp. 122 (E.D.Mich. 1992); *Nordic Bank PLC, supra*; *Dannhausen v. First Nat'l Bank of Sturgeon Bay*, 538 F.Supp. 551 (E.D.Wis.1982).

7. On the meaning of "furnishing a service" for these purposes, see *Shulman, supra*.

8. On the meaning of the term "customer" for these purposes, see *Swerdloff, supra*; *Hargus v. First Nat'l Bank in Port Lavaca*, 666 F.Supp. 111 (S.D.Tex.1987), *aff'd*, 835 F.2d 286 (5th Cir.).

9. 12 U.S.C.A. § 1972(1)(A). On the meaning and application of the term "additional credit, property or service," see *Integon Life Ins. Corp. v. Browning*, 989 F.2d 1143 (11th Cir.1993); *Gulf States Land & Dev. Inc. v. Premier Bank N.A.*, 956 F.2d 502 (5th Cir.1992); *Bieber v. State Bank of Terry*, 928 F.2d 328 (9th Cir.1991); *Palermo v. First Nat'l Bank and Trust Co. of Oklahoma City*, 894 F.2d 363 (10th Cir.1990); *Tose v. First Pennsylvania Bank, N.A.*, 648 F.2d 879 (3d Cir.1981), *cert. denied*, 454 U.S. 893, 102 S.Ct. 390; *B.C. Recreational Ind. v. First Nat'l Bank of Boston*, 639 F.2d 828 (1st Cir.1981); *Duryea v. Third Northwestern Nat'l Bank of Minneapolis*, 606 F.2d 823 (8th Cir.1979); *Hargus, supra*; *Federal Deposit Ins. Corp. v. Eagle Props., Ltd.*, 664 F.Supp. 1027 (W.D.Tex. 1985); *Pappas v. NCNB Nat'l Bank of North Carolina*, 653 F.Supp. 699 (M.D.N.C.1987); *Sharkey v. Security Bank & Trust Co.*, 651 F.Supp. 1231 (D.Minn.1987); *Nordic Bank PLC, supra*; *Freidco, supra*.

10. 12 U.S.C.A. § 1972(1)(B).

trust service.[11] Similarly, the customer cannot be required to provide additional credit, property, or service to the holding company of the bank, or to another subsidiary of the holding company.[12]

Finally, the bank cannot prohibit or restrict the customer from obtaining some other credit, property, or service from a competitor of the bank, its holding company, or any subsidiary of the holding company, other than as a reasonable condition or requirement imposed in a credit transaction to assure the soundness of the credit.[13]

The Fed has the authority, by regulation or order, to permit exceptions to these five prohibitions, as it considers not contrary to the purposes of the anti-tying provisions.[14] The Fed currently has three exceptions to the tying restrictions.[15] (1) The regulations extend statutory exceptions for traditional banking relationships to affiliates of banks.[16] Thus, a bank may extend credit, lease or sell property of any kind, or furnish any service, or fix or vary the consideration for any of these financial services, on the condition that the customer obtain a loan, discount, deposit, or trust service from an affiliate of the bank, or provide to the affiliate some additional credit, property, or service that the bank could require to be provided to itself pursuant to the anti-tying provisions. (2) A bank may vary the consideration for any financial service or group of services based on a customer's maintaining a combined minimum balance in certain products specified by the bank if the bank offers deposits, and of which are eligible under this rule; and, balances in deposits count at least as much as nondeposits toward the minimum balance required by the bank.[17] (3) A bank may engage in any transaction with a customer if that customer is a corporation, business, or other person (other than an individual) that is incorporated, chartered, or otherwise organized outside the United States and has its principal place of business outside the

---

11. *Id.* § 1972(1)(C). On the issue of whether a bank demand for additional security is a usual banking practice for these purposes, see *New England Co., supra*; *Quintana v. First Nat'l Bank of Santa Fe*, 851 F.Supp. 407 (D.N.M. 1994), *rev'd*, 64 F.3d 670 (10th Cir. 1995). On what constitutes a "traditional banking practice" for these purposes, see *Alpine Elec. Co., supra*; *Gulf States, supra*; *Sanders, supra*; *Bieber, supra*; *McCoy v. Franklin Sav. Ass'n*, 636 F.2d 172 (7th Cir.1980); *Mid–State Fertilizer Co. v. Exchange Nat'l Bank of Chicago*, 693 F.Supp. 666 (N.D.Ill.1988), *aff'd*, 877 F.2d 1333 (7th Cir.1989); *Federal Deposit Ins. Corp. v. Linn*, 671 F.Supp. 547 (N.D.Ill.1987); *Continental Ill. Nat.*

Bank & Trust Co. v. Windham, 668 F.Supp. 578 (E.D.Tex.1987), *reconsideration denied*, 685 F.Supp. 152 (E.D.Tex. 1988); *Nordic Bank PLC, supra*; *Bank of Am. Nat'l Trust & Sav. Ass'n v. Hotel Rittenhouse Assocs.*, 595 F.Supp. 800 (E.D.Pa.1984); *Peterson v. Wells Fargo Bank*, 556 F.Supp. 1100 (N.D.Cal.1981).

12. 12 U.S.C.A. § 1972(1)(D).

13. *Id.* § 1972(1)(E).

14. *Id.* § 1972(1).

15. 12 C.F.R. § 225.7(b).

16. *Id.* § 225.7(b)(1).

17. *Id.* § 225.7(b)(2).

United States; or, the customer is an individual who is a citizen of a foreign country and is not resident in the United States.[18]

Any of these exceptions terminates if the Fed finds that the arrangement results in anti-competitive practices.[19] The eligibility of a bank to operate under any of these exceptions also terminates upon a finding by the Fed that its exercise of this authority is resulting in anti-competitive practices.[20]

A person "injured in his business or property" by reason of a violation of these prohibitions may sue in any U.S. district court in which the defendant resides or is found or has an agent, without regard to the amount in controversy.[21] Plaintiff is entitled to recover treble damages and costs and reasonable attorneys' fees in such an action.[22] Injunctive relief for threatened loss or damages is also available, under traditional equitable principles for injunctive relief and under the statutory rules governing such proceedings.[23] In such actions, preliminary injunctions may issue on execution of a bond against damages for an injunction improvidently granted and a showing that the danger of irreparable loss or damage is immediate.[24]

§ 5.10   Usury Rules

Statutory usury provisions, limiting the amount of interest that may be charged on a loan or extension of credit, appear in both federal and state law.[1] Federal law is peculiar in this regard because, under certain circumstances, it references over to state law to determine the maximum allowable interest rate.[2]

The rates of interest permitted under the National Bank Act (NBA) present a somewhat complex series of alternatives. The series of alternative rates is illustrated in Figure 5–2, *infra*. They represent entirely distinct tests, and, according to *Tiffany v. National Bank of Missouri*,[3] it is the purpose of the statute to treat

---

18. *Id.* § 225.7(b)(3).

19. *Id.* § 225.7(c).

20. *Id.*

21. 12 U.S.C.A. § 1975.

22. *Id.* Attorneys' fees are apparently not available to a bank successfully defending against a counterclaim based on the anti-tying provisions. *Cohen v. United Am. Bank of Central Fla.*, 83 F.3d 1347 (11th Cir.1996) (interpreting Florida law).

23. 12 U.S.C.A. § 1976.

24. Id.

§ 5.10

1. For analysis of the state law provisions that restrict the interest that may be charged, see 6 Fed. Banking L. Rep. (CCH) ¶¶ 64,052–64,053.

2. 12 U.S.C.A. § 85. There is also a federal statutory provision prohibiting usury by federally insured, state-chartered depository institutions. *Id.* § 1831d. See Mamot Feed Lot and Trucking v. Hobson, 539 F.3d 898 (8th Cir. 2008) (interpreting and applying § 1831d in accordance with § 85 cases).

3. 85 U.S. (18 Wall.) 409 (1873).

national banks as "national favorites"[4] in this regard, so that they are entitled to use the most favored rate available under the statute, whether the rate is derived from the NBA directly or from state law.[5]

Nevertheless, the rate, even if *derived* from state law, is governed by federal law.[6] Hence, if a national bank is operating an

---

4. Despite the "national favorites" formulation of *Tiffany*, some courts have spoken of Section 85 in terms of national banks achieving "competitive equality" with other lenders in their respective states. *See, e.g., Roper v. Consurve, Inc.*, 578 F.2d 1106 (5th Cir.1978), *aff'd sub nom. Deposit Guar. Nat'l Bank v. Roper*, 445 U.S. 326, 100 S.Ct. 1166 (1980), *reh'g denied*, 446 U.S. 947, 100 S.Ct. 2177 *on remand sub nom. Roper v. Consurve, Inc.*, 777 F.Supp. 508 (D.Miss. 1990), *aff'd*, 932 F.2d 965 (5th Cir.), *cert. denied*, 502 U.S. 861, 112 S.Ct. 181 (1991); *First Nat'l Bank in Mena v. Nowlin*, 509 F.2d 872 (8th Cir.1975); *Brown v. First Nat'l City Bank*, 503 F.2d 114 (2d Cir.1974); *Hiatt v. San Francisco Nat'l Bank*, 361 F.2d 504 (9th Cir. 1966), *cert. denied*, 385 U.S. 948, 87 S.Ct. 323, *reh'g denied*, 385 U.S. 1021, 87 S.Ct. 702 (1967); *United Missouri Bank of Kansas City, N.A. v. Danforth*, 394 F.Supp. 774 (W.D.Mo.1975); *Monongahela Appliance Co. v. Community Bank & Trust, N.A.*, 393 F.Supp. 1226 (N.D.W.Va.1975), *aff'd*, 532 F.2d 751 (4th Cir.1976), *cert. denied*, 425 U.S. 960, 96 S.Ct. 1742; *Meadow Brook Nat'l Bank v. Recile*, 302 F.Supp. 62 (D.La. 1969).

Cases like *Northway Lanes v. Hackley Union Nat'l Bank & Trust Co.*, 334 F.Supp. 723 (W.D.Mich.1971), *aff'd*, 464 F.2d 855 (6th Cir.1972), endorse the full implications of *Tiffany* in favoring national banks over competing state banks in the application of usury provisions. If we accept the *Tiffany* preference in favor of national banks, then the "reference over" required by Section 85 is intended not to ensure "competitive equality," but rather to ensure the greatest available advantage to the national bank. Reasonable people may differ about the answer here, but *Nowlin* does not appear to be reconcilable with *Tiffany*, which seems to counsel a policy of competitive *advantage* in favor of national banks.

Northway and *Nowlin* represent a fundamental clash at a number of levels.

Northway gives national banks the best of both worlds. If a specialized state rate is to the national bank's advantage, then that rate applies, but as calculated under federal rules, not state rules. Hence, under longstanding (but arguably outdated) federal rules, the *nominal* rate could be applied by discounting (*i.e.*, taking the interest up front), even though this would mean that the *effective* rate applied to the loan is higher than the permitted rate. The *Nowlin* court, reinterpreting section 85 in light of later "competitive equality" notions, finds this objectionable. Read in this fashion, *Nowlin* argues, Section 85 leaves the national bank at a competitive advantage over state banks working with the same rate. The better authority appears to be that which remains true to *Tiffany*.

5. *Daggs v. Phoenix Nat'l Bank*, 177 U.S. 549, 20 S.Ct. 732 (1900); *Union Nat'l Bank of Chicago v. Louisville, N.A. & C. Ry. Co.*, 163 U.S. 325, 16 S.Ct. 1039 (1896); *Ray v. American Nat'l Bank & Trust Co. of Chattanooga*, 443 F.Supp. 883 (E.D.Tenn.1978).

6. *Marquette Nat'l Bank of Minneapolis v. First of Omaha Serv. Corp.*, 439 U.S. 299, 99 S.Ct. 540 (1978); *Schuyler Nat'l Bank v. Gadsden*, 191 U.S. 451, 24 S.Ct. 129 (1903); *Barnet v. Muncie Nat'l Bank*, 98 U.S. (8 Otto) 555 (1878); *Farmers' & Mechanics' Nat'l Bank v. Dearing*, 91 U.S. (1 Otto) 29 (1875); *Ray, supra; American Auto. Ins. Co. v. Albert*, 102 F.Supp. 542 (D.Minn.1952). This does not necessarily preempt other state claims related to the loan or extension of credit. *See, e.g., Hunter v. Beneficial Nat'l Bank USA*, 947 F.Supp. 446 (M.D.Ala.1996) (involving state law fraud claims); *State ex rel. McGraw v. Parrish Automobile Training Co.*, 147 F.Supp.2d 470 (N.D.W.Va.2001) (holding state consumer credit and protection act, requiring disclosure to consumers that automobile dealer was adding interest points to rate quoted by bank and

interstate credit card business, for example, the maximum rate to be charged is still the rate of the state in which the *bank* is located, if that is the highest permissible rate under the federal statute.[7] Similarly, the Gramm–Leach–Bliley Act[8] provides that, if an interstate bank based in State X can charge a particular interest rate at its branch in State Y, then a local bank in State Y may charge a comparable rate.[9]

In *Beneficial National Bank v. Anderson*,[10] the Supreme Court considered the preemptive effects of the usury penalty provisions of the NBA. Borrowers had obtained from Beneficial "tax refund anticipation loans," advancing to them sums calculated on the basis of the amount of tax refunds that they expected to receive from the IRS. The borrowers brought suit in state court against, *inter alia*,

was receiving difference back from bank, not preempted by § 85). *But cf. Basile v. H & R Block, Inc.*, 897 F.Supp. 194 (E.D.Pa.1995) (preempting claim under state unfair trade practices and consumer protection act).

7. *Smiley v. Citibank (South Dakota) N.A.*, 517 U.S. 735, 116 S.Ct. 1730 (1996); *Marquette Nat'l Bank, supra*; *Tikkanen v. Citibank (South Dakota) N.A.*, 801 F.Supp. 270 (D.Minn.1992). *See also Cades v. H & R Block, Inc.*, 43 F.3d 869 (4th Cir.1994), *cert. denied*, 515 U.S. 1103, 115 S.Ct. 2247 (1995) (permitting use of home-state rate for out-of-state loan); *Fisher v. First Nat'l Bank of Chicago*, 538 F.2d 1284 (7th Cir. 1976), *cert. denied*, 429 U.S. 1062, 97 S.Ct. 786 (1977) (involving out-of-state revolving credit at higher home-state rate). *But cf. Meadow Brook Nat'l Bank, supra* (finding loan made in Louisiana by New York bank subject to law of state of transaction); *Haas v. Pittsburgh Nat'l Bank*, 60 F.R.D. 604 (W.D.Pa. 1973) (same).

The Supreme Court's June 1996 decision in *Smiley* follows up on *Marquette* by considering whether late charges should be included within the meaning of the term "interest" for purposes of Section 85. If they should be (as the Court ultimately decides that they are), then the statutory decision of the *home* state of the bank—here, South Dakota— to authorize such a higher permissible rate of interest trumps the attempt of the transaction state—here, California— to prohibit certain late charges on credit cards. The key to the decision is the Court's deference to the Comptroller's interpretation of Section 85 as including

such charges. That being established, the *Marquette* analysis takes hold, and the enhanced rate can be "exported" by the home state of the bank. The combined practical effect of *Marquette* and *Smiley* is that usury policy with respect to credit card transactions will be equalized nationally, in accordance with the most liberal home state policy. Since national bank credit card operations will migrate to the liberal home states, like South Dakota, banks in other home states will not have the same flexibility in pricing credit card services unless either: (1) they also migrate to liberal home states (robbing their current home states of influence over credit card operations); or (2) their current home states also liberalize their credit card policies to retain such business within their jurisdiction.

One possible implication of *Marquette Nat'l Bank* in the merger context (*see generally supra* §§ 4.10–4.14 (discussing bank merger law)) is that it could lead to the delineation of a larger geographic market for certain products, such as credit cards. This might be an advantage to the bank, if it results in dilution of its apparent market share. On the other hand, it may place two merging banks from different states within the same broad geographic market for these purposes.

8. Pub. L. No. 106–102, Nov. 12, 1999, 113 Stat. 1338 (1999) (codified at scattered sections of 12, 15, 16, 18 U.S.C.A.).

9. GLBA, § 731 (codified at 12 U.S.C.A. § 1831u(f)).

10. 539 U.S. 1, 123 S.Ct. 2058 (2003).

the lending national bank for violations of a common law usury doctrine and an Alabama usury statute. On the defendants' motion, the action was removed to federal court,[11] and the borrowers moved to remand. The district court denied the motion, and the borrowers appealed. The Eleventh Circuit reversed and remanded.[12] On certiorari, the Supreme Court reversed, holding that the NBA provided the exclusive cause of action for usury against national banks,[13] and that, under the "complete preemption" doctrine,[14] the cause of action arose only under federal law and could therefore be removed.[15]

11. See 28 U.S.C.A. § 1441 (federal removal provision).

12. *Anderson v. H & R Block, Inc.*, 287 F.3d 1038 (11th Cir. 2002). The Eleventh Circuit majority held that under the "well-pleaded complaint" rule, removal was generally not permitted unless the complaint explicitly alleged a federal claim. (On the "well-pleaded complaint" rule, see *Rivet v. Regions Bank of La.*, 522 U.S. 470, 118 S.Ct. 921 (1998), *Franchise Tax Bd. of Cal. v. Construction Laborers Vacation Trust for Southern Cal.*, 463 U.S. 1, 103 S.Ct. 2841 (1983); *Taylor v. Anderson*, 234 U.S. 74, 34 S.Ct. 724, 58 L.Ed. 1218 (1914); *Louisville & Nashville R. Co. v. Mottley*, 211 U.S. 149, 152, 29 S.Ct. 42, 53 L.Ed. 126 (1908).) The Eleventh Circuit also held that a narrow exception known as the "complete preemption doctrine" did not apply, because the court could "find no clear congressional intent to permit removal under §§ 85 and 86." *Id.*, at 1048. This holding conflicted with the Eighth Circuit decision in *Krispin v. May Dept. Stores Co.*, 218 F.3d 919 (8th Cir. 2000).

13. *Beneficial National Bank*, 539 U.S. at 9–10, 123 S.Ct. at 2064.

14. *Id.* at 8, 123 S.Ct. at 2063 ("[A] state claim may be removed to federal court in only two circumstances—when Congress expressly so provides ..., or when a federal statute wholly displaces the state-law cause of action through complete pre-emption.").

15. *Id.* at 10–11, 123 S.Ct. at 2064.

Figure 5-2

Usury Rates: National Bank Act Alternatives

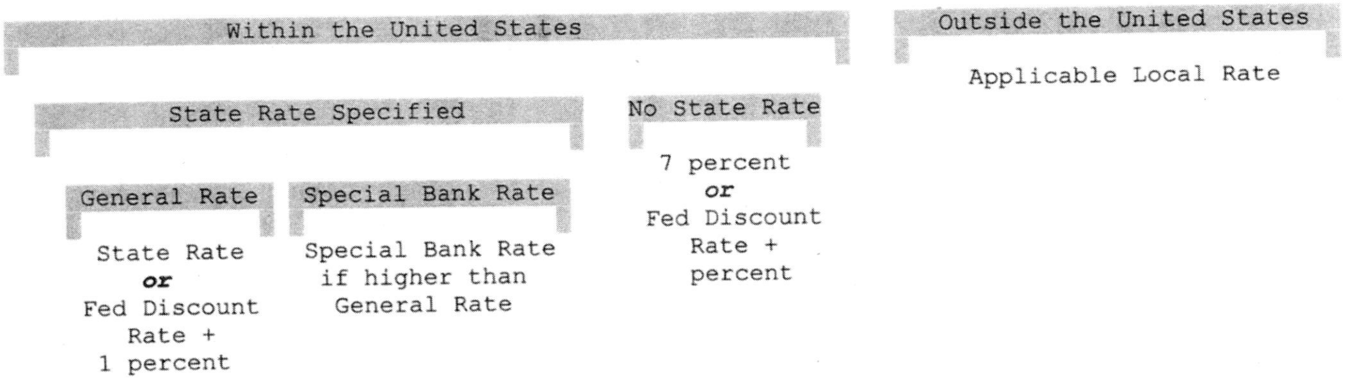

Within the United States

- State Rate Specified
  - General Rate
    - State Rate **or** Fed Discount Rate + 1 percent
  - Special Bank Rate
    - Special Bank Rate if higher than General Rate
- No State Rate
  - 7 percent **or** Fed Discount Rate + percent

Outside the United States

- Applicable Local Rate

A national bank "may take, receive, reserve, and charge on any loan or discount made, or upon any notes, bills of exchange, or other evidence of debt" interest at a rate allowed by the laws of the state where it is located.[16] In the alternative, the bank may charge interest at a maximum rate of one percent above the discount rate on 90–day commercial paper in effect at the Federal Reserve Bank in the district where it is located, "whichever may be the greater, and no more."[17]

Second, in situations in which the state provides a different rate for banks organized under state law, that rate "shall be allowed" for national banks within the state.[18] However, if some other financial institution is given a more favorable rate under state law, the NBA has been interpreted to allow national banks to use that higher rate.[19]

Third, if no rate is fixed by the laws of the state, a national bank is limited to a maximum rate of seven percent, or one percent above the discount rate on 90–day commercial paper in effect at its Federal Reserve Bank, "whichever may be the greater."[20]

Fourth, for a national bank branch outside of the United States and the District of Columbia, the maximum rate is that "allowed by the laws of the country, territory, dependency, province, dominion, insular possession, or other political subdivision where the branch

---

16. 12 U.S.C.A. § 85. Elsewhere the section explicitly indicates that "such interest may be taken in advance." *Id.* See, *e.g., Evans v. National Bank of Savannah,* 251 U.S. 108, 40 S.Ct. 58 (1919) (permitting up-front discounting of short-term note, despite fact that effective rate of interest charged would thereby exceed the nominal rate permitted); *National Bank v. Johnson,* 104 U.S. (14 Otto) 271 (1881) (recognizing no difference between loan and discount for purposes of § 85); *Northway Lanes, supra* (permitting reserving of interest in advance). *But cf. First Nat'l Bank in Mena, supra* (rejecting reserving in advance as permissible method of calculation). Other methods of calculating interest, though using the nominal rate permitted, may still violate the statute based on the effective rate charged. *See, e.g., American Timber & Trading Co. v. First Nat'l Bank of Oregon,* 511 F.2d 980 (9th Cir.1973), *cert. denied,* 421 U.S. 921, 95 S.Ct. 1588 (1975) (involving use of 360–day computation of interest). The maximum allowable state rate referenced over by the statute includes any

exceptions to that rate permitted by state law. *Monongahela Appliance Co., supra.* In defining "interest" for purposes of calculating the maximum allowable rate under state law, the bank may include other charges permitted by local state law. *See, e.g., Smiley, supra* (including late-payment fees). It does not matter whether or not state lenders are in fact charging the maximum allowable rate, but only that rate is legally available. *United Missouri Bank, supra.*

17. 12 U.S.C.A. § 85. On the use of the 90–day discount rate, see *Kimball v. National Bank of N. Am.,* 468 F.Supp. 1069 (E.D.N.Y.), *aff'd,* 614 F.2d 1288 (2d Cir.1979).

18. 12 U.S.C.A. § 85.

19. *Northway Lanes, supra* (referring to rate for savings and loan associations). *But cf. United States v. Palmer,* 28 F.Supp. 936 (S.D.N.Y.1939) (limiting national banks to rate for state banks and trust companies, not industrial banks).

20. 12 U.S.C.A. § 85.

is located."[21]

Federal law specifies its own penalties for charging interest at a usurious rate, even if the applicable maximum rate for national banks is derived from state law.[22] There is apparently no *de minimis* defense to a penalty action under the NBA.[23] The validity of the underlying contract is not affected, however, by the penalties imposed by the NBA.[24]

When knowingly done,[25] taking, receiving, reserving, or charging a usurious rate is "deemed a forfeiture of the entire interest."[26] If the usurious rate has been paid,[27] the debtor (or the legal representative[28] thereof) may recover from the national bank twice the amount of the interest paid.[29] A two-year limitation on such

---

21. *Id.*

22. 12 U.S.C.A. § 86. *See generally Schuyler Nat'l Bank, supra* (discussing penalty provision); *Farmers' & Mechanics' Nat'l Bank, supra* (invalidating application of higher state penalty to national bank); *Beatrice Prod. Credit Ass'n v. Vieselmeyer,* 376 F.Supp. 1391 (D.Neb. 1973) (noting penalties governed by federal law); *First Nat'l Bank in Mena, supra* (same); *American Auto. Ins. Co., supra* (same). This does not preempt possible state law penalties for other claims based on state law. *See, e.g., Hunter, supra. But cf. Watson v. First Union Nat'l Bank of South Carolina,* 837 F.Supp. 146 (D.S.C.1993) (arguing for complete preemption).

23. *Citizens' Nat'l Bank of Kansas City v. Donnell,* 195 U.S. 369, 25 S.Ct. 49 (1904).

24. *Oates v. First Nat'l Bank of Montgomery,* 100 U.S. (10 Otto) 239 (1879).

25. On the *mens rea* requirement of this provision, see *Wheeler v. Union Nat'l Bank of Pittsburg,* 96 U.S. (6 Otto) 268 (1877) (discussing requirement); *American Timber & Trading Co., supra* (same); *McAdoo v. Union Nat'l Bank of Little Rock, Ark.,* 535 F.2d 1050 (8th Cir.1976) (same).

26. 12 U.S.C.A. § 86. *See Brown v. Marion Nat'l Bank of Lebanon, Ky.,* 169 U.S. 416, 18 S.Ct. 390 (1898) (discussing forfeiture provision); *Barnet, supra* (same); *Anderson v. Hershey,* 127 F.2d 884 (6th Cir.1942) (same). *But cf. Wheeler v. Union Nat'l Bank of Pittsburg,* 96 U.S. (6 Otto) 268 (1877) (disfavoring forfeiture unless facts clearly established).

27. If the interest has been paid, it cannot be reapplied to principal to avoid the double penalty provision. *Walsh v. Mayer,* 111 U.S. 31, 4 S.Ct. 260 (1884). *But cf. Danforth v. National State Bank,* 48 F. 271 (3d Cir.1891) (allowing unallocated payments to be applied to principal). Rollover of a previous note does not in itself constitute a payment of the usurious interest for purposes of this penalty provision. *First Nat'l Bank v. Lasater,* 196 U.S. 115, 25 S.Ct. 206 (1905); *National Bank of Daingerfield v. Ragland,* 181 U.S. 45, 21 S.Ct. 536 (1901).

28. On the meaning of the term "legal representative" for these purposes, see *Louisville Trust Co. v. Kentucky Nat'l Bank,* 87 F. 143 (D.Ky.1898) (including assignee for benefit of creditors); *Barnet, supra* (excluding indorser of bill of exchange).

29. 12 U.S.C.A. § 86. *See McCollum v. Hamilton Nat'l Bank of Chattanooga,* 303 U.S. 245, 58 S.Ct. 568 (1938) (applying "knowingly" requirement to double penalty provision); *Talbot v. First Nat'l Bank of Sioux City,* 185 U.S. 172, 22 S.Ct. 612 (1902) (discussing double penalty provision); *First Nat'l Bank of Lake Benton v. Watt,* 184 U.S. 151, 22 S.Ct. 457 (1902) (applying double penalty to entire interest paid, not only to usurious portion); *Anderson, supra* (discussing double penalty provision).

Class actions may be appropriate for certain issues with respect to double penalty actions. *American Timber & Trading Co., supra. See also Cosgrove v. First & Merchants Nat'l Bank,* 68 F.R.D. 555 (E.D.Va.1975) (involving cash advance fees); *Partain v. First Nat'l Bank*

actions applies, calculated from the time the usurious transaction occurred.[30]

§ 5.11 Deposits

Depository institutions have express statutory authority to take deposits.[1] In the case of commercial banks like national banks, this power typically extends to all types of deposits, including demand deposits, time deposits, and deposits for all types of depositors whether individuals, business entities, nonprofit organizations, or governmental.[2] While the deposit-taking activities of other depository institutions have generally been limited to time and savings deposits of individuals,[3] the emergence of NOW accounts and other modern developments gradually blurred the distinctions between the different types of financial institutions with respect to deposit-taking.[4] Currently the range of deposits and depositors that these institutions, and particularly savings associations, may service has expanded significantly.[5]

§ 5.12 Deposit Insurance

One of the distinctive features of deposit-taking in the post-Depression United States has been the availability of federal deposit insurance. Today the reach of the deposit insurance regime is broad in two important respects. First, all depository institutions are eligible in principle for federal deposit insurance, either through

of Montgomery, 59 F.R.D. 56 (M.D.Ala. 1973) (limiting class to current holders of credit cards issued by bank). *But cf. Landau v. Chase Manhattan Bank, N.A.*, 367 F.Supp. 992 (S.D.N.Y.1973) (denying class action treatment); *Koos v. First Nat'l Bank of Peoria*, 358 F.Supp. 890 (S.D.Ill.1973), *aff'd*, 496 F.2d 1162 (7th Cir.1974) (same).

30. 12 U.S.C.A. § 86. *See M. Nahas & Co., Inc. v. First Nat'l Bank of Hot Springs*, 930 F.2d 608 (8th Cir.1991) (discussing limitation provision in light of subsequent state legislation); *First Nat'l Bank of Birmingham v. Daniel*, 239 F.2d 801 (5th Cir.1956) (discussing effect of two-year limitation provision on double penalty provision). *See generally McCarthy v. First Nat'l Bank*, 223 U.S. 493, 32 S.Ct. 240 (1912) (beginning limitation period from date of payment of usurious interest); *National Bank of Daingerfield, supra* (rejecting view that rollover of previous note starts limitation period); *Panos v. Smith*, 116 F.2d 445 (6th Cir.1940) (discussing effect of

rollovers of notes on running of limitation period); *Cronkleton v. Hall*, 66 F.2d 384 (8th Cir.1933) (starting limitation period on first payment of interest); *Louisville Trust Co., supra* (starting limitation period with respect to discounted note at full payment of note or its renewals).

§ 5.11

1. *See, e.g.*, 12 U.S.C.A. § 24 (Seventh) (national banks); 1464 (federal savings associations); 1757 (federal credit unions).

2. 12 U.S.C.A. § 24 (Seventh).

3. *See, e.g.*, 12 U.S.C.A. §§ 1464, 1757 (1968).

4. *See La Caisse Populaire Ste–Marie (St. Mary's Bank) v. United States*, 425 F.Supp. 512 (D.N.H.1976) (discussing changes).

5. *See, e.g.*, 12 U.S.C.A. § 1464(b). For permissible deposits of federal credit unions (known as "shares"), see *id.* § 1757(6).

the FDIC,[1] or through the NCUA.[2] Second, the concept of what constitutes a "deposit" for purposes of federal deposit insurance is markedly broader than our ordinary application of the term.[3]

The first point is illustrated by the breadth of coverage of the FDIA, as recently amended, to include a wide range of institutions within the scope of its eligibility, and its broadened impact on uninsured deposits as well. Under the Federal Deposit Insurance Corporation Improvements Act ("FDICIA"),[4] FDIC insurance of deposits of any depository institution now generally requires a specific application to and approval by the FDIC.[5] New rules also apply to depository institutions that are not insured by the FDIC.[6] Private deposit insurers are required to obtain an annual audit from an independent auditor, using generally accepted auditing standards.[7] The audit must include a determination by the auditor of whether or not the private insurer follows generally accepted accounting principles, and whether or not it has set aside sufficient reserves for losses.[8] The FDICIA also required the establishment of a risk-based assessment system for federal deposit insurance.[9]

Under section 5 of the FDIA,[10] an applicant for deposit insurance must be "engaged in the business of receiving deposits other than trust funds."[11] The statute does not explain whether a depository institution must hold any particular dollar amount of deposits.[12] Similarly, it does not specify whether a depository institution

---

§ 5.12

1. 12 U.S.C.A. §§ 1813(c)(1), 1815 (providing for FDIC deposit insurance for "depository institutions," defined as banks and savings associations).

2. *Id.* §§ 1781–1789 (providing for NCUA deposit insurance for credit unions).

3. *See id.* § 1813(*l*) (defining "deposit" for purposes of FDIA).

4. Pub. L. No. 102–242, 105 Stat. 2236 (Dec. 19, 1991) (codified at scattered sections of 12 U.S.C.A.).

5. FDICIA, § 115(a) (codified at 12 U.S.C.A. § 1815(a)).

6. *See* FDICIA, § 151(a)(1), (b) (codified at 12 U.S.C.A. § 1831t), *as amended*, Riegle Community Development and Regulatory Improvement Act of 1994 ("CDRIA"), Pub. L. No. 103–325, § 340(a), 108 Stat. 2160, 2237–2238 (Sept. 23, 1994) (codified at 12 U.S.C.A. § 1831t(b)(3)) (simplified disclosure for existing depositors). *See also* CDRIA, § 304(b), 108 Stat. at 2238 (codified at 12 U.S.C.A. § 1831t note) (effective date).

7. 12 U.S.C.A. § 1831t(a)(1).

8. *Id.*

9. FDICIA, § 302 (codified at 12 U.S.C.A. § 1817(b)). *Cf.* 12 C.F.R. Pt. 330 (FDIC deposit insurance coverage regulations).

10. 12 U.S.C.A. § 1815.

11. *Id.* § 1815(a)(1). The language used by section 5 also appears in sections 3 and 8 of the FDIA. In section 3, the term "state bank" is defined to include only those state banking institutions "engaged in the business of receiving deposits, other than trust funds...." *Id.* § 1813(a)(2). In section 8, the FDIC is obligated to terminate the insured status of any depository institution "not engaged in the business of receiving deposits, other than trust funds...." *Id.* § 1818(p).

12. The leading case on the subject indicates that a depository institution may be "engaged in the business of receiving [non-trust] deposits" even though the institution holds a very small amount of non-trust deposits. *Meriden Trust and Safe Deposit Co. v. FDIC*, 62

must accept any particular number of deposits within any particular period. In addition, it does not specify whether a depository institution must accept non-trust deposits from the general public, as opposed to accepting deposits only from one or more members of a particular group.[13]

In applying the statutory standard, the FDIC has approved applications from many institutions that did not intend to accept non-trust deposits from the general public.[14] The FDIC has also approved applications from institutions that only intended to hold one type of deposit account (*e.g.*, certificates of deposit) or that did not intend to hold more than one or a few non-trust deposit accounts. The FDIC's long-standing practice of approving applications from such non-traditional depository institutions has not been sufficient to remove uncertainty as to the meaning of being "engaged in the business of receiving deposits other than trust funds." In order to clarify its interpretation of the law, the FDIC published General Counsel Opinion No. 12 in March 2000.[15] The Opinion took the position that the statutory requirement could be satisfied by the continuous maintenance of one or more non-trust deposit accounts in the aggregate amount of $500,000. Unfortunately, the effort of the Opinion to remove uncertainty as to the meaning of being "engaged in the business of receiving deposits other than trust funds" was not successful. In January 2001, the statutory interpretation endorsed by the Opinion was rejected by a federal district court.[16] The Eastern District of Louisiana took the position

F.3d 449 (2d Cir.1995). *Cf. United States v. Jenkins*, 943 F.2d 167 (2d Cir.1991), *cert. denied*, 502 U.S. 1014, 112 S.Ct. 659 (holding defendant in violation of Glass–Steagall Act, 12 U.S.C.A. § 378(a), by engaging "in the business of receiving deposits" without proper state or federal authorization by receiving single deposit of $150,000).

13. The Bank Holding Company Act (BHCA) appears to contemplate the existence of depository institutions that are insured by the FDIC even though they do not accept a continuing stream of non-trust deposits from the general public. 12 U.S.C.A. § 1841(c). In the BHCA, the definition of "bank" includes banks insured by the FDIC. *Id*. § 1841(c)(1). A list of exceptions from the BHCA definition of "bank" includes institutions functioning solely in a trust or fiduciary capacity if several conditions are satisfied. However, the conditions related to deposit-taking are, *inter alia*, that all or substantially all of the deposits of the institution must be trust funds, and that

insured deposits of the institution must not be offered through an affiliate. *Id*. § 1841(c)(2)(D)(i), (ii). The first condition provides that all *or substantially all* of the deposits of the institution must be trust funds; the second condition involves "insured deposits". Thus, the BHCA suggests that a trust company— functioning solely as a trust company and holding substantially no deposits except trust deposits—could hold "insured deposits." Hence, the BHCA contemplates (without requiring) that an institution could be insured by the FDIC even though the institution does not accept non-trust deposits from the general public.

14. Examples of past FDIC actions in this regards are discussed in 66 Fed. Reg. 20,102, 20,103 (2001).

15. 65 Fed. Reg. 14,568 (2000).

16. *Heaton v. Monogram Credit Card Bank of Georgia*, 2001 WL 15635 (E.D.La.2001), *reversed*, 297 F.3d 416 (5th Cir.2002).

that the interpretation ignored the statute, because the statute refers to "deposits" in the plural. In the court's opinion, a depository institution could not be "engaged in the business of receiving *deposits* other than trust funds" unless the it maintained more than one deposit account.

In April 2001, the FDIC proposed to replace the Opinion with a regulation,[17] to clarify the requirement. As with the Opinion, the proposed regulation would consider the statutory requirement satisfied by continuous maintenance of one or more non-trust deposit accounts in the aggregate amount of $500,000. The FDIC hoped that the proposed regulation would resolve the ambiguity created by the ongoing litigation in *Heaton v. Monogram Credit Card Bank of Georgia.*[18] The FDIC has since issued the rule in final form.[19] On 8 July 2002, the Fifth Circuit reversed the District Court's decision in *Heaton.*[20]

The second point is illustrated by *Federal Deposit Insurance Corp. v. Philadelphia Gear Corp.,*[21] which considered whether the term "deposit" under the FDIA was sufficiently broad to include a standby letter of credit backed by a contingent promissory note. Both the majority and the dissent in *Philadelphia Gear* acknowledged the very broad language and potential scope of the definition of "deposit" in the FDIA, which as amended, states:

> The term "deposit" means ... the unpaid balance of money or its equivalent received or held by a bank or savings association in the usual course of business and for which it has given or is obligated to give credit, either conditionally or unconditionally, to a commercial, checking, savings, time, or

---

17. 66 Fed. Reg. 20,102 (2001) (to be codified at 12 C.F.R. § 303.14).

18. *Supra* note 17. As to the appropriateness of proposing such a regulation in the face of ongoing litigation, the FDIC argued:

> The FDIC does not agree that the initiation of the rulemaking process would constitute an "abuse of discretion". On the contrary, the FDIC believes that rulemaking is necessary in order to remove the existing uncertainty and confusion. *See Smiley v. Citibank, N.A.,* 517 U.S. 735, 116 S.Ct. 1730 (1996). Accordingly, the FDIC has decided to publish this notice of proposed rulemaking.
>
> Of course, the publication of this notice does not mean that the FDIC necessarily will adopt the proposed rule as a final rule. The FDIC is interested in receiving comments from all interested members of the public—not just the plaintiff and the defendant in the *Heaton* litigation—because the final rule (if any) will be effective nationwide. The comments may address all aspects of the proposed rule.

66 Fed. Reg. at 20,104. No doubt with an eye towards the pending appeal of the *Heaton* decision, the FDIC appended to the publication of its proposed rulemaking General Counsel's Opinion No. 12, which had been repudiated by *Heaton. Id.* at 20,106–20,111.

19. 66 Fed. Reg. 54,645 (2001) (codified at 12 C.F.R. § 303.14) (clarifying meaning of phrase "engaged in the business of receiving deposits other than trust funds" in FDIA).

20. *Heaton, supra* note 17.

21. 476 U.S. 426, 106 S.Ct. 1931 (1986).

thrift account, or which is evidenced by its certificate of deposit, thrift certificate, investment certificate, certificate of indebtedness, or other similar name, or a check or draft drawn against a deposit account and certified by the bank or savings association, or a letter of credit or a traveler's check on which the bank or savings association is primarily liable: Provided, That, without limiting the generality of the term "money or its equivalent", any such account or instrument must be regarded as evidencing the receipt of the equivalent of money when credited or issued in exchange for checks or drafts or for a promissory note upon which the person obtaining any such credit or instrument is primarily or secondarily liable, or for a charge against a deposit account, or in settlement of checks, drafts, or other instruments forwarded to such bank or savings association for collection.[22]

To a significant extent, of course, this definitional concept is circular. At base, "deposit" represents a credit relationship in favor of a person dealing with a bank, "in the usual course of [the bank's] business and for which it has given or is obligated to give credit," but since deposit-taking (along with lending) *is* a bank's usual course of business, this barely delineates the concept. Presumably, "deposit" does not include a bank's account outstanding for window washing services, or for rent on its business premises, or for other similar undertakings. However, any credit created in favor of a person dealing with the bank *qua* bank is potentially within this broad definition.

Philadelphia Gear focused on the "purpose behind the insurance of deposits in general, and especially in the [FDIA] section defining deposits as 'money or its equivalent,' [as] the protection of assets and hard earnings entrusted to a bank."[23] Applying its understanding of the significance of the term "money or its equivalent"—as understood against the background of this purpose—the Court concluded that the "purpose [was] not furthered by extending deposit insurance to cover a standby letter of credit backed by a contingent promissory note, which involves no surrender of assets or hard earnings to the custody of the bank."[24]

Justice Marshall, in a dissenting opinion joined by Justices Blackmun and Rehnquist, acknowledged the "considerable common sense backing the Court's opinion,"[25] but could not find the qualifications that the Court wanted to read into the definition of "deposit" in the statutory language itself.[26] That definition explicitly

---

22. 12 U.S.C.A. § 1813(*l*)(1).

23. *Philadelphia Gear Corp.*, 476 U.S. at 435, 106 S.Ct. at 1936.

24. *Id.*

25. 476 U.S. at 440, 106 S.Ct. at 1939 (Marshall, J., dissenting).

26. 476 U.S. at 440–441, 106 S.Ct. at 1939.

included letters of credit within the scope of the term, and the instruments in question clearly fit within the concepts of a note and a "letter of credit" for purposes of, for example, the Uniform Commercial Code ("UCC").[27]

However, it is misleading to focus on whether or not the instrument involved is governed, as a matter of transactional law, by Article 5 of the UCC.[28] Rather, the question is whether the arrangement represents the kind of obligation or instrument covered by the language of the FDIA definition of "deposit," as informed by its legislative history, which is not necessarily coterminous with its treatment in the UCC in any event.

Beyond these two general considerations, there is a web of technical rules concerning the maximum insurable amount per depositor.[29] In 1999, the FDIC streamlined these rules, and to some extent relaxed them.[30] After legislative deliberations over a period of years, the deposit insurance system was significantly amended in 2006. The Federal Deposit Insurance Reform Act of 2005 (FDIRA)[31] and the Federal Deposit Insurance Reform Conforming Amendments Act of 2005 (FDIRCAA)[32] together brought about a major change in the structure of the insurance system. The principal legislative changes are as follows.

FDIRA § 2102[33] mandated the merger of the Bank Insurance Fund (BIF) and the Savings Association Insurance Fund (SAIF) into a Depository Insurance Fund (DIF).[34] As of March 31, 2006, the FDIC merged the BIF and the SAIF into the new DIF, and the separate existence of the two former funds ceased on the effective date of the merger.[35]

---

27. 476 U.S. at 442, 106 S.Ct. at 1940. *See generally* UCC §§ 3–104(1), 5–117 (dealing with notes and letters of credit, respectively).

28. *Cf. First Empire Bank–New York v. Federal Deposit Ins. Corp.*, 572 F.2d 1361 (9th Cir.1978), *cert. denied*, 439 U.S. 919, 99 S.Ct. 293, *appeal after remand*, 634 F.2d 1222 (9th Cir.1980), *cert. denied*, 452 U.S. 906, 101 S.Ct. 3032 (1981) (dealing with treatment of letters of credit by FDIC in failing bank situation).

29. *See, e.g., Lambert v. FDIC*, 847 F.2d 604 (9th Cir.1988) (discussing limitations on insurable amount of deposit).

30. *See* 64 Fed. Reg. 15,653, 15,656–15,657 (1999) (codified at 12 C.F.R. §§ 330.5(b)(1), 330.10(a), (e)) (recognizing interests of beneficiaries as insurable under certain circumstances).

31. Pub. L. No. 109–171, tit. II, §§ 2101–2109, 120 Stat. 4, 9–21 (Feb. 8, 2006) (FDIRA).

32. Pub. L. No. 109–173, 119 Stat. 3601 (Feb. 15, 2006).

33. 120 Stat. at 9 (codified at 12 U.S.C.A. § 1821 note; 2 U.S.C.A. § 905, 12 U.S.C.A. §§ 24, 338a, 347b, 1431, 1441a, 1441b, 1464, 1467a, 1723i, 1735f–14, 1813, 1815, 1817, 1816, 1821, 1821a, 1823, 1824, 1825, 1827, 1828, 1831a, 1831e, 1831h, 1831m, 1831o, 1833a, 1834, 1841, 3341).

34. FDIRA, § 2102(a)(1) (codified at 12 U.S.C.A. § 1821 note).

35. *Id.* § 2102(a)(3). *See id.* § 2102(c) (establishing effective date). On risk-based assessment rules and procedures with respect to deposit insurance under the DIF, see *id.* §§ 2104–2106, 120 Stat. at 12–16 (codified at 12 U.S.C.A. §§ 1817 note, 1817(b)(1)(E)–

FDIRA § 2103[36] made three important substantive changes to the insurance coverage provisions of the Federal Deposit Insurance Act.[37] First, FDIRA § 2103(a)(2) provided for an inflation index to be applied to the then current maximum deposit insurance amount of $100,000,[38] defined in the act as the "standard maximum deposit insurance amount" (SMDIA).[39] Beginning April 1, 2010, and every succeeding five years, subject to approval by the Board of Directors of the FDIC and the National Credit Union Administration Board, the current SMDIA can be increased by a cost-of-living adjustment.[40] Second, the section provides per-participant coverage to employee benefit plan accounts, even if the depository institution at which the deposits are placed is not authorized to accept employee benefit plan deposits.[41] (The FDIRA eliminates the former requirement that an insured depository institution meet prescribed capital requirements before employee benefit plan deposits accepted by that institution would be eligible for per-participant coverage.) Third, the section increases the deposit insurance limit for "certain retirement accounts" from $100,000 to $250,000, also subject to the inflation adjustment described above.[42]

§ 5.13   Reserve Requirements

With the enactment of section 103 of the Depository Institutions Deregulation and Monetary Control Act of 1980,[1] all depository institutions, including savings associations and credit unions generally became subject to the deposit reserve requirements administered by the Fed.[2] The complex transitional period generally ended in September 1987,[3] so that currently all depository institutions, whether or not federally chartered or insured, became fully subject to the Fed's deposit reserve requirements.

Hence, all depository institutions are currently subject to the

---

(F), 1817(b)(2)(A)–(B), (D), (b)(3), (b)(5), (g), 1828(h)). On deposit insurance reserve ratio requirements, see *id.* §§ 2107–2108, 120 Stat. at 16–20 (codified at 12 U.S.C.A. §§ 1813(y), 1817(b)(3)(E), (e)).

36. *Id.* § 2103, 120 Stat. at 9–12 (codified at 12 U.S.C.A. §§ 1821(a)(1)(B), (D)–(F), (a)(3)(A), 1821 note).

37. 12 U.S.C.A. §§ 1811 *et seq.*

38. FDIRA, § 2103(a)(2) (codified at 12 U.S.C.A. 1821(a)(1)(F)).

39. 12 U.S.C.A. § 1821(a)(1)(E).

40. *Id.* § 1821(a)(1)(F).

41. FDIRA, § 2103(b) (codified at 12 U.S.C.A. 1821(a)(1)(D)).

42. *Id.* § 2103(c) (codified at 12 U.S.C.A. § 1821(a)(3)(A)).

§ 5.13

1. *See* Pub. L. No. 96–221, tit. I, § 103, 94 Stat. 133 (1980) (codified *at* 12 U.S.C.A. § 461(b)), *as amended*, Financial Institutions Reform, Recovery, and Enforcement Act of 1989 ("FIRREA"), Pub. L. No. 101–73, § 744(i)(2), 103 Stat. 183, 439 (1989).

2. *See* 12 U.S.C.A. § 461(b)(1), (b)(2)–(4). *See also* 12 C.F.R. Pt. 204 (setting forth Fed's Regulation D reserve requirements).

3. *See* 12 U.S.C.A. § 461(b)(8). *Cf.* 12 C.F.R. § 204.4.

Fed's Regulation D concerning deposit reserve requirements.[4] These regulations cover the technical issues of computation and maintenance of reserves.[5]

Most issues that might be raised under the reserve requirements have been mechanized outside of the lawyer's normal scope, e.g., the calculation of reserves, which is normally prepared on detailed Fed forms. Nevertheless, there are certain aspects of importance from a legal and policy point of view that should be noted. Foremost among these is the scope of the current reserve requirements. The statutory provisions mandating Fed jurisdiction over reserves of all depository institutions represent a rather dramatic jurisdictional assertion.[6] The provisions sweep within direct federal jurisdiction the reserve requirements applicable to all depository institutions *eligible for* federal deposit insurance, not just those actually insured by the FDIC.[7] However, a state bank that has a direct depositor relationship with the Federal Reserve with respect to required deposit reserves does not thereby have a compensable property interest in earnings or income generated by the Federal Reserve through its open market operations.[8]

Nevertheless, effective 1 October 2011,[9] the Fed is authorized to pay interest on deposit reserves.[10] The Fed also has increased flexibility to establish reserve requirements from 0 percent to 3 percent for the first tranche of total transaction accounts (rather

---

4. 12 C.F.R. Pt. 204.

5. Pursuant to 12 U.S.C.A. § 461(b)(2), the reserve rate is amended before December 31 of each year (usually, in the mid-Fall of each year), to index the specified amounts of total deposits that trigger reserve ratios by reference to an amount equal to 80 percent of the percentage increase or decrease in net transaction accounts at all depository institutions over the one-year period that ends on the June 30 prior to the adjustment. *See, e.g.,* 12 C.F.R. §§ 204.4, as *amended,* 74 Fed. Reg. 52,873 (2009) (codified at 12 C.F.R. § 204.4(f)) (annual indexing of low reserve tranche, from $44.4 million to $55.2 million, and of reserve requirement exemption amount, from $10.3 million to $10.7 million; annual indexing of non-exempt deposit cut-off level, to $243.1 million for 2010., and reduced reporting limit to $1.362 billion for 2010, effective November 16, 2009.). *See also.* 12 C.F.R. §§ 204.5 (maintenance of required reserves), 204.6 (concerning charges for reserve deficiencies); 204.7 (concerning authority to impose supplemental reserve requirements, not currently in use); 204.9 (concerning au-

thority to impose emergency reserve requirements, not currently in use).

6. 12 U.S.C.A. § 461(b)(1)(A), (c).

7. *Id.* § 461(b)(1)(A).

8. *Texas State Bank v. United States,* 423 F.3d 1370, 1379–1380 (Fed. Cir. 2005), *cert. denied,* 547 U.S. 1206, 126 S.Ct. 2889 (2006). Nevertheless, Section 201(a) of the Financial Services Regulatory Relief Act (FSRRA), Pub. L. No. 109–351, 120 Stat. 1966 (2006) (codified at 12 U.S.C.A. § 461(b)(12)), has authorized the Fed to pay interest on reserves. *Cf.* 73 Fed. Reg. 59,482 (Oct. 9, 2008) (codified at 12 C.F.R. § 204.10; removing and reserving § 204.4) (directing Federal Reserve Banks to pay interest on balances held at Reserve Banks to satisfy reserve requirements and on balances held in excess of required reserve balances and clearing balances).

9. Financial Services Regulatory Relief Act, § 203, Pub. L. No. 109–351, 120 Stat. 1966, 1969 (2006) (codified at 12 U.S.C.A. § 461 note).

10. *Id.* § 201(a)–(b), 120 Stat. at 1968–1969 (codified at 12 U.S.C.A. § 461(b)(4)(C)–(D), (b)(12), (c)(1)(A)).

than a required 3 percent) and 0 percent and greater for the second tranche (rather than a required minimum of 8 percent).[11]

§ 5.14   Interest Rates

Traditionally, the rate of interest that depository institutions could pay on deposits was restricted.[1] Pursuant to changes in federal statute beginning in 1980,[2] however, interest rate limitations were gradually eliminated with the transitional process completed by March 31, 1986.[3]

§ 5.15   Brokered Deposits

The practice of brokering deposits, in which an intermediary consolidates funds of prospective depositors and negotiates *en bloc* with a depository institution for a jumbo rate for placement of the consolidated deposit,[1] represents a danger for depository institutions that may be in danger of default. These institutions are particularly vulnerable to overbidding on the consolidated deposits, since they often desperately need the liquidity that the deposits would offer. Since these deposits tend to be particularly rate-sensitive, they are also relatively volatile; they will follow the bidding-up of rates to other institutions, thus leaving the vulnerable depository with an immediate liquidity crisis. As a result, the practice of brokering deposits was also a serious problem for deposit insurers like the FDIC and the now defunct FSLIC.

Attempts to deal with this problem at the regulatory level—for example, by treating such deposits as defined FDIA "deposits" only up to $100,000 per broker—were struck down in *FAIC Securities v. United States*[2] as unauthorized by the statute. In response, the Financial Institutions Reform, Recovery, and Enforcement Act of 1989 ("FIRREA")[3] established a statutory scheme of regulation for brokered deposits,[4] which is essentially based upon supervision of these activities as a matter of "safe and sound banking" under the

---

11. *Id.* § 202, 120 Stat. at 1969 (codified at 12 U.S.C.A. § 461(b)(2)(A)(I)–(ii)).

§ 5.14

1. *See, e.g.,* 12 C.F.R. Pt. 208 (1979) (restricting interest rates under Fed Regulation Q).

2. 12 U.S.C.A. §§ 3501 *et seq.*

3. *Id.* Elimination of interest rate limitation on insured credit union shares was effected by regulatory action by the NCUA in 1982. 47 Fed. Reg. 17,979 (1982) (codified at 12 C.F.R. § 701.35).

§ 5.15

1. For a curious early case involving a "solicitor" of deposits for a national bank, see *Case v. First Nat'l Bank of City of Brooklyn*, 109 N.Y.S. 1119, 59 Misc. 269 (Sup.Ct.1908) (finding the practice permissible, on a one-year basis, under 12 U.S.C.A. § 24 (Third), (Seventh)).

2. 768 F.2d 352 (D.C.Cir.1985).

3. Pub. L. No. 101–73, § 744(i)(2), 103 Stat. 183, 439 (1989) (codified at scattered sections of 12 U.S.C.A.).

4. 12 U.S.C.A. § 1831f.

FDIA,[5] an approach neither tried by the FDIC nor addressed by *FAIC Securities*. The end result is probably the equivalent of the result under the approach invalidated in the case: troubled institutions are excluded from the brokered deposit market.

In the Financial Regulatory Relief and Economic Efficiency Act of 2000,[6] Congress repealed section 29A of the FDIA,[7] which had imposed notification, recordkeeping, and reporting requirements on deposit brokers. In April 2001, the FDIC published a rescission of the regulations implementing § 29A.[8]

Currently, the FDIC rules provide for three distinct tiers of depository institutions within the scheme of regulation of brokered deposits.[9] First, a "well capitalized" insured depository institution (*e.g.*, one with capital equal to at least ten percent of its risk-weighted assets[10]) may solicit and accept, renew or roll over any brokered deposit without restriction.[11]

Second, an "adequately capitalized" insured depository institution (*e.g.*, one with capital equal to eight to ten percent of assets[12]) may not accept, renew or roll over any brokered deposit, unless it has been granted a waiver by the FDIC.[13] However, an adequately capitalized insured depository institution that has been granted a waiver may not pay an effective yield on any such deposit which, at the time the deposit is accepted, renewed or rolled over, exceeds by more than 75 basis points (1) the effective yield paid on deposits of comparable size and maturity in such institution's normal market area for deposits accepted from within its normal market area; or (2) the national rate[14] paid on deposits of comparable size and

---

5. 12 U.S.C.A. § 1818(b).

6. Pub. L. 106–569, Title XII, § 1203, 114 Stat. 2944 (2000).

7. 12 U.S.C.A. § 1831f–1 (1999).

8. 66 Fed. Reg. 17,621 (2001) (rescinding 12 C.F.R. § 337.6(e)).

9. 12 C.F.R. § 337.6.

10. *See id.* §§ 325.103(b)(1), 337.6(a)(3)(i) (discussing "well capitalized" institution).

11. *Id.* § 337.6(b)(1).

12. *Id.* §§ 325.103(b)(2), 337.6(a)(3)(i).

13. *Id.* § 337.6(b)(2)(i). Waivers are available on a case-by-case basis, as follows:

The FDIC may, on a case-by-case basis and upon application by an adequately capitalized insured depository institution, waive the prohibition on the acceptance, renewal or rollover of brokered deposits upon a finding that such acceptance, renewal or rollover does not constitute an unsafe or unsound practice with respect to such institution. The FDIC may conclude that it is not unsafe or unsound and may grant a waiver when the acceptance, renewal or rollover of brokered deposits is determined to pose no undue risk to the institution. Any waiver granted may be revoked at any time by written notice to the institution.

Id. § 337.6(c).

14. For these purposes, the national rate is considered to be:

(1) 120 percent of the current yield on similar maturity U.S. Treasury obligations; or

(2) In the case of any deposit at least half of which is uninsured, 130 percent of such applicable yield.

Id. § 337.6(b)(2)(ii).

maturity for deposits accepted outside the institution's normal market area.[15]

Third, an "undercapitalized" insured depository institution (*e.g.*, one with capital equal to less than eight percent of assets[16]) may not accept, renew or roll over any brokered deposit.[17] An undercapitalized insured depository institution may not solicit deposits by offering an effective yield that exceeds by more than 75 basis points the prevailing effective yields on insured deposits of comparable maturity in its normal market area, or in the market area in which the deposits are being solicited.[18] In June 2009, the FDIC amended its regulations relating to the interest rate restrictions that apply to insured depository institutions that are not well capitalized.[19] As amended, the regulations generally permit such an institution to offer a "national rate" plus 75 basis points. The "national rate" will be defined, for deposits of similar size and maturity, as the simple average of rates paid by all insured depository institutions and branches for which data are available. For those cases in which the FDIC determines that the national rate as published on the FDIC Web site does not represent the prevailing rate in a particular market as indicated by available evidence, the institution will be permitted to offer the prevailing rate in that market plus 75 basis points. The amendment was effective on January 1, 2010.[20]

§ 5.16 Tying Arrangements

As noted previously,[1] the anti-tying provisions prohibit involuntary tying of bank products and services in specified instances. In addition, the provisions prohibit a bank that maintains a correspondent account in the name of another bank from making an extension of credit to an executive officer or director of, or to a significant insider of,[2] the other bank, or to any related interest of such person, except on specified conditions.[3] The extension of credit must be made on substantially the same terms (including interest

---

15. *Id.* § 337.6(b)(2)(ii)(A)–(B).

16. *Id.* § 325.103(b)(3), 337.6(a)(3)(i).

17. *Id.* § 337.6(b)(3)(i).

18. *Id.* § 337.6(b)(3)(ii).

19. 74 Fed. Reg. 27,679 (2009) (codified at § 337.6(b)(2)(ii)(B), (e); removing § 337.6(b)(4)).

20. 74 Fed. Reg. at 27,679.

§ 5.16

1. *See supra* § 5.9 (discussing anti-tying provisions as applied to lending activities).

2. The statutory formulation for this "significant insider" is "any person who directly or indirectly or acting through or in concert with one or more persons owns, controls, or has the power to vote more than 10 per centum of any class of voting securities of, such other bank." 12 U.S.C.A. § 1972(2)(A).

3. *Id.* § 1972(2)(A).

rates and collateral requirements) as those prevailing at the time for comparable transactions with other persons.[4] In addition, the extension of credit may not involve more than the normal risk of repayment or present other unfavorable features.[5]

Furthermore, a bank is generally prohibited from opening a correspondent account at another bank, if the other bank has an outstanding extension of credit in favor of an executive officer or director of, or significant insider of, the bank wishing to open the account, or to any related interest of such person.[6] Again, the opening of the correspondent account will be permitted if the existing extension of credit was made on substantially the same terms (including interest rates and collateral requirements) as those prevailing at the time for comparable transactions with other persons, and the credit does not involve more than the normal risk of repayment or present other unfavorable features.[7]

Civil money penalties may be assessed for violation of these prohibitions of the anti-tying provisions.[8] The civil money penalty provision does not itself create a private right of action.[9] However, private civil actions for treble damages[10] and injunctive relief against threatened loss or damage[11] are authorized elsewhere in the anti-tying provisions.

§ 5.17 Guarantees and Letters of Credit

It may be reasonably argued that the regulatory law and lore surrounding the treatment of third-party guarantees and letters of credit represent the triumph of form over substance. Starting with the proposition that national banks lacked the statutory authority to issue third-party guarantees,[1] the courts and the regulators have fashioned a series of end-runs and near-misses around this proposition, which typically continues to be cited as a starting point for analysis. The trend in the cases appears to suggest that, even if a transaction is for all economic purposes a third-party guarantee, calling it something else (*e.g.*, a standby letter of credit) will suffice

---

4. *Id.* § 1972(2)(A).

5. *Id.*

6. *Id.* § 1972(2)(B). *See also id.* § 1972(2)(D).

7. *Id.* § 1972(2)(B).

8. *Id.* § 1972(2)(F).

9. *Baggett v. First Nat'l Bank of Gainesville*, 117 F.3d 1342 (11th Cir. 1997).

10. 12 U.S.C.A. § 1975.

11. *Id.* § 1976.

§ 5.17

1. *See, e.g., Federal Intermediate Credit Bank of Omaha v. L'Herisson*, 33 F.2d 841 (8th Cir.1929) (holding national bank may not lend its credit); *Border Nat'l Bank of Eagle Pass, Tex. v. American Nat'l Bank of San Francisco*, 282 F. 73 (5th Cir.1922), *error dismissed and cert. denied*, 260 U.S. 732, 43 S.Ct. 96 (noting that guaranty by national bank is *ultra vires*); *C.E. Healey & Son v. Stewardson Nat'l Bank*, 285 Ill.App. 290, 1 N.E.2d 858 (1936) (finding no power in national bank to guarantee).

to escape the basic proposition that third-party guarantees are unauthorized.

§ 5.18 Guarantees

The judicial treatment of third-party guarantees exhibits much ambiguity and is generally unsatisfying from an analytical point of view. Since the courts originally decided that national banks lacked the power to issue third-party guarantees,[1] the project of the case law developments has generally been to find ways to back away from that position. Hence, the courts are often quite willing to distinguish the arrangement under consideration from a forbidden third-party guarantee—even when "guarantee" language is explicitly used by the bank, as in *Border National Bank of Eagle Pass, Texas v. American National Bank of San Francisco*.[2]

While the proposition that national banks cannot issue third-party guarantees is often stated quite baldly, it is in fact subject to many refinements and qualifications. Thus, a guaranty issued by a bank in the furtherance of its own rights or incidental to a transaction in which it has an interest is authorized.[3] Guarantees may also be validly issued in favor of a failing bank in order to protect the banking business of the guaranteeing banks.[4] Likewise, a national bank may indorse or guarantee negotiable paper in connection with its transfer or discount,[5] in the ordinary course of the bank's business.[6]

Current regulatory policy expressly permits the use of third-party guarantees, whether styled as a guaranty, surety on an

§ 5.18

1. *See, e.g., Federal Intermediate Credit Bank of Omaha v. L'Herisson*, 33 F.2d 841 (8th Cir.1929) (holding national bank may not lend its credit); *Border Nat'l Bank of Eagle Pass, Tex. v. American Nat'l Bank of San Francisco*, 282 F. 73 (5th Cir.1922), *error dismissed and cert. denied*, 260 U.S. 732, 43 S.Ct. 96 (noting that guaranty by national bank is *ultra vires*); *C.E. Healey & Son v. Stewardson Nat'l Bank*, 285 Ill.App. 290, 1 N.E.2d 858 (1936) (finding no power in national bank to guarantee).

2. *Border Nat'l Bank, supra. See also Federal Deposit Ins. Corp. v. Freudenfeld*, 492 F.Supp. 763 (E.D.Wis.1980) (finding that letter of credit, even if impermissible guaranty, can only be challenged by federal government).

3. *Second Nat'l Bank of Parkersburg, W. Va. v. U.S. Fidelity & Guar. Co.*, 266 F. 489 (4th Cir.1920), *appeal dismissed*, 254 U.S. 660, 41 S.Ct. 10;

Dunn v. McCoy, 113 F.2d 587 (3d Cir. 1940); *American Nat'l Bank v. National Wall–Paper Co.*, 77 F. 85 (8th Cir.1896).

4. *McCoy v. Adams*, 29 F.Supp. 815 (E.D.Pa.1939).

5. *People's Bank v. Manufacturers' Nat'l Bank*, 101 U.S. (11 Otto) 181 (1879); *Farmers' & Miners' Bank v. Bluefield Nat'l Bank*, 11 F.2d 83 (4th Cir.1926), *cert. denied*, 271 U.S. 669, 46 S.Ct. 483; *Hanover Nat'l Bank v. First Nat'l Bank of Burlingame*, 109 F. 421 (8th Cir.1901); *Bowen v. Needles Nat'l Bank*, 94 F. 925 (9th Cir.1899), *cert. denied*, 176 U.S. 682, 20 S.Ct. 1024 (1900); *Commercial Nat'l Bank v. Pirie*, 82 F. 799 (8th Cir.1897).

6. *Barron v. McKinnon*, 179 F. 759 (C.C.D.Mass.1910) (finding guarantee not in ordinary course of business of banking).

indemnity bond, or otherwise, subject to certain conditions.[7] The national bank must have a substantial interest in the performance of the underlying transaction involved,[8] or the transaction must be for the benefit of a customer from whom the bank obtains a segregated deposit sufficient to cover the bank's total potential liability.[9] In addition, a national bank is permitted to guarantee obligations of a customer, subsidiary or affiliate that are financial in character, provided that the amount of the bank's obligation is "reasonably ascertainable and otherwise consistent with applicable law."[10] Essentially, these conditions create a situation likely to enhance the safety and soundness of a bank's practice in issuing third-party guarantees.

§ 5.19   Documentary Letters of Credit

Issuance and confirmation of documentary letters of credit are incidental powers of a bank in which the transaction itself is governed by state law. Currently, Article 5 of the Uniform Commercial Code covers these transactions.[1] These activities are permissible even if the bank has characterized what it is doing as a "guaranty."[2] The primary regulatory concern here is that the bank's practices in issuing and confirming letters of credit are conducted in a safe and sound manner.[3]

§ 5.20   Standby Letters of Credit

Standby letters of credit operate, in terms of their economic reality, are third-party guarantees, yet to the extent they are structured as letters of credit, they share the legal treatment of

---

7. 12 C.F.R. § 7.1017.

8. 12 C.F.R. § 7.1017(a)(1).

9. *Id.* § 7.1017(a)(2). The segregated deposit can include collateral consisting of cash or specified liquid securities in which the bank has perfected its security interest and which has a market value, at the close of each business day, equal to the bank's total potential liability. Id. § 7.1017(a)(2)(i)–(ii)(A)–(D). Alternatively, it should have a market value, at the close of each business day, equal to 110 percent of the bank's exposure and be composed of obligations of a state or political subdivision of a state. *Id.* § 7.1017(a)(2)(iii).

10. *Id.* § 7.1017(b).

§ 5.19

1. *Prudential Ins. Co. of Am. v. Marquette Nat'l Bank of Minneapolis*, 419 F.Supp. 734 (D.Minn.1976). *See also*

American Ins. Ass'n v. Clarke, 865 F.2d 278, 282 (D.C.Cir.1988) (discussing characteristics of letters of credit as incidental activities of national banks); *United Bank Ltd. v. Cambridge Sporting Goods Corp.*, 41 N.Y.2d 254, 360 N.E.2d 943, 392 N.Y.S.2d 265 (1976) (discussing documentary letters of credit under applicable state law); *Maurice O'Meara Co. v. National Park Bank of New York*, 239 N.Y. 386, 146 N.E. 636 (1925) (same).

2. *Border Nat'l Bank of Eagle Pass, Tex. v. American Nat'l Bank of San Francisco*, 282 F. 73 (5th Cir.1922), *error dismissed and cert. denied*, 260 U.S. 732, 43 S.Ct. 96.

3. 12 C.F.R. § 7.1016(b).

documentary letters of credit.[1] Because of their dual nature as functional guarantees and as letters of credit, standby letters of credit raise some peculiar issues concerning their proper treatment for regulatory purposes; this problem is discussed in Chapter 9, *infra*.[2]

§ 5.21   Real Property

The power of banks to hold real property, aside from a headquarters and branches, was traditionally limited because of concerns about the need for liquidity, the dangers of land speculation, and the fear of large aggregations of economic power that banks' control of land naturally exacerbated in an agrarian society.[1] An additional complication for national banks arose from the fact that the original provision of the NBA dealing with real property[2] did not permit the taking of a mortgage interest in a transaction extending credit, but only to secure a debt previously contracted. Positive authority for real estate holdings did not enter the federal statutes until the 20th century, permitting contemporaneous mortgages under specified conditions.[3]

However, courts resisted voiding of lending transactions on the basis of the existence of an impermissible mortgage, instead limiting the remedy of voidability to the chartering authority.[4] *Ultra vires* notwithstanding, where a bank has already enjoyed the benefits of an executed real estate transaction—*e.g.*, occupation of leased premises—the courts have had little difficulty in requiring payment by the bank for the benefit received.[5]

The original NBA provision, as amended, generally limits the power of a national bank to purchase, own, and convey real property to the following specified purposes: (1) It may do so to the extent "necessary for its accommodation in the transaction of its

§ 5.20

1. *Legality of Guaranty Letters of Credit*, [1974 Transfer Binder] Fed. Banking L. Rep. (CCH) ¶ 96,301 (July 1, 1974); *American Ins. Ass'n v. Clarke*, 865 F.2d 278, 282 (D.C.Cir.1988) (comparing documentary and standby letters of credit); *Federal Deposit Ins. Corp. v. Freudenfeld*, 492 F.Supp. 763 (E.D.Wis. 1980) (discussing standby letters of credit).

2. *See infra* § 9.21 (discussing regulatory policy concerning standby letters of credit).

§ 5.21

1. *Union National Bank v. Matthews*, 98 U.S. (8 Otto) 621, 626 (1878); *First Nat'l Bank of Bellaire v. Comptrol-*

ler of the Currency, 697 F.2d 674, 681 (5th Cir.1983) (quoting *Matthews*).

2. 12 U.S.C.A. § 29. For a modern case interpreting and applying this provision, see *First Nat'l Bank of Bellaire*, *supra*.

3. 12 U.S.C.A. § 371.

4. *Kerfoot v. Farmers' & Merchants' Bank*, 218 U.S. 281, 31 S.Ct. 14 (1910); *National Bank v. Whitney*, 103 U.S. (13 Otto) 99 (1880); *Matthews, supra*.

5. *Houston v. Drake*, 97 F.2d 863 (9th Cir.1938).

business.''[6] (2) It may accept mortgages on real property ''in good faith by way of security for debts previously contracted.''[7] (3) It may accept conveyance of real estate ''in satisfaction of debts previously contracted in the course of its dealings.''[8] (4) It may purchase real estate at sales, ''under judgments, decrees, or mortgages held by [it], or [it may] purchase to secure debts due to it.''[9]

By its own terms, these provisions give no authority for taking of a mortgage contemporaneous with the making of a real estate loan. Furthermore, under these provisions, national banks are generally not permitted to hold any real estate under mortgage, or the title and possession of any real estate purchased to secure any debts due to it, for longer than five years.[10]

This restrictive situation is ameliorated by a provision of the Federal Reserve Act (''FRA'') dealing with real estate loans.[11] Among other things, the FRA authorizes national banks to make real estate loans secured by liens on interests in real estate, subject to any requirements that the Comptroller may prescribe.[12] The Comptroller has consolidated regulatory provisions drawing on the authority of both the NBA and the FRA provision.[13]

§ 5.22   Trust Powers

Approval of the formation of a commercial bank does not necessarily include an inherent grant of authority to engage in trust activities. Under one statutory model, this authority must be

---

6. 12 U.S.C.A. § 29 (First).

7. *Id.* § 29 (Second).

8. *Id.* § 29 (Third).

9. *Id.* § 29 (Fourth).

10. *Id.* § 29. However, upon application, the Comptroller may approve possession of such real property for a longer period, not to exceed an additional five years, if one of the following conditions is met: (1) the bank must have made a good faith attempt to dispose of the real property within the original five-year period; or, (2) disposal of the real property within the original five-year period would be detrimental to the bank. *Id.* § 29(1)–(2). The Comptroller may also approve expenditure of funds by the bank for the development and improvement of the property, subject to conditions and limitations imposed by the Comptroller in his discretion. *Id.* § 29. Limited grandfathering of certain property holdings is also provided, as follows:

Notwithstanding the five-year holding limitation of this section or any other provision of this chapter, any national [bank that] on October 15, 1982, held, directly or indirectly, real estate, including any subsurface rights or interests therein, that since December 31, 1979, had not been valued on the books of such association for more than a nominal amount, may continue to hold such real estate, rights, or interests for such longer period of time as would be permitted a State chartered bank by the law of the State in which the association is located if the aggregate amount of earnings from such real estate, rights, or interests is separately disclosed in the annual financial statements of the association.

Id.

11. 12 U.S.C.A. § 371.

12. *Id.* § 371(a).

13. 12 C.F.R. §§ 5.37 (requiring application for investment in bank premises); 7.1000 (providing interpretive guidance with respect to national bank ownership of property).

specifically granted by the chartering authority.[1] Other statutes may authorize exercise of such powers by either a bank or trust company at the applicant's option, subject to approval by the appropriate regulator,[2] or by a bank or trust company limited to fiduciary activities.[3] Nevertheless, most commercial banks apply for and obtain those powers, typically incorporating the trust activities within a trust department or division of the bank itself.

For national banks, the NBA authorizes the Comptroller to grant trust powers to national banks.[4] The NBA limits the availability of trust powers for national banks by reference over to state law; the Comptroller may only grant trust powers if, and to the extent that, the state of a national bank's locality permits such powers to state-chartered entities.[5] In passing upon applications for trust powers, the Comptroller may consider the following factors: (1) the amount of capital and surplus of the applicant bank;[6] (2) the needs of the community to be served;[7] and, (3) any other facts and circumstances that seem appropriate to the Comptroller.[8]

In the 1970s, the OCC initiated a policy of chartering a national bank limited to the exercise of trust powers only, and the policy was challenged as outside the authority of the Comptroller under the NBA.[9] However, in the interim, Congress amended the NBA specifically to ratify such charters.[10] Hence, it is now clear that national banks limited to trust powers may be chartered by

---

§ 5.22

1. *See, e.g.,* 12 U.S.C.A. § 92a (authorizing approval of trust powers for national bank).

2. Cal. Fin. Code §§ 1500, 1500.1 (specifying prerequisites for engaging in trust business).

3. 12 U.S.C.A. § 27; N.Y. Banking Law §§ 94, 96.

4. 12 U.S.C.A. § 92a(a).

5. *Id. See St. Louis County Nat'l Bank v. Mercantile Trust Co. Nat'l Ass'n*, 548 F.2d 716 (8th Cir.1976), *cert. denied*, 433 U.S. 909, 97 S.Ct. 2975 (1977) (applying "local law" requirement); *American Trust Co., Inc. v. South Carolina State Bd. of Bank Control*, 381 F.Supp. 313 (D.S.C.1974) (discussing "local law" requirement).

6. 12 U.S.C.A. § 92a(i). Specifically, the Comptroller may consider "whether or not such capital and surplus is sufficient under the circumstances of the case...." *Id.* Despite the permissive tone of the language of Section 92a(i),

the Comptroller is specifically prohibited from issuing a trust powers permit "to any national [bank] having a capital and surplus less than the capital and surplus required by State law of State banks, trust companies, and corporations exercising such powers." *Id.*

7. *Id.*

8. *Id.* For discussion of the Comptroller's implementing regulations, see 1 Michael P. Malloy, Banking Law and Regulation § 2.2.4.1 (1994 & Cum. Supp.).

9. *National State Bank of Elizabeth, N.J. v. Smith*, 591 F.2d 223 (3d Cir. 1979).

10. Pub. L. No. 95–630, § 1504, 92 Stat. 3713 (1978) (codified at 12 U.S.C.A. § 27(a)), which provided that

A [national bank], to which the Comptroller of the Currency has heretofore issued or hereafter issues [a] certificate [of authority to commence banking], is not illegally constituted solely because its operations are or have been required by the Comptroller of the Currency to be limited to those of

the OCC.[11] Charter applications for such banks resemble those for any *de novo* national bank.

The trust activities of commercial banks are governed by principles of the law of trusts, as they would affect any fiduciary. Overlaying the operation of these principles, however, is a system of federal regulation of trust activities.[12] The Comptroller will in the first instance supervise and examine the trust departments and activities of national banks;[13] the Fed will do the same for state member banks,[14] the FDIC for state nonmember insured banks,[15] and the OTS for savings associations.[16]

§ 5.23   Incidental Powers

Since state-chartered insured banks are significantly limited in their activities to those permissible for national banks,[1] the scope of national bank incidental powers has become increasingly important for all participants in the depository institutions industry.[2] The concept of incidental powers, in fact, serves as the authority for many traditional banking activities.

With ever greater frequency, however, it is also the basis for many nontraditional activities. There are certain inherent analytical difficulties here. In large part, what constitutes a "traditional" banking activity for these purposes is whatever banks have historically done, beyond the core functions of deposit-taking and lending. Attempts can be made to organize this group of activities under a generic concept such as "incidental powers," but problems arise in that regard.

a trust company and activities related thereto.

11. *Cf.* OCC Trust Interpretation No. 175, *reprinted in*, [1988–1989 Transfer Binder] Fed. Banking L. Rep. (CCH) ¶ 84,942 (Oct. 21, 1988) (concerning separation of national bank's trust department into national trust company); OCC Interpretive Letter No. 436, *reprinted in*, [1988–1989 Transfer Binder] Fed. Banking L. Rep. (CCH) & 85,660 (Aug. 19, 1988) (permitting establishment of limited national trust company affiliated with investment adviser and registered broker-dealer).

12. For a case exploring this overlay of state substantive law and federal supervisory rules, see *Humane Soc'y of Austin and Travis County v. Austin Nat'l Bank*, 531 S.W.2d 574 (Tex.1975), *cert. denied*, 425 U.S. 976, 96 S.Ct. 2177 (1976).

13. 12 C.F.R. Pt. 9.

14. *See, e.g.*, Board of Governors, Division of Banking Supervision and Regulation, Memorandum SR–83–2 (SA) (Jan. 11, 1983), *reprinted in*, 4 Fed. Banking L. Rep. (CCH) ¶ 37–659.

15. 12 C.F.R. Pt. 330.

16. 12 C.F.R. Pt. 550.

§ 5.23

1. 12 U.S.C.A. § 1831a.

2. On incidental powers of federal credit unions (FCUs), see 12 U.S.C.A. § 1757(17). *See also* American Bankers Association v. Connell, 447 F.Supp. 296, 298 (D.D.C.1978) (applying national bank test for determining incidental powers to FCUs), *citing* Arnold Tours, Inc. v. Camp, 472 F.2d 427 (1st Cir. 1972). *Cf.* 65 Fed. Reg. 70,526 (2000) (to be codified at 12 C.F.R. §§ 721.1–721.7) (proposing NCUA revised rules to categorize activities deemed within incidental powers of FCU).

First of all, it is not at all clear that certain traditional banking powers necessarily fit under this concept at all. (For example, is the issuance of letters of credit an "incidental power?" Trust activities?) Second, in its contemporary guise, the "incidental powers" approach has resulted in the prospective addition of new powers that are in no realistic sense banking powers at all.

The "incidental powers" concept has often been used as the justification for the prospective addition of new powers that we might not think of intuitively as banking powers. Yet, in the framework of the NBA,[3] incidental powers could be viewed as a natural and integral part of banking powers. Indeed, if we take seriously the notion that a bank is a creature of its enabling statute, so that "powers not conferred . . . are denied,"[4] then we must find a way to locate "new" powers within the statutory concept of incidental powers.

An initial question concerns the character of the incidental powers provision. Is it a limiting concept, or an enabling concept? Early cases seem to be ambiguous on this issue.[5] One might suggest that a court inclined towards a "limiting" characterization is more likely to withhold power, particularly for an activity that is not historically one performed by banks, whereas a court that is inclined towards an "enabling" characterization may be more likely to recognize a power.[6] Yet cases that speak of incidental powers as those "convenient and useful in connection with the performance of one of [a] bank's established activities" may just as well refuse to recognize a particular activity as an incidental power.[7] Similarly, is there a practical difference between the view that an incidental power must be directly related to an express power,[8] and one that insists that an incidental power may simply be convenient and useful in connection with established activities?[9]

The fact is that none of the formulations of the incidental powers concept that float through the cases has added any precision

---

3. 12 U.S.C.A. § 24 (Seventh).

4. *Texas & Pac. Ry. v. Pottorff*, 291 U.S. 245, 253, 54 S.Ct. 416, 417 (1934), *amended sub nom. Texas & Pac. Ry. v. First Nat'l Bank of El Paso, Tex.*, 291 U.S. 649, 54 S.Ct. 525, *reh'g denied sub nom. Texas & Pac. Ry. v. Pottorff*, 292 U.S. 600, 54 S.Ct. 627.

5. *See, e.g., First Nat'l Bank v. National Exch. Bank*, 92 U.S. (2 Otto) 122 (1875) (finding incidental power to compromise contested claim, while speaking of incidental powers concept as limiting).

6. *See, e.g., M & M Leasing Corp. v. Seattle First Nat'l Bank*, 563 F.2d 1377 (9th Cir.1977), *cert. denied*, 436 U.S. 956, 98 S.Ct. 3069 (1978) (upholding lease financing as incidental power, with certain exceptions).

7. *See, e.g., Arnold Tours, Inc. v. Camp*, 472 F.2d 427 (1st Cir.1972) (disapproving operation of travel agency under incidental powers doctrine).

8. *See, e.g., Arnold Tours, Inc., supra* (using both the "directly related" and the "convenient and useful" formulations).

9. *See, e.g., M & M Leasing Corp., supra* (upholding lease financing as incidental power, while citing *Arnold Tours* with approval).

to what is essentially a case-by-case inquiry. *Arnold Tours, Inc. v. Camp*[10] clears away some of the underbrush by providing some relatively unprovocative examples of incidental powers, but it speaks successively about the incidental powers concept as "directly related to one or another of a national bank's express powers,"[11] as bearing a "great similarity" to an express power,[12] and as "virtually identical to" an express power.[13] Obviously, these varying formulations could lead to rather different results in a close case.

Ultimately, each of these formulations leads us back to the same question: what is the power incidental *to*, or "directly related *to*," or bearing a "great similarity *to*," or "virtually identical *to*"? The short answer is "the business of banking."[14] But what is the "business of banking" for these purposes? The long answer, or one version, is presented by *M & M Leasing Corp. v. Seattle First National Bank.*[15] The business of banking is *represented* by the series of express powers mentioned in the same section of the NBA,[16] but this does not necessarily freeze banking powers in a single historical moment. Opting for a fluid approach that seeks to identify functional equivalence between express statutory powers and challenged incidental powers, the court noted:

> [T]he National Bank Act did not freeze the practices of national banks in their nineteenth century forms.... [W]hatever the scope of [incidental] powers may be, we believe the powers of national banks must be construed so as to permit the use of new ways of conducting the very old business of banking.[17]

"Functional equivalence" or "interchangeability" would appear to open up incidental powers analysis to include a connection between an express power and an asserted incidental power based, not on a weak causal or supportive link between the two ("convenient or useful" to the exercise of the express power), but rather an independent connection of practical equivalence or identity between the two powers.[18]

10. 472 F.2d 427 (1st Cir.1972).

11. *Id.* at 431.

12. *Id.*

13. *Id.* at 432.

14. 12 U.S.C.A. § 24 (Seventh).

15. 563 F.2d 1377 (9th Cir.1977), *cert. denied*, 436 U.S. 956, 98 S.Ct. 3069 (1978).

16. 12 U.S.C.A. § 24 (Seventh). *See NationsBank of North Carolina, N.A. v. Variable Annuity Life Ins. Co.*, 513 U.S. 251, 115 S.Ct. 810 (1995) (interpreting express powers mentioned in § 24 (Seventh) as not exclusive).

17. *M & M Leasing Corp.*, 563 F.2d at 1382.

18. *See, e.g., NationsBank of North Carolina, N.A., supra* (reading "business of banking" in NBA as open-ended term of art, to be fleshed out through functional analysis); *American Ins. Ass'n v. Clarke*, 865 F.2d 278 (D.C.Cir.1988) (suggesting "functional equivalence" test for incidental powers). The *Clarke* opinion rejects the "convenient or useful" formulation of the test of incidental powers as being "a narrow and artificially rigid view of both the business of banking and the [NBA]." *Id.* at 281. To the contrary, the opinion recognizes the

To the extent that incidental powers analysis remains a case-by-case inquiry, Figure 5–3, *infra*, is an illustrative, selective list of activities held to be within the incidental powers concept.

Figure 5–3

Incidental Powers: Selected Examples

Incidental Power	*Authority*
Acceptance of assignment of judgment for collection	*Miller v. King*, 223 U.S. 505, 32 S.Ct. 243 (1912).
Agent for depositor or customer	*Wylie v. Northampton Nat'l Bank*, 119 U.S. 361, 7 S.Ct. 268 (1886); *Brooklyn Nat'l Bank of New York v. Keystone Bond & Mortgage Co.*, 150 Misc. 571, 268 N.Y.S. 485 (N.Y.Sup.1933); *Bock v. First Nat'l Bank*, 123 Kan. 304, 255 P. 68 (1927).[19]
Annuities, variable, sale of	*NationsBank of North Carolina, N.A. v. Variable Annuity Life Ins. Co.*, 513 U.S. 251, 115 S.Ct. 810 (1995).
Assignment or sale of judgment	*Emory v. Joice*, 70 Mo. 537 (1879).
Bill of lading, purchase of	*Citizens' Bank & Trust Co. v. Harpeth Nat'l Bank of Franklin*, 120 Miss. 505, 82 So. 329 (1919).[20]
Borrowing	*Wyman v. Wallace*, 201 U.S. 230, 26 S.Ct. 495 (1906); *Frenzer v. Wallace*, 201 U.S. 244, 26 S.Ct. 498 (1906); *Aldrich v. Chemical Nat'l Bank*, 176 U.S. 618, 20 S.Ct. 498 (1900); *Auten v. U.S. Nat'l Bank*, 174 U.S. 125, 19 S.Ct. 628 (1899).

municipal bond insurance business as an incidental part of the business of banking, because it is "sufficiently similar to credit services routinely performed by banks," *id*. at 282, and is "functionally equivalent to the issuance of a standby letter of credit, a device long recognized as within the business of banking." *Id*.

19. *But cf. Pollock v. Lumbermen's Nat'l Bank of Portland*, 86 Or. 324, 168 P. 616 (1917) (denying power to negoti-

ate loan for another); *Hotchkin v. Third Nat'l Bank of Syracuse*, 219 Mass. 234, 106 N.E. 974 (1914) (acting as broker for sale of stock *ultra vires*).

20. *But cf. First Nat'l Bank of Mifflintown v. First Nat'l Bank of New Kensington*, 247 Pa. 40, 92 A. 1076 (1915) (finding no power to purchase bills of lading, in contrast to purchase of sight drafts).

Incidental Power	*Authority*
Borrowing, Interbank	*Armstrong v. Chemical Nat'l Bank*, 83 F. 556 (6th Cir. 1897).
Certification of checks	*Merchants' Nat'l Bank v. State Nat'l Bank*, 77 U.S. (10 Wall.) 604 (1870); *Fidelity & Deposit Co. of Md. v. National Bank of Commerce of Dallas*, 48 Tex.Civ.App. 301, 106 S.W. 782 (1907) (limiting power).
Charge-backs	*Bryant v. Williams*, 16 F.2d 159 (E.D.N.C.1926).
Check protection	*Thompson v. St. Nicholas Nat'l Bank*, 113 N.Y. 325, 21 N.E. 57 (1889), *aff'd*, 146 U.S. 240, 13 S.Ct. 66 (1892).
Collection of judgment on behalf of depositor	*Miller v. King*, 223 U.S. 505, 32 S.Ct. 243 (1912).
Collection of negotiable instruments	*Logan County Nat'l Bank v. Townsend*, 139 U.S. 67, 11 S.Ct. 496 (1891); *Brandenburg v. First Nat'l Bank of Casselton*, 48 N.D. 176, 183 N.W. 643 (1921); *Hanson v. Heard*, 69 N.H. 190, 38 A. 788 (1897).
Compromise of debts	*First Nat'l Bank v. National Exchange Bank*, 92 U.S. (2 Otto) 122 (1875).
Data processing services	*National Retailers Corp. of Ariz. v. Valley Nat'l Bank of Ariz.*, 604 F.2d 32 (9th Cir. 1979) (limiting services).
Debt cancellation contracts	*First Nat'l Bank of Eastern Ark. v. Taylor*, 907 F.2d 775 (8th Cir.1990), *cert. denied*, 498 U.S. 972, 111 S.Ct. 442.
Debt, evidences of, sale of	*First Nat'l Bank v. Hartford*, 273 U.S. 548, 47 S.Ct. 462 (1927).
Electronic interbank communications systems, operation of	*State of Oklahoma ex rel. State Banking Bd. v. Bank of Okla.*, 409 F.Supp. 71 (N.D.Okla.1975).
Financial advice	*Norwest Bank of Minn. Nat'l Ass'n v. Sween Corp.*, 916 F.Supp. 1494 (D.Minn.1996), *aff'd in part and remanded*

Incidental Power	*Authority*
	in part, *118 F.3d 1255 (8th Cir.1997)*.
Individual Retirement Accounts, management of	*Investment Co. Inst. v. Clarke*, 793 F.2d 220 (9th Cir.1986), *cert. denied*, 479 U.S. 939, 107 S.Ct. 422.
Investment securities, purchase and sale of	*City Nat'l Bank v. McCann*, 193 Ark. 967, 106 S.W.2d 195 (1937).
Lease financing	*M & M Leasing Corp. v. Seattle First Nat'l Bank*, 563 F.2d 1377 (9th Cir.1977), *cert. denied*, 436 U.S. 956, 98 S.Ct. 3069 (1978).[21]
Mortgage, agreements and compromises concerning	*Morris v. Third Nat'l Bank*, 142 F. 25 (8th Cir.1905), *cert. denied*, 201 U.S. 649, 26 S.Ct. 762 (1906); *Guth v. First Nat'l Bank*, 137 Wash. 280, 242 P. 42 (1926); *Security Nat'l Bank v. Home Nat'l Bank*, 106 Kan. 303, 187 P. 697 (1920).
Mortgage pass-through certificates, sale of	*Securities Indus. Ass'n v. Clarke*, 885 F.2d 1034 (2d Cir.1989), *cert. denied*, 493 U.S. 1070, 110 S.Ct. 1113 (1990).
Mortgage, sale of	*First Nat'l Bank v. Hartford*, 273 U.S. 548, 47 S.Ct. 462 (1927).
Municipal bond insurance	*American Ins. Ass'n v. Clarke*, 656 F.Supp. 404 (D.D.C.1987), *aff'd*, 865 F.2d 278 (D.C.Cir.1988).
Pension fund, creation of	*Heinz v. National Bank of Commerce of St. Louis*, 237 F. 942 (8th Cir.1916).
Pledged property, acceptance of as security	*California Nat. Bank v. Kennedy*, 167 U.S. 362, 17 S.Ct. 831 (1897); *Thompson v. St. Nicholas Nat'l Bank*, 146 U.S. 240, 13 S.Ct. 66 (1892); *Crescent City Nat'l Bank v.*

21. On rules governing leasing activities of national banks, see 12 C.F.R. pt. 23. *See also* 66 Fed. Reg. 8178 (2001) (to be codified at 12 C.F.R. pts. 1, 7, 23) (proposing, *inter alia*, to vary percentage limit on extent to which national banks may rely on estimated residual value to recover costs in personal property leasing arrangements).

Incidental Power	*Authority*
	Case, *99 U.S. (9 Otto) 628 (1878);* Hayward v. Eliot Nat'l Bank, *96 U.S. (6 Otto) 611 (1877);* First Nat'l Bank v. National Exchange Bank, *92 U.S. (2 Otto) 122 (1875).*
Pledged property, sale of	*Merchants' Nat'l Bank v. State Nat'l Bank,* 77 U.S. (10 Wall.) 604 (1870).
Pledged property, transfer of	*U.S. Securities Corp. v. Exchange Nat'l Bank of Shreveport,* 15 La.App. 23, 130 So. 818 (1930).
Pledging assets for deposits	*Lewis v. Fidelity & Deposit Co. of Md.,* 292 U.S. 559, 54 S.Ct. 848 (1934);[22] *Nebraska v. First Nat'l Bank,* 88 F. 947 (C.C.D.Neb.1898).[23]
Real property, maintenance of	*Cooper v. Hill,* 94 F. 582 (8th Cir.1899).
Rediscounting	*Auten v. U.S. Nat'l Bank,* 174 U.S. 125, 19 S.Ct. 628 (1899); *U.S. Nat'l Bank v. First Nat'l Bank,* 79 F. 296 (8th Cir.1897).
Resale of mortgages	*First Nat'l Bank v. City of Hartford,* 273 U.S. 548, 47 S.Ct. 462 (1927).
Safe deposit and other "special deposits"	*Colorado Nat'l Bank of Denver v. Bedford,* 310 U.S. 41, 60 S.Ct. 800 (1940); *First Nat'l Bank of Carlisle, Pa. v. Graham,* 100 U.S. (10 Otto) 699 (1879); *Cooper v. National Bank of Savannah,* 21 Ga. App. 356, 94 S.E. 611 (1917), *aff'd sub nom. Evans v. National Bank of Savannah,* 251 U.S. 108, 40 S.Ct. 58 (1919); *U.S. Shipping Bd. Emcy. Fleet Corp. v. Atlantic Corp.,* 5 F.2d 529 (D.Mass.

22. *But cf. City of Marion, Ill. v. Sneeden,* 291 U.S. 651, 54 S.Ct. 557 (1934) (limiting pledge to public deposits of United States).

23. *But cf. Texas & Pac. Ry. Co. v. Pottorff,* 291 U.S. 245, 54 S.Ct. 416 (1934), *amended sub nom. Texas & Pac. Ry. v. First Nat'l Bank of El Paso, Tex.,* 291 U.S. 649, 54 S.Ct. 525, *reh'g denied sub nom. Texas & Pac. Ry. v. Pottorff,* 292 U.S. 600, 54 S.Ct. 627; *Griffin v. Royall,* 70 F.2d 103 (4th Cir.1934) (same); *Third Nat'l Bank and Trust Co. of Scranton v. McMahon,* 17 F.Supp. 869 (M.D.Pa.1937) (same).

Incidental Power	Authority
	1925), *error dismissed*, 16 F.2d 27 (1st Cir.1926).
Savings deposits, advertisement of	*Franklin Nat'l Bank v. New York*, 347 U.S. 373, 74 S.Ct. 550 (1954).
Seed grain lien, acceptance of	*First Nat'l Bank of Parker v. Peavy Elevator Co.*, 10 S.D. 167, 72 N.W. 402 (S.D. 1897).
Setoff	*Lawrence v. Lincoln County Trust Co.*, 123 Me. 273, 122 A. 765 (1923).[24]
Stock, acquisition of by foreclosure of pledge	*First Nat'l Bank v. Federal Land Bank of Louisville*, 93 Ind.App. 15, 177 N.E. 462 (1931); *McBoyle v. Union Nat'l Bank*, 162 Cal. 277, 122 P. 458 (1911).
Stock, acquisition of in settlement of claim	*First Nat'l Bank v. National Exchange Bank*, 92 U.S. (2 Otto) 122 (1875).
Taxes, payment of on behalf of depositor	*Clement Nat'l Bank v. Vermont*, 231 U.S. 120, 34 S.Ct. 31 (1913).
Thrift bonds, sale of	*Adams v. Compo Bond Corp.*, 282 F. 894 (S.D.N.Y.1922).
Title, warrant of	*Farmers' & Miners' Bank v. Bluefield Nat'l Bank*, 11 F.2d 83 (4th Cir.1926), *cert. denied*, 271 U.S. 669, 46 S.Ct. 483.

Under the incidental powers authority in the Federal Credit Union Act (FCUA), a federal credit union (FCU) may "exercise such incidental powers as shall be necessary or requisite to enable it to carry on effectively the business for which it was incorporated."[25] The NCUA implementing incidental powers rule[26] provides a standard derived from well-established case law for recognizing an activity that constitutes an incidental power. It incorporates into general "preapproved" categories the activities recognized by NCUA legal opinions,[27] and it describes the application process for

24. *But cf. Appleton v. National Park Bank of N.Y.*, 122 Misc. 248, 202 N.Y.S. 516 (N.Y.Sup.1924) (allowing no setoff where subject note not matured). *Contra Parker v. First Nat'l Bank*, 96 Okla. 70, 220 P. 39 (1923).

25. 12 U.S.C.A. § 1775(17).

26. 12 C.F.R. pt. 721.

27. The rule specifically states the examples of activities within each category are provided as illustrations and "not as an exclusive or exhaustive list." 12 C.F.R. § 721.3.

adding new activities and for seeking advisory opinions from the NCUA Office of the General Counsel on the incidental powers status of an activity. Currently recognized categories of FCU incidental powers are identified in Figure 5–4, *infra*.

Figure 5–4
FCU Incidental Powers

Activity	Authority: 12 C.F.R. §
certification services	721.3(a)
correspondent services	721.3(b)
electronic financial services	721.3(c)
excess capacity	721.3(d)
financial counseling services	721.3(e)
finder activities	721.3(f)
loan-related products	721.3(g)
marketing activities	721.3(h)
monetary instrument services	721.3(i)
operational programs	721.3(j)
stored value products	721.3(k)
trustee and custodial services	721.3(*l*)

In May 2008, the NCUA proposed to amend its regulations governing the incidental powers of FCUs by adding illustrations of permissible activities with respect to correspondent services, operational programs, and finder activities.[28] The amendment was adopted in final form, without changes, in October 2008.[29] The amendment was effective November 21, 2008.[30]

§ 5.24 Bank Service Companies

The establishment or acquisition of a bank service company subsidiary or affiliate represents another method by which a bank may diversify into nonbanking activities. Analysis of the authority of the bank to diversify in this fashion under the Bank Service Company Act ("BSCA"),[1] does not differ greatly from that applied

---

28. 73 Fed. Reg. 30,818 (2008) (to be codified at 12 C.F.R. § 721.3(b), (f), (j)).

29. 73 Fed. Reg. 62,854 (Oct. 22, 2008) (codified at 12 C.F.R. §§ 721.3(b), (f), (j)) (adding illustrations of permissible FCU activities under categories of correspondent services, operational programs, and finder activities).

30. 73 Fed. Reg. at 62,854.

§ 5.24

1. 12 U.S.C.A. §§ 1861 *et seq.* The Act was originally known as the Bank Service Corporation Act, and only authorized the creation of a corporate subsidiary of a national bank. The Act was amended in 1996 to authorize bank service "companies" to be organized as limited liability partnerships. *See* Economic Growth and Regulatory Paperwork Reduction Act, Pub. L. No. 104–208, title II, § 2613, 110 Stat. 3009 (1996) (codi-

to its direct exercise of incidental powers.[2] Nonbanking competitors have standing to challenge such activities.[3]

An FDIC-insured bank has the authority under the BSCA to invest an amount not more than ten percent of its paid in and unimpaired capital and unimpaired surplus in a bank service company.[4] However, the amount invested must not exceed five percent of the bank's total assets.[5] The company may perform any and all of the following services exclusively for depository institutions: (1) check and deposit sorting and posting; (2) computation and posting of interest and other credits and charges; (3) preparation and mailing of checks, statements, notices, and similar items; and, (4) any other clerical, bookkeeping, accounting, statistical, or similar functions performed for a depository institution.[6]

Beyond these rather modest services, a bank service company may offer a wide range of services to the public—except deposit-taking[7]—subject to a complex set of requirements and limitations,[8] discussed below. The service company, and any person performing contracted-out services for the company, are also subject to regulation and periodic examination by the appropriate federal regulator of the principal investor of the company.[9]

fied at 12 U.S.C.A. §§ 1861–1867) (renaming Bank Service Corporation Act as Bank Service Company Act; authorizing bank service companies to organize as limited liability partnerships; conforming amendments).

2. *Arnold Tours v. Camp*, 400 U.S. 45, 91 S.Ct. 158 (1970) (incidental powers analysis applied to activities under § 4 of BSCA).

3. *Association of Data Processing Serv. Orgs. v. Camp*, 397 U.S. 150, 90 S.Ct. 827 (1970); *Arnold Tours, supra*.

4. 12 U.S.C.A. § 1862. A "bank service company" by definition includes a limited liability company. *Id.* § 1861(b)(2)(B). Authorization of limited liability companies as a permitted form of organization of the bank service company is significant, since under prior case law, national banks had been held to be legally incapable of entering into a partnership agreement. *See, e.g., First Nat'l Bank v. Stokes*, 134 Ark. 368, 203 S.W. 1026 (1918); *Pronger v. Old Nat'l Bank*, 20 Wash. 618, 56 P. 391 (1899); *Cameron v. First Nat'l Bank*, 34 S.W. 178 (Tex.Civ.App.1896). Since 2006, insured savings associations have also been authorized to invest in bank service companies. Financial Services Regulatory Relief Act, § 602, Pub. L. No.

109–351, 120 Stat. 1966, 1978–1980 (2006) (codified at 12 U.S.C.A. §§ 1861(b)(2)(A)(ii), (B)(ii), (4)–(5), (7)–(9), 1862–1863, 1864(b)–(f), 1865(a)–(c), 1867(b)–(c)).

5. 12 U.S.C.A. § 1862.

6. *Id.* § 1863.

7. *See id.* § 1864(a) (prohibiting deposit-taking by bank service companies).

8. *Id.* §§ 1864–1866.

9. *Id.* § 1867(a), (c). The principal investor is required to inform the appropriate federal regulator of any contracting-out within 30 days of entry into the contract or performance, whichever occurs first. *Id.* § 1867(c)(2). For these purposes, the BSCA uses the term "appropriate Federal banking agency," which is defined to have the same meaning as the term is given in 12 U.S.C.A. § 1813(q). In other words, the appropriate regulator is the Comptroller of the Currency, in the case of a national bank; the Fed, in the case of a state-chartered member bank; and the FDIC, in the case of a state-chartered, insured nonmember bank. *Id.* The agencies are authorized to issue regulations and orders necessary to administer the BSCA, to carry out its purposes, and to prevent evasions. *Id.* § 1867(d).

If the company confines itself to services performed in the state in which its shareholders or members are located[10]—and all insured bank shareholders or members must be located in the same state[11]—then investment of an insured bank is permitted with prior notice to the bank's appropriate federal regulator.[12] The following services may be performed. (1) *Where the shareholder or member is a state bank*: The company may perform services that the state bank is permitted to perform under state law, at locations where the bank would be authorized to perform them under state law.[13] (2) *Where the shareholder or member is a national bank*: The company may perform services that the national bank is permitted to perform under federal law, at locations where the bank would be authorized to perform them under federal law.[14] (3) *Where the shareholders or members are state and national banks*: The company may perform services that both the national bank and the state bank are permitted to perform under federal and state law respectively, at locations where either bank would be authorized to perform them under federal and state law respectively.[15]

Notwithstanding these or any other provision of law,[16] a company may offer any service (except deposit-taking) that the Fed has determined to be a "closely related" activity under the Bank Holding Company Act ("BHCA")[17] at *any* geographic location.[18] However, an insured bank may not invest in a service company performing any such service, nor may the company perform such a service, without the prior approval of the Fed.[19]

Prior approval of the Fed, and approval of prior notice by any appropriate federal regulator, is subject to the following factors:

> the financial and managerial resources and future prospects of the bank or banks and bank service company involved, including the financial capability of the bank to make a proposed investment under this chapter, and possible adverse effects such as undue concentration of resources, unfair or decreased competition, conflicts of interest, or unsafe or unsound banking practices.[20]

The service company is subject to the administrative enforcement powers of 12 U.S.C.A. § 1818 to the same extent as if it were an insured bank. *Id.* § 1867(b).

10. *Id.* § 1864(b)(1).

11. *Id.* § 1864(b)(2).

12. *Id.* § 1865(a).

13. *Id.* § 1864(c).

14. *Id.* § 1864(d).

15. *Id.* § 1864(e).

16. With the exception of limitations on interstate branching. *Id.* § 1864(f).

17. *Id.* § 1843(c)(8).

18. *Id.* § 1864(f).

19. *Id.* § 1865(b).

20. *Id.* § 1865(c). In addition, bank service companies are prohibited from "unreasonably discriminat[ing] in the provision of any services ... to any depository institution" that is not a shareholder or member, on the basis that the institution is in competition with an institution that is a shareholder or member. *Id.* § 1866. However, the following

Failure on the part of the regulatory agency to act on a prior notice or application for prior approval within 90 days of submission of a complete notice or application is deemed to be approval.[21]

If the bank that owns or controls the service company is itself a subsidiary of a holding company, then the bank subsidiary's control of the nonbanking activity constitutes "indirect" control of the activity by the holding company, and is therefore subject to the BHCA.[22] Direct or indirect control of the service company by a bank holding company may require approval under the BHCA.[23]

On the other hand, a service corporation owned directly by a bank holding company, rather than by a bank subsidiary is not a "bank service company" for purposes of the BSCA.[24] For service companies owned or controlled by subsidiary banks, the BSCA applies.[25]

§ 5.25   Securities Activities

The securities sector is one area of the financial services industry that has exhibited significant crossover of depository institutions.[1] Depository institutions may also be securities market professionals, that is, persons who underwrite, purchase, sell, and otherwise deal in securities in the securities markets. These activities have been significantly limited, until relatively recently, by the

exceptions apply to this nondiscrimination rule:

(1) it shall not be considered unreasonable discrimination for a bank service company to provide services to a nonstockholding or nonmember institution only at a price that fully reflects all of the costs of offering those services, including the cost of capital and a reasonable return thereon; and

(2) a bank service company may refuse to provide services to a nonstockholding or nonmember institution if comparable services are available from another source at competitive overall costs, or if the providing of services would be beyond the practical capacity of the service company.

Id. § 1866(1)–(2).

21. *Id.* § 1865(d).

22. 12 C.F.R. §§ 225.101(c), 225.102 (interpreting indirect bank holding company control through subsidiaries). *See* 12 U.S.C.A. § 1843 (BHCA provision governing holding company control of nonbanking activities). *See also American Ins. Ass'n v. Clarke,* 865 F.2d 278 (D.C.Cir.1988) (discussing indirect hold-

ing company "control" of bank subsidiary's controlled subsidiary operations).

23. 12 C.F.R. § 225.115(c)(3)–(4), (d).

24. *Id.* § 225.115(b)(2). Accordingly, only Section 5 of the BSCA applies to such service corporations.

25. *Id.* § 225.115(c)(2).

§ 5.25

1. Note that the discussion in this section focuses primarily on the effect of Sections 16 and 21 of the Glass–Steagall Act, 12 U.S.C.A. § 24 (Seventh), 378, on depository institutions. Restrictions may also apply to an enterprise of which a depository institution is a subsidiary or affiliate, under Section 4(c) and (k)–(*o*) of the Bank Holding Company Act ("BHCA"), *id.* § 1843(c), (k)–(*o*). The effects of and interaction among these provisions are discussed in Chapter 6, *infra.* For more detailed treatment of securities activities of depository institutions, see 2 MICHAEL P. MALLOY, BANKING LAW AND REGULATION §§ 7.3–7.3.10.3 (1994 & CUM. SUPP.).

Glass–Steagall Act,[2] but these limitations had been progressively eroded by administrative interpretation and court decisions. In 1999, two major changes occurred in this area as a result of the enactment of the Gramm–Leach–Bliley Act ("GLBA").[3] First, the GLBA repealed Glass–Steagall prohibitions on affiliations between commercial and investment banking enterprises and on interlocking directorates between such enterprises.[4] Second, the GLBA permits bank holding companies that qualify as "financial holding companies" ("FHCs") to engage in activities, and acquire companies engaged in activities, that are "financial in nature"[5] or that are incidental to such activities.[6] FHCs are also permitted to engage in activities that are complementary to financial activities,[7] if the Fed determines that the activity does not pose a substantial risk to the safety or soundness of depository institutions or the financial system in general.[8] Subject to certain statutory restrictions, activities financial in nature may also be performed by direct subsidiaries of banks themselves.[9]

This section focuses on the Glass–Steagall Act, since it has been the major concern of much recent litigation and congressional consideration. However, to be understood adequately, securities activities of depository institutions need to be seen in conjunction with the overall federal policy on securities regulation, which in part applies to depository institutions, as well as to all other securities issuers and securities professionals. In Chapter 7, *infra*, this subject is discussed from the perspective of securities regulation. Performance of activities financial in nature, either by a direct subsidiary of a bank[10] or by a subsidiary of an FHC,[11] are discussed elsewhere in this book.

The Glass–Steagall Act was enacted in the wake of the financial crisis that burgeoned during the period from 1929 to 1933. As

---

2. 48 Stat. 162 (1933) (codified at scattered sections of 12 U.S.C.A.).

3. Pub. L. No. 106–102, Nov. 12, 1999, 113 Stat. 1338 (1999) (codified at scattered sections of 12, 15, 16, 18 U.S.C.A.).

4. GLBA, § 101 (repealing 12 U.S.C.A. §§ 78 & 377). The GLBA also authorized national banks to deal in, underwrite, and purchase municipal bonds for their own investment accounts. GLBA, § 151 (codified at 12 U.S.C.A. § 24). *See* 66 Fed. Reg. 8178 (2001) (to be codified at 12 C.F.R. pt. 1) (proposing to incorporate GLBA authority to underwrite, deal in, and purchase certain municipal bonds by well capitalized national banks).

5. 12 U.S.C.A. § 1843(k)(1).

6. *Id.* § 1843(k)(1)(A).

7. *Id.* § 1843(k)(1)(B). The term "complementary" is undefined.

8. The integrity of the deposit insurance funds is preserved by prohibiting the use of deposit insurance funds to benefit any shareholder, subsidiary or nondepository affiliate of an FHC. GLBA, § 117 (codified at 12 U.S.C.A. § 1821(a)(4)(B)).

9. *See, e.g.*, 12 U.S.C.A. § 24a.

10. On activities of bank subsidiaries that are financial in nature, see § 5.26, *infra*.

11. On activities of FHC subsidiaries that are financial in nature, see § 6.5, *infra*.

Investment Company Institute v. Camp[12] explained, during the 1920s close affiliation between investment and commercial banks resulted in a great potential for harm in the activities of each. The congressional solution was a radical break between the two, in many situations involving divestiture of the investment banking affiliates of major commercial banks.[13] In the years since its enactment in 1933, and particularly since the 1960s, banks and bank regulators have been crossing over into investment banking and the securities business with increasing vigor. Until relatively recently, however, this was a slow development.

Congress has also assisted this development, although until 1999, only inadvertently. Section 16, one of the key provisions of the Glass–Steagall Act,[14] has been amended repeatedly to allow more and more exceptions to the basic rule that depository institutions are generally prohibited from underwriting, purchasing and dealing in securities.[15]

Reviewing the key provisions of Glass–Steagall,[16] one can see that the limitations on the securities activities overlap for national

12. 401 U.S. 617, 91 S.Ct. 1091 (1971).

13. *See United States v. Morgan*, 118 F.Supp. 621, 646 (S.D.N.Y.1953):

Institutions which had previously engaged both in commercial and deposit banking on the one hand and investment banking on the other were required to elect prior to June 16, 1934, which of the two functions they would pursue to the exclusion of the other. This resulted in the complete elimination of the commercial banks and trust companies from the investment banking business; and the various bank affiliates were dissolved and liquidated.

On the basis of the Glass–Steagall Act, the Court in *Investment Company Institute* therefore held that the Comptroller's regulations permitting a national bank to market "participations" in a collective investment fund, 12 C.F.R. Pt. 9 (1963), were prohibited. A second generation of the Comptroller's regulations was promulgated in 1982, authorizing "common trust funds," 12 C.F.R. § 9.18(a)(1), (collective investment and reinvestment of funds contributed to a common trust fund maintained by a national bank) and "collective investment funds," *id.*

§ 9.18(a)(2) (collective investment in a fund consisting solely of assets of retirement, pension, profit-sharing, stock bonus or other trusts exempt from federal income taxation). These regulations were upheld despite a challenge under the Glass–Steagall Act. *Investment Co. Inst. v. Conover*, 790 F.2d 925 (D.C.Cir.1986), *cert. denied sub nom. Investment Co. Inst. v. Clarke*, 479 U.S. 939, 107 S.Ct. 421; *accord, Investment Co. Inst. v. Clarke*, 789 F.2d 175 (2d Cir.1986), *cert. denied*, 479 U.S. 940, 107 S.Ct. 422; *Investment Co. Inst. v. Clarke*, 793 F.2d 220 (9th Cir.1986), *cert. denied*, 479 U.S. 939, 107 S.Ct. 422.

14. 12 U.S.C.A. § 24 (Seventh). For an interesting interpretation of the meaning and applicability of 12 U.S.C.A. § 24 (Seventh), see *NationsBank of North Carolina, N.A. v. Variable Annuity Life Ins. Co.*, 513 U.S. 251, 115 S.Ct. 810 (1995).

15. *See, e.g.,* 12 C.F.R. Pt. 1 (interpreting and applying investment securities provisions of 12 U.S.C.A. § 24 (Seventh)). *See also* 2 MICHAEL P. MALLOY, BANKING LAW AND REGULATION §§ 7.3–7.3.2.3 (1994 & CUM. SUPP.) (discussing investment securities activities of depository institutions).

16. 12 U.S.C.A. §§ 24, 378.

banks,[17] member banks,[18] and "financial institutions" generally.[19] It may be useful to take a walk through these statutory provisions. As currently applicable, there are actually three surviving sections of the Glass–Steagall Act that are relevant. The first is Section 16,[20] which provides for, *inter alia*, the regulation of investment activities of national banks.[21]

The second relevant section is Section 21 of the Glass–Steagall Act, under which it became unlawful, as of June 16, 1934,

> [f]or *any person*, firm, corporation, association, business trust, or other similar organization, *engaged in the business of* issuing, underwriting, *selling*, or distributing, *at wholesale or retail*, or through syndicate participation, *stocks, bonds, debentures, notes, or other securities*, to engage at the same time to any extent whatever in the business of receiving deposits subject to check or to repayment upon presentation of a passbook, certificate of deposit, or other evidence of debt, or upon request of the depositor....[22]

This provision, which might raise serious questions concerning the legality of traditional bank securities activities, was modified in 1935, definitively mooting these questions. The original prohibition was qualified by the following proviso:

> [T]he provisions of this paragraph shall not prohibit *national banks or State banks or trust companies (whether or not members of the Federal Reserve System) or other financial institutions or private bankers* from dealing in, underwriting, purchasing, and selling investment securities to the extent permitted to national banking associations by the provisions of [12 U.S.C.A. § 24]....[23]

This language has the effect of broadening the scope of Section 16 to reach all depository institutions and financial intermediaries, limiting them to the securities activities permitted to national banks under Section 16 of the Act.[24] This restriction on securities activities of "financial institutions" would seem to be the broadest of the Glass–Steagall Act provisions. Under a third provision of

---

17. *See id.* § 24 (Seventh) (restricting securities activities of national banks).

18. *See id.* § 335 (expressly imposing same limitations on state member banks that apply to national banks).

19. *See id.* § 378 (prohibiting certain securities activities of "financial institutions").

20. *Id.* § 24 (Seventh).

21. *See* 12 C.F.R. Pt. 1.

22. 12 U.S.C.A. § 378(a)(1) (emphasis added).

23. *Id.* § 378(a)(1) (emphasis added).

24. For an interpretation of the applicability of this prohibition to the activities of an insured state nonmember bank, see FDIC Advisory Opinion 83–20, *reprinted in* [1988–1989 Transfer Binder] Fed. Banking L. Rep. (CCH) ¶ 81,194 (Feb. 3, 1989) (application of prohibition of Section 21 to bank's operation of collective investment pool).

Glass–Steagall, Fed member banks, whether national or state-chartered, are subject to all of these provisions, by cross-reference in the pertinent provision to the restrictions applicable to national banks under section 16 of the Act.[25] However, the reach of the Glass–Steagall Act extends to *all* national and state-chartered banks by limiting securities activities of such entities to those permitted to national banks under section 16.[26] Indeed, as the language quoted above indicates, all "financial institutions" that receive demand or savings deposits are subject to the restrictions of section 16 on investment activities.[27] The interrelationship among these prohibitions is illustrated in Figure 5–5, *infra*.

Figure 5–5

Scope of Glass–Steagall Prohibitions (post–GLBA)

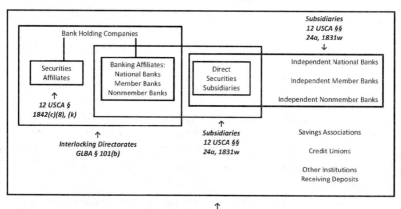

In-House Securities Activities
Permitted under Glass-Steagall §§ 16, 21

Even before the passage of the GLBA in 1999, judicial interpretation of the scope the Glass–Steagall Act had become increasingly favorable to involvement by depository institutions in securities activities. The contrasts in judicial attitudes over time are striking.

At the turn of the century, well before Glass–Steagall, judicial pronouncements rejecting securities powers for banks were unequivocal.[28] Similarly, for almost 50 years following the enactment of Glass–Steagall, courts took a relatively strict approach to the

---

25. *See id.* §§ 335, 378.

26. *See id.* § 378.

27. *See id.* § 378(a)(1).

28. *See, e.g., California Nat'l Bank v. Kennedy*, 167 U.S. 362, 17 S.Ct. 831 (1897) (allowing *ultra vires* defense, even where bank received benefits from stock purchases).

separation of banking and securities.[29] As Glass–Steagall has become viewed as more and more anachronistic, however, the courts have begun to relax their view of the precise contours of that separation.

Thus, the courts have permitted private placement of short-term notes.[30] They have upheld the Comptroller's second version of collective investment regulations,[31] despite the clear language of a prior Supreme Court decision to the contrary.[32] Courts have permitted bank in-house operation of securities brokerage services without registration as a broker under the Securities Exchange Act of 1934.[33] Similar developments have occurred in the bank holding company context, discussed in Chapter 6, *infra*. Figure 5–6, *infra*, provides selected examples of judicial interpretations under the Glass–Steagall Act permitting certain securities activities.

Figure 5–6

Glass–Steagall: Selected Judicial Interpretations

Security Activity	*Authority*
Annuities, variable, sale of	*NationsBank of North Carolina, N.A. v. Variable Annuity Life Ins. Co.*, 513 U.S. 251, 115 S.Ct. 810 (1995).
Brokerage services	*Clarke v. Securities Indus. Ass'n*, 479 U.S. 388, 107 S.Ct. 750 (1987); *American Bankers Ass'n v. Securities Exchange Comm'n*, 804 F.2d 739 (D.C.Cir.1986).
Collective investment funds	*Investment Co. Inst. v. Conover*, 790 F.2d 925 (D.C.Cir. 1986), *cert. denied sub nom. Investment Co. Inst. v. Clarke*, 479 U.S. 939, 107 S.Ct. 421; *Investment Co. Inst. v. Clarke*, 789 F.2d 175 (2d Cir.1986), *cert. denied*,

29. *See, e.g., Investment Co. Inst. v. Camp*, 401 U.S. 617, 91 S.Ct. 1091 (1971) (rejecting Comptroller's collective investment regulations).

30. *Securities Indus. Ass'n v. Board of Governors*, 468 U.S. 137, 104 S.Ct. 2979 (1984), *on remand*, 807 F.2d 1052 (D.C.Cir.1986), *cert. denied*, 483 U.S. 1005, 107 S.Ct. 3228 (1987) (holding placement of commercial paper by member banks permissible under section 16).

31. *See supra* note 13 (discussing *Investment Co. Institute v. Conover* and related cases). *See also* 12 C.F.R. § 9.18 (establishing OCC collective investment regulations).

32. *Investment Co. Inst., supra* note 12 (striking previous version of OCC collective investment regulations).

33. *American Bankers Ass'n v. Securities and Exch. Comm'n*, 804 F.2d 739 (D.C.Cir.1986).

Security Activity	Authority
	479 U.S. 940, 107 S.Ct. 422; *Investment Co. Inst. v. Clarke*, 793 F.2d 220 (9th Cir.1986), *cert. denied*, 479 U.S. 939, 107 S.Ct. 422.
Commercial paper, distribution of	*Securities Indus. Ass'n v. Board of Governors*, 807 F.2d 1052 (D.C.Cir.1986), *cert. denied*, 483 U.S. 1005, 107 S.Ct. 3228 (1987).
Investment advisory services	*Board of Governors v. Investment Co. Inst.*, 450 U.S. 46, 101 S.Ct. 973 (1981).
Investment securities, purchase and sale of	*Marx v. Centran Corp.*, 747 F.2d 1536 (6th Cir.1984), *cert. denied*, 471 U.S. 1125, 105 S.Ct. 2656 (1985); *City Nat'l Bank v. McCann*, 193 Ark. 967, 106 S.W.2d 195 (1937).
Mortgage pass-through certificates, sale of	*Securities Indus. Ass'n v. Clarke*, 885 F.2d 1034 (2d Cir.1989), *cert. denied*, 493 U.S. 1070, 110 S.Ct. 1113 (1990).
Stock of bank, dealing in	*Oppenheimer v. Harriman Nat'l Bank & Trust Co.*, 301 U.S. 206, 57 S.Ct. 719 (1937).
Stock transfers in connection with reorganization	*Independent Bankers Ass'n of Ga. v. Board of Governors*, 516 F.2d 1206 (D.C.Cir. 1975).

In contrast to the prior situation, in which a statutory provision for incidental powers of *banking* was one of the main authorities for *securities* activities of banks, the GLBA generally endorses the principle of functional regulation, positing that similar activities should be regulated by the same regulator.[34] Hence, banking activities are regulated by federal and state bank regulators, securities activities by federal and state securities regulators, and insurance activities by state insurance regulators.[35] More specifically, the

34. *But cf.* Michael P. Malloy, *Functional Regulation: Premise or Pretext? in* PATRICIA A. McCOY (ed.), FINANCIAL MODERNIZATION AFTER GRAMM-LEACH-BLILEY (LexisNexis 2002) (arguing that GLBA does not consistently or completely apply principle of functional regulation).

35. *See, e.g.,* GLBA, §§ 111–112, 115, 301 (codified at 12 U.S.C.A. §§ 1820a, 1831v, 1844(c)(4)(A)–(B), (g), 15 U.S.C.A. § 6711).

GLBA imposes functional regulation on bank securities activities by eliminating the "bank exception" from the definitions of "broker" and "dealer" in the Securities Exchange Act of 1934,[36] thus subjecting an incidental banking power to the generally applicable securities regulation regime.

This development may alter the significance of the incidental powers concept, at least prospectively, since the claim that an activity is an incidental power will not necessarily shield bank operations from rigorous regulation by other regulators. "Incidental powers" remain a source of authority for engaging in nonbanking activities, but the emergence of the concept of the activity financial in nature[37] may draw some attention away from incidental powers and towards the relatively new concept of "financial activities."

In addition to permitting a national bank to engage through a financial subsidiary in "financial activities" authorized by the act,[38] the GLBA permits bank holding companies (BHCs) that qualify as "financial holding companies" (FHCs) to engage in, and to acquire companies engaged in, activities that are "financial in nature" or that are incidental to such activities.[39]

The financial crisis that followed the collapse of the subprime mortgage market[40] has forced the Congress to rethink its uncritical release of securities powers into the hand of banks. Among other things, proprietary securities trading by banks will be restricted, but not eliminated.[41] It also imposed new standards with respect to securitization of pools of financial instruments,[42] one of the critical

36. GLBA, §§ 201–202 (codified at 15 U.S.C.A. § 78c(a)(4)–(5)). *See also* GLBA, § 221(a) (codified at 15 U.S.C.A. § 77c(a)(2)) (concerning treatment of bank common trust funds under Securities Act of 1933); GLBA, § 221(b) (codified at 15 U.S.C.A. § 78c(a)(12)(A)(iii)) (concerning treatment under Securities Exchange Act of 1934).

37. *See* § 5.26, 6.5, *infra* (discussing activities financial in nature in context of direct subsidiaries of banks and FHC subsidiaries, respectively).

38. GLBA § 121(a)(2), 113 Stat. at 1373 (codified at 12 U.S.C.A. § 24a). For discussion of this authorization, *see* § 5.26, *infra*.

39. GLBA § 103(a), 113 Stat. at 1342 (codified at 12 U.S.C.A. § 1843(k)). For discussion of FHCs under the GLBA, *see* § 6.5, *infra*.

40. For background on the subprime mortgage crisis, see 1 MICHAEL P. MALLOY, BANKING LAW AND REGULATION § 1.4 (1994

& Cum. Supp.). For a timeline of the current financial crisis, see http://www.stlouisfed.org/timeline/default.cfm.

41. Dodd–Frank Wall Street Reform and Consumer Protection Act (DFA), § 619, Pub. L. No. 111–203, 124 Stat. 1376, 1620–1631 (2010) (codified at 12 U.S.C.A. § 1851).

42. *Id.* §§ 941–945 (codified at 15 U.S.C.A. §§ 77d(5), 77g(c)–(d), 78c(a)(4)(B)(vii)(I), 78c(a)(77), 78o(d), 78o–11). See also DFA § 621(a) (codified at 15 U.S.C.A. § 77z–2a) (concerning conflicts of interest with respect to securitizations). Cf. DFA § 619(g)(2) (codified at 12 U.S.C.A. § 1851(g)(2)) (protecting otherwise authorized sale or securitization of loans by banking entity or systemically significant nonbank financial company from prohibitions on proprietary trading).

processes prior to the collapse for moving mortgage obligations into the capital markets as securities. It has required hedge and private equity fund advisers to register with the SEC, and it subjects them to SEC inspection and examination.[43]

The Congress has also directly addressed the structural need for comprehensive regulation of swaps and security-based swaps. In what may turn out to be a parlous compromise, Congress has authorized the Commodity Futures Trading Commission (CFTC) and the SEC to coordinate their regulation of swaps and security-based swaps respectively,[44] in consultation with the Fed.[45] The SEC and the CFTC have already jointly issued proposed rules "further defining" key terms and regulating "mixed swaps."[46] Institutions deemed to be swap dealers—typically, large banks that make markets in swaps by creating and selling them—as well as "major swap participants" are required to register with either the SEC or CFTC, depending on the nature of their products.[47] At the same time, a "de minimis" exception from designation as a swap dealer is available to "an entity that engages in a de minimis quantity of swap dealing in connection with transactions with or on behalf of customers."[48] This clause is important for regional banks and other smaller financial institutions such as savings associations and credit unions and will enable them to avoid the regulatory burdens likely to be associated with being identified as a swap dealer.

§ 5.26 Activities Financial in Nature

The Gramm–Leach–Bliley Act ("GLBA")[1] provides for financial

---

43. DFA §§ 401–412, 419 (codified at 15 U.S.C.A. §§ 80b–2(a)(11), (29)–(30), 80b–3(b), (*l*)–(n), 80b–3a(a), 80b–4, 80b–10(c), 80b–11, 80b–18b). As a general rule, these registration requirements are effective as of 21 July 2011, except that an investment adviser may, in its discretion, register with the SEC under the Investment Advisers Act of 1940 during this one-year transition period, subject to rules to be promulgated by the SEC. 15 U.S.C.A. § 80b–2 note.

44. DFA §§ 711–716, 718 (codified at 7 U.S.C.A. §§ 6d(h), 24(c); 15 U.S.C.A. §§ 78o(c)(3)(C), 8301–8306).

45. DFA § 712(a)(8) (codified at 15 U.S.C.A. § 8302(a)(8)). The SEC and the CFTC have joint responsibility for swap products, to be allocated between the two agencies depending on whether the underlying product is a "security" or not. *Id.* § 717 (codified at 7 U.S.C.A. § 2(a)(1)(C), 7a–2(c)(1); 15 U.S.C.A.

§§ 78c–1, 78s(b)(10)). Cf. *id.* § 720 (codified at 15 U.S.C.A. § 8308) (memorandum of understanding to be negotiated between CFTC and Federal Energy Regulatory Commission).

46. 75 Fed. Reg. 51,429 (2010) (to be codified at 17 C.F.R. pt. 1 (CFTC rules); *id.* pt. 240 (SEC rules)). Public comments were due September 20, 2010. 75 Fed. Reg. at 51,429.

47. DFA §§ 721–724 (codified at 7 U.S.C.A. §§ 1a, 1b, 2(a)(1), (c)(2)(A), (i)–(j), 6(c)(1), (6), 6d(f) 6m, 6q, 6s(*l*), 7—7a–1, 13–1(a), 16(h), 27; 11 U.S.C.A. 761; 15 U.S.C.A. §§ 78f, 8321–8322).

48. DFA § 721(a)(49)(D) (codified at 7 U.S.C.A. § 1a(a)(49)(D)).

§ 5.26

1. Pub. L. No. 106–102, Nov. 12, 1999, 113 Stat. 1338 (1999) (codified at scattered sections of 12, 15, 16, 18 U.S.C.A.).

services subsidiaries of national and insured state banks.[2] The GLBA permits a national bank to engage through a financial subsidiary[3] only in financial activities authorized by the act, with certain exceptions.[4] The GLBA itself identifies certain activities that are "financial in nature,"[5] and the Secretary of the Treasury, in consultation with the Fed, has statutory authority to determine whether other activities are also "financial in nature."[6] Section 24a specifically excludes four types of activities for these subsidiaries: insurance or annuity underwriting, insurance company portfolio investments, real estate investment and development, and merchant banking. These types of financial activities may only be done in FHC affiliates.[7] Substantial "firewalls" are established, intended to limit exposure of a state or national bank to the risk of the activities of the bank's financial subsidiary.[8] Federal banking regulators are prohibited from interpreting these provisions to provide for any expansion of these activities contrary to the express language of the GLBA.[9] The legislative history of the act indicates that

2. GLBA § 121(a)(2), (d)(1) (codified at 12 U.S.C.A. §§ 24a, 1831w), *as amended* Dodd–Frank Wall Street Reform and Consumer Protection Act (DFA), § 728, Pub. L. No. 111–203, 124 Stat. 1376, 1697–1701 (2010) (codified at 12 U.S.C.A. § 24a) (providing for swap data repositories).

3. For these purposes, the term "financial subsidiary" is defined to mean a company controlled by one or more insured depository institutions *other than a subsidiary that*:

> (A) engages solely in activities that national banks are permitted to engage in directly and are conducted subject to the same terms and conditions that govern the conduct of such activities by national banks; or

> (B) a national bank is specifically authorized . . . to control . . . by . . . the Bank Service Company Act.

12 U.S.C.A. § 24a(g)(3)(A)–(B). The first category would seem to include incidental activities under 12 U.S.C.A. § 24(Seventh) . . On the relationship between powers authorized under 12 U.S.C.A. § 24(Seventh) and those authorized under § 24a, see *Watters v. Wachovia Bank, N.A.*, 550 U.S. 1, 16–18, 127 S.Ct. 1559, 1570 (2007).

4. GLBA § 121(a)(2) (codified at 12 U.S.C.A. § 24a).On the meaning of the term "financial activity" for these purposes, see 12 U.S.C.A. §§ 24a(b), 1843(k)(4).

5. 12 U.S.C.A. § 1843(k)(4). For a list of these "K4 activities," see *infra* Figure 6–2.

6. The Treasury Department published an interim rule in March 2000, 65 Fed. Reg. 14,819 (2000) (codified at 12 C.F.R. pt. 1501), after consultation with the Fed, establishing a procedure for a national bank or other interested parties to request that the Secretary make a determination whether an activity is "financial in nature" or incidental to a financial activity, and therefore permissible for a financial subsidiary of a national bank. 12 C.F.R. § 1501.1.

7. On FHC activities financial in nature, see § 6.5, *infra*. However, after a five-year period from enactment of the GLBA, the Fed and the Secretary of the Treasury are authorized jointly to adopt rules permitting merchant banking by financial subsidiaries, subject to the conditions that the agencies may jointly determine. GLBA, § 122 (codified at 12 U.S.C.A. § 1843 note).

8. GLBA, § 121(b)–(d) (codified at 12 U.S.C.A. §§ 335, 371c(b)(11), (e)–(f), 1831w, 1971).

9. 12 U.S.C.A. § 24a(b)(2)(A), (b)(3). *See, e.g.*, 66 Fed. Reg. 257 (2001) (codified at 12 C.F.R. pts. 225, 1501) (promulgating joint Fed–Treasury interim rule finding three general types of activities to be "financial in nature" and creating mechanism by which FHCs, financial subsidiaries of national banks, and

Congress intended to prevent the kind of broad interpretative approach that grew up around the "incidental powers" language of section 24, and specifically to supersede and replace the Comptroller's broad rules[10] on operating subsidiaries of national banks.[11]

To qualify for "financial activities," a national bank and each depository institution affiliate of the national bank must be well capitalized[12] and well managed.[13] Failure by the national bank or its affiliate to continue to meet these requirements would result in issuance of a notice by the Comptroller of the Currency to the national bank, describing the conditions that triggered the notice.[14] Within 45 days of receipt of the notice,[15] the national bank must execute an agreement with the Comptroller,[16] and any other involved insured depository institution affiliate must execute an agreement with its appropriate federal banking agency to comply with these requirements.[17] Until the deficiencies are corrected, the

---

others may request that Fed or Treasury Secretary define particular activities within one of three categories); 66 Fed. Reg. 307 (2001) (to be codified at 12 C.F.R. pts. 225, 1501) (proposing joint Fed–Treasury rule determining that real estate brokerage is activity "financial in nature" or incidental to financial activity).

10. 12 C.F.R. pt. 5 (1999).

11. *See Conference Report on S. 900, reprinted in* 145 Cong. Rec. H11255–01, H11296 (1999) (discussing congressional intent concerning GLBA section 121). Pursuant to the GLBA, the Comptroller's operating subsidiary regulations were amended in March 2000. 65 Fed. Reg. 12,905, 12,911–12,913 (2000) (codified at 12 C.F.R. § 5.34).

12. For these purposes, the term "well capitalized" is given the same meaning as in section 38 of the Federal Deposit Insurance Act. *Id.* § 24a(g)(5). *See id.* § 1831o. *Cf. id.* 24a(c)(1)(A) (requiring deduction of aggregate amount of outstanding equity investment, including retained earnings, in all financial subsidiaries from assets and tangible equity of national bank, in determining compliance with applicable capital standards). Assets and liabilities of financial subsidiaries and parent bank are not to be consolidated for purposes of capital requirements. *Id.* § 24a(c)(1)(B). Published financial statements must include separate financial information for the parent bank, in addition to any information prepared in accordance with GAAP. *Id.* § 24a(c)(2).

13. *Id.* § 24a(a)(2)(C). For these purposes, the term "well managed" is defined to mean:

(A) in the case of a depository institution that has been examined, unless otherwise determined in writing by the appropriate Federal banking agency—

(i) the achievement of a composite rating of 1 or 2 under the Uniform Financial Institutions Rating System (or an equivalent rating under an equivalent rating system) in connection with the most recent examination or subsequent review of the depository institution; and

(ii) at least a rating of 2 for management, if such rating is given; or

(B) in the case of any depository institution that has not been examined, the existence and use of managerial resources that the appropriate Federal banking agency determines are satisfactory.

Id. § 24a(g)(6).

14. *Id.* § 24a(e)(1).

15. The Comptroller may permit an "additional period." *Id.* § 24a(e)(2).

16. Any action under this provision by the Comptroller requires consultation "with all relevant Federal and State regulatory agencies and authorities." *Id.* § 24a(e) (5).

17. *Id.* § 24a(e)(2).

Comptroller may impose limits on the conduct or activities of the national bank or any subsidiary thereof, as the Comptroller deems appropriate under the circumstances and consistent with the statutory purposes.[18] Other appropriate federal banking agencies may impose similar limits on the conduct or activities of other involved insured depository institution affiliates or subsidiaries, as such agencies deem appropriate.[19] If the conditions are not corrected within 180 days of receipt of the notice, the Comptroller may require the national bank, under terms, conditions and timing imposed by the Comptroller, to divest control of any financial subsidiary.[20]

The aggregate consolidated total assets of all financial subsidiaries of the national bank may not exceed the lesser of 45 percent of consolidated total assets of the parent bank,[21] or $50,000,000,000.[22] This dollar amount will be indexed and adjusted in accordance with a mechanism to be established jointly by regulation by the Secretary of the Treasury and the Fed.[23]

The national bank must meet certain rating requirements made applicable by the act.[24] In general, if the national bank is one of the fifty largest insured banks,[25] then it must have no fewer than one issue of outstanding eligible debt[26] currently rated within the three highest investment grade rating categories by a nationally recognized statistical rating organization.[27] If it is one of the second fifty largest insured banks, then it must meet either the foregoing criteria "or such other criteria as the Secretary of the Treasury and the [Fed] may jointly establish by regulation and determine to be comparable to and consistent with the purposes of" those criteria.[28]

---

18. *Id.* § 24a(e)(3)(A).

19. *Id.* § 24a(e)(3)(B).

20. *Id.* § 24a(e)(4).

21. *Id.* § 24a(a)(2)(D)(i).

22. *Id.* § 24a(a)(2)(D)(ii).

23. *Id.* § 24a(a)(6).

24. *Id.* § 24a(a)(2)(E).

25. For these purposes, the size of an insured bank is to be determined on the basis of consolidated total assets of the bank as of calendar-year-end. *Id.* § 24a(a)(3)(B).

26. For these purposes, the term "eligible debt" is defined to mean unsecured long-term debt that—

   (A) is not supported by any form of credit enhancement, including a guarantee or standby letter of credit; and

   (B) is not held in whole or in any significant part by any affiliate, officer, director, principal shareholder, or employee of the bank or any other person acting on behalf of or with funds from the bank or an affiliate of the bank.

Id. § 24a(g)(4).

27. *Id.* § 24a(a)(3)(A)(i).

28. *Id.* § 24a(a)(3)(A)(ii). *See* 65 Fed. Reg. 15,050 (2000) (codified at 12 C.F.R. §§ 208.71(c), 208.77(e)–(g), 1501.2; redesignating § 208.77(e)–(f) as (f)–(g)) (setting forth joint Fed–Treasury alternative criteria); 65 Fed. Reg. 16,460 (2000) (codified at 12 C.F.R. pts. 208, 1501) (interim rule establishing alternative criteria), *superseded by* 66 Fed. Reg. 8748 (2001) (codified at 12 C.F.R. pts. 208, 1501) (promulgating joint Fed–Treasury rules permitting national bank or state member bank in second 50 largest insured banks to own or control a financial subsidiary only if bank meets § 121 eligible debt requirement or alter-

This rating requirement does not apply to financial subsidiaries that engage in financial activities solely as agent and not directly or indirectly as principal.[29] A national bank's failure to maintain the public rating or to meet other applicable criteria would effectively bar the bank, directly or through a subsidiary, from purchasing or acquiring any additional equity capital[30] of any financial subsidiary until the bank again meets the requirements.[31]

The national bank must receive approval of the Comptroller of the Currency before its subsidiary may engage in financial activities.[32] The Comptroller promulgated final rules prescribing application procedures in March 2000.[33]

No approval of a financial subsidiary's financial activities is permitted if the parent bank, its holding company, or any insured depository institution affiliate has received in its most recent CRA examination a rating of less than "satisfactory."[34]

The GLBA also mandates risk-analysis safeguards.[35] Failure by a national bank or its affiliate to continue to meet these safeguards requirements would trigger the notice and correction procedures discussed previously.[36]

native criteria of current long-term issuer credit rating from nationally recognized statistical rating organization within organization's three highest investment grade rating categories).

29. 12 U.S.C.A. § 24a(a)(4).

30. For these purposes, the term "equity capital" is defined to include in addition to any equity instrument, any debt instrument issued by a financial subsidiary, if the instrument qualifies as capital of the subsidiary under any Federal or State law, regulation, or interpretation applicable to the subsidiary. *Id.* § 24a(f)(2).

31. *Id.* § 24a(f)(1).

32. *Id.* § 24a(a)(2)(F).

33. *See* 65 Fed. Reg. 12,905 (2000) (codified at 12 C.F.R. §§ 5.24(d)(2)(ii)(G), 5.33(e)(3)(i)–(ii), 5.34, 5.35(e), (f)(1)–(5), (g)(2), (h), (i)(2), 5.36(c)–(f), 5.39; removing § 5.35(f)(3); redesignating § 5.35(f)(4)–(6) as (f)(3)–(5); redesignating § 5.36(c)–(d) as (d), (f)) (promulgating rules under 12 U.S.C.A. § 24a(a)(5))). Parallel rules are also in place for state member banks and insured state nonmember banks. *See* 65 Fed. Reg. 14,810 (2000) (codified at 12 C.F.R. §§ 208.71–208.77) (interim rule authorizing activities "financial in nature" for state member banks); 65 Fed.

Reg. 15,526 (2000) (codified at 12 C.F.R. §§ 303.120–303.121, 303.122(a), 303.-123(b), 362.16–362.18) (interim rule establishing procedure for authorizing activities of insured state nonmember banks that national bank can conduct through financial subsidiary).

34. *Id.* §§ 24a(a)(7), 1843(*l*)(2) (applying CRA requirements of § 1843(*l*) to national bank that controls financial subsidiary).

35. *See id.* § 24a(d), which requires that a national bank establishing or maintaining a financial subsidiary assure that:

(1) the procedures of the national bank for identifying and managing financial and operational risks within the national bank and the financial subsidiary adequately protect the national bank from such risks;

(2) the national bank has, for the protection of the bank, reasonable policies and procedures to preserve the separate corporate identity and limited liability of the national bank and the financial subsidiaries of the national bank; and

(3) the national bank is in compliance with this section.

The GLBA amended the Federal Deposit Insurance Act[37] by adding section 46,[38] which roughly parallels the authority of section 24a of the NBA. The new section provides that an insured non-member state bank[39] may control or hold an interest in a subsidiary that engages *as principal* in activities that would be permissible for a national bank to conduct only through a "financial subsidiary," subject to certain conditions.[40] In January 2001, the FDIC implemented the new authority by adopting final rules governing the activities and investments of insured state banks.[41]

The FDIC has adopted a streamlined certification process for insured state nonmember banks to follow before they may conduct activities as principal through a financial subsidiary.[42] State nonmember banks will self-certify that they meet the requirements to carry out these activities, thus allowing the banks to conduct the new activities immediately.[43] There will be no delay for administrative approval or review, although the FDIC will evaluate these activities as part of its normal supervision process for safety and soundness standards pursuant to FDIC authority under section 8 of the FDIA.[44] The final rule confirms, with minor modifications, an interim rule that had been in effect since 11 March 2000.[45] To eliminate unnecessary provisions and make technical amendments, the FDIC also revised its rule implementing sections 18(m)[46] and 24[47] of the FDIA, dealing with other activities and investments of insured state banks.[48] The new rules are effective as of 5 January 2001.[49] The FDIC has taken the position that, because new FDIA section 46(a) applies only to "as principal" activities, state nonmember banks may engage in agency activities without considering the new requirements.[50]

§ 5.27　Insurance Activities

Banks, and particularly national banks, have made significant inroads into the insurance industry.[1] *NationsBank of North Car-*

36. *See* text and accompanying notes 14–20, *supra* (discussing procedure).

37. 12 U.S.C.A. §§ 1811 *et seq.*

38. 12 U.S.C.A. § 1831w.

39. For rules governing financial subsidiaries of state-chartered member banks, see 66 Fed. Reg. 42,929 (2001) (codified at 12 C.F.R. §§ 208.71–208.77).

40. *Id.* § 1831w(a).

41. 66 Fed. Reg. 1018 (2001) (codified at 12 C.F.R. pts. 303, 337, 362).

42. 66 Fed. Reg. at 1018.

43. *Id.*

44. 12 U.S.C.A. § 1818.

45. 65 Fed. Reg. 15,526 (2000).

46. 12 U.S.C.A. § 1828(m).

47. *Id.* § 1831.

48. 66 Fed. Reg. at 1018.

49. *Id.*

50. *Id.*

§ 5.27

1. *See, e.g., NationsBank of North Carolina v. Variable Annuity Life Insurance Co.,* 513 U.S. 251, 115 S.Ct. 810

olina v. Variable Annuity Life Insurance Co.[2] upheld the Comptroller's authorization[3] of the brokerage of variable annuities[4] by national banks as an incidental power. *Barnett Bank of Marion County, N.A. v. Nelson*,[5] upheld insurance agency powers of national banks under a specialized section of the National Bank Act (NBA).[6] *NationsBank* and *Barnett Bank* are significant as part of a broader range of developments expanding the involvement of banking enterprises in insurance services. Despite the modest limitations on bank holding company involvement in insurance services suggested by *Alabama Ass'n of Ins. Agents v. Board of Governors*,[7] a range of insurance activities were later imbedded in the amended Bank Holding Company Act[8] as closely related to banking, and as such permissible in principle for bank holding companies.[9] The Court's decision in *NationsBank* extended the reach of national banks into insurance services by upholding the Comptroller's authorization of sales of variable annuities as an "incidental power" under the NBA.[10] In this perspective, *Barnett Bank* confirms the direction and quickens the speed of the march of commercial banks into insurance services.

The pace of change quickened again with the decision in

(1995) (approving national bank offering of variable annuities); *Barnett Bank of Marion County, N.A. v. Nelson*, 517 U.S. 25, 116 S.Ct. 1103 (1996) (approving national bank insurance agency activities). For a discussion of the longstanding issues between commercial banking and insurance services, see Schweitzer & Halbrook, *Insurance Activities of Banks and Banks Holding Companies: A Survey of Current Issues and Regulations*, 29 Drake L. Rev. 743 (1979/1980); Hemmer, *Insurance Underwriting Activities of BHC's*, 100 Banking L.J. 700 (1983); Note, *The Merger of Banking and Insurance: Will Congress Close the South Dakota Loophole?*, 60 Notre Dame L. Rev. 762 (1985); Malloy, *The Sound of Two Hands Flapping: Insurance–Related Activities of National Banks*, 41 St. Louis U. L.J. 75 (1997).

2. *Supra* note 1.

3. 12 C.F.R. § 5.34 (1996).

4. For these purposes, an "annuity" may be understood as follows:

Annuities are contracts under which the purchaser makes one or more premium payments to the issuer in exchange for a series of payments, which continue either for a fixed period or for the life of the purchaser or a desig-

nated beneficiary. When a purchaser invests in a "variable" annuity, the purchaser's money is invested in a designated way and payments to the purchaser vary with investment performance. In a classic "fixed" annuity, in contrast, payments do not vary.

NationsBank, 513 U.S. at 254, 115 S.Ct. at 812.

5. *Supra* note 1.

6. 12 U.S.C.A. § 92. *See Association of Banks in Insurance, Inc. v. Duryee*, 55 F.Supp.2d 799 (S.D.Ohio 1999), *affirmed and remanded*, 270 F.3d 397 (6th Cir. 2001) (holding that § 92 preempted "principal purpose" requirement and other provisions of Ohio statutes regulating licensing of insurance agents).

7. 533 F.2d 224 (5th Cir.1976), *amended*, 558 F.2d 729 (1977), *cert. denied*, 435 U.S. 904, 98 S.Ct. 1448 (1978) (questioning authorization by Federal Reserve of general insurance agency activities by bank holding companies).

8. 12 U.S.C.A. § 1843(c)(8)(A)–(G).

9. *But cf. id.* § 1843(c)(8) ("closely related" activity subject to showing that activity is "proper incident" of banking).

10. 12 U.S.C.A. § 24 (Seventh).

American Council of Life Ins. v. Ludwig,[11] which explores the interplay of section 92 with section 35, providing for conversions of state banks to national bank charters. The case upheld OCC approval of a conversion of state-chartered bank with two insurance subsidiaries that did not conform to the requirements of section 92.[12] In allowing the converted bank to retain the nonconforming subsidiaries, the OCC relied on section 35, which gives the Comptroller the discretion to permit a converting state bank to "retain and carry" certain nonconforming assets.[13] The court found that

> The terms "retain and carry," are plain enough, and given their ordinary meaning, do not suggest to the Court that ultimate divesture of nonconforming assets is a built in, yet unstated component of section 35. The legislative history also supports the Comptroller's interpretation, showing that the purpose of section 35 was to remove impediments from state banks seeking to convert to national bank status by allowing them to retain their nonconforming assets.[14]

The court thus held that the Comptroller has the express authority to permit a converting bank to retain its nonconforming assets "subject to such conditions as he may prescribe," including the permanent retention of the nonconforming assets.[15] In *dicta,* the court went on to suggest that, even if the language of section 35 were not clear on its face, it "would still find the Comptroller's interpretation to be proper insofar as it was reasonable."[16] In any event, the court further held that the Comptroller's decision to allow the converting bank to retain its nonconforming assets was not arbitrary, capricious or an abuse of discretion and therefore upheld it

It appeared that state law policymakers are without power to slow the rising trend of OCC policy with respect to bank insurance activities. In *New York Bankers Ass'n, Inc. v. Levin,*[17] the court held that section 92 preempted contrary New York law prohibiting banking institutions from negotiating real or personal property insurance policies that are the subject matter of, or security for, a loan from the institution.

The Gramm–Leach–Bliley Act ("GLBA")[18] finally intervened. The GLBA permits affiliations among banking, securities and in-

11. 1 F.Supp.2d 24 (D.D.C.1998), *vac'd and remanded as moot,* 194 F.3d 173 (D.C.Cir.1999).

12. The insurance subsidiaries operated in part in offices situated in communities with populations that exceeded 5,000. *American Council of Life Ins.,* 1 F.Supp.2d at 26.

13. 12 U.S.C.A. § 35.

14. *American Council of Life Ins.,* 1 F.Supp.2d at 28.

15. *Id.* at 29.

16. *Id.*

17. 999 F.Supp. 716 (W.D.N.Y.1998).

18. Pub. L. No. 106–102, Nov. 12, 1999, 113 Stat. 1338 (1999) (codified at scattered sections of 12, 15, 16, 18 U.S.C.A.).

surance firms, but it provides explicitly that the McCarran–Ferguson Act[19] is still operative to require federal deference in most cases to state regulation of the insurance activities carried on by these firms.[20] Subject to special rules concerning permissible affiliations and activities and nondiscrimination in state treatment of affiliated firms, the GLBA requires a state license for any firm to engage in the business of insurance as a principal or agent,[21] and so insurance regulation post-GLBA remains primarily a matter of individual state concern.[22]

National banks and their subsidiaries are prohibited from underwriting insurance, except for authorized products.[23] To prevent evasion of state insurance regulation through the use of non-U.S. reinsurance subsidiaries or offices of U.S. banks, the GLBA explicitly states that providing insurance (including reinsurance) *outside* the United States to indemnify an insurance product or firm *within* a state is considered to be providing insurance as principal in that state.[24]

National banks are prohibited from engaging in any activity involving underwriting or sale of title insurance, except that national banks may sell title insurance products in any state in which state-chartered banks are authorized to do so (other than through a state "wild card" provision).[25] Sales by national banks must be undertaken in the same manner, to the same extent, and under the same restrictions as apply to state-chartered banks. Certain extant, lawfully conducted title insurance activities of banks are grandfathered.[26] Preexisting state laws prohibiting all persons from providing title insurance are preserved.[27] As to conflicts between federal and state regulators regarding insurance issues, GLBA establishes an expedited and equalized dispute resolution mechanism, originating in the federal courts of appeals, to guide the courts in deciding such conflicts.[28]

The GLBA preempts state laws that prevent or otherwise significantly interfere with the ability of an insurer to affiliate, become a financial holding company ("FHC"),[29] or demutualize, except as provided in the GLBA itself.[30] GLBA also preempts state

---

19. 15 U.S.C.A. §§ 1011 *et seq.*

20. GLBA, § 104(a) (codified at 15 U.S.C.A. § 6701(a)).

21. *Id.*, § 104(b)–(f) (codified at 15 U.S.C.A. § 6701(b)–(f)).

22. GLBA, § 301 (codified at 15 U.S.C.A. § 6711).

23. GLBA, § 302 (codified at 15 U.S.C.A. § 6712).

24. 15 U.S.C.A. § 6712(d).

25. GLBA, § 303 (codified at 15 U.S.C.A. § 6713).

26. 15 U.S.C.A. § 6713(c).

27. *Id.* § 6713(e).

28. GLBA, § 304 (codified at 15 U.S.C.A. § 6714).

29. On FHCs and their regulation under the GLBA, see § 6.5, *infra*.

30. GLBA, § 306 (codified at 15 U.S.C.A. § 6715). On GLBA require-

laws limiting the investment of an insurer's assets in a depository institution, except to the extent that the GLBA permits an insurer's domicile state to limit such investments.

GLBA allows mutual insurance companies to "redomesticate" to another state and reorganize into a mutual holding company or stock company.[31] This rule only applies to insurers in states that have not established reasonable terms and conditions for allowing mutual insurance companies to reorganize into a mutual holding company. All licenses of the insurer are preserved.[32] All outstanding policies, contracts, and forms remain in effect.[33] A redomesticating insurer must provide notice to the state insurance regulators of each state for which the company is licensed.[34] A mutual insurer may redomesticate under this rule only if the state insurance regulator of the new domicile affirmatively determines that the company's reorganization plan meets certain reasonable terms and conditions.[35] The reorganization must be approved by a majority of the insurer's board of directors and voting policyholders (after notice and disclosure of the reorganization and its effects on contract rights of policyholders). The policyholders must have equivalent voting rights in the new mutual holding company, and all contractual rights of the policyholders must be preserved. Any initial public offering of stock must be in accordance with applicable securities laws, and under the supervision of the state insurance regulator of the new domicile. The new mutual holding company may not award any stock options or grants to its elected directors or officers for six months. The reorganization must be approved as fair and equitable to the policyholders by the insurance regulators of new domicile. GLBA generally preempts state laws that otherwise restrict redomestication.[36]

The GLBA encourages the states to establish uniform or reciprocal requirements for the licensing of insurance agents.[37] If a majority of the states do not establish uniform or reciprocal licensing provisions within a three-year period, as determined by the National Association of Insurance Commissioners ("NAIC"), then the National Association of Registered Agents and Brokers ("NARAB") would be established as a private, non-profit entity managed

ments in this regard (especially the requirement that states not discriminate in their treatment of insurance firms), see text and accompanying notes 20–21, *supra.*

31. GLBA, § 312(a)–(b) (codified at 15 U.S.C.A. § 6732(a)–(b)).

32. *Id.,* § 312(c) (codified at 15 U.S.C.A. § 6732(c)).

33. *Id.,* § 312(d) (codified at 15 U.S.C.A. § 6732(d)).

34. *Id.,* § 312(e) (codified at 15 U.S.C.A. § 6732(e)).

35. *Id.,* § 312(f) (codified at 15 U.S.C.A. § 6732(f)).

36. *Id.,* § 313 (codified at 15 U.S.C.A. § 6733).

37. *Id.,* § 321 (codified at 15 U.S.C.A. § 6751).

and supervised by the state insurance regulators.[38] State insurance laws and regulations are not affected, except to the extent that they are inconsistent with any specific requirement of these rules.

If the NAIC determines that the states have not met the uniformity or reciprocity requirements, then the NAIC has two years to establish the NARAB.[39] The NAIC is to appoint the NARAB board of directors, some of whom must have significant experience with the regulation of commercial insurance lines in the twenty states with the most commercial lines business.[40] If within the time period allotted for creation of the NARAB, the NAIC has still not appointed the initial board of directors for NARAB, then the initial directors shall be the state insurance regulators of the seven states with the greatest amount of commercial lines insurance. NARAB bylaws are required to be filed with the NAIC, taking effect 30 days after filing unless disapproved by the NAIC as being contrary to the public interest or requiring a public hearing.[41] The NAIC may require NARAB to adopt or repeal additional bylaws or rules as it determines appropriate to the public interest. The NAIC is given the responsibility of overseeing the NARAB, and is authorized to examine and inspect NARAB records, and to require the NARAB to furnish it with any reports.[42]

If at the end of the two years after the NARAB is required to be established, a majority of the states representing at least 50 percent of the total commercial lines insurance premiums in the United States have not established uniform or reciprocal licensing regulations, or the NAIC has not approved NARAB bylaws or is unable to operate or supervise the NARAB (or if the NARAB is not conducting its activities under the GLBA), then the NARAB is to be created and supervised by the President, and would exist without NAIC oversight.[43] The President would be required to appoint the NARAB board, with the advice and consent of the Senate, from lists of candidates submitted by the NAIC. If the President determines that the NARAB board is not acting in the public interest, the President may replace the entire board with new members (subject to the advice and consent of the Senate). The President may also

38. *Id.,* § 322 (codified at 15 U.S.C.A. § 6752). Significant progress has been made on licensing. See U.S. Government Accountability Office, Insurance Reciprocity and Uniformity: NAIC and State Regulators Have Made Progress in Producer Licensing, Product Approval, and Market Conduct Regulation, but Challenges Remain (GAO-09-372, Apr. 6, 2009), available at 2009 WL 1262871.

39. *Id.,* § 321(d)(1) (codified at 15 U.S.C.A. § 6751(d)(1)).

40. On the NARAB board of directors and officers, see GLBA, §§ 326–327 (codified at 15 U.S.C.A. § 6756–6757).

41. GLBA, § 328 (codified at 15 U.S.C.A. § 6758).

42. *Id.,* § 324 (codified at 15 U.S.C.A. § 6754).

43. *Id.,* § 332 (codified at 15 U.S.C.A. § 6762).

suspend the effectiveness of any rule or action by the NARAB that the President determines to be contrary to the public interest. The NARAB would be required to report annually to the President and Congress on its activities.

Membership in the NARAB is voluntary and does not affect the rights of a firm under each individual state license. Any state-licensed insurance firm whose license has not been suspended or revoked is eligible to join the NARAB.[44] The NARAB is required to base its membership criteria on the highest qualification levels set by the states on standards such as integrity, personal qualification, education, training, and experience. NARAB members must continue to pay the appropriate fees required by each state in which they are licensed, and must renew their membership annually. The NARAB may inspect member records, and revoke membership where appropriate. The NARAB must establish an Office of Consumer Complaints to receive and investigate consumer complaints and recommend disciplinary actions. The Office must maintain records of such complaints, and these records must be made available to the NAIC and individual state insurance regulators. The NARAB must refer complaints where appropriate to the regulators.

The GLBA preempts state laws regulating insurance licensing that discriminate against NARAB members based on non-residency, and state laws and regulations that impose additional licensing requirements on non-resident NARAB members beyond those established by the NARAB board.[45] However, state unfair trade practice and consumer protection laws are protected from preemption. The NARAB is required to coordinate its multistate licensing with the various states, and to coordinate with the states on establishing a central clearinghouse for license issuance and renewal and for the collection of regulatory information on insurance firm activities.[46] The NARAB is also required to coordinate with the NASD to facilitate joint membership.[47]

Any dispute involving the NARAB must be brought in the appropriate U.S. District Court under federal law.[48] All administrative remedies through the NARAB and the NAIC must first be exhausted.[49]

To provide additional safeguards for the sale of insurance by any depository institution, or by a person at or on behalf of such an

---

44. *Id.*, § 325 (codified at 15 U.S.C.A § 6755).

45. *Id.*, § 333 (codified at 15 U.S.C.A. § 6763).

46. *Id.*, § 334(a) (codified at 15 U.S.C.A. § 6764(a)).

47. *Id.*, § 334(b) (codified at 15 U.S.C.A. § 6764(b)).

48. *Id.*, § 335(a), (c) (codified at 15 U.S.C.A. § 6765(a), (c)).

49. *Id.*, § 335(b) (codified at 15 U.S.C.A. § 335(b)).

institution, GLBA requires the federal banking agencies to issue final consumer protection regulations within one year.[50]

The Dodd–Frank Wall Street Reform and Consumer Protection Act ("Dodd–Frank Act")[51] takes federal inroads into insurance regulation a step further. As of July 21, 2011,[52] the Dodd–Frank Act imposes basic oversight on state regulatory and tax treatment of "nonadmitted insurance,"[53] i.e., property and casualty insurance permitted by a state to be placed directly or through a surplus lines broker with an insurer not licensed to engage in the insurance business within the state.[54] The act also provides for federal regulation of credit for reinsurance and reinsurance activities.[55]

50. *Id.*, § 305 (codified at 12 U.S.C.A. § 1831x).

51. Pub. L. No. 111–203, 124 Stat. 1376 (2010) (codified at scattered sections of 2, 5, 7, 11, 12, 15, 18, 20, 22, 26, 28, 31, 42, 44 U.S.C.A.) (DFA).

52. DFA § 512 (codified at 15 U.S.C.A. § 8201 note).

53. DFA §§ 521–527 (codified at 15 U.S.C.A. §§ 8201–8206).

54. 15 U.S.C.A. § 8206(9), (11).

55. DFA §§ 531–533 (codified at 15 U.S.C.A. §§ 8221–8223).

Chapter 6

HOLDING COMPANY ACTIVITIES

Table of Sections

§ 6.1 Introduction

As a general rule, holding companies are expected to limit their activities to ownership and control of banks[1] (in the case of bank holding companies) or of savings associations[2] (in the case of savings and loan holding companies). However, an extensive set of statutory provisions provide exemptions from this general rule. This chapter examines the effect of those exemptive provisions on the activities of holding companies. The most recent development in this regard is the enactment of the Gramm–Leach–Bliley Act ("GLBA")[3] in November 1999. Among other things, the GLBA permits bank holding companies that qualify as "financial holding companies" ("FHCs") to engage in activities, and acquire companies engaged in activities, that are "financial in nature"[4] or that are incidental[5] or complementary to such activities.[6] This new

---

§ 6.1

1. 12 U.S.C.A. § 1843(a)(1)–(2), (b).

2. 12 U.S.C.A. § 1467a(c)(1).

3. Pub. L. No. 106–102, Nov. 12, 1999, 113 Stat. 1338 (1999) (codified at scattered sections of 12, 15, 16, 18 U.S.C.A.)

4. GLBA, § 103(a) (codified at 12 U.S.C.A. § 1843(k)(1)).

5. 12 U.S.C.A. § 1843(k)(1)(A).

6. *Id.* § 1843(k)(1)(B). *See* 65 Fed. Reg. 80,384 (2000) (to be codified at 12 C.F.R. pt. 225) (proposing certain financial and nonfinancial data processing activities as "complementary" to financial activities).

authority marks a potentially dramatic change in bank regulatory policy; these provisions are discussed later in this chapter.[7]

§ 6.2 Bank Holding Company Act

Sections 6.2–6.5 focus on the Bank Holding Company Act ("BHCA") provisions governing nonbanking activities of holding companies,[1] as implemented by the Fed.[2] However, at the outset we should note the relationship between the Comptroller's power to approve incidental powers (including the acquisition or creation of a bank subsidiary to engage in incidental powers) under the National Bank Act ("NBA")[3] and the Fed's power to approve direct or indirect control of nonbanking activities under the BHCA.[4]

If a national bank proposes to conduct an activity as an "incidental power" in a wholly owned subsidiary, but the subsidiary is "indirectly controlled" by the bank's own holding company parent, does the Comptroller get to approve the activity, or must it also (or first) be approved by the Fed? As the D.C. Circuit's opinion in *American Insurance Association v. Clarke*[5] illustrates, this has been a particularly complex inquiry.[6] Essentially, the Fed has exclusive jurisdiction to interpret and apply the BHCA.[7] If the Comptroller, in applying the NBA, must interpret the BHCA, its interpretation is not entitled to deference, since the Comptroller is not charged with administration of that statute.[8] Hence, in "exceptional circumstances," the Comptroller may be required to defer his *final* approval under the NBA pending completion of the Fed's review under the BHCA.[9]

---

7. *See* § 6.3, *infra* (discussing regulation of FHCs).

§ 6.2

1. 112 U.S.C.A. §§ 1843–1844, 1848, *as amended*, Gramm–Leach–Bliley Act of 1999 (GLBA), Pub. L. No. 106–102, §§ 102(a), 103(a), (c)(2), (d), 107(a)–(b), (d)–(f), 111, 112(a), 116, 122, 113 Stat. 1338, 1341–1351, 1359–1367, 1372, 1381 (Nov. 12, 1999) (codified at 12 U.S.C.A. §§ 1843 note, 1843(c)(8), (f)(2)–(4), (f)(14), (j)(1)(A), (E), (j)(3), (k)–(o), 1844(a), (c), (e)(1), (g)); Dodd–Frank Wall Street Reform and Consumer Protection Act (DFA), §§ 354(2)–(3), 604(a)–(b), (c)(1)–(2), (e)(1)–(2), 606(a), 616(a), 623(b)(1)(A)–(B), Pub. L. No. 111–203, 124 Stat. 1376, 1546–1547 1599–1602, 1607, 1615–1635 1640–1641 (2010) (codified at 12 U.S.C.A. §§ 1843(i)(8), 1843(j)(2)(A), 1843(k)(6) (B), 1843(*l*)(1), 1844(b), 1844(c)(1)– (2), 1844(c)(5)(B)).

2. *See, e.g.,* 12 C.F.R. §§ 225.2, 225.21–225.28 (implementing 12 U.S.C.A. § 1843(c)); *id.* §§ 225.81– 225.94 (implementing 12 U.S.C.A. § 1843(k)–(o)).

3. 12 U.S.C.A. § 24 (Seventh).

4. *Id.* § 1843(a)(1)–(2), (c).

5. 865 F.2d 278 (D.C.Cir.1988).

6. The D.C. Circuit's first opinion, *American Ins. Ass'n v. Clarke*, 854 F.2d 1405 (D.C.Cir.1988), was later withdrawn, and its superseding opinion was itself later modified.

7. *See generally Whitney Nat'l Bank v. Bank of New Orleans & Trust Co.*, 379 U.S. 411, 85 S.Ct. 551 (1965).

8. *Department of the Treasury v. Federal Labor Relations Auth.*, 837 F.2d 1163, 1167 (D.C.Cir.1988) (citing cases).

9. *Whitney Nat'l Bank*, 379 U.S. at 426 n.7, 85 S.Ct. at 560 n. 7. *Whitney Nat'l Bank* has been interpreted to require the Comptroller to defer the issuance of a bank charter pending comple-

What seems clear from *American Insurance Association* is that the BHCA *does* apply to the acquisition of a nonbanking subsidiary by a national bank that is itself owned by a bank holding company, since the holding company is prohibited from acquiring "direct *or indirect* ownership or control of any voting shares of any company which is not a bank," unless an exception applies.[10] Hence, in cases that present a "substantial" question under the BHCA, "analysis must be undertaken by the [Fed] in the first instance."[11]

§ 6.3 Structure of the Statute

The Bank Holding Company Act ("BHCA") generally prohibits direct and indirect acquisition by a bank holding company of a company that is not a bank.[1] However, the typical question is whether or not a proposed acquisition of a nonbanking company meets the requirements of one of the exemptions specified in the BHCA.[2] Aside from some transitional and grandfathering exemptions,[3] there are 14 principal exemptions to the nonbanking prohibition.[4] The scope of each of these exemptions is illustrated in Figure 6–1, *infra*.

tion of the Fed's BHCA review when the transaction in question presents a "substantial" question under the BHCA. *American Bank of Tulsa v. Smith*, 503 F.2d 784, 789 (10th Cir.1974).

10. *See, e.g.,* 12 U.S.C.A. § 1843(a)(1) (emphasis added). *See also Security Pacific Corp.*, 72 Fed. Res. Bull. 800, 801 (1986) (acquisition of voting shares by subsidiary bank of bank holding company treated as acquisition by bank holding company and thus subject to § 1843); *Merchants Nat'l Corp.*, 73 Fed. Res. Bull. 876, 880 (1987) (same), *vacated in part on other grounds sub nom. Independent Ins. Agents of Am. v. Board of Governors*, 838 F.2d 627 (2d Cir.1988). *But cf. Citicorp v. Board of Governors*, 589 F.2d 1182 (2d Cir.1979), *cert. denied*, 442 U.S. 929, 99 S.Ct. 2860 (finding BHCA inapplicable to bank insurance subsidiary).

11. *American Ins. Ass'n*, 865 F.2d at 285. However, on rehearing, the D.C.

Circuit concluded that "the facts of this case do not present the 'exceptional circumstances' that would warrant our reaching the merits of the AIA's contention that the challenged acquisition is prohibited by the BHCA." *Id.* at 288. This issue was left to possible future petition by the American Insurance Association to the Fed. *Id.* at 287.

§ 6.3

1. 12 U.S.C.A. § 1843(a)(1)–(2). On acquisitions of savings associations by bank holding companies, see 12 U.S.C.A. § 1843(i). *See Citicorp v. Board of Governors*, 589 F.2d 1182 (2d Cir.1979), *cert. denied*, 442 U.S. 929, 99 S.Ct. 2860 (discussing nature of prohibition).

2. 12 U.S.C.A. § 1843(c).

3. 12 U.S.C.A. § 1843(c)(i)–(ii). *Cf. Patagonia Corp. v. Board of Governors*, 517 F.2d 803 (9th Cir.1975) (discussing grandfathering under § 1843).

4. 12 U.S.C.A. § 1843(c)(1)–(14).

Figure 6–1

BHCA: Principal Exemptions of Nonbanking Activities

12 U.S.C.A.	Exempted Activity
§ 1843(c)(1)	providing intra-company services; conducting safe deposit business; liquidating assets acquired from the parent holding company or banking subsidiaries, or acquired from any other source prior to becoming a bank holding company
§ 1843(c)(2)	holding shares acquired in satisfaction of a debt previously contracted (shares must be disposed of within two years, plus extensions granted by Fed)
§ 1843(c)(3)	acquiring shares from subsidiary requested to dispose of shares by federal or state examining authority (holding company must dispose of shares within two years)
§ 1843(c)(4)	holding or acquiring shares by bank in good faith in a fiduciary capacity[5]
§ 1843(c)(5)	holding "bank eligible" shares; i.e., "investment securities" eligible for investment by national banks under 12 U.S.C.A. § 24(Seventh)
§ 1843(c)(6)	holding not more than five percent of the outstanding voting shares of any company
§ 1843(c)(7)	holding shares of any investment company that is not a bank holding company and is not engaged in any business other than investing in securities (securities held by the investment company not to involve more than five percent of the outstanding voting shares of any company)
§ 1843(c)(8)	holding shares of any company the activities of which the Fed had determined, as of the day before enactment of the GLBA (November 12, 1999), to be *so closely related* to banking or managing or controlling banks as to be a *proper incident* thereto[6]
§ 1843(c)(9)	holding shares of or conducting activities by a company organized under laws of foreign country, with a majority of its business conducted outside the United States (application of the

5. This exemption does not cover shares held under a trust that itself constitutes a "company" for BHCA purposes For these purposes, "company" is defined in 12 U.S.C.A. § 1841(b). *See also id.* § 1841(g)(2)–(3) (stating exceptions).

6. *See* GLBA, § 102(a) (codified at 12 U.S.C.A. § 1843(c)(8)) (limiting prospective effect of "closely related" exception).

12 U.S.C.A.	Exempted Activity
	exemption must not be substantially at variance with the purposes of BHCA and must be in the public interest)
§ 1843(c)(10)	holding shares lawfully acquired and owned prior to May 9, 1956, by a bank that is bank holding company, or by its wholly owned subsidiary
§ 1843(c)(11)	holding shares owned directly or indirectly by a company that became a bank holding company under 1970 BHCA amendments, of a company that engages only in activities permissible for a bank holding company or subsidiaries (shares must have been owned as a subsidiary on June 30, 1968)[7]
§ 1843(c)(12)	ten-year transitional exemption generally allowing company that became a bank holding company under 1970 BHCA amendments, or its subsidiary, to retain shares if within ten years it ceases to be a bank holding company, divests shares,[8] or ceases activities not authorized under § 1843 (must comply with other conditions prescribed by Fed)[9]
§ 1843(c)(13)	holding shares of or conducting activities by, a company that does no U.S. business except incident to international or foreign business (application of the exemption must not be substantially at variance with the purposes of BHCA and must be in the public interest)
§ 1843(c)(14)	holding shares of an export trading company whose acquisition or formation by bank holding company has not been disapproved by Fed (the investment, direct or indirect, must not exceed five percent of holding company's consolidated capital and surplus)

Prior to the enactment of the Gramm–Leach–Bliley Act ("GLBA")[10] in November 1999, the key exemptive provision was, as a practical matter, "closely related" exemption.[11] The GLBA freezes

---

7. *Cf.* 12 U.S.C.A. § 1843(d) (providing special exemption for certain companies that controlled one bank prior to 1 July 1968).

8. *Cf. id.* § 1843(e) (providing generally for divestiture of non exempted shares).

9. *Cf. id.* § 1843(d).

10. Pub. L. No. 106–102, Nov. 12, 1999, 113 Stat. 1338 (1999) (codified at

scattered sections of 12, 15, 16, 18 U.S.C.A.).

11. *Id.* § 1843(c)(8). For cases interpreting the meaning and applicability of § 1843(c)(8), see *Securities Indus. Ass'n v. Board of Governors*, 468 U.S. 207, 104 S.Ct. 3003 (1984); *National Courier Ass'n v. Board of Governors*, 516 F.2d 1229, 1232 (D.C.Cir.1975); *Alabama Ass'n of Ins. Agents v. Board of Governors*, 533 F.2d 224 (5th Cir.1976),

in place the "closely related" exemption as of GLBA enactment.[12] A new section permits BHCs that qualify as "financial holding companies" ("FHCs") to engage in activities, and acquire companies engaged in activities, that are "financial in nature"[13] or that are incidental to such activities.[14] FHCs are also permitted to engage in activities that are complementary to financial activities,[15] if the Fed determines that the activity does not pose a substantial risk to the safety or soundness of depository institutions or the financial system in general.[16] The integrity of the deposit insurance funds is preserved by prohibiting the use of deposit insurance funds to benefit any shareholder, subsidiary or nondepository affiliate of an FHC.[17]

amended, 558 F.2d 729 (5th Cir.1977), *cert. denied*, 435 U.S. 904, 98 S.Ct. 1448 (1978); *Association of Bank Travel Bureaus, Inc. v. Board of Governors*, 568 F.2d 549 (7th Cir.1978); *Independent Ins. Agents of Am., Inc. v. Board of Governors*, 658 F.2d 571 (8th Cir.1981), *reh'g denied*, 664 F.2d 177, *appeal after remand*, 736 F.2d 468 (8th Cir.1984); *Association of Data Processing Serv. Orgs. v. Board of Governors*, 745 F.2d 677 (D.C.Cir.1984).

12. GLBA, § 102(a) (codified at 12 U.S.C.A. § 1843(c)(8)). For an example of the post-GLBA policy of the Fed with respect to this exemption, see 65 Fed. Reg. 80,384 (2000) (to be codified at 12 C.F.R. pt. 225) (proposing to change conditions governing conduct of financial data processing activities previously found to be closely related to banking, to permit all BHCs to conduct greater amount of nonfinancial data processing in connection with processing financial data).

13. GLBA, § 103(a) (codified at 12 U.S.C.A. § 1843(k)(1)). For an example of implementation by the Fed and Treasury of the concept of an activity "financial in nature," see 66 Fed. Reg. 307 (2001) (to be codified at 12 C.F.R. pts. 225, 1501) (proposing joint Fed–Treasury rule determining that real estate brokerage is *either* activity "financial in nature" *or* activity "incidental" to financial activity; also considering whether real estate management activities should be considered "financial in nature" or "incidental" to financial activity).

14. 12 U.S.C.A. § 1843(k)(1)(A). For an example of the Fed's implementation of the authority for activities "incidental" to financial activities, see 65 Fed. Reg. 80,735 (2000) (codified at 12 C.F.R. pt. 225), determining by rule that acting as finder (*i.e.*, bringing together buyer and seller of product or service, with buyer and seller negotiating and concluding transaction) incidental to activity "financial in nature". *See also* 66 Fed. Reg. 307 (2001) (discussed in note 14, *supra*).

15. 12 U.S.C.A. § 1843(k)(1)(B). The term "complementary" is not defined. For an example of the Fed's implementation of the authority for "complementary" activities, see 65 Fed. Reg. 80,384 (2000) (to be codified at 12 C.F.R. pt. 225) (proposing to allow FHC to own company engaged in specified types of data storage, internet and portal hosting activities, and broad advisory activities involving data processing activities, if company also provides financial data processing or other financial products and services; also considering whether to permit FHC to invest in company engaged in developing new technologies that might support the sale and availability of financial products and services, company providing communication links for delivery of financial products and services, and/or company engaged in electronic sale and delivery of products and services).

16. Complementary activities must be approved by the Fed case-by-case under BHCA notice procedures. GLBA, § 103(c)(2) (codified at 12 U.S.C.A. § 1843(j)). *Cf.* 65 Fed. Reg. 80,384, *supra* (proposing certain complementary activities).

17. GLBA, § 117 (codified at 12 U.S.C.A. § 1821(a)(4)(B)).

The Fed is required (by regulation or order) to define, consistent with the purposes of the GLBA, the activities described as financial in nature, and the extent to which such activities are financial in nature or incidental to a financial activity.[18] The described activities are as follows:

(i) Lending, exchanging, transferring, investing for others, or safeguarding financial assets other than money or securities.

(ii) Providing any device or other instrumentality for transferring money or other financial assets.

(iii) Arranging, effecting, or facilitating financial transactions for the account of third parties.[19]

In determining what activities are financial in nature or incidental,[20] the Fed must notify the Secretary of the Treasury—*not* the Comptroller—of applications or requests to engage in new financial activities.[21] The Fed may not determine that an activity is financial or incidental to a financial activity if the Secretary objects.[22] The Secretary may also propose to the Fed that the Fed find that a particular activity is financial in nature or incidental.[23] Section 1843(k)(4) does contain a list of activities that are *per se* considered to be financial in nature.[24] These "K4 activities" are identified in Figure 6–2, *infra*. An FHC may engage in the activities on this list without obtaining prior approval from the Fed,[25] but with notice to

18. 12 U.S.C.A. § 1843(k)(5)(A). On the implementation of § 1843(k)(5), see 66 Fed. Reg. 257 (2001) (codified at 12 C.F.R. pts. 225, 1501) (joint Fed–Treasury interim rule identifying three general types of activities as "financial in nature;" creating mechanism for FHCs, financial subsidiaries of national banks, and others to request that Fed or Treasury Secretary define particular activities within one of three categories).

19. *Id.* § 1843(k)(5)(B)(i)–(iii).

20. In making such determinations, the Fed is required to consult the following factors:

(A) the purposes of this Act and the [GLBA];

(B) changes or reasonably expected changes in the marketplace in which financial holding companies compete;

(C) changes or reasonably expected changes in the technology for delivering financial services; and

(D) whether such activity is necessary or appropriate to allow a financial holding company and the affiliates of a financial holding company to—

(i) compete effectively with any company seeking to provide financial services in the United States;

(ii) efficiently deliver information and services that are financial in nature through the use of technological means, including any application necessary to protect the security or efficacy of systems for the transmission of data or financial transactions; and

(iii) offer customers any available or emerging technological means for using financial services or for the document imaging of data.

Id. § 1843(k)(3)(A)–(D)(iii).

21. *Id.* § 1843(k)(2)(A)(i).

22. *Id.* § 1843(k)(2)(A)(ii).

23. *Id.* § 1843(k)(2)(B).

24. *Id.* § 1843(k)(4).

25. *Id.* § 1843(k)(6)(B), as amended, Dodd–Frank Wall Street Reform and Consumer Protection Act §§ 604(e)(2), 623(B)(1)(b), Pub. L. No. 111–203, 124 Stat. 1376,1601–1602, 1635 (2010).

the Fed within 30 days after the activity is commenced or a company is acquired.[26]

Figure 6–2

Activities "Financial in Nature"

12 U.S.C.A. § 1843(k)(4)	*Activity*
(A)	Lending, exchanging, transferring, investing for others, or safeguarding money or securities.
(B)	Insuring, guaranteeing, or indemnifying against loss, harm, damage, illness, disability, or death, or providing and issuing annuities, and acting as principal, agent, or broker for purposes of the foregoing, in any State.
(C)	Providing financial, investment, or economic advisory services, including advising an investment company.
(D)	Issuing or selling instruments representing interests in pools of assets permissible for a bank to hold directly.
(E)	Underwriting, dealing in, or making a market in securities.
(F)	Engaging in "closely related" activity (as in effect on 12 November 1999).
(G)	Engaging, in the United States, in any activity that a BHC could engage in outside the United States, as usual in connection with the transaction of banking or other financial operations abroad, as in effect on 11 November 1999.
(H)	Directly or indirectly acquiring or controlling, whether as principal, on behalf of one or more entities (including entities, other than a depository institution or subsidiary of a depository institution, that the BHC controls), or otherwise, shares, assets, or ownership interests (including debt or equity securities, partnership interests, trust certificates, or other instruments representing ownership) of a securities or investment firm engaged in any activity not authorized pursuant to 12 U.S.C.A. § 1843, subject to specified conditions.
(I)	Directly or indirectly acquiring or controlling, whether as principal, on behalf of one.

---

26. *Id.* § 1843(k)(6)(A).

12 U.S.C.A. § 1843(k)(4)	Activity
	or more entities (including entities, other than a depository institution or subsidiary of a depository institution, that the BHC controls) or otherwise, shares, assets, or ownership interests (including debt or equity securities, partnership interests, trust certificates or other instruments representing ownership) of an insurance firm engaged in any activity not authorized pursuant to 12 U.S.C.A. § 1843,[27] subject to specified conditions.

A BHC may elect to become an FHC if all of its subsidiary banks are well capitalized and well managed.[28] A BHC that meets these requirements may file a certification to that effect with the Fed and a declaration electing to be an FHC.[29] After this filing an FHC may engage, either *de novo* or by acquisition, in any activity that has been determined by the Fed to be financial in nature or incidental.[30] BHCs that elect to become FHCs by meeting the statutory requirements and filing a declaration and a certification are not required to file a duplicative BHC registration statement under section 1844.[31] FHCs may engage in K4 activities, and any other financial activity approved by the Fed without prior notice.[32] Complementary activities must be approved by the Fed case-by-case under BHCA notice procedures.[33]

As events have overtaken the act's FHC provisions, it turns out that not just BHCs but also other financial services firms—like investment banks and insurance companies—have been attracted

27. On insurance activities of BHCs under § 1843, see *National Ass'n of Cas. & Sur. Agents v. Board of Governors*, 856 F.2d 282 (D.C.Cir.1988), *reh'g denied*, 862 F.2d 351, *cert. denied*, 490 U.S. 1090, 109 S.Ct. 2430 (1989); *Florida Ass'n of Ins. Agents, Inc. v. Board of Governors*, 591 F.2d 334 (5th Cir.1979); *Alabama Ass'n of Ins. Agents v. Board of Governors*, 533 F.2d 224 (5th Cir.1976), *amended*, 558 F.2d 729 (5th Cir.1977), *cert. denied*, 435 U.S. 904, 98 S.Ct. 1448 (1978); *Independent Bankers Ass'n of Ga. v. Board of Governors*, 516 F.2d 1206 (D.C.Cir.1975); *National Ass'n of Ins. Agents, Inc. v. Board of Governors*, 489 F.2d 1268 (D.C.Cir.1974). *See also* Michael P. Malloy, *The Sound of Two Hands Flapping: Insurance–Related Activities of National Banks*, 41 St. Louis U. L.J. 75 (1997).

28. GLBA, § 103(a) (codified at 12 U.S.C.A. § 1843(*l*)).

29. 12 U.S.C.A. § 1843(*l*)(1)(C).

30. *Id.* § 1843(*l*)(1).

31. *Id.* § 1844(a), *as amended*, Dodd–Frank Wall Street Reform and Consumer Protection Act, § 354(3), Pub. L. No. 111–203, 124 Stat. 1376, 1547 (codified at 12 U.S.C.A. § 1844).

32. *Id.* § 1843(k)(6)(B).

33. *Id.* § 1843(j). *See* 65 Fed. Reg. 80,384 (2000) (to be codified at 12 C.F.R. pt. 225) (proposing certain financial and nonfinancial data processing activities as "complementary" to financial activities).

to the idea of reorganizing and diversifying as FHCs. Insurance companies have shown increasing interest in acquiring or establishing de novo banking and financial services affiliates under the FHC structure.[34] Since 1999, over fifteen insurance companies have established such affiliates, including State Farm Group (State Farm Bank), MetLife (MetLife Bank NA), American International Group (AIG Federal Savings Bank), and Allstate Corp. (Allstate Bank), with total assets of $28 billion. With large bank-based FHCs possibly withdrawing from the insurance sector and selling off insurance assets,[35] insurance companies have an opportunity to diversify into a sector with a higher return on equity. Efficiencies are also being achieved by these insurance companies by maintaining their banking affiliates as "virtual banks," accessed by customers through the Internet, ATMs, and mail.[36]

In late 2008, two major investment banks, Goldman Sachs and Morgan Stanley, reorganized their operations to convert to bank holding company status, with a full service bank as an operating subsidiary.[37] Goldman Sachs converted some of its operations to a full service bank approved by New York State, and Morgan Stanley similarly converted some of its operations to a national bank approved by the Comptroller of the Currency.

As originally enacted, the GLBA imposed restrictions on certain cross-marketing activities between a depository institution affiliated with an FHC and the FHC's securities or insurance affiliates[38] but with specified exceptions for certain insurance affiliates of the FHC.[39] Section 611 of the Financial Services Regulatory Relief Act of 2006[40] modified the cross marketing restrictions, allowing an FHC's depository institution subsidiary to engage in specified cross-marketing with securities affiliates to the same extent that cross-marketing is permitted for insurance affiliates.[41]

If the Fed finds that an FHC is engaged in an activity financial in nature (other than a "closely related" activity) at a time when it is not well capitalized or well managed, or before it has filed an FHC election and certification, the Fed is required to give notice to

34. See Shefali Anand, U.S. Insurers Acquire A Foothold in Banking, Wall St. J. Europe, July 18, 2005, at M1, col. 5 (discussing insurance companies establishing retail banking units).

35. See id. at M1, col. 6, M5, col. 5 (describing movement of banks away from insurance).

36. Id. at M5, col. 6.

37. See Stephen Joyce, Last Two Investment Banks Receive Charters, Foreshadow Regulatory Debate, BNA BANKING DAILY (Dec. 1, 2008), available at http://news.bna.com (discussing approv-

als of reorganizations and conversions by state and federal authorities).

38. 12 U.S.C.A. § 1843(n)(5)(A) (2000). See id. § 1843(k)(4)(H)–(I) (identifying K4 securities and insurance activities),

39. 12 U.S.C.A. § 1843(n)(5)(B) (2000).

40. Pub. L. No. 109–351, § 611, 120 Stat. 1966, 1984 (2006) (codified at 12 U.S.C.A. § 1843(n)(5)(B)),

41. 12 U.S.C.A. § 1843(n)(5)(A)–(B).

the FHC to that effect, describing the conditions giving rise to the notice.[42] Within 45 days of receipt of the notice,[43] the FHC must execute an agreement with the Fed[44] to comply with these requirements.[45] Until the deficiencies are corrected, the Fed may impose limits on the conduct or activities of the FHC or any affiliate thereof, as the Fed deems appropriate under the circumstances and consistent with the statutory purposes.[46] If the conditions are not corrected within 180 days of receipt of the notice, the Fed may require the FHC, under terms, conditions and timing imposed by the Fed to divest control of any depository institution subsidiary[47] or to cease activities that are not "closely related" to banking.[48]

Any person aggrieved by an order of the Fed under the BHCA may obtain judicial review in the U.S. court of appeals in any circuit in which the person has a principal place of business, or in the D.C. Circuit.[49] Petition for review must be filed within 30 days after entry of the Fed's order.[50] The standard of judicial review with respect to Fed action under the BHCA is generally whether the action was arbitrary, capricious, an abuse of discretion, or otherwise not in accordance with law.[51] However, the Fed's factual findings under the act are conclusive only if supported by substantial evidence.[52]

§ 6.4   Structure of the Regulations

The current regulations mirror the structure of the statute, but in certain respects they are skewed in favor of the statute's application in practice. For example, while the statute gives formally equivalent status to all of the exemptions in § 1843(c), the regulations emphasize the role of the closely related exemption and almost trivializes the others.[1] In addition, the regulations under-

---

42. *Id.* § 1843(m)(1).

43. The Fed may permit an "additional period." *Id.* § 1843(m)(2).

44. Any action under this provision by the Fed requires consultation "with all relevant Federal and State regulatory agencies and authorities." *Id.* § 1843(m)(5).

45. *Id.* § 1843(m)(2).

46. *Id.* § 1843(m)(3).

47. *Id.* § 1843(m)(4)(A).

48. *Id.* § 1843(m)(4)(B).

49. 12 U.S.C.A. § 1848. On the options available to a "party aggrieved," see *BankAmerica Corp. v. Board of Governors,* 596 F.2d 1368 (9th Cir.1979).

50. 12 U.S.C.A. § 1848. *See Memphis Trust Co. v. Board of Governors,*

584 F.2d 921 (6th Cir.1978) (discussing filing requirement and exclusive jurisdiction of courts of appeal).

51. *See, e.g., Securities Indus. Ass'n v. Board of Governors,* 468 U.S. 207, 104 S.Ct. 3003 (1984) (upholding Fed action under standard); *NCNB Corp. v. Board of Governors,* 599 F.2d 609 (4th Cir. 1979).

52. 12 U.S.C.A. § 1848. On application of the substantial evidence standard of review, see *Association of Data Processing Serv. Orgs. v. Board of Governors,* 745 F.2d 677 (D.C.Cir.1984); *Independent Bankers Ass'n of Ga., supra*: *American Bancorporation, Inc. v. Board of Governors,* 509 F.2d 29 (8th Cir.1974).

§ 6.4

1. *See, e.g.* 12 C.F.R. § 225.21(a):

standably give some prominence to the implementation of the activities "financial in nature" that may be engaged in by financial holding companies ("FHCs") under the Gramm–Leach–Bliley Act into law ("GLBA").[2] The structure is illustrated in Figure 6–3, *infra*.

(a) Prohibited nonbanking activities and acquisitions. Except as provided in § 225.22 ..., a bank holding company or a subsidiary may not engage in, or acquire or control, directly or indirectly, voting securities or assets of a company engaged in, any activity other than:

(1) Banking or managing or controlling banks and other subsidiaries authorized under the [BHCA]; and

(2) An activity that the [Fed] determines to be so closely related to banking, or managing or controlling banks as to be a proper incident thereto, including any incidental activities that are necessary to carry on such an activity, if the bank holding company has obtained the prior approval of the [Fed] for that activity in accordance with the requirements of this regulation.

In fact, of course, § 225.21(a)(1) collapses into 14 words, the provisions of 12 U.S.C.A. § 1843(a)(1)–(2), while § 225.21(a)(2) memorializes 12 U.S.C.A. § 1843(c)(8). The other 13 exemptions of § 1843(c) are picked up by various paragraphs of 12 C.F.R. § 225.22. *But see* 12 U.S.C.A. § 1843(j)(1)(A) (requiring written notice and often prior approval for closely related activities). The nonbanking activities "financial in nature" that are authorized under 12 U.S.C.A. § 1843(k) are treated in 12 C.F.R. § 225.86.

2. Pub. L. No. 106–102, Nov. 12, 1999, 113 Stat. 1338 (1999) (codified at scattered sections of 12, 15, 16, 18 U.S.C.A.).

Figure 6-3
Nonbanking Activities: Structure of the Regulations

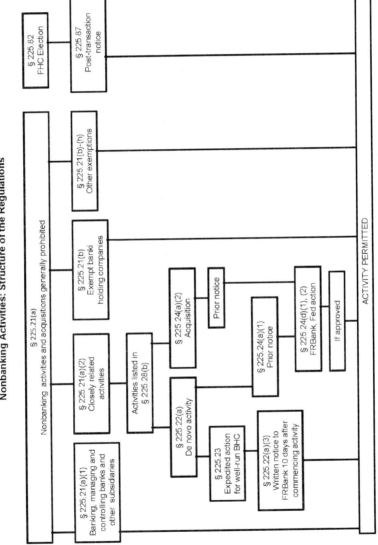

Both the statute and the implementing regulations provide for a limited period of time for action on an application (or "notice," in current Fed practice).[3] In general, a notice is deemed approved 60 days after filing of a complete notice with the Fed, unless the Fed acts on the notice before the end of that period.[4] The period may be extended for an additional 30 days by the Fed, with additional extensions subject to agreement with the bank holding company that has filed the notice.[5] In addition, if a hearing is requested or the Fed determines that a hearing is warranted,[6] the period may be extended for a time not exceeding 91 days after the hearing record is complete.[7] For notices involving nonlisted activities (*i.e.*, activities not listed in the regulations as being closely related to banking[8]), the Fed has the authority to extend the period for an additional 90 days.[9]

In reviewing a notice, the Fed is required by the statute to consider whether the public benefits of the activity outweigh the possible adverse effects.[10] In addition, the Fed has the statutory authority to disapprove any notice if the bank holding company

---

3. *Cf. BankAmerica Corp. v. Board of Governors*, 596 F.2d 1368 (9th Cir. 1979) (discussing statutory objective of prompt consideration of applications).

4. 12 U.S.C.A. § 1843(j)(1)(C)(i). *See* 12 C.F.R. § 225.25(b)(1) (providing for approval through failure to act on notice).

5. 12 U.S.C.A. § 1843(j)(1)(C)(ii).

6. *See* 12 C.F.R. § 225.25(a)(2) (providing that Fed "shall order a hearing only if there are disputed issues of material fact that cannot be resolved in some other manner").

7. 12 U.S.C.A. § 1843(j)(1)(C)(iii). *See* 12 C.F.R. § 225.25(a)(3) (providing for extension of period for hearing).

8. *See* 12 C.F.R. § 225.28(b) (listing activities predetermined to be closely related).

9. 12 U.S.C.A. § 1843(j)(1)(E).

10. 12 U.S.C.A. § 1843(j)(2)(A). *See* 12 C.F.R. § 225.26, which provides in part as follows:

(a) In general. In evaluating a notice ... the [Fed] shall consider whether the notificant's performance of the activities can reasonably be expected to produce benefits to the public (such as greater convenience, increased competition, and gains in efficiency) that outweigh possible adverse effects (such as undue concentration of resources, decreased or unfair competition, conflicts of interest, and unsound banking practices).

(b) Financial and managerial resources. Consideration of the factors in paragraph (a) of this section includes an evaluation of the financial and managerial resources of the notificant, including its subsidiaries and any company to be acquired, the effect of the proposed transaction on those resources, and the management expertise, internal control and risk-management systems, and capital of the entity conducting the activity.

(c) Competitive effect of de novo proposals. Unless the record demonstrates otherwise, the commencement or expansion of a nonbanking activity de novo is presumed to result in benefits to the public through increased competition....

(e) Conditional approvals. The [Fed] may impose conditions on any approval, including conditions to address permissibility, financial, managerial, safety and soundness, competitive, compliance, conflicts of interest, or other concerns to ensure that approval is consistent with the relevant statutory factors and other provisions of the [BHCA].

submitting the notice neglects, fails, or refuses to furnish all the information required by the Fed.[11]

In January 2000, the Fed published interim final rules implementing the new GLBA authority for FHCs.[12] The interim rule was effective 11 March 2000, but the Fed indicated that it would allow BHCs and foreign banks to file FHC elections immediately, in anticipation of the effective date of the GLBA provisions and the interim rule, and that it would review elections as promptly as possible after the effective date.[13] This interim final rule was replaced by a final rule in January 2001.[14]

In March 2000, the Fed published three interim rules that amended the January rules and also provided further detail and implementation of GLBA. On 17 March 2000, the Fed published an interim rule amending the FHC rules to include a list of financial activities permissible to FHCs under the GLBA.[15] This interim final rule was also replaced by a final rule in January 2001.[16]

Also on 17 March 2000, the Fed published an interim rule[17] that imposed two operating standards on FHCs.[18] Under this interim rule, intra-day extensions of credit to a securities affiliate must be on market terms, and affiliate transactions of foreign bank FHCs are also restricted.[19] This interim rule is also effective as of 11 March 2000.[20]

On 21 March 2000, the Fed published an interim rule amending the January 2000 rule to make a number of changes concerning FHC election by a foreign bank.[21] This interim rule was also replaced by a final rule in January 2001.[22] Among other things, the final rule establishes the procedures a domestic bank holding company and a foreign banking organization must follow and the

---

11. 12 U.S.C.A. § 1843(j)(2)(B).

12. 65 Fed. Reg. 3785 (2000) (codified at 12 C.F.R. pt. 225) (adopting interim final rule on FHC election and operation).

13. 65 Fed. Reg. at 3785. The Fed anticipated that it would begin notifying qualifying companies as early as 13 March 2000 of FHC effectiveness. *Id.*

14. 66 Fed. Reg. 400 (2001) (codified at 12 C.F.R. pt. 225).

15. 65 Fed. Reg. 14,433 (2000) (codified at 12 C.F.R. pt. 225). *See also* 65 Fed. Reg. 47,696 (2000) (to be codified at 12 C.F.R. pt. 225) (proposing activity of acting as "finder" as "financial in nature," permissible for FHCs); 65 Fed. Reg. 80,384 (2000) (to be codified at 12 C.F.R. pt. 225) (proposing certain financial and nonfinancial data processing ac-

tivities as "complementary" to financial activities). By final rule, acting as a finder was later added to the list of activities that are permissible for an FHC under a streamlined, post-transaction notice procedure. 65 Fed. Reg. 80,735 (2000) (codified at 12 C.F.R. pt. 225).

16. 66 Fed. Reg. 400 (2001) (codified at 12 C.F.R. pt. 225).

17. 65 Fed. Reg. 14,440 (2000) (codified at 12 C.F.R. pt. 225).

18. 12 C.F.R. § 225.200.

19. *Id.* § 225.4(g)(1)–(2).

20. 65 Fed. Reg. at 14,440.

21. 65 Fed. Reg. 15,053 (2000) (codified at 12 C.F.R. pt. 225).

22. 66 Fed. Reg. 400 (2001) (codified at 12 C.F.R. pt. 225).

capital, management, and CRA requirements that they must meet in order to qualify as an FHC.[23] It also contains provisions that apply to an FHC that subsequently ceases to meet the applicable requirements.[24] In addition, the final rule lists the activities that the GLBA defines as "financial in nature" and thus authorized for an FHC to conduct.[25] It establishes a post-transaction notice procedure;[26] a procedure that allows any interested party to request that the Fed determine, in consultation with the Secretary of the Treasury, that additional activities are "financial in nature" or incidental to a financial activity and thus permissible for an FHC;[27] and a procedure that allows an FHC to request Fed prior approval to conduct an activity that is complementary to a financial activity.[28] The final rule is effective as of 2 February 2001.[29]

Also in January 2001, the Fed and the Secretary of the Treasury jointly adopted a final rule governing merchant banking investments made by FHCs.[30] The rule implements provisions of the GLBA that permit FHCs to make investments as part of a *bona fide* securities underwriting or merchant or investment banking activity. It is effective as of 15 February 2001.[31]

§ 6.5   Permissible Activities

Through a combination of formal rulemaking, administrative determinations based on specific notices, and litigation concerning Fed policies, a core list of "closely related" activities emerged, up through the enactment of the Gramm–Leach–Bliley Act ("GLBA").[1] For the most part, it is codified in the Fed's BHCA regulations.[2] Figure 6–4, *infra*, illustrates the current list of closely related activities. Although the inclusion of a particular activity in the list creates certain procedural advantages in the processing of a notice,[3] it does not predetermine the outcome of a notice.[4] The public

23. 12 C.F.R. §§ 225.82, 225.90–225.92.

24. *Id.* §§ 225.84, 225.93–225.94.

25. *Id.* § 225.86.

26. *Id.* § 225.87.

27. *Id.* § 225.88.

28. *Id.* § 225.89.

29. 66 Fed. Reg. at 400.

30. 66 Fed. Reg. 8466 (2001) (codified at 12 C.F.R. pts. 225, 1500).

31. 66 Fed. Reg. at 8466.

§ 6.5

1. Pub. L. No. 106–102, Nov. 12, 1999, 113 Stat. 1338 (1999) (codified at scattered sections of 12, 15, 16, 18

U.S.C.A.). The GLBA freezes in place the "closely related activity" exception as of the date of the act's enactment. GLBA, § 102(a) (codified at 12 U.S.C.A. § 1843(c)(8)).

2. 12 C.F.R. § 225.28(b).

3. *See, e.g.,* 12 C.F.R. §§ 225.22(a), 225.24(a)(1)–(2) (concerning treatment of notices involving listed activities).

4. *Independent Bankers Ass'n of Ga. v. Board of Governors,* 516 F.2d 1206 (D.C.Cir.1975).

benefits of the proposed activity, outweighing its possible adverse affects, must still be demonstrated on a case-by-case basis.[5]

Permissible activities that are "financial in nature" are authorized by the GLBA by inclusion of an activity in the list of "K4 activities,"[6] or by the Fed's determination that an unlisted activity is "financial in nature."[7] K4 activities are identified in Figure 6–2, *supra*. In March 2000, the Fed published an interim rule amending the FHC rules to include a list of financial activities permissible for FHCs under the GLBA.[8] In addition to K4 activities, the rule identified the following activities as determined to be permissible for FHCs: (*i*) Activities previously determined by Fed regulation[9] or order[10] to be "closely related to banking"[11] prior to November 12, 1999; and, (*ii*) Activities that are usual in connection with the transaction of banking abroad, as determined by Fed regulation in effect on November 11, 1999.[12] A joint Fed–Treasury rule later expressly added securities underwriting, merchant banking, and investment banking activities to the permitted activities of FHCs.[13] By final rule, the Fed later added acting as a finder to the list of activities that are permissible for an FHC, under a streamlined, post-transaction notice procedure.[14]

Figure 6–4
Activities Predetermined to be Closely Related[15]

12 C.F.R.	Activity
§ 225.28(b)(1)	extending credit and servicing loans
§ 225.28(b)(2)	activities related to extending credit (*e.g.*, property appraising; arranging financing; check-guaranty services; collection agency services; credit bureau services; asset management; acquiring debt in default; real estate settlement servicing)
§ 225.28(b)(3)	leasing personal or real property, under specified circumstances

5. 12 C.F.R. § 225.26(a). *Cf. Independent Bankers Ass'n of Ga.*, *supra* (emphasizing right of interested parties to full adjudicatory hearing).

6. 12 U.S.C.A. § 1843(k)(4).

7. *Id.* 1843(k)(1).

8. 65 Fed. Reg. 14,433, 14,438–14,439 (2000) (codified at 12 C.F.R. § 225.86).

9. 12 C.F.R. § 225.86(a)(1). *See id.* § 225.28 (identifying closely related activities).

10. *Id.* § 225.86(a)(2).

11. *Per* 12 U.S.C.A. § 1843(c)(8).

12. 12 C.F.R. § 225.86(b). *See id.* § 211.5(d) (identifying activities usual in connection with transaction of banking abroad).

13. 65 Fed. Reg. 16,460 (2000) (codified at 12 C.F.R. §§ 225.1(c)(9)–(15), 225.170–225.175, 1500.1–1500.7; redesignating 225.1(c)(9)–(13) as (c)(11)–(15); reserving 225.1(c)(9)).

14. 65 Fed. Reg. 80,735 (2000) (codified at 12 C.F.R. pt. 225).

15. *Source*: 12 C.F.R. § 225.28(b).

12 C.F.R.	Activity
§ 225.28(b)(4)	operating nonbank depository institutions, including industrial banks and savings associations
§ 225.28(b)(5)	trust company functions
§ 225.28(b)(6)	financial and investment advisory activities
§ 225.28(b)(7)	transactional services as agent for customer investments (*e.g.*, securities brokerage;[16] "riskless principal" transactions;[17] private placement services; futures commission merchant, under specified circumstances; services with respect to swaps and similar transactions); permitted activities do not include selling "bank-ineligible" securities[18] at the order of a customer that is the issuer of the securities, selling bank-ineligible securities in a transaction where the company has a contractual agreement to place the securities as agent of the issuer, or acting as a principal in a transaction involving a bank-ineligible security for which the company or any of its affiliates acts as underwriter (during the period of the underwriting or for 30 days thereafter) or dealer
§ 225.28(b)(8)	investment transactions as principal (*e.g.*, underwriting and dealing in government obligations and money market instruments; investing and trading activities involving foreign exchange, forward contracts, options, futures, options on futures, swaps, and similar contracts, under specified circumstances; buying and selling bullion, and related activities)
§ 225.28(b)(9)	management consulting and counseling activities (*e.g.*, employee benefits consulting services; career counseling services)
§ 225.28(b)(10)	support services such as courier services, under specified circumstances;[19] and printing and selling MICR-encoded items

16. *See Securities Indus. Ass'n v. Board of Governors*, 468 U.S. 207, 104 S.Ct. 3003 (1984) (upholding Fed position).

17. *I.e.*, buying and selling all types of securities in the secondary market, on the order of a customer, by "purchas[ing] (or sell[ing]) the security for [the company's] own account to offset a contemporaneous sale to (or purchase from) the customer." 12 C.F.R. § 225.28(b)(7)(ii).

18. A bank-ineligible security is any security that a national or state member bank is not permitted to underwrite or deal in under 12 U.S.C.A. §§ 24 and 335.

19. *Cf. National Courier Ass'n v. Board of Governors*, 516 F.2d 1229 (D.C.Cir.1975) (approving certain courier services); *Cameron Fin. Corp. v. Board of Governors*, 497 F.2d 841 (4th Cir.1974) (discussing courier services spun off from holding company).

12 C.F.R.	Activity
§ 225.28(b)(11)	insurance agency and underwriting, under specified circumstances[20]
§ 225.28(b)(12)	community development activities, including financing and investment activities, advisory activities
§ 225.28(b)(13)	money orders, savings bonds, and traveler's checks
§ 225.28(b)(14)	data processing, under specified circumstances[21]

§ 6.6   Home Owners' Loan Act

The savings and loan holding company provisions of the Home Owners' Loan Act ("HOLA")[1] generally parallel the Bank Holding Company Act "(BHCA") provisions, although there are some significant differences. Figure 6–5, *infra*, gives a schematic comparison of the two sets of provisions.

Figure 6–5
Holding Company Activities: BHCA and HOLA

Provision	BHCA Section	HOLA Section
General prohibition on non-banking/non-S & L activities	§ 1843(a)	§ 1467a(c)(1), (4)

20. *See* 12 U.S.C.A. § 1843(c)(8)(A)–(G) (1998) (providing statutory limits on insurance activities of bank holding companies). *See also National Ass'n of Cas. & Sur. Agents v. Board of Governors*, 856 F.2d 282 (D.C.Cir.1988), *reh'g denied*, 862 F.2d 351, *cert. denied*, 490 U.S. 1090, 109 S.Ct. 2430 (1989) (discussing § 1843(c)(8)(D)). *Cf. Florida Ass'n of Ins. Agents, Inc. v. Board of Governors*, 591 F.2d 334 (5th Cir.1979) (interpreting prior statutory language); *Alabama Ass'n of Ins. Agents v. Board of Governors*, 533 F.2d 224 (5th Cir.1976), *amended*, 558 F.2d 729 (5th Cir.1977), *cert. denied*, 435 U.S. 904, 98 S.Ct. 1448 (1978); *Independent Bankers Ass'n of Ga. v. Board of Governors*, 516 F.2d 1206 (D.C.Cir.1975); *National Ass'n of Ins. Agents, Inc. v. Board of Governors*, 489 F.2d 1268 (D.C.Cir.1974). *See generally* Michael P. Malloy, *The Sound of Two Hands Flapping: Insurance–Relat-ed Activities of National Banks*, 41 St. Louis U. L.J. 75 (1997) (discussing insurance activities).

21. *See National Courier Ass'n, supra; Association of Data Processing Serv. Orgs. v. Board of Governors*, 745 F.2d 677 (D.C.Cir.1984).

§ 6.6

1. 12 U.S.C.A. § 1467a, *as amended* Dodd–Frank Wall Street Reform and Consumer Protection Act, §§ 367(2), 604(g), (h)(2), (i), 606(b), 616(b), 623(c), 624, 625, Pub. L. No. 111–203, § 312(b)(2)(C)(ii), 124 Stat. 1376, 1556, 1564–1565, 1602–1604, 1607, 1615–1616, 1635–1638 (2010) (codified at 12 U.S.C.A. §§ 1467a note, 1467a(a)(1) (D)(ii), 1467a(b)(2), (b)(4), 1467a(c) (2)(H), 1467a(e)(2)(E), 1467a(g)(1), 1467a(m)(3)(A), (m)(3)(B)(i)(III)–(IV), 1467a(o)(11)).

Provision	BHCA Section	HOLA Section
Treatment of share certificates	§ 1843(b)	
Exceptions	§ 1843(c)	§ 1467a(c)(2)
Special organizations	§ 1843(c)(i)	[§ 1467a(c)(2)(F), (4)]
Family companies	§ 1843(c)(ii)	[§ 1467a(c)(2)(F), (4)]
Special services	§ 1843(c)(1)	§ 1467a(c)(2)(A), (C), (D), (F), (4)
Debt previously contracted	§ 1843(c)(2)	§ 1467a(c)(2)(F), (4)
Divesting subsidiaries	§ 1843(c)(3)	§ 1467a(c)(2)(C), (F), 4
Fiduciary activities	§ 1843(c)(4)	§ 1467a(c)(2)(E), (F), (4)
Investment securities	§ 1843(c)(5)	§ 1467a(c)(2)(F), (4)
Five percent holdings	§ 1843(c)(6)	§ 1467a(c)(2)(F), (4)
Diversified investment company	§ 1843(c)(7)	§ 1467a(c)(2)(F), (4)
Closely related activities	§ 1843(c)(8)	§ 1467a(c)(2)(B), (F), (4)
Foreign corporation	§ 1843(c)(9)	§ 1467a(c)(2)(F), (4)
Grandfathered bank subsidiary	§ 1843(c)(10)	[§ 1467a(c)(2)(F), (4)]
Grandfathered 1970 activities	§ 1843(c)(11)	[§ 1467a(c)(2)(F), (4)]
Transition for 1970 companies	§ 1843(c)(12)	[§ 1467a(c)(2)(F), (4)]
Foreign-based company activities	§ 1843(c)(13)	§ 1467a(c)(2)(F), (4), (7)
Export trading company	§ 1843(c)(14)	§ 1467a(c)(2)(F), (4)
Financial holding companies	§ 1843(k)–(o)^2	§ 1467a(c)

2. 12 U.S.C.A. § 1843(k)–(*o*), *as* amended, Dodd–Frank Wall Street Reform and Consumer Protection Act §§ 604(e)(2), 606(a), 623(B)(1)(b), Pub. L. No. 111–203, 124 Stat. 1376,1601–1602, 1607, 1635 (2010) (codified at 12 U.S.C.A. § 1843(k)(6)(B), (*l*)(1)). In a memorandum publicly released on 15 May 2001, the OTS Chief Counsel has taken the position that multiple SLHCs had authority to engage in activities that are permissible for FHCs. *FHC Activities*

Provision	BHCA Section	HOLA Section
Qualified stock issuance		§ 1467a(b)(4), (c)(2)(G)
Unitary stock issuance		§ 1467a(c)(3)(A)
Qualified thrift lender holding companies		§ 1467a(c)(3)(B)
Bank holding companies		§ 1467a(c)(B), (t)
Grace period for compliance		§ 1467a(c)(5)
Special provisions for 1987 amendments		§ 1467a(c)(6)
Judicial review	§ 1848	§ 1467a(j)
Mutual holding companies		§ 1467a(o)(5), (6)

One important structural difference is that the HOLA incorporates by reference activities approved by the Fed for bank holding companies.[3] These activities are authorized for savings and loan holding companies unless the Office of Thrift Supervision ("OTS") prohibits or limits such an activity by regulation for savings and loan holding companies.[4] However, BHCA-authorized activities still require the prior approval of the OTS.[5]

Under section 313 of the Dodd–Frank Wall Street Reform and Consumer Protection Act,[6] the OTS and the position of the OTS Director are scheduled to be abolished. This dramatic event is effective 90 days after the "transfer date"[7]—21 July 2011—on which the functions and authority of the DOTS and the OTS are first exercised by the other federal regulators.[8] After the transfer

---

Allowed for Thrift Firms, Federal Savings and Loan Regulator Says, BNA Banking Daily, May 16, 2001, at d4. The text of the OTS document may be found online at: http://www.ots.treas.gov/docs/56102.pdf. Arguably, the authority is to be found in HOLA § 10(c), 12 U.S.C.A. § 1467a(c), as amended by the GLBA. The OTS has since proposed amendments to its regulation to authorize certain S & L holding companies to engage in financial activities post-GLBA. 66 Fed. Reg. 56,488 (2001) (to be codified at 12 C.F.R. §§ 584.1–584.2a, 584.100, 584.110, 584.120, 584.130).

3. *Id.* § 1467a(c)(2)(F)(i).

4. *Id.*

5. *Id.* § 1467a(b)(4)(A), *as amended* DFA § 604(g), (h)(2) (codified at 12 U.S.C.A. § 1467a(b)(4)) (providing for use of existing SLHC reports and examination of SLHCs by Fed).

6. Pub. L. No. 111–203, § 313, 124 Stat. 1376, 1523 (2010) (codified at 12 U.S.C.A. § 5413) (DFA). For discussion of the impact of the DFA, see 1 Michael P. Malloy, Banking Law and Regulation § 1.4.11 (1994 & Cum. Supp.).

7. DFA §§ 311(a), 313, 124 Stat. at 1520, 1523 (codified at 12 U.S.C.A. §§ 5411(a), 5413).

8. See *id.* § 312(b), 124 Stat. at 1522 (codified at 12 U.S.C.A. § 5412(b)) (mandating transfer of functions).

date, supervision of SLHCs will be the responsibility of the Fed.[9]

In reviewing an application for approval of such activities, the OTS is required to consider the following statutory factors: (1) Whether the performance of the activity described in the application by the company or the subsidiary can reasonably be expected to produce benefits to the public (such as greater convenience, increased competition, or gains in efficiency) that outweigh possible adverse effects of such activity (such as undue concentration of resources, decreased or unfair competition, conflicts of interest, or unsound financial practices).[10] (2) The managerial resources of the companies involved.[11] (3) Finally, the adequacy of the financial resources, including capital, of the companies involved.[12]

Unlike the situation under the BHCA, the HOLA exempts from regulation the non-savings association activities of any holding company that controls only one savings association.[13] This exemption is available so long as the savings association subsidiary is a "qualified thrift lender"[14]—in effect, an association specializing to a significant degree in traditional savings association activities of home mortgage lending and savings deposits.[15] However, in 1999 the Gramm–Leach–Bliley Act ("GLBA")[16] prohibited *new* unitary savings and loan holding companies from engaging in nonfinancial activities or affiliating with nonfinancial entities.[17] The prohibition applies to a company that becomes a unitary savings and loan holding company pursuant to an application filed with the OTS after 4 May 1999.[18] A grandfathered unitary thrift holding company retains its authority to engage in nonfinancial activities.[19] In addition, the prohibition does not apply to corporate reorganizations.[20]

An exemption from the application requirement is also available for a holding company controlling more than one savings association, on the following conditions.[21] (1) All or all but one of the savings association subsidiaries must have been acquired initially by the holding company, or an individual controlling the company, either in an FDIC-assisted transaction,[22] an emergency

9. *Id.* § 369(8), 124 Stat. at 1564–1565 (codified at 12 U.S.C.A. § 1467a) (conforming amendments).

10. *Id.* § 1467a(c)(4)(B)(i).

11. *Id.* § 1467a(c)(4)(B)(ii).

12. *Id.* § 1467a(c)(4)(B)(iii).

13. *Id.* § 1467a(c)(3)(A).

14. *Id.*

15. *See id.* § 1467a(m) (establishing qualified thrift lender test), *as amended* DFA § 624 (codified at 12 U.S.C.A. § (m)(3)(A), (m)(3)(B)(i)(III)–(IV)) (restricting operation of savings association not maintaining status as qualified thrift lender).

16. Pub. L. No. 106–102, Nov. 12, 1999, 113 Stat. 1338 (1999) (codified at scattered sections of 12, 15, 16, 18 U.S.C.A.).

17. GLBA, § 401(a) (codified at 12 U.S.C.A. § 1467a(c)(9)).

18. 12 U.S.C.A. § 1467a(c)(9)(A).

19. *Id.* § 1467a(c)(9)(C).

20. *Id.* § 1467a(c)(9)(D).

21. *Id.* § 1467a(c)(3)(B).

22. *Id.* § 1823(c) (providing for FDIC "open bank" assistance).

acquisition,[23] or an FSLIC-approved acquisition;[24] or in an acquisition in which capital assistance to the savings association was continued under the FDIA.[25] (2) All of the savings association subsidiaries must be qualified thrift lenders.[26]

One final set of differences between the BHCA and HOLA provisions concerns the applicability of HOLA to certain entities. First, upon application, a savings bank or cooperative bank[27] may be treated as a savings association for purposes of the holding company provisions of the HOLA, if the OTS determines that the bank is a qualified thrift lender.[28] Second, a bank holding company subject to the BHCA, or a company controlled by such a bank holding company, is exempt from the HOLA provisions.[29]

§ 6.7   Structure of the Regulations

The structure of the regulations implementing the HOLA provisions[1] roughly tracks the structure of the statute. Figure 6–6, *infra*, illustrates the structure of the regulations.

23. *Id.* § 1823(k) (providing for FDIC-approved emergency acquisitions).

24. *Id.* § 1467a(c)(3)(B)(i)(I). *See* 12 U.S.C.A. § 1730a(m) (1988) (providing since repealed emergency acquisitions authority for now abolished FSLIC).

25. 12 U.S.C.A. § 1467a(c)(3)(B)(i)(II). *See id.* § 1823(i) (concerning purchase of "net worth certificates" from troubled depository institution by FDIC as support for institution's capital position).

26. *Id.* § 1467a(c)(3)(B)(ii).

27. *See id.* § 1813(h) (defining "cooperative bank").

28. *Id.* § 1467a(*l*)(1). However, failure to maintain qualified thrift lender status will disqualify the bank for treatment as such a lender (and, hence, as a savings association for these purposes) for a period of five years. *Id.* § 1467a(*l*)(2).

29. *Id.* § 1467a(t).

§ 6.7

1. 12 C.F.R. Pt. 584.

Figure 6-6

HOLA: Structure of the Holding Company Regulations

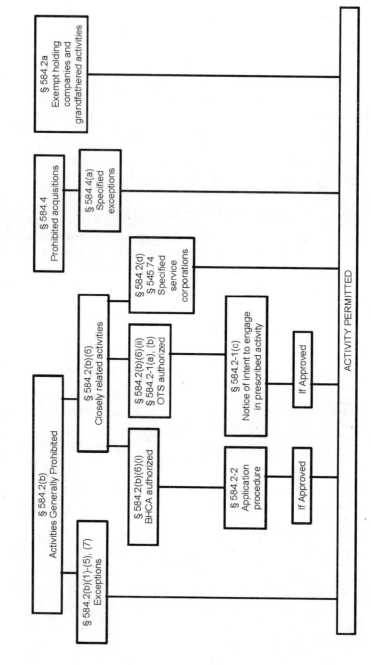

§ 6.8   Permissible Activities

A core list of prescribed or permissible activities is codified in the various provisions of the OTS regulations.[1] In addition, the regulations incorporate by reference permissible activities under the Fed's BHCA regulations.[2] Figure 6–7, *infra*, illustrates these prescribed or permissible activities. However, certain activities included in the list may require notice or application and OTS approval.

Figure 6–7

HOLA: Prescribed or Permitted Activities

12 C.F.R.	*Required Filing*	*Activity*
§ 584.2(b)(1)		furnishing or performing management services for savings association subsidiary
§ 584.2(b)(2)		conducting insurance agency or escrow business
§ 584.2(b)(3)		holding, managing, or liquidating assets owned by or acquired from subsidiary savings association
§ 584.2(b)(4)		holding or managing properties used or occupied by subsidiary savings association
§ 584.2(b)(5)		acting as trustee under deed of trust
§ 584.2(b)(6)(i), § 584.2(b)(6)(ii)	Application[3]	BHCA closely related activities
§ 584.2–1(b)	Notice[4]	HOLA closely related activities
§ 584.2(b)(7)		purchasing, holding, or disposing of stock acquired in connection with qualified stock issuance, if prior approval for acquisition is granted by the OTS (in the case of a savings and loan holding company)[5]
§ 584.2–1(d)		service or activity conducted by service corporation subsidiary

§ 6.8

1. 12 C.F.R. §§ 584.2(b)(1)–(7), 584.2–1(b), 584.4(a)(1)–(7).

2. *Id.* § 584.2–2(a). *Cf.* Figure 6–3, *supra* (identifying predetermined "closely related" activities under BHCA).

3. 12 C.F.R. § 584.2–2.

4. *Id.* § 584.2–1(c).

5. *Per id.* § 574.8.

12 C.F.R.	Required Filing	Activity
		of subsidiary savings association, if service corporation has legal power to do so
§ 584.4(a)		acquisition or retention of more than five percent of voting stock or shares of nonsubsidiary savings association, or of nonsubsidiary savings and loan holding company, or, in the case of multiple savings and loan holding company (other than an exempted multiple savings and loan holding company[6]); acquisition or retention of more than five percent of voting shares of nonsubsidiary company engaged in specified business activities if the voting shares acquired or retained are held as a bona fide fiduciary or in other specified limited or temporary capacity

§ 6.9   State Law

By its own terms, the BHCA reserves to the states the right to exercise jurisdiction over bank holding companies.[1] Presumably, under this authority states laws could be *more* restrictive than the BHCA on the question of the scope of nonbanking activities of bank holding companies,[2] but it is doubtful whether a state could expand the permissible nonbanking activities of a bank holding company beyond the limits established by the BHCA. Hence, the BHCA effectively defines the outer limits of nonbanking activities of bank holding companies.

6. *Per id.* § 584.2a(a)(ii).

§ 6.9

1. 12 U.S.C.A. § 1846(a), which provides:

No provision of this chapter shall be construed as preventing any State from exercising such powers and jurisdiction which it now has or may hereafter have with respect to companies, banks, bank holding companies, and subsidiaries thereof.

See Security Nat'l Bank & Trust Co. v. First W. Va. Bancorp., Inc., 166 W.Va. 775, 277 S.E.2d 613 (1981), *appeal dismissed,* 454 U.S. 1131, 102 S.Ct. 986 (1982) (finding state authority not preempted).

2. *Cf., e.g., Commercial Nat'l Bank of Little Rock v. Board of Governors,* 451 F.2d 86 (8th Cir.1971) (finding state free to prohibit formation of bank holding companies).

Chapter 7

SECURITIES REGULATION

Table of Sections

§ 7.1 Introduction

This chapter deals with two interrelated areas of concern: (1) the regulation of depository institutions as *issuers* of securities, a topic usually neglected in the literature;[1] and, (2) the regulation (or restriction) of depository institutions as *participants* in the securi-

---

§ 7.1

1. *But see* 1 MICHAEL P. MALLOY, THE CORPORATE LAW OF BANKS 367–544 (1988) (providing seminal study of securities regulation of depository institutions); Michael P. Malloy, *Public Disclosure as a Tool of Federal Bank Regulation*, 9 Ann. Rev. Banking L. 229 (1990) (dis-cussing implications of disclosure-orient-ed securities regulation on depository in-stitutions); Michael P. Malloy, *The 12(i)'ed Monster: Administration of the Securities Exchange Act of 1934 by the Federal Bank Regulatory Agencies*, 19 Hofstra L. Rev. 269 (1990) (criticizing regulators).

ties markets, an area still dominated by the Glass–Steagall Act,[2] since 1999 by the Gramm–Leach–Bliley Act ("GLBA"),[3] and now by the Dodd–Frank Wall Street Reform and Consumer Protection Act (Dodd–Frank)[4] as well.

Aside from regulatory restrictions on securities activities, banks and other depository institutions are also subject to securities regulation, like other issuers and traders in securities. However, as issuers, they are not fully subject to the Securities Act of 1933 ("1933 Act"),[5] the federal regulatory statute generally applicable to the issuance of securities.[6] In addition, until 1964, the generally applicable SEC regulations[7] governing periodic disclosure and trading in securities in the secondary market were also, as a practical matter, inapplicable to bank- and thrift-issued securities.[8] In 1964, banks and savings associations with publicly traded securities became subject to the requirements of the Securities Exchange Act of 1934 ("1934 Act"),[9] but these requirements are administered in their case *not* by the SEC, but by their respective primary federal banking regulators.[10]

Depository institutions may also be securities market professionals—enterprises that underwrite, purchase, sell, and otherwise deal in securities—subject to the limits of the Glass–Steagall Act, the GLBA, and Dodd–Frank. However, only since 1999 have banks acting as market professionals been significantly subject to SEC supervision of their activities in that capacity.[11]

The financial crisis that followed the collapse of the subprime mortgage market[12] forced the Congress to rethink its uncritical

---

2. On the Glass–Steagall Act restrictions on participation of depository institutions in the securities market, see *supra* § 5.24.

3. Pub. L. No. 106–102, Nov. 12, 1999, 113 Stat. 1338 (1999) (codified at scattered sections of 12, 15, 16, 18 U.S.C.A.).

4. Pub. L. No. 111–203, 124 Stat. 1376 (2010) (codified at scattered sections of 2, 5, 7, 11, 12, 15, 18, 20, 22, 26, 28, 31, 42, 44 U.S.C.A.) (DFA). For an overview of the DFA, see 1 MICHAEL P. MALLOY, BANKING LAW AND REGULATION § 1.4.11 (1994 & Cum. Supp.).

5. 15 U.S.C.A. §§ 77a *et seq.*

6. *See* 12 U.S.C.A. § 77c(a)(2), (5) (exempting bank- and thrift-issued securities from registration requirements of Securities Act of 1933).

7. 15 C.F.R. Pt. 240.

8. *See* 2 MICHAEL P. MALLOY, BANKING LAW AND REGULATION § 6.2.1 (1994 & CUM.

SUPP.) (discussing pre–1964 scope of SEC regulations).

9. 15 U.S.C.A. §§ 78a *et seq.*

10. *Id.* § 78*l*(i).

11. *See* GLBA, §§ 201–202 (codified at 15 U.S.C.A. § 78c(a)(4)(A)–(E), (5)(A)–(C)) (subjecting bank broker-dealer activities to SEC regulation, with specified exceptions). *See also* GLBA, § 221(a) (codified at 15 U.S.C.A. § 77c(a)(2)) (concerning treatment of bank common trust funds under Securities Act of 1933); GLBA, § 221(b) (codified at 15 U.S.C.A. § 78c(a)(12)(A)(iii)) (concerning treatment under Securities Exchange Act of 1934). *See generally infra* §§ 7.14–7.30 (discussing regulation of securities market activities of depository institutions).

12. For background on the subprime mortgage crisis, see 1 MICHAEL P. MALLOY, BANKING LAW AND REGULATION § 1.4 (1994 & Cum. Supp.). For a timeline of the

release of securities powers into the hand of banks. The full implications of Dodd–Frank, which is the product of this congressional rethinking, are as yet undetermined, since the bulk of the act does not become effective for at least a year after enactment (*i.e.*, after 21 July 2010). Furthermore, an extensive range of implementing regulations will need to be proposed and promulgated in final form before the practical impact of the act will be unfolded. As to the implications for securities regulation, we do know a number of important aspects of Dodd–Frank already. First, the act restricts "proprietary securities trading"[13] by banks, in which banks deal in securities for their own accounts.[14]

Second, the act does not confine itself to the impact of securities regulation on banks alone. For all market participants, it imposes new standards with respect to securitization of pools of financial instruments,[15] a process in which interests in a pool of mortgage obligations are marketed to investors as securities. Prior to the 2008 collapse of the mortgage market, this was one of the critical processes for moving mortgage obligations into the capital markets as securities.

Third, Dodd–Frank requires hedge fund and private equity fund advisers to register with the SEC, and will subject them to SEC inspection and examination.[16] A *hedge fund* is an investment fund, usually organized as a private investment partnership, open to a limited number of investors and requiring a very large initial minimum investment, with the investment committed to the fund for a relatively long period, typically at least one year. The fund's

---

current financial crisis, see http://www.stlouisfed.org/timeline/default.cfm.

13. *See* DFA § 619 (codified at 12 U.S.C.A. § 1851(h)(4)), which defines the term *proprietary trading* for these purposes to mean:

> engaging as a principal for the trading account of the banking entity or non-bank financial company supervised by the [Fed] in any transaction to purchase or sell, or otherwise acquire or dispose of, any security, any derivative, any contract of sale of a commodity for future delivery, any option on any such security, derivative, or contract, or any other security or financial instrument that the appropriate Federal banking agencies, the Securities and Exchange Commission, and the Commodity Futures Trading Commission may, by rule as provided in [§ 1851(b)(2)], determine.

14. DFA § 619 (codified at 12 U.S.C.A. § 1851).

15. *Id.* §§ 941–945 (codified at 15 U.S.C.A. §§ 77d(5), 77g(c)–(d), 78c(a)(4)(B)(vii)(I), 78c(a)(77), 78o(d), 78o–11). See also DFA § 621(a) (codified at 15 U.S.C.A. § 77z–2a) (concerning conflicts of interest with respect to securitizations). Cf. DFA § 619(g)(2) (codified at 12 U.S.C.A. § 1851(g)(2)) (protecting otherwise authorized sale or securitization of loans by banking entity or systemically significant nonbank financial company from prohibitions on proprietary trading).

16. *Id.* §§ 401–412, 419 (codified at 15 U.S.C.A. §§ 80b–2(a)(11), (29)–(30), 80b–3(b), (*l*)–(n), 80b–3a(a), 80b–4, 80b–10(c), 80b–11, 80b–18b). As a general rule, these registration requirements are effective as of 21 July 2011, except that an investment adviser may, in its discretion, register with the SEC under the Investment Advisers Act of 1940 during this one-year transition period, subject to rules to be promulgated by the SEC. 15 U.S.C.A. § 80b–2 note.

investment strategies are usually very aggressive, making use of leveraged and derivative trading in targeted securities in order to increase the rate of return when the securities perform well. (This also means, of course, that losses can be exacerbated if the securities perform poorly.) A *private equity fund* is an investment fund that specializes in investments not quoted on public exchanges. The fund typically makes an investment directly into an existing private company or it may buy up a public company and take it private, "delisting" it from public exchanges in the process. Participants in a private equity fund are typically high-end investors (institutions and sophisticated, wealthy individuals) who commit a relatively large amount to the fund for a long period of time.[17]

Fourth, the act provides for comprehensive regulation of swaps and security-based swaps[18] by the Commodity Futures Trading

17. The DFA treats these definitional issues less helpfully. *See* DFA § 619 (codified at 12 U.S.C.A. § 1851), which defines both terms as follows:

> The terms 'hedge fund' and 'private equity fund' mean an issuer that would be an investment company, as defined in the Investment Company Act of 1940 (15 U.S.C.A. 80a–1 *et seq.*), but for [the Investment Company Act exemptive provisions in 15 U.S.C.A. § 80a–3(c)(1) or (c)(7)], or such similar funds as the appropriate Federal banking agencies, the Securities and Exchange Commission, and the Commodity Futures Trading Commission may, by rule, as provided in subsection (b)(2), determine.

12 U.S.C.A. § 1851(h)(2). The exemptive provisions referred to in the quoted excerpt actually provide a more informative description of these types of funds as follows:

> [N]one of the following persons is an investment company within the meaning of [the Investment Company Act]:
>
> (1) Any issuer whose outstanding securities (other than short-term paper) are beneficially owned by not more than one hundred persons and which is not making and does not presently propose to make a public offering of its securities . . .
>
> (7)(A) Any issuer, the outstanding securities of which are owned exclusively by persons who, at the time of acquisition of such securities, are qualified purchasers [*i.e.*, sophisticated investors], and which is not making and does not at that time propose to

make a public offering of such securities . . .

> (E) For purposes of determining compliance with this paragraph and paragraph (1), an issuer that is otherwise excepted under this paragraph and an issuer that is otherwise excepted under paragraph (1) shall not be treated by the Commission as being a single issuer for purposes of determining whether the outstanding securities of the issuer excepted under paragraph (1) are beneficially owned by not more than 100 persons or whether the outstanding securities of the issuer excepted under this paragraph are owned by persons that are not qualified purchasers. . . .

See Clemente Global Growth Fund, Inc. v. Pickens, 705 F.Supp. 958 (S.D.N.Y. 1989) (interpreting § 80a–3(c)(1)).

18. For purposes of the DFA, the terms *swap* and *securities-based swap* have the same meaning as they do under the Commodity Exchange Act (CEA), 7 U.S.C.A. §§ 1a *et seq.* DFA, § 711, (codified at 15 U.S.C.A. § 8301). A *swap* is essentially a derivative arrangement in which two parties exchange cash flows or benefits (and the attendant risks) in respective financial instruments in which each has invested. *See* Gramm–Leach–Bliley Act, § 206(b), 113 Stat. at 1393 (15 U.S.C.A. § 78c note). A *security-based swap* is a swap agreement in which a material term is based on the price, yield, value, or volatility of a security or group or index of securities, or an interest therein. 15 U.S.C.A. § 78c note.

Commission (CFTC) and the SEC,[19] in consultation with the Fed.[20] The two agencies have joint responsibility for swap products, to be allocated between them depending on whether the underlying product is a "security" or not.[21] Institutions deemed to be swap dealers,[22] as well as "major swap participants" are required to register with either the SEC or CFTC, depending on the nature of their products.[23]

§ 7.2　Issuance of Securities

Issuance of securities in a public offering, involving the use of interstate instrumentalities, normally is subject to regulation by the SEC under the 1933 Act.[1] However, despite the enactment of the Gramm–Leach–Bliley Act of 1999 (GLBA),[2] and its endorsement of functional regulation as a basic organizing principle,[3] bank- and thrift-issued securities are exempt from the registration requirements of the 1933 Act.[4]

Section 3(a)(2) of the 1933 Act exempts any security issued by a "bank" from the registration requirements of the act.[5] Section 3(a)(5) exempts any security issued by a savings and loan association, building and loan association, cooperative bank, homestead

---

19. DFA §§ 711–716, 718 (codified at 7 U.S.C.A. §§ 6d(h), 24(c); 15 U.S.C.A. §§ 78o(c)(3)(C), 8301–8306).

20. *Id.* § 712(a)(8) (codified at 15 U.S.C.A. § 8302(a)(8)).

21. *Id.* § 717 (codified at 7 U.S.C.A. § 2(a)(1)(C), 7a–2(c)(1); 15 U.S.C.A. §§ 78c–1, 78s(b)(10)). Cf. DFA § 720 (codified at 15 U.S.C.A. § 8308) (memorandum of understanding to be negotiated between CFTC and Federal Energy Regulatory Commission). The SEC and the CFTC have already jointly issued proposed rules "further defining" key terms and regulating "mixed swaps." 75 Fed. Reg. 51,429 (2010) (to be codified at 17 C.F.R. pt. 1 (CFTC rules); *id.* pt. 240 (SEC rules)). Public comments are due September 20, 2010. 75 Fed. Reg. at 51,429.

22. These typically include large banks that make markets in swaps by creating and selling them. A "de minimis" exception from designation as a swap dealer is available to "an entity that engages in a de minimis quantity of swap dealing in connection with transactions with or on behalf of customers." DFA § 721(a)(49)(D) (codified at 7 U.S.C.A. § 1a(a)(49)(D)). This clause is important for regional banks and other smaller financial institutions such as savings associations and credit unions

and will enable them to avoid the regulatory burdens likely to be associated with being identified as a swap dealer.

23. *Id.* §§ 721–724 (codified at 7 U.S.C.A. §§ 1a, 1b, 2(a)(1), (c)(2)(A), (i)–(j), 6(c)(1), (6), 6d(f) 6m, 6q, 6s(*l*), 7–7a–1, 13–1(a), 16(h), 27; 11 U.S.C.A. 761; 15 U.S.C.A. §§ 78f, 8321–8322).

§ 7.2

1. 15 U.S.C.A. §§ 77a *et seq.*

2. Pub. L. No. 106–102, Nov. 12, 1999, 113 Stat. 1338 (1999) (codified at scattered sections of 12, 15, 16, 18 U.S.C.A.).

3. *See supra* § 1.9, text and accompanying notes 1–3 (discussing functional regulation under GLBA).

4. 15 U.S.C.A. § 77c(a)(2), (5). *See Dougherty v. Carver Fed. Sav. Bank*, 112 F.3d 613, 617, 619 (2d Cir.1997) (discussing exemption).

5. "Bank" for these purposes means "any national bank, or any banking institution organized under the laws of any State, territory, or the District of Columbia, the business of which is substantially confined to banking and is supervised by the State or territorial banking commission or similar official." 15 U.S.C.A. § 77c(a)(2).

association, or similar thrift institution.[6] The reason for these exemptions appears to be that Congress assumed that depository institutions would be adequately supervised by their primary federal and state regulators, making application of the 1933 Act requirements unnecessary.[7] However, on its own terms, the general anti-fraud provision of the 1933 Act[8] applies to *any* security, exempted or not.[9]

§ 7.3 Regulatory Parallels to the 1933 Act

The Office of the Comptroller of the Currency ("OCC") and—until July 2011—the Office of Thrift Supervision ("OTS") administer parallel systems of securities regulation for issuance of bank and thrift-issued securities into the public market. Taken as a whole, the parallel systems that apply to depository institutions are broader than that of the 1933 Act, and many of their elements are informed primarily by policy concerns peculiar to the depository institutions regulators: namely, maintenance of safety and soundness of the depository institutions sector, not protection of investors and stability of the securities markets. Under section 313 of the Dodd–Frank Wall Street Reform and Consumer Protection Act,[1] the OTS and the position of the DOTS are scheduled to be abolished. This dramatic event is effective 90 days after the "transfer date"[2]—21 July 2011—on which the functions and authority of the DOTS and the OTS are first exercised by the other federal regulators.[3]

Nevertheless, even with the abolishment of the OTS, the problem of duplicative regulatory structure persists in U.S. securities regulation to date. Notwithstanding the enactment of the Gramm–Leach–Bliley Act of 1999 (GLBA),[4] and its endorsement of functional regulation as a basic organizing principle,[5] the GLBA did

---

6. 15 U.S.C.A. § 77c(a)(5)(A). An institution must be "supervised and examined by State or Federal authority having supervision over such institution" to qualify for the exemption. *Id.*

7. *See* MICHAEL P. MALLOY, BANKING LAW AND REGULATION §§ 5.2.1–5.2.2 (1994 & CUM. SUPP.) (discussing exemption and legislative history of 1933 Act).

8. 15 U.S.C.A. § 77q.

9. *See Dougherty*, 112 F.3d at 619 (stating that common stock of savings bank not exempt from antifraud provisions of 1933 and 1934 Acts).

§ 7.3

1. Pub. L. No. 111–203, § 313, 124 Stat. 1376, 1523 (2010) (codified at 12 U.S.C.A. § 5413) (DFA). For discussion of the impact of the DFA, see 1 MICHAEL

P. MALLOY, BANKING LAW AND REGULATION § 1.4.11 (1994 & Cum. Supp.).

2. DFA §§ 311(a), 313 (codified at 12 U.S.C.A. §§ 5411(a), 5413).

3. See *id.* § 312(b) (codified at 12 U.S.C.A. § 5412(b)) (mandating transfer of functions).

4. Pub. L. No. 106–102, Nov. 12, 1999, 113 Stat. 1338 (1999) (codified at scattered sections of 12, 15, 16, 18 U.S.C.A.) (GLBA).

5. *See supra* § 1.9, text and accompanying notes 1–3 (discussing functional regulation under GLBA).

not disturb the exemption of bank- and thrift-issued securities from the scope of regulation under the Securities Act of 1933 (1933 Act),[6] with the result that the parallel OCC and OTS systems continue by default.

§ 7.4   Securities Disclosure Requirements

The first element of each parallel system is in fact concerned with adequate disclosure to investors in bank- and thrift-issued securities. Each is, in most respects, virtually identical to the SEC's regulations under the 1933 Act,[1] but each is also based upon the general statutory authority of each regulator to supervise the capital of institutions subject to their respective authority.[2]

These disclosure requirements can be illustrated by the regulations of the OCC. (The OTS has a corresponding set of regulations requiring material disclosure in the issuance of securities by savings associations subject to its supervision.[3]) As regulator of national banks, the Comptroller has promulgated detailed Securities Offering Disclosure Rules that require material disclosure in connection with the issuance of securities by national banks.[4] These regulations generally require that any direct or indirect offer or sale by a national bank of any security[5] issued by it be made through the use of an "offering circular" filed with and declared effective by the Comptroller.[6] Like the 1933 Act requirements applicable to non-bank issuers,[7] the offering circular requirements contemplate three separate stages in the process leading to distribution of securities: (1) prior to filing the circular, offers and sales are prohibited;[8] (2) between filing and the effective date of the circular, offers to sell, but not sales, may be made through under-

---

6. *But cf.* GLBA, § 221(a), 113 Stat. at 1401 (codified at 15 U.S.C.A. § 77c(a)(2)) (modifying treatment of bank common trust funds under 1933 Act); 12 U.S.C.A. § 77q(a) (applying antifraud provision of 1933 Act to "any security").

§ 7.4

1. *Compare, e.g.*, 17 C.F.R. Pt. 230 (SEC 1933 Act regulations), *with* 12 C.F.R. Pts. 16 (OCC securities disclosure regulations); 563g (OTS securities disclosure regulations).

2. 12 U.S.C.A. §§ 57 (concerning capital of national banks); 1464 (concerning savings associations). *See, e.g.*, 42 Fed. Reg. 2200 (1977) (promulgating Comptroller regulations, *citing* 12 U.S.C.A. § 57 as statutory authority).

3. 12 C.F.R. Pt. 563g.

4. *Id.* Pt. 16.

5. The regulations define "security" to mean:

> any common stock, preferred stock, or other equity security, or right to subscribe to any of the foregoing, or subordinated note or debenture. The term "security" shall not include any deposit loan, participation, letter of credit or other form of bank indebtedness incurred in the ordinary course of business.

Id. § 16.2(d).

6. *Id.* § 16.3(a)

7. *See* 15 U.S.C.A. § 77e (setting forth 1933 Act registration requirements).

8. *Compare* 12 C.F.R. § 16.3(a)–(b), *with* 15 U.S.C.A. § 77e(a), (c).

writers, under certain conditions;[9] and (3) after the effective date of the offering circular, offers and sales of the securities may generally be made.[10] The effective period of the offering circular is generally six months.[11]

What is notable about the OCC and OTS regulations is the degree to which they resemble, and in many respects directly incorporate, the coordinate provisions of the regulations promulgated by the SEC under the 1933 Act. Securities disclosure would appear to be "an area of unnecessary duplication of government resources."[12] In an effort to promote more consistent functional regulation of financial services generally and to streamline unnecessary regulatory controls, the Task Group on Regulation of Financial Services made the recommendation that "[t]he registration requirements of the [1933 Act] should be made applicable to publicly offered securities of banks and thrifts (but not deposit instruments)."[13] However, the Task Group would have allowed the Federal Home Loan Bank Board ("FHLBB"), the predecessor to the OTS, to continue to exercise securities jurisdiction over the conversion of savings associations banks from the mutual to the stock form of organization.[14]

In addition, the Task Group would have left such jurisdiction with the FHLBB with respect to "other matters involving the safety and soundness of [Federal Savings and Loan Insurance Corporation ("FSLIC")] insured thrift institutions [*i.e.*, savings associations] or affecting the operations of the [FSLIC]."[15] The Task Group offered no cogent reason why it would split off securities jurisdiction for conversions. As to the retention of this jurisdiction by the FHLBB with respect to safety and soundness matters and FSLIC operations, the Task Group argued:

> The issuance of securities by thrift institutions sometimes differs from securities offerings by other financial institutions because of the unique mortgage-related nature of many types of thrift securities. For example, thrifts issue a variety of

---

9. *Compare* 12 C.F.R. § 16.3(b), *with* 15 U.S.C.A. § 77e(b)(1), (c). The conditions are: (1) prior authorization must be obtained from the Comptroller, 12 C.F.R. § 16.3(b)(1), and an appropriate "preliminary offering circular" must be used, *id.* § 16(b); (2) prior to consummation of the actual sale, a copy of the offering circular as finally effective, must be furnished to each purchaser, *id.* § 16.3(b)(2).

10. *Compare* 12 C.F.R. § 16.3(a), (e), *with* 15 U.S.C.A. § 77e.

11. 12 C.F.R. § 16.3(e).

12. REPORT OF THE TASK GROUP ON REGULATION OF FINANCIAL SERVICES 93 (1984) ("TASK GROUP REPORT").

13. TASK GROUP REPORT at 91. In light of the Supreme Court's holding in *Marine Bank v. Weaver*, 455 U.S. 551, 102 S.Ct. 1220 (1982), that a bank-issued certificate of deposit was not a "security" for purposes of the 1934 Act, 15 U.S.C.A. §§ 78a *et seq.*, it seems doubtful whether the parenthetical limitation in the quoted text is necessary.

14. TASK GROUP REPORT at 91.

15. *Id.*

securities that represent interests in pools of mortgages, or that are collateralized by mortgages. Thrifts also have developed other debt and equity financing techniques that use mortgage-related securities that have been obtained in exchange for mortgages in their portfolio.

While other types of firms issue mortgage-backed securities that are registered with the SEC under the 1933 Act, such issuances by thrifts are unique because the mortgages backing such securities issued by thrifts may directly affect the assets available to the FSLIC in the event of insolvency or have other direct impacts on safety and soundness. Therefore, the FHLBB should have authority to limit securities offerings by thrift institutions that would adversely affect thrift safety and soundness or the FSLIC [insurance] fund.[16]

This distinction between savings associations and other issuers is unconvincing. Realignment of securities disclosure regulation under the administration of the SEC does not have any impact upon regulatory considerations such as safety and soundness and the integrity of the FSLIC's deposit insurance fund. Since securities regulation is disclosure-oriented, not primarily substantive, it is a weak argument to assert that the FHLBB needs to retain disclosure regulation authority in order to "to limit [certain] securities offerings by thrift institutions." Such direct authority does not exist under the federal securities laws; it remains with the regulator of the substantive activities of the depository institution in question.[17]

§ 7.5 Minimum Capital Requirements

The second element in the parallel system of securities regulation that applies to the issuance of securities by depository institutions is concerned with minimum capital requirements for entry into the depository institutions industry. Minimum capital requirements relate to safety and soundness of *de novo* depository institutions. Until 2001, national banks were required to be organized with no less than a statutorily required amount of capital, keyed to the size of the community in which the bank would be located.[1] These requirements were completely impractical in light of current economic conditions, and they have been repealed.[2] Minimum capi-

---

16. *Id.* at 93.

17. *See, e.g.,* 12 U.S.C.A. §§ 57, 1464 (providing general supervisory authority over capital of national banks and savings associations); *id.* §§ 1818(b)(1), 3907(b) (providing enforcement authority with respect to capital of insured depository institutions).

§ 7.5

1. 12 U.S.C.A. § 51 (2000).

2. *See* American Homeownership and Economic Opportunity Act of 2000, Pub. L. No. 106–569, § 1233(c), 114 Stat. 2944 (2000) (repealing 12 U.S.C.A. § 51). Under the literal terms of 12 U.S.C.A. § 51 (2000), a national bank could have been organized in San Fran-

tal requirements for formation are now found only in the OCC regulations,[3] and routinely require generally not less than $1 million in initial capital.

The NBA also required that a national bank have a paid-in surplus equal to 20 percent of capital before it would be authorized to commence business.[4] The requirement could be waived for state banks converting to a national charter.[5] Since this amounted to no more than $40,000 for a bank proposed for the largest metropolitan areas, it was obviously a negligible requirement, and has been repealed.

The Fed also imposes minimum capital requirements for Fed membership.[6] To be eligible for membership, state-chartered banks must possess capital and surplus adequate for their assets and deposit liabilities and other obligations.[7]

For state-chartered banks to be eligible for deposit insurance, adequacy of capital is also a requirement.[8]

§ 7.6 Regulation of Capital Formation

The third element in the parallel system of securities regulation that applies to the issuance of securities by depository institutions regulates the process of capital formation itself. Capital formation by a depository institution is subject to prior approval by its chartering agency—on the merits of the securities offering planned by the institution—quite apart from any applicable public disclosure requirements imposed in connection with the issuance of securities. The practice of the agencies varies. In the case of national banks, for example, the NBA permits the issuance of common stock,[1] and, since 1933, preferred stock,[2] with the approval of the Comptroller.

What is the relationship between securities disclosure requirements and capital formation requirements? Capital formation requires merit review of the proposed issuance on the merits. And yet the two federal chartering agencies require in their respective offering circular rules that the circular include a boldface disclaimer to the effect that:

cisco with a minimum required capital of only $200,000.

3. 12 C.F.R. § 5.20(f)(2)(i)(C), (h)(4).

4. 12 U.S.c.A. § 51 (2000).

5. *Id.*

6. *See Continental Bank & Trust Co. of Salt Lake City v. Woodall,* 239 F.2d 707 (10th Cir.1957), *cert. denied,* 353

U.S. 909, 77 S.Ct. 663 (1957) (upholding Fed membership requirements).

7. 12 C.F.R. Pt. 208.

8. 12 U.S.C.A. § 1816.

§ 7.6

1. 12 U.S.C.A. § 51.

2. *Id.* § 51a.

THESE SHARES HAVE NOT BEEN APPROVED OR DISAP-
PROVED BY THE OFFICE OF THRIFT SUPERVISION NOR
HAS SUCH OFFICE PASSED UPON THE ACCURACY OR
ADEQUACY OF THIS OFFERING CIRCULAR. ANY REPRE-
SENTATION TO THE CONTRARY IS UNLAWFUL.[3]

If the issuance has been approved by the agency under capital formation rules, how can it require this kind of disclaimer under its securities disclosure rules? Essentially, *Dougherty v. Carver Federal Savings Bank*[4] has taken the position that there is no relationship between the securities disclosure and merit review (capital formation) aspects of securities regulation applicable to depository institutions. While this position may underplay the significance of merit review, it does have the result of leaving it open to investors to proceed to appropriate remedies for, *e.g.*, securities fraud, notwithstanding the merit review process.[5]

§ 7.7   Securities Exchange Act of 1934

Until 1964, the Securities Exchange Act did not cover over-the-counter securities (*i.e.*, securities not listed on a national securities exchange)[1] except for the antifraud provisions of Section 10(b),[2] which covers all securities, whether listed or not.[3] As a matter of fact, most, if not all, bank-issued securities fell into this over-the-counter category, and hence they were not generally subject to the 1934 Act.

Based on a special study performed by the SEC,[4] Congress decided to bring over-the-counter securities—and specifically, bank-issued securities—under the 1934 Act.[5] The bank regulators resisted this change in the law.[6] Their efforts were unsuccessful, but the bank regulators did extract one significant concession: they were

---

3. 12 C.F.R. § 563b.102 Item 3 (1994) (OTS rules). *See also* 12 C.F.R. § 16.7(c), Item 1(d) (OCC rules).

4. 112 F.3d 613 (2d Cir.1997).

5. *Id.*

§ 7.7

1. *See, e.g.*, 15 U.S.C.A. § 78*l*(a) (1960) (applying registration requirements of 1934 Act to securities listed on national securities exchange).

2. 15 U.S.C.A. § 78j(b).

3. *See, e.g., id.* § 78j(b) (authorizing SEC to promulgate rules with respect to securities fraud). *See also* 17 C.F.R. § 240.10b–5 (establishing generally applicable antifraud prohibition). *See generally Dougherty v. Carver Fed. Sav. Bank,* 112 F.3d 613, 619 (2d Cir.1997)

(stating that common stock of savings bank not exempt from antifraud provisions of 1933 and 1934 Acts).

4. *Report of the Special Study of the Securities Markets of the Securities and Exchange Commission,* H.R. Doc. No., 95, 88th Cong., 1st Sess. (1963).

5. *See* 15 U.S.C.A. § 78*l*(g) (subjecting publicly traded securities to registration requirements of 1934 Act).

6. *See, e.g., Letter from the Federal Reserve Board to the Chairman, House Interstate and Foreign Commerce Committee,* June 21, 1963, *reprinted in* H.R. Rep. No. 1418, 88th Cong., 1st Sess. (1963). *See also Reports on Bank Securities Activities of the Securities and Exchange Commission,* 95th Cong., 1st Sess. 307–8 (1977).

granted administrative authority over the 1934 Act provisions that applied to depository institutions, with one important exception. With respect to securities issued by banks and savings associations, the registration,[7] reporting,[8] proxy,[9] tender offer[10] and insider reporting provisions[11] of the 1934 Act are administered by the depository institutions regulatory agencies, not by the SEC.[12] Section 12(i) of the 1934 Act,[13] added in 1964, contains a statutory mandate that, within 60 days of any amendments to pertinent SEC rules, these regulatory agencies issue regulations substantially similar to those issued by the SEC, unless such regulations would not be "necessary or appropriate in the public interest or for the protection of investors."[14] Notwithstanding the enactment of the Gramm–Leach–Bliley Act of 1999 (GLBA),[15] and its endorsement of functional regulation as a basic organizing principle,[16] the act did not eliminate section 12(i), with the result that the duplicative shadow systems of 1934 Act regulation "administered" by the banking agencies persists.

Despite this statutory mandate, by the end of the 1980s, the regulatory agencies were generally at least one year—and often as much as seven years—behind in adopting appropriate analogs to SEC amendments,[17] with one longstanding exception: the FHLBB (and, since 1989, its successor, the OTS), whose 1934 Act regulations simply incorporate by reference the SEC regulations.[18] Hence, neither the FHLBB nor the OTS has ever had occasion to amend this section in any significant respect. In 1988, the Fed followed the FHLBB's lead, and converted to an incorporation-by-reference approach as well.[19] The Fed was later joined by the OCC,[20] and, in February 1997, by the FDIC.[21]

If the federal bank and saving association regulators are simply incorporating 1934 Act rules into their own regulations, one might reasonably ask what the point is in delegating authority to them

---

7. 15 U.S.C.A. § 78*l*.

8. *Id*. § 78m.

9. *Id*. § 78n.

10. *Id*. § 78n(d), (f).

11. *Id*. § 78p.

12. *Id*. § 78*l*(i). *See* Michael P. Malloy, *The 12(i)'ed Monster: Administration of the Securities Exchange Act of 1934 by the Federal Bank Regulatory Agencies*, 19 Hofstra L. Rev. 269 (1991) (discussing § 78*l*(i) and its implementation by depository institution regulators).

13. 15 U.S.C.A. § 78*l*(i).

14. *Id*.

15. Pub. L. No. 106–102, Nov. 12, 1999, 113 Stat. 1338 (1999) (codified at scattered sections of 12, 15, 16, 18 U.S.C.A.) (GLBA).

16. *See supra* § 1.9, text and accompanying notes 1–3 (discussing functional regulation under GLBA).

17. *See* Malloy, *The 12(i)'ed Monster*, *supra* (reviewing performance of regulatory agencies under § 12(i)).

18. 12 C.F.R. § 563d.1.

19. *See id*. 208.16.

20. *See id*. Pt. 11 (incorporating SEC 1934 Act rules into OCC rules).

21. *See* 62 Fed. Reg. 6852 (1997) (codified at 12 C.F.R. Pt. 335) (incorporating 1934 Act rules into FDIC rules).

under Section 12(i). The SEC administers the 1934 Act with respect to bank and savings and loan holding companies,[22] and it could do the same directly with respect to banks and savings associations. In any event, with respect to antifraud violations involving securities issued by banks and savings associations, only the SEC has the authority to bring action for violations of Section 10(b) of the 1934 Act.[23]

§ 7.8　Sarbanes–Oxley Act

On 30 July 2002, the president signed into law the Sarbanes–Oxley Act of 2002 (Sarbanes–Oxley).[1] Largely in response to the corporate accounting scandals that erupted during late 2001,[2] titles III and IV of Sarbanes–Oxley included a number of provisions designed to improve the corporate governance and financial disclosures of issuers that have a class of securities registered under sections 12(b) or 12(g) of the 1934 Act,[3] or that are required to file periodic reports with the SEC under section 15(d)[4] of the act. Sarbanes–Oxley also amended section 12(i) of the 1934 Act to vest the banking agencies with authority to administer and enforce Sarbanes–Oxley §§ 302–304, 306(a), 401(b), 404 and 406–407, as well as 1934 Act § 10A(m) (added by Sarbanes–Oxley § 301), with respect to insured banks and savings associations registered under the 1934 Act.[5] The Fed's implementing regulations are illustrative. In September 2002, the Fed adopted an interim rule to implement the revisions made by Sarbanes–Oxley to 1934 Act § 12(i).[6] On January 28, 2003, the Fed published an identical final rule.[7] The

---

22. *See* 15 U.S.C.A. § 78*l*(i) (limiting delegation to regulatory agencies to securities of banks and savings associations, not holding companies thereof).

23. *See* 15 U.S.C.A. §§ 78j(b), 78*l*(i) (providing no delegated authority to regulatory agencies with respect to antifraud violations). *Cf. Peoples Bank of Danville v. Williams*, 449 F.Supp. 254 (W.D.Va.1978) (discussing antifraud provision). *But cf.* 12 U.S.C.A. § 1818(b)(1) (providing administrative enforcement authority to regulatory agencies for "violations of law").

§ 7.8

1. Pub. L. 102–204, 116 Stat. 745 (2002).

2. For background on the scandals, see *Special Report Enron: One Year On*, THE ECONOMIST, Nov. 30, 2002, at 59.

3. 15 U.S.C.A. § 78*l*(a), (g).

4. *Id.* § 78o(d).

5. The impact of the section 12(i) amendment is limited. For example, as of December 2002, seventeen state member banks had a class of securities registered under section 12(b) or 12(g) of the Exchange Act. 68 Fed. Reg. 4092, 4093 n. 1 (2003).

6. 67 Fed. Reg. 57,938 (2002) (codified at 12 C.F.R. § 208.36(a)) (Fed interim final rule modifying regulations implementing 1934 Act § 12(i) to reflect Sarbanes–Oxley Act amendments to § 12(i)). The Fed also issued supervisory guidance designed to assist registered member banks and other public banking organizations supervised by the Fed in understanding and complying with the requirements of Sarbanes–Oxley. *See The Sarbanes–Oxley Act of 2002*, SR Letter 02–20 (Oct. 29, 2002).

7. 68 Fed. Reg. 4092 (2003) (codified at 12 C.F.R. § 208.36(a)).

rule was effective as of April 1, 2003.[8] As required by § 12(i), the final rule provides that the Fed will administer and enforce the Sarbanes–Oxley provisions with respect to registered member banks. The final rule also generally requires registered member banks to comply with any rules, regulations and forms adopted by the SEC to implement the Sarbanes–Oxley sections, unless such rules, regulations or forms are modified by the Fed. If the SEC rules require the filing of any documents with the SEC, registered member banks must file such documents with the Fed, rather than the SEC.[9]

§ 7.9 Capital Adequacy

A fourth element in the parallel system of securities regulation that applies to the issuance of securities by depository institutions represents the most recent development in this regard. It concerns the supervision of capital adequacy of existing institutions (usually measured in a ratio to the assets of the institutions). Recently, the regulators have increased their attention to capital adequacy of depository institutions. If inadequate capital maintenance constitutes an "unsafe and unsound practice,"[1] the bank regulators have broad statutory authority progressively to define and remedy capital inadequacy.[2] This authority was questioned in *First National Bank of Bellaire v. Comptroller of the Currency,*[3] but the authority was quickly confirmed by congressional action.[4]

The International Lending Supervision Act ("ILSA"),[5] enacted in 1983, requires each agency to "cause banking institutions to achieve and maintain adequate capital by establishing minimum levels of capital for such banking institutions."[6] What constitutes "adequate capital" remains a question within the discretion of the agencies, and ILSA explicitly gives them authority to establish capital adequacy levels as they deem "necessary or appropriate in light of the particular circumstances of the banking institution."[7]

In a legislative reversal of *Bellaire,* ILSA also provides that the failure of a bank to maintain prescribed capital adequacy levels may

---

8. *Id.* at 4092.

9. 12 C.F.R. § 208.36(a)

§ 7.9

1. *See* 12 U.S.C.A. §§ 1818(b)(1), 3907(b) (providing enforcement authority with respect to "unsafe and unsound" practices).

2. 12 U.S.C.A. §§ 1818(b)(1), 3907(b). *Cf., e.g., Groos Nat'l Bank v. Comptroller of the Currency,* 573 F.2d 889 (5th Cir.1978); *First Nat'l Bank of Eden v. Department of the Treasury,* 568

F.2d 610 (8th Cir.1978). Similar authority exists in the bank holding company context. *See Board of Governors v. First Lincolnwood Corp.,* 439 U.S. 234, 99 S.Ct. 505 (1978).

3. 697 F.2d 674 (5th Cir.1983)

4. Pub. L. No. 98–181, tit. IX, § 908, 97 Stat. 1280 (1983) (codified at 12 U.S.C.A. § 3907).

5. 12 U.S.C.A. §§ 3901 *et seq.*

6. *Id.* § 3907(a)(1).

7. *Id.* § 3907(a)(2).

be deemed to constitute an unsafe and unsound practice.[8] Failure to maintain capital adequacy may also lead to the issuance of a directive requiring the bank to submit and comply with a capital plan to reform capital levels.[9] Pursuant to their statutory authority, the federal bank regulators have developed specific capital adequacy policies.

The regulators have progressively focused their attention on refining their capital adequacy policies to take into account, in an explicit way, the relative degrees of risk among the various elements composing the assets of depository institutions, and to define more precisely the elements of "capital." This effort has become more particularly directed at the establishment of convergent capital adequacy regimes among the United States and it major trading partners.

The regulators had freely admitted that their pre–1992 rules did not adequately or efficiently realize the capital adequacy goals of ILSA.[10] The new approach attempts to quantify and account for, *within* the capital ratio, financial factors that significantly affect capital adequacy, but that are not necessarily apparent from the face of the balance sheet.[11]

Guidelines for international convergence of capital measurement and capital standards developed by the Basel Committee on Banking Regulations and Supervisory Practices,[12] now known as the Committee on Banking Regulation, set forth "the details of the agreed framework for measuring capital adequacy and the minimum standard to be achieved that the national supervisory authorities represented on the Committee[13] intend to implement in their

---

8. *Id.* § 3907(b)(1).

9. *See id.* § 3907(b)(2). Such directives and plans submitted pursuant to such directives are enforceable to the same extent as an effective and outstanding final cease and desist order under Section 8(b) of the Federal Deposit Insurance Act, *id.* § 1818(b). *See id.* § 3907(b) (2)(B)(ii).

10. For example, in issuing its 1985 capital adequacy regulations, the OCC acknowledged that the minimum capital ratio rules did not rigorously account either for differences in a given bank's balance sheet composition or for the presence of off-balance-sheet activities. *See* 50 Fed. Reg. 10,207, 10,214 (1985) (so stating). The OCC therefore announced its intention to give further consideration to alternatives for incorporating risk-related criteria into its capital adequacy rules. *Id.*

11. *See generally* 2 MICHAEL P. MALLOY, BANKING LAW AND REGULATION 5.99–5.112 (1994 & CUM. SUPP.) (discussing capital adequacy guidelines).

12. *See* BANK FOR INTERNATIONAL SETTLEMENTS, FINAL REPORT FOR INTERNATIONAL CONVERGENCE OF CAPITAL MEASUREMENT AND CAPITAL STANDARDS, *reprinted in* 4 Fed. Banking L. Rep. (CCH) ¶ 47–105 (Mar. 15, 1996) ("FINAL REPORT").

13. At the time, the Basel Committee consisted of representatives of central bank and supervisory authorities of Belgium, Canada, France, Federal Republic of Germany, Italy, Japan, Luxembourg, the Netherlands, Sweden, Switzerland, United Kingdom, and the United States. Final Report at 51,166 n.1. For background on the proposals leading to the adoption of the Final Report, *see id.* at 51,166.

respective countries."[14] The basic focus of this multilateral framework is "assessing capital in relation to credit risk (the risk of counterparty failure)."[15] However, the framework acknowledges that "other risks, notably interest rate risk and the investment risk on securities, need to be taken into account by supervisors in assessing overall capital adequacy."[16]

The multilateral framework consists of a minimum required ratio of certain specified constituents of capital to risk-weighted assets. "Capital" has two types of constituents: (1) "core capital;"[17] and (2) "supplementary capital."[18] Core capital, the so-called Tier 1 of capital elements, consists of: (a) equity capital;[19] and (b) disclosed reserves from post-tax earnings.[20]

Tier 1 capital elements are the only ones common to the banking systems of all the countries represented on the Committee.[21] Nevertheless, a number of other significant elements of capital are often recognized. The framework therefore identified two tiers of capital elements. The Tier 1 elements must account for at least 50 percent of a bank's capital base for purposes of the risk-weighted ratio.[22] Constituents of supplementary capital, the so-called Tier 2 of capital elements, may be included for these purposes, up to an amount equal to the amount of Tier 1 capital

---

14. FINAL REPORT at 51,166.

15. *Id.*

16. *Id.* The agencies have since released guidance with respect to interest rate risk. 61 Fed. Reg. 33,166 (1996) (OCC, FRS, and FDIC joint policy statement providing guidance on sound practices for managing interest rate risk). *See also* 62 Fed. Reg. 68,064 (1997) (codified at 12 C.F.R. Pts. 3, 208, 225, 325) (amending market risk provisions in risk-based capital standards); 63 Fed. Reg. 30,369 (1998) (codified at 12 C.F.R. pt. 225) (amending Tier 1 leverage ratio for bank holding companies; incorporating market risk capital rule into leverage standard). *See generally* FDIC, *Differences in Capital and Accounting Standards Among the Federal Banking and Thrift Agencies, reprinted in,* 63 Fed. Reg. 20,633 (1998) (discussing treatment of capital adequacy by federal agencies).

17. *See* FINAL REPORT at 51,166. (discussing meaning of "core capital"). *See generally id.* at 51,173, Annex 1 (defining capital in terms of capital base after transitional period).

18. *See id.* at 51,167–51,168 (discussing meaning of "supplementary capital"). *See generally id.* at 51,173, Annex

1 (defining capital in terms of capital base after transitional period). *See id.* at 51,167–51,168 (discussing meaning of "supplementary capital"). *See generally id.* at 51,173, Annex 1 (defining capital in terms of capital base after transitional period).

19. The term "equity capital" is defined for these purposes as "[i]ssued and fully paid ordinary shares/common stock and non-cumulative perpetual preferred stock (but excluding cumulative preferred stock)." *Id.* at 51,167 n. 2. *See also id.* at 51,174, Annex 1, § D(i) (definition of "Tier 1" capital elements). In the case of consolidated accounts, Tier 1 capital would also include the minority interests in the equity of subsidiaries of the bank which are less than wholly owned. *Id.*

20. *Id.* at 51,167. For these purposes, disclosed reserves are reserves that are "created or increased by appropriations of retained earnings or other surplus, *e.g.* share premiums, retained profit, general reserves and legal reserves." *Id.* at 51,174. Tier 1 does not include revaluation reserves. *Id.*

21. *Id.* at 51,167.

22. *See id.*

elements.[23] Supplementary capital consists of: (1) undisclosed reserves;[24] (2) revaluation reserves;[25] (3) general provisions or loan loss reserves;[26] (4) certain hybrid debt capital instruments;[27] and (5) subordinated term debt.[28]

23. *Id.*

24. *Id.* at 51,167–51,168 (discussing undisclosed reserves). *See also id.* at 51,-174, Annex 1, § D(ii)(a) (defining capital in terms of capital base). Inclusion of undisclosed reserves in the capital base is contemplated by the framework only to the extent permitted by local regulatory and accounting arrangement. *Id.* at 51,167. In any event, undisclosed reserves are included in supplementary capital only to the extent that they "have been passed through the profit and loss account and [have been] accepted by [a] bank's supervisory authorities." *Id.* at 51,168.

25. *Id.* at 51,168 (discussing revaluation reserves). *See also id.* at 51,174, Annex 1, § D(ii)(b) (defining capital in terms of capital base). Inclusion of revaluation reserves in the capital base is contemplated by the framework only to the extent permitted by local regulatory and accounting arrangement. *Id.* at 51,-167. Revaluation reserves, whether arising from a formal revaluation or from a "latent revaluation" (a notional additional to capital of hidden values with respect to securities carried at historic cost), may be included in the capital base only if "the assets are considered by the supervisory authority to be prudently valued, fully reflecting the possibility of price fluctuations and forced sale." *Id.* at 51,168. In addition, latent revaluation reserves are subject to a substantial discount reflecting, for example, market volatility and any tax effect of realization of the gain. *Id.* The framework indicates that a 55 percent discount on the difference between historical cost book value and current market value has been agreed to be appropriate in this regard. *See id.*

26. *Id.* at 51,168 (discussing general provisions and general loan loss reserves). *See also id.* at 51,174, Annex 1, § D(ii)(c) (defining capital included in capital base). Reserves against identified losses or with respect to "known deterioration in the valuation of particular assets" are not included in this category. *Id.* at 51,168. *See generally* 65 Fed. Reg. 54,268 (2000) (proposing policy statement on allowance for loan and lease losses methodologies and documentation).

27. Final Report at 51,168 (discussing "hybrid debt capital instruments"). *See also id.* at 51,175, Annex 1, § D(ii)(d) (defining capital included in capital base). Generally, this category includes elements that "combine certain characteristics of equity and certain characteristics of debt." *Id.* at 51,168. Characteristics vary from country to country, but to be included the instruments should exhibit the following specifications:

- they are *unsecured, subordinated and fully paid-up*;

- they are *not redeemable* at the initiative of the holder or without prior or consent of the supervisory authority;

- they are *available to participate in losses* without the bank being obliged to cease trading (unlike conventional subordinated debt); [and]

- although the capital instrument may carry an obligation to pay interest that cannot permanently be reduced or waived (unlike dividends on ordinary share holders' equity), *it should allow service obligations to be deferred* (as with cumulative preference shares) where the profitability of the bank would not support payment.

Id. at 51,175 (emphasis in original). Such instruments as mandatory convertible debt instruments (in U.S. practice), perpetual debt and preference shares (in U.K. practice), long-term preferred shares (in Canadian practice), *titres participatifs* and *titres subordonnes a duree indeterminee* (in French practice), or *Genussscheine* (in German practice) would qualify for inclusion in this category of Tier 2 capital. *See id.* at 51,168. *See also id.* at 51,175.

28. *Id.* at 51, 168–51, 169 (discussion of subordinated term debt). *See also id.* at 51,175, Annex 1, § D(ii)(e) (definition of capital included in the capital base).

The eligible constituents of Tier 1 and Tier 2 capital are subject to certain deductions under the framework.[29] The amount of goodwill must be deducted from the figure for Tier 1 capital.[30] The amount of investments in unconsolidated banking and financial subsidiaries, if any,[31] must be deducted from the total capital base.[32] The Committee considered, but ultimately rejected, requiring deduction of banks' holdings of capital issued by other banks or depository institutions.[33] Nevertheless, the framework does reflect the agreement that individual supervisory authorities retain the discretion to require such deductions.[34] If no deduction is applied, then the full value of such holdings must be included in assessing capital adequacy of the holding bank.[35]

The framework endorses a risk-weighted approach to the assets denominator of the capital-assets ratio utilized in assessing capital adequacy.[36] The framework establishes a relatively simplified methodology for risk-weighting, with only five basic risk weights being employed.[37] The basic methodology effectively captures only credit risk.[38] It is left to the discretion of individual supervisory authori-

---

This category includes "conventional unsecured subordinated debt capital instruments with a minimum original fixed term to maturity of over five years and limited life redeemable preference shares." *Id.* Such instruments are not normally available to participate in the losses of an issuing bank that continues trading (*see id.*), they are viewed as having "significant deficiencies as constituents of capital in view of their fixed maturity and inability to absorb losses except in liquidation." *Id.* at 51,168. Accordingly, these instruments may be included only up to an amount equal to 50 percent of the total amount of core capital (*id.* at 51,169), and they are subject to a cumulative discount or amortization of twenty percent per year during the last five years of maturity "to reflect the diminishing value of these instruments as a continuing source of strength." *Id.* at 51,175.

29. *See id.* at 51,169.

30. *Id.* In December 2008, the agencies amended their regulatory capital rules to permit banks, bank holding companies, and savings associations to reduce the amount of goodwill that a banking organization must deduct from tier 1 capital by the amount of any deferred tax liability associated with that goodwill. 73 Fed. Reg. 79,602 (2008) (codified at 12 C.F.R. pts. 3 (OCC rules), 208, 225 (Fed rules), 325 (FDIC rules),

567 (OTS rules)). The amendment was effective January 29, 2009. *Id.* at 79,603.

31. The framework generally assumes as the normal practice that subsidiaries will be consolidated for the purpose of assessing capital adequacy, but "[w]here this is not done, deduction is essential to prevent multiple use of the same capital resources in different parts of [a banking] group." FINAL REPORT at 51,169.

32. *Id.*

33. *See id.*

34. *Id.* Conceivably, these discretionary policies may require deduction of the amount of all such holdings, holdings to the extent that they exceed some determined limit in relation to the holding bank's or the issuing bank's capital, or on a case-by-case basis. *Id.* The framework also reflects the agreement that, "in applying these policies, member countries [should] consider that reciprocal cross-holdings of bank capital designed artificially to inflate the capital position of the banks concerned should not be permitted." *Id.*

35. *Id.* at 51,169.

36. *See id.*

37. *See id.* at 51,175–51,176, Annex 2 (establishing risk weights by categories of on-balance-sheet asset).

38. *Id.* at 51,169.

ties to decide whether to attempt to account for more methodologically difficult types of risk, such as investment risk, interest rate risk, exchange rate risk, or concentration risk.[39] Furthermore, the individual supervisory authorities also retain discretion to supplement the framework's risk-weighted methodology with "other methods of capital measurement,"[40] such as capital-assets ratios. In addition, to account for country transfer risk, the Basel Committee ultimately adopted an approach that applied differing risk weights to defined groups of countries.[41]

The framework also recognizes the importance of bringing off-balance-sheet risk into the analysis of capital adequacy (*e.g.*, contingent letter of credit exposure).[42] Off-balance-sheet risk is brought within the framework by conversion into appropriate credit risk equivalents.[43]

Some uncertainty remained about the appropriate approach to interest rate and exchange rate related items, such as swaps, options, and futures.[44] As to these contingencies, the framework takes the position that special treatment is necessary, "because banks are not exposed to credit risk for the full face value of their

---

39. *Id.* at 51,169–51,170.

40. *Id.* at 51,169.

41. *Id.* at 51,170–51,171:

[T]he Committee has concluded that a defined group of countries should be adopted as the basis for applying differential weighting coefficients[.] The framework also recognizes the importance of and that this group should be full members of the OECD or countries which have concluded special arrangements with the [International Monetary Fund] associated with the Fund's General Arrangements to Borrow. . . .

. . . This decision has the following consequences for the weighting structure. Claims on central governments within the OECD will attract a zero weight (or a low weight if the national supervisory authority elects to incorporate interest rate risk); and claims on OECD non-central government public-sector entities will attract a low weight. . . . Claims on central governments and central banks outside the OECD will also attract a zero weight (or a low weight if the national supervisory authority elects to incorporate investment risk), provided such claims are denominated in the national currency and funded by liabilities in the same currency. . . .

. . . As regards the treatment of interbank claims, in order to preserve the efficiency and liquidity of the international interbank market[,] there will be no differentiation between short-term claims on banks incorporated within or outside the OECD. However, the Committee draws a distinction between . . . short-term placements with other banks . . . and . . . longer-term cross-border loans to banks which are often associated with particular transactions and carry greater transfer and/or credit risks. A 20 per cent [*sic*] weight will therefore be applied to claims on all banks, wherever incorporated, with a residual maturity of up to an[d] including one year; longer-term claims on OECD incorporated banks will be weighted at 20 per cent [*sic*]; and longer-term claims on banks incorporated outside the OECD will be weighted at 100 percent.

42. *See id.* at 51,171–51,172 (discussing treatment of off-balance-sheet obligations).

43. *See id.* at 51,176, Annex 3 (establishing credit conversion factors for off-balance-sheet items).

44. *See id.* at 51,172.

contracts, but only to the cost of replacing the cash flow if the counterparty defaults."[45]

Once the credit equivalent amounts of such contingencies have been calculated, the amounts are to be weighted in accordance with the risk weights applicable to the category of counterparties involved. However, in anticipation of the fact that most counterparties in the market for such contingencies, particularly long-term contracts, "tend to be first-class names,"[46] the FINAL REPORT reflects general agreement that such contingencies will be assigned a 50 percent risk weight, rather than the 100 percent risk weight that might otherwise be applicable.[47]

The final element in the risk-weighted methodology, as with any capital-assets ratio requirement, is the required minimum level of the ratio. The framework adopted a target standard ratio of eight percent, of which core capital must constitute at least four percent.[48] This target ratio became fully applicable by year-end 1992.[49]

The 1988 Capital Accord is currently used by regulators in over 100 countries to determine minimum capital reserves of banks subject to their supervision.[50] In brief, the risk-weighted methodology is applied as follows:

> (1) Identification of Tier 1 capital elements must be made, with the amount of goodwill deducted from the gross amount of Tier 1 capital.

> (2) Tier 2 capital elements must be identified. The total of Tier 2 capital may be included for ratio purposes only up to an amount equal to the amount of Tier 1 capital. Furthermore, among the Tier 2 capital elements, subordinated term debt is limited to a maximum of 50 percent of the amount of Tier 1 elements, and certain amounts for general provisions or general loan loss reserves are generally limited to an amount equal to 1.25 percent of risk-weighted assets.

> (3) From the total capital base (Tier 1 plus eligible Tier 2), there must be deducted any investments in unconsolidated banking and finance subsidiaries of the banking enterprise under consideration. Furthermore, in the discretion of the individual supervisory authorities, investments in the capital of other banks and depository institutions may also be required to be deducted from the total capital base.

---

45. *Id.*

46. *Id.* at 51,178.

47. *Id.* However, some member countries have apparently reserved the right to apply the full 100 percent risk weight. *See id.* n. 9.

48. *Id.* at 51,172.

49. *Id.* at 51,172–51,173.

50. Daniel Pruzin, *Basel Committee Cites Mixed Results for Meeting Proposed Capital Accord*, BNA Int'l Bus. & Fin. Daily, Apr. 24, 2001, at d2.

The result of these first three steps yields the numerator of the risk-weighted ratio.

(4) The on-balance-sheet assets must be weighted according to the general categories of risk set forth in Annex 2 of the FINAL REPORT. (Figure 7–1, *infra*, illustrates the risk weights by asset category.)

Figure 7–1

Risk Weights by Category of On–Balance–Sheet Asset

Risk Weight	*Category of Assets*
0%	Cash[51]
	Claims on central governments and central banks denominated in national currency and funded in that currency
	Other claims on OECD[52] central governments[53] and central banks
	Claims collateralized by cash or OECD central-government securities or guaranteed by OECD central governments[54]
0, 10, 20, or 50%[55]	Claims on domestic public-sector entities, excluding central government, and loans guaranteed by such entities
20%	Claims on multilateral development banks[56] and claims guaranteed by or collateralized by securities issued by such banks
	Claims on banks incorporated in the OECD and loans guaranteed by OECD incorporated banks

51. Includes (at national discretion) gold bullion held in own vaults or on an allocated basis to the extent backed by bullion liabilities.

52. The OECD comprises countries which are full members of the OECD or which have concluded special lending arrangements with the International Monetary Fund ("IMF") associated with the IMF General Arrangements to Borrow.

53. Some member countries intend to apply weights to securities issued by OECD central governments to take account of investment risk. These weights would, for example, be ten percent for all securities or ten percent for those maturing in up to one year and twenty percent for those maturing in over one year.

54. Commercial loans partially guaranteed by these bodies will attract equivalent low weights on that part of the loan that is fully covered. Similarly, loans partially collateralized by cash or securities issued by OECD central governments and multilateral development banks will attract low weights on that part of the loan which is fully covered.

55. In the discretion of individual supervisory authorities.

56. *I.e.*, International Bank for Reconstruction and Development; Inter–American Development Bank; Asian Development Bank; African Development Bank; European Investment Bank. Claims on other multilateral development banks of which G–10 countries are shareholding members may, at national discretion, also attract a twenty percent weight.

Risk Weight	Category of Assets
	Claims on banks incorporated in countries outside the OECD with a residual maturity of up to one year and loans with a residual maturity of up to one year guaranteed by banks incorporated in countries outside the OECD
	Claims on non-domestic OECD public-sector entities, excluding central government, and loans guaranteed by such entities
	Cash items in process of collection
50%	Loans fully secured by mortgage on residential property that is or will be occupied by the borrower or that is rented[57]
100%	Claims on the private sector
	Claims on banks incorporated outside the OECD with a residual maturity of over one year
	Claims on central governments outside the OECD (unless denominated in national currency—and funded in that currency—see above)
	Claims on commercial companies owned by the public sector
	Premises, plant, and equipment and other fixed assets
	Real estate and other investments (including non-consolidated investment participations in other companies)
	Capital instruments issued by other banks (unless deducted from capital)

57. The continuing subprime mortgage crisis has put pressure on this risk weight policy. (On the subprime mortgage crisis, see 1 MICHAEL P. MALLOY, BANKING LAW AND REGULATION § 1.4 (1994 & Cum. Supp.).) For example, on March 4, 2009, Treasury announced guidelines under its Making Home Affordable Program (MHA Program) to promote sustainable loan modifications for homeowners at risk of losing their homes due to foreclosure. See http://www.making homeaffordable.gov (providing program details). The MHA Program provided a detailed framework for mortgage servicers to modify mortgages on owner-occupied residential properties and offers financial incentives to lenders and servicers that participate in the Program. It also provided financial incentives for homeowners whose mortgages are modified pursuant to Program guidelines to remain current on their mortgages after modification. To support and facilitate the timely implementation and acceptance of the program, and to promote the stability of depository institutions, holding companies, and the financial system generally, the OCC, the Fed, the FDIC, and the OTS adopted interim final rules in June 2009 providing that mortgage loans modified under the MHA Program would retain the risk weight assigned to the loan prior to the modification, so long as the loan continued to meet other applicable prudential criteria. 74 Fed. Reg. 31,160 (2009) (codified at 12 C.F.R. pts. 3, App. A, § 3(a)(3)(iii), 208, App. A, § III. C.3., 225, App A, § III.C.3. (Fed rules), 325, App. A (FDIC rule), 576.1(4) (OTS rule)) (amending risk-based capital guidelines as applied to residential mortgage loans modified under MHA Program).

Risk Weight	Category of Assets
	All other assets

(5) Off-balance-sheet items must be converted to their credit equivalents. (Figure 7–2, *infra*, illustrates the credit conversion factors.) The credit equivalent amounts are then risk-weighted in accordance with the generally applicable rules governing risk weighting.

Figure 7–2
Credit Conversion Factors for Off–Balance–Sheet Items

Factor	Type of Instrument[58]
100%	Direct credit substitutes, *e.g.*, general guarantees of indebtedness (including standby letters of credit serving as financial guarantees for loans and securities) and acceptances (including endorsements with the character of acceptances)
50%	Certain transaction-related contingent items (*e.g.*, performance bonds, bid bonds, warranties, and standby letters of credit related to particular transactions)
20%	Short-term self-liquidating trade-related contingencies (such as documentary credits collateralized by the underlying shipments)
100%	Sale and repurchase agreements and asset sales with recourse,[59] where the credit risk remains with the bank
100%	Forward asset purchases, forward deposits, and partly-paid shares and securities, that represent commitments with certain drawdown
50%	Note issuance facilities and revolving underwriting facilities
50%	Other commitments (*e.g.*, formal standby facilities and credit lines) with an original maturity of over one year

58. "Member countries will have some limited discretion to allocate particular instruments into [the above] items ... according to the characteristics of the instrument in the national market." FINAL REPORT, Annex 3.

59. These items are to be weighted according to the type of asset and not according to the type of counterparty with whom the transaction has been entered into. Reverse repos (*i.e.*, purchase and resale agreements—where the bank is the receiver of the asset) are to be treated as collateralized loans, reflecting the economic reality of the transaction. The risk is therefore to be measured as an exposure to the counterparty. Where the asset temporarily acquired is a security that attracts a preferential risk weighting, this would be recognized as collateral and the risk weighting would be reduced accordingly.

Factor	Type of Instrument[58]
0%	Similar commitments with an original maturity of up to one year, or that can be unconditionally canceled at any time

(6) The denominator of the risk-weighted ratio, total risk-weighted assets, is derived by adding the risk-weighted on-balance-sheet amounts to the risk-weighted credit equivalents of the off-balance-sheet items. The ratios of Tier 1 capital to total risk-weighted assets and of total capital (Tier 1 plus eligible Tier 2 amounts) to total risk-weighted assets are then calculated and assessed in relation to the required minimum ratios under the framework.

The Basel Committee has continued to refine the details and mechanics of risk management and supervision.[60] Correspondingly, implementation of the guidelines in the United States has not been a static project; the guidelines have been the subject of almost continuous reassessment and refinement by the regulators.[61] By the

---

60. *See, e.g.*, BIS, Committee on Banking Supervision, *The Treatment of the Credit Risk Associated with Certain Off–Balance–Sheet Items* (July 1994); BIS, Committee on Banking Supervision, *Risk Management Guidelines for Derivatives* (July 1994); BIS, Committee on Banking Supervision, *Amendment to the Capital Accord of July 1988* (July 1994); BIS, Committee on Banking Supervision, *Prudential Supervision of Banks' Derivatives Activities* (Dec. 1994); BIS, Committee on Banking Supervision, *Basle Capital Accord: Treatment of Potential Exposure for Off–Balance–Sheet Items* (April 1995); BIS, Committee on Banking Supervision, *An Internal Model–Based Approach to Market Risk Capital Requirements* (April 1995); BIS, Committee on Banking Supervision, *Public Disclosure of the Trading and Derivatives Activities of Banks and Securities Firms* (Nov. 1995); BIS, Committee on Banking Supervision, *Supervisory Framework for the Use of "Backtesting" in Conjunction with the Internal Models Approach to Market Risk Capital Requirements* (Jan. 1996); BIS, Committee on Banking Supervision, *Amendment to the Basle Capital Accord to Incorporate Market Risks* (Jan. 1996); BIS, Committee on Banking Supervision, *Interpretation of the Capital Accord for the Multilateral Netting of Forward Value Foreign Exchange Transactions* (April 1996).

61. *See, e.g.*, 62 Fed. Reg. 55,686 (1997) (to be codified at 12 C.F.R. pts. 3, 208, 325, 567) (proposing uniform treatment of certain construction and real estate loans and investments in mutual funds; simplifying Tier 1 capital standards); 62 Fed. Reg. 55,692 (1997) (to be codified at 12 C.F.R. pt. 225) (proposing similar amendments with respect to treatment of capital of bank holding companies); 62 Fed. Reg. 59,944 (1997) (to be codified at 12 C.F.R. pts. 3, 208, 225, 325, 567) (proposing regulatory capital treatment of recourse obligations and direct credit substitutes); 64 Fed. Reg. 10,194 (1999) (codified at 12 C.F.R. pts. 3, 208, 325, 567) (OCC, Fed, FDIC and OTS rules for construction loans on presold residential properties, junior liens on one-to four-family residential properties, investments in mutual funds, and tier 1 leverage ratio); 64 Fed. Reg. 10,201 (1999) (codified at 12 C.F.R. pt. 225) (corresponding Fed rule applicable to bank holding companies); 65 Fed. Reg. 12,320 (2000) (to be codified at 12 C.F.R. pts. 3, 208, 225, 325, 567) (proposing changes in risk-based capital standards to address recourse obligations and direct credit substitutes); 65 Fed. Reg. 16,480 (2000) (to be codified at 12 C.F.R. pt. 225, Appendices A, D) (proposing regulatory capital treatment of certain investments in nonfinancial com-

mid–1990s, the agencies were seriously focusing upon management of interest-rate risk, which was not within the purview of the original guidelines.[62] Similarly, the regulators have folded market-risk provisions into the framework of the guidelines.[63]

Over the past decade, the BIS Committee began working on amendments to the 1988 Guidelines in order to take account of new globalized financial practices and to create a more flexible, risk-sensitive framework for determining minimum capital require-ments.[64] In June 1999, the BIS issued a proposal that would significantly revise the capital adequacy accord,[65] in two basic ways: by extensively refining the 1988 guidelines, and by providing a dramatic alternative approach. The new approach had three basic principles: (*i*) International banks would be required to establish their own internal methods for assessing the relative risks of their assets. (*ii*) Supervisory authorities would be expected to exercise greater oversight of these capital assessments by banks. (*iii*) Great-er transparency in banking operations would be required, *e.g.*, the creditworthiness of borrowing governments and corporations would be assessed by credit-rating agencies, and these ratings would be used by banks in pricing loans to such borrowers. Financial institu-tions had until 31 March 2000 to respond to the proposed revisions,

panies by bank holding companies); 66 Fed. Reg. 59,176 (2001) (to be codified at 12 C.F.R. pt. 208, App. A, pt. 225, App. A) (proposing amendments to Fed capi-tal adequacy guidelines; clarifying that deferred tax assets in excess of allowable amount are included in items deducted from Tier 1 capital for purpose of deter-mining maximum allowable amount of Tier 2 capital); 67 Fed. Reg. 3783 (2002) (codified at 12 C.F.R. § 3.2(a), pt. 3 App. A, pt. 208 App. A, App. B, pt. 225 App. A, App. D, §§ 325.2(v), (x), 325.2(f)(3)–(4), (g)(2)(i), pt. 325 App. A) (amending OCC, Fed and FDIC capital adequacy guidelines to establish special minimum capital requirements for equity invest-ments in nonfinancial companies); 67 Fed. Reg. 16,971 (2002), *corrected*, 67 Fed. Reg. 34,991 (2002) (codified at 12 C.F.R. pts. 3, 208, 225, 325, 567) (reduc-ing risk weight applicable to claims on, and claims guaranteed by, qualifying U.S. securities firms and securities firms incorporated in OECD member coun-tries from 100 percent to 20 percent; conforming FDIC and OTS rules to ex-isting OCC and Fed to permit zero per-cent risk weight for certain claims on qualifying securities firms collateralized by cash on deposit in lending institution or by securities issued or guaranteed by

the United States or other OECD cen-tral governments).

62. *See, e.g.*, 61 Fed. Reg. 33,166 (1996) (publishing OCC, FRS & FDIC joint policy statement providing guid-ance on sound practices for managing interest rate risk). *But see* 67 Fed. Reg. 31,722 (2002) (codified at 12 C.F.R. §§ 516.40(a)(2), 567.1, 567.5(b)(4), 567.6(a)(1)(iv)(G)–(H); *removing* § 567.7) (imposing 50 percent risk weight for certain qualifying mortgage loans; eliminating interest rate risk com-ponent of risk-based capital regulations; making technical amendments).

63. *See, e.g.*, 62 Fed. Reg. 68,064 (1997) (codified at 12 C.F.R. pts. 3, 208, 225, 325) (amending market risk provi-sions in risk-based capital standards).

64. *See* Daniel Pruzin, *Basel Com-mittee Sets Out Changes to Risk Calcu-lations Under Capital Accord*, BNA Int'l Bus. & Fin. Daily, Oct. 3, 2001, at d3 (discussing BIS motivations for proposed Capital Accord). *See also* note 58, *supra* (citing BIS issuances concerning refine-ment of capital adequacy framework).

65. *See, e.g.*, Alan Cowell, *An Inter-national Banking Panel Proposes Ways to Limit Risk*, N.Y. Times, June 4, 1999, at C4, col. 2 (describing proposed revi-sion).

which the BIS anticipated would be effective no sooner than 2001.[66]

A revised version of the proposal was issued for comment in January 2001.[67] This latest version takes the three-pronged approach to capital adequacy for international banks that are qualified to use it: capital adequacy requirements (largely revised from the 1988 guidelines);[68] increased supervision of bank capital maintenance policies;[69] and greater transparency through disclosure to the market, with resulting market discipline.[70] These elements are referred to as the three "pillars" of minimum capital requirements, the supervisory review process, and market discipline.

Of the three pillars, by far the most extensively discussed in the proposal is the first pillar, which will involve significant changes in capital adequacy regulation. First, capital requirements would be extensively revised from the original framework version and would offer banks two alternative approaches to capital adequacy. The standardized approach[71] is essentially the 1988 guidelines, as revised by the new Accord.[72] The revisions represent refinements of the guidelines, including for example more articulated risk weights with respect to claims on sovereign borrowers based upon their credit assessments by export credit agencies.[73] Furthermore, the Accord imposes a requirement that internationally active banks account for internal or operational risk (arising from poor documentation, fraud, infrastructural failure and the like),[74] in addition to credit and market risk.[75] Generally, the charge for operational risk would involve approximately 20 percent of overall

66. *Id.* at C4, col. 4.

67. BIS Committee on Banking Supervision, *Consultative Document: The New Capital Accord* (Jan. 2001) ("*Accord*").

68. *See Accord* at 6–103 (discussing approaches to capital requirements).

69. *See id.* at 104–112 (discussing supervision).

70. *See id.* at 114–133.

71. *Id.* at 7–31.

72. *Id.* at 7.

73. *Id.* at 7–8.

74. The term *operational risk* may be defined as "the risk of direct or indirect loss resulting from inadequate or failed internal processes, people and systems or from external events." *Accord* at 94. As used in the BIS proposed Accord, the term does not include strategic and reputational risk. *Id.* For discussion of reputational risk, see BIS, Committee on

Banking Supervision, *Core Principles for Effective Banking Supervision* § IV.A, *reprinted in*, Michael P. Malloy, International Banking: Cases, Materials, and Problems 291 (2001–2002 Supp.) ("*Core Principles*"). A working paper of the BIS Committee's Risk Management Group has proposed the deletion of the phrase "direct or indirect" from the definition of operational loss, because it was too vague. Risk Management Group, BIS Committee on Banking Supervision, *Working Paper on the Regulatory Treatment of Operational Risk, available at*, http://www.bis.org ("*RMG Working Paper*"). In June 2002, the Basel Committee announced that it would be seeking detailed information from internationally active banks with respect to operational risk exposures for 2001. Daniel Pruzin, *Basel Committee Seeks More Bank Data on Operational Risk Exposures for FY 2001*, BNA Int'l Bus. & Fin. Daily, June 7, 2002, at d7.

75. *Accord, supra* note 65, at 95.

capital requirements.[76] The capital requirements would be applied to consolidated and sub-consolidated elements of larger financial services enterprises.[77]

As an alternative to the standardized approach, banks that demonstrate to their supervisors an internal methodology for assigning exposures to different classes of assets consistently over time[78] will be able to maintain capital in accordance with an internal credit ratings system (the so called "internal ratings based," or "IRB" approach).[79] The IRB approach is based upon sophisticated computer modeling or other in-house analytical tools to determine credit risk on a borrower-by-borrower basis that includes an estimate of future losses on assets.[80] Two methodologies are available in this regard. The foundation methodology would allow the bank to estimate internally the probability of default on the asset, while using regulator-imposed analysis of other risk components associated with the asset.[81] Under the advanced methodology, a sophisticated bank would be permitted to use internally generated estimates for other risk components.[82]

76. *Id.* at 95 n.51.

77. *Id.* at 1:

1. The New Basel Capital Accord ... will be applied on a consolidated basis to internationally active banks. . . .

2. The scope of application of the Accord will be extended to include, on a fully consolidated basis, holding companies that are parents of banking groups to ensure that it captures risks within the whole banking group. . . .

3. The Accord will also apply to all internationally active banks at every tier within a banking group. . . .

(Footnote omitted.) However, the parent holding company of a banking group's holding company may not itself be subject to the Accord if it is not viewed as a parent of a banking group. *Id.* at 1 n.1. For an illustration of the consolidation and sub-consolidation requirements of the Accord, see Figure 7–3, *infra*.

78. *Accord, supra* note 65, at 32.

79. *Id.* at 32–86.

80. *Id.* at 34.

81. *Id.* In October 2001, a task force of the BIS Committee questioned whether the foundation approach was necessary and asked for comment from the banking industry on this issue. Models Task Force, BIS Committee on Banking Supervision, *Working Paper on the Internal Ratings–Based Approach to Specialized Lending Exposures, available at,* http://www.bis.org [hereinafter *MTF Working Paper*].

82. *Accord, supra* note 65, at 34.

Figure 7–3
Consolidation and Sub–Consolidation Requirements

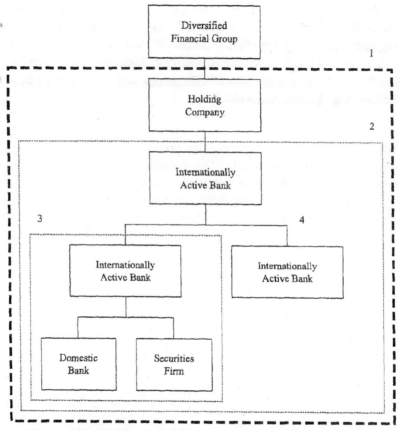

1. Boundary of predominately banking group. The Accord is to be applied at this level on a consolidated basis, i.e. up to holding company level.

2, 3, 4. The Accord is also to be applied at lower levels to all internationally active banks on a consolidated basis.

The revised proposal was highly criticized by banking industry commentators,[83] mainly because of reporting requirements perceived as excessive, and the level of capital charges viewed as unnecessarily high. In addition, in the Spring 2001, the annual report of the BIS Committee on Banking Supervision, reviewing the public disclosure practices of international banks, criticized the relative lack of disclosure in areas related to credit risk modeling and use of internal and external ratings by major banks.[84] This seriously implicates the proposed Accord, since disclosure of infor-

83. *See* Daniel Pruzin, *supra* note 62, at d3 (noting industry opposition).

84. Daniel Pruzin, *Basel Committee Cites Mixed Results for Meeting Proposed Capital Accord*, BNA Int'l Bus. & Fin. Daily, Apr. 24, 2001, at d2. However, in a May 2002 report, the Basel Committee indicated that internationally active banks had modestly increased their

mation with respect to use of internal ratings is necessary for banks to qualify for the IRB approach proposed in "Pillar 1" of the new accord.[85]

In fact, as a result of its assessment of the critical comments that were received in response to the last version of the proposal and the need for further study and adjustment of the proposal in light of those comments, in June 2001 the BIS Committee decided to delay implementation of the proposed Capital Accord until 2005.[86] The delay was particularly welcomed by the European Commission, which had launched a consultative process for a parallel EU proposal based on the Basel Committee's recommendations.[87] The Commission noted that, during its own consultation process, the proposed calibration of risk weights and the potential impact of the proposed ratio of regulatory capital to operational risk (20 percent) had been consistently criticized by various branches of the banking and financial services sector.[88] Concerns had also been raised about the relatively tight timetable for finalizing the new capital regime.[89]

In a working paper issued Sept. 28, 2001, the Risk Management Group of the BIS Committee on Banking Supervision outlined changes to the proposed Capital Accord.[90] The proposed changes to the Accord's "Pillar 1" would include, *inter alia*, a significant lowering of the operational risk charge as a percentage of a bank's overall capital set-aside requirements and greater flexibility in the use of advanced internal risk estimate methods for determining a bank's minimum capital requirements.[91] Comments on the proposed changes were to be received by 31 October 2001.[92]

On 5 October 2001, the BIS Committee released another working paper, proposing further changes to the revised Accord.[93] The working paper focused on issues concerning the application of IRB

public disclosure of such information during 2000. Daniel Pruzin, *Basel Committee Cites "Modest" Improvement in Information Disclosures*, BNA Int'l Bus. & Fin. Daily, May 16, 2002, at d5. Nevertheless, it did caution that most banks still failed to provide such information with respect to the use of credit derivatives and other sophisticated instruments subject to reporting requirements under the proposed accord. *Id.*

85. Pruzin, *Basel Committee Cites Mixed Results, supra* note 82.

86. Daniel Pruzin, *Capital Accord Draft Completion Delayed as Basel Committee Eyes New Revisions*, BNA Int'l Bus. & Fin. Daily, June 26, 2001, at d3.

87. Joe Kirwin, *EC Welcomes Basel Committee Delay in Implementing New*

Capital Accord, BNA Banking Daily, June 26, 2001, at d3.

88. *Id.*

89. *Id.*

90. *RMG Working Paper, supra* note 72. *See* Daniel Pruzin, *supra* note 62 at d3 (reporting on implications of *RMG Working Paper*).

91. Daniel Pruzin, *supra* note 62 at d3 (discussing proposed changes).

92. *Id.*

93. *MTF Working Paper, supra* note 79. *See* Daniel Pruzin, *Basel Committee Outlines Further Changes to IRB Approach in Proposed Capital Accord*, Int'l Bus. & Fin. Daily, Oct. 10, 2001, at d5 (reporting on *MTF Working Paper*).

approaches to risk assessment, and specifically on the treatment of "specialized loans" such as project finance undertakings.[94] The working paper proposed a specific framework for treatment of specialized loans that relied upon a stream of income generated by an asset rather than the creditworthiness of the borrower for repayment of the loan. Such a loan arrangement does not conform to assumptions underlying the IRB approach of the revised Accord, which tends to focus on the ongoing operations of the borrower as the source of repayment.[95] The proposed treatment of specialized loans would include any loans that exhibited the following characteristics: (*i*) loan is intended for the acquisition or financing of an asset; (*ii*) asset cash flow is the sole or almost sole source of repayment; (*iii*) loan represents a significant liability for the borrower; and, (*iv*) variability of asset cash flow, rather than the independent creditworthiness of the borrower's overall enterprise, is the key determinant of credit risk.[96]

According to the MTF Working Paper, four loan products clearly meet these criteria. Project finance, "in which the lender looks primarily to the revenues generated by a single project"[97] for security and repayment, would be subject to the proposed treatment of specialized loans. A second product would be income-producing real estate, in which construction or acquisition of such assets as office buildings, retail properties, hotels, and the like, is financed and repayment depends upon income generated by the property.[98] Big-ticket lease financing (or "object financing," in the vocabulary of the MTF Working Paper), in which the acquisition of significant capital equipment such as vessels, aircraft, satellites and railcars, is financed on the strength of the lease income that the asset will generate, is a third category included in specialized loans.[99] Finally, commodity financing, involving "short-term lending to finance reserves, inventories, or receivables of exchange-traded commodities,"[100] would be included since repayment is dependent upon subsequent sale of the commodity. These (and possibly other loan products) would be subject to a single framework, with a specified set of components generating minimum capital requirements related to the specialized loan products.

No deadline for comments on the MTF Working Paper was formally set by the task force, although it reportedly would antici-

94. *MTF Working Paper, supra* note 79.

95. *See, e.g., Accord, supra* note 65, at 50–51 (discussing risk assessment criteria applicable to corporate exposures).

96. Daniel Pruzin, *supra* note 91, at d5.

97. *MTF Working Paper, supra* note 79.

98. *Id.*

99. *Id.*

100. *Id.*

pate receiving such comments by mid-November 2001.[101] Since the industry reaction has played an important role in the content and timing of the proposed Accord, it is reasonable to conclude that we are potentially some considerable distance from a final version of the revised Accord.

In December 2001, the BIS Committee announced that it had decided to carry out a comprehensive "quantitative impact study" (QIS) immediately, to assess the overall impact of the proposed capital accord on banks and the banking system.[102] The revised version of the accord, which the Committee had planned to circulate in early 2002, has been postponed indefinitely.[103] Conceivably, the results of the QIS could adversely affect the likelihood that the new accord will be finalized during 2002 and implemented by 2005.[104]

In August 2003, the OCC, the Fed., the FDIC and the OTS issued an advance notice proposing a new risk-based regulatory capital framework based on the Basel Committee's April 2003 consultative paper, *New Basel Capital Accord*.[105] The proposal solicited public comments on certain advanced approaches to regulatory capital contained in the proposed a new accord that the agencies believed were appropriate for large, internationally active U.S. banks—the internal ratings based (IRB) approach for credit risk, and the advanced measurement approaches (AMA) for operational risk. The agencies received approximately 100 public comments on the proposal from banks, trade associations, supervisory authorities, and other interested parties.[106] The comments were generally favorable, while raising a number of conceptual and technical issues.

However, the momentum behind the Basel II proposal continued to dissipate.[107] Finally, on May 11, 2004, the Basel Committee

---

101. Daniel Pruzin, *supra* note 91 (citing statements by unnamed official).

102. Daniel Pruzin, *Basel Committee Announces Further Delay to Completion of Revised Capital Accord*, Int'l Bus. & Fin. Daily, Dec. 14, 2001, at d9.

103. *Id.*

104. *Id.* (quoting statement issued by the Committee).

105. 68 Fed. Reg. 45,900 (2003) (to be codified at 12 C.F.R. pt. 3, App. A, B (OCC rules applicable to national banks), pt. 208, App. A, E (Fed rules applicable to state member banks), pt. 225, App. A, E (Fed rules applicable to bank holding companies), pt. 325, App. A, C (FDIC rules applicable to state non-

member banks), pt. 567 (OTS rules applicable to savings associations)).

106. 71 Fed. Reg. at 55832.

107. *See, e.g.*, R. Christian Bruce, Regulators Must Supply More Answers Before Basel Can Be Adopted, Shelby, Sarbanes Say, BNA Banking Daily, June 19, 2003, at 1 (reporting on congressional dissatisfaction with Basel II deliberations); Patrick Tracey and Karen Werner, British Banking Groups Seek Delay In Basel II Capital Accord Until 2010, BNA Banking Daily, Aug. 11, 2003, at 1 (reporting on request by British Bankers' Association and London Investment Banking Association for "less prescriptive and more principles-based" rules); Richard Cowden, Regulators, Lawmak-

on Banking Supervision announced that it had reached agreement on outstanding issues that had impeded the finalizing of the Basel II accord.[108] The Committee stated that it would adhere to the proposed year-end 2006 target date for banks to adopt the more basic "standardized" and "foundation IRB" approaches for assessing minimum capital charges.[109] However, for banks adopting the most advanced IRB approaches—most, if not all, major internationally-active banks—the Committee expected that a year-end 2007 target date was necessary to allow further impact analysis and parallel running before full implementation.[110]

On June 26, 2004, the Committee approved the final version of the revised accord.[111] The committee emphasized that it would continue to review the calibration of the accord prior to its implementation and adjust it as necessary to ensure that the new capital rules did not result in a sharp increase in overall minimum capital requirements.[112] As with the previous guidelines, the committee expected that the revised accord would become the global standard for minimum capital requirements.[113] However, India and China, among other major developing countries, have already indicated that they did not intend to adopt the revised accord,[114] and U.S. regulators—including the SEC as well as the OCC, Fed, FDIC and OTS—decided that it would only be required for the relatively small number of the largest internationally-active U.S. banks.[115] Nevertheless, according to the secretary-general of the Basel Committee, Basel II would make financial markets healthier by giving accountants, investors, and other interested parties more information on which to base critical decisions.[116]

ers, Industry Cautious As Basel II Accord Staggers to Finish Line, BNA Banking Daily, April 26, 2004 (reporting on preference of U.S. banks, regulators, and lawmakers probably to delay Basel II implementation past 2006).

108. Daniel Pruzin, Basel Committee Announces Deal on Key Remaining Accord Issues, BNA Banking Daily, May 12, 2004. These issues included calibration of minimum capital requirements, the proposed capital charge for operational risk, and the use of advanced internal ratings-based (IRB) systems for assessing bank capital charges. *Id*

109. *Id.*

110. *Id.*

111. Committee on Banking Supervision, Bank for International Settlements, International Convergence of Capital Measurement and Capital Standards: A Revised Framework (June 26,

2004), *available at* http://www.bis.org/publ/bcbs107.htm.

112. Daniel Pruzin, Basel Committee Approves "Final" Version of Capital Accord; Criteria Could Still "Evolve," BNA Banking Daily, June 29, 2004.

113. *Id.*

114. *Id.*

115. Five Federal Agencies Announce Plans to Implement Basel II over Four–Year Period, BNA Banking Daily, June 29, 2004.

116. Ryozo Himino, Basel II—Towards a New Common Language, BIS Quarterly Review (Sept. 2004) *available at* http://www.bis.org/press/p040906.htm. As an example, Secretary–General Himino argued that Basel II will mean more transparency, allowing investors to know, for example, whether the bank's assets are risk-free cash or high-risk securities. *Id.*

Uncertainty continued to dog the prospective implementation of Basel II. In June 2005, George French, FDIC Deputy Director for Policy and Examination Oversight, was reported as suggesting that differences between U.S. and European approval procedures could inhibit the flexibility and cooperation needed to move ahead with the effort to revise global capital standards.[117] In addition, there was substantive concern whether implementation of Basel II—applicable to the fullest extent only for the largest U.S. internationally active banks[118]—might result in significant capital reductions for those banks.[119] This could stratify the effects of bank regulation as between the largest U.S. banks and other financial institutions.

In August 2006, concern over the stratification of U.S. banks was renewed by the industry group America's Community Bankers (ACB).[120] In a letter to federal regulators, ACB President and CEO Diane Casey–Landry urged that regulators give U.S. depository institutions the option of adopting the standardized approach to the Basel II capital accord, rather than just the advanced approaches, arguing that U.S. institutions needed the same degree of flexibility enjoyed by non-U.S. institutions. The letter also argued that most U.S. banks, which were slated to operate under the revised standardized approach, "Basel IA," should be given flexibility to continue to operate under the original 1988 Basel I accord or Basel IA. In October 2006—after the Basel II proposed rules were issued by the federal regulators—the FDIC chairman suggested that she would remain "open-minded" about flexible options for determining the risk-based capital requirements of large banks, including the use of the "Standardized Approach" for calculating risk-based capital requirements as an alternative to the more rigorous "Advanced Approach" at the center of the proposed rules.[121] Similarly, in a letter made public on March 21, 2007, four trade associations—the Independent Community Bankers of America, ACB, the Financial Services Roundtable, and the American Bankers Association—asked the federal regulators to give U.S. banks the choice of using

---

117. See R. Christian Bruce, *FDIC Official Cites Basel II Disconnect Between U.S., European Bank Regulators*, BNA Banking Daily (June 28, 2005), *available at* http://pubs.bna.com/ip/BNA/bbd.nsf/is/A0B1A2F1A3 (reporting on Mr. French's remarks). U.S. supervisors are using the regulatory process to implement Basel II, whereas in Europe implementation is expected to be effected through legislative amendment. *Id.*

118. Ten to fifteen U.S. banks are likely to be required to adopt Basel II, with perhaps another fifteen or so being permitted to move to the Basel II system. *Id.* The vast majority of U.S. banks

are expected to continue to operate subject to Basel I. *Id.*

119. *Id.*

120. R. Christian Bruce, *ACB Joins Bankers' Calls for Option To Use Standardized Basel Approach*, BNA Banking Daily (Aug. 10, 2006), *available at* http://pubs.bna.com/ip/bna/bbd.nsf/eh/A0B3D4M2M6.

121. Michael Bologna, *Bair Promises Open–Minded Assessment Of Standard Approach to Basel II Accord*, BNA Banking Daily (Oct. 10, 2006), *available at* http://pubs.bna.com/ip/bna/bbd.nsf/eh/A0B3M9V9V1.

the standardized approach to comply with Basel II, as a less costly and less complicated alternative to the IRB approach requiring expensive computer modeling.[122]

The potential for stratification also engaged the attention of state regulators. In a statement delivered in September 2006, New York Superintendent of Banks Diana Taylor said that state bank supervisors wanted an opportunity to say how the Basel II accord will be implemented in the United States.[123] She voiced concern that the Basel II rulemaking process, dominated by federal regulators, could further erode the dual banking system. So far, state bank supervisors have not been consulted by federal regulators on proposed rules for the U.S. version of Basel II or on preliminary efforts to draft Basel IA, the separate initiative to be designed for the large majority of U.S. banks not covered by the U.S. version of Basel II.

Exacerbating these concerns about regulatory stratification, a July 2005 study of the capital impact of the Basel II prepared by Standard & Poor's[124]33 suggested that the regulators may have to impose additional capital charges to address problems identified in the study.[125] This problem may be precipitated by the most recent quantitative impact study (QIS 4), which indicated that Basel II would significantly reduce aggregate bank regulatory capital. As a result, the regulators must consider whether to add capital charges under "pillar 2"—the enhanced supervisory review process—for noncredit risks (*e.g.*, interest rate risk, concentration risk, strategic risk, liquidity risk).[126]

Also in July 2005, the Basel Committee and the International Organization of Securities Commissions (IOSCO) finalized rules on capital set-aside requirements for bank exposures related to trading in securities, derivatives, and other financial instruments, as well as the treatment of "double default effects" (the risk that both a borrower and its guarantor might default on the same obligation).[127]

---

122. R. Christian Bruce, *Bank Industry, Showing United Front, Calls for More Options in Capital Rules*, BNA Banking Daily (Mar. 22, 2007), *available at* http://pubs.bna.com/ip/bna/bbd.nsf/eh/A0B4E2Z1E7.

123. R. Christian Bruce, *States Demand Role in Basel II Plans, New York State Banking Regulator Says* BNA Banking Daily (Sept. 14, 2006), *available at* http://pubs.bna.com/ip/bna/bbd.nsf/eh/A0B3H7F4N7.

124. Standard & Poor's, *Latest Test Run of Basel II Raises Troubling Issues for Regulators, available* at http://www2.standardandpoors.com.

125. *See S & P Report Predicts New Capital Charges to Address Questions*

Posed by Latest Study, BNA Banking Daily (July 7, 2005), *available at* http://pubs.bna.com/ip/BNA/bbd.nsf/is/A0B1B4F4R4 (discussing S & P quantitative impact study).

126. For guidance regarding the Pillar 2 supervisory review process for capital adequacy provided in the advanced approaches final rule, see 73 Fed. Reg. 44,620 (2008) (codified at 12 C.F.R. pts. 3 (OCC rules), 208, 225 (Fed rules), 325 (FDIC rules), 567 (OTS rules)).

127. Daniel Pruzin, *Basel Committee, IOSCO Finalize Rules on Treatment of Trade–Related Exposures*, BNA Banking Daily, July 19, 2005, *available at* http://pubs.bna.com/ip/BNA/bbd.nsf/is/A

The new rules amended several aspects of Basel II, to increase significantly the risk-sensitivity of regulatory capital requirements for these exposures.[128] In September 2005, the Basel Committee issued a paper offering suggestions on the treatment of low-default loan portfolios under Basel II.[129]

U.S. regulators had expected to ask for comment on proposed rules implementing Basel II during the Summer 2005, but the QIS 4 demonstrated that banks adopting the accord would on balance hold significantly less capital than previously assumed. The data also raised questions about the ability of banks relegated to the revised Basel I—the so-called "Basel IA"—to compete with banks that are permitted to adopt the Basel II methodologies. That situation would give Basel II banks significant competitive advantages over Basel IA banks, and might leave the latter vulnerable to acquisition by the former. As a result, the regulators put their plans on hold in May 2005 to allow more time to analyze the QIS 4 results. Nevertheless, one Federal Reserve Governor publicly indicated in September 2005 that the Fed planned to move forward with the rulemaking process to implement Basel II, despite continued uncertainty about its impact in the United States.[130] Fed Governor Bies, as well as Comptroller Dugan, have called for "substantial[ly] overlapping comment periods" for the proposed rules intended to implement Basel IA and Basel II.[131]

During a September 2005 hearing before the House Financial Institutions Subcommittee, an ACB representative urged that U.S. bank regulators refrain from making any commitments concerning implementation of Basel II during upcoming discussions with European financial authorities.[132] The Subcommittee Chair, Spencer Bachus, and Representative Barney Frank, the ranking Democrat on the full House Financial Services Committee, criticized the Fed's

0B1D1N8C5. The Basel Committee/IOSCO paper, *The Application of Basel II to Trading Activities and the Treatment of Double Default Effects*, is *available at* http://www.bis.org.

128. Pruzin, *supra*.

129. *Validation of Low–Default Portfolios in the Basel II Framework* (Basel Committee Newsletter No. 6), *available at* http://www.bis.org/publ/bcbs_nl6.htm. See Daniel Pruzin, *Basel Committee Issues Recommendations on Treatment of Low-default Loan Portfolios*, BNA Int'l Bus. & Fin. Daily (Sept. 7, 2005), *available at* http://pubs.bna.com/ip/BNA/ibd. nsf/is/A0B1K2Y1F0 (reporting on Basel paper).

130. *See Fed Wants to Move Ahead on Basel II Despite Uncertainty from QIS 4, Bies Says*, BNA Banking Daily (Sept. 27, 2005), *available at* http://pubs. bna.com/ip/BNA/bbd.nsf/is/A0B1M9Z5E5 (reporting on implications of QIS 4). The text of Governor Bies' remarks are *available at* http://www.federalreserve. gov/boarddocs/speeches/2005/20050926/ default.htm.

131. *Fed Wants to Move Ahead*, *supra*. The text of the Comptroller's speech is *available at* http://www.occ. treas.gov/ftp/release/2005–95a.pdf.

132. R. Christian Bruce, *Hold Off on New Basel II Commitments in Basel Meeting, ACB Urges Regulators*, BNA Int'l Bus. & Fin. Daily, Sept. 28, 2005, *available at* http://pubs.bna.com/ip/BNA/ ibd.nsf/is/A0B1N2X1B1.

intention to prepare for U.S. implementation of the Basel II.[133] Two days after the hearing, U.S. bank and savings association regulators announced that they would delay implementation of Basel II by at least one year and would develop extra safeguards to address the problems identified by the QIS 4.[134]

In the meantime, on the day of the House subcommittee hearing, the European Parliament adopted Basel II rules for investment firms, banks, and other credit institutions.[135] Once EU directives entered into force, member states would have until January 1, 2008, to adjust their national legislation.[136] However, there may be exemptions from the new rules until December 31, 2017, in certain areas such as ten-year grandfathering provisions for equity.[137] The likely benefit to EU banks from implementation of Basel II was estimated to amount to between €80 billion and €120 billion ($96 billion to $144 billion), while capital requirements for loans to small and medium-sized firms would likely be reduced by as much as 50 percent.[138]

Throughout the Spring of 2006, the federal regulators continued in their efforts to contain anxiety about the potential negative effects of Basel II. In March 2006, Comptroller Dugan acknowledged that the QIS4 did indicate that implementation of Basel II in 2007 would result in a substantial overall drop in and dispersion of capital standards.[139] He indicated that U.S. supervisors will impose a one-year delay before promulgating a final rule, and a three-year transition period to allow affected banks to prepare for the new accord.[140] In May 2006, the FDIC Acting Chairman assured state bank regulators that, as federal regulators move toward implementation of Basel II, they would preserve current safeguards in the

133. R. Christian Bruce, *Bachus, Frank Criticize Federal Reserve, Fear U.S. May Adopt Flawed Basel Accord,* BNA Banking Daily (Sept. 29, 2005), *available at* http://pubs.bna.com/ip/BNA/bbd.nsf/is/A0B1N6Y3T0.

134. R. Christian Bruce, *Regulators Delay Basel II Implementation, Promising New Roadmap, Extra Safeguards,* BNA Banking Daily (Oct. 3, 2005), *available at* http://pubs.bna.com/ip/BNA/bbd.nsf/is/A0B1P0X1Q1.

135. Arthur Rogers, *European Parliament Adopts Basel II Rules Expedited Approval in Member States Seen,* BNA Banking Daily (Sept. 29, 2005), *available at* http://pubs.bna.com/ip/BNA/bbd.nsf/is/A0B1N6Y3N3. *See also European Commission Lauds Basel II Vote by Parliament, Urges Member State Approval,* BNA Banking Daily (Sept. 29, 2005),

available at http://pubs.bna.com/ip/BNA/bbd.nsf/is/A0B1N6Y3Q5 (reporting on European Parliament adoption of Basel II). The original texts and the supporting report are *available at* http://www.europarl.eu.int/oeil/file.jsp?id=5205372 and http://www.europarl.eu.int/oeil/file.jsp?id=5206932.

136. Rogers, *supra.*

137. *Id.*

138. *Id.*

139. *See* Richard Cowden, *Regulators Intent on Cautious Approach To Final Rules, Implementation of Basel II,* BNA Banking Daily (Mar. 14, 2006), *available at* http://pubs.bna.com/ip/bna/bbd.nsf/eh/A0B2M7N3B0 (reporting on speech at meeting of Institute of International Bankers).

140. *Id.*

U.S. financial system, and specifically that implementation would not be allowed to drain away regulatory capital from the financial system.[141]

Nevertheless, since European banks were still scheduled to start implementing the new risk-based capital standards on January 1, 2007,[142] U.S. plans to delay implementation of Basel II until January 2008[143] could give EU banks a competitive advantage.[144] In early July 2006, Fed Governor Susan S. Bies acknowledged as much in remarks before the Risk Capital 2006 Forum in Paris, when she asked bankers for comments on expected conflicts as bank regulators begin implementing different versions of the Basel II capital accord on different timetables.[145] Potential home-host inconsistencies are expected to be major concerns for transnational financial institutions. "For example, even if the Fed approves a U.S.-regulated banking conglomerate's capital plan, regulators in other countries that supervise the bank's overseas subsidiaries may have additional demands."[146]

More negative news assaulted confidence in Basel II. QIS–5, based on data submitted by banks in G–10 countries plus Luxembourg, Spain, and Switzerland, was intended to test outcomes using the three main methods under Basel II for determining capital requirements.[147] The study found that the advanced IRB approach would result in an average 7.1 percent reduction in the current capital required for the largest affected banks—the so-called "Group 1 banks"—and the foundation approach would result in an average 1.3 percent reduction. While very few Group 1 banks are expected to use the standardized approach, it appeared to *increase* required capital by 1.7 percent. For smaller "Group 2" banks, the results showed a greater reduction in required capital under all three approaches. For banks outside the G–10 that had submitted data, the BIS Committee indicated that the results showed "sub-

141. *Gruenberg Assures That Capital Safeguards Will Remain With Implementation of Basel II*, BNA Int'l Bus. & Fin. Daily (May 22, 2006), *available at* http://pubs.bna.com/ip/bna/ibd.nsf/eh/A0B2V0N1N1.

142. R. Christian Bruce, *U.S. Delay on Basel II May Give Advantage To European Banks, EU Commissioner Says*, BNA Banking Daily (Feb. 10, 2006), *available at* http://pubs.bna.com/ip/bna/bbd.nsf/eh/A0B2G9W3C5 (reporting on remarks by European Commissioner for Internal Market and Services McCreevy).

143. *See Fed Sets March 30 Meeting To Vote on Basel II Proposal*, BNA Banking Daily (Mar. 27, 2006), *available*

at http://pubs.bna.com/ip/bna/bbd.nsf/eh/A0B2N8T8C5 (suggesting January 2008 implementation date for U.S. banks).

144. R. Christian Bruce, *U.S. Delay, supra.*

145. *Bies Calls for Bankers' Input On Basel II Home–Host Conflicts*, BNA Banking Daily (July 6, 2006), *available at* http://pubs.bna.com/ip/bna/bbd.nsf/eh/A0B2Z1K6F9.

146. *Id.*

147. Daniel Pruzin, *Basel Committee to Maintain Calibration For Risk–Weighting Under New Capital Accord*, BNA Banking Daily (May 25, 2006), *available at* http://pubs.bna.com/ip/bna/bbd.nsf/eh/A0B2V4W0A7.

stantial dispersion" both within and between countries. In May 2006, the BIS Committee announced that it would not recalibrate the risk-weighting under Basel II, despite these results.[148] In late September 2006, the Chair and ranking minority member of the Senate Banking Committee both expressed serious concern about the QIS data, warning federal regulators that Basel II could result in unsafe capital levels similar to the situation leading to the savings and loan crisis of the 1980s.[149] In July 2007, Standard & Poor's released a detailed set of recommendations that called for additional disclosure under Basel II, specifically more data on credit risk, operational risk, trading operations, pricing, securitization, as well as interest rate and foreign exchange risks.[150] While these recommendations are not binding on banks or regulators, they were intended to enhance the ability of financial markets to judge risk profiles of individual banks.[151] It is implicit in the proposal that higher S & P credit ratings would depend upon compliance with the higher disclosure standards, and the ratings are at the heart of Pillar Three market discipline through more disclosure and transparency.[152]

The federal regulators nevertheless appeared to remain committed to implementation of Basel II on their own timetable. Following testimony before the House Financial Institutions Subcommittee in mid-September 2006, Fed Governor Bies expressed serious skepticism about any last-minute restructuring of Basel II, arguing that it would take years to adopt and implement any such new approach.[153] She also argued that the delays attendant on developing a new approach would put U.S. banks even further behind their European competitors, which were implementing the EU version of Basel II as of January 1, 2007. In September 2006, the agencies issued a joint notice proposing a new risk-based capital adequacy framework that would require some, and permit other, qualifying depository institutions (*i.e.*, banks, savings associations and bank holding companies) to use an internal ratings-based approach to calculate regulatory credit risk capital requirements and advanced measurement approaches to calculate regulatory operational risk capital requirements.[154] The proposed rule described

148. *Id.*

149. R. Christian Bruce, *Basel II Could Spawn S & L Déja Vu, Senators Warn Federal Bank Regulators*, BNA Banking Daily (Sept. 27, 2006), *available at* http://pubs.bna.com/ip/bna/bbd.nsf/eh/A0B3J7H1D9.

150. R. Christian Bruce, *S & P Wants More Disclosure Under Basel II, Urges More Transparency, Market Discipline*, BNA Banking Daily (July 12, 2007), *available at* http://pubs.bna.com/ip/bna/bbd.nsf/eh/A0B4W5U7N9.

151. *Id.*

152. *Id.*

153. R. Christian Bruce, *Pressing for Another Basel II Alternative Puts U.S. Bankers Further Behind, Fed's Bies Says*, BNA Banking Daily (Sept. 15, 2006), *available at* http://pubs.bna.com/ip/bna/bbd.nsf/eh/A0B3H8M5Y1.

154. 5871 Fed. Reg. 55,830 (2006) (to be codified at 12 C.F.R. pts. 3 (OCC rules), 208, 225 (Fed rules), 325 (FDIC rules), 566 (OTS rules)).

the qualifying criteria for banks required or seeking to operate under the proposed framework and the applicable risk-based capital requirements for banks that operate under the framework. Comments on the proposal were due January 23, 2007.[155]

However, on November 1, 2006, the American Bankers Association requested more time to comment on the proposed Basel II rules, in light of the delay in issuing a proposal for Basel IA rules.[156] (Federal regulators had planned overlapping comment periods for the Basel II and Basel IA rules, but issuance of the Basel IA proposal had been delayed by a review by the Office of Management and Budget, which conceivably could last for as long as 90 days.) In December 2006, the regulators announced proposed Basel IA rules,[157] and extended the comment period on the Basel II proposed rules an additional two months.[158] The regulators were specifically seeking comment on the question whether Basel II banks—the largest internationally active banks—should have the option of adopting Basel IA rules instead of being required to follow Basel II.[159] If adopted as proposed, the Basel IA revisions would apply to banks, bank holding companies, and savings associations (collectively, "banking organizations"). A banking organization would be permitted to elect to comply with the proposed Basel IA revisions or remain subject to the existing risk-based capital rules, unless it uses the Basel II Advanced Capital Adequacy Framework proposed in September 2006.[160] Despite these developments, at a February 2007 industry conference, Fed Governor Bies insisted that the Fed was intent on promulgating final Basel II rules in time to allow for the targeted January 2008 implementation.[161]

The extended comment period for the proposal to implement Basel II ended on March 26, 2007. Although the OCC, the Fed, the FDIC, and the OTS had agreed to issue jointly the September 2006 proposed rules for comment, clear differences among the regulators have surfaced over what the final version of the Basel II rules would look like.[162] In a July 2007 letter to the four regulators,

155. *Id.* at 55,830.

156. R. Christian Bruce, *ABA Asks Regulators for More Time To File Comments on Basel II Proposal* (Nov. 2, 2006), *available at* http://pubs.bna.com/ip/bna/ibd.nsf/eh/A0B3P9T7A5.

157. 71 Fed. Reg. 77,446 (2006) (to be codified at 12 C.F.R. pts. 3 (OCC rules), 208, 225 (Fed rules), 325 (FDIC rules) 567 (OTS rules)); *as corrected*, 72 Fed. Reg. 1266 (2007).

158. 71 Fed. Reg. 77,518 (2006) (extending comment period until March 26, 2007).

159. R. Christian Bruce, *Regulators Unveil Basel IA Proposal, Will Consider*

Adoption by Basel II Banks (Dec. 6, 2006), *available at* http://pubs.bna.com/ip/bna/bbd.nsf/eh/A0B3U6D7U2.

160. 71 Fed. Reg. at 77,446.

161. Kip Betz, *Fed Intent on Timely Completion of Final Basel II Rule, Bies Says*, BNA Banking Daily (Feb. 27, 2007), *available at* http://pubs.bna.com/ip/bna/bbd.nsf/eh/A0B4C2M8M9.

162. *See, e.g.,* Michael Bologna, *Federal Reserve Working Quickly To Implement Basel II Final Rules* (May 22, 2007), *available at* http://pubs.bna.com/ip/bna/bbd.nsf/125731d8816a84d385256297005f336a/e5d6955c1be1c48d

Senators Christopher Dodd and Richard Shelby, respectively the chairman and ranking member of the Senate Banking Committee, asked the regulators to come to a consensus on regulations implementing Basel II.[163] Within a week, the regulators announced that they had reached a compromise agreement on a final rule that cleared the way for U.S. implementation of Basel II in early 2008.[164]

In December 2007, the four regulators jointly published final rules implementing Basel II for the largest, internationally active U.S. banks.[165] The final rules were effective April 1, 2008.[166] In unanimously approving the Fed's version of the final regulations in November 2007,[167] several governors said that the recent turmoil in the credit markets, particularly the emerging subprime mortgage crisis,[168] highlighted the need for a more effective set of capital standards and addressed weaknesses in current rules by requiring a more risk-sensitive assessment of creditworthiness and capital needs.[169] Banks were to start a preliminary phase of the U.S. implementation effort early in 2008, but required Basel II compliance would not initiate until January 1, 2009, when the new

852572e30001c0cc?OpenDocument (discussing Fed concerns that review of Basel II proposal was falling increasingly behind "in terms of industry practice, which continues to evolve;" suggesting that Basel II proposal was "a very dynamic process" subject to continuing revision).

163. *Dodd, Shelby Ask Regulators to Reach Consensus on Capital Standards in Basel II*, BNA Banking Daily (July 19, 2007), *available at* http://pubs.bna.com/ip/bna/bbd.nsf/eh/A0B4X2R5M6.

164. R. Christian Bruce, *Regulators Reach Agreement on Basel II, Clearing Path for 2008 U.S. Implementation*, BNA Banking Daily (July 23, 2007), *available at* http://pubs.bna.com/ip/bna/bbd.nsf/125731d8816a84d385256297005f336a/c228220131a5bb868525731f000184b5?OpenDocument.

165. 72 Fed. Reg. 69,288 (2007) (codified at 12 C.F.R. pts. 3 (OCC rules), 208, 225 (Fed rules), 325 (FDIC rules), 559–560, 563, 567 (OTS rules)). For simplicity, the final rule uses the term "bank" to include banks, savings associations, and bank holding companies (BHCs). 72 Fed. Reg. at 69,288 n.1. The terms "bank holding company" and "BHC" do not include savings and loan holding companies regulated by the OTS. *Id.* For interagency guidance on qualification for and implementation of

an internal ratings-based approach and other methodologies to calculate risk-based capital requirements for credit risk and advanced measurement approaches (AMA) to calculate risk-based capital requirements for operational risk, *see* http://www.federalreserve.gov/boarddocs/srletters/2008/SR0804a1.pdf.

166. 72 Fed. Reg. at 69,288.

167. R. Christian Bruce, *Fed's Governors, Eyeing Credit Turmoil, Welcome New Capital Rules Under Basel II*, BNA Banking Daily (Nov. 5, 2007), *available at* http://pubs.bna.com/ip/bna/bbd.nsf/eh/A0B5H8M7E8.

168. On the subprime mortgage crisis, *see* 1 MALLOY, *supra*, § 1.4, text and accompanying notes 33–47.

169. *See* Bruce, *Fed's Governors, supra* note 171 (reporting on remarks of Fed Gov. Randall S. Kroszner). Ironically, the likely tightening of risk-sensitive standards will become effective as assets are being repriced to reflect higher risk and major banks are experiencing capital shortfalls while their risk models predicted profits. *See* R. Christian Bruce, *Basel Rules, Set to Be Phased In, Will Feel Impact from Credit Market Turmoil*, BNA Banking Daily (Jan. 22, 2008), *available at* http://pubs.bna.com/ip/bna/bbd.nsf/eh/A0B5R7G6A1 (discussing emerging problem).

standards would begin to be phased in over a three-year period.[170] At that point, it was anticipated that only about 25 U.S. banking institutions will be required to adopt Basel II, with another small group of relatively large U.S. banking institutions having the option to do so.[171]

The overwhelming majority of U.S. banking institutions would be required either to continue to apply the 1988 Basel I standards, or the new and more risk-sensitive Basel IA.[172] In July 2008, the agencies proposed a new risk-based capital framework based on the standardized approach for credit risk and the basic indicator approach for operational risk described in the new Accord, the "Basel IA."[173] The standardized framework, which would generally would be available, on an optional basis, to banks, BHCs, and savings associations (banking organizations) that apply the general risk-based capital rules, "essentially refines the risk-weighting framework of the 1988 Accord."[174] The deadline for comments on the proposed Basel Ia rules was October 27, 2008,[175] by which time the financial services industry was in complete disarray.

With the emergence of the current financial crisis, the revisewd capital regime was criticized by some commentators for its failure to account adequately for various risks, particularly off-balance-sheet exposures and the treatment of trading book assets.[176] In early January 2009 the Basel Committee issued a new consultative paper outlining recommendations for the improvement of bank "stress testing" (i.e., risk analysis and assessment, including risk mitigation and risk transfer) to assess whether they can withstand extended periods of severe financial crisis.[177] Among the problems identified by the consultative paper were the following: (i) most bank stress tests have not been designed to model extreme market events; (ii) at most banks, stress testing was relegated to non-executive, operational levels and did not receive prominent attention from senior management; and, (iii) most banks were too reliant on historical data for their stress testing models, which as a result

170. *See* R. Christian Bruce, *Fed's Governors, supra.*

171. *Id.*

172. *Id.*

173. 73 Fed. Reg. 43,982 (2008) (to be codified at 12 C.F.R. pts. 3 app. D (OCC rules), 208 app. G, 225 app. H (Fed rules), 325 app. E (FDIC rules), 567 app. B, § 567.0(a)–(c), (c)(2)(ii) (OTS rules)).

174. 73 Fed. Reg. at 44,025.

175. *Id.* at 44,026.

176. See, e.g., Daniel Pruzin, Basel Panel Issues Recommendations On Improving Stress Testing for Banks, BNA

Banking Daily, Jan. 7, 2009, available at http://news.bna.com (commenting on criticism); Daniel Pruzin, Basel Committee Unveils Plan to Alter Capital Rules in Wake of Financial Crisis, BNA Banking Daily, Nov. 21, 2008, available at http://news.bna.com (reporting on to reform Basel II to address weaknesses revealed by ongoing crisis).

177. *Id.* The text of the consultative paper, Principles for Sound Stress Testing Practices and Supervision, is available at http://www.bis.org.

tended not to identify the possibility of severe, systemic vulnerabilities. The committee has also reacted to the criticism of excessive executive compensation, which created perverse incentives for banks to engage in high-risk strategies in favor of short-term financial results.[178] Basel II itself has been amended to require national regulators to monitor executive compensation structures consistent with principles of effective risk management.[179] Doubts have even been raised about the capital ratio itself. In November 2009, the Swiss National Bank announced that it would urge the committee to raise the minimum 8 percent ratio of capital to risk-weighted assets to 16 percent.[180]

In March 2009, the Fed announced[181] that it would delay for two years the March 31, 2009, implementation date for certain amendments to the its capital adequacy guidelines for BHCs on trust preferred securities and the definition of capital.[182] As the Fed explained, it was imposing the delay "[d]ue to the continuing stressed conditions in the financial markets and in order to promote stability in the financial markets and the banking industry as a whole. . . . ."[183] The delay was effective upon publication, March 23, 2009.[184] Given the past enthusiasm of the Fed for Basel II and its permutations, this announcement may well be read as the end of the Fed's long enchantment with the risk-based capital guidelines.

Technically, the Basel II Capital Accord was incorporated—but not fully implemented—into domestic regulations in the United States on December 7, 2007.[185] In the wake of the financial collapse, however, a cascading series of efforts to refine the accord ensued.[186] Among those efforts, the Basel Committee produced revisions to the

178. For discussion of this criticism and extensive analysis, see Lucian A. Bebchuk & Holger Spamann, Regulating Bankers' Pay, 98 Geo. L.J. 247 (2010).

179. Bank for International Settlements, Committee on Banking Supervision, Enhancements to the Basel II Framework 25–27 (2009).

180. Daniel Pruzin, Swiss Central Bank Official Calls for Doubling Of Basel II Minimum Capital Requirements, BNA Banking Daily, Nov. 6, 2009, available at http://www.bna.com.

181. 74 Fed. Reg. 12,076 (Mar. 23, 2009) (amending 12 C.F.R. pt. 225, App. A, ¶¶ II.A.1.b.ii., II.A.2.d.iv.).

182. See 70 Fed. Reg. 11,827 (Mar. 10, 2005) (amending risk-based capital standards for BHCs to allow continued inclusion of outstanding and prospective issuances of trust preferred securities in the BHC tier 1 capital, subject to stricter

requirements, and to revise requirements generally applied to aggregate amount of restricted core capital elements (including trust preferred securities) included in the BHC tier 1 capital, scheduled to become effective March 31, 2009).

183. 74 Fed. Reg. at 12,076.

184. Id. at 12,077.

185. 72 Fed. Reg. 69,288 (2007).

186. For a summary, see Basel Committee on Banking Supervision, Strengthening the Resilience of the Banking Sector (Consultative Document, Dec. 17, 2009) (including proposed changes to definition of capital, proposed introduction of leverage ratio, and proposed changes to treatment of counterparty credit risk).

market risk framework,[187] and guidelines on incremental risk in an institution's trading book,[188] including incremental risk capital charge, a comprehensive risk measure for correlation trading portfolios, new rules for securitization exposures in the trading book, and revised capital charges for equity exposures subject to a standardized measurement method for market risk. Given the significance of securitization in the collapse, enhancements to the Basel II framework included revised risk weights for re-securitizations held by a bank.[189] Finally, in December 2009 the Committee raised the issue of the need to increase liquidity in institutions subject to the Accord.[190] It was becoming clearer that a new "Basel III" arrangement was emerging from the consultative process.

§ 7.10   Capital Supervision

"Capital supervision," the use of capital adequacy ratios for supervisory purposes, has become a central focus of current federal bank regulatory policy. This is mainly the result of three developments: (1) the emergence of the international capital adequacy guidelines; (2) the issuance in February 1991 of a study by the Department of the Treasury that advanced certain recommendations to strengthen capital supervision of banks;[1] and, (3) the enactment of the Federal Deposit Insurance Corporation Improvement Act of 1991 ("FDICIA") in December 1991.[2]

FDICIA includes a series of provisions intended to improve supervision of insured depository institutions, with a significant emphasis on capital supervision as a primary tool. For example, it adopted a general rule requiring annual on-site examinations of all insured depository institutions,[3] effective one year after enactment (December 19, 1991). However, well-capitalized and well-managed institutions, with total assets of less than $100 million and with no recent change in control, are exempt from this rule. They are to be examined only every 18 months.[4]

187. Basel Committee on Banking Supervision, Revisions to the Basel II Market Risk Framework (July 2009).

188. Basel Committee on Banking Supervision, Guidelines for Computing Capital for Incremental Risk in the Trading Book (July 2009).

189. See Basel Committee on Banking Supervision, Enhancements to the Basel Ii Framework (July 2009).

190. See Basel Committee on Banking Supervision, International Framework for Liquidity Risk Measurement, Standards and Monitoring (Consultative Document, Dec. 17, 2009).

§ 7.10

1. See U.S. DEPARTMENT OF THE TREASURY, MODERNIZING THE FINANCIAL SYSTEM: U.S. TREASURY DEPARTMENT RECOMMENDATIONS FOR SAFER, MORE COMPETITIVE BANKS (FEBRUARY 1991), reprinted in Fed. Banking L. Rep. (CCH) No. 1377, Part II (Feb. 14, 1991) ("MODERNIZATION STUDY").

2. Pub. L. No. 102–242, 105 Stat. 2236 (Dec. 9, 1991) (codified at scattered sections of 12 U.S.C.A.).

3. FDICIA, § 111(a) (codified at 12 U.S.C.A. § 1820(d)(1)–(3)).

4. FDICIA, § 111(a) (codified at 12 U.S.C.A. § 1820(d)(4)). But see FDICIA, § 111(c) (transition rule).

The FDICIA generally requires "prompt corrective action"[5] intended to "resolve the problems of insured depository institutions at the least possible long-term loss to the deposit insurance fund,"[6] including the imposition of capital requirements.[7]

On the subject of safety and soundness of insured depository institutions, the FDICIA authorizes federal banking agencies to impose more stringent treatment of capital of institutions that are in an unsafe and unsound condition or are engaged in an unsafe and unsound practice.[8]

The emphasis on capital supervision is not intuitively justifiable. Even banks that fully comply with capital requirements are still highly leveraged, far beyond the levels of viable general business corporations. (Thus, in a capital-intensive industry like automotive manufacturing debt-to-equity ratios might be above 2/1, but in a "well capitalized" bank, it would not be surprising to find a debt-to-equity ratio of 11/1 or 12/1.) This prompts the question whether the capital levels of banks are an appropriate benchmark at all for judging the safety and soundness of banks.[9]

§ 7.11   Market Activities

In the remainder of this chapter, we examine some of the principal market activities of depository institutions. It should be kept in mind that this is an open-ended set of activities, since the principal sources of authority in this regard do not limit the incidental powers of banks, the closely related activities of bank holding companies, or "activities financial in nature" to specified activities.[1] As a result, this is an area of remarkable growth for

---

5. FDICIA, § 131 (codified at 12 U.S.C.A. § 1831o(a)(2)).

6. *Id.* (codified at 12 U.S.C.A. § 1831o(a)(1)).

7. *Id.* (codified at 12 U.S.C.A. § 1831o(c)–(f), (h)–(i), (k), (n)). These rules do not apply to depository institutions in conservatorship, or to bridge banks the stock of which is owned only by the FDIC. *Id.* (codified at 12 U.S.C.A. § 1831o(j)). The act also contains provisions requiring the periodic review and improvement of applicable capital standards. *See* FDICIA, § 305.

8. FDICIA, § 131(a) (codified at 12 U.S.C.A. § 1831o(g)).

9. *See, e.g.,* Michael P. Malloy, *Capital Regulation and International Banking: A Questionable Strategy,* in GREGORY T. PAPANIKOS (ed.), ESSAYS ON THE ECONOMICS OF LAW AND INDUSTRIAL ORGANIZATION

155 (2006) (expressing doubts about efficacy of capital supervision).

§ 7.11

1. Section 16 of the Glass–Steagall, 12 U.S.C.A. § 24 (Seventh), authorizes—but does not specifically identify— "incidental activities," a concept which has been interpreted to include many securities activities. *See also* 61 Fed. Reg. 60,342, 60,374–60,379 (1996) (codified at 12 C.F.R. §§ 5.34–5.36) (amending OCC rules, policies, and procedures for corporate activities; establishing rules for operating subsidiaries, service companies, and other equity investments of national banks, *per* 12 U.S.C.A. § 24 (Seventh)). Securities activities of operating subsidiaries are now governed by 12 U.S.C.A. § 24a, added by the Gramm–Leach–Bliley Act ("GLBA"), Pub. L. No. 106–102, Nov. 12, 1999, § 121(a)(2), 113 Stat. 1338, 1373 (1999).

diversification of banking enterprises into related nonbanking activities. Nevertheless, the activities highlighted in the following sections remain of continuing importance.

§ 7.12   Broker–Dealer Activities

Discount brokerage services are one area in the securities sector where banks have become active.[1] In 1982, the Comptroller abandoned a longstanding interpretation—that Section 16 of the Glass–Steagall Act limited bank brokerage activities to current customers of traditional banking services—by allowing a national bank to establish a subsidiary to offer retail discount brokerage services to any customer at branch offices of the bank.[2] The Comptroller's decision was upheld in *Securities Industry Association v. Comptroller of Currency.*[3] The Comptroller subsequently made clear that his new interpretation of Section 16 applied to brokerage activities undertaken directly by a bank itself, in addition to those of a bank subsidiary.[4]

Bank service companies[5] also are authorized by the Bank

Likewise, until 1999 § 4(c)(8) of the Bank Holding Company Act ("BHCA"), 12 U.S.C.A. § 1843(c)(8), authorized—but did not specifically identify—"closely related activities," determined by the Federal Reserve Board to include many securities activities. *See also* 12 U.S.C.A. §§ 1861–1867 (authorizing bank service companies). *Cf.* 61 Fed. Reg. at 60,377–60,379 (1996) (codified at 12 C.F.R. § 5.35(f)(5)) (amending OCC rules, policies, and procedures for corporate activities; requiring Fed approval of certain service companies of national banks, *per* Bank Service Company Act ("BSCA") and § 4(c)(8) of BHCA). In 1999, the GLBA froze in place the "closely related activity" exception as of the date of GLBA enactment. GLBA, § 102(a) (codified at 12 U.S.C.A. § 1843(c)(8)). However, a new section permits BHCs that qualify as FHCs to engage in activities, and acquire companies engaged in activities, that are "financial in nature" or that are incidental to such activities. GLBA, § 103(a) (codified at 12 U.S.C.A. § 1843(k)). The GLBA did not specifically identify all activities that might be considered "financial in nature" for these purposes, leaving it generally to the Federal Reserve Board progressively to identify such activities. *But cf.* 12 U.S.C.A. § 1843(k)(4) (identifying certain activities as "financial in nature").

§ 7.12

1. *See* 12 U.S.C.A. §§ 24 (Seventh), 378 (governing permissibility of securities activities of banks and other financial institutions). *See supra* § 5.24 (discussing Glass–Steagall Act §§ 16 and 21 as applied to national banks and member banks).

2. *In re Security Pacific Nat'l Bank, reprinted in* [1982–1983 Transfer Binder] Fed. Banking L. Rep. (CCH) ¶ 99,-284 (Aug. 26, 1982), at 86,255.

3. 577 F.Supp. 252 (D.D.C.1983), *aff'd,* 758 F.2d 739 (D.C.Cir.1985) (per curiam), *cert. denied sub nom. Securities Indus. Ass'n v. Comptroller of Currency,* 474 U.S. 1054, 106 S.Ct. 790 (1986), *cert. granted on other grounds and aff'd sub nom. Clarke v. Securities Indus. Ass'n,* 479 U.S. 388, 107 S.Ct. 750 (1987).

4. *See, e.g.,* Comptroller of the Currency Opinion Letter No. 363 (May 23, 1986); *see also* 50 Fed. Reg. 31,605 (Aug. 5, 1985) (withdrawing proposed rule requiring national bank engaging in discount brokerage services to do so through nonbanking subsidiary).

5. *See supra* § 5.23 (discussing bank service companies).

Service Company Act ("BSCA")[6] to engage in discount brokerage activities.[7] However, a bank's investment in a bank service company is limited to not more than 10 percent of its paid-in and unimpaired capital and unimpaired surplus, and not more than 5 percent of its total assets may be invested in such a company.[8] Engaging in this activity would require prior approval of either the Comptroller[9] or the Fed.[10] Approval would be based upon a consideration of

> the financial and managerial resources and future prospects of the bank or banks and [company] involved, including the financial capability of the bank to make a proposed investment ..., and possible adverse effects such as undue concentration of resources, unfair or decreased competition, conflicts of interest, or unsafe or unsound banking practices.[11]

Furthermore, discount brokerage services are also permitted by a nonbanking subsidiary of a bank holding company. In *Securities Industry Association v. Board of Governors ("SIA II")*,[12] the Supreme Court allowed an affiliation between a broker (registered with the SEC) and a bank holding company (and, hence, indirectly an affiliation with a commercial bank).

If a banking enterprise operated a brokerage service through a separately incorporated affiliate, the brokerage affiliate would be required to register with the SEC.[13] However, prior to 1999 banks themselves were not covered by the definitions of "broker" and "dealer" in the 1934 Act, and so were not be subject to supervision by the SEC in that regard.[14]

The GLBA eliminated this "bank exception" from the definitions of "broker" and "dealer" in the Securities Exchange Act of 1934.[15] However, the GLBA retains limited exemptions to facilitate

---

6. 12 U.S.C.A. §§ 1861–1865.

7. *See* 12 U.S.C.A. § 1864(f) (authorizing bank service company to engage in any activity "permissible for a bank holding company" under 12 U.S.C.A. § 1843(c)(8)).

8. 12 U.S.C.A. § 1862.

9. *See* 12 C.F.R. § 5.35(f)(1)–(4) (establishing rules for approval of service companies of national banks, *per* BSCA).

10. 12 U.S.C.A. § 1865(b). *See* 12 C.F.R. § 5.35(f)(5) (requiring Fed approval of certain service companies of national banks, *per* BSCA and § 4(c)(8) of BHCA).

11. 12 U.S.C.A. § 1865(c).

12. 468 U.S. 207, 104 S.Ct. 3003 (1984).

13. *See* 15 U.S.C.A. § 78o (authorizing supervision of broker-dealers by SEC).

14. *American Bankers Association v. Securities and Exchange Commission*, 804 F.2d 739 (D.C.Cir.1986).

15. GLBA, §§ 201–202 (codified at 15 U.S.C.A. § 78c(a)(4)–(5)) (defining "broker" and "dealer," for purposes of Securities Exchange Act of 1934, to include banks, with certain exceptions for specified traditional banking activities such as trust services). *See also* GLBA, § 221(a) (codified at 15 U.S.C.A. § 77c(a)(2)) (concerning treatment of bank common trust funds under Securities Act of 1933); GLBA, § 221(b) (codified at 15 U.S.C.A. § 78c(a)(12)(A)(iii)) (concerning treatment under Securities Exchange Act of 1934).

certain traditional bank activities such as third-party networking arrangements, trust activities, commercial paper and exempted securities, employee and shareholder benefit plans, sweep accounts, affiliate transactions, private placements, safekeeping and custody services, asset-backed securities, derivatives, and "identified banking products."[16] The GLBA does not amend the Commodity Exchange Act ("CEA"); no transaction or person that is otherwise subject to the jurisdiction of the Commodity Futures Trading Commission pursuant to the CEA is exempted from that jurisdiction because of the GLBA.[17]

To the extent that bank trust department activities are the functional equivalent of certain securities activities, they are of concern to the GLBA, which subjects financial activities to "functional regulation" by appropriate regulators of the activity involved.[18] Conceivably, trust department activities may be the equivalent of securities brokerage, and as such would result in the bank being treated as a "broker" under the Securities Exchange Act of 1934 (1934 Act).[19] However, the GLBA excepts from the 1934 Act definition of "broker" a bank that effects transactions in a trustee or fiduciary capacity in its trust department or other department, regularly examined by bank examiners for compliance with fiduciary principles and standards, if the bank meets the following conditions:

(i) The bank is "chiefly compensated" for the transactions, consistent with fiduciary principles and standards, on the basis of an administration or annual fee (payable on a monthly, quarterly, or other basis); a percentage of assets under management; a flat or capped per order processing fee equal to not more than the cost incurred by the bank in connection with executing securities transactions for trustee and fiduciary customers; or, any combination of such fees;[20] and,

(ii) The bank does not publicly solicit brokerage business, other than by advertising that it effects transactions in securities in conjunction with advertising its other trust activities.[21]

Similarly, trust department activities may be the equivalent of securities dealing, and as such would result in the bank being

---

16. 15 U.S.C.A. § 78c(a)(4)–(5). On the definition of "identified banking products," see GLBA, § 206 (codified at 15 U.S.C.A. § 78c note).

17. GLBA, § 210 (codified at 12 U.S.C.A. § 1811 note).

18. See supra § 1.9, text and accompanying notes 1–3 (discussing functional regulation under GLBA).

19. See 15 U.S.C.A. §§ 78c(a)(4) (defining "broker" in 1934 Act),

78c(a)(12)(A)(iii) (concerning treatment of bank common trust funds under 1934 Act). See also GLBA, § 221(a), 113 Stat. at 1401 (codified at 15 U.S.C.A. § 77c(a)(2)) (concerning treatment of bank common trust funds under Securities Act of 1933).

20. 15 U.S.C.A. § 78c(a)(4)(B)(ii)(I).

21. Id. § 78c(a)(4)(B)(ii)(II).

treated as a "dealer" under the 1934 Act.[22] However, the GLBA excepts from the 1934 Act definition of "dealer" a bank that buys or sells securities, for investment purposes, for the itself or for accounts for which it acts as trustee or fiduciary.[23]

In implementing the GLBA, the SEC had taken the position that the act meant that banks engaging in securities trading activities would generally need to register with the SEC as broker dealers. Because of intense opposition from affected depository institutions and from federal bank regulatory agencies, the SEC had never been able to issue a final rule implementing such requirements. The Financial Services Regulatory Relief Act (FSRRA)[24] resolved this long-standing dilemma about the proper application of the GLBA to securities trading activities traditionally carried out by banks. The FSSRA required a joint rulemaking by the SEC and the Fed for a revised definition of "broker" under the Securities Exchange Act of 1934.[25] This rulemaking superseded previous rulemaking efforts undertaken by the SEC.[26] Prior to adopting a joint set of final rules, the SEC and the Fed were required to consult with and seek the concurrence of the "federal banking agencies"[27] concerning the content of the rulemaking.[28] In addition, FSRRA § 401 gave savings association trust activities the same exemptions that are available for bank trust activities under the 1934 Act[29] and the Investment Advisors Act of 1940.[30]

In October 2007, the Fed and the SEC published a single set of jointly adopted rules[31] to implement GLBA exceptions for banks

22. *See* 15 U.S.C.A. §§ 78c(a)(5) (defining "dealer" in 1934 Act), 78c(a)(12)(A)(iii) (concerning treatment of bank common trust funds under 1934 Act).

23. *Id.* § 78c(a)(5)(C)(ii).

24. Pub. L. No. 109–351, 120 Stat. 1966 (2006).

25. FSRRA, § 101(a)(1), 120 Stat. at 1968 (codified at 15 U.S.C.A. § 78c(a)(4)(F)). Not later than 180 days after the date of the enactment of the FSRRA, the SEC and the Fed were required jointly to issue a proposed single set of rules or regulations to define the term "broker" in accordance with the 1934 Act § 3(a)(4), 15 U.S.C.A. § 78c(a)(4). FSRRA, § 101(a)(2), 120 Stat. at 1968 (codified at 15 U.S.C.A. § 78c note).

26. FSRRA, § 101(a)(3), 120 Stat. at 1968 (codified at 15 U.S.C.A. § 78c note).

27. The term "federal banking agencies" is defined for these purposes as "Office of the Comptroller of the Currency, the Office of Thrift Supervision, and the Federal Deposit Insurance Corporation." *Id.* § 101(c), 120 Stat. at 1968 (codified at 15 U.S.C.A. § 78c note).

28. *Id.* § 101(b), 120 Stat. at 1968 (codified at 15 U.S.C.A. § 78c note).

29. *Id.* § 401(a)(1)–(2), 120 Stat. at 1971–1973 (codified at 12 U.S.C.A. § 78c(a)(6)(A), (C), (a)(34)(A)–(D), (F)–(H)). *See also id.* § 401(a)(3), 120 Stat. at 1973 (codified at 12 U.S.C.A. § 78w(b)(1)) (conforming exemption to reporting requirement).

30. *Id.* § 401(b)(1)–(2), 120 Stat. at 1973 (codified at 12 U.S.C.A. §§ 80b–2(a)(2)(A), (c), 80b–10a(a)(1)(A)(I), (B), (a)(2), (b)). *See also id.* § 401(c), 120 Stat. at 1973 (codified at 12 U.S.C.A. § 80a–10(c)) (conforming amendment to 1940 Act).

31. 72 Fed. Reg. 56,514 (2007) (codified at 12 C.F.R. §§ 218.100, 218.700–218.701, 218.721–218.723, 218.740–

from the definition of the term "broker."[32] The rules define terms used in these statutory exceptions and include certain related exemptions. The rules became fully effective in December 2007, as did the amendments removing and reserving certain superseded provisions of 17 C.F.R. pt. 240.[33] As to required compliance, a bank would be exempt from complying with the rules and the "broker" exceptions in 1934 Act until the first day of its first fiscal year commencing after September 30, 2008.[34]

At the same time that the joint rule was issued, the SEC adopted rules and rule amendments regarding exemptions from the definitions of "broker" and "dealer" under the 1934 Act for bank securities activities.[35] These new rules and rule amendments were effective November 2, 2007.[36] Intended to complement Regulation R, the rules and rule amendments for the most part reflect changes that the GLBA made to the 1934 Act with respect to the status of banks as "dealers."[37] In particular, the SEC adopted a conditional exemption[38] that will allow banks to effect riskless principal transactions with non-U.S. persons pursuant to Regulation S[39] under the 1933 Act. The exemption will apply only to purchases and sales of "eligible securities,"[40] *i.e.*, securities that are not in the inventory of

218.741, 218.760, 218.771–218.772, 218.775–218.776, 218.780–218.781; 12 C.F.R. §§ 247.100, 247.700–247.701, 247.721–247.723, 247.740–247.741, 247.760, 247.771–247.772, 247.775–247.776, 247.780–247.781; *removing* 17 C.F.R. §§ 240.3a4–2—240.3a4–6, 240.3b–17, 240.15a–7, 240.15a–8). Identical sets of the final rules were adopted by the Fed and the SEC, codified by the Fed in 12 C.F.R. pt. 218 and by the SEC in 17 C.F.R. pt. 247. The final rules adopted by the two agencies within their respective C.F.R. titles were intentionally numbered identically from § —.100 to § —.781. 72 Fed. Reg. 56,514, 56,516 & n.27 (2007).

32. 15 U.S.C.A. § 78c(a)(4). Pursuant to the FSRRA § 101, this single set of final rules supersedes any and all other proposed or final rules issued by the SEC on or after the date of enactment of the GLBA with regard to the definition of "broker." 72 Fed. Reg. at 56,516.

33. *Id.*

34. 72 Fed. Reg. at 56,514.

35. 72 Fed. Reg. 56,562 (2007).

36. 72 Fed. Reg. at 56,562.

37. 72 Fed. Reg. at 56,562–56,563.

38. *See* 17 C.F.R. § 240.3a5–2 (providing conditional exemption from defi-

nition of "dealer" to allow banks to engage in certain transactions involving securities exempted from registration by Reg S). This new 1934 Act rule corresponds to Rule 771 of Regulation R under the 1933 Act, which permits banks to engage in certain Regulation S transactions on an agency basis without being "brokers." Rule 771 "recognizes that non-U.S. persons generally will not rely on the protections of the U.S. securities laws when purchasing Regulation S securities from U.S. banks, and that non-U.S. persons can purchase the same securities from banks located outside of the U.S." 72 Fed. Reg. at 56,563 (citing 71 Fed. Reg. at 77,552, discussing proposed version).

39. 17 C.F.R. §§ 230.901 *et seq.*

40. The rule specifically defines an "eligible security" as a security that is not being sold from the inventory of the bank or an affiliate of the bank, and not being underwritten by the bank or an affiliate of the bank on a firm-commitment basis unless the bank acquired the security from an unaffiliated distributor that did not purchase the security from the bank or an affiliate of the bank. 17 C.F.R. § 240.3a5–2(b)(2). For these purposes, the term "distributor" is defined to have the same meaning as in Rule

the bank or an affiliate, and that are not underwritten by the bank or an affiliate on a firm commitment basis (apart from securities acquired from an unaffiliated distributor). In addition, this exemption will apply only to Reg S transactions that a bank makes on a "riskless principal" basis.[41] This focus permits U.S. banks to sell securities overseas that foreign banks themselves sell, "thus helping to avoid placing U.S. banks at a competitive disadvantage with respect to eligible securities, while also helping to safeguard against investor protection risks associated with unregistered entities distributing eligible securities."[42] The exemption is available when a bank purchases a newly issued eligible security from an issuer or a broker-dealer and sells that security in compliance with the requirements of Rule 903[43] to a purchaser who is not in the United States.[44] The exemption is also available when a bank purchases, from a person who is not a "U.S. person" under Reg S,[45] an eligible security after its initial sale with a reasonable belief that the eligible security was initially sold outside of the United States within the meaning of and in compliance with the requirements of Rule 903, and resells that security to a purchaser who is not in the

902(d). *Id.* § 230.902(d) (defining "distributor" to mean any underwriter, dealer, or other person who participates, pursuant to contractual arrangement, in distribution of securities offered or sold in reliance on Regulation S).

41. The rule defines a "riskless principle transaction" as a transaction in which, after receiving an order to buy from a customer, the bank purchased the security from another person to offset a contemporaneous sale to such customer or, having received an order to sell from a customer, the bank sold the security to another person to offset a contemporaneous purchase from such customer. *Id.* § 3a5–2(b)(4).

42. 72 Fed. Reg. at 56,563.

43. 17 C.F.R. § 230.903. Rule 903 provides that an offer or sale of securities by the issuer, a distributor, or an affiliate or a person acting on their behalf shall be deemed to occur outside the U.S. within the meaning of Rule 901 if the offer or sale is made in an offshore transaction, and no directed selling efforts are made in the U.S. by the issuer, a distributor, affiliate, or person acting on their behalf. However, other conditions may also apply, depending upon the place of incorporation and reporting status of the issuer, and the amount of U.S. market interest in the securities. *Cf. id.* § 230.901 (providing generally that, for purposes of 1933 Act § 5, the terms "offer," "offer to sell," "sell," "sale" and "offer to buy" include offers and sales that occur within United States, and excludes those occurring outside United States).

44. *Id.* § 240.3a5–2(a)(1).

45. *See id.* § 230.902(k) (defining "U.S. person" to mean: (*i*) any natural person resident in United States; (*ii*) any partnership or corporation organized or incorporated under the U.S. laws; (*iii*) any estate of which any executor or administrator is U.S. person; (*iv*) any trust of which any trustee is U.S. person; (*v*) any agency or branch of foreign entity located in United States; (*vi*) any non-discretionary account or similar account (other than estate or trust) held by dealer or other fiduciary for benefit or account of U.S. person; (*vii*) any discretionary account or similar account (other than estate or trust) held by dealer or other fiduciary organized, incorporated, or (if individual) resident in United States; and, (*viii*) any partnership or corporation if organized or incorporated under laws of any foreign jurisdiction and formed by U.S. person principally for purpose of investing in securities not registered under 1933 Act, unless organized or incorporated, and owned, by accredited investors (as defined in *id.* § 230.501(a)) who are not natural persons, estates or trusts).

United States or to a registered broker-dealer.[46] If that resale is made prior to any applicable distribution compliance period specified in Rules 903(b)(2) or (b)(3),[47] the resale must be made in compliance with the requirements of Rule 904.[48] Finally, the exemption is available when a bank purchases, from a registered broker-dealer, an eligible security after its initial sale with a reasonable belief that the eligible security was initially sold outside of the United States within the meaning of and in compliance with the requirements of Rule 903, and resells that security to a purchaser who is not in the United States.[49] This provision also requires compliance with Rule 904 if the resale is made prior to the expiration of the security's distribution compliance period.[50] It should be emphasized that nothing in these amendments modifies the 1934 Act § 3(a)(6) definition of "bank"[51] as it applies to foreign banks. "Generally, foreign banks doing business with U.S. customers will not meet this definition and would be considered broker-dealers under the U.S. securities laws."[52] Accordingly, a foreign bank would generally be required to register as a U.S. broker-dealer unless it qualified for an exemption from registration under Rule 15a–6.[53]

The SEC also amended and redesignated an existing exemption from the definition of "dealer"[54] for bank securities lending activi-

---

46. *Id.* § 240.3a5–2(a)(2).

47. Rules 903(b)(2) and (b)(3), *id.* § 230.903(b)(2)–(3), subject "Category 2" securities and "Category 3" debt securities to a 40–day distribution compliance period, and subject "Category 3" equity securities to a one-year distribution compliance period. Under Rule 903, "Category 1" encompasses certain securities (*i*) issued by a foreign issuer, for which there is no substantial U.S. market interest; (*ii*) that are offered and sold in an overseas directed offering; (*iii*) that are backed by the full faith and credit of a foreign government; or, (*iv*) that are offered and sold to employees of the issuer or its affiliates pursuant to certain foreign employee benefit plans. "Category 2" encompasses securities not eligible for Category 1 that are equity securities of a reporting foreign issuer, or debt securities of a reporting issuer or of a non-reporting foreign issuer. "Category 3" applies to all offerings of securities that do not fall within Category 1 or 2.

48. Rule 904, *id.* § 230.904, provides that an offer or sale of securities by any person other than the issuer, a distributor, an affiliate (except an officer or director who is an affiliate solely by virtue

of that position) or person acting on their behalf will be deemed to occur outside the United States within the meaning of Rule 901 if the offer or sale are made in an offshore transaction, and no directed selling efforts are made in the U.S. by the seller, an affiliate or person acting on their behalf. Additional conditions apply in the case of resales of Category 2 or 3 securities by dealers and persons receiving selling concessions, and in the case of resales by certain affiliates of the issuer or a distributor.

49. *Id.* § 240.3a5–2(a)(3).

50. On distribution compliance periods, see note 47, *supra*.

51. 15 U.S.C.A. § 78c(a)(6).

52. 72 Fed. Reg. at 56,565.

53. *See id.* (expressing SEC view to this effect).

54. *See id.* § 240.3a5–3 (former Rule 15a–11, concerning bank securities lending activities). In February 2003, the SEC adopted 1934 Act Rule 15a–11 to provide an exemption from the definitions of both "broker" and "dealer" for banks engaging in securities lending transactions. *See* 68 Fed. Reg. 8686

ties as a conduit lender.[55] In addition, the SEC conformed the rule[56] that grants a limited exemption from U.S. broker-dealer registration for foreign broker-dealers to the amended definitions of "broker" and "dealer" under the 1934 Act.[57]

The SEC withdrew an earlier rule defining the term "bank" for purposes of the 1934 Act definitions of "broker" and "dealer,"[58] since it had been judicially invalidated.[59] A time-limited exemption for bank securities activities was withdrawn due to the passage of time.[60] Finally, the exemption from the definitions of "broker" and "dealer" for savings associations and savings banks was withdrawn, since it was no longer necessary in light of enactment of the FSRRA.[61]

In the wake of the financial crisis precipitated by the collapse of the subprime mortgage market,[62] the Dodd–Frank Wall Street Reform and Consumer Protection Act[63] has restricted, but not eliminated, proprietary securities trading by banks.[64]

§ 7.13 Investment Management

The two ends of the spectrum of commercial bank involvement in sponsoring and advising investment companies are occupied by

(2003) (codified at 17 C.F.R. § 240.15a–11). As applicable to bank broker activities, the Rule 15a–11 exemption was never operable, because of the temporary exemptions applicable to all bank broker activities. In accordance with the mandate of the FSRRA, the SEC and the Fed jointly proposed rules governing bank broker activities, and the SEC adopted Rule 772 of Regulation R jointly with the Fed to exempt banks from the "broker" definition for certain securities lending activities. However, the FSRRA did not directly affect the operation of the rules the SEC adopted concerning banks' dealer activities.

55. Rule 3a5–3(d) defines the term "conduit lender" to mean a bank that borrows or loans securities, as principal, for its own account, and contemporaneously loans or borrows the same securities, as principal, for its own account. The rule further states that a bank that qualifies under this definition as a conduit lender at the commencement of a transaction will continue to qualify, notwithstanding whether (*i*) the lending or borrowing transaction terminates and so long as the transaction is replaced within in one business day by another lending or borrowing transaction involving the same securities; and, (*ii*) any substitu-

tions of collateral occur. 17 C.F.R. § 240.3a5–3(d).

56. *Id.* § 240.15a–6(a)(4)(i).

57. The amendment "does not change the substance of Rule 15a–6." 72 Fed. Reg. at 56,565.

58. 17 C.F.R. § 240.3b–9 (2007).

59. *See American Bankers Ass'n v. S.E.C.*, 804 F.2d 739 (D.C.Cir. 1986) (striking down Rule 3b–9 regulating bank broker-dealer activities). *See also* Michael P. Malloy, *The Regulation of Bank Brokerage Activities: Was Rule 3b–9 Benign?* 6 ANN. REV. BANKING L. 181 (1987) (discussing and criticizing *American Bankers Ass'n*).

60. 17 C.F.R. § 240.15a–8 (2007).

61. *Id.* § 240.15a–9.

62. On the subprime mortgage crisis, see 1 MALLOY, *supra* § 1.4.

63. Pub. L. No. 111–203, 124 Stat. 1376 (2010) (codified at scattered sections of 2, 5, 7, 11, 12, 15, 18, 20, 22, 26, 28, 31, 42, 44 U.S.C.A.) (DFA). For discussion of the DFA, 1 MALLOY, *supra*, § 1.4.11.

64. DFA § 619 (codified at 12 U.S.C.A. § 1851).

the Supreme Court's decisions in *Investment Company Institute v. Camp* ("*ICI* I")[1] and *Board of Governors v. Investment Company Institute* ("*ICI* II").[2] *ICI* I established the basic framework that has been used in interpreting the prohibitions of securities activities in Glass–Steagall Act in judicial decisions since the case was decided in 1971.[3] It also established the premise that commercial banks were generally prohibited from sponsoring open-end investment companies, also known as mutual funds,[4] which are continuous issuers of redeemable securities. Since open-end investment companies are defined in terms of certain of their key functions (*e.g.*, continuous issuance and redemption of securities), rather than by a mere formal label, this case has fostered the continuing concern in the analysis of securities-related activities of banks that the bank might be inadvertently involved in the sponsorship of an activity which is, functionally, an open-end investment company.[5]

On the other hand, *ICI* II, distinguishing itself from *ICI* I, held that the affiliation prohibition of the Glass–Steagall Act[6] did not bar a bank holding company from control of a nonbanking subsidiary that acted as an investment adviser[7] to a closed-end investment company,[8] which issues (nonredeemable) securities only from time to time as capital needs dictate. As a result, a closed-end investment company would not be "engaged principally" in the issuance of securities, a key feature that would trigger the affiliation prohibition of the Act.[9] The Court suggested, though it did not decide, that advising a closed-end investment company would not necessarily be prohibited to Fed member banks that undertook the service directly.[10] A similar result would be expected in the case of savings and loan associations and nonmember, state-chartered banks, which, not being "member banks," were not subject to the Glass–Steagall Act's affiliation prohibition by its own terms.[11]

§ 7.13

1. 401 U.S. 617, 91 S.Ct. 1091 (1971).

2. 450 U.S. 46, 101 S.Ct. 973 (1981).

3. *See, e.g., supra* § 5.24 (discussing *ICI I*).

4. On the definition of "open-end investment company," see 15 U.S.C.A. § 80a–5(a)(1).

5. *Cf., e.g.*, Michael P. Malloy & James T. Pitts, *Post–Mortem on Retail Repurchase Agreements: Where Were the Regulators*, 3 Ann. Rev. Banking L. 89, 102, 114 (1984) (discussing implications of investment company definition for bank activities).

6. 12 U.S.C.A. § 377, *repealed*, GLBA, § 101.

7. On the definition of "investment adviser," see 15 U.S.C.A. § 80b–2(a)(11).

8. *ICI II*, 450 U.S. at 66–67, 101 S.Ct. at 986–987.

9. *See* 450 U.S. at 63–64, 101 S.Ct. at 985–986.

10. *See* 450 U.S. at 59–60, 62–63, 101 S.Ct. at 983, 984–985.

11. *See* 12 U.S.C.A. § 377 (prohibited affiliations between investment firms and member banks). *See also* FDIC Advisory Opinion FDIC–83–14 (Oct. 11, 1983), *reprinted in* [1988–1989 Transfer Binder] Fed. Banking L. Rep. (CCH) & 81,159 (Feb. 10, 1989) (permitting state nonmember insured bank discount brokerage service to act as agent for customers in purchase of units of closed-end mutual fund). *Cf.* FDIC Advisory

Continuing member bank involvement with mutual funds re-emerged, but generally within the confines established by *ICI* I. For example, the OCC indicated in March 1985 that a national bank would be permitted to offer investment services to its customers, in which the bank would execute customer orders to buy and sell shares in tax-exempt mutual funds.[12] While the service contemplated bank use of continuing facilities at the mutual funds involved,[13] as well as fee income from the funds,[14] the primary activity of the bank was analogized to bank discount brokerage services previously approved by the OCC.[15] Other proposed services, such as the provision of information on current yields and values, immediate cash credits for redemptions, and automatic purchases and redemptions (including customer-predetermined "sweeps" of accounts), were also considered by the OCC to be authorized banking activities.[16] The OCC found no danger of the "subtle hazards" identified by *ICI* I as the intended target of the prohibitions of the Glass–Steagall Act.[17]

Similarly, the OCC has offered no objection to a national bank's plan to sell units in a unit investment trust[18] on a second-tier, agency basis only.[19] The OCC justified its position by analogy to permitted bank discount brokerage activities,[20] since the bank's involvement would be limited to activities as agent on behalf of customers.[21]

The OCC has also approved proposed subsidiary activities of a national bank operating through a third-tier subsidiary as a co-investment adviser to a closed-end mutual fund.[22] The subsidiary

---

Opinion FDIC 83–20 (Nov. 17, 1983), *reprinted in* [1988–1989 Transfer Binder] Fed. Banking L. Rep. (CCH) ¶ 81,194 (Feb. 3, 1989), at 55,310 (applying prohibition of Section 21 to insured state nonmember bank's operation of collective investment pool).

12. OCC Interpretive Letter No. 332, [1984–85 Transfer Binder] Fed. Banking L. Rep. (CCH) ¶ 85,502 (March 8, 1985).

13. *See id.* at 77,777.

14. *See id.* at 77,777–77,778.

15. *Id.* at 77,778–77,779, *citing Decision of the Comptroller of the Currency on the Application of Security Pacific National Bank to Establish an Operating Subsidiary to be Known as Security Pacific Discount Brokerage Services, Inc.* (Aug. 26, 1982), *reprinted in* [1982–83 Transfer Binder] Fed. Banking L. Rep. (CCH) ¶ 99,284.

16. OCC Interpretive Letter No. 332 at 77,779–77,780.

17. *Id.* at 77,780–77,782.

18. On the definition of "unit investment trust," see 15 U.S.C.A. § 80a–4(2).

19. OCC Interpretive Letter No. 363 (May 23, 1986), [1985–86 Transfer Binder] Fed. Banking L. Rep. (CCH) & 85,533 at 77,828.

20. *Id.* at 77,829–77,830, *citing Securities Indus. Ass'n v. Board of Governors*, 468 U.S. 207, 104 S.Ct. 3003 (1984), and *Securities Indus. Ass'n v. Comptroller of the Currency*, 577 F.Supp. 252 (D.D.C.1983), *aff'd* 758 F.2d 739 (D.C.Cir.1985) (per curiam), *cert. denied*, 474 U.S. 1054, 106 S.Ct. 790 (1986), *cert. granted on other grounds and aff'd in part and reversed in part sub nom. Clarke v. Securities Indus. Ass'n*, 479 U.S. 388, 107 S.Ct. 750 (1987).

21. OCC Interpretive Letter No. 363 at 77,830.

22. OCC Interpretive Letter No. 515 (July 9, 1990), *reprinted in* 3 OCC Interpretations and Actions (Aug. 1990).

would be registered as an investment adviser under the Investment Advisers Act of 1940.[23] The subsidiary would provide investment research, identifying municipal bonds for fund purchase, monitoring market and credit risks of bonds in the portfolio, and identifying trading opportunities.[24] The fund would be sponsored by the other co-investment adviser, and also would serve as the administrator of the fund.[25] In approving the proposal, the OCC reaffirmed its administrative position, adopted at least as early as September 1983, that investment advice was a permissible activity under the incidental powers provision of the National Bank Act.[26]

The Fed has authorized similar mutual fund and unit investment trust activities by bank holding companies through nonbanking discount brokerage subsidiaries.[27] It has also ruled similarly under the BHCA[28] on related activities.

Under the GLBA, affiliations between banks and investment firms are no longer prohibited.[29] Indeed, many investment company and investment advising activities may now be considered activities "financial in nature," and thus authorized by the GLBA for nonbanking subsidiaries of banks[30] and for nonbanking subsidiaries of financial holding companies (FHCs).[31] However, the GLBA also amended the Investment Advisers Act of 1940[32] and the Investment Company Act of 1940[33] to subject banks that advise mutual funds to the same regulatory scheme, administered by the SEC, as other advisers to mutual funds.[34] Subsequently, the Dodd–Frank Wall Street Reform and Consumer Protection Act ("Dodd–Frank Act"),[35] in response to the financial crisis precipitated in 2008 by the failure

---

23. 15 U.S.C.A. §§ 80b–1 *et seq. See* OCC Interpretive Letter No. 515 at 2.

24. OCC Interpretive Letter No. 515 at 1–2.

25. *Id.* at 2.

26. *See id.* at 2 (citing previous interpretations).

27. *See Fed Approves Sovran Plan to Offer Mutual Funds, UITs Through Subsidiary,* 18 Sec. Reg. & L. Rep. 1057 (1986).

28. *See id.* at 1058. *See generally* 12 U.S.C.A. § 1843(c)(8) (authorizing activities "closely related" to banking).

29. *See supra* note 6 (noting repeal of prohibition).

30. *See, e.g.,* 12 U.S.C.A. § 24a. On financial activities of operating subsidiaries, see *infra* § 7.18.

31. 12 U.S.C.A. § 1843(k). On FHCs, see *infra* § 7.20.

32. 15 U.S.C.A. §§ 80b–1 *et seq.*

33. *Id.* §§ 80a–1 *et seq.*

34. GLBA, §§ 211–220, 222–224 (codified at 15 U.S.C.A. §§ 80a–2(a)(5), (a)(6), (a)(11), (a)(19)(A)(v)–(vii), (a)(19)(B)(v)–(vii), 80a–9(a)(1)–(2), 80a–10(c), 80a–17(a)(4), (f)(1)–(6), 80a–26(b)–(f), 80a–34(a), 80b–2(a)(3), (a)(7), (a)(11)(A), (a)(26), (c), 80b–10a). *See also* GLBA, § 221(c) (codified at 15 U.S.C.A. § 80a–3(c)(3)) (treatment of bank common trust funds under Investment Company Act of 1940).

35. Pub. L. No. 111–203, 124 Stat. 1376 (2010) (codified at scattered sections of 2, 5, 7, 11, 12, 15, 18, 20, 22, 26, 28, 31, 42, 44 U.S.C.A.) (DFA). For discussion of the DFA, see 1 MICHAEL P. MALLOY, BANKING LAW AND REGULATION § 1.4.11 (1994 & Cum. Supp.).

of the subprime mortgage market,[36] further amended the Investment Company Act[37] and the Investment Advisers Act.[38]

§ 7.14 Investment Securities

Section 16 of the Glass–Steagall Act provides that a national bank "may purchase for its own account investment securities under such limitations and restrictions as the Comptroller of the Currency may by regulation prescribe."[1] Purchasing, underwriting, and dealing in "investment securities"[2] is a longstanding exception to the prohibition against commercial bank involvement in securities activities.[3] All other financial institutions that accept deposits are also subject to the Comptroller's regulation of bank activities involving investment securities,[4] essentially a class of high-grade debt securities.

§ 7.15 Municipal Securities

The Glass–Steagall Act has long permitted banks to engage in underwriting of "general obligation bonds"[1] of state and local

36. For background on the subprime mortgage crisis, see 1 MALLOY, *supra*, § 1.4. For a timeline of the current financial crisis, see http://www.stlouisfed.org/timeline/default.cfm.

37. 15 U.S.C.A. §§ 80a–1 *et seq.*, amended, DFA, §§ 769, 923(a)(2), 929E(c), 929F(f), 929I(b), 929M(b), 929P(a)(3), 929Q(a), 939(c), 985(d)(1)–(5), 986(c)(1)–(4), Pub. L. No. 111–203, 124 Stat. 1376, 1801, 1849, 1853–1854, 1858, 1861–1864, 1865–1866, 1886, 1934–1936 (2010) (codified at 15 U.S.C.A. §§ 80a–2(a)(19), 80a–2(a)(44), 80a–2(a)(54), 80a–6(a)(5)(A)(iv)(I), 80a–9(b)(4)(B), 80a–9(d)(1), 80a–12(d)(1)(J), 80a–17(f), 80a–30, 80a–35(a), 80a–37(b), 80a–41(e)(3)(A), 80a–43, 80a–48, 80a–49, 80a–60(a)(3)(B)(iii); repealing 15 U.S.C.A. § 80a–3(c)(8)).

38. 15 U.S.C.A. §§ 80b–1 *et seq.*, amended, DFA §§ 402(a)–(b), 403–408, 409(a)–(c), 410–411, 414, 418, 419, 770, 913(g)(2), (h)(2), 921(b), 923(a)(3), 925(b), 928(1)–(2), 929E(d), 929I(c), 929N, 929P(a)(4), (b)(3), 929Q(b), 985(e)(1)–(4), 986(d), Pub. L. No. 111–203, 124 Stat. at 1570–1580, 1801, 1828–1830, 1841, 1849, 1851–1853, 1858–1859, 1861–1862, 1864–1866, 1936 (2010) (codified at 15 U.S.C.A. §§ 80b–2 note, 80b–2(a)(11), 80b–2(a)(21), 80b–2(a)(29)–(30), 80b–3, 80b–3a(a), 80b–3(b), 80b–3(f), 80b–3(i)(1), 80b–3(*l*),

80b–3(m)–(n), 80b–4, 80b–5(a), (e)–(f), 80b–6(3), 80b–9(e)(3)(A), 80b–9(f), 80b–10(c), 80b–10(d), 80b–11(g), (i), 80b–13(a), 80b–14, 80b–18a, 80b–18b, 80b–18c).

§ 7.14

1. 12 U.S.C.A. § 24(Seventh).

2. The term "investment securities" is defined by Section 16 of the Glass–Steagall Act to mean:

> marketable obligations evidencing indebtedness of any person, copartnership, association, or corporation in the form of bonds, notes and/or debentures commonly known as investment securities under such future definition of the term "investment securities" as may by regulation be prescribed by the Comptroller of the Currency.

Id.

3. For a discussion of the regulatory implementation and supervision of this exception, see 2 MICHAEL P. MALLOY, BANKING LAW AND REGULATION § 7.3.2 (1994 & CUM. SUPP.).

4. 12 U.S.C.A. § 378.

§ 7.15

1. On the meaning of the term "general obligations," see 12 C.F.R. § 1.3(g) (1995).

governments.[2] Revenue bonds, which depend upon revenue of the financed public project and are not backed by the full faith and credit of the governmental issuer, were not be included within this concept. The Comptroller had identified exceptions to this general exclusion, thus permitting underwriting of certain municipal revenue bonds, as early as the 1960s.[3]

The Comptroller's position was challenged in *Baker, Watts & Co. v. Saxon,*[4] and the Federal District Court for the District of Columbia invalidated the Comptroller's interpretations, ruling that permissible underwriting of "general obligations" did not include bonds issued by governmental units lacking general taxing power.[5] On appeal by the governmental issuer of the bonds, the D.C. Circuit affirmed.[6]

In 1999, the GLBA authorized national banks to deal in, underwrite, and purchase municipal bonds for their own investment accounts.[7] Even before this amendment, commercial banks could and did *deal* in municipal securities. The Securities Acts Amendments of 1975[8] explicitly required the registration of municipal securities dealers under the 1934 Act,[9] including any department or division of a bank engaged in purchasing and selling municipal securities for its own account.[10]

The pattern of regulation applicable to municipal securities dealers is byzantine. The bank regulatory agencies are to be primarily responsible for enforcement and inspection with respect to the municipal securities operations of commercial banks,[11] but the SEC has broad power over the registration of municipal securities dealers.[12] In addition, the Municipal Securities Rulemaking Board ("MSRB") is given authority to regulate the activities of municipal securities dealers.[13] However, registration tests and periodic examinations of *bank* municipal securities dealers are performed by the appropriate bank regulatory agency.[14]

2. 12 U.S.C.A. § 24 (Seventh).

3. *See, e.g.,* 27 Fed. Reg. 10,251 (1962); 28 Fed. Reg. 8280 (1963). *See also* 12 C.F.R. §§ 1.127, 1.167 (1963), *removed* 44 Fed. Reg. 76,264 (1979).

4. 261 F.Supp. 247 (D.D.C.1966), *aff'd sub nom. Port of N.Y. Auth. v. Baker, Watts & Co.,* 392 F.2d 497 (D.C.Cir.1968).

5. *Id.*

6. *See Port of N.Y. Auth.,* 392 F.2d at 504.

7. GLBA, § 151 (codified at 12 U.S.C.A. § 24). *See* 66 Fed. Reg. 8178 (2001) (to be codified at 12 C.F.R. pt. 1) (proposing to incorporate GLBA authority to underwrite, deal in, and purchase certain municipal bonds by well capitalized national banks).

8. Pub. L. No. 94–29, 89 Stat. 97 (1975) (codified at scattered sections of 15 U.S.C.A.).

9. *See* 15 U.S.C.A. § 78o–4(a)(1).

10. *See* 15 U.S.C.A. § 78c(a)(30) (defining municipal securities dealer).

11. *See* S. Rep. No. 94–75, 94th Cong., 1st Sess. 52 (1975) (so stating).

12. 15 U.S.C.A. § 78o–4(a)(1).

13. *See id.* § 78o–4(b).

14. *See id.* § 78o–4(b)(2)(A)(iii), (E), (c)(7)(A). *See also id.* § 78c(a)(34)(A)(i)–(iii) (defining "appropriate regulatory agency").

In addition to implementing regulations promulgated by the SEC and the MSRB, the appropriate bank regulatory agencies have also implemented the municipal securities provisions of the 1934 Act by issuing regulations. Those regulations issued by the Comptroller are applicable to national bank municipal securities dealers.[15] Those issued by the Fed apply to state-chartered member bank municipal securities dealers.[16] Those issued by the FDIC apply to state-chartered nonmember insured bank municipal securities dealers.[17]

§ 7.16   Transfer Agent

A commercial bank acting as a transfer agent[1] for purchases and sales of securities may be subject to regulation of its activities both by a clearing agency[2] and by its "appropriate regulatory

---

15. *See* 12 C.F.R. Pt. 10.

16. *See* 12 C.F.R. § 208.8(j).

17. *See* 12 C.F.R. Pt. 343 (1998), *rescinded,* 64 Fed. Reg. 62,103 (1999) (determining that rule is unnecessary and duplicative of many requirements in MSRB Rule G–7).

§ 7.16

1. The term "transfer agent" is defined for these purposes by the 1934 Act as:

> any person who engages on behalf of an issuer of securities or on behalf of itself as an issuer of securities in (A) countersigning such securities upon issuance; (B) monitoring the issuance of such securities with a view to preventing unauthorized issuance, a function commonly performed by a person called a registrar; (C) registering the transfer of such securities; (D) exchanging or converting such securities; or (E) transferring record of ownership of securities by bookkeeping entry without physical issuance of securities certificates. . . .

15 U.S.C.A. § 78c(a)(25).

2. For these purposes, the term "clearing agency" is defined as:

> any person who acts as an intermediary in making payments or deliveries or both in connection transactions in securities or who provides facilities for comparison of data respecting the terms of settlement of securities transactions, to reduce the number of settlements of securities transactions, or for the allocation of securities settlement responsibilities. Such term

also means any person, such as a security depository, who (i) acts as a custodian of securities in connection with a system for the central handling of securities whereby all securities of a particular class or series of any issuer deposited within the system are treated as fungible and may be transferred, loaned, or pledged by bookkeeping entry without physical delivery of securities certificates, or (ii) otherwise permits or facilitates the settlement of securities transactions or the hypothecation or lending of securities without physical delivery of securities certificates.

Id. § 78c(a)(23)(A). Clearing agencies making use of the mails or any means or instrumentality of interstate commerce to perform a clearing function with respect to securities not exempt under the 1934 Act must register under that Act. *Id.* § 78q–1(b)(1). As to exempted securities under the 1934 Act, see *id.* § 78c(a)(12). (Municipal securities are not exempted securities for purposes of clearing agency registration. *Id.*) The term "clearing agency" does not include

> any bank . . . building and loan, savings and loan, or homestead association, or cooperative bank if such bank . . . association, or cooperative bank would be deemed to be a clearing agency solely by reason of functions performed by such institution as part of customary banking, . . . association, or cooperative banking activities, or solely by reason of acting on behalf of a clearing agency or a participant therein in connection with the fur-

agency." For purposes of transfer agent regulation of commercial banks, the "appropriate regulatory agencies" are: (1) the Comptroller, for national banks and D.C. banks, and subsidiaries of such banks; (2) the Fed, for state member banks, subsidiaries thereof, bank holding companies, and subsidiaries of bank holding companies that are banks other than banks subject to the authority of the Comptroller or the FDIC; and, (3) the FDIC, for state-chartered nonmember insured banks and subsidiaries thereof.[3]

Regulation of transfer agent activities of commercial banks by the "appropriate regulatory agency" is authorized by Section 17A(c)–(d) of the 1934 Act.[4] Among other things, the appropriate regulatory agency has the authority to review final actions of a clearing agency imposing sanctions or limitations with respect to a bank's participation in the clearing agency.[5] In addition, banks acting as transfer agents may be liable for negligence or conversion with respect to its actions as transfer agent.[6]

Any commercial bank making use, directly or indirectly, of the mails or any means or instrumentality of interstate commerce in connection with transfer agent functions with respect to securities registered under the 1934 Act[7] must register as a transfer agent in accordance with the regulations of the bank's appropriate regulatory agency.[8] The registration requirement is also triggered if transfer agent activities involve securities that would be required to be registered under the 1934 Act but for the exemption provided[9] for certain investment company securities and for certain securities issued by insurance companies.[10]

The appropriate regulatory agencies are given statutory authority to exempt by rule or order any person, security, or class of

---

nishing by the clearing agency of services to its participants or the use of services of the clearing agency by its participants. . . .

Id. § 78c(a)(23)(B). However, the SEC has statutory authority to include such institutions within the term by rule, "as necessary and appropriate to assure the prompt and accurate clearance and settlement of securities transactions or to prevent evasion of [the 1934 Act]." *Id.* Clearing agency regulation of its participants is authorized by Section 17A(b)(4)–(5) of the 1934 Act. 15 U.S.C.A. § 78q–1(b)(4)–(5). A clearing agency's supervisory authority over its participants includes the power to impose such sanctions as summary suspension (*see id.* § 78q–1(b)(5)(C)) and denial of participation in the clearing agency, or prohibition or limitation with respect

to access to clearing agency services. *See id.* § 78q–1(b)(4)(A)–(B).

3. *Id.* § 78c(a)(34)(B)(i)–(iii).

4. 15 U.S.C.A. § 78q–1(c)–(d). *Cf., e.g.,* 12 C.F.R. § 9.20 (Comptroller's regulations; registration of national bank transfer agents).

5. *See, e.g.,* 12 C.F.R. § 9.22 (applications for review).

6. *See generally Woods v. Bank of N.Y.,* 806 F.2d 368 (2d Cir.1986) (holding duty of bank, acting as mutual fund transfer agent, to follow instructions on check dependent upon obligations assumed by bank under its procedures).

7. *See* 15 U.S.C.A. § 78*l*(a)–(b), (g).

8. *Id.* § 78q–1(c)(1)–(2).

9. *Id.* § 78*l*(g)(2)(B), (G)

10. *See id.* § 78q–1(c)(1).

persons or securities from the transfer agent provisions of the 1934 Act.[11] Such an exemption, resulting from the agency's motion or from an application by the agent, requires a finding by the regulatory agency to the effect that:

> (1) the exemption is in the public interest and is consistent with the general statutory goal of protection of investors and the specific goals of prompt and accurate clearance and settlement of transactions and the safeguarding of securities and funds; and

> (2) the SEC does not object to the exemption.[12]

The procedure for registration is governed by the regulations promulgated by the regulatory agencies.[13] The regulatory agencies have the statutory authority, by order, to deny registration applications,[14] and to censure,[15] place limitations on,[16] suspend (for periods not exceeding 12 months),[17] or revoke the registration of,[18] registered transfer agents subject to their respective authorities under the 1934 Act.[19]

The imposition of these sanctions requires findings on the record, after notice and opportunity for hearing, that the sanction is in the public interest and that the transfer agent has either willfully violated or is unable to comply with the transfer agent provisions or the recordkeeping, reporting and examinations provisions of Section 17 of the 1934 Act,[20] or any rules or regulations

---

11. *Id.*

12. *Id.*

13. *See id.* § 78q–1(c)(2). *Cf., e.g.,* 12 C.F.R. § 9.20 (Comptroller's regulations; registration of national bank transfer agents; incorporating SEC rule, 17 C.F.R. § 240.17Ac2–1).

14. 15 U.S.C.A. § 78q–1(c)(3). *See, e.g.,* 12 C.F.R. §§ 19.132(a)(5) (providing for denial of national bank transfer agent registration by Comptroller); 208.8(f)(1) (providing for denial of insured state nonmember bank transfer agent registration by Fed); 341.3(c) (providing for denial of insured state nonmember bank transfer agent registration by FDIC).

15. 15 U.S.C.A. § 78q–1(c)(3). *See, e.g.,* 12 C.F.R. § 19.130(a)(3) (Comptroller's rules for disciplinary proceedings involving the federal securities laws; applying procedures to registered bank transfer agent under § 78q–1(c)(3)(A)); *id.* § 19.132(a)(6) (providing for censure of person associated or seeking to become associated with bank transfer

agent). *Cf. Bradford Nat'l Clearing Corp. v. Securities and Exch. Comm'n,* 590 F.2d 1085 (D.C.Cir.1978) (concerning disciplinary actions under § 78q–1 against clearing agent).

16. 15 U.S.C.A. § 78q–1(c)(3). *See, e.g.,* 12 C.F.R. § 19.132(a)(5) (providing for limitations on registered bank transfer agent).

17. 15 U.S.C.A. § 78q–1(c)(3). *See, e.g.,* 12 C.F.R. § 19.132(a)(5)–(6) (providing for suspension of registered bank transfer agent or associated person).

18. 15 U.S.C.A. § 78q–1(c)(3). *See, e.g.,* 12 C.F.R. § 19.132(a)(5) (providing for revocation of registered bank transfer agent).

19. 15 U.S.C.A. § 78q–1(c)(3)(A)–(B).

20. 15 U.S.C.A. § 78q. For a staff interpretation clarifying the transfer agent recordkeeping requirements, see OCC Interpretive Letter No. 473 (Jan. 13, 1989), *reprinted in* [1988–1989 Transfer Binder] Fed. Banking L. Rep. (CCH) & 83,010 (May 26, 1989).

promulgated under these provisions.[21] The regulatory agencies may also enforce compliance with the transfer agent provisions of the 1934 Act by use of the cease-and-desist authority of the FDIA.[22]

§ 7.17   Underwriting and Placement

The Glass–Steagall Act notwithstanding, banking enterprises have authority to engage in a wide range of securities underwriting activities. Even before the enactment of the Gramm–Leach–Bliley Act (GLBA),[1] banks and bank holding company securities subsidiaries were permitted to underwrite "bank-eligible" securities.[2] In addition, so long as it did not account for more than 25 percent of its business, a bank holding company securities subsidiary was also permitted to underwrite "bank-ineligible" securities, *e.g.*, corporate equities.[3]

---

21. 15 U.S.C.A. § 78q–1(c)(3)(A).

22. *See* 15 U.S.C.A. § 78q–1(d)(2), which provides:

[T]he appropriate regulatory agency for such clearing agency or transfer agent may, in accordance with section 8 of the Federal Deposit Insurance Act (12 U.S.C.A. 1818), enforce compliance by such clearing agency or transfer agent with the provisions of this section, sections 17 [concerning recordkeeping, reporting and examinations] and 19 [concerning self-regulatory organizations] of [the 1934 Act], and the rules and regulations thereunder. For purpose of the preceding sentence, any violation of any such provision shall constitute adequate basis for the issuance of an order under [12 U.S.C.A. § 1818(b) or (c)], and the participants in any such clearing agency and the persons doing business with any such transfer agent shall be deemed to be "depositors" as that term is used in [12 U.S.C.A. § 1818(c)].

See, e.g., 12 C.F.R. § 19.130(b) (retaining authority in Comptroller to apply § 1818 to transfer agent violations). For examples of enforcement actions against commercial banks acting as transfer agents, see *The Chase Manhattan Bank*, Administrative Proceeding No. 3–8518, Securities Exchange Act Release No. 34784 (October 4, 1994), 57 SEC Docket 2195 (joint SEC–OCC action against transfer agent for failure to report stolen cancelled certificates pursuant to Rule 17f–1 and failure to safeguard securities in its possession pursuant to Rule

17Ad–12; transfer agent consented to civil penalty of $100,000 and cease and desist order); *Seattle–First National Bank*, Securities Exchange Act Release No. 34293 (July 1, 1994), 57 SEC Docket 146 (joint SEC–OCC action against transfer agent for failure to report missing securities to SEC Lost and Stolen Securities Program; transfer agent consented to civil penalty of $75,000 and cease and desist order). *See also* 65 Fed. Reg. 59,766, 59,766–59767 (2000) (to be codified at 17 C.F.R. §§ 240.17f–1(a)(6)–(8), (c)(2)(i)–(ii), (d)(3), 240.17Ad–7(i), 240.17Ad–12(a)(1), (b), 240.17Ad–19; redesignating former § 240.17f–1(c)(2)(ii)–(iii) as (c)(2)(iii)–(iv)) (proposing amendments to SEC rules; discussing supervision and enforcement with respect to transfer agents).

§ 7.17

1. Pub. L. No. 106–102, Nov. 12, 1999, 113 Stat. 1338 (1999) (codified at scattered sections of 12, 15, 16, 18 U.S.C.A.). On the effects of the GLBA, see *infra* §§ 7.18–7.20.

2. *I.e.*, securities in which banks may deal, purchase and underwrite under section 16 of the Glass–Steagall Act, 12 U.S.C.A. § 24 (Seventh).

3. *See, e.g.*, 73 FED. RES. BULL. 473 (1987); *id.* at 607; *id.* at 616; *id.* at 620; *id.* at 622 (announcing Fed authorization of "bank-ineligible" securities by BHC subsidiaries, subject to specified conditions). *See also Securities Industry Ass'n v. Board of Governors*, 839 F.2d 47 (2d Cir.1988) (upholding Fed policy with

Commercial banks have also been involved in the private placement of securities,[4] typically, a non-public offering directly negotiated with large, institutional investors.[5] As such, these distributions are generally exempt from the registration requirements of the 1933 Act.[6] Authority to engage in these activities, in a relatively aggressive manner, was confirmed by the D.C. Circuit in *Securities Industry Association v. Board of Governors*.[7]

With the enactment of the GLBA, national and state member banks were no longer prohibited from affiliating with investment banking firms.[8] Banking involvement in securities underwriting and placement is further enhanced by the GLBA authorization of bank subsidiaries[9] and subsidiaries of financial holding companies ("FHCs")[10] to engage in a wide range of securities activities, including underwriting and placement.

§ 7.18 Financial Services Activities

Since November 1999, a new category of permissible activities has become available to banks and bank holding companies, "activities financial in nature." The next two sections examine this grant of authority, as it applies to financial subsidiaries of banks[1] and to bank holding companies that have elected to operate as financial holding companies.[2]

§ 7.19 Financial Services Activities by Bank Subsidiaries

The Gramm–Leach–Bliley Act ("GLBA")[1] permits a national bank[2] or an insured state bank[3] to engage, through a financial

respect to "bank-ineligible" securities activities).

4. *See* 3 SECURITIES AND EXCHANGE COMMISSION, REPORTS ON BANK SECURITIES ACTIVITIES 57–60 (1977); FEDERAL RESERVE BOARD, COMMERCIAL BANK PRIVATE PLACEMENT ACTIVITIES 29–31 (1977). *See generally* Miller, *Participation of National Banks in Private Placements of Corporate Securities*, 13 New England L. Rev. 63 (1977).

5. *See, e.g.*, [1978–79 Transfer Binder] Fed. Banking L. Rep. (CCH) ¶ 85,-107; OCC Interpretive Letter No. 212, [1981–82 Transfer Binder] Fed. Banking L. Rep. ¶ 85,293.

6. *See* 15 U.S.C.A. §§ 77d(2), 77e (exempting nonpublic offerings). *See also* 17 C.F.R. §§ 230.501–230.503, 230.506 (Regulation D provisions with respect to non public offerings).

7. 807 F.2d 1052 (D.C.Cir.1986), *cert. denied*, 483 U.S. 1005, 107 S.Ct. 3228 (1987).

8. GLBA, § 101 (repealing affiliation prohibition of 12 U.S.C.A. § 377).

9. *See, e.g., id.*, § 121(a)(2) (codified at 12 U.S.C.A. § 24a).

10. *Id.*, § 103(a) (codified at 12 U.S.C.A. § 1843(k)–(*o*)). On the regulation of FHCs, see *infra* § 7.20.

§ 7.18

1. 12 U.S.C.A. §§ 24a, 1831w.

2. *Id.* § 1843(k).

§ 7.19

1. Pub. L. No. 106–102, Nov. 12, 1999, 113 Stat. 1338 (1999) (codified at scattered sections of 12, 15, 16, 18 U.S.C.A.).

2. GLBA, § 121(a)(2) (codified at 12 U.S.C.A. § 24a).

subsidiary, only in financial activities authorized by the act, with certain exceptions. Section 24a specifically excludes four types of activities for these subsidiaries of national banks[4]: insurance or annuity underwriting, insurance company portfolio investments, real estate investment and development, and merchant banking.[5] These types of financial activities may only be done in financial holding company ("FHC") affiliates.[6] Substantial "firewalls" were established, intended to limit exposure of a state or national bank to the risk of the activities of the bank's financial subsidiary.[7] Federal banking regulators are prohibited from interpreting these provisions to provide for any expansion of these activities contrary to the express language of the GLBA.[8]

In January 2000, the Comptroller published proposed regulations implementing the new GLBA authority.[9] In January 2001, the FDIC implemented the new authority by adopting final rules governing the activities and investments of insured state banks.[10]

§ 7.20   Financial Services Activities by FHCs

The Gramm–Leach–Bliley Act ("GLBA")[1] permits bank hold-

---

3. *Id.*, § 121(d)(1) (codified at 12 U.S.C.A. § 1831w).

4. On the corresponding provisions applicable to insured state banks, see *supra* § 5.25, text and accompanying notes 37–50.

5. However, after a five-year period from enactment of the GLBA, the Federal Reserve Board and the Secretary of the Treasury are authorized jointly to adopt rules permitting merchant banking by financial subsidiaries, subject to the conditions that the agencies may jointly determine. GLBA, § 122 (codified at 12 U.S.C.A. § 1843 note).

6. On financial services activities of FHCs, see *infra* § 7.20.

7. GLBA, §§ 121(b)–(d) (codified at 12 U.S.C.A. §§ 335, 371c(b)(11), (e)–(f), 1831w, 1971).

8. The legislative history of the act indicates that Congress intended to prevent the kind of broad interpretative approach that grew up around the "incidental powers" language of section 24, and specifically to supersede and replace the Comptroller's broad rules on operating subsidiaries of national banks contained in 12 C.F.R. pt. 5 (1999). *See Conference Report on S. 900, reprinted in* 145 Cong. Rec. H11255-01, H11296 (1999) (discussing congressional intent concerning GLBA section 121).

9. *See* 65 Fed. Reg. 3157 (2000) (proposing implementing regulations; authorizing national banks to conduct expanded financial activities through financial subsidiaries). *Cf., e.g.*, 64 Fed. Reg. 69,071 (1999) (publishing OCC operating subsidiary notice, proposing expansion of activities of national bank operating subsidiary, to underwrite and deal in, to limited extent, all types of debt and equity securities (other than ownership interests in open-end investment companies)). The OCC noted that the applicant's proposal "will be permissible under the standards of the recently enacted [GLBA]. The Bank meets (and where applicable, all its insured depository institution affiliates meet) the standards set forth in [12 U.S.C.A. § 24a] for a national bank to have a 'financial subsidiary' engaged in the types of activities that include those proposed by the Bank." 64 Fed. Reg. at 69,072 n.1.

10. 66 Fed. Reg. 1018 (2001) (codified at 12 C.F.R. pts. 303, 337, 362).

§ 7.20

1. Pub. L. No. 106–102, Nov. 12, 1999, 113 Stat. 1338 (1999) (codified at scattered sections of 12, 15, 16, 18 U.S.C.A.).

ing companies ("BHCs")[2] that qualify as financial holding companies ("FHCs") to engage in activities, and acquire companies engaged in activities, that are "financial in nature" or that are incidental to such activities.[3] To qualify for these new financial activities and affiliations, a BHC may elect to become an FHC, if all of its subsidiary banks are well capitalized and well managed.[4] A BHC that meets these requirements may file a certification to that effect with the Board of Governors of the Federal Reserve System ("the Fed") and a declaration electing to be an FHC. After this filing an FHC may engage, either *de novo* or by acquisition, in any activity that has been determined by the Fed to be financial in nature or incidental to such an activity.

As amended by the GLBA, the BHCA now contains a list of "K4 activities" that are considered to be financial in nature.[5] An FHC may engage in listed activities without prior approval from the Fed,[6] but with notice to the Fed within 30 days after the activity is commenced or a company is acquired.[7] The list includes securities underwriting, dealing, and market-making, without any revenue limitation; sponsoring and distributing all types of mutual funds and investment companies; insurance underwriting and agency activities; merchant banking, and insurance company portfolio investments.[8] In addition, the Fed has authority to determine that other, unlisted activities are "financial in nature."[9] In determining what activities are financial in nature or incidental, the Fed must notify the Secretary of the Treasury of applications or requests to engage in new financial activities.[10] The Fed may not determine that an activity is financial or incidental to a financial activity if the Secretary objects.[11] The Secretary may also propose to the Fed that the Fed find that a particular activity is financial in nature or incidental.[12] Early in 2000, a joint Fed–Treasury rule expressly

2. On the formation and regulated activities of BHCs, see *supra* §§ 4.3, 6.2–6.5.

3. GLBA, § 103(a) (codified at 12 U.S.C.A. § 1843(k)). FHCs are also permitted to engage in activities that are complementary to financial activities, if the Fed determines that the activity does not pose a substantial risk to the safety or soundness of depository institutions or the financial system in general. GLBA, § 103(c)(2) (codified at 12 U.S.C.A. § 1843(j)). *See* 65 Fed. Reg. 80,384 (2000) (to be codified at 12 C.F.R. pt. 225) (proposing certain financial and nonfinancial data processing activities as "complementary" to financial activities). The integrity of the deposit insurance funds is preserved by prohibiting the use of deposit insurance funds to benefit any

shareholder, subsidiary or nondepository affiliate of an FHC. GLBA, § 117 (codified at 12 U.S.C.A. § 1821(a)(4)(B)).

4. GLBA, § 103(a) (codified at 12 U.S.C.A. § 1843(*l*)).

5. 12 U.S.C.A. § 1843(k)(4). For a list of the K4 activities, see *supra* Figure 6–2.

6. *Id.* § 1843(k)(6)(B).

7. *Id.* § 1843(k)(6)(A).

8. *See supra* Figure 6–2 (identifying K4 activities).

9. 12 U.S.C.A. § 1843(k).

10. *Id.* § 1843(k)(2)(A)(i).

11. *Id.* § 1843(k)(2)(A)(ii).

12. *Id.* § 1843(k)(2)(B).

identified securities underwriting, merchant banking, and investment banking as permissible FHC activities.[13]

13. 65 Fed. Reg. 16,460 (2000) (codified at 12 C.F.R. §§ 225.1(c)(9)–(15), 225.170–225.175, 1500.1–1500.7; redesignating 225.1(c)(9)–(13) as (c)(11)–(15); reserving 225.1(c)(9)). For more detailed discussion of the regulations implementing the FHC provisions of the GLBA, see *supra* § 6.4, text and accompanying notes 12–30.

Chapter 8

RESOLUTION OF INSTITUTION FAILURES

Table of Sections

---

§ 8.1 Introduction

This chapter examines the various ways in which the bank regulatory agencies supervise troubled and failing depository institutions.[1] It begins with an examination of the statutory and regula-

---

§ 8.1

1. In statutory terms, "troubled" and "failing" institutions are now referred to as "institutions in danger of default" and "institutions in default," respectively. *See* 12 U.S.C.A. § 1813(x) (definitions relating to default).

tory devices available to the agencies to identify, monitor, and rehabilitate institutions that are troubled. Some institutions in danger of default may not be susceptible to reasonable efforts to rehabilitate them, however, and these institutions may eventually fail. The chapter therefore continues with a discussion of the statutory and regulatory alternatives available to the agencies to "resolve" the situation of a failing depository institution.

§ 8.2   The Subprime Mortgage Crisis

Beginning in late 2008, a financial crisis overwhelmed the capital markets, resulting from the failure of the subprime mortgage market.[1] The crisis continued to deepen and spread in 2009.[2] As of year-end 2009, 140 banks had been placed in receivership administered by the Federal Deposit Insurance Corporation (FDIC), at a likely cumulative cost to the Deposit Insurance Fund (DIF) of more than $1.8 billion.[3] In the first quarter of 2010, the FDIC was appointed receiver for 41 failed banks and savings associations with a total exposure for the Deposit Insurance Fund of more than $320 million.[4] By contrast, five credit unions failed during approximately the same period.[5]

U.S. Government responses to the crisis have generally fallen into one of three categories. The Government has initiated certain

---

§ 8.2

1. For background on the subprime mortgage crisis, see 1 MICHAEL P. MALLOY, BANKING LAW AND REGULATION § 1.4 (1994 & Cum. Supp.). On December 22, 2008, the St. Louis Federal Reserve Bank launched a website, *The Financial Crisis: A Timeline of Events and Policy Actions*, which tracks the current financial crisis. *See* http://www.stlouisfed.org/timeline/default.cfm.

2. See Thecla Fabian, *DIF Dips Sharply; Bank Profit Falls 61% Comparing '08, '09 1st Quarters, FDIC Says*, BNA Banking Daily (May 28, 2009), available at http://www.bna.com (reporting on results of FDIC Quarterly Banking Profile and related statistical information).

3. Thecla Fabian, Failed Federally Insured Banks Now 140; Insurance Fund Falls by $1.8 Billion Dec. 18, BNA Banking Daily, Dec. 22, 2009, available at http://www.bna.com.

4. 75 Fed. Reg. 6667 (2010); Thecla Fabian, Minnesota Bank Becomes 16th Failure In 2010; Costs Insurance Fund $3.1 Million, BNA Banking Daily, Feb. 9, 2010, available at http://www.bna. com.

5. Thecla Fabian, Virginia's Chartway Buys Utah Credit Union; Fifteenth and Last 2009 Failed Credit Union, BNA Banking Daily, Jan. 6, 2010, available at http://www.bna.com. According to the latest call report data released by the NCUA, credit union membership increased 1.3 percent in the first six months of 2009, to 89.7 million members (from 88.6 million), and member share growth (i.e., deposit growth) increased 8.0 percent to $735.5 billion (from $681.1 billion). http://www.ncua.gov/news/press_releases/2009/MR09–0825. htm ("Call Report Announcement"). See Thecla Fabian, NCUA Sees Strong Member, Share Growth, But Lending Down, Defaults Up for First Half, BNA Banking Daily (Aug. 26, 2009), available at http://news.bna.com (reporting on NCUA announcement). However, lending growth was slow—0.7 percent to $570.0 billion (from $566.0 billion). Call Report Announcement, supra. Investment activity by the 7,691 federally insured credit unions grew significantly as lending lagged, increasing 22.9 percent to $203.0 billion (from $165.7 billion). Id.

transactional responses to assuage the crisis by injecting credit into the financial markets. The Government has also amended regulations to ease the situation of market participants or to encourage private parties to participate in troubled markets. Finally, the Government undertook supervisory responses to correct conditions or behavior in the financial markets.

What was missing at first, however, was any significant reform of the financial services sector or the regulatory structure that supervises it. Gaps in the U.S. regulatory structure were at least partly responsible for the crisis—in particular, the fragmented structure of regulation, with specialized regulatory agencies operating across artificially segregated lines of services, such as banking, insurance, securities and futures.[6] However, until the enactment of the Dodd–Frank Wall Street Reform and Consumer Protection Act,[7] almost two years after the crisis erupted, little if anything concrete was done to address structural problems in the regulatory system that failed to supervise adequately the financial services sector and the risks it was generating. The first structural response to the crisis by the Congress, the Housing and Economic Recovery Act of 2008 (HERA),[8] transferred the supervisory and oversight responsi-

6. See Organisation for Economic Cooperation and Development (OECD), *Economic Survey of the United States 2008* (Dec. 9, 2008) (identifying structural causes of crisis). For a summary of the OECD economic survey of the United States, see http://www.oecd.org/document/32/0,3343,en_2649_33733_41803296_1_1_1_1,00.html. Similarly, a January 2009 GAO study cogently argued that the U.S. financial services regulatory system required a significant restructuring. U.S. Government Accountability Office, *Financial Regulation: A Framework for Crafting and Assessing Proposals to Modernize the Outdated U.S. Financial Regulatory System* (GAO-09-216, Jan. 8, 2009), available at 2009 WL 52168.

7. Pub. L. No. 111-203, 124 Stat. 1376 (2010) (codified at scattered sections of 2, 5, 7, 11, 12, 15, 18, 20, 22, 26, 28, 31, 42, 44 U.S.C.A.) (DFA).

8. Pub. L. 110-289, div. A (Federal Housing Finance Regulatory Reform Act of 2008), §§ 1001-1605, 122 Stat. 2654, 2659-2830 (July 30, 2008) (codified at 5 U.S.C.A. §§ 3132 note, 3132(a)(1)(B), (D)-(F), 5313, app. 3 § 11, 11 U.S.C.A. § 783, 12 U.S.C.A. §§ 250, 1422(11)-(12), 1423-1424, 1426(a)(3)(A), (B), (b)(1), (c)(4)(B), (d)(2), 1426a, 1427(a)-(d), (f), (i)(1), (*l*), 1428, 1430(a)-(b),

(j)(2)(A), (B)-(C), (12)(C)-(D), (k), 1430c, 1431(b)-(c), (f), (*l*), 1432, 1435, 1436, 1440, 1440a, 1441(b)(5), 1441a-1441b, 1442-1446, 1452 note, 1452(a)(2)(A)-(C), (b)(2), (d)(4), (h)(2), (4), 1454 note, 1454(a)(2), 1455(c)(2), (i), (j)(2), (*l*), 1456(e)-(f), 1701 note, 1701x note, 1708(e)(5), 1715z-23, 1717 note, 1717(b)(2), 1718(c)(2), 1719(g), 1723 note, 1723(b), 1723a(d)(3)(B), (k)(1), (m)-(n), 1787(c)(10(C)(i), 1813(I), 1820(d)(5)(B), 1821(d)(2)(F), (G), (e)(10)(C)(i), (m)(1), (6), (9), (15)-(16), (18), (n)(1)(A)-(B)(i), (E), (2)(A), (4)(C)-(D), (H), (5)(D), (8)(A)-(B), (11)-(13), (t)(2)(A)(vii), 1822, 1831o(j)(2), 1833(a)(3), (b)-(c), 3413(*o*), 4501 note, 4502(2), (8)-(11), (13), (19)-(20), (24), (25)-(31), 4511 note, 4511-4513, 4513a, 4513b, 4514, 4514a, 4515(a), (c)-(f), 4516-4521, 4523-4526, 4541-4548, 4561-4569, 4581-4588, 4588(c), 4611, 4612(a)-(f), 4613 note, 4613(a)-(b), 4614 note, 4614(a)-(f), 4615(b)(1)-(2), (c), 4616(a)(2), (b)(5), (7), (c), 4617, 4618, 4619(a)(3), 4622-4623(a)(1), 4624 note, 4624, 4631(a)-(e), 4632(a)-(e), 4633, 4634(a), 4635(a)-(b), 4636(a)-(d), (g), 4636a, 4636b, 4637-4642, 4715(a)(1), (4)-(5), 4716, 5101 note, 5101-5116, 15 U.S.C.A. §§ 78oo, 1639a, 7215(b)(5)(B)(ii)(II), 18 U.S.C.A. §§ 212, 657, 1006, 1014, 1905, 26 U.S.C.A.

bilities of the Office of Federal Housing Enterprise Oversight (OFHEO) over Fannie Mae and Freddie Mac[9] and the oversight responsibilities of the FHFB over the FHLBanks and the Office of Finance (which acts as the FHLBanks' fiscal agent) to a new independent executive branch agency, the Federal Housing Finance Agency (FHFA).[10]

Transactional responses. Much of the initial response by the Government was a series of attempts to spend its way out of the crisis. In September 2008, for example, the Treasury Department entered into senior preferred stock purchase agreements with the Federal National Mortgage Association (Fannie Mae) and the Federal Home Loan Mortgage Corporation (Freddie Mac), providing in effect protection to the holders of senior debt, subordinated debt, and mortgage-backed securities (MBS) issued or guaranteed by Fannie and Freddie.[11]

On October 3, 2008, Title I of the Emergency Economic Stabilization Act of 2008 (EESA)[12] created the Troubled Assets Relief Program (TARP) for the purchase of troubled assets from financial institutions. From the onset of the TARP, Treasury appeared to be improvising, unsure of even basic issues such as how to price the targeted assets.[13] By mid-October 2008, Treasury shifted

§ 414(*l*)(2)(G), 42 U.S.C.A. §§ 1437f note, 4012a(f)(3)(A), 44 U.S.C.A. § 3502(5)); redesignating 12 U.S.C.A. § 1422(2)–(9), (12)–(13) as § 1422(1)–(10); redesignating 12 U.S.C.A. § 4502(2)–(7), (8)–(12), (16)–(19) as § 4502(5)–(7), (12), (14)–(18), (21)–(23); redesignating 12 U.S.C.A. § 4614(c)–(d) as § 4614(d), (f); redesignating 12 U.S.C.A. § 4616(b)(5) as § 4616(b)(6); redesignating 12 U.S.C.A. § 4715(a)(1)–(2) as § 4715(a)(2)–(3); repealing 12 U.S.C.A. §§ 1422(1), (9)–(10), 1422a–1422b, 1427(f)(2), 1438(b), 1451 note, 4502(13)–(15), 4520(b), 4541, 4542, 4547–4548, 4562 note, 4589, 4616(b)(6), 4619–4621, 42 U.S.C.A. § 3534(d)).

9. See, e.g.,74 Fed. Reg. 2347 (Jan 15, 2009) (codified at 12 C.F.R. pt. 1250) (codifying FHFA authority and responsibility to oversee and enforce statutory requirements affecting flood insurance operations of Federal National Mortgage Association and Federal Home Loan Mortgage Corporation under the Flood Disaster Protection Act of 1973 (FDPA); implementing congressionally mandated adjustments to the civil money penalties applicable to violations of FDPA; replacing prior HUD regulations, 12 C.F.R. pt. 1773).

10. For extended discussion of the FHFA and its functions, see 1 MICHAEL

P. MALLOY, BANKING LAW AND REGULATION § 1.3.4 (1994 & Cum. Supp.).

11. U.S. Department of Treasury Office of Public Affairs, Fact Sheet: Treasury Senior Preferred Stock Purchase Agreement (Sept 7, 2008) available at http://www.treas.gov/press/releases/reports/pspa—factsheet—090708hp1128.pdf. In early September 2008, the Government placed Fannie Mae and Freddie Mac in conservatorship and replaced their management. Stephen Labaton & Edmund L. Andrews, *In Rescue to Stabilize Lending, U.S. Takes Over Mortgage Finance Titans*, N.Y. Times, Sept. 8, 2008, at A1. As in a bank conservatorship or receivership, the end result of the process could be the elimination of the value of private investment in the each of the two enterprises. *Id.*

12. Pub. L. No. 110–343, tit. I, §§ 101–136. 122 Stat. 3765, 3767–3800 (2008) (codified at 5 U.S.C.A. § 5315, 12 U.S.C.A. §§ 461 note, 1715z–23, 1823(c)(11), 1828(a), (c), 5211–5241, 15 U.S.C.A. § 1638 note, 1638(b)(2), 31 U.S.C.A. §§ 301, 3101).

13. See, e.g., Stephen Joyce, *Treasury Official Discusses Implementation Of $700 Billion Program to Buy Bad Assets*, BNA Banking Daily (Oct. 7,

direction[14] and began using TARP funds to purchase equity in troubled financial institutions (primarily nine large institutions) rather than purchasing troubled assets. The new approach prompted criticism[15] that Treasury has failed to require beneficiaries of its funding to use the capital infusions to strengthen the weak credit market.[16] The criticism was exacerbated by the apparent failure of government-assisted banks to increase lending. Treasury's Bank Lending Survey indicated that overall lending by financial institutions that received the largest amount of government investment had declined in February 2009.[17]

Treasury officials insisted that the Capital Purchase Program (CPP), under which Treasury was buying shares of preferred stock in selected financial institutions, taking in most cases a five percent dividend for the first few years, with an increase to nine percent, would be profitable in the long run.[18] Congressional concern grew over the excessive levels of executive compensation at institutions benefitting from the CPP.[19] By mid-November 2008, Treasury was

2008), available at http://news.bna.com (reporting on efforts of Treasury to implement TARP).

14. Cf. Thecla Fabian, Senate Finance Ranking Member Grassley Hammers Paulson on EESA Implementation, BNA Banking Daily (Nov. 14, 2008), available at http://news.bna.com (criticizing "repeated[ ] change[s] [of] direction" by Treasury and the Fed under EESA).

15. See, e.g., Levin: Treasury Needs Firm Commitment From Banks to Use New Funds for Loans, BNA Banking Daily, Oct. 20, 2008, available at http://news.bna.com; Malini Manickavasagam, Pelosi, Reid, Other Lawmakers Share Concern Over Banks' Possible TARP Misuse, BNA Banking Daily (Oct. 30, 2008), available at http://news.bna.com.

16. For contrary studies, arguing that bank lending had increased during the credit crisis, see V. Chari, L. Christiano, & P. Kehoe, Facts and Myths about the Credit Crisis (Federal Reserve Bank of Minneapolis Working Paper 666, Oct. 2008), available at http://www.minneapolisfed.org/publications_papers/pub_display.cfm?id=4062; Octavio Marenzi et al., Flawed Assumptions about the Credit Crisis: A Critical Examination of US Policymakers (Celent, Dec. 2009) (arguing that U.S. Government responses to credit crisis based on assumptions contradicted by government's own data), available at http://www.celent.com/PressReleases/20081210/

CreditCrisis20081212DRAFT.pdf. But see Ethan Cohen–Cole, Burcu Duygan–Bump, Jose Fillat, & Judit Montoriol–Gerriga, Minneapolis: Looking Behind the Aggregates:A Reply to "Facts and Myths About the Financial Crisis of 2008" (Federal Reserve Bank of Boston Working Paper No. QAU08–5, Nov. 2008) (disputing Minneapolis Fed paper), available at http://www.bos.frb.org/bankinfo/qau/wp/2008/qau0805.htm.

17. Mike Ferullo, *Survey Shows Slight Decline in Lending Among Banks Receiving Government Capital*, BNA Banking Daily (Apr. 16, 2009), available at http://www.bna.com. The February lending survey is available at http://www.financialstability.gov/latest/tg_041509.html.

18. The text of prepared remarks on the CPP by Interim Assistant Secretary for Financial Stability Neel Kashkari is available at: http://www.treas.gov/press/releases/hp1314.htm. See also Capital Purchases Will Turn a Profit For Taxpayers, Treasury's Kashkari Says, BNA Banking Daily (Dec. 8, 2008), available at http://news.bna.com (reporting on Assistant Secretary Kashkari's remarks).

19. See Pelosi, Reid Concerned About Excessive CEO Compensation at Banks Getting EESA Funds, BNA Banking Daily (Oct. 30, 2008), available at http://news.bna.com (reporting on congressional criticism of CEO compensation at EESA-aided firms participating

publicly moving away from its plan to buy mortgage-related assets. Instead, it was reportedly considering other uses for what remained of the original $700 billion in TARP funds.[20] Coincidentally, on November 14, 2008, the Administration reached agreement with congressional leaders to establish a TARP inspector general, and congressional leaders appointed three experts to the Congressional Oversight Panel, another EESA-mandated watchdog.[21] (The CPP officially ended on December 29, 2009, after Treasury closed the last ten CPP investments, worth about $29.3 million.[22])

By late November 2008, Treasury had completed a $40 billion purchase of American International Group (AIG) preferred stock and warrants through the TARP.[23] That transaction was part of a restructured rescue of AIG, in which the Fed reworked loans to the insurance company, relaxing some terms and offered two new lending facilities. In effect, AIG would use the proceeds from the Treasury transaction to reduce the credit extended by the Fed in September 2008.[24] In addition, the Fed initiated two programs to boost lending and limit damage from the weakening economy—(i) the Term Asset–Backed Securities Loan Facility (TALF), a $200 billion lending facility to facilitate purchases of loan-backed securities, with a Treasury pledge of $20 billion to assist the Fed in hedging the credit risk of possible defaults on the underlying credit exposure; and, (ii) a program to purchase up to $600 billion in

---

in CPP). Concern over excessive executive compensation in financial services firms led Treasury to issue an interim final rule, pursuant to EESA §§ 101 and 111, 12 U.S.C.A. §§ 5211, 5221, providing "guidance" about the EESA executive compensation and corporate governance provisions that apply to entities that receive TARP assistance. 74 Fed. Reg. 28,394 (2009) (codified at 31 C.F.R. pt. 30).

20. Aaron Lorenzo & R. Christian Bruce, Treasury Pulls Back From TARP Purchase Of Mortgage–Related Assets, Paulson Says, BNA Banking Daily (Nov. 13, 2008), available at http://news.bna.com.

21. R. Christian Bruce, Oversight of TARP Comes Into Focus With Action by White House, Pelosi, Reid, BNA Banking Daily (Nov. 17, 2008), available at http://news.bna.com. The members of the five-member TARP Congressional Oversight Panel are appointed by Speaker of the House (who appointed Richard H. Neiman, the N.Y. Superintendent of Banks), the House Republican Leader (Rep. Jeb Hensarling (R–Texas)), the Senate Majority Leader (Harvard Law

Professor Elizabeth Warren, who serves as chair) and the Senate Republican Leader (former Sen. John Sununu) each selecting one member. The fifth member is jointly selected by the Speaker and the Majority Leader (Damon Silvers, AFL–CIO associate general counsel). See R. Christian Bruce, McConnell Names Sununu to TARP Panel; Thacher, Proffitt Tapped to Advise Treasury, BNA Banking Daily (Dec. 18, 2008) (reporting on TARP panel).

22. Aaron Lorenzo, *Treasury Closes CPP Program With 10 Final Investments in Community Banks*, BNA Banking Daily, Jan. 5, 2010, available at http://www.bna.com.

23. Aaron Lorenzo, Treasury Completes $40 Billion Equity Buy In AIG; Transaction Proceeds to Repay Fed, BNA Banking Daily, Nov. 28, 2008, available at http://news.bna.com (reporting on AIG rescue).

24. For details concerning Treasury transactions conducted under the Emergency Economic Stabilization Act of 2008 see http://www.treasury.gov/initiatives/eesa/transactions.shtml.

mortgage-related assets, involving a commitment to buy up to $100 billion in direct debt issued by Fannie Mae, Freddie Mac, and the FHLBanks, and a commitment to purchase up to $500 billion in MBS guaranteed by Fannie Mae, Freddie Mac, and the Government National Mortgage Association (Ginnie Mae).[25] It was expected that the TALF would continue to operate through the Federal Reserve Bank of New York until Dec. 31, 2009.[26]

Also in November 2008, an economic assistance package for ailing Citigroup was finalized.[27] It involved an agreement by the Government to purchase approximately $27 billion in Citigroup stock, and the issuance of over $300 billion in guarantees with respect to mortgage-back securities. Combining features of the Capital Purchase Program (CPP), financial assistance such as AIG received, and troubled asset purchases under the TARP, the transaction required Citigroup to assume up to $29 billion in portfolio losses, and 10 percent of all losses thereafter, with Treasury, the FDIC, and the Fed each successively responsible for all remaining losses.[28] The arrangement banned dividend payments on common stock for three years without the consent of the regulators, established new regulatory approval requirements for executive compensation, and required Citigroup to adopt FDIC mortgage modification procedures.

TARP recipients have been paying back TARP loans in full since April 2009.[29] In June, American Express Co. repurchased a warrant it had issued to Treasury as a condition for receiving a total of $3.39 billion in TARP funds, including $74.4 million in dividends (an annualized return on investment of approximately 26 percent). In August 2009, Morgan Stanley announced that it would pay $950 million for warrants that it had issued to Treasury in exchange for TARP funds, a 20 percent annualized return.[30] With TARP funds being repaid, by November 2009 the Administration was beginning to consider other uses for TARP proceeds.[31] Under

---

25. See R. Christian Bruce & Aaron Lorenzo, Fed, Treasury Announce New Actions, BNA Banking Daily (Nov. 26, 2008), available at http://news.bna.com (reporting on TALF and MBS facility). For background information on Ginnie Mae, see www.ginniemae.gov.

26. Bruce & Lorenzo, supra.

27. R. Christian Bruce, Regulators Unveil Assistance Package To Back $300 Billion in Citigroup Assets, BNA Banking Daily (Nov. 25, 2008), available at http://news.bna.com.

28. For an interagency statement the Citigroup assistance, see http://www.

on federalreserve.gov/newsevents/press/bcreg/20081123a.htm.

29. Stephen Joyce, American Express Fully Repays TARP Loan By Making $340 Million Warrant Payment, BNA Banking Daily, July 31, 2009, available at http://www.bna.com.

30. Mike Ferullo, Morgan Stanley Buys TARP Warrants From Treasury Department for $950 Million, BNA Banking Daily, Aug. 10, 2009, available at http://www.bna.com.

31. Jonathan Nicholson, OMB's Orszag Says Administration Mulling "Reorienting" TARP to Help Cut Debt Load, BNA Banking Daily, Nov. 13, 2009, available at http://www.bna.com.

EESA § 120(b),[32] the TARP would expire on December 31, 2009, unless the Secretary of the Treasury submitted to Congress a written certification extending the program for two years from the date of enactment, i.e., October 3, 2010. On December 9, 2009, the Secretary extended TARP.[33] Controversy quickly grew over whether or not repaid TARP funds created renewed authority to initiate fresh rescues, i.e., whether TARP was a revolving fund.[34]

In the meantime, on February 17, 2009, the President signed the American Recovery and Reinvestment Act (ARRA) into law.[35] The ARRA was primarily a $787 billion economic stimulus package intended to create or preserve approximately 3.5 million jobs and to jump start the failing economy, but it does not address the serious problems affecting regulatory and supervisory structure applicable to the financial services industry.[36] Even Title V of the ARRA,[37] specifically dealing with financial services, has no intended effect on the regulatory structure itself.

Regulatory responses. In some instances, the regulatory response to the crisis adjusted regulatory requirements to create incentives for private firms to invest in troubled financial assets. For example, in September 2008, the Fed established a special lending facility that enabled depository institutions and bank holding companies (BHCs) to borrow from the Federal Reserve Bank of Boston on a nonrecourse basis if they used the proceeds of the loan to purchase certain types of asset-backed commercial paper (ABCP) from money market mutual funds.[38] To support this program, the Fed adopted, on an interim final basis, an exemption from its leverage and risk-based capital rules for ABCP held by a state member bank or BHC as a result of participation in the program.[39]

---

32. 12 U.S.C.A. § 5230(b).

33. http://www.treasury.gov/press/releases/tg433.htm.

34. Aaron Lorenzo, *Sens. Hatch, Lincoln, Corker Push to Block Treasury From Recycling Repaid TARP Funds,* BNA Banking Daily, June 23, 2009, available at http://www.bna.com.

35. Pub. L. No. 111–5, 111th Cong., 1st. Sess., 123 Stat. 115 (2009) (codified at scattered sections of 1, 6, 7, 12, 15, 16, 19, 20, 26, 28, 29, 31, 33, 38, 42, 47 U.S.C.A.) (ARRA).

36. See Ralph Lindeman, Obama Signs Stimulus Plan Into Law In Effort to Revive Slumping Economy, BNA Banking Daily (Feb. 18, 2009), available at http://news.bna.com (discussing ARRA). Additional details on the economic stimulus package is available at http://www.whitehouse.gov/assets/

documents/Recovery_Act_Health_Care_2–17.pdf.

37. ARRA, tit. V, 123 Stat. at 148–161 (2009) (codified at scattered sections of 15 U.S.C.A.).

38. See 73 Fed. Reg. 55,706 (2008) (discussing ABCP lending facility). See also 73 Fed. Reg. 55,708 (2008) (codified at 12 C.F.R. §§ 223.42(*o*), 223.56) (exempting on interim basis member banks from certain provisions of FRA §§ 23A, 23B to increase authority of member bank to purchase ABCP from affiliated money market mutual funds in connection with ABCP Lending Facility).

39. 73 Fed. Reg. at 55,707 (codified at 12 C.F.R. pt. 208, App. A, § III.C.1, App. B, § II; id. pt. 225, App. A, § III.C.1, App. D, § II) (implementing ABCP purchase policy for member banks and BHCs, respectively).

Effective January 30, 2009, the exemption was made permanent.[40]

On September 22, 2008, the Fed announced that Morgan Stanley and Goldman Sachs Group would convert immediately from investment banks to BHCs.[41] The move would subject the firms to Fed supervision, but it would also give them access to Fed credit facilities, and the extensive liquidity and funding resource of deposit-taking. There is no indication so far that the Fed has utilized its extensive supervisory authority over BHCs to shape the behavior of these investment banks. American Express followed the same path to BHC status in November 2008, again with no specific constraints on its behavior.[42]

Supervisory responses. In November 2008, the Office of the Comptroller of the Currency (OCC) created a new procedure for chartering—a "shelf charter"—that allows a well capitalized investor group to pre-qualify for a national bank charter, so that the group may actively compete in FDIC auctions of troubled institutions, secure in the knowledge that the group already has preliminary approval for a national charter into which it would fold the acquired entity.[43] If the FDIC accepts an investor group bid, the OCC would almost invariably grant a final charter, and if the bid is not accepted, the preliminary approval of the charter remains "on the shelf" to be used for other bids for up to 18 months.[44]

In February 2009, the interested regulators—Treasury, the OCC, the Fed, the FDIC, and the Office of Thrift Supervision (OTS), but not the National Credit Union Administration (NCUA)—unveiled the details of Treasury's Capital Assistance Plan (CAP),[45] which required "stress testing"[46] of, primarily, the 19 largest U.S. banking enterprises that held more than $100 billion in

---

40. 74 Fed. Reg. 6226 (2009) (codified at 12 CFR §§ 223.42(*o*), 223.56).

41. Malini Manickavasagam & Joe Tinkelman, Changing Face of Wall Street, Goldman, Morgan Become Banks, BNA Banking Daily, Sept. 23, 2008, available at http://pubs.bna.com/ip/bna/bbd.nsf/eh/A0B7C3F1Y3.

42. See Eric Dash, American Express to Become A Bank to Access the Bailout, N.Y. Times, Nov. 11, 2008, at B2 (reporting on American Express reorganization as BHC, in order to gain eligibility to Fed financial assistance).

43. Mike Ferullo, OCC Move to Create 'Shelf Charter' For Investors Welcomed by Banking Industry, BNA Banking Daily (Nov. 26, 2008), available at http://www.bna.

44. Id.

45. For background information on the CAP, see http://www.treas.gov/press/releases/tg40.htm. See also R. Christian Bruce, Capital Plan Gives Bank Firms Six Months To Raise Private Funds Following New Tests, BNA Banking Daily (Feb. 26, 2009), available at http://news.bna.com. (discussing CAP).

46. I.e., submission to "forward-looking economic assessments" that will test the ability of a subject enterprise to function and lend under two different macroeconomic scenarios: (i) a "consensus estimate" that forecasts an economic upturn in 2010; and (ii) a further significant economic downturn, factoring in

an environment with unemployment as high as 10.3 percent. For the methodology used in the stress tests,

assets. The release of the results of the stress tests on May 7, 2009, indicated that ten of the largest U.S. banking enterprises would need more capital to withstand worse-than-expected economic conditions (see Figure 8–1, *infra*), assuming a requirement of a Tier 1 capital-to-assets risk-based ratio of at least six percent, of which at least four percent must be common equity by the end of 2010.[47] The banks had thirty days to develop capital plans and six months to complete recapitalization. Stressed banking enterprises that failed to raise enough private capital would then be eligible for a federal capital injection if the pertinent supervisor approved. Enterprises that have already received funds under the CPP, which involved Treasury purchases of nonvoting preferred bank shares with a 5 percent dividend, would be permitted to exchange those sharees for the new CAP instruments—convertible 9 percent preferred shares, convertible, at the issuer's option, to common stock.

By contrast, based on a 2009 "stress test" survey by the Committee for European Banking Supervisors that gauged the capital adequacy of 22 of the largest EU cross-border banks, if the economy in 2009 declined by 5.7 percent of GDP and a projected 2.7 percent in 2010, their aggregate Tier 1 capital-assets ratio would remain above 8 percent.[48] Nor would any bank experience a decrease in Tier I ratio below 6 percent.[49]

Figure 8–1

2009 Stress Test Results—Ten Most Critical Financial Services Enterprises*

Enterprise	Capital Needs under stress (in $billions)
Bank of America Corp.	$33.9
Wells Fargo & Co.	$13.7
GMAC LLC	$11.5
Citigroup Inc.	$5.5
Regions Financial Corp.	$2.5
SunTrust Banks Inc.	$2.2
Morgan Stanley & Co. Inc.	$1.8
KeyCorp	$1.8
FifthThird Bancorp	$1.1
PNC Financial Services Group Inc.	$0.6

* Source: http://www.federalreserve.gov/newsevents/press/bcreg/bcreg2009 0507a1.pdf.

see http://www.federalreserve.gov/news events/press/bcreg/bcreg20090424a1.pdf.

47. For stress test results, see http:// www.federalreserve.gov/newsevents/ press/bcreg/bcreg20090507a1.pdf.

48. Joe Kirwin, *EU Declares Banking Sector Sound After Stress Tests on 22 Large Banks*, BNA Banking Daily, Oct. 2, 2009, *available at* http://www. bna.com. For background information on the CEBS stress tests, see http:// www.c-ebs.org.

49. Irwin, EU Declares, supra. Basel II capital adequacy requirements would require a minimum Tier I ratio of 4 percent. Id.

One neglected aspect of the response to the subprime crisis is state consumer protection law. This neglect stems in large part from the Federal Government's aggressive preemption initiative against state regulation of financial services,[50] epitomized by Watters v. Wachovia Bank, N.A.[51] The initiative blunted any "early warning response" that state regulation might have provided. In those instances where state authorities were able to intervene, the results have often been dramatic.[52]

§ 8.3   Institutions in Danger of Default

The federal bank regulatory agencies have a variety of statutory powers available to them to deal with troubled institutions,[1] from relatively informal techniques, through formal, statutorily established enforcement measures, and ending with formal resolution of failed institutions. Any combination of these may come into play with respect to an institution in danger of default. The optimal goal is to activate an appropriate power at an early enough stage to avoid more costly supervisory measures at a more advanced stage of the problem.[2] Figure 8–2, infra, illustrates the principal devices found along the continuum of techniques available to the regulators.

50. On the effect of federal preemption policies on state financial services regulation, see 1 MICHAEL P. MALLOY, BANKING LAW AND REGULATION § 1.3.9 (1994 & Cum. Supp.). *See generally* Mark E. Budnitz, *The Federalization and Privatization of Public Consumer Protection Law in the United States: Their Effect on Litigation and Enforcement*, 24 GA. ST. U. L. REV. 663 (2008).

51. 550 U.S. 1, 127 S.Ct. 1559 (2007). *See* Amanda Quester & Kathleen Keest, *Looking Ahead after Watters v. Wachovia Bank: Challenges for Lower Courts, Congress, and the Comptroller of the Currency*, 27 REV. BANKING & FIN. L. 187 (2007) (criticizing *Watters* for "deal[ing] a major blow to consumers by shielding operating subsidiaries of national banks from the reach of state banking officials, despite the states' demonstrated vigilance and success in consumer protection").

52. See, e.g., *Cuomo v. Clearing House Ass'n, L.L.C.*, ___ U.S. ___, 129 S.Ct. 2710 (2009) (holding state investigation of banking practices not preempted; rejecting preemption argument based on *Watters*); LaSalle Bank, N.A. v. Shearon, 19 Misc.3d 433, 850 N.Y.S.2d 871 (N.Y.Sup. 2008) (vindicating state

consumer protection policy in private suit involving home owner's claims against foreclosing bank).

§ 8.3

1. *See, e.g.*, OFFICE OF THE COMPTROLLER OF THE CURRENCY, THE DIRECTOR'S BOOK 7075 (1987) (describing supervisory tools available) ("DIRECTOR'S BOOK"). See generally MICHAEL P. MALLOY, BANKING AND FINANCIAL SERVICES LAW 557–570 (Durham, N.C.: Carolina Academic Press, 2d ed. 2005) (analyzing supervisory tools).

2. See, e.g., 12 U.S.C.A. §§ 1823(c)(4) (mandating least-cost resolution through use of FDIC financial assistance authority); 1823(c)(8) (concerning least-cost resolution); 1831o (mandating prompt regulatory action for troubled insured depository institutions); Credit Union Membership Access Act (CUMAA), Pub. L. No. 105–219, § 301(a), 112 Stat. 913, 923–929 (1998) (codified at 12 U.S.C.A. § 1790d) (requiring NCUA system of prompt corrective action indexed to each of five capital categories for federally insured credit unions).

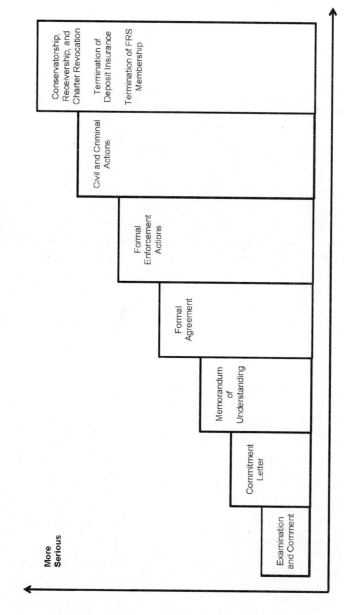

Figure 8-2

Supervisory Responses to Troubled Depository Institutions

(excluding financial assistance under, *inter alia*, 12 U.S.C.A. § 1823(c))

National banks are required by statute to submit periodic reports to the Comptroller of the Currency,[3] which should give early warning of potential problems in the condition of national banks. The Comptroller also has the authority to examine national banks on a periodic basis, generally once a year.[4] The examination process is given teeth by the enforcement powers available to the Comptroller under the Federal Deposit Insurance Act ("FDIA"),[5] to deal with violations of law and unsafe and unsound practices of national banks that may be uncovered in the course of an examination.[6]

Problems that suggest that an institution may be in danger of default often implicate the adequacy of its financial resources.[7] In cases where the capital of a national bank is impaired by losses, there exists—theoretically, but not in current practice—the power to require that any deficiencies in capital be paid in.[8] In addition, where the problem involves capital inadequacy, the statutory provisions for increases in capital may be invoked.[9]

If the problems of a national bank are caused by or are directly related to violations of the National Bank Act ("NBA") by or with the assent of the directors, personal liability provisions of the NBA may be invoked against management.[10] Violations of the NBA may also result in the imposition of civil money penalties under a provision of the NBA that is essentially the same as the general civil money penalty provision of the FDIA.[11] If the troubled condition of the institution is markedly moving towards "failing" status, there exists statutory authority, similar to that found in the general bankruptcy context, to frustrate transfers in contemplation of insolvency.[12]

The Fed has corresponding authority to deal with problem situations involving state-chartered Fed-member banks. Among

---

3. *Id.* § 161. See also *id.* § 1831m (requiring annual report on financial condition and management).

4. *Id.* § 1820(d)(1)–(3).

5. *Id.* § 1818, as amended, Dodd–Frank Wall Street Reform and Consumer Protection Act (DFA) §§ 172(b), 363(3), 367(7), 1090(1) Pub. L. No. 111-203, 124 Stat. 1376, 1439, 1522–1523, 1557, 2093–2094 (2010) (codified at 12 U.S.C.A. §§ 1818 note, 1818, 1818(t)(6)).

6. For discussion of the Comptroller's authority in this regard, see Chavers v. Fleet Bank (RI), N.A., 844 A.2d 666, 672–684 (R.I. 2004).

7. Some cases have argued that "problem" status is limited to financial

considerations. *Cf., e.g., First Nat'l Bank of Bellaire v. Comptroller of the Currency*, 697 F.2d 674 (5th Cir.1983) (limiting concept of "safety and soundness" under § 1818(b) to issues of financial soundness); *Gulf Fed. Sav. & Loan Ass'n v. Federal Home Loan Bank Bd.*, 651 F.2d 259 (5th Cir.1981), *cert. denied*, 458 U.S. 1121, 102 S.Ct. 3509 (1982) (same).

8. *Id.* § 55.

9. *See id.* § 57, 3907.

10. *Id.* § 93(a).

11. *Compare id.* § 93(b) (NBA civil money penalty provision), *with id.* § 1818(i)(2) (FDIA provision).

12. *See id.* § 91.

other things, knowing violations of many bank regulatory provisions of federal law (both civil and criminal) can result in personal liability of participating directors and officers of a member bank for all damages sustained by the bank, its shareholders, and other persons damaged by the violation.[13] Violations of certain provisions of the Federal Reserve Act ("FRA") may also result in the imposition of civil money penalties under a provision of the FRA that is essentially the same as the general civil money penalty provision of the FDIA.[14]

The Fed also has supervisory authority over bank holding companies ("BHCs"), and it has long followed a policy of requiring a BHC to act as a "source of strength" for its subsidiary banks.[15] The Fifth Circuit rejected the validity of the doctrine, as not based upon the BHCA, in MCorp Financial, Inc. v. Board of Governors.[16] However, there are indications in the Gramm–Leach–Bliley Act ("GLBA")[17] that the Congress has implicitly accepted the validity of the doctrine. The GLBA enhances the source of strength doctrine[18] by, in certain circumstances, protecting the federal banking agencies and the deposit insurance funds from claims brought by the bankruptcy trustee of the holding company or any other interested person for the return of capital infusions made by the company to the banking subsidiaries—i.e., it gives priority to source-of-strength capital transfers from a BHC to its subsidiary banks.[19] Such transferred assets must be those of an affiliate or a controlling shareholder of an insured depository institution (i.e., the BHC parent), and the transfer must be made by an affiliate or controlling shareholder of such insured depository institution.[20] The transfer must be to or for the benefit of an insured depository institution.[21] Claims barred by this provision would include a claim against a federal banking agency for monetary damages, return of assets, or

---

13. *See id.* § 503.

14. *Compare id.* § 504 (FRA provision), *with id.* § 1818(i)(2) (FDIA provision).

15. *See, e.g., Board of Governors v. First Lincolnwood Corp.,* 439 U.S. 234, 99 S.Ct. 505 (1978) (requiring source of strength showing by BHC resulting from spin-up from an existing bank). *See also* 12 C.F.R. § 225.4(a)(1) (articulating doctrine in Fed's BHC regulations); 52 Fed. Reg. 15,707 (1987) (setting forth statement of policy with respect to doctrine). See generally James F. Groth, Comment, *Can Regulators Force Bank Holding Companies to Bail Out Their Failing Subsidiaries?—An Analysis of the Federal Reserve Board's Source-of-Strength Doctrine,* 86 Nw. U.L. Rev. 112 (1991) (discussing doctrine).

16. 900 F.2d 852 (5th Cir.1990), *affirmed in part and reversed in part on other grounds,* 502 U.S. 32, 112 S.Ct. 459 (1991).

17. Pub. L. No. 106–102, Nov. 12, 1999, 113 Stat. 1338 (1999) (codified at scattered sections of 12, 15, 16, 18 U.S.C.A.).

18. It also clarifies situations in which a holding company is in bankruptcy proceedings to which its banking subsidiaries are not directly subject—precisely the situation at issue in *MCorp Financial, Inc.*

19. GLBA, § 730 (codified at 12 U.S.C.A. § 1828(t)).

20. 12 U.S.C.A. § 1828(t)(1).

21. *Id.*

for other legal or equitable relief in connection with such transfer, consistent with certain limitations.[22] The legislative history of the GLBA indicates that this provision is not intended to limit any right to seek direct review of an order or directive of a federal banking agency under the Administrative Procedure Act[23] in accordance with various banking statutes,[24] or to limit the rights of a claimant to bring suit against the United States for a breach of contract[25] or a taking under the Fifth Amendment to the Constitution.[26]

As to insured nonmember state banks, the FDIA also contains reporting provisions that give the Federal Deposit Insurance Corporation ("FDIC") an opportunity to identify potential problems at an early stage.[27] The FDIC also has available to it a variety of explicit statutory powers, ranging from denial or termination of insurance[28] to the ability to take enforcement action against the bank to reform its unsafe and unsound practices.[29]

In situations where a bank or savings association is in danger of default, the FDIC has fairly broad authority to act to aid an

---

22. *Id.* For purposes of this provision, a claim is defined as a cause of action based on federal or state law providing for the avoidance of preferential or fraudulent transfers or conveyances, or providing for similar remedies. The definition, however, explicitly excepts any claim based on actual intent to hinder, delay or defraud pursuant to such fraudulent transfer or conveyance law. *Id.* § 1828(t)(2).

23. *See, e.g.,* 5 U.S.C.A. §§ 551–559, 701–706 (setting forth APA provisions for rulemaking and adjudication, and for judicial review of agency action).

24. *See* 12 U.S.C.A. § 1848 (providing for judicial review of Fed action under BHCA).

25. *Cf. United States v. Winstar Corp.,* 518 U.S. 839, 116 S.Ct. 2432 (1996) (plurality opinion) (rejecting retrospective application of 1989 capitalization requirements to savings and loan holding company operating under pre–1989 rules; upholding contract liability in favor of company); *Admiral Financial Corp. v. United States,* 378 F.3d 1336 (Fed. Cir. 2004) (finding no contract liability); *La Van v. United States,* 382 F.3d 1340 (Fed.Cir. 2004) (holding *inter alia* that investors could recover expectancy damages under implied-in-fact contract); *Fifth Third Bank v. United States,* 518 F.3d 1368 (Fed. Cir. 2008) (finding contract liability); *Slattery v. United States,*

583 F.3d 800 (Fed.Cir. 2009) (upholding failed bank shareholder derivative action against FDIC for breach of contract). For discussion of the implications of *Winstar,* see Andrew Kull, *Disgorgement for Breach, the "Restitution Interest," and the Restatement of Contracts,* 79 Tex. L. Rev. 2021 (2001); Michael P. Malloy, *When You Wish Upon Winstar: Contract Analysis and the Future of Regulatory Action,* 42 St. Louis U. L.J. 409 (1998).

26. *See Conference Report on S. 900, reprinted in* 145 Cong. Rec. H11255–01, H11302 (1999) (discussing effect of GLBA section 730). *Cf. Castle v. United States,* 301 F.3d 1328 (Fed.Cir.2002) (holding neither enactment of FIRREA nor regulatory seizure of savings association for capital inadequacies constituted Fifth Amendment taking of property). *See generally* Susan Rose–Ackerman & Jim Rossi, *Disentangling Deregulatory Takings,* 86 Va. L. Rev. 1435 (2000) (discussing implications of *Winstar* for takings).

27. *See* 12 U.S.C.A. § 1817(a)(1). *See also id.* § 1831m (requiring annual report on financial condition and management).

28. *Id.* § 1818(a).

29. *See, e.g. id.* § 1818(b) (providing for cease and desist orders).

institution to avoid insolvency.[30] Should insolvency be unavoidable, the FDIC, as the federally designated receiver, has authority to act to resolve the insolvency and liquidate the bank.[31]

As to federally chartered or insured savings associations, the supervisory system currently administered by the Office of Thrift Supervision ("OTS") parallels that of the other federal regulators.[32] Under DFA § 312,[33] the functions and authority of the DOTS and the OTS will be transferred to the other federal regulators on the "transfer date,"[34] *i.e.*, 21 July 2011. Under DFA § 313,[35] the OTS and the position of the DOTS are then scheduled to be abolished 90 days after the transfer date.

Even without this transition, there is now a more or less unified body of federal enforcement provisions, the enforcement provisions of the FDIA, applicable regardless of the type of depository institution involved.[36] These enforcement provisions include the power to issue administrative cease and desist orders against violations of law or unsafe and unsound banking practices,[37] the power to suspend or remove members of management,[38] and the power to impose civil money penalties.[39]

30. *See, e.g. id.* § 1823(c) (providing for "open bank" financial assistance).

31. *See, e.g. id.* § 1821(d), (e), (j) (concerning powers of FDIC). *See also id.* 1823(f) (concerning assisted emergency interstate acquisitions). On the limits of FDIC authority to manage and resolve the liabilities of a failed institution, see *Battista v. F.D.I.C.*, 195 F.3d 1113 (9th Cir.1999), *cert. denied*, 531 U.S. 812, 121 S.Ct. 44 (2000) (holding that severance pay claims arising from FDIC repudiation, as receiver, of insolvent bank's employment contracts were subject to distribution priority scheme under § 1821(e), not distribution priority under § 1821(d)(11)(A)).

32. *See, e.g. id.* § 1464(d)(1)(A) (providing authority of Director of OTS under § 1818); 1467(a)–(b) (mandating periodic examinations of savings associations and affiliates); 1831m (requiring annual reports on financial condition and management).

33. See *id.* § 312(b) (codified at 12 U.S.C.A. § 5412(b)) (mandating transfer of functions).

34. *Id.* §§ 311(a), 313 (codified at 12 U.S.C.A. §§ 5411(a), 5413).

35. DFA § 313 (codified at 12 U.S.C.A. § 5413).

36. This includes not only insured banks but also insured savings associations, for the present primarily regulated at the federal level by the OTS. Until the transfer of authority to the OCC in July 2011, the Director of the OTS is the "appropriate Federal banking agency" authorized to impose formal enforcement measures with respect to insured savings associations. *Id.* §§ 1813(q), 1818(b)–(n), as amended, DFA, §§ 172(b), 312(c), 363(3), 367(7), 1090(1) (codified at 12 U.S.C.A. §§ 1813(q), 1818 note, 1818, 1818(t)(6)). However, the FDIC has authority to take formal enforcement action against savings associations, in certain specified circumstances, in the absence of action by the Director of the OTS. 12 U.S.C.A. § 1818(t).

The one exception to this unified body of federal enforcement provisions is the credit union, federally or state-chartered, which is subject to a parallel set of enforcement powers contained in the Federal Credit Union Act, *id.* 1786, administered by the National Credit Union Administration ("NCUA").

37. *See id.* § 1818(b).

38. *See id.* § 1818(e) (providing for removal authority).

39. *See id.* § 1818(i)(2).

§ 8.4   The Examination Process

Effective supervision is grounded on the process of annual on-site examinations and other specialized examinations conducted from time to time. A bank may first be apprised of its regulator's concerns over a particular practice or problem at the examiner's exit interview, when the examiner in charge of the periodic examination meets with management to discuss generally the supervisory concerns.[1] At that point, the bank's board of directors usually begins to formulate a response and to carry out a reasonable plan to correct any problems noted by the examiners.[2] The bank's regulator generally will encourage it to submit a response indicating the bank's proposed corrective plan with respect to any problems identified by the examination.[3] Most problems can be rectified during the period immediately following the end of the examination through informal discussion and correspondence with the regulator. This is the normal process of regulatory oversight.

§ 8.5   Remedial Actions

Occasionally, the significance of a given problem or the circumstances in which it arises may require more specific action to be taken by the regulator. The usual approach then is remedial action on the part of the regulator short of formal enforcement measures. Remedial action may take a variety of forms: a commitment letter, a memorandum of understanding, or a "formal agreement" between the depository institution and its regulator.[1] In the typical case, the remedial action specifies corrective measures that the institution or individuals affiliated with it need to take with respect to identified problems.

The commitment letter is the least severe remedial action taken by the regulators. The typical commitment letter is initiated by the institution's board of directors or trustees. The letter is signed by the board; identifies problems that require corrective action; and establishes a plan and timetable to remedy the problems.[2] The commitment letter is recommended by the regulator in situations in which the problems do not appear to represent a serious threat to the safety and soundness of the institution.[3]

---

§ 8.4

1. *See* Director's Book at 70.
2. *See id.* at 71.
3. *See, e.g., id.*

§ 8.5

1. The terminology varies somewhat from agency to agency, but the three devices discussed in this section are used in the practice of each of the agencies.

2. *See, e.g.,* OCC Quarterly Journal 122–123 (1991) (describing enforcement practices).

3. *See, e.g.,* Director's Book at 72 (noting that commitment letter "may be used by a bank that has been responsive and does not have a history of serious problems and when the problems identified do not pose an immediate or serious threat to the bank's health").

If the identified problems "do not pose an immediate or serious threat to the [institution] and when the agency expects that the [institution] will cooperate in correcting the problems so that legal enforcement will not be required to achieve compliance,"[4] a memorandum of understanding may be initiated by the regulator.[5] It memorializes the understanding between the regulator and the institution's board or an affiliated individual.[6] The memorandum, which is more formal than the commitment letter, is drafted by the regulator and lays out the institution's or individual's agreement to take specified actions within specified time periods to correct violations of law or unsafe and unsound practices.[7]

If the institution has more serious problems, but such problems are not critical and the institution's management is cooperative, the agency may use a "formal agreement."[8] A formal agreement is similar in form to a memorandum of understanding, but it has special statutory significance. Violation of the terms of a formal agreement constitutes grounds for the issuance of a cease and desist order,[9] and judicial enforcement of the order may then ensue.[10]

§ 8.6   Formal Enforcement Actions

In situations in which the problem is serious or the safety and soundness of the institution is threatened, and in situations in which the institution or affiliated individuals have not been cooperative or have already violated the terms of a remedial action, formal enforcement action may ensue.[1] Jurisdiction to take any formal

---

4. *Id.*

5. *See, e.g., Greene County Bank v. Federal Deposit Ins. Corp.,* 92 F.3d 633 (8th Cir.1996), *cert. denied,* 519 U.S. 1109, 117 S.Ct. 944 (1997) (upholding cease and desist order issued on basis of violation of memorandum of understanding regarding futures and securities activities that constituted unsafe and unsound banking practices).

6. DIRECTOR'S BOOK at 72.

7. *Id.*

8. *See generally* Deal, *Bank Regulatory Enforcement—Some New Dimensions,* 40 Bus. Law. 1319 (1985) (discussing status of formal agreements).

9. *See* 12 U.S.C.A. § 1818(b)(1) (providing for issuance of cease and desist order for violation of "any written agreement entered into with the agency"). For cases involving issuance of cease and desist orders based upon violation of formal agreements, see *Rapaport v. United States Dep't of Treasury, Office*

of Thrift Supervision, 59 F.3d 212 (D.C.Cir.1995), *cert. denied,* 516 U.S. 1073, 116 S.Ct. 775 (1996); *Groos Nat'l Bank v. Comptroller of Currency,* 573 F.2d 889 (5th Cir.1978). *Cf. CityFed Fin. Corp. v. Office of Thrift Supervision,* 58 F.3d 738 (D.C.Cir.1995) (involving net worth maintenance agreement); *Akin v. Office of Thrift Supervision, Dep't of Treasury,* 950 F.2d 1180 (5th Cir.1992) (same).

10. *See Groos Nat'l Bank,* 573 F.2d at 896–897 (involving cease and desist order issued for violation of written agreement concerning extensions of credit).

§ 8.6

1. *See generally* Michael P. Malloy, *Nothing to Fear but FIRREA Itself: Revising and Reshaping the Enforcement Process of Federal Bank Regulation,* 50 Ohio St. L. J. 1117 (1989) (discussing formal enforcement powers of federal depository institutions regulators).

enforcement action against insured depository institutions and persons affiliated with them is divided up among the federal regulatory agencies. This division of authority is illustrated in Figure 8–3, infra.

Figure 8–3

Principal Formal Enforcement Powers:
Division of Authority[2]

Agency	Institutions Subject to Agency's Enforcement Authority
Comptroller of the Currency	▶ national banks ▶ District of Columbia banks ▶ federal branches or agencies of foreign banks
Board of Governors of the Federal Reserve System ("Fed")	▶ state member insured banks (except District of Columbia banks) ▶ branches or agencies of foreign banks, with respect to provisions of FRA, 12 U.S.C.A. §§ 221 *et seq.*, made applicable under International Banking Act of 1978 ("IBA"), 12 U.S.C.A. §§ 3101 *et seq.*, and with respect to supervisory or regulatory proceedings arising from the authority given to the Fed under Section 7(c)(1) of the IBA, 12 U.S.C.A. § 3105(c)(1) ▶ foreign banks that do not operate insured branches ▶ agencies and commercial lending companies, other than federal agencies ▶ bank holding companies and subsidiaries of bank holding companies (other than a bank)
Federal Deposit Insurance Corporation	▶ state nonmember insured banks (except District of Columbia banks) ▶ foreign banks that operate insured branches
Director of the Office of Thrift Supervision[3]	▶ any savings associations ▶ savings and loan holding companies

For each type of institution covered by each regulatory agency's enforcement authority, "institution-affiliated persons" (IAPs) are also subject to that enforcement authority. The IAP term is a statutorily broadened concept of "insider" for purposes of formal enforcement authority under the federal banking laws. Figure 8–4, infra, illustrates the broad scope of this defined term.

2. Source: 12 U.S.C.A. § 1813(q), as amended, Dodd–Frank Wall Street Reform and Consumer Protection Act (DFA) § 312(c), Pub. L. No. 111–203, 124 Stat. 1376, 1522–1523 (2010) (codified at 12 U.S.C.A. § 1813(q)) (conforming amendments).

3. Under DFA § 312(b) (codified at 12 U.S.C.A. § 5412(b)) (the functions and authority of the DOTS and the OTS will be transferred to the OCC (for federal savings associations), the FDIC (for state savings associations), and the Fed (for savings and loan holding companies) on the "transfer date," *i.e.*, 21 July 2011. *Id.* §§ 311(a), 313 (codified at 12 U.S.C.A. §§ 5411(a), 5413). Under DFA § 313 (codified at 12 U.S.C.A. § 5413), the OTS and the position of the DOTS are scheduled to be abolished 90 days after the transfer date.

Figure 8–4

Institution–Affiliated Persons of Insured Depository Institutions[4]

Traditional Insiders	▶ directors ▶ officers ▶ employees ▶ controlling stockholders (other than a bank holding company) ▶ agents
Acquiring Individuals	▶ persons who have filed or are required to file change-in-control notice under 12 U.S.C.A. § 1817(j)
Management Participants	▶ any of the following persons who participates in the conduct of the affairs of an insured depository institution: —shareholder (other than a bank holding company) —consultant —shareholder (other than a bank holding company) —consultant —joint venture partner —any other person determined by the appropriate federal banking agency (*see supra* Figure 8–2) to be a participant
Independent Contractors	▶ any independent contractor, *including any attorney, appraiser, or accountant*, who *knowingly or recklessly* participates in: —any violation of any law or regulation —any breach of fiduciary duty —any unsafe or unsound practice that caused or is likely to cause more than minimal financial loss to, or significant adverse effect on, insured depository institution

The category of independent contractors who may be considered IAPs may raise questions about outside counsel's involvement in a depository institution's business decisions. The "u4" IAPs are as much subject to administrative enforcement by the banking agencies as the institutions that they serve, but there are few cases considering the application of the IAP definition to them.[5]

4. Source: 12 U.S.C.A. 1813(u), as amended, DFA, § 312(c), (codified at 12 U.S.C.A. § 1813(u)) (conforming amendment).

5. *See, e.g.*, Grant Thornton, LLP v. Office of Comptroller of the Currency, 514 F.3d 1328 (D.C.Cir. 2008) (holding accounting firm merely performing external audit not IAP); *Lindquist & Vennum v. F.D.I.C.*, 103 F.3d 1409 (8th Cir. 1997), *cert. denied sub nom. Donohoo v. Federal Deposit Ins. Corp.*, 522 U.S. 821, 118 S.Ct. 77 (holding attorney and law firm not IAP in absence of knowledge of critical facts); *Cavallari v. Office of Comptroller of Currency*, 57 F.3d 137 (2d Cir. 1995) (holding outside counsel as IAP when actively advising bank and bank president in structuring series of loans); *Oberstar v. F.D.I.C.*, 987 F.2d 494 (8th Cir. 1993) (holding potential investor in bank with proxies to vote controlling shareholders' shares constituted IAP); *Paul v. Office of Thrift Supervision*, 763 F.Supp. 568 (S.D.Fla. 1990), *affirmed sub nom. Paul v. Ryan*, 948 F.2d 1297 (1991) (holding IAP definition encompassed depository institution officer-shareholder after receivership initiated).

The principal formal enforcement powers that may be applied by the appropriate federal regulatory agency against an insured depository institution or institution-affiliated person are discussed in the sections that follow. Figure 8–5, *infra*, identifies the major, generally applicable enforcement powers available to the regulators.

Figure 8–5

Generally Applicable Enforcement Authorities[6]

Formal Enforcement Power	Authority
Termination of Insurance	▶ authority granted to FDIC under 12 U.S.C.A. § 1818(a)(2); termination of insurance for money laundering or cash transaction reporting offenses under 12 U.S.C.A. § 1818(w)
Termination of Federal Reserve Membership	▶ termination required on termination of deposit insurance, *per* 12 U.S.C.A. § 1818(*o*)
Cease-and-Desist Orders	▶ proceedings authorized for each agency, *per* 12 U.S.C.A. § 1818(b) ▶ temporary cease-and-desist orders available under 12 U.S.C.A. § 1818(c)
Capital Directive	▶ § 1818 powers available to remedy unsafe and unsound capital levels, by capital directive *per* 12 U.S.C.A. § 3907(b)
Suspension and Removal of Management, Insiders, and Participants	▶ general authority includes power to prohibition participation, as well as removal from office, under 12 U.S.C.A. § 1818(e) ▶ Summary suspension or removal of institution-affiliated party charged with felony authorized under 12 U.S.C.A. § 1818(g)
Civil Money Penalties	▶ First tier (12 U.S.C.A. § 1818(i)(2)(A)): —applicable to violation of law or regulation, final order or temporary order, condition imposed in writing by agency, written formal agreement —civil penalty of not more than $5,000 per day, per violation ▶ Second tier (12 U.S.C.A. § 1818(i)(2)(B)): —pattern of misconduct that causes or is likely to cause more than a minimal loss, or results in pecuniary gain or other benefit —involves first-tier violation; *recklessly* engages in unsafe or unsound practice; or breaches fiduciary duty; —civil penalty of not more than $25,000 per day per violation, practice, or breach ▶ Third tier (12 U.S.C.A. § 1818(i)(2)(C)): —knowing first-or second-tier violation *and* knowingly or recklessly causes substantial loss or substantial pecuniary gain or other benefit —civil penalty not more than maximum amount, per day, per violation, practice, or breach, of $1,000,000 or (in case of institution) the lesser of $1,000,000 or one percent of total assets

6. Source: 12 U.S.C.A. §§ 1818, 3907(b), as amended, DFA, §§ 172(b), 363(3), 367(7), 1090(1) (codified at 12 U.S.C.A. §§ 1818 note, 1818, 1818(t)(6)).

§ 8.7 Cease and Desist Orders

The cease and desist order[1] is the administrative equivalent of an injunction. It is the typical response of the regulator when there is a need to increase the formality and seriousness of the supervisory response to the problem activities of an institution.[2] The regulators can also issue temporary cease and desist orders.[3] Temporary orders are effective upon service, and they remain in effect (absent court action to the contrary[4]) until the completion of the cease and desist proceedings, or in certain cases, until the regulator determines by examination or otherwise that the books and records are accurate and reflect the institution's financial condition.[5]

Prior to 1989, temporary cease and desist orders were available to deal with such exigencies as violations or threatened violations of law or unsafe or unsound practices that were "likely to cause insolvency or substantial dissipation of assets or earnings" of a depository institution or were "likely to seriously weaken [its] condition ... or otherwise seriously prejudice the interests of its depositors" during the pendency of a cease and desist proceeding.[6] However, the Financial Institutions Reform, Recovery, and Enforcement Act of 1989 ("FIRREA")[7] amended this authority so that issuance of a temporary order is now possible not only where the violation or practice is likely to cause insolvency of the depository institution involved, but also where (1) the violation or order is likely to cause "*significant*," rather than "substantial," dissipation of assets or earnings of the depository institution, a change in standard that was intended to "lower the agencies' burden of proof ... and ... cover anything more than a minimal or nominal dissipation of assets;"[8] or (2) the violation or practice is likely to

§ 8.7

1. See 12 U.S.C.A. §§ 1786(e) (credit unions); 1818(b) (all other insured depository institutions). *See generally Wachtel v. Office of Thrift Supervision*, 982 F.2d 581 (D.C.Cir.1993) (holding order for restitution of failed bank's asset deficit requires showing of recklessness or unjust enrichment under 1818(b)(6)(a)).

2. *See, e.g.*, DIRECTOR'S BOOK at 73 (noting that such orders issue "most often when the agency is not confident that bank management will take the necessary corrective action or when the problems are so severe that a lesser action cannot be justified").

3. *See* 12 U.S.C.A. §§ 1786(f) (credit unions); 1818(c)(1) (all other insured depository institutions). On the use of temporary cease and desist orders, see *Landmark Land Co., Inc. v. Office of Thrift Supervision*, 990 F.2d 807 (5th Cir.1993).

4. *See* 12 U.S.C.A. §§ 1786(f)(2) (credit unions); 1818(c)(3)(B)(ii) (all other insured depository institutions). On review of temporary cease and desist orders, see *CityFed Fin. Corp. v. Office of Thrift Supervision*, 58 F.3d 738 (D.C.Cir.1995); *Parker v. Ryan*, 959 F.2d 579 (5th Cir.1992).

5. *Id.* §§ 1786(f)(3)(B)(ii)(I)–(II) (credit unions); 1818(c)(3)(B)(ii)(I)–(II) (all other insured depository institutions).

6. 12 U.S.C.A. § 1818(c)(1) (1982).

7. Pub. L. No. 101–73, 103 Stat. 183 (1989) (codified at scattered sections of 12 U.S.C.A.).

8. H. R. Conf. Rep. No. 222, 101st Cong., 1st Sess. 444 (1989).

"weaken" (rather than "seriously weaken") the condition of the bank or otherwise *"prejudice"* (rather than "seriously prejudice") the interests of the institution's depositors.[9]

Temporary cease and desist orders can include an order restricting the growth of the depository institution involved.[10] They are also available where the books and records of an institution are so inaccurate that the enforcing regulator cannot determine, in the normal supervisory process, the financial condition of the involved depository institution, or cannot determine the details or purpose of a transaction that may have a material effect on the financial condition of the institution.[11]

§ 8.8 Suspension and Removal of Management and Affiliated Persons

Suspension and removal of management and affiliated control persons are also specifically authorized.[1] This authority was substantially amended by FIRREA in 1989.[2] Removal or prohibition of participation of an institution-affiliated person requires a determination, *inter alia*, of actual or probable "financial loss or other damage," "prejudice[ ]" to depositors' interests, or "financial gain or other benefit" to such person,[3] rather than "substantial financial loss" or "serious prejudice[ ]" as was the case prior to FIRREA.[4] These changes were intended to "allow[ ] the regulatory agencies to proceed with a removal or prohibition action . . . without requiring the agencies to quantify the harm or prejudice."[5]

In situations in which a director, officer, or affiliated person of an insured depository institution has been charged with a felony involving dishonesty or breach of trust, summary suspension or removal is also a possibility.[6] FIRREA expanded this authority to

---

9. 12 U.S.C.A. §§ 1786(f)(1) (credit unions); 1818(c)(1) (all other insured depository institutions).

10. *Id.* §§ 1786(f)(1) (credit unions); 1818(c)(1) (all other insured depository institutions). *See Spiegel v. Ryan*, 946 F.2d 1435 (9th Cir.1991), *cert. denied*, 503 U.S. 970, 112 S.Ct. 1584 (1992) (discussing § 1818(c) (1)).

11. 12 U.S.C.A. §§ 1786(f)(3)(A) (credit unions); 1818(c)(3)(A) (all other insured depository institutions).

§ 8.8

1. 12 U.S.C.A. §§ 1786(g) (credit unions); 1818(e)(1)–(2) (all other insured depository institutions). There is also authority for the federal regulators to disapprove the proposed addition of any individual to the board of directors or

the employment of any individual as a senior executive officer of depository institutions in certain specified circumstances. *See id.* § 1790a (credit unions); § 1831i (all other insured depository institutions).

2. *See id.* §§ 1786(g)(1) (amended FCUA); 1818(e)(1) (corresponding FDIA provisions).

3. *Id.* §§ 1786(g)(1)(B)(i)–(iii) (credit unions); 1818(e)(1)(B)(i)–(iii) (all other insured depository institutions).

4. 12 U.S.C.A. §§ 1786(g)(1), 1818(e)(1) (1982).

5. H. R. Conf. Rep. No. 222, 101st Cong., 1st Sess., at 444.

6. 12 U.S.C.A. §§ 1786(i) (credit unions); 1818(g) (all other insured depository institutions).

include state criminal proceedings as a ground for initiating summary suspension or removal.[7]

§ 8.9 Civil Money Penalties

Civil money penalties may also be imposed by the regulators in appropriate cases.[1] These penalties were expanded and increased in 1989.[2] Three tiers of civil money penalties against depository institutions and institution-affiliated parties now exist. These penalties are periodically adjusted for inflation.[3] Among other things, the penalties apply to failures to submit timely and accurate reports as required by federal law.[4]

The first tier imposes penalties not exceeding $5,000 per day during the continuation of a violation of any law or regulation, of any order or temporary order, of any written condition imposed in connection with the grant of an application or other request, or of any written agreement between any agency and a depository institution.[5]

The second tier imposes penalties not exceeding $25,000 per day during the continuation of any such violation, recklessly engaging in an unsafe or unsound practice, or breach of a fiduciary duty, where the violation, practice, or breach is part of a "pattern of

---

7. See FIRREA, § 906(a)(1) (codified at 12 U.S.C.A. § 1818(g)(1)) (FDIA provision); *id.* § 906(b)(1) (codified at 12 U.S.C.A. § 1786(i)(1)) (corresponding FCUA provision).

§ 8.9

1. 12 U.S.C.A. §§ 1786(k)(2) (credit unions); 1818(i)(2) (all other insured depository institutions).

2. See FIRREA, § 907 (codified at 12 U.S.C.A. §§ 93(b), 481, 504, 505(1), 1467a(i), 1786(k)(2), 1817(j) (16), 1818(i)(2), 1828(j)(4)–(5), 1847, 1972(2)(F)). *See generally Pharaon v. Board of Governors*, 135 F.3d 148 (D.C.Cir.1998), *cert. denied*, 525 U.S. 947, 119 S.Ct. 371 (discussing civil money penalty provision under Bank Holding Company Act, 12 U.S.C.A. § 1847); *Greenberg v. Comptroller of the Currency*, 938 F.2d 8 (2d Cir.1991) (involving OCC suit against director after separation from service); *United States v. Godbout–Bandal*, 232 F.3d 637 (8th Cir. 2000), *cert. denied sub nom. Donohoo v. United States*, 534 U.S. 825, 122 S.Ct. 63 (2001) (holding that, where assessment of civil penalty provides administrative procedure for assessing penalty, general statute of limitations for collection of civil penalties does not run until final determination in administrative process).

3. See, e.g., 69 Fed. Reg. 56,929 (2004) (codified at 12 C.F.R. 263.65) (amending Fed rules of practice for hearings to adjust maximum CMP amounts); 69 Fed. Reg. 60,077 (2004) (codified at 12 C.F.R. 747.1001) (amending NCUA CMP provisions); 69 Fed. Reg. 61,301 (2004) (codified at 12 C.F.R. 308.116, 308.132(c)) (amending FDIC rules of practice and procedure); 69 Fed. Reg. 64,249 (2004) (codified at 12 C.F.R. 509.103(c)) (amending OTS rules of practice and procedure in adjudicatory proceedings); 69 Fed. Reg. 65,067 (2004) (codified at 12 C.F.R. 19.240; removing 12 C.F.R. 19.241) (amending OCC rules of practice and procedure), per the Federal Civil Penalties Inflation Adjustment Act of 1990, as amended by the Debt Collection Improvement Act of 1996, 28 note.

4. See 12 U.S.C.A. §§ 161, 164, 324, 1782(a)(3), 1817(a)(1), 1847(d).

5. See, e.g., id. U.S.C.A. § 1818(i)(2)(A) (providing for civil money penalties applicable to insured depository institutions under FDIA).

misconduct," causes more than minimal loss to the depository institution, or results in pecuniary gain or other benefit to such party.[6]

The third tier imposes maximum civil money penalties, which may amount to as much as $1 million per day[7] during the continuance of such a violation, practice, or breach, in situations where the depository institution or institution-affiliated party knowingly or recklessly causes substantial loss to the institution or substantial pecuniary gain or other benefit through the violation, practice, or breach.[8]

§ 8.10   Capital Directives

Because of the critical importance of adequate capital supervision, in appropriate circumstances a regulator may issue to an individual institution a capital directive that establishes higher capital requirements for the individual institution than might otherwise apply under generally applicable regulations.[1] The institution is required by the order to achieve these capital levels within a specified period of time.[2]

§ 8.11   Other Specialized Enforcement Devices

There is a broader range of enforcement authorities available to the federal regulators of depository institutions than the generally applicable devices discussed above.[1] Among the more extreme are such enforcement powers as charter revocation[2] and deposit insurance termination.[3]

Other more specialized enforcement powers available to these federal regulators include, *inter alia*, (1) civil money penalty provisions for violations of specified provisions of the Federal Reserve Act;[4] (2) criminal and civil penalty provisions for violations of the Bank Holding Company Act ("BHCA");[5] (3) civil money penalties

---

6. *See, e.g., id.* U.S.C.A. § 1818(i)(2)(B).

7. On the determination of the maximum penalties, *see, e.g., id.* U.S.C.A. § 1818(i)(2)(D). Mitigating factors with respect to the determination of any specific penalty under any of the three tiers are specified in the statutory provisions. *See, e.g., id.* U.S.C.A. § 1818(i)(2)(G).

8. *See, e.g., id.* § 1818(i)(2)(C).

§ 8.10

1. 12 U.S.C.A. § 3907(a)(1), (b)(2).

2. *See* DIRECTOR'S BOOK at 74.

§ 8.11

1. *See generally* Stephen Huber, *Enforcement Powers of the Federal Banking Agencies*, 7 Ann. Rev. Banking L. 123 (1988) (providing exhaustive discussion of state and federal criminal and formal and informal civil enforcement authorities).

2. *See, e.g.,* 12 U.S.C.A. §§ 93 (national bank charters); 1766 (federal credit union charters).

3. *See id.* § 1818(a).

4. *Id.* §§ 504, 505.

5. *Id.* § 1847.

provisions for violations of the antitying provisions of the BHCA;[6] (4) enforcement authority under the Depository Institutions Management Interlocks Act ("DIMIA"),[7] which intersects the authority granted under the FDIA and the FCUA;[8] (5) authority under Section 12(i) of the Securities Exchange Act of 1934[9] with respect to the securities of depository institutions registered under that Act; and, (6) federal criminal penalties for knowing participation in any institution's affairs in violation of a removal or prohibition order,[10] and criminal penalties for knowing unauthorized participation by a convicted person.[11]

§ 8.12   Institutions in Default

The remainder of this chapter explores regulatory problems with respect to the failure of a depository institution, *i.e.*, an "institution in default."[1] As in the case of the bankruptcy of a general business corporation, a depository institution failure usually involves a situation of insolvency.[2] However, the process for

---

6. *Id.* § 1972(2)(F).

7. *Id.* §§ 3201 et seq.

8. *See, e.g. id.* §§ 1786(g)(3) (concerning violations of DIMIA; suspension and removal authority of FCUA); 1818(e)(3) (same; suspension and removal authority of FDIA).

9. 15 U.S.C.A. § 78*l*(i).

10. *See* 12 U.S.C.A. §§ 1786(*l*) (credit unions); 1818(j) (all other insured depository institutions).

11. *See id.* §§ 1785(d) (credit unions); 1829 (all other insured depository institutions).

§ 8.12

1. *See, e.g.*, 12 U.S.C.A. § 1813(x)(1) (defining "default" as adjudication or other official determination under which conservator, receiver, or other custodian is appointed for insured depository institution). Such a situation should be distinguished from one in which a depository institution decides voluntarily to dissolve. *See, e.g. id.* §§ 181–182 (providing for voluntary dissolution of national bank).

2. *See, e.g. id.* §§ 191(1) (specifying grounds for appointment of receiver of national bank, referring to § 1821(c)(5)); 1821(c)(5)(A) (specifying depository institution's obligations greater than assets as grounds for appointment of receiver); 1821(c)(5)(F) (specifying inability to meet obligations as they come due as grounds for appointment of receiver); 1821(c)(5)(G) (specifying depletion of capital as grounds for appointment of receiver); 1821(c)(5)(H) (specifying violation of law or regulation, or unsafe or unsound practice or condition likely to cause insolvency as grounds for appointment of receiver). Other grounds for the appointment of a receiver or conservator do not directly relate to a condition of insolvency. These grounds are:

    (1) substantial dissipation of assets or earnings due to violation of any statute or regulation or any unsafe or unsound practice (*id.* § 1821(c)(5)(B));

failing depository institutions is distinguishable from a general business bankruptcy in two important respects.

First, depository institutions are not subject to the general federal law with respect to bankruptcy.[3] Determination of default by the depository institution's primary regulator in this regard is exclusive, and results in the institution being placed into conservatorship[4] or receivership.[5]

Second, with the exception of "systemically significant financial institutions,"[6] a holding company of a depository institution is focuses exclusively on the regulatory regime applicable to the failing depository institution.

---

(2) unsafe or unsound condition to transact business (*id.* § 1821(c)(5)(C));

(3) willful violation of a final cease-and-desist order (*id.* § 1821(c)(5)(D));

(4) concealment of the institution's books, papers, records or assets, or any refusal to submit the institution's books, papers, records or affairs for inspection to any examiner or to any lawful agent of the appropriate federal or state supervisor (*id.* § 1821(c)(5)(E));

(5) consent to the appointment by resolution of board of director or of shareholders or members (*id.* § 1821(c)(5)(I); *see also id.* § 1821(c)(12) (directors not liable for such consent or acquiescence));

(6) cessation of insured status of the institution (*id.* § 1821(c)(5)(J));

(7) undercapitalization, under specified circumstances (*id.* § 1821(c)(5)(K)); or,

(8) critical undercapitalization or substantially insufficient capital (*id.* § 1821(c)(5)(L)).

In situations of undercapitalization (grounds (7) and (8), *supra*), additional authority exists for the appropriate federal banking agency to appoint the FDIC as conservator or receiver of any insured state depository institution. *See* 12 U.S.C.A. § 1821(c)(9). *See also id.* § 1821(c)(11) (providing FDIC opportu-

nity to appoint itself as receiver before appropriate federal banking agency may appoint conservator). The FDIC has additional authority to appoint itself as conservator or receiver under any of the grounds identified, if such appointment is necessary to reduce or prevent a loss to the deposit insurance fund. *See id.* § 1821(c)(10).

Appointment of a conservator or receiver does not violate the Fifth Amendment takings clause, since those who enter the banking industry do so voluntarily. *California Housing Sec. v. United States*, 959 F.2d 955, 958 (Fed.Cir.), *cert. denied*, 506 U.S. 916, 113 S.Ct. 324 (1992). Use of the appointment authority is "entitled to a presumption of regularity," and judicial review is narrow. *Franklin Sav. Ass'n v. Director, Office of Thrift Supervision*, 934 F.2d 1127, 1141 (10th Cir.1991), *cert. denied*, 503 U.S. 937, 112 S.Ct. 1475 (1992).

3. *See* 11 U.S.C.A. § 109 (expressly exempting banks and other depository institutions from recourse to bankruptcy protection).

4. *See, e.g.,* 12 U.S.C.A. §§ 202–206, 209, 211 (providing conservatorship rules for national bank).

5. *See, e.g. id.* §§ 191–199 (receivership rules for national bank). *See also id.* § 91 (transfers in contemplation of insolvency).

6. *See* § 8.20, *infra* (discussing SSFIs).

itself subject to the general federal bankruptcy laws.[7] However, since the financial condition of the principal operating subsidiary of such a holding company (*i.e.*, its subsidiary bank or savings association) is likely to be the cause of the parent's insolvency, the situation will naturally be a very complicated one, with the parent subject to the Bankruptcy Code and the principal subsidiary subject exclusively to federal statutes governing the default of depository institutions.[8] For the sake of clarity, the discussion that follows

§ 8.13   Insured Deposit Payoff

The ultimate liability of the federal government with respect to a depository institution in default is its obligation for the insured deposits of the institution.[1] However, the resolution of failures by the FDIC has varied, and since 1945 the insured deposit payoff approach has not been favored.[2]

Originally, the FDIC tended to resolve failures by either paying off its deposit insurance obligation or by allowing the failing bank to be acquired by another institution.[3] In a deposit payoff transaction, illustrated in Figure 8–6, *infra*, the FDIC as receiver would hold any net assets of the failed institution, against which uninsured depositors, other unsecured creditors, and the FDIC itself as insurer became general creditors.

7. *Cf.* 11 U.S.C.A. § 109 (providing exemption does not explicitly apply to holding company). *See generally MCorp Fin., Inc. v. Board of Governors*, 900 F.2d 852 (5th Cir.1990), *aff'd in part and rev'd in part on other grounds*, 502 U.S. 32, 112 S.Ct. 459 (1991) (discussing 109 of the Bankruptcy Code).

8. *See, e.g., MCorp Fin., supra* (illustrating complications inherent in failure of depository institution and holding company parent).

§ 8.13

1. *See* 12 U.S.C.A. § 1821(a)(1), *as amended*, Dodd–Frank Wall Street Reform and Consumer Protection Act (DFA) §§ 343(a), 363(5), Pub. L. No.

111–203, 124 Stat. 1376, 1544–1545, 1552–1553 (2010) (codified at 12 U.S.C.A. §§ 1821, 1821(a)(1)) (providing for insurance of deposit to statutory maximum).

2. *See generally* U.S. DEPARTMENT OF THE TREASURY, MODERNIZING THE FINANCIAL SYSTEM, DISCUSSION CHAPTER I, AT I–30–I–45 (FEB. 1991), *reprinted in* Fed. Banking L. Rep. (CCH) No. 1377, Pt. II (Feb. 14, 1991) (discussing FDIC treatment of bank failures) ("MODERNIZATION REPORT").

3. MODERNIZATION REPORT at I–30. Between 1935 to 1945, approximately 390 failures were resolved by either payoff or merger. *Id.*

Figure 8–6

Deposit Payoff

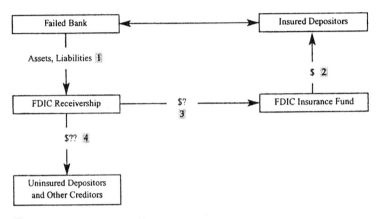

1 Failed bank placed in receivership
2 Insured deposits paid off by FDIC
3 Fund repaid out of net assets
4 Other obligations repaid out of net assets

The FDIA was amended in August 1993, to provide a national depositor preference for amounts realized from the liquidation or other resolution of FDIC-insured depository institutions.[4] The amendment requires that distributions from all future receivership estates be made in the following order: (1) administrative expenses of the receiver; (2) deposit liability claims; (3) other general or

4. Pub. L. No. 103–66, 107 Stat. 312 (1993) (codified at 12 U.S.C.A. § 1821(d)(11)).

senior liabilities of the institution, other than subordinated obligations or shareholder claims; (4) subordinated obligations; and, (5) shareholder claims.[5]

The legislation applies to all receiverships of insured institutions established after its enactment date (August 10, 1993),[6] and it supersedes any inconsistent state or other federal distribution provisions.[7]

§ 8.14 Modified Insured Deposit Payoff

In 1984, the FDIC initiated a "modified payoff" approach as a variation on the traditional insured deposit payoff.[1] Under this approach, insured deposits would be paid off, and a sum equal to a relatively conservative estimate of the net realizable assets in the receivership would be paid out to the uninsured deposits, with additional payments to be made in the future if collections exceeded the estimate.[2] This approach eventually led to the development of the "insured deposit transfer,"[3] in which an acquiring bank would pay a premium for insured deposits and certain assets of a failed bank, thus realizing the net asset value up front. These related approaches are illustrated in Figure 8–7, *infra.*

---

5. 12 U.S.C.A. § 1821(d)(11).

6. *Id.* § 1821 note.

7. *Id.* § 1821(d)(11). For FDIC rules interpreting and implementing the amendment, see 58 Fed. Reg. 43,069 (1993) (codified at 12 C.F.R. Pt. 360) (interim rule); 58 Fed. Reg. 67,662 (1993) (redesignating 12 C.F.R. §§ 360.1–360.3 as §§ 360.2–360.4) (final rule), *as amended*, 60 Fed. Reg. 35,487 (1995) (codified at 12 C.F.R. §§ 360.3(f), 360.4).

§ 8.14

1. MODERNIZATION REPORT at I–32.

2. *Id.*

3. *Id.*

Figure 8–7
Modified Deposit Payoff

A. Modified Payoff

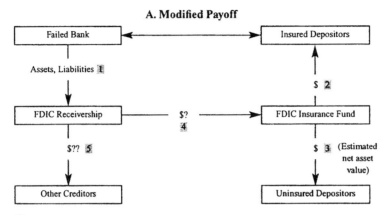

1. Failed bank placed in receivership
2. Insured deposits paid off by FDIC
3. Uninsured deposits paid out of estimated net assets value
4. Fund reimbursed out of liquidated net assets
5. Other obligations (and any remaining uninsured deposits) paid out of liquidated net assets

B. Transfer

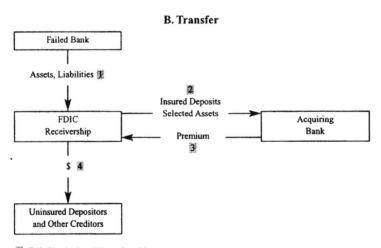

1. Failed bank placed in receivership
2. Insured deposits and selected assets transferred to acquiror
3. Premium paid by acquiror
4. Other obligation paid out of liquidated net assets

§ 8.15   Purchase and Assumption

Originally, the typical acquisition transaction involving a failed bank was not a merger, strictly speaking, but a purchase of assets (*i.e.*, loans) and assumption of liabilities (*i.e.*, deposits) of the failing bank by the acquiring bank, with the FDIC making up the shortfall between the value of liabilities assumed and assets purchased.[1] Before the 1960s, these resolutions took place without the creation of a receivership, and so approval of the shareholders and the chartering authority of the acquired bank would be required.[2] During the latter part of the 1960s, the FDIC adopted a different approach to these transactions, by first placing the institution into receivership, so that the FDIC as receiver could approve the transaction directly, without the costly delays of shareholder and chartering authority approval.[3] Figure 8–8, *infra*, illustrates the transaction.

Figure 8–8
Purchase and Assumption (post-1964)

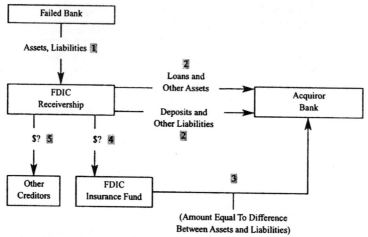

■ Failed bank placed in receivership
② Assets and liabilities transferred to acquiror
③ Sweetener paid to acquiror
④ Fund repaid out of liquidated net assets
⑤ Other creditors repaid out of liquidated net assets

If successful, the effect of this transaction is similar to a payoff of *all* depositors, not just insured depositors.[4] On the other hand, assuming that the cost of the "sweetener" provided by the FDIC to the acquiror bank is less than its total insured deposits liability, the purchase and assumption method could be less costly to the FDIC.[5]

§ 8.15

1. MODERNIZATION REPORT at I–30.

2. *Id.* at I–31.

3. *Id.*

4. *Cf.* MODERNIZATION REPORT at I–31 (describing criticism by Senator Fulbright to this effect).

5. For a discussion of alternative methods for fulfilling the FDIC's obligation to depositors, including deposit payoffs and purchase-and-assumption

(However, the FDIC as receiver is left, almost inevitably, with a nearly worthless shell within the receivership.) To narrow its exposure still further, since 1968 the FDIC has sought premiums from potential acquiror banks in proposed purchase and assumption transactions through an explicit bidding process.[6]

§ 8.16 "Open–Bank" Assistance

In the various approaches to failed bank resolution adopted by the FDIC, the FDIC has almost invariably sought to avoid the rigors of insured deposit payoff, and the resulting disruption of the local economy that the closing of a bank would cause. An important device in this regard, first seriously used by the FDIC in 1971,[1] is "open-bank assistance,"[2] in which the FDIC lends, contributes, invests, or otherwise utilizes its financial resources to assist an institution in default or in danger of default to regain financial stability. This approach proceeds on the assumption that it will be less costly to the FDIC to lend financial assistance to a troubled institution than to close and liquidate it in receivership.[3] Since 1982 in particular, with the broadening of the FDIC's open bank assistance authority, open-bank assistance has become an extremely important and frequently used option.

One obvious difficulty with this approach is that it sometimes appeared to allow a "walking dead" institution to continue to incur further obligations, followed by a possibly inevitable failure of the institution at a greater net cost to the insurer.[4] With the passage of

transactions, see *NCNB Tex. Nat'l Bank v. Cowden*, 895 F.2d 1488 (5th Cir.1990).

6. MODERNIZATION REPORT at I–31.

§ 8.16

1. *See* MODERNIZATION REPORT at I–34 (discussing "open-bank" assistance).

2. 12 U.S.C.A. § 1823(c).

3. Previously, § 1823(c) had only authorized loans, deposits, and purchase of assets by the FDIC to prevent closing or to reopen a bank. 12 U.S.C.A. § 1823(c) (1980). Section 111 of the Garn–St Germain Act, Pub. L. No. 97–320, § 111, 96 Stat.1469 (1982), fundamentally amended the formerly narrow option presented by 12 U.S.C.A. § 1823(c). The amended section also explicitly authorized the FDIC to engage in a range of actions in order to facilitate a merger or consolidation of an insured bank, or to arrange a purchase and assumption transaction. *See* 12 U.S.C.A. § 1823(c)(2).

4. Two variations on this "walking dead" approach to failing bank resolution should be mentioned. One was the

"capital forbearance" program, in which capital and other supervisory requirements were not enforced against financially troubled institutions viewed as "viable" by the FDIC. MODERNIZATION REPORT at I–37–I–38. *Cf.* 12 U.S.C.A. § 1823(i) (concerning purchase of "net worth certificates" from troubled depository institution by FDIC as support for institution's capital position). This approach has been severely criticized as increasingly the ultimate cost of unavoided (and possibly unavoidable) collapse of such "viable" but troubled institutions. MODERNIZATION REPORT at I–37. Presumably, this situation is less likely to occur since the FDIC is now required to refrain from invoking Section 1823 unless:

(i) the [FDIC] determines that the exercise of such authority is necessary to meet the obligation of the [FDIC] to provide insurance coverage for the insured deposits in such institution; and

(ii) the total amount of the expenditures by the [FDIC] and obligations

FIRREA[5] and the Federal Deposit Insurance Corporation Improvements Act of 1991 ("FDICIA"),[6] the statutory framework for dealing prospectively[7] with institutions[8] in default was significantly reformed. As to open bank assistance, the current framework is as follows.

To prevent the default of an insured depository institution,[9] to restore a closed insured bank to normal operation,[10] or to lessen the risk to the FDIC from the instability of a significant number of insured depository institutions or of institutions with significant financial resources,[11] the FDIC has the sole authority and discretion to give financial assistance to such institutions.[12] This assistance may take the form of loans to, deposits in, purchase of assets or securities of, assumption of liabilities of, or contributions to any

incurred by the [FDIC] (including any immediate and long-term obligation of the [FDIC] and any direct or contingent liability for future payment by the [FDIC]) in connection with the exercise of any such authority with respect to such institution is the least costly to the deposit insurance fund of all possible methods for meeting the [FDIC's] obligation under [§ 1823].
12 U.S.C.A. § 1823(c)(4)(A)(i)(ii).

Until 1991, another "walking dead" approach existed that involved an FDIC equity investment in the troubled institution. MODERNIZATION REPORT at I–38–I–39. This often involved extreme, and arguably questionable measures, such as the 75 to 80 percent equity interests assumed by the FDIC in large, failing regional banks such as the MCorp subsidiary and Continental Illinois. *See, e.g., id.* at I–39 (discussing equity investments in failing regional banks). The FDIC is now significantly limited by statute in its use of equity investment as a means of open-bank assistance. *See* 12 U.S.C.A. § 1823(c)(5), (i)(11) (limiting FDIC authority to make equity investments).

5. Pub. L. No. 101–73, 103 Stat. 183 (1989) (codified at scattered sections of 12 U.S.C.A.).

6. Pub. L. No. 102–242, 105 Stat. 2236 (1991) (codified at scattered sections of 12 U.S.C.A.).

7. *See United States v. Winstar Corp.,* 518 U.S. 839, 116 S.Ct. 2432 (1996) (plurality opinion) (rejecting retrospective application of FIRREA capitalization requirements to savings and loan holding company operating under

pre-FIRREA rules). *Cf. Bluebonnet Sav. Bank, F.S.B. v. United States,* 266 F.3d 1348 (Fed.Cir.2001) (holding damages resulting from government's breach of forbearances granted to thrift to be foreseeable); California Federal Bank, FSB v. United States, 245 F.3d 1342 (Fed.Cir. 2001), *cert. denied,* 534 U.S. 1113, 122 S.Ct. 920 (2002) (finding enforceable *Winstar*-type contracts existed between United States and savings bank); *Castle v. United States,* 301 F.3d 1328 (Fed.Cir. 2002) (holding neither enactment of FIRREA nor regulatory seizure of savings association for capital inadequacies constituted Fifth Amendment taking of property).

8. On the involuntary liquidation of federal credit unions, see 12 U.S.C.A. § 1787(c); 12 C.F.R. pt. 709, *as amended,* 66 Fed. Reg. 11,229 (2001) (codified at 12 C.F.R. §§ 709.0, 709.12).

9. 12 U.S.C.A. § 1823(c)(1)(A).

10. *Id.* § 1823(c)(1)(B).

11. *Id.* § 1823(c)(1)(C).

12. *Id.* § 1823(c)(1). For discussion of the implications of an open bank assistance arrangement, see *Senior Unsecured Creditors' Comm. v. Federal Deposit Ins. Corp.,* 749 F.Supp. 758 (N.D.Tex.1990). In December 1992, the FDIC published a policy statement indicating the circumstances under which it would extend assistance to a troubled insured depository institution that was still open. 57 Fed. Reg. 60,203 (1992). *See also* 61 Fed. Reg. 34,814 (1996) (proposed revision of policy statement).

such institution.[13] FDIC financial assistance may also take the form of assistance to facilitate a merger, consolidation, or other acquisition of a troubled or closed insured depository institution by another insured institution.[14] FDIC decisions to render assistance are generally subject to a requirement that the FDIC make a determination that the assistance provided be "necessary to meet the obligation of the [FDIC] to provide insurance coverage,"[15] and that it be the least-cost approach to resolving the problem; *i.e.*, that

> the total amount of the expenditures by the [FDIC] and obligations incurred by the [FDIC] (including any immediate and long-term obligation of the [FDIC] and any direct or contingent liability for future payment by the [FDIC]) in connection with the exercise of any such [assistance] authority with respect to such institution is the least costly to the deposit insurance fund of all possible methods for meeting the [FDIC's] obligation....[16]

The FDIC may not use its assistance authority to purchase voting or common stock of an insured depository institution.[17] The financial assistance provided may be made subordinated to the rights of depositors and other creditors.[18]

§ 8.17 Appointment of Conservator or Receiver

It is generally within the discretion of the chartering authority[1] of a failing depository institution to determine whether or not to

13. 12 U.S.C.A. § 1823(c)(1). On purchase of assets by the FDIC, see *id.* § 1823(d). On parallel FDIC assistance authority for savings associations, see *id.* § 1823(k)(5).

14. *Id.* § 1823(c)(2).

15. *Id.* § 1823(c)(4)(A)(i).

16. *Id.* § 1823(c)(4)(A)(ii).

17. *Id.* § 1823(c)(5).

18. *Id.* § 1823(c)(9).

§ 8.17

1. *But see* 12 U.S.C.A. § 1821(c)(4) (authorizing FDIC self-appointment as conservator or receiver, notwithstanding other state or federal law, under specified statutory conditions). On judicial review of these FDIC self-appointments, see *id.* § 1821(c)(7). On FDIC replacement of a conservator with itself in such situations, see *id.* § 1821(c)(8). *See also id.* § 1821(c)(10) (providing other grounds for FDIC self-appointment as conservator or receiver of insured depository institution). Heightened involvement of the regulators in the burgeon-

ing thrift crisis beginning in the early 1980s placed additional strains on the regulatory system and raised questions about the discretion and good faith of the regulators themselves. For a case considering a challenge to federal regulatory discretion in the face of claims of basic property rights of thrift owners, see *Biscayne Fed. Sav. & Loan v. Federal Home Loan Bank Bd.*, 720 F.2d 1499 (11th Cir.1983), *cert. denied*, 467 U.S. 1215, 104 S.Ct. 2656 (1984). *Cf. Hindes v. F.D.I.C.*, 137 F.3d 148 (3d Cir.1998) (barring actions affecting FDIC exercise of powers as receiver, where claims based on allegedly improper notification by FDIC in corporate capacity that bank was operating in unsafe and unsound condition); *Auction Co. of America v. F.D.I.C.*, 132 F.3d 746 (D.C.Cir.1997), *clarified on denial of rehearing*, 141 F.3d 1198 (allowing breach of contract action where auction company was to auction assets of failed thrifts for FDIC receiver; reading statutory reference to FDIC "as receiver" to mean as receiver for specific institution, not situation un-

place it in conservatorship or receivership.[2] In a conservatorship, the basic statutory assumption is that the institution may well return to the transaction of its business.[3] In a receivership, the basic statutory assumption is that the institution will be liquidated, or that it will be merged with or otherwise acquired by a healthy depository institution.[4] In either event, a conservator or receiver, respectively, will be appointed. Almost inevitably in either case, this will be the FDIC.[5]

der auctioneer's contract); *Bolduc v. Beal Bank, SSB*, 994 F.Supp. 82 (D.N.H. 1998), *remanded*, 167 F.3d 667 (1st Cir. 1999) (allowing certain affirmative claims of debtors' invalid indorsement relating to transfers arising long after FDIC received promissory notes at issue; case remanded on insufficiency of factual record); *First Pacific Bancorp, Inc. v. Helfer*, 224 F.3d 1117 (9th Cir. 2000) (*contra Hindes*; allowing private action under § 1821(d)(15) against FDIC to compel financial accounting in conformity with FDIC accounting and reporting practices and procedures; barring corresponding private action under state law).

2. *See, e.g.*, 12 U.S.C.A. §§ 191 (providing Comptroller with authority to declare conservatorship of national bank); 1464(d)(2)(A) (providing OTS with same authority with respect to federal savings association). *See Sinclair v. Hawke*, 314 F.3d 934 (8th Cir. 2003) (affirming dismissal of claim by owner of failed national bank declared insolvent by Comptroller). On the procedures governing a conservatorship, see generally *In re Conservatorship of Wellsville Nat'l Bank*, 407 F.2d 223 (3d Cir.1969), *cert. denied sub nom. Miller v. Camp*, 396 U.S. 832, 90 S.Ct. 85, *reh'g denied*, 396 U.S. 949, 90 S.Ct. 371. *See also Central W. Rental Co. v. Horizon Leasing*, 740 F.Supp. 1109 (E.D.Pa.1990) (involving challenge to conservator's actions, notwithstanding 1464(d)(7)(C) prohibition on judicial action restraining or affecting conservator's power). On the procedures governing the decision to place an institution in receivership, see generally *Federal Deposit Ins. Corp. v. McKnight*, 769 F.2d 658 (10th Cir.1985), *cert. denied sub nom. All Souls Episcopal Church v. FDIC and sub nom. Rocket Oil Co. v. FDIC*, 475 U.S. 1010, 106 S.Ct. 1184. The receivership process has primarily been an administrative one, with a limited role for courts. *See Shemonsky v. Office of Thrift Supervision*, 733 F.Supp.

892 (M.D.Pa.1990); *Matter of Receivership of Penn Square Bank, N.A.*, 556 F.Supp. 494 (D.Okla.1983). On conservatorship and liquidation procedures for insured credit unions, see, *e.g.*, 66 Fed. Reg. 40,574 (2001) (codified at 12 C.F.R. §§ 709.0, 709.12) (clarifying that, as conservator or liquidating agent of federally-insured credit union, NCUA will honor claim for prepayment fees by FHLBank under specified circumstances).

3. *See, e.g.*, 12 U.S.C.A. § 205(a)(1) (providing for termination of conservatorship of national bank permitting bank "to resume the transaction of its business subject to such terms, conditions, and limitations as the Comptroller may prescribe"). *See also Minichello v. Saxon*, 337 F.2d 75 (3d Cir.1964), *cert. denied*, 380 U.S. 952, 85 S.Ct. 1084 (1965) (concerning Comptroller's authority and minority shareholder rights). *Cf.* 12 U.S.C.A. § 1821(d)(2)(D) (providing general power of FDIC as conservator to put institution on sound and solvent condition and to conserve its assets). But note, as discussed *infra*, conservatorship may become receivership.

4. *See, e.g.*, 12 U.S.C.A. § 1821(c)(2)(A)(ii) (authorizing appointment of FDIC as receiver "for the purpose of liquidation or winding up the affairs of an insured Federal depository institution"). *See also id.* § 1821(d)(2)(E) (providing general power of FDIC as receiver to place institution in liquidation). Despite its starting assumption (*see supra* preceding note), a conservatorship may also ultimately conclude with the liquidation or winding up of the affairs of the institution in conservatorship. *See* 12 U.S.C.A. § 205(a)(2).

5. *See generally* 12 U.S.C.A. § 1821(c) (providing for appointment of FDIC as conservator or receiver).

The statutory rules governing the appointment of the FDIC in either capacity override any contrary provision of federal law, state constitution, or state law.[6] In the case of federal depository institutions,[7] appointment of the FDIC as conservator is within the discretion of the institution's supervisor.[8] Appointment of the FDIC as receiver is mandatory whenever the institution's supervisor decides to place it in receivership.[9]

When acting as conservator or receiver, the FDIC is not subject to the direction or supervision of any other state or federal agency in the exercise of its rights, powers, or privileges.[10] However, in the conservatorship context, the institution in conservatorship itself remains subject to the supervision of its appropriate federal banking agency, *i.e.*, the Comptroller (for national banks and District banks) and the Director of the Office of Thrift Supervision (for federal savings associations).[11]

In the case of insured state depository institutions,[12] appointment of the FDIC as conservator or receiver is within the discretion of the appropriate state authority.[13] When acting as conservator or receiver under appointment by the state authority, the FDIC is not subject to the direction or supervision of any other state or federal

---

6. *Id.* § 1821(c)(1).

7. For these purposes, the term "federal depository institution" is defined by the FDIA to mean "any national bank, any Federal savings association, and any Federal branch" of a foreign bank. *Id.* § 1813(c)(4). On the meaning of "Federal savings association," see *id.* § 1813(b)(2). On the meaning of the term "Federal branch," see *id.* § 1813(s)(2).

8. *Id.* § 1821(c)(2)(A)(i) (concerning conservatorship in general); 1821(c)(6)(A) (providing for OTS appointment of FDIC as conservator and FDIC acceptance of appointment). *But see id.* § 1821(c)(11) (authorizing FDIC self-appointment as receiver, under certain conditions, before federal agency may appoint a conservator).

9. *Id.* §§ 1821(c)(2)(A)(ii) (receivership in general); 1821(c)(6)(B)(i)–(ii) (providing for OTS appointment of FDIC).

10. *Id.* § 1821(c)(2)(C).

11. *Id.* § 1821(c)(2)(D).

12. For these purposes, the term "insured State depository institution" is derived from two terms defined by the FDIA: "insured depository institution," defined to mean "any bank or savings association the deposits of which are insured by the [FDIC]" and "State depository institution," defined to mean "any State bank, any State savings association and any insured branch which is not a Federal branch" of a foreign bank. *Id.* § 1813(c)(2), (c)(4). On the meaning of the term "State bank," see *id.* § 1813(a)(2). On the meaning of the term "State savings association," see *id.* § 1813(b)(3). On the meaning of the term "insured branch," see *id.* § 1813(s)(3).

13. *Id.* § 1821(c)(3)(A). This discretionary aspect of the appointment of a federal agency as receiver has occasionally created tension between the state authority and the federal agency. *See, e.g., Fidelity Sav. & Loan Ass'n v. Federal Home Loan Bank*, 689 F.2d 803 (9th Cir.1982) (describing tension between California Savings and Loan Commissioner and now defunct FSLIC). For grounds for appointment of FDIC as conservator or receiver of state depository institution by its appropriate *federal* banking agency (after consultation with the state authority), see 12 U.S.C.A. § 1821(c)(9).

agency in the exercise of its rights, powers, or privileges.[14] However, in the conservatorship context, the institution in conservatorship itself remains subject to the supervision of its state authority.[15]

As conservator or receiver, the FDIC has a wide range of statutory powers.[16] The FDIC gains control of the entity as its successor by operation of law.[17] As such, the FDIC has full authority to operate the institution.[18] Whether serving as conservator or receiver, it also has the power to effect the merger of the institution with another insured depository institution,[19] or arrange a purchase or assumption transaction with another insured depository institution.[20] The FDIC may, where it determines that it is "practicable, efficient, and cost effective"[21] utilize the resources of the private sector to carry out its responsibilities for management and disposition of the assets of an insured depository institution. In addition to these general powers, there is also a range of specific powers available to the FDIC in either of its capacities.

As conservator, the FDIC has the power to take any action necessary to put the institution in a sound and solvent condition.[22] It also has the power to take any action appropriate to carry on the institution's business and to preserve or conserve the institution's assets.[23]

As receiver, the FDIC has the power to liquidate the institution and realize on the institution's assets, "having due regard [for] the conditions of credit in the locality" of the institution.[24] In this

---

14. 12 U.S.C.A. § 1821(c)(3)(C).

15. *Id.* § 1821(c)(3)(D).

16. This grant of authority includes all incidental powers "as shall be necessary to carry out [its] powers" as conservator or receiver. *Id.* § 1821(d)(2)(I). *See also id.* §§ 1821(c)(2)(B), (c)(3)(B) (providing additional powers to FDIC as conservator or receiver); 1821(c)(13) (providing additional powers to FDIC when self-appointed under § 1821(c)(4), appointed by the OTS under § 1821(c)(6), appointed because of undercapitalization under § 1821(c)(9), or self-appointed because of potential loss to deposit fund under § 1821(c)(10)).

17. *Id.* § 1821(d)(2)(A).

18. *Id.* § 1821(d)(2)(B). On the functions of the institution's directors, officers, and shareholders by FDIC regulation or order, see *id.* § 1821(d)(2)(C). In operating the institution, the FDIC also has the responsibility to pay all valid obligations of the institutions, "in accordance with the prescriptions and limita-

tions of [the FDIA]." *Id.* § 1821(d)(2)(H).

19. *Id.* § 1821(d)(2)(G)(i)(I).

20. *Id.* § 1821(d)(2)(G)(i)(II). *See SCFC ILC, Inc. v. Visa USA, Inc.*, 936 F.2d 1096, 1099–1100 (10th Cir.1991) (interpreting statute). This transaction would be subject to the approval of the appropriate federal banking agency that supervises the acquiring institution. 12 U.S.C.A. § 1821(d)(2)(G)(ii). The FDIC also has the authority to purchase assets of an insured depository institution in default from any conservator, receiver or liquidator, including itself, or to take assets as security for loans from the FDIC. *Id.* § 1823(d).

21. 12 U.S.C.A. § 1821(d)(2)(K).

22. *Id.* § 1821(d)(2)(D)(i).

23. *Id.* § 1821(d)(2)(D)(ii).

24. *Id.* § 1821(d)(2)(E). On the status of the FDIC as receiver, see *id.* § 1822.

respect, it may organize a new savings association,[25] a new national bank,[26] or transitional "bridge bank"[27] to take over assets and liabilities of the institution in receivership, as it deems appropriate.

To operate effectively as receiver, the FDIC needs an accurate picture of those assets and liabilities. The growth of interstate banking and branching over the past two decades and the increasing complexity of bank products and practices (such as sweep accounts[28]) have made the determination of closing account balances much more complicated for a receiver. The industry is more concentrated than in the past, and increasingly, consolidated financial institutions have become much larger, factors further complicating the determination. These complications make it more difficult for the FDIC to determine potential deposit insurance liability quickly and accurately in the event of a bank closing.

In July 2008, the FDIC adopted a final rule requiring the largest insured depository institutions to adopt mechanisms that would, in the event of the institution's failure, provide the FDIC with standard deposit account and other customer information; and allow the placement and release of holds on liability accounts, including deposits.[29] The requirement applies only to insured depository institutions having at least $2 billion in domestic deposits[30] and either more than 250,000 deposit accounts[31] (currently estimated to be 152 institutions) or total assets over $20 billion, regardless of the number of deposit accounts[32] (currently estimated to be seven institutions).

The final rule also requires that covered institutions have in place practices and procedures for providing the FDIC, in a stan-

---

25. *Id.* § 1821(d)(2)(F)(i).

26. *Id.* § 1821(d)(2)(F)(ii), (m).

27. *Id.* § 1821(d)(2)(F)(ii), (n). *See generally Bell & Murphy and Assocs., Inc. v. Interfirst Bank Gateway, N.A.,* 894 F.2d 750 (5th Cir.1990) (discussing role of bridge banks).

28. *See* 73 Fed. Reg. 2364, 2366 (2008):

Most agreements between sweep customers and a depository institution expressly provide that the institution's liability, once the sweep occurs [from a designated account], is not a deposit (as defined in [12 U.S.C.A. § 1813(*l*)]) and that the institution will pay interest (typically overnight) while the liability remains a non-deposit liability. These sweep agreements allow an institution to pay interest without violating the statutory prohibition on the payment of interest

on demand deposits. [*See, e.g.,* 12 U.S.C.A. §§ 371a, 1828(g) (so providing); *see also* 12 C.F.R. pts. 217; 329 (implementing regulations)] These sweep agreements also relieve insured institutions from having to maintain reserve requirements for the swept liabilities under the regulations issued by the Board of Governors of the Federal Reserve System. [12 C.F.R. pt. 204.] In addition, the agreements relieve institutions from having to pay deposit insurance assessments (or premiums) on the swept liabilities, since only deposits are included in the base upon which institutions pay assessments. [*Id.* § 327.5.]

29. 73 Fed. Reg. 41,180 (2008) (codified at 12 C.F.R. § 360.9, apps. A–H).

30. 12 C.F.R. § 360.9(b)(1).

31. *Id.* § 360.9(b)(1)(i).

32. *Id.* § 360.9(b)(1)(ii).

dard format upon the close of any day's business, with required depositor and customer data for all deposit accounts held in domestic and foreign offices and interest-bearing investment accounts connected with sweep and automated credit arrangements.[33] At the same time, the FDIC adopted an interim rule establishing practices for determining deposit and other liability account balances at a failed insured depository institution.[34] In February 2009, the FDIC published a final version of that rule.[35] For the most part, the practices defined in the rule represent "a continuation of long-standing FDIC procedures in processing such balances,"[36] though it does initiate disclosure requirements with respect to sweep accounts.

The FDIC has authority to determine the validity of claims against the institution in accordance with an administrative procedure created by statute.[37] As was demonstrated in *First Empire Bank–New York v. Federal Deposit Insurance Corporation*,[38] resolving the problems of a failing institution can often be considerably complicated, and the costs markedly increased, by the claims of third parties that have dealt with the institution. In this regard, the now defunct Federal Home Loan Bank Board and the Federal Savings and Loan Insurance Corporation ("FSLIC") experienced great difficulty in attempting to deal with such claims by way of an expedited administrative process for claims resolution created by regulation.[39] The FDIA was subsequently amended to provide an elaborate administrative procedure for the resolution of third-party claims.[40]

33. *Id.* § 360.9(d)(1). Such data files must be created "through a mapping of pre-existing data elements and internal institution codes into standard data formats. Deposit account and customer data provided must be current as of the close of business for that day." *Id.*

34. *See* 73 Fed. Reg. 41,170 (2008) (codified at 12 C.F.R. §§ 360.8).

35. 74 Fed. Reg. 5797 (2009) (codified at 12 C.F.R. § 360.8).

36. 74 Fed. Reg. at 5797.

37. 12 U.S.C.A. § 1821(d)(3)–(10). On the adjudication of creditor claims involving federally-insured credit unions in liquidation, see 12 U.S.C.A. 1787(c); 12 C.F.R. pt. 709, *as amended*, 66 Fed. Reg. 11,229 (2001) (codified at 12 C.F.R. §§ 709.0, 709.12).

38. 572 F.2d 1361 (9th Cir.1978).

39. *See Coit Independence Joint Venture v. Federal Sav. and Loan Ins. Corp.*, 489 U.S. 561, 109 S.Ct. 1361 (1989) (invalidating administrative

claims process). *See also Carrollton–Farmers Branch Indep. Sch. Dist. v. Johnson & Cravens*, 889 F.2d 571 (5th Cir.1989) (rehearing on claims following *Coit*); *Triland Holdings & Co. v. Sunbelt Serv. Corp.*, 884 F.2d 205 (5th Cir. 1989) (remand under *Coit*); *Central W. Rental Co. v. Horizon Leasing*, 740 F.Supp. 1109 (E.D.Pa.1990) (applying *Coit*). *See generally* Lawrence Baxter, *Life in the Administrative Track: Administrative Adjudication of Claims against Savings Institution Receivers*, 1988 Duke L.J. 422 (discussing *Coit* and making recommendations for reform).

40. *See* Pub. L. No. 101–73, § 212(a), 103 Stat. 183, 225–234 (1989) (codified at 12 U.S.C.A. § 1821(d)), *as amended*, Pub. L. No. 102–242, §§ 123(a), 141(b), 161(a)(1)–(2), 416, 105 Stat. 2236 (1991) (codified at 12 U.S.C.A. § 1821(d)(3)(A), (d)(4), (d)(5)(D), (d)(11)(B), (d)(13)(E)). *See Tuxedo Beach Club Corp. v. City Fed. Sav. Bank*, 737 F.Supp. 18 (D.N.J.1990)

§ 8.18 Claims Against Third Parties

As conservator or receiver, the FDIC stands in a position to prosecute claims of the depository institution against third parties.[1]

(discussing statutory policy and legislative intent of 1989 amendments); *Meliezer v. Resolution Trust Co.*, 952 F.2d 879 (5th Cir.1992) (discussing administrative claims procedures).

Generally, the 1989 legislation is retroactively applicable to cases pending at the time of its enactment. *Demars v. First Serv. Bank for Sav.*, 907 F.2d 1237 (1st Cir.1990). However, the claims determination provisions, and specifically § 1821(d)(13)(D), do not require dismissal of all pending claims against failed institutions at the time of the enactment of the legislation. *Marquis v. Federal Deposit Ins. Corp.*, 965 F.2d 1148 (1st Cir.1992) (efficiency goal of statute promoted by this approach). Proceedings may be stayed under 12 U.S.C.A. § 1821(d)(12), pending the completion of the administrative claims process. *Marquis, supra* (interpreting § 1821(d) to allow more than one 90-day stay). *But cf. Praxis Properties, Inc. v. Colonial S.B., S.L.A.*, 947 F.2d 49 (3d Cir.1991) (stay expires 90 days after FDIC appointment); *Hunter's Run v. Arapahoe County Pub. Trustee*, 741 F.Supp. 207 (D.Colo.1990) (stay of proceedings under § 1821(d)(12) inappropriate where FDIC has had sufficient time to prepare case and plaintiff will suffer irreparable harm); *Tuxedo Beach Club Corp. v. City Fed. Sav. Bank*, 729 F.Supp. 1508 (D.N.J.1990) (same result as to RTC as receiver); *Federal Deposit Ins. Corp. v. Taylor*, 727 F.Supp. 326 (S.D.Tex.1989) (same; FDIC as receiver).

Failure to file a timely claim bars the claim before the administrative agency and the courts. *Althouse v. Resolution Trust Corp.*, 969 F.2d 1544, 1546 (3d Cir.1992). On the relationship between the administrative claims procedure and pending litigation involving the claim, see *Resolution Trust Corp. v. Mustang Partners*, 946 F.2d 103 (10th Cir.1991).

State law claims may be preempted by the administrative claims provisions. *Meliezer*, 952 F.2d at 883 (involving negligence claim by home mortgage owners against failed bank that issued loan); *Bueford v. Resolution Trust Corp.*, 991 F.2d 481, 484 (8th Cir.1993) (employment discrimination claims by former employees of failed bank); *Henderson v. Bank of New England*, 986 F.2d 319, 321 (9th Cir.1993) (claims by denied credit card applicant); *McCarthy v. FDIC*, 348 F.3d 1075, 1081 (9th Cir. 2003) (claims by debtors of failed bank arising out of acts of receiver, rather than bank in receivership); *Freeman v. FDIC*, 56 F.3d 1394, 1402 (D.C.Cir.1995) (claims by debtors of failed bank alleging fraudulent restructuring of home mortgage loan). There are few types of claims that the courts have retained for judicial resolution. *See, e.g., Homeland Stores, Inc. v. Resolution Trust Corp.*, 17 F.3d 1269, 1273–75 (10th Cir.1994) (holding claims against receiver, not failed bank, in connection with receiver's management of shopping center asset of failed institution, not subject to administrative claims process); *Rosa v. Resolution Trust Corp.*, 938 F.2d 383, 394–95 (3d Cir.1991), *cert. denied*, 502 U.S. 981, 112 S.Ct. 582 (1991) (claim by pension plan participants seeking order barring retroactive termination of plan). *Resolution Trust Corp. v. Elman*, 949 F.2d 624, 627 (2d Cir.1991) (involving attorney retaining lien). *Federal Deposit Ins. Corp. v. Shain, Schaffer & Rafanello*, 944 F.2d 129 (3d Cir.1991) (same). *See also Circle Indus. v. City F.S.B.*, 931 F.2d 7 (2d Cir.1991).

As to standing under the administrative claims procedure, it has been held that a union has standing to represent claims of its members, pursuant to 12 U.S.C.A. § 1821(d)(6). *Transohio S.B. v. Director, Office of Thrift Supervision*, 967 F.2d 598 (D.C.Cir.1992); *Office and Prof'l Employees Int'l Union, Local 2 v. Federal Deposit Ins. Corp.*, 962 F.2d 63, 67 (D.C.Cir.1992).

§ 8.18

1. *See, e.g.*, 12 U.S.C.A. 1821(d)(2)(B)(ii) (power of FDIC as conservator or receiver to collect obligation and money due the institution). *See also Federal Deposit Insurance Corporation v. Schuchmann*, 235 F.3d 1217 (10th Cir.2000) (acknowledging limitation of negligence theories in FDIC suit against director of failed savings association for director's alleged breach of fiduciary

The amended FDIA continues, in expanded form, the codification of the *D'Oench, Duhme* rule against secret agreements[2] against the

duty and negligence in allegedly causing association to enter into transactions in which director had personal interest); *In re Sunrise Sec. Litig.*, 916 F.2d 874, 889 (3d Cir.1990) (FDIC as receiver has power to pursue derivative claims against officers and directors of failed institution); *Hindes v. F.D.I.C.*, 137 F.3d 148 (3d Cir.1998) (barring derivative actions by shareholders); *Pareto v. F.D.I.C.*, 139 F.3d 696 (9th Cir.1998) (holding that claims asserted by stockholders were derivative to which FDIC had acceded; stockholders lacked standing to sue). *But see Hayes v. Gross*, 982 F.2d 104 (3d Cir.1992) (1989 legislation did not amend or subordinate federal securities law cause of action). *See generally Telematics Int'l, Inc. v. NEMLC Leasing Corp.*, 967 F.2d 703 (1st Cir.1992) (FDIC attachment of certificate of deposit as security on loan agreement within FDIC's discretion under 1821(j)). Under 12 U.S.C.A. § 1821(j), courts are generally prohibited from taking "any action, except at the request of the [FDIC] Board of Directors by regulation or order, to restrain or affect the exercise of power or functions of the [FDIC] as a conservator or a receiver." The provision has been interpreted to restrict injunctions and other equitable relief against the FDIC (or the now-defunct RTC) when it acts as a receiver or conservator, even if it were to violate its own procedures or to behave unlawfully. *Bank of America National Association v. Colonial Bank*, 604 F.3d 1239 (11th Cir. 2010); *281–300 Joint Venture v. Onion*, 938 F.2d 35, 39 (5th Cir.1991), *cert. denied*, 502 U.S. 1057, 112 S.Ct. 933 (1992); *Rosa*, 938 F.2d at 397–400; *In re Landmark Land Co. of Okla.*, 973 F.2d 283 (4th Cir.1992); *Gross v. Bell Sav. Bank PaSA*, 974 F.2d 403 (3d Cir.1992); *Telematics Int'l, Inc. v. NEMLC Leasing Corp.*, 967 F.2d 703, 705–706 (1st Cir. 1992); *United Liberty Life Ins. Co. v. Ryan*, 985 F.2d 1320, 1328–1329 (6th Cir.1993); *Harkness Apt. Owners Corp. v. Federal Deposit Ins. Corp.*, 999 F.2d 538 (2d Cir.1993); *National Trust for Historic Preservation v. Federal Deposit Ins. Corp.*, 21 F.3d 469 (D.C.Cir.1994); *Bursik v. One Fourth Street North, Ltd.*, 84 F.3d 1395 (11th Cir.1996); *Hindes, supra* (barring actions affecting FDIC exercise of powers as receiver, where

claims based on allegedly improper notification by FDIC in corporate capacity that bank was operating in unsafe and unsound condition). *But cf. Auction Co. of America v. F.D.I.C.*, 132 F.3d 746 (D.C.Cir.1997), *clarified on denial of rehearing*, 141 F.3d 1198 (D.C.Cir.1998) (allowing breach of contract action where auction company was to auction assets of failed thrifts for FDIC receiver; reading statutory reference to FDIC "as receiver" to mean as receiver for specific institution, not situation under auctioneer's contract); *Bolduc v. Beal Bank, SSB*, 994 F.Supp. 82 (D.N.H.1998), remanded, 167 F.3d 667 (1st Cir.1999) (allowing certain affirmative claims of debtors' invalid indorsement relating to transfers arising long after FDIC received promissory notes at issue; case remanded on insufficiency of factual record); *National Loan Investors L.P. v. Town of Orange*, 204 F.3d 407 (2d Cir. 2000), *cert. denied*, 531 U.S. 828, 121 S.Ct. 77 (holding municipal water pollution control authority's assessment of additional fee for late sewer charges, for period when FDIC was receiver for an insolvent mortgagee-bank, not a "penalty;" FDIC exemption from liability for penalties under FIRREA not applicable).

2. *See D'Oench, Duhme & Co., Inc. v. Federal Deposit Ins. Corp.*, 315 U.S. 447, 62 S.Ct. 676 (1942) (holding such agreements unenforceable against the FDIC). Section 1823(e) codifies but does not preempt the *D'Oench, Duhme* decision. *Murphy v. F.D.I.C.*, 208 F.3d 959 (11th Cir.2000), *cert. granted sub nom. Murphy v. Beck*, 530 U.S. 1306, 121 S.Ct. 30, *cert. dismissed*, 531 U.S. 1107, 121 S.Ct. 849 (2001); *Federal Sav. and Loan Ins. Corp. v. Griffin*, 935 F.2d 691, 698 (5th Cir.1991), *cert. denied sub nom. Griffin v. First Gibraltar Bank*, 502 U.S. 1092, 112 S.Ct. 1163 (1992); *Adams v. Madison Realty & Dev., Inc.*, 746 F.Supp. 419 (D.N.J.1990), *affirmed*, 937 F.2d 845 (3d Cir.1991). *But see Murphy v. F.D.I.C.*, 829 F.Supp. 3 (D.D.C.1993), *affirmed in part and reversed in part*, 61 F.3d 34 (D.C.Cir.1995) (holding *contra*). *See also Federal Deposit Ins. Corp. v. Wainer*, 4 Ill.App.2d 233, 124 N.E.2d 29 (1955) (interpreting § 1823(e)); *Central W. Rental Co. v. Horizon Leasing*, 967

interests of the FDIC.[3] Under this rule, any agreement between a depository institution and a third party that would tend to diminish or defeat the interest of the FDIC in any asset acquired by it under the financial assistance provisions of the FDIA[4] or the conservatorship and receivership provisions of the FDIA,[5] either as security for a loan, by purchase, or as receiver, is invalid unless it meets certain specified conditions:[6]

(1) The agreement must be in writing.[7]

(2) The agreement must have been executed by the depository institution and the third party contemporaneously with the acquisition by the institution of the asset in question.[8]

(3) The agreement must have been approved by the institution's board of directors or its loan committee.[9]

F.2d 832, 840 (3d Cir.1992) (doctrine prevents use of "oral undocumented agreements" as defense against enforcement of FDIC judgment); *Federal Deposit Ins. Corp. v. Kasal*, 913 F.2d 487 (8th Cir.1990) (applying 1823(e)); *Oliver v. Resolution Trust Corp.*, 747 F.Supp. 1351 (E.D.Mo.1990) (applying 1823(e)); *Morgan v. Heights Sav. Ass'n*, 741 F.Supp. 620 (E.D.Tex.1990) (applying doctrine to alleged pre-insolvency settlement of action on mortgage); *Mery v. Universal Sav. Ass'n*, 737 F.Supp. 1000 (S.D.Tex.1990) (applying § 1823(e) to partner's liability for partnership notes to failed institution); *Carico v. First Nat'l Bank of Bogata*, 734 F.Supp. 768 (E.D.Tex.1990) (applying § 1823(e)). The doctrine applies to affirmative claims as well as to defenses. *Jackson v. Federal Deposit Ins. Corp.*, 981 F.2d 730 (5th Cir.1992). *Accord Bruneau v. Federal Deposit Ins. Corp.*, 981 F.2d 175 (5th Cir.1992); *Federal Deposit Ins. Corp. v. Byrne*, 736 F.Supp. 727 (N.D.Tex.1990) (rule precludes affirmative claims as well as defenses). *But cf. Murphy v. Federal Deposit Ins. Corp.*, supra (suggesting that 1823(e) supersedes *D'Oench, Duhme*). *See generally Federal Deposit Ins. Corp. v. Kucera Builders, Inc.*, 503 F.Supp. 967, 970 (N.D.Ga.1980) (collecting cases); Frank Skillern, *Federal Deposit Insurance Corporation and the Failed Bank: The Past Decade*, 99 Banking L.J. 292, 295–305 (1982) (discussing cases interpreting § 1823(e)); J. Michael Echevarria, *A Precedent Embalms a Principle: The Expansion of the* D'Oench, Duhme *Doctrine*, 43 Cath. U. L. Rev. 745 (1994) (reviewing and criticizing application of doctrine).

3. 12 U.S.C.A. § 1823(e), *as amended*, Pub. L. No. 101–73, § 217(4), 103 Stat. at 256. *See Timberland Design v. Federal Deposit Ins. Corp.*, 745 F.Supp. 784 (D.Mass.1990) (applying amended 1823(e) retroactively to the benefit of FDIC as receiver); *Federal Deposit Ins. Corp. v. Sullivan*, 744 F.Supp. 239 (D.Colo.1990) (applying amended 1823(e) retroactively); *Resolution Trust Corp. v. Camp*, 965 F.2d 25, 31 (5th Cir.1992) (avoiding question of retroactivity). *Cf. Resolution Trust Corp. v. Murray*, 935 F.2d 89, 94 (5th Cir.1991) (extension of doctrine to RTC claims); *Olney Sav. & Loan Ass'n v. Trinity Banc Sav. Ass'n*, 885 F.2d 266 274 (5th Cir. 1989), *reh'g denied*, 892 F.2d 78 (extension of doctrine to FSLIC claims).

4. 12 U.S.C.A. § 1823(c).

5. *Id.* § 1821, *as amended*, Dodd–Frank Wall Street Reform and Consumer Protection Act (DFA) §§ 335(a), 343(a), 363(5), Pub. L. No. 111–203, 124 Stat. 1376, 1540, 1544–1545, 1552–1553 (2010) (codified at 12 U.S.C.A. §§ 1821, 1821(a)(1)(E)).

6. *Id.* § 1823(e). The doctrine may even be raised in the first instance on appeal in exceptional circumstances. *In re 604 Columbus Ave. Realty Trust*, 968 F.2d 1332, 1343–1344 (1st Cir.1992) (discussing circumstances).

7. *Id.* § 1823(e)(1).

8. *Id.* § 1823(e)(2).

9. *Id.* § 1823(e)(3). This approval must be reflected in the minutes of the board or committee. *Id.*

(4) The agreement must have been, continuously from the time of its execution, an official record of the institution.[10]

A depository institution's alleged negligence in failing to meet these conditions is not imputable to the FDIC.[11] The doctrine bars defenses and affirmative claims whether characterized as contract or tort.[12] However, a defense of fraud in the inducement on the part of the depository institution may constitute a good defense despite 12 U.S.C.A. 1823(e).[13]

§ 8.19 Claims Against Directors and Officers

Directors and officers of insured depository institutions in default may be held subject to personal liability in a civil action by or on behalf of the FDIC[1] for gross negligence under applicable state law.[2] Such actions may be brought by or on behalf of the FDIC on the basis of its status as conservator or receiver of the institution, on the basis of a claim purchased from, assigned by, or otherwise conveyed by the conservator or receiver, or on the basis of a claim purchased from, assigned by, or otherwise conveyed by an insured depository institution or its affiliate in connection with financial assistance extended by the FDIC under the "open bank" provisions of the FDIA.[3]

---

10. *Id.* § 1823(e)(4). In February 1997, the FDIC adopted a policy statement that sets forth circumstances under which the FDIC would assert the *D'Oench, Duhme* doctrine to bar certain agreements or arrangements entered into with an institution prior to its receivership. FDIC, *Statement of Policy Regarding Federal Common Law and Statutory Provisions Protecting FDIC, as Receiver or Corporate Liquidator, Against Unrecorded Agreements or Arrangements by a Depository Institution Prior to Receivership, reprinted in* 62 Fed. Reg. 5984 (1997).

11. *Federal Deposit Ins. Corp. v. Alker,* 164 F.2d 469 (3d Cir.1947). *See also Timberland Design, Inc. v. First Serv. Bank for Sav.,* 932 F.2d 46, 50 (1st Cir. 1991) (actual knowledge of agreement by FDIC not bar to application of doctrine).

12. *Alker, supra. But see Federal Deposit Ins. Corp. v. Meo,* 505 F.2d 790 (9th Cir.1974) (third party's defenses valid under § 1823(e) if misrepresentation of bank's records not the result of action or inaction of the third party).

13. *Black v. Federal Deposit Ins. Corp.,* 640 F.2d 699 (5th Cir.1981); *Federal Deposit Ins. Corp. v. Hoover–Morris,*

642 F.2d 785 (5th Cir.1981). *Cf. Federal Deposit Ins. Corp. v. Selaiden Builders,* 973 F.2d 1249, 1254–1255 (challenging ownership by FDIC of notes in question); *Resolution Trust Corp. v. Oaks Apts. Joint Venture,* 966 F.2d 995, 999–1001 (5th Cir.1992), *reh'g denied,* 974 F.2d 1337 (defenses based on obligations contained in integral loan agreement documents); *Federal Sav. and Loan Ins. Corp. v. Mackie,* 962 F.2d 1144, 1150–1151 (5th Cir.1992) (same); *Garrett v. Commonwealth Mortgage Corp. of Am.,* 938 F.2d 591, 594–595 (5th Cir.1991) (defenses involving breach of fiduciary duty or negligence not necessarily dependent on "secret agreement"); *Cadle Company v. Patoine,* 172 Vt. 178, 772 A.2d 544 (2001) (holding that buyer of promissory note from FDIC was not holder in due course under federal law and that "no-asset" exception to statutory *D'Oench, Duhme* doctrine applied to bar accommodation maker's liability on note).

§ 8.19

1. 12 U.S.C.A. § 1821(k)(1)–(3).

2. *Id.* § 1821(k).

3. *Id.* § 1821(k)(1)–(3). On open bank assistance, see *id.* § 1823.

The statute explicitly states that this standard of conduct does not exclude a claim based on action by a director or officer involving a greater disregard of the fiduciary duty of care than gross negligence, such as, for example, intentional torts.[4] Concepts such as "gross negligence," "duty of care," and "intentional tortious conduct" are to be determined under applicable state law.[5]

In *Atherton v. Federal Deposit Insurance Corporation,*[6] the Supreme Court considered the implications of this gross negligence standard. The FDIC as receiver had brought an action against former officers and directors of a failed federal savings association, alleging negligence, breach of fiduciary duty, and gross negligence. The district court dismissed all claims except the gross negligence claim.[7] On interlocutory appeal, the Third Circuit reversed, concluding that the government could pursue any claims for negligence or breach of fiduciary duty available as a matter of federal common law.[8] In an opinion by Justice Breyer, the Court held that there was no federal common law providing a standard of care for officers and directors of federally insured savings institutions.[9] However, the FIRREA provision[10] setting forth a gross negligence standard for directors or officers of federally insured savings institutions provided only a minimum standard of conduct, a floor that guaranteed that officers and directors were required to meet at least a gross negligence standard.[11] Consequently, the FIRREA provision did not bar the application of any stricter state standard making directors and officers liable for such conduct, as simple negligence.[12]

In a separate opinion joined by Justices Scalia and Thomas, Justice O'Connor concurred in part and concurred in the judgment.[13] She found that "the most natural reading of the savings clause in 12 U.S.C.A. § 1821(k) covers both state and federal rights."[14] Consequently, in light of the plain statutory language, she could not endorse the Court's reliance on admittedly ambivalent legislative history to support the holding.[15]

4. *Id.* § 1823(k).

5. *Id. See Federal Deposit Ins. Corp. v. Canfield,* 967 F.2d 443, 448 (10th Cir.1992), *cert. dismissed,* 506 U.S. 993, 113 S.Ct. 516 (discussing statute's reliance on state law for definition of gross negligence); *Federal Deposit Ins. Corp. v. McSweeney,* 976 F.2d 532 536–537 (9th Cir.1992), *cert. denied,* 508 U.S. 950, 113 S.Ct. 2440 (1993) (citing *Canfield*).

6. 519 U.S. 213, 117 S.Ct. 666 (1997).

7. *Atherton,* 519 U.S. at 216, 117 S.Ct. at 669.

8. 57 F.3d 1231 (3d Cir.1995).

9. *Atherton,* 519 U.S. at 218, 117 S.Ct. at 669.

10. 12 U.S.C.A. § 1821(k).

11. *Atherton,* 519 U.S. at 227, 117 S.Ct. at 674.

12. 519 U.S. at 227, 117 S.Ct. at 675.

13. 519 U.S. at 231, 117 S.Ct. at 676 (O'Connor, J., concurring in part and concurring in the judgment).

14. 519 U.S. at 232, 117 S.Ct. at 677.

15. *Id.*

A cause of action may also be pursued by the FDIC against any director, officer, employee, agent, attorney, accountant, appraiser, or other employee or provider of services for damages for "the improvident or otherwise improper use or investment of an insured depository institution's assets."[16]

§ 8.20 Treatment of Systemically Significant Financial Companies

Traditionally, failures in the financial services sector have been divided along broad regulatory lines. Depository institutions were subject to an administratively supervised resolution process, while holding companies of depository institutions—as well as securities and insurance enterprises—were subject to the generally applicable federal bankruptcy law. In the wake of the failure of the subprime mortgage market in 2008,[1] the question naturally arises whether it makes sense to organize the financial services sector in this way for purposes of failure and resolution. An April 2009 report issued by the Congressional Research Service[2] argued that Congress must consider whether there was a better way to handle the failure of "systemically significant financial companies" (SSFCs) that are not themselves depository institutions. Congressional proposals for regulatory reform included such measures.[3]

The reform legislation that was being shaped in Congress during 2009 and 2010 included these proposals in a broader package of measures intended to respond to the financial crisis that had erupted in September 2008. Long, intense discussions culminated in a conference committee led by Representative Frank. Early on June 25, 2010, an approved Conference bill emerged from the committee, based largely on the Senate version.[4] After further

---

16. 12 U.S.C.A. § 1821(*l*). Such damages include losses of principal and appropriate interest. *Id.* For a pre-FIRREA cause of action against accountants of a failed savings association, see *Federal Deposit Ins. Corp. v. Cherry, Bekaert & Holland*, 742 F.Supp. 612 (M.D.Fla. 1990).

§ 8.20

1. For background on the subprime mortgage crisis, see 1 MICHAEL P. MALLOY, BANKING LAW AND REGULATION § 1.4 (1994 & Cum. Supp.). For a timeline of the current financial crisis, see http://www.stlouisfed.org/timeline/default.cfm.

2. David H. Carpenter, *Insolvency of Systemically Significant Financial Companies: Bankruptcy vs. Conservatorship/Receivership* (Cong. Res. Serv. Apr. 20, 2009).

3. Both H.R. 4173, the Wall Street Reform and Consumer Protection Act of 2009, and the Administration's proposed Resolution Authority for Systemically Significant Financial Companies Act of 2009 contemplated resolution procedures modeled on FDIC conservatorship/receivership authority under 12 U.S.C.A. § 1821. *See* Diane Davis, *CRS Report Compares Bankruptcy Process With Conservatorship/Receivership Regimes*, BNA Banking Daily, Jan. 19, 2010, available at http://www.bna.com (discussing proposals).

4. H.R. Conf. Rep. 111–517, 111th Cong., 2d Sess. (June 29, 2010). *See* Malini Manickavasagam, *Lawmakers Reach Consensus on Bill To Modernize Capital Markets Regulation*, BNA Banking Daily (June 28, 2010), *available at* http://www.

negotiations with outriding Senators, the conference bill, H.R. 4173, was approved by both houses and signed into law by the President on July 21, 2010. The Dodd–Frank Wall Street Reform and Consumer Protection Act ("Dodd–Frank Act")[5] has as its twin themes new supervision and controls over large and "systemically significant" financial companies and creation of genuine consumer protection mechanisms at the federal level.

In terms of the supervision of troubled financial companies, the Dodd–Frank Act includes the following principal features. First, it mandates the transfer of enforcement functions and responsibilities of the Office of Thrift Supervision to the other federal regulators,[6] effective July 21, 2011.[7] The abolishment of the OTS and the position of its director follows 90 days after that effective date.[8]

Second, the act establishes a new Financial Stability Oversight Council (FSOC), a committee of financial services regulators[9] to identify systemic risks, to promote market discipline, and to respond to emerging threats to the U.S. financial system.[10] Under Dodd–Frank § 113[11] the FSOC has the authority to require that a nonbank financial company be supervised by the Fed and subject to prudential standards, if the FSOC determines that material financial distress at such a firm, or the nature, scope, size, scale, concentration, interconnectedness, or mix of the activities of the firm, could pose a threat to the financial stability of the United States. In October 2010, the FSOC issued a proposed rule identifying the criteria that should inform its designation of nonbank financial companies under the Dodd–Frank Act.[12] In addition, under Dodd–Frank § 619[13] the FSOC is required to study and make recommendations on implementing the "Volcker Rule," which prohibits banking entities from engaging in proprietary trading and

bna.com (reporting on conference approval).

5. Pub. L. No. 111–203, 124 Stat. 1376 (2010) (codified at scattered sections of 2, 5, 7, 11, 12, 15, 18, 20, 22, 26, 28, 31, 42, 44 U.S.C.A.) (DFA).

6. DFA §§ 312(b), 314 (codified at 12 U.S.C.A. §§ 1, 4a, 11 5412(b)(2)(B) (OCC authority); 12 U.S.C.A. 5412(b)(1), (2)(A) (Fed authority); 12 U.S.C.A. § 5412(b)(2)(C) (FDIC authority)).

7. DFA § 311(a) (codified at 12 U.S.C.A. § 5411(a)). The effective date may be extended under certain specified circumstances. 12 U.S.C.A. § 5411(b). Technical details of the transfer are handled by DFA §§ 302, 312(a)–(b), 317, 319, 322–327.

8. DFA § 313 (codified at 12 U.S.C.A. 5413).

9. DFA § 111(a)–(h) (codified at 12 U.S.C.A. § 5321(a)–(h)).

10. DFA § 112(a)(1) (codified at 12 U.S.C.A. § 5322(a)(1)).

11. DFA § 113 (codified at 12 U.S.C.A. § 5323).

12. Financial Stability Oversight Council, *Advance Notice of Proposed Rulemaking Regarding Authority To Require Supervision and Regulation of Certain Nonbank Financial Companies*, 75 Fed. Reg. 61,653 (October 6, 2010) (to be codified at 12 C.F.R. ch. XIII). Comments were due by by November 5, 2010. 75 Fed. Reg. at 61,653.

13. DFA § 619 (codified at 12 U.S.C.A. § 1851).

from maintaining certain relationships with hedge funds and private equity funds. Accordingly, in October the FSOC published a notice initiating that study.[14]

Third, the Dodd–Frank Act gives the Fed authority to supervise the nonbank financial companies[15] identified by the FSOC as systemically significant.[16] This authority is in addition to Fed authority over bank holding companies and financial holding companies.[17]

Fourth, the act gives the FDIC authority to supervise the "orderly liquidation" of any systemically significant financial company that is at risk.[18] This authority is in addition to the separate and distinct FDIC resolution authority over insured depository institutions.[19] In late October 2010, the FDIC published a proposed rule to implement its authority to "resolve" the failure of any covered financial companies.[20]

§ 8.21 Emergency Interstate Acquisitions

At a time when interstate expansion of banks was subject to significant limitation,[1] the administratively arranged interstate acquisition of a failing depository institution was an important device. From the point of view of the acquiring institution, the transaction

---

14. Financial Stability Oversight Council, *Public Input for the Study Regarding the Implementation of the Prohibitions on Proprietary Trading and Certain Relationships With Hedge Funds and Private Equity Funds*, 75 Fed. Reg. 61,758 (October 6, 2010).

15. DFA §§ 161–169 (codified at 12 U.S.C.A. §§ 5361–5369). See also *id.* § 170 (codified at 12 U.S.C.A. § 5370) (providing for safe harbor exemptions for certain types or classes of U.S. nonbank financial companies or foreign nonbank financial companies from supervision by Fed).

16. DFA § 113 (codified at 12 U.S.C.A. § 3523).

17. *See* 12 U.S.C.A. §§ 1841 *et seq.*, *as amended*, Dodd–Frank Wall Street Reform and Consumer Protection Act (DFA), §§ 354(1)–(3), 355, 604(a)–(b), (c)(1)–(2), (d), (e)(1)–(2), 606(a), 607(a), 616(a), 618–619, 622, 623(b)(1)(A)–(B), (b)(2), 628, Pub. L. No. 111–203, 124 Stat. 1376, 1546–1547 1599–1602, 1607, 1615–1635 1640–1641 (2010) (codified at 12 U.S.C.A. §§ 1841(c)(2)(F)(v), 1841(j)(3), 1841(o)(4), 1842(c)(7), 1842(d)(1)(A), 1843(i)(8), 1843(j)(2)(A), 1843(k)(6)(B), 1843(*l*)(1), 1844(b), 1844(c)(1)–(2), 1844(c)(5)(B), 1850a, 1851, 1852, 1872(1); repealing 12 U.S.C.A. § 1848a).

18. DFA §§ 201–214 (codified at 12 U.S.C.A. §§ 4403, 5381–5394; 18 U.S.C.A. § 1032(1)).

19. DFA § 201(a)(8)(B) (codified at 12 U.S.C.A. § 5381(a)(8)(B)).

20. Federal Deposit Insurance Corporation, *Notice of Proposed Rulemaking Implementing Certain Orderly Liquidation Authority Provisions of the Dodd–Frank Wall Street Reform and Consumer Protection Act*, 75 Fed. Reg. 64,173 (October 19, 2010) (to be codified at 12 C.F.R. pt. 380). Comments on the proposal were due by November 18, 2010. 75 Fed. Reg. at 64,173. Written responses to certain additional questions posed by the FDIC were due by January 18, 2011. *Id.*

§ 8.21

1. *See, e.g.,* 12 U.S.C.A. §§ 36(c), 1843(d) (1988) (imposing restrictions on national bank branching and on interstate bank holding company acquisitions).

had the added attractiveness of giving it access to interstate markets that might otherwise be unavailable.[2]

Such acquisitions are typically arranged through a bidding process. In emergency circumstances an out-of-state acquiror may be the only feasible candidate to take over the failing institution and avoid an expensive regulatory resolution of the institution's eventual default. The FDIA provides for such acquisitions.

§ 8.22   Target Banks in Default

In the case of an insured bank or a holding company, assisted[1] emergency interstate acquisitions by an out-of-state bank, savings association, or holding company are authorized under certain specified conditions.[2] Under certain circumstances, an emergency interstate acquisition may be authorized even though the § 1823(c) financial assistance *preceded* the proposed acquisition, rather than being an integral part of it.[3] The FDIC may require consideration for its previous assistance as a condition for approval of such an acquisition.[4]

If the target insured bank is in default, the target must have total assets of $500 million or more to qualify for an assisted interstate acquisition.[5] The FDIC must consult the target's state bank supervisor before making a determination to take action.[6] The supervisor must be given a reasonable opportunity (not less than 48

---

2. *See, e.g.,* Bennett, *Citicorp Acquires Fidelity: New York Bank Allowed into California,* N.Y. Times, Sept. 29, 1982, at D1 (describing Citicorp's entry into California market through acquisition of failing Fidelity Savings and Loan Association).

§ 8.22

1. *I.e.,* financially assisted by the FDIC under 12 U.S.C.A. § 1823(c). *See id.* § 1823(f)(1) (conditioning acquisitions on provision of FDIC assistance).

2. *Id.* § 1823(f)(1). No assistance is authorized for a holding company subsidiary, other than a subsidiary that is itself an insured depository institution, in connection with any assisted emergency interstate acquisition. *Id.* § 1823(f)(9)(A). However, this does not prohibit an intermediate holding company or an affiliate of an insured depository institution from being a conduit for assistance ultimately intended for an insured bank. *Id.* § 1823(f)(9)(B).

3. *Id.* § 1823(f)(3)(D), which provides:

if—

(i) at any time after August 10, 1987, the [FDIC] provides any assistance under [§ 1823(c)] to an insured bank; and

(ii) at the time such assistance is granted, the insured bank, the holding company which controls the insured bank (if any), or any affiliated insured bank is eligible to be acquired by an out-of-State bank or out-of-State holding company under this paragraph,

the insured bank, the holding company, and such other affiliated insured bank shall remain eligible, subject to such terms and conditions as the [FDIC] (in the [FDIC's] discretion) may impose, to be acquired by an out-of-State bank or out-of-State holding company under this paragraph as long as any portion of such assistance remains outstanding.

4. *Id.* § 1823(f)(3)(G).

5. *Id.* § 1823(f)(2)(A). Total assets are determined as of the most recent report of condition. *Id.*

6. *Id.* § 1823(f)(2)(B)(i).

hours) to object to the proposed acquisition.[7] If there is an objection, the FDIC may still proceed, but only on an affirmative vote of 75 percent of the FDIC Board of Directors.[8]

Assuming all applicable conditions are met, the FDIC is authorized to arrange a purchase and assumption transaction involving the insured bank in default.[9] Such transactions are also generally subject to the approval of the primary federal or state supervisor of each party to the transaction.[10] However, these transactions are generally not subject to the interstate banking provisions of the Bank Holding Company Act, state law, or the savings and loan holding company provisions of the Home Owner's Loan Act.[11] Any subsidiary created as a result of the transaction may retain existing branches of the target institution,[12] but this does not authorize any move of a principal office or branch.[13] Any subsequent nonemergency interstate acquisitions would be subject to applicable state law.[14]

In determining whether or not to arrange such a transaction, the FDIC is authorized in its discretion to solicit offers or acquisition proposals from any prospective purchasers or merger partners.[15] Intra-industry in-state bidders are favored in this process.[16]

---

7. *Id.* § 1823(f)(2)(B)(ii).

8. *Id.* § 1823(f)(2)(B)(iii).

9. *Id.* § 1823(f)(2)(A).

10. *Id.*

11. *Id.* § 1823(f)(4)(A), (E), provides:

(4)(A) Acquisitions not subject to certain other laws

Section 1842(d) of this title, any provision of State law, and section 1730a(e)(3) of this title shall not apply to prohibit any acquisition under paragraph (2) or (3), except that an out-of-State bank may make such an acquisition only if such ownership is otherwise specifically authorized....

(E) Certain State interstate banking laws inapplicable

Any holding company which acquires control of any insured bank or holding company under paragraph (2) or (3) or subparagraph (D) of this paragraph shall not, by reason of such acquisition, be required under the law of any State to divest any other insured bank or be prevented from acquiring any other bank or holding company.

12. *Id.* § 1823(f)(4)(B).

13. *Id.* § 1823(f)(4)(C).

14. *Id.* § 1823(f)(4)(D)(i). This provision does not apply to any out-of-state

bank holding company before the end of the earlier of the following two periods:

(1) the end of the two-year period beginning on the date the acquisition is consummated; or

(2) the end of any period established under state law during which the out-of-state bank holding company may not be treated as a bank holding company whose insured bank subsidiaries' operations are "principally conducted" in the state for purposes of acquiring other insured banks or establishing bank branches.

Id. § 1823(f)(4)(D)(ii)(I)–(II). For these purposes, the state where the operations are "principally conducted" means "the State in which the operations of a holding company's insured bank subsidiaries are principally conducted is the State determined under [§ 1842(d)] with respect to such holding company." *Id.* § 1823(f)(4)(D) (iii).

15. *Id.* § 1823(f)(5). Such prospective purchasers or partners must be "both qualified and capable of acquiring the assets and liabilities of the bank in default or in danger of default." *Id.*

16. *See, e.g., id.* § 1823(f)(6)(A):

If, after receiving offers, the offer presenting the lowest expense to the

In considering bids, the FDIC is to give consideration to minimizing the cost of its financial assistance and to the maintenance of specialized depository institutions.[17] Generally, a disappointed bidder for bank assets does not have standing to challenge the FDIC's selection of the successful bidder.[18]

In deciding to authorize any particular assisted emergency acquisition, the FDIC is directed to apply the following priorities, in the following order:

(1) Transactions should be authorized, if possible, between depository institutions of the same type within the same state.[19]

(2) Transactions should be authorized between depository institutions of the same type, but in different states that authorize such transactions, or failing that, at least in states that are contiguous.[20]

(3) If not in such states, then transactions should be authorized between depository institutions at least of the same type but in different states.[21]

(4) If not such institutions, then transactions should be authorized between depository institutions of different types in the same state.[22]

(5) If not in the same state, then transactions should be authorized between depository institutions of different types, but in different states that authorize such transactions, or failing that, at least in states that are contiguous.[23]

(6) If not in such states, then transactions should be authorized between depository institutions of different types

---

[FDIC]. that is in a form and with conditions acceptable to the [FDIC] (hereinafter referred to as the "lowest acceptable offer"), is from an offeror that is not an existing in-State bank of the same type as the bank that is in default or is in danger of default (or, where the bank is an insured bank other than a mutual savings bank, the lowest acceptable offer is not from an in-State holding company), the [FDIC] shall permit the offeror which made the initial lowest acceptable offer and each offeror who made an offer the estimated cost of which to the [FDIC] was within 15 per centum or $15,000,000, whichever is less, of the initial lowest acceptable offer to submit a new offer.

The FDIC's calculations and estimations of the cost of offers and reoffers are determinative. *Id.* § 1823(f)(6)(D). The FDIC is authorized to set reasonable time limits on offers and reoffers. *Id.*

17. *Id.* § 1823(f)(6)(B). In other words, the FDIC is directed to favorably consider transactions that would not result in a savings association being absorbed by a commercial bank. *Id.*

18. *Gosnell v. Federal Deposit Ins. Corp.*, 938 F.2d 372, 376 (2d Cir.1991).

19. 12 U.S.C.A. § 1823(f)(6)(B)(i).

20. *Id.* § 1823(f)(6)(B)(ii)(I)–(II).

21. *Id.* § 1823(f)(6)(B)(iii).

22. *Id.* § 1823(f)(6)(B)(iv).

23. *Id.* § 1823(f)(6)(B)(v)(I)–(II).

but in different states.[24]

However, in the case of a minority-controlled target bank, before the FDIC proceeds to these bidding priorities, it is required to seek an offer from other minority-controlled banks.[25] In any event, a transaction is prohibited if it would result in, or further a scheme to create, a monopoly or attempt to monopolize the business of banking in any part of the United States.[26] A transaction is also prohibited if its effect in any section of the country would be anticompetitive, unless the FDIC finds that the anticompetitive effects would be clearly outweighed by the probable effect of the transaction in meeting the convenience and needs of the community to be served by the target institution.[27] Finally, a transaction is prohibited if, in the opinion of the FDIC, the acquisition would threaten the safety and soundness of the acquiror or would not result in the future viability of the resulting institution.[28]

§ 8.23   Target Banks in Danger of Default

If the target is in danger of default, somewhat different conditions apply. In this case, one or more out-of-state banks or holding companies are permitted to acquire and retain shares or assets of an insured bank in danger of default if it has total assets of $500 million or more.[1] In addition, such banks or holding companies may acquire two or more affiliated insured banks in danger of closing if the targets have aggregate total assets of $500 million or more, or if the aggregate total is equal to or greater than 33 percent of the aggregate total assets of all such affiliated insured banks.[2] In either case, if the 33 percent test is met, the acquirors may also acquire and retain shares or assets of the holding company that controls the affiliated target banks or any other affiliated insured banks.[3]

Assisted emergency acquisitions of banks in danger of default are only permitted if the board of directors or trustees of each target requests FDIC assistance in writing.[4] In addition to any other applicable approval requirements under state or federal law,[5]

---

24. *Id.* § 1823(f)(6)(B)(vi).

25. *Id.* § 1823(f)(6)(C). On the acquisition of a minority-controlled bank by a minority bank holding company, see *id.* § 1823(f)(12).

26. *Id.* § 1823(f)(7)(A).

27. *Id.* § 1823(f)(7)(B).

28. *Id.* § 1823(f)(7)(C).

§ 8.23

1. 12 U.S.C.A. § 1823(f)(3)(A)(i).

2. *Id.* § 1823(f)(3)(A)(ii).

3. *Id.* § 1823(f)(3)(B).

4. *Id.* § 1823(f)(3)(C).

5. *Id.* § 1823(f)(3)(F). However, these transactions are generally not subject to § 1842(d), state law, or the S & L holding company provisions of the Home Owner's Loan Act. *Id.* § 1823(f)(4)(A), (E). Any subsidiary created as a result of the transaction may retain existing branches of the target institution, *id.* § 1823(f)(4)(B), but this does not authorize any move of a principal office or branch. *Id.* § 1823(f)(4)(C). Subsequent nonemergency interstate acquisitions would be subject to applicable state law. *Id.* § 1823(f)(4)(D).

no final action can be taken by the FDIC unless the state bank supervisor in the state in which the target bank is located approves the acquisition.[6] These acquisitions are subject to the same bidding rules and priorities as apply to acquisitions of banks in default. They are also subject to the same prohibitions with respect to monopoly, anticompetitiveness, and safety and soundness.

§ 8.24   Target Savings Associations

Similar rules apply to emergency acquisitions of savings associations.[1] However, unlike the corresponding provisions with respect to emergency acquisitions of insured banks and holding companies, these provisions do not specifically require that the acquisition transaction involve financial assistance by the FDIC under § 1823(c).[2] They do include specific provisions for financial assistance before grounds exist for appointment of a conservator or receiver.[3]

Notwithstanding contrary state law provisions,[4] the FDIC may authorize certain acquisitions if it determines that severe financial conditions threaten the stability of a significant number of savings associations, or of savings associations with significant financial resources, and that authorization of an emergency acquisition would lessen the FDIC's risk.[5] Eligible transactions under this provision are:

(1) Merger, consolidation, or purchase and assumption of a savings association eligible for financial assistance under § 1823(c) with any other savings association or any insured bank;[6]

(2) Acquisition of control of such a savings association by any other savings association;[7] or,

---

6. *Id.* § 1823(f)(3)(E).

§ 8.24

1. 12 U.S.C.A. § 1823(k), *as amended*, Dodd–Frank Wall Street Reform and Consumer Protection Act (DFA) § 363(6), Pub. L. No. 111–203, 124 Stat. 1376, 1553 (2010) (codified at 12 U.S.C.A. § 1823(k)(1)(A)(iv)).

2. *Id.*

3. *Id.* § 1823(k)(5).

4. Nothing in this authorization overrides or supersedes state laws restricting or limiting the activities of savings associations undertaken on behalf of another entity. *Id.* § 1823(k)(1)(A)(vi).

5. *Id.* § 1823(k)(1)(A)(i).

6. *Id.* § 1823(k)(1)(A)(i)(I). With the concurrence of the Comptroller of the Currency, such an acquisition by a federal savings association where the target becomes a subsidiary of the acquiror is permitted without regard to investment percentage limitations of § 1464(c)(4)(B). *Id.* § 1823(k)(1)(A)(iv), as amended, DFA § 363(6) (striking "Director of the Office of Thrift Supervision" and inserting "Comptroller of the Currency").

7. *Id.* § 1823(k)(1)(i)(A)(II). With the concurrence of the Comptroller, such an acquisition by a federal savings association where the target becomes a subsidiary of the acquiror is permitted without regard to investment percentage limitations of § 1464(c)(4)(B). *Id.* § 1823(k)(1)(A)(iv), *as amended*.

(3) Acquisition of control, or purchase and assumption of such a savings association by any company.[8]

The FDIC may only authorize such a transaction if it determines that the authorization will not present a substantial risk to the safety and soundness of the target and the acquiror.[9] The transaction may be authorized on such terms as the FDIC provides.[10] The transaction is subject to any required approval of the appropriate federal banking agency of each party to the transaction.[11] Dual service of management officials otherwise prohibited by the Depository Institutions Management Interlocks Act[12] may continue for a period of 10 years after the acquisition, with the approval of the FDIC.[13]

The FDIC must consult the target's state supervisor before making a determination to take action.[14] The supervisor must be given a reasonable opportunity (not less than 48 hours) to object to the proposed acquisition.[15] The FDIC may still proceed, but only on an affirmative vote of 75 percent of the FDIC Board of Directors.[16]

The FDIC is expressly authorized in its discretion to solicit practicable offers and proposals from prospective purchasers or merger partners.[17] Such bidders must be "qualified and capable of acquiring the assets and liabilities of the [target] savings association."[18] However, in the case of a minority-controlled institution, the FDIC is required to seek offers from other minority-controlled bidders before seeking offers from other bidders.[19]

Special provisions exist with respect to the retention of branches.[20] If a merger, consolidation, transfer, or acquisition involves a savings association eligible for FDIC assistance and a bank or bank holding company, the savings association may retain and operate any existing branch or branches or any other existing facilities.[21] If the savings association continues to exist as a separate entity, it may establish and operate new branches to the same extent as any savings association that is not affiliated with a bank holding company, and the home office of which is located in the same state.[22] Notwithstanding this branching authorization, however, certain

---

8. *Id.* § 1823(k)(1)(i)(A)(III).

9. *Id.* § 1823(k)(1)(A)(i).

10. *Id.* § 1823(k)(1)(A)(ii).

11. *Id.* § 1823(k)(1)(A)(iii).

12. *Id.* §§ 3201 *et seq*, as amended, DFA § 360 (codified at 12 U.S.C.A. §§ 3206–3207, 3208).

13. *Id.* § 1823(k)(1)(A)(v).

14. *Id.* § 1823(k)(1)(B)(i).

15. *Id.* § 1823(k)(1)(B)(ii).

16. *Id.* § 1823(k)(1)(B)(iii).

17. *Id.* § 1823(k)(2)(A).

18. *Id.*

19. *Id.* § 1823(k)(2)(B).

20. *Id.* § 1823(k)(4). *Cf. Arkansas State Bank Comm'r v. Resolution Trust Corp.*, 911 F.2d 161 (8th Cir.1990) (upholding operation of branches by acquiror despite contrary state law).

21. 12 U.S.C.A. § 1823(k)(4)(A).

22. *Id.*

limitations apply.[23] If the savings association does not have its home office in the state of the bank holding company bank subsidiary, and it does not qualify as a "domestic building and loan association" for tax purposes,[24] the savings association is subject to the same conditions imposed on a bank seeking to retain, operate, and establish branches in the state in which the insured association is located.[25] The FDIC is authorized, for good cause, to allow the association up to two years to comply with these requirements.[26]

23. *Id.* § 1823(k)(4)(B)(i).

24. 26 U.S.C.A. § 7701(a)(19). The same result would apply if the association does not meet the asset composition test imposed by *id.* § 7701(a)(19)(C).

25. 12 U.S.C.A. § 1823(k)(4)(B)(i) (I)(II).

26. *Id.* § 1823(k)(4)(B)(ii).

Chapter 9

INTERNATIONAL BANKING

Table of Sections

---

§ 9.1 Introduction

The development of international banking by U.S.-based banks has tended to be reactive.[1] For the most part, U.S. international banking has followed the expansion of transnational business interests of U.S. banks' larger customers. By 1914, however, European banks still dominated foreign bank branching over U.S. banks by a margin of almost 100 to 1.[2]

Four developments during the second decade of the Twentieth Century gradually changed the balance of power in international banking. First, in 1913 the Federal Reserve Act ("FRA") was enacted with provisions that for the first time permitted foreign branching by national banks.[3] Second, the beginning of World War I in 1914 began to realign the relative influence of U.S. and European banks.[4] Third, in 1916 the FRA was amended to authorize the Board of Governors of the Federal Reserve System ("Fed") to enter into agreements with state-chartered member banks to incorporate under state law subsidiaries specializing in international and foreign banking, so-called Agreement corporations.[5] Fourth, the Edge Act amended the FRA again in 1919 to permit the Fed to authorize the incorporation under federal law of subsidiaries specializing in international and foreign banking.[6]

The emerging influence of U.S.-based banks in international banking continued through the post-World War II period, in no small part due to the development of the Eurodollar market in offshore dollar-denominated deposits.[7] As the post-war dominance of U.S. commercial and financial strength diminished with reemergence of European economies and the development of newly emerging economies in Asia, and as financial problems of U.S. banks themselves developed in the late 1980s, overall international pres-

---

§ 9.1

1. Nevertheless, a select number of U.S. banks did venture offshore in pursuit of their own strategies by the end of the nineteenth century, such as J.P. Morgan and Company and Lazard Freres among others. *See* SARKIS J. KHOURY, DYNAMICS OF INTERNATIONAL BANKING 38 (New York: Praeger Special Studies, 1980) (discussing offshore expansion of certain U.S. banks in the 1800s). Citibank followed this trend after the enactment of international branching provisions in the Federal Reserve Act in 1913, 12 U.S.C.A. §§ 601 *et seq.*, establishing a network of offshore branches by the onset of World War I. *See* Haley & Seligman, *The Development of International Banking by the United States, in* W. H. BAUGHN & D. R. MANDICH, THE INTERNATIONAL BANKING HANDBOOK (1983) (discussing Citibank's expansion into 13 countries).

2. F. JOHN MATHIS, ED., OFFSHORE LENDING BY U.S. BANKS 23 (PHILADELPHIA: ROBERT MORRIS ASSOCIATES, 1981).

3. 12 U.S.C.A. §§ 601 *et seq.*

4. Haley & Seligman, *supra* note 1.

5. 12 U.S.C.A. §§ 613 *et seq. See* Neil Pinsky, *Edge Act and Agreement Corporations: Mediums for International Banking, in* Economic Perspective 28 (Federal Reserve Bank of Chicago, September–October 1978) (discussing slow historical beginning of use of state-incorporated "Agreement" corporations and federally incorporated Edge Act corporations).

6. 12 U.S.C.A. §§ 613 *et seq.*

7. *See, e.g.,* WORLD FINANCIAL MARKETS 3, 15 (New York: Morgan Guaranty Trust Co., October 1980) (noting the expanding importance of the Eurodollar market).

ence of U.S. banks also diminished.[8] However, during the 1990s, U.S. financial centers have reemerged as stable havens of economic activity,[9] and as a result the strength and influence of those centers have been renewed.[10]

§ 9.2　The Regulatory Environment

Permissible international banking activities vary significantly from country to country, largely due to the differing regulatory environments in their respective home states.[1] As a general rule, in less developed countries banking is subject to more severe controls than in developed economies. However, given the increasingly "globalized" nature of the banking markets, the regulatory environment facing a bank involved in international banking tends to be a complex mix of home-state supervision, host-state regulation, and specialized international or multinational rules enforced by both states.

A number of important contemporary trends have shaped the contours of the regulatory environment of international banking. First, an increasingly important role has been taken by the European Union ("EU") in the regulation of banking, and adjustments in the regulatory environment of the individual EU member states have become necessary.[2] Second, the transition from socialist to

---

8. *See* Kraus, *Overseas Pullback by US Banks Portends Reduced Global Role,* Am. Banker, Sept. 21, 1988, at 1, col. 2 (discussing changes in international role of U.S. banks).

9. *See, e.g.,* Sharon R. King, *Watchful Waiting on Japan,* N.Y. Times, Nov. 26, 1997, at C1, col. 2 (discussing the relative stability of U.S. financial markets).

10. *Cf.* Richard W. Stevenson, *Clinton Presses Asians at Summit To Remedy the Economic Turmoil,* N.Y. Times, at A1, col. 4 (discussing relative influence of U.S. economic policy); John M. Broder, *Asia Pacific Talks Vow Tough Action on Economic Crisis,* N.Y. Times, at A1, col. 6 (illustrating effects of U.S. financial and economic strength).

§ 9.2

1. *See* Wendt, *The Role of Foreign Banks in International Banking, in* W. H. Baughn & D. R. Mandich, The International Banking Handbook (1983) (discussing varying roles of non-U.S. banks in international banking).

2. *See. e.g.,* M. Galy, G. Pastor & T. Pujol, Spain: Converging with the European Community (IMF Occasional Paper

101, Feb. 1993) (discussing effects of ongoing convergence of the Spanish banking system with the EU). The structure of European bank regulation has remained largely a dual system, with the role of primary safety-and-soundness supervisor carried out by individual member state authorities. Emergencies involving transborder financial services firms operating across the EU—a more frequent occurrence during the financial crisis that erupted in 2008 (see § 9.26, *infra* (discussing the international implications of the crisis))—have put considerable strain on the dual-level regulatory structure. In response, the European Commission has established an expert advisory group to assist in improving supervision of financial services, as a possible precursor to EU-wide supervision of transborder banking. *See* Joe Kirwin, *EC to Set Up Expert Group to Chart Path For Revamping of EU Banking Supervision,* BNA Int'l Bus. & Fin. Daily (Oct. 9, 2008), available at http:// pubs.bna.com/ (discussing developments).

market economies in central and eastern Europe and the transformation of the former Soviet Union into the loose confederation of the Commonwealth of Independent States has had important consequences for banking and bank regulation.[3] Third, something approaching genuine international regulation has emerged primarily under the auspices of the Bank for International Settlements ("BIS") and the "Group of Ten," the major industrialized democracies. Each of these developments has had a marked impact on the conduct of international banking activities.[4]

§ 9.3　National　Supervision　of　International　Banking

One fundamental objective is shared by bank supervisors worldwide: to support the "lender of last resort" function triggered by significant financial instability, in order to maintain public confidence in the depository institutions system.[1] Since domestic banking systems are interlinked—if not integrated—on a transborder basis, significant instability in any one market is potentially a problem for other markets. Yet there often appears to be little if any agreement among national regulators as to approaches to regulation and supervision of depository institutions subject to their respective jurisdictions, particularly on a day-to-day basis. In the case of U.S. bank supervision and regulation, the approach has been one of relatively close oversight of the banking system, including maintenance of public confidence and stability by the establishment of restrictions on industry structure (e.g., entry, competition,

---

3. *See, e.g.,* Inna Vysman, *The New Banking Legislation in Russia: Theoretical Adequacy, Practical Difficulties, and Potential Solutions,* 62 Fordham L. Rev. 265 (1993) (describing and assessing transformation of banking and bank regulation in the Russian Federation).

4. For example, in May 2001, European Commissioner Frederik Bolkestein announced that the consumer financial information privacy provisions of the Gramm–Leach–Bliley Act (GLBA), Pub. L. No. 106–102, Nov. 12, 1999, §§ 501–505, 113 Stat. 1338, 1436–1440 (1999) (codified at 15 U.S.C.A. §§ 6801–6805), were not sufficient to guarantee privacy protections afforded citizens of EU member states. Charles Bogino & Anandashankar Mazumdar, *EU Commissioner Says Current U.S. Law Inadequate to Protect Financial Services,* BNA Banking Daily, May 14, 2001, at d4. (The text of documents related to the data protection issue is available at the European Union's Europa Web site, http://europa.

eu.int, and at the U.S. Department of Commerce's Export Portal Web site, http://www.export.gov.) The EU position may result in a reassessment of U.S. financial information privacy policy, in order to avoid compromising the activities of U.S.-based banks in the EU market. On GLBA rules governing privacy and disclosure of nonpublic personal information, see *infra* 10.6.

§ 9.3

1. In the United States, the lender of last resort function—providing financial assistance to institutions experiencing the most significant financial crises— has traditionally been performed by the Federal Reserve System. The National Credit Union Administration also performs a similar function with respect to credit unions, as did the now defunct Federal Home Loan Bank Board, until 1989, with respect to savings associations.

products,) and operations (e.g., capital adequacy, lending limits, liquidity, interest rates). In other jurisdictions, supervision may be comparatively passive, or it may largely consist of self-regulation, at least on a day-to-day basis.

§ 9.4 U.S. Supervision of International Banking

The regulatory structure governing U.S. domestic banking is extremely complex. That complexity carries over into U.S. regulation of international banking activities. However, additional complications are introduced into the regulatory structure specifically because of the international dimension of these activities. A basic overview of U.S. regulation of international banking activity is provided in Figure 9–1, *infra.*

Foreign-based banks operate in the United States within the same supervisory structure as U.S.-based banks, consistent with the policy of "national treatment" established by the International Banking Act of 1978.[1] (Different modes of operation are explained in § 9.11, *infra.*) A foreign-based bank that wishes to operate a representative office in the United States must obtain the prior approval of the Fed.[2] To operate an agency, branch, affiliate, or subsidiary in the United States it must apply to the Fed, and a U.S. agency or branch of a foreign-based bank must be licensed and supervised either by a state supervisor or the Comptroller of the Currency. In addition, all U.S. agencies or branches must be approved and supervised by the Fed. The FDIC approves deposit insurance coverage for U.S. branches of foreign banks.

In general, any foreign bank that maintains a branch or agency within the United States, and any company of which the foreign bank is a subsidiary, are subject to the requirements of the Bank Holding Company Act ("BHCA")[3] with respect to restrictions on nonbanking activities.[4] Nonconforming activities are grandfathered as of the pertinent date that the BHCA became applicable to the foreign enterprise's activities.[5] However, the grandfather authority lasts only two years after the date on which the foreign bank or

---

§ 9.4

1. On the concept of national treatment, see *Conference of State Bank Supervisors v. Conover*, 715 F.2d 604 (D.C.Cir.1983), *cert. denied*, 466 U.S. 927, 104 S.Ct. 1708 (1984).

2. *See, e.g.,* Andhra Bank Hyderabad, India: Order Approving Establishment of a Representative Office (July 23, 2008), available at http://www.federalreserve.gov/newsevents/press/orders/orders20080723a1.pdf; International Bank of Azerbaijan, Baku, Azerbaijan:

Order Approving Establishment of a Representative Office, available at http://www.federalreserve.gov/pubs/bulletin/2008/legal/q308/order7.htm.

3. *See* 12 U.S.C.A. § 1843 (prohibiting nonbanking activities of bank holding companies absent applicable exception).

4. *Id.* § 3106(a)(1), (3). On BHCA restrictions on nonbanking activities, see *supra* §§ 6.2–6.5.

5. 12 U.S.C.A. § 3106(c)(1).

other company became a "bank holding company,"[6] except that the Fed may, upon application of the foreign bank or company, extend the period for not more than one year at a time, "if, in its judgment, such an extension would not be detrimental to the public interest."[7] These extensions may not exceed three years in the aggregate.[8] The Gramm–Leach–Bliley Act ("GLBA")[9] permits termination of the financial grandfathering authority granted by federal statute to foreign banking enterprises to engage in certain financial activities.[10] Foreign banking enterprises with grandfathered financial affiliates would be permitted to retain these affiliates on the same terms that domestic "financial holding companies" ("FHCs") are permitted to establish them.[11]

A significant change in the supervision of international banking occurred in December 1991, the President signed into law the Federal Deposit Insurance Corporation Improvement Act of 1991 ("FDICIA").[12] In brief, the principal features of the FDICIA that affect international banking are as follows.

a. *Capital supervision.* The FDICIA requires the federal banking agencies to revise their risk-based capital standards for insured depository institutions to ensure, among other things, that these standards take account of interest-rate risk, concentration of credit risk, and the risks of nontraditional activities.[13] The agencies are also required to discuss the development of comparable standards with members of the supervisory committee of the BIS.[14]

b. *Payments on foreign deposits.* FDICIA prohibits the agencies from making, directly or indirectly, any payment, or from providing any financial assistance in connection with any insured depository institution that would have the direct or indirect effect of satisfying any claim, in whole or in part, against the institution for its obligations on foreign deposits.[15] This prohibition does not apply to "open bank assistance" provided by the FDIC.[16] Nor does the prohibition bar a Federal Reserve bank from making advances or other extensions of credit consistent with the Federal Reserve Act (so-called discount window lending).[17]

---

6. *See id.* § 1841(a) (defining "bank holding company" for purposes of BHCA).

7. *Id.* § 3106(c)(2).

8. *Id.*

9. Pub. L. No. 106–102, Nov. 12, 1999, 113 Stat. 1338 (1999) (codified at scattered sections of 12, 15, 16, 18 U.S.C.A.).

10. GLBA, § 141 (codified at 12 U.S.C.A. § 3106(c)(3)).

11. *Id.* On the establishment and regulation of FHCs, see *supra* §§ 6.3–6.4.

12. Pub. L. No. 102–242, 105 Stat. 2236 (Dec. 19, 1991) (codified at scattered sections of 12 U.S.C.A.).

13. FDICIA, § 305(b)(1) (12 U.S.C.A. § 1828 Note).

14. FDICIA, § 305(b)(2).

15. 12 U.S.C.A. § 1831r(a).

16. *Id.* § 1831r(b). On "open-bank" assistance, see *id.* § 1823(c).

17. *Id.* § 1831r(c).

c. *Establishment and operation of federal branches and agencies of foreign-based banks.* Under FDICIA, the Comptroller is required, in considering any application for approval of an initial federal branch or agency, to include any condition imposed by the Fed as a condition for the approval of the application.[18] The Comptroller is also required to coordinate examinations of such branches and agencies with examinations conducted by the Fed, to the extent possible, to participate in any simultaneous examinations of U.S. operations of foreign banks requested by the Fed.[19] Furthermore, in considering any application to establish an additional federal branch or agency of a foreign-based bank, the Comptroller is required to provide the Fed with notice and opportunity for comment on the application.[20]

d. *Broadened Fed supervisory authority.* The Fed is given authority to approve the establishment of any branch or agency, or the acquisition or control of any commercial lending company by a foreign-based bank.[21] The Fed also has the authority, under specified circumstances to order the closing of any state-licensed office of a foreign-based bank,[22] and to recommend to the Comptroller the termination of the license of any federally-licensed office of a foreign-based bank.[23] The FDICIA also gives the Fed broad authority to examine U.S. branches, agencies and affiliates of foreign-based banks, whether state-or federally-approved.[24]

e. *Limitation of powers of state-licensed branches and agencies.* The FDICIA prohibits a state-licensed branch or agency from engaging in any type of activity that is not permissible for a federally-licensed branch, unless the Fed determines that the activity is consistent with sound banking practice, and (in the case of an insured branch), the FDIC determines that the activity would pose no significant risk to the deposit insurance fund.[25] In addition, such branches and agencies are subject to the same limits on lending to a single borrower that apply to federally-licensed branches and agencies.[26]

f. *Establishment and supervision of representative offices.* Prior to the FDICIA, a foreign bank operating a representative office in the United States was only required to register the office with the Department of the Treasury.[27] Under the FDICIA and the 1999 GLBA, establishment of a representative office now requires prior

---

18. *Id.* § 3102(a)(2).

19. *Id.* § 3102(b).

20. *Id.* § 3102(h)(2).

21. *Id.* § 3105(d)(1), (g).

22. *Id.* § 3105(e)(1)–(4), (g).

23. *Id.* § 3105(e)(5).

24. *Id.* § 3105(b)(1).

25. *Id.* § 3105(h)(1).

26. *Id.* § 3105(h)(2). In fact, the FDICIA allows the Fed or the state supervisory authority to impose more stringent restrictions than apply to federally-licensed branches and agencies. *Id.* § 3105(h)(3).

27. 12 U.S.C.A. § 3107 (1988).

approval of the Fed.[28] The Fed also has the authority to terminate the activities of any representative office.[29] It also has the authority to examine representative offices.[30]

g. *Cooperation with foreign supervisors.* The FDICIA explicitly authorizes disclosure of supervisory information by the federal bank agencies to foreign bank regulatory or supervisory authorities.[31]

h. *Retail deposit-taking by foreign banks.* To accept or maintain deposit accounts with balances of less than $100,000, foreign banks are required to establish one or more U.S. banking subsidiaries for that purpose, and to obtain federal deposit insurance for any such subsidiary.[32] However, if the foreign bank had a U.S. branch that was an insured branch prior to FDICIA, the branch may continue to accept or maintain retail deposits.[33]

i. *New penalties.* The FDICIA established authority for civil money penalties (administrative fines) to be assessed against any foreign bank, and any office or subsidiary of a foreign bank, that violates, and any individual who participates in a violation of, any provision of the International Banking Act, or any regulation prescribed or order issued under the act.[34] In addition, the FDICIA established criminal penalties for the knowing violation of any provision of the International Banking Act or any regulation or order issued by a federal banking agency under the act, with the intent to deceive, to gain financially, or to cause financial gain or loss to any person.[35]

Where do the U.S. state bank regulators fit into this regulatory structure? International Banking Act ("IBA") provisions concerning federal branches and agencies have minimized the role of state bank regulators as policy makers, since entry into the U.S. market through federal licensing of a branch or agency is a preemptive possibility in most cases.[36] FDICIA amendments of the IBA have further affected the relative importance of the state regulators with respect to international banking. The Fed's authority over state-licensed branches and agencies has increased dramatically. Powers of state-licensed branches and agencies are now directly limited by the IBA.[37] The Fed may even impose more stringent restrictions

---

28. 12 U.S.C.A. § 3107(a). *See also* GLBA, § 142 (codified at 12 U.S.C.A. §§ 3101(b)(15), 3107(c)) (requiring prior approval by Fed for establishment of any representative office that is subsidiary of foreign bank). Compliance with any applicable state law requirements is still required. 12 U.S.C.A. § 3107(d).

29. *Id.* § 3107(b).

30. *Id.* § 3107(c).

31. *Id.* § 3109(a).

32. *Id.* § 3104(c)(1).

33. *Id.* § 3104(c)(2).

34. *Id.* § 3110.

35. *Id.* § 3111.

36. *Conference of State Bank Supervisors, supra.*

37. 12 U.S.C.A. § 3105(h).

than those that apply to federally-licensed branches and agencies.[38] The establishment of representative offices is also subject to prior Fed approval, and the Fed has the authority to examine and to terminate such offices.[39]

Figure 9–1

Depository Institutions and their Regulators: International Banking Activities[40]

A.   Organization & Expansion

Type of Institution	Chartering/ Licensing	Branching Intrastate	Branching Interstate	Acquisitions Intrastate	Acquisitions Interstate
Foreign Branch of U.S. Bank					
National Bank	Federal Reserve	N/A	N/A	N/A	N/A
State Fed–Member Bank	Federal Reserve and States	N/A	N/A	N/A	N/A
Insured State Non–Member Bank	FDIC & States	N/A	N/A	N/A	N/A
Edge Act Corporation	Federal Reserve	Federal Reserve	Federal Reserve	Federal Reserve	Federal Reserve
Agreement Corporation	State and Federal Reserve	Federal Reserve	Federal Reserve	State and Federal Reserve	Federal Reserve
International Banking Facility	N/A	N/A	N/A	N/A	N/A
U.S. Branches & Agencies of Foreign Banks					
Federal	Comptroller & Federal Reserve	Comptroller & Federal Reserve	Comptroller & FDIC	Comptroller & Federal Reserve	Comptroller & Federal Reserve
State	States & Federal Reserve	States & FDIC	States & Federal Reserve	States, Federal Reserve, & FDIC	States & Federal Reserve

B.   Transactional

Type of Institution	Reserve Requirements	Access to Discount Window	Discount Deposit
Foreign Branch of U.S. Bank			
National Bank	Federal Reserve	N/A	N/A
State Fed–Member Bank	Federal Reserve	N/A	N/A

---

38. *Id.* § 3105(h)(3).

39. *Id.* § 3107.

40. Source: Adapted from Federal Reserve Bank of New York, *Depository Institutions and Their Regulators* (1987).

Type of Institution	Reserve Requirements	Access to Discount Window	Discount Deposit
Insured State Non–Member Bank	Federal Reserve	N/A	N/A
Edge Act Corporation	Federal Reserve	N/A	N/A
Agreement Corporation	Federal Reserve	N/A	N/A
International Banking Facility	Federal Reserve	N/A	N/A
U.S. Branches & Agencies of Foreign Banks			
Federal	Federal Reserve	Federal Reserve	FDIC
State	Federal Reserve	Federal Reserve	FDIC

C. Supervision & Regulation

Type of Institution	Supervision and Examination	Prudential Limits, Safety & Soundness	Consumer Protection	Enforcement
Foreign Branch of U.S. Bank				
National Bank	Comptroller	Comptroller	N/A	Comptroller
State Fed–Member Bank	Federal Reserve & States	Federal Reserve & States	N/A	Federal Reserve & States
Insured State Non–Member Bank	FDIC & States	FDIC & States	N/A	FDIC & States
Edge Act Corporation	Federal Reserve	Federal Reserve	N/A	Federal Reserve
Agreement Corporation	States & Federal Reserve	States & Federal Reserve	N/A	States & Federal Reserve
International Banking Facility	Federal Reserve	Federal Reserve	N/A	N/A
U.S. Branches & Agencies of Foreign Banks				
Federal	Comptroller & Federal Reserve	Comptroller & Federal Reserve	Comptroller & Federal Reserve	Comptroller & Federal Reserve
State	States, Federal Reserve, & FDIC	States, Federal Reserve, & FDIC	States & Federal Reserve	States, Federal Reserve, & FDIC

§ 9.5 Host State Regulation of International Banking

The international activities of U.S. banks are also affected by the regulation of other host states. International banking is subject to a diverse array of restrictions imposed by host states, in many cases severely limiting and in some cases actually prohibiting entry of nonindigenous banking enterprises into the local market.[1] As a

§ 9.5

1. REPORT TO CONGRESS ON FOREIGN

GOVERNMENT TREATMENT OF U.S. BANKING ORGANIZATIONS (Washington, D.C.: U.S.

result, the regulatory laws and policies of host states represent a significant factor in the decision to enter the international market and in the determination of the scope and nature of a bank's international operations. In some cases, differential treatment by the host country will impair the competitive position of an international bank.[2]

From the perspective of the United States as a host state, the International Banking Act ("IBA") endorses a policy "national treatment" of foreign banks seeking entry into the U.S. banking market. However, despite the U.S. policy of encouraging "national treatment" for U.S. banks within other local markets, transnational competitive disadvantages remain. Generally, the U.S. policy has resulted in no improvement in most host state markets.[3]

Another approach to the problem of treatment of foreign investment by nonindigenous enterprises is embodied in the concept of reciprocity. As mentioned in *Conference of State Bank Supervisors v. Conover*,[4] U.S. state bank regulatory provisions may include reciprocity as a condition on entry of foreign banks into the state's banking market. As with the national treatment concept, the precise meaning of "reciprocity" will vary from jurisdiction to jurisdiction, ranging from a strict reciprocity (or "one-for-one") approach, to more flexible approaches. However, in the United States the federal national treatment policy has the effect of

Government Printing Office, 1979). In the years since this "National Treatment" study, the range of competitive disadvantages facing U.S. banks in the international market has remained broad. Competitive disadvantages may result from artificially imposed limitations on capital formation, asset growth, and product and market expansion. In addition, host country regulation remains a source of competitive disadvantage, resulting from differential treatment of multinational banking enterprises. Although the 1986 update of the study, DEPARTMENT OF THE TREASURY, NATIONAL TREATMENT STUDY: 1986 UPDATE (1986) indicates improvement in the competitive climate, this improvement is far from complete or uniform. The 1986 Update was intended to examine the improvement, if any, in the competitive climate for U.S. banks and other financial institutions in foreign markets since the issuance of the first update was issued in July 1984. 1986 UPDATE at 1. Senator Garn, then Chairman of the Senate Banking Committee, had re-

quested that the 1986 Update be broadened to include, *inter alia*, the treatment of U.S. securities firms in foreign markets. *See id.* The primary finding of the 1986 Update in this regard was that, overall,

> the degree of national treatment received by U.S. banks abroad has somewhat improved since the 1984 Update. Over the eight years subsequent to passage of the [IBA], the record reflects sporadic and slow improvement in treatment.

Id. at 3.

2. *See* REPORT TO CONGRESS, *supra* (detailing disparate treatment).

3. *See* 1986 UPDATE at 5–9 *passim*. Furthermore, even significant improvement in a particular host state market "do[es] not necessarily mean that national treatment has been approached or achieved—substantial areas of discrimination may still remain." *Id.* at 3.

4. 715 F.2d 604 (D.C.Cir.1983), *cert. denied*, 466 U.S. 927, 104 S.Ct. 1708 (1984).

preempting any state reciprocity requirements that impede the federal policy.[5]

§ 9.6 International Regulation of International Banking

International banking regulation and supervision is formulated in a domestic context, with certain limited exceptions. Important examples of regional arrangements for the regulation of financial services are the provided by the European Union[1] and the North American Free Trade Agreement (NAFTA).[2] At the international level, the most notable exceptions to the domestic orientation of banking regulation involve the work of the Bank for International Settlements ("BIS"), and the General Agreement on Trade in Services ("GATS"). Each is intended to produce supervisory initiatives based on multilateral undertakings that respond to the need for regulation of international activities on an international basis.[3] Curiously, the increasing interdependence of international banks and their activities cause domestic regulators to fashion *multilateral* undertakings to secure what are still essentially *domestic* objectives.

§ 9.7 The Bank for International Settlements

The BIS has been a leader in initiating genuine international bank regulation. The BIS, located in Basel, Switzerland, is a multilateral bank for national central banks. It is primarily supported by the "Group of Ten" large industrialized democracies, consisting of Belgium, Canada, France, Germany, Italy, Japan, the Netherlands, Sweden, United Kingdom, and the United States, with Switzerland as an additional significant participant. The BIS assists these central banks in the transfer and investment of monetary reserves

---

5. See, e.g., *National Commercial Banking Corp. of Australia, Ltd. v. Harris*, 125 Ill.2d 448, 532 N.E.2d 812 (1988) (preempting application of state nonreciprocal license fee to foreign banks which "do[ ] not provide reciprocal licensing authority" to state or national banks).

§ 9.6

1. See, e.g., *Reorganisation and Winding up of Credit Institutions*, Directive 2001/24/EC (4 April 2001) (providing for EU supervision and resolution of failing banks). For a comparative analysis including EU financial services regulation, see Joel P. Trachtman, *Trade in Financial Services Under GATS, NAFTA and the EC: A Regulatory Jurisdiction Analysis*, 34 Colum. J.

Transnat'l L. 37 (1995). *See also* Michael P. Malloy, International Banking 17–19 (2d ed. 2005) (discussing effect of EU regulation of banking).

2. For discussion of the impact of NAFTA on banking regulation, see Michael P. Malloy, *Financial Services Regulation After NAFTA, in* Kevin Kennedy (ed.), The First Decade of NAFTA: The Future of Free Trade in North America (2004).

3. On multilateral efforts to foster convergence in bank regulatory standards, see Brian P. Volkman, *The Global Convergence of Bank Regulation and Standards for Compliance*, 115 Banking L.J. 550 (1998).

and often plays a role in settling international loan arrangements. Of increasing significance is its role as a forum or catalyst for international monetary cooperation and policy development.

§ 9.8   Coordination of International Supervision

The dramatic failure of Herstatt Bank in Germany and Franklin National Bank in New York in 1974—with its financial repercussions throughout the increasingly "internationalized" banking market—led the Group of Ten to sponsor an informal understanding on resolution of international bank failures, now known as the Basel Concordat (1974). The Governors of the BIS acknowledged the need to establish a framework of multilateral bank supervision, and so they formed the Committee on Banking Regulations and Supervisory Practices, now known as the Committee on Banking Supervision. The committee originally consisted of foreign exchange and supervisory officials from the Group of Ten, plus Luxembourg and Switzerland, but its membership has grown over time.[1]

This standing committee of the BIS is intended to promote cooperation among national regulators. It looks to the establishment of broadly delineated principles to guide the differing national supervisory systems in establishing their own detailed arrangements. Thus, the 1974 Concordat established the following set of broad principles. All foreign banking institutions should be subject to supervision. Supervision should be adequate, judged by the standards of both host and home (parent) authorities. Supervision of a joint venture involving parent institutions in more than one country should be undertaken by the host authorities of the venture. Achievement of these objectives calls for cooperation between host and parent authorities. In general, supervising liquidity (*i.e.*, the ability to meet obligations as they mature) must rest first with the local authorities. Supervision for solvency (*i.e.*, the condition in which assets exceed net liabilities) must rest primarily with the host authority for foreign subsidiaries and joint ventures, while in the case of branches, solvency was principally the concern of the home supervisory authority of the parent bank.

§ 9.8

1. The Basel Committee on Banking Supervision has increased the size of its membership several times. With Spain joining on 1 February 2001, the Committee consisted of thirteen participant states: the G–10 countries plus Luxembourg, Spain and Switzerland. See BIS website, http://www.bis.org. In March 2009 the Basel Committee extended membership to Australia, Brazil, China, India, Mexico, Russia, and South Korea.

See Daniel Pruzin, *Basel Committee Announces Expansion Of Membership to Emerging Economies*, BNA INT'L BUS. & FIN. DAILY (June 11, 2009), *available at* http://pubs.bna.com/ (discussing implications of expanded membership). In June 2009, Argentina, Indonesia, Saudi Arabia, South Africa, and Turkey joined the committee. The Basel Committee has also invited Hong Kong and Singapore to take part in the committee's deliberations.

The generality of the guiding principles articulated in the 1974 Concordat encountered harsh reality and lost in 1982, when Banco Ambrosiano failed. The bank was based in Italy and had a subsidiary in Luxembourg. Italian authorities at first indicated that, from the lender of last resort perspective, they would honor only Ambrosiano's domestic (*i.e.*, Italian) obligations. This caused great distress in the banking world, although a large group of creditor banks of the subsidiary did eventually reach a settlement with Italian central bank involving more than $300 million in subsidiary obligations.

One result of the experience of resolving the difficulties of this multinational bank failure was the revision of the Concordat in 1983.[2] The revision articulated in relatively greater detail supervisory responsibilities with respect to multinational banking enterprises. The 1983 Concordat identifies principles for the supervision of the foreign operations of international banking enterprises. It deals exclusively with the responsibilities of banking supervisors for monitoring the prudential conduct and soundness of these foreign operations; it does not address itself to lender-of-last-resort functions of central banks. The "principles" are not, strictly speaking, legally binding. Rather, they are "recommended guidelines of best practices . . . , which all members have undertaken to work towards implementing, according to the means available to them."[3] The Concordat established certain basic, thematic principles. First, effective cooperation between home-country and host-country authorities is essential to the supervision of international banking operations. The next two principles follow from the first. Second, no banking establishment should escape supervision. Third, supervision must be adequate.

Hence, home-country and host-country authorities must keep each other effectively informed of serious problems that arise in or affect a parent bank's foreign operations. The Concordat identified three categories of operation in international banking: branches, subsidiaries, and joint ventures or consortia. As to each of these categories, the Concordat recommends certain principles for the resolution of liquidity and solvency problems. Essentially, these principles attempt to establish relative roles that home-country and host country authorities should undertake.

As to the supervision of a bank's foreign exchange operations, the Concordat takes the position that these should be the joint responsibility of the home-country and host-country authorities.

---

2. Bank for International Settlements, Committee on Banking Regulations and Supervisory Practices, Principles for the Supervision of Banks' Foreign Establishments (1983), *reprinted in* Michael P.

Malloy, International Banking 79–83 (2d ed. 2005).

3. *Id.* at 79.

Home-country authorities are expected to monitor the internal controls of their international banking enterprises. Host-country authorities are expected to monitor the foreign exchange exposure of foreign bank operations within their territories.

Since the issuance of the Basel Concordat, the BIS Committee has given further attention to the problems of supervising transnational banking enterprises. An April 1990 Supplement to the Concordat sought to strengthen the principle of effective information flow between home-country and host-country authorities,[4] by making the rules on information transfer more explicit and detailed. Part D of the 1990 Supplement deals with the problem of domestic bank secrecy laws that might otherwise impede information flows necessary for effective transnational regulation and supervision of banking.

The scandal surrounding the collapse of the Bank of Credit and Commerce International ("BCCI")[5] subsequently caused the BIS Committee to review the arrangements for coordination of international bank supervision, which was sorely lacking in the events surrounding the BCCI collapse. Hence, in June 1992, the BIS Committee took the further significant step of issuing a report establishing binding minimum standards on the supervision of international banking enterprises.[6] While the standards are not, on their own terms, binding on states, BIS participating states are expected to implement them, and other states are encouraged to do so. In the United States, implementation has occurred primarily in connection with the enactment of the FDICIA.[7]

These issuances are intended to foster better information flows between national regulators and better national controls over the entry of a multinational banking enterprise into the national market supervised by the regulator. If these policies are effective, presumably the supervision of multinational bank failures could be

---

4. BANK FOR INTERNATIONAL SETTLEMENTS, COMMITTEE ON BANKING REGULATION AND SUPERVISORY PRACTICES: SUPPLEMENT TO THE BASEL CONCORDAT ENSURING OF ADEQUATE INFORMATION FLOWS BETWEEN BANKING SUPERVISORY AUTHORITIES (1990), *reprinted in* MALLOY, INTERNATIONAL BANKING, *supra*, at 84–87.

5. For a review of the BCCI scandal and the legislative reaction to the scandal in the United States, see RAJ K. BHALA, FOREIGN BANK REGULATION AFTER BCCI (1994).

6. BANK FOR INTERNATIONAL SETTLEMENTS, BASEL COMMITTEE ON BANKING REGULATION AND SUPERVISORY PRACTICES: REPORT ON MINIMUM STANDARDS FOR THE SUPERVISION OF INTERNATIONAL BANKING GROUPS AND THEIR CROSS-BORDER ESTABLISHMENT (1992), *reprinted in*, MALLOY, INTERNATIONAL BANKING, *supra*, at 87–91.

7. *See, e.g.*, 12 U.S.C.A. §§ 3105(d)(2)(1)(A) (approval of U.S. branch of foreign bank; comprehensive supervision of applicant on consolidated basis by home state authorities required); 3105(d)(3)(A) (same; consent of home state to establishment of U.S. branch as standard of approval by U.S. authorities); 3105(e)(1)(A) (termination of U.S. office of foreign bank when foreign bank not subject to comprehensive supervision on consolidated basis by home state authorities).

more efficiently anticipated or managed. More recently, the Basel Committee on Banking Supervision, in conjunction with the International Monetary Fund and the International Bank for Reconstruction and Development, developed a set of core principles for effective banking supervision.[8] The Core Principles consisted of twenty-five basic principles, ranging from preconditions for effective banking supervision (Principle 1) to principles for cross-border banking (Principles 23–25).

The principles were, of course, not binding, but they did provide a basic reference point for supervisors. In April 2006, the Committee issued a proposed revision of the CORE PRINCIPLES.[9] After a comment period for banks and other institutions, the revised version of the CORE PRINCIPLES was issued in October 2006. The basic focus remains the same as in the original version, but a new "umbrella principle" advises banks to establish integrated risk management systems across the range of different risks that banks face (Principle 7). Criteria for evaluating liquidity (Principle 14), operational (Principle 15), and interest rate (Principle 16) risks have also been enhanced, and criteria with respect to money laundering, terrorist financing, and fraud prevention (Principle 18) have been strengthened. Bank supervisors from central banks and supervisory agencies in 120 countries endorsed the updated version of the Basel Core Principles.

In June 2009, the BIS Committee and the International Association of Deposit Insurers (IADI) issued a final version of *Core Principles for Effective Deposit Insurance Systems*, a set of joint voluntary guidelines for the establishment and maintenance of an effective deposit insurance system.[10] Core Principles identifies eighteen recommendations concerning, inter alia, the objectives and powers of deposit insurance systems, governance issues, relationships with other safety-net participants, cross-border issues, coverage and funding, and reimbursing depositors.[11]

---

8. BASEL COMMITTEE ON BANKING SUPERVISION, BASEL CORE PRINCIPLES FOR EFFECTIVE BANKING SUPERVISION (SEPT. 22, 1997), *reprinted in* 37 Int'l Leg. Mat. 405 (1998) ("CORE PRINCIPLES"). The principles are, of course, not binding and "serve as a basic reference for supervisory and other public authorities in all countries and internationally." CORE PRINCIPLES, 37 Int'l Leg. Mat. at 407.

9. *See* CORE PRINCIPLES METHODOLOGY–CONSULTATIVE DOCUMENT (2006), *available at* http://www.bis.org/publ/bcbs124.htm. A paper comparing the 1999 and 2006 versions of the METHODOLOGY is available at http://www.bis.org/publ/bcpmaster

mapping.pdf. *See generally* Daniel Pruzin, *Basel Committee Issues Revised Supervisory Principles for Comment*, BNA INT'L BUS. & FIN. DAILY (April 10, 2006), *available at* http://pubs.bna.com/ip/bna/ibd.nsf/eh/A0B2Q2G8G2 (discussing proposed revision).

10. Daniel Pruzin, Basel Committee, Deposit Insurers Issue Final Version of Deposit Insurer Guidelines, BNA Banking Daily (June 19, 2009), available at http://www.bna.com. The Core Principles is available on the BIS website at http://www.bis.org/publ/bcbs156.htm.

11. Basel Committee, supra.

§ 9.9   Capital Adequacy

The BIS is also responsible for what is perhaps the most significant recent development in terms of substantive international supervision of banking—the formulation of uniform guidelines governing the measurement and enforcement of capital adequacy of banks.[1] In U.S. practice, capital adequacy requirements predate the BIS efforts in this regard.[2] However, the rules developed under BIS auspices are aimed not only at a capital adequacy regime that is effective as a purely regulatory matter, but also one that will encourage a multilateral convergence of regulatory standards.[3]

In 2004, after five years of study and controversy, the BIS Committee approved the final version of a dramatic replacement for the capital adequacy guidelines.[4] Among other things, the new version, known as Basel II, was intended to address the four basic problems that affected the original guidelines, now known as Basel I. At its most basic level, it extensively refined the Basel I guidelines. In addition, the new approach, Basel II, (*i*) would require international banks to establish their own internal methods for assessing the relative risks of their assets that would be more precise than the previous guidelines; (*ii*) would mandate that supervisory authorities exercise greater oversight of capital assessments by banks; and, (*iii*) would require greater transparency in banking operations, *e.g.*, the creditworthiness of borrowing governments and corporations would be assessed by credit-rating agencies, and these ratings would be used by banks in pricing loans to such borrowers.

The BIS Committee expected that Basel II would become the global standard for minimum capital requirements, as had Basel I before it.[5] However, India and China, among other major developing countries, had already indicated that they did not intend to adopt Basel II,[6] and U.S. supervisors—including the SEC as well as

---

§ 9.9

1. Bank for International Settlements, Final Report for International Convergence of Capital Measurement and Capital Standards, *reprinted in* 4 Fed. Banking L. Rep. (CCH) ¶ 47105 (Mar. 15, 1996) ("Final Report"). For discussion of the BIS capital adequacy rules and their implementation in U.S. law, see *supra* § 7.9.

2. *See* Michael P. Malloy, *U.S. International Banking and the New Capital Adequacy Requirements: New, Old and Unexpected*, 7 Ann. Rev. Banking L. 75, 75–76, 81–87 (1988) (discussing pre-BIS U.S. regulatory practice).

3. For discussion of the evolving BIS approaches to capital adequacy, see Michael P. Malloy, *Capital Adequacy and Regulatory Objectives*, 25 Suffolk Trans-nat'l L. Rev. 299 (2002).

4. Daniel Pruzin, *Basel Committee Announces Deal On Key Remaining Accord Issues*, BNA Banking Daily, May 12, 2004.

5. *Id.*

6. *Id.* However, in April 2006, the head of China's Banking Regulatory Commission stated that China would adopt Basel II standards within four to six years for domestic banks with substantial numbers of overseas branches.

the four principal federal bank supervisors—decided that Basel II would only be applied to the relatively small number of the largest internationally-active U.S. banks.[7] The vast majority of U.S. financial institutions would continue to be governed by a modified version of Basel I, referred to as "Basel IA." This could stratify U.S. bank supervision, as between the largest banks and all other financial institutions, for the first time in the history of modern U.S. bank supervision. Exacerbating concerns about regulatory stratification, a BIS quantitative impact study ("QIS 4") indicated that Basel II would significantly reduce aggregate bank regulatory capital of the banks to which it applied. As a result, supervisors had to consider whether to add capital charges under their enhanced supervisory review authority to account for noncredit risks (*e.g.*, interest rate risk, concentration risk, strategic risk, liquidity risk).[8]

The QIS 4 data indefinitely delayed the plans of U.S. supervisors to ask for comment on proposed rules implementing Basel II during the Summer 2005. The data also raised questions about the ability of banks relegated to Basel IA to compete with banks that are permitted to adopt the Basel II methodologies. This situation would give Basel II banks significant competitive advantages over Basel IA banks, and might leave the latter vulnerable to acquisition by the former, a result that would be politically unacceptable to many in the U.S. Congress. As a result, the supervisors put their plans on hold in May 2005, to allow more time to analyze the QIS 4 results. In September 2005, after further congressional hearings on Basel II, U.S. supervisors announced that they would delay implementation by at least one year and would develop extra safeguards to address the problems identified by the QIS 4.[9]

By March 2006, the Comptroller of the Currency acknowledged that the QIS4 did indicate that implementation of Basel II in 2007

Kathleen E. McLaughlin, *CBRC Chair Says China Will Adopt Basel II Standards Starting in 2010*, BNA BANKING DAILY (April 13, 2006), *available at* http://pubs.bna.com/ip/bna/bbd.nsf/eh/A0 B2Q6C7R7.

7. *Five Federal Agencies Announce Plans to Implement Basel II over Four-year Period*, BNA Banking Daily, June 29, 2004.

8. Also in July 2005, the Basel Committee and the International Organization of Securities Commissions (IOSCO) finalized rules on capital set-aside requirements for bank exposures related to trading in securities, derivatives, and other financial instruments, as well as the treatment of "double default effects," *i.e.*, the risk that both a borrower and a guarantor could default on the

same obligation. Daniel Pruzin, *Basel Committee, IOSCO Finalize Rules On Treatment of Trade–Related Exposures*, BNA Banking Daily, July 19, 2005, *available at* http://pubs.bna.com/ip/BNA/ bbd.nsf/is/A0B1D1N8C5. The Basel Committee/IOSCO paper, *The Application of Basel II to Trading Activities and the Treatment of Double Default Effects*, is available at http://www.bis.org. The new rules amend several aspects of Basel II, to increase significantly the risk-sensitivity of capital requirements for these exposures.

9. R. Christian Bruce, *Regulators Delay Basel II Implementation, Promising New Roadmap, Extra Safeguards*, BNA BANKING DAILY (Oct. 3, 2005), *available at* http://pubs.bna.com/ip/BNA/bbd. nsf/is/ A0B1P0X1Q1.

would result in a substantial overall drop in and dispersal of capital standards.[10] He indicated that U.S. supervisors would impose a one-year delay before promulgating a final rule, and a three-year transition period to allow affected banks to prepare for the new accord.[11] Throughout the Spring of 2006, the federal regulators tried to contain the growing anxiety about the potential negative effects of Basel II. In May 2006, the FDIC Acting Chairman assured state bank regulators that, as federal regulators moved toward implementation of Basel II, they would preserve current safeguards in the U.S. financial system, and specifically that implementation would not be allowed to drain away regulatory capital from the financial system.[12]

In August 2006, concern over the stratification of U.S. banks was renewed by the industry group America's Community Bankers (ACB).[13] In a letter to federal regulators, ACB President and CEO Diane Casey–Landry urged that regulators give U.S. depository institutions the option of adopting the standardized approach to the Basel II capital accord, rather than just the advanced approaches, arguing that U.S. institutions needed the same degree of flexibility enjoyed by non-U.S. institutions. The letter also argued that most U.S. banks, which are slated to operate under the revised standardized approach, "Basel IA," should be given flexibility to continue to operate under the original 1988 Basel I accord or Basel IA. In October 2006—after the Basel II proposed rules were issued by the federal regulators[14]—the FDIC chairman suggested that she would remain "open-minded" about flexible options for determining the risk-based capital requirements of large banks, including the use of the "Standardized Approach" for calculating risk-based capital requirements as an alternative to the more rigorous "Advanced Approach" at the center of the proposed rules.[15] In a letter made public on March 21, 2007, four trade associations—the Independent

---

10. See Richard Cowden, *Regulators Intent on Cautious Approach To Final Rules, Implementation of Basel II*, BNA Banking Daily (Mar. 14, 2006), *available at* http://pubs.bna.com/ip/bna/bbd.nsf/eh/ A0B2M7N3B0 (reporting on speech at meeting of Institute of International Bankers).

11. *Id.*

12. *Gruenberg Assures That Capital Safeguards Will Remain With Implementation of Basel II*, BNA Int'L Bus. & Fin. Daily (May 22, 2006), *available at* http://pubs.bna.com/ip/bna/ibd.nsf/eh/A0 B2V0N1N1.

13. R. Christian Bruce, *ACB Joins Bankers' Calls for Option To Use Standardized Basel Approach*, BNA Banking

Daily (Aug. 10, 2006), *available at* http:// pubs.bna.com/ip/bna/bbd.nsf/eh/A0B3D4 M2M6.

58*See* 71 Fed. Reg. 55,830 (2006) (to be codified at 12 C.F.R. pts. 3 (OCC rules), 208, 225 (Fed rules), 325 (FDIC rules), 566 (OTS rules)).

14. *See* 71 Fed. Reg. 55,830 (2006) (to be codified at 12 C.F.R. pts. 3 (OCC rules), 208, 225 (Fed rules), 325 (FDIC rules), 566 (OTS rules)).

15. Michael Bologna, *Bair Promises Open–Minded Assessment Of Standard Approach to Basel II Accord*, BNA Banking Daily (Oct. 10, 2006), *available at* http://pubs.bna.com/ip/bna/bbd.nsf/eh/A0 B3M9V9V1.

Community Bankers of America, ACB, the Financial Services Roundtable, and the American Bankers Association—asked the federal regulators to give U.S. banks the choice of using the standardized approach to comply with Basel II, as a less costly and less complicated alternative to the IRB approach requiring expensive computer modeling.[16] With rising criticism directed at the new capital rules, the U.S. regulators began to consider delaying implementation of Basel II until January 2008.[17]

Negative news continued to assault Basel II. QIS–5, based on data submitted by banks in G–10 countries plus Luxembourg, Spain, and Switzerland, tested outcomes using the three main methods under Basel II for determining capital requirements.[18] The study found that the advanced IRB approach would result in an average 7.1 percent reduction in the current capital required for the largest affected banks—the so-called "Group 1 banks"—and the foundation approach would result in an average 1.3 percent reduction. The standardized approach appeared to *increase* required capital by 1.7 percent, but very few Group 1 banks are expected to use it. For smaller "Group 2" banks, the results showed a greater reduction in required capital under all three approaches. For banks outside the G–10 that had submitted data, the BIS Committee indicated that the results showed "substantial dispersion" both within and between countries. In May 2006, the BIS Committee announced that it would not recalibrate the risk-weighting under Basel II, despite these results.

In September 2006, the regulators issued a joint notice proposing a new risk-based capital adequacy framework that would require some, and permit other, qualifying depository institutions (*i.e.*, banks, savings associations and bank holding companies) to use an internal ratings-based approach to calculate regulatory credit risk capital requirements and advanced measurement approaches to calculate regulatory operational risk capital requirements.[19] The proposed rule described the qualifying criteria for banks required or seeking to operate under the proposed framework and the applicable risk-based capital requirements for banks that operate under the framework. However, with the proposal for

---

16. R. Christian Bruce, *Bank Industry, Showing United Front, Calls for More Options in Capital Rules*, BNA Banking Daily (Mar. 22, 2007), *available at* http://pubs.bna.com/ip/bna/bbd.nsf/eh/ A0B4E2Z1E7.

17. *See Fed Sets March 30 Meeting To Vote on Basel II Proposal*, BNA Banking Daily (Mar. 27, 2006), *available at* http://pubs.bna.com/ip/bna/bbd.nsf/eh/ A0B2N8T8C5 (suggesting January 2008 implementation date for U.S. banks).

18. Daniel Pruzin, *Basel Committee to Maintain Calibration For Risk–Weighting Under New Capital Accord*, BNA Banking Daily (May 25, 2006), *available at* http://pubs.bna.com/ip/bna/ bbd.nsf/eh/A0B2V4W0A7.

19. 71 Fed. Reg. 55,830 (2006) (to be codified at 12 C.F.R. pts. 3 (OCC rules), 208, 225 (Fed rules), 325 (FDIC rules), 566 (OTS rules)).

Basel IA rules delayed until December 2006,[20] the regulators extended the comment period on the Basel II proposed rules an additional two months.[21]

The comment period for the proposed rules implementing Basel II ended on March 26, 2007. Because of sharp differences among the OCC, the Fed, the FDIC, and the OTS, it was not until July 2007 that the regulators announced a compromise on a final rule for U.S. implementation of Basel II in early 2008.[22]

In December 2007, the four regulators jointly published final rules implementing Basel II for the largest, internationally active U.S. banks,[23] effective April 1, 2008. While U.S. banking institutions were expected to begin a preliminary phase of implementation early in 2008, compliance with Basel II was not required until January 1, 2009, when the new standards would begin to be phased in over a three-year period.[24] It was anticipated that only 25 or so of the largest U.S. banking institutions would be required to adopt Basel II, with another small group of relatively large U.S. banking institutions having the option to do so. The overwhelming majority of U.S. banking institutions would be required either to continue to apply the 1988 Basel I standards, or to comply with the new, more risk-sensitive Basel IA standards expected to be promulgated by the regulators within a few months of the final rule.

By late 2008, however, the subprime mortgage crisis[25] had begun to emerge as a worldwide financial meltdown.[26] In March 2009, the Basel Committee conceded that, at least in the immediate future, there would be no increase in its minimum capital requirements for banks, at a time when banks are having serious difficulty maintaining liquidity.[27]

---

20. 71 Fed. Reg. 77,446 (2006) (to be codified at 12 C.F.R. pts. 3 (OCC rules), 208, 225 (Fed rules), 325 (FDIC rules) 567 (OTS rules)); *as corrected*, 72 Fed. Reg. 1266 (2007).

21. 71 Fed. Reg. 77,518 (2006) (extending comment period until Mar. 26, 2007).

22. R. Christian Bruce, *Regulators Reach Agreement on Basel II, Clearing Path for 2008 U.S. Implementation*, BNA Banking Daily (July 23, 2007), *available at* http://pubs.bna.com/ip/bna/bbd.nsf/125731d8816a84d385256297005f336a/c228220131a5bb868525731f000184b5?OpenDocument.

23. 72 Fed. Reg. 69,288 (2007) (codified at 12 C.F.R. pts. 3 (OCC rules), 208, 225 (Fed rules), 325 (FDIC rules), 559–560, 563, 567 (OTS rules)). For simplicity, the final rule uses the term "bank" to include banks, savings associations,

and bank holding companies (BHCs). 72 Fed. Reg. at 69,288 n.1. The terms "bank holding company" and "BHC" do not include savings and loan holding companies regulated by the OTS. *Id.*

24. R. Christian Bruce, *Fed's Governors, Eyeing Credit Turmoil, Welcome New Capital Rules Under Basel II*, BNA Banking Daily (Nov. 5, 2007), *available at* http://pubs.bna.com/ip/bna/bbd.nsf/eh/A0B5H8M7E8.

25. On the subprime crisis, see 2 MICHAEL P. MALLOY, BANKING LAW AND REGULATION §§ 4A.2.5–4A.2.5.3 (1994 & Cum. Supp.).

26. On the international implications of the subprime mortgage crisis, see *id.* § 12.5.1.

27. Daniel Pruzin, *Basel Committee Rules Out Increases For Minimum Capital Set–Aside Requirements*, BNA INT'L

Criticism of Basel II escalated, with EU Single Market Commissioner Charlie McCreevy calling for a fundamental revision of Basel II in light of the current financial crisis.[28] Further, the Organization for Economic Cooperation and Development (OECD) suggested that the Basel capital rules had supported a trend among banks to increase their exposure to mortgages, which were subject to a lower risk weighting.[29] The deputy director of the OECD Directorate for Financial and Enterprise Affairs went so far as to urge that Basel II be abandoned.[30] In its place he urged the adoption of a simple leverage ratio of bank equity to the unweighted sum of total bank assets—precisely the pre-Accord method employed in the United States and other major banking jurisdictions.[31]

It should be obvious at this point that at least one reason that the current economic and financial crisis[32] became so severe was that the financial services sector in many countries accumulated excessive on- and off-balance sheet leverage, accompanied by a gradual erosion of the level and quality of their capital base. Despite the capital adequacy requirements, the international banking system was simply not capable of absorbing the systemic losses that bled into it. In the aftermath of the crisis, the Basel Committee announced in July 2009 that it had agreed in principle to three significant sets of changes in the Basel II capital accord.[33]

First, "Pillar 1" capital requirements would be significantly revised. The committee would require a leverage ratio of core capital to assets as a backup measure to the Basel II capital-assets ratio.[34] In addition, banks would be expected to build up capital above the required ratio as a reserve against future systemic crises. Finally, banks would be required to improve the quality of capital maintained in these reserves, possibly by increasing the percentage

BUS. & FIN. Daily (Mar. 13, 2009), *available at* http://www.bna.com.

28. Joe Kirwin, *European Commission Calls for Major Basel II Capital Requirements Overhaul*, BNA INT'L BUS. & FIN. DAILY (Mar. 24, 2009), available at http://www.bna.com.

29. Daniel Pruzin, *OECD Official Slams Basel II Accord For Contributing to Financial Meltdown*, BNA INT'L BUS. & FIN. DAILY (Apr. 29, 2009), available at http://www.bna.com.

30. *Id.* (quoting Adrian Blundell–Wignal recommending "The best thing to do with Basel II is to put it into the shredding machine and start again").

31. Id.

32. For discussion of the crisis, see § 9.26, *infra*.

33. See http://www.bis.org/press/p 090713.htm (setting forth committee statements on revisions). *See also* Daniel Pruzin, *Basel Committee Announces Changes To Supervisory Pillar of Capital Accord*, BNA BANKING DAILY, July 14, 2009, available at http://www.bna.com (reporting on revisions).

34. Committee participants such as the United States, Canada, and Switzerland have already introduced such leverage ratios. Pruzin, supra. In the case of Switzerland, for example, the two largest banks, UBS and Credit Suisse, are required to maintain a minimum capital-core assets ratio of 3 percent for the consolidated group and 4 percent for the operating bank. Id.

of core capital required in the calculation of the capital to assets ratio. The actual calibration of the leverage ratio and of the systemic reserve was deferred until later in 2010.[35] Banks would be expected to comply with the newly revised requirements by December 31, 2010, with Basel I capital requirements remaining in place in the interim. The committee was also introducing higher risk weights for securitization exposures such as collateralized debt obligations of asset-backed securities—subprime mortgage-related investments—to reflect the higher risk inherent in such products, and it was raising the credit conversion factor for short-term liquidity facilities with respect to off-balance sheet conduits.

Second, the committee planned to issue supplemental guidance under "Pillar 2" of Basel II, governing enhanced supervision of banks, to address the flaws in risk management revealed by the financial crisis.[36] In particular, the supplemental guidance was expected to raise the standards for enterprise-wide governance and risk management of internationally active banks, to improve the identification of off-balance sheet risks and the management of risk concentrations within banks, and to provide incentives for banks to manage long-term risk and returns better. The committee expects these changes to be implemented immediately.

Third, "Pillar 3," establishing disclosure requirements, would be revised to strengthen disclosure requirements for securitizations, off-balance sheet exposures and trading activities.[37] Banks would have until December 31, 2010, to implement the revised Pillar 3 requirements.

In December 2009, the committee fleshed out the agreement in principle by issuing two proposals to revise the Basel Accord further to strengthen capital requirements and improve risk management of liquidity.[38] At that point, however, the committee acknowledged that a fully calibrated set of revised standards would only be phased in over a period of years, with implementation by year-end 2012, as financial conditions improved and economic recovery fell into place.[39] The committee expected to initiate phase-in

---

35. There are some indications that the committee would use the Canadian leverage ratio as a model; it includes on-balance sheet assets as well as off-balance sheet assets (including derivatives) in the leverage ratio. Pruzin, supra.

36. Id.

37. Id.

38. Basel Committee on Banking Supervision, *Strengthening the Resilience of the Banking Sector* (2009); Basel Committee on Banking Supervision, *International Framework for Liquidity Risk Measurement, Standards and Mon-*

itoring (2009), available at http://www.bis.org. For the U.S. Government position encouraging Basel II revisions for higher regulatory capital and liquidity standards by the end of 2010, see http://www.treasury.gov/press/releases/tg274.htm. See also R. Christian Bruce, *Treasury Department Eyes Global Accord On Bank Regulatory Capital by End of 2010*, BNA Banking Daily, Sept. 4, 2009, available at http://www.bna.com.

39. Daniel Pruzin, Basel Committee Unveils Proposals For Strengthening Global Financial System, BNA Banking

measures and grandfathering provisions for a sufficiently long transitional period to assure a smooth implementation of the revisions.[40] The intention was to create a situation leading to "more resilient banks and a sounder banking and financial system."[41] The proposals still lacked specific calibration of the leverage ratio and the revised core capital requirements. Calibration would await public comment on the proposals and committee assessment of the impact the proposals on the global financial system during the first six months of 2010.[42] A final version of the proposals was expected to be issued before year-end 2010. However, requirements approved in July 2009 for the trading book, securitizations, and exposures to off-balance sheet conduits were due to be implemented by year-end of 2010.[43] The Committee was in effect headed towards a "Basel III" arrangement.[44] The problem, however, was that the added capital costs of markedly stronger liquidity requirements could well be prohibitive for most banks.[45] Furthermore, in light of the fact that the U.S. regulators never fully implemented Basel II, the very real possibility that they might abandon "Basel III" in whole or in part has been a source of serious concern among European regulators in particular.[46]

Strong criticism has also emerged concerning the patterns of excessive executive compensation at major financial services firms that created perverse incentives for these firms to engage in high-risk strategies in favor of short-term financial results.[47] Basel II itself has been amended to require national regulators to monitor executive compensation structures consistent with principles of effective risk management.[48]

Doubts have also been raised about the capital ratio itself. In November 2009, the Swiss National Bank announced that it would

Daily, Dec. 18, 2009, available at http://www.bna.com.

40. Id.

41. *Id.* (quoting Nout Wellink, chairman of Basel Committee).

42. *Id.*

43. Pruzin, supra.

44. Cf. 2 Michael P. Malloy, Banking Law and Regulation § 5.3.3.4.2 (1994 & Cum. Supp.) (discussing extensive proposed revisions to Basel II).

45. See Daniel Pruzin, *Research Group Says Banks Would "Struggle" To Meet Liquidity Standards of Basel III Draft*, BNA Int'l Bus. & Fin. Daily (May 10, 2010) (reporting on analysts' concerns about consequences of "Basel III" liquidity proposals).

46. See, e.g., Aaron Lorenzo, *European Officials Worry U.S. Regulators Might Not Heed New Basel Standards*, BNA Int'l Bus. & Fin. Daily (June 9, 2010), available at www.bna.com. (reporting on European concerns over possible failure of capital harmonization efforts).

47. For discussion of this criticism and extensive analysis, see Lucian A. Bebchuk & Holger Spamann, *Regulating Bankers' Pay*, 98 Geo. L.J. 247 (2010).

48. Bank for International Settlements, Committee on Banking Supervision, *Enhancements to the Basel II Framework* 25–27 (2009).

urge the committee to raise the minimum 8 percent ratio of capital to risk-weighted assets to 16 percent.[49]

§ 9.10 General Agreement on Trade in Services

In April 1994, the Uruguay Round of GATT multilateral trade negotiations finalized the General Agreement on Trade in Services ("GATS").[1] The GATS establishes "a multilateral framework of principles and rules for trade in services with a view to the expansion of such trade under conditions of transparency and progressive liberalization,"[2] by applying GATT nondiscrimination principles to trade in services.[3] The GATS specifically applies to financial services.[4] The requirements of nondiscriminatory treatment do not, however, prevent WTO member states from enforcing domestic regulations for "prudential reasons, including for the protection of ... depositors, ... or persons to whom a fiduciary duty is owed by a financial service supplier, or to ensure the integrity and stability of the financial system."[5]

As a transitional matter, a second Annex to the GATS, concerning financial services, permitted temporary withdrawal from the GATS commitments.[6] Nevertheless, it was anticipated that inclusion of financial services under the GATS regime would "likely ... result in increased market access"[7] for international banks. This expectation received a setback when the United States with-

---

49. Daniel Pruzin, *Swiss Central Bank Official Calls for Doubling Of Basel II Minimum Capital Requirements*, BNA BANKING DAILY, Nov. 6, 2009, available at http://www.bna.com.

§ 9.10

1. General Agreement on Trade in Services, 15 April 1994, Agreement Establishing the World Trade Organization, Annex 1B, 33 Int'l Leg. Materials 1167 (1994) ("GATS"). WTO members are not permitted to derogate from adherence to Annex 1B. Agreement Establishing the World Trade Organization, art. XVI, ¶ 5. For an excellent review of the GATS and its implications for banking, see Kristin Leigh Case, Recent Development, *The Daiwa Wake–Up Call: The Need for International Standards for Banking Supervision*, 26 Ga. J. Int'l & Comp. L. 215 (1996).

2. GATS, preamble.

3. *See, e.g.*, GATS, art. II, ¶ 1 (applying most-favored-nation treatment to services and service suppliers); GATS, art. XVII, ¶ 1 (applying national treat-

ment to services and service suppliers of other WTO member states).

4. GATS, Annex on Financial Services.

5. GATS, Annex on Financial Services, § 2(a).

6. GATS, Second Annex on Financial Services. Case suggests that temporary withdrawal or modification is permitted in the Second Annex to allow for continued negotiation on market liberalization "because at the conclusion of the Uruguay Round, the United States was unsatisfied with other countries' commitments. The United States was not willing to lock in its own liberal policies without reciprocal guarantees of full market access on a most-favored nation basis." Case, *supra* note 1, at 220, n.32 (citing Joel P. Trachtman, *Trade in Financial Services Under GATS, NAFTA and the EC: A Regulatory Jurisdiction Analysis*, 34 Colum. J. Transnat'l L. 37, 54 (1995)).

7. Case, *supra* note 1, at 221.

drew from the GATS transitional process with respect to the Agreement on Financial Services in June 1995.[8]

In withdrawing from the transitional arrangement, the U.S. Government opted for a policy of measured reciprocity, prospectively limiting access to U.S. markets to financial services firms from home countries that provided reciprocal treatment to U.S. firms.[9] Essentially, the government had decided to seek market-access liberalization through bilateral negotiations, rather than through the multilateral mechanism of the WTO and the GATS.[10]

Matters remained in play, however, because the commitments of WTO member states participating in the transitional arrangement were to expire at the end of 1997.[11] Thereafter, WTO member states were expected to renegotiate GATS financial services commitments.[12] In advance of the expiration date, however, the United States joined in the signing of a global accord to govern international trade in services.[13]

Under the GATS, each WTO member is required to accord most-favored-nation treatment to services and service suppliers of other WTO members.[14] Current restrictions on trade in services of each member must be transparent.[15] Members are also required to administer current restrictions "in a reasonable, objective and impartial manner."[16]

Two factors may cut against broad effects for the GATS. First, the agreement itself provides a series of general exceptions that apply to GATS obligations, similar to the general exceptions under the GATT.[17] More importantly, perhaps, the GATS includes a self-

---

8. *See* Paul Lewis, *Trade Accord Without U.S. Set in Geneva*, N.Y. Times, July 27, 1995, at D1, col. 6 (reporting U.S. refusal to join transitional arrangement). In July 1995, over 80 states—including Japan, but not the United States—concluded a transitional agreement to liberalize international trade in financial services. *Id.*

9. Bob Davis & John R. Wilke, *Trade Official Is 'Close' to Limited Pact To Liberalize Global Financial Services*, Wall St. J., July 25, 1995 at A2.

10. *See, e.g.,* Frances Williams, *EU Eager to Salvage Financial Services Pact*, Fin. Times, July 1, 1995, at A1 (noting U.S. position).

11. Joel P. Trachtman, *Trade in Financial Services Under GATS, NAFTA and the EC: A Regulatory Jurisdiction Analysis*, 34 Colum. J. Transnat'l L. 37, 55 (1995).

12. *Id.*

13. *See* Edmund L. Andrews, *Accord Is Reached To Lower Barriers In Global Finance*, N.Y. Times, Dec. 13, 1997, at A1, col. 6 (discussing GATS accord).

14. GATS, art. II, ¶ 1.

15. *See* GATS, art. III (requiring publication and reporting of restrictive measures).

16. GATS, art. VI, ¶ 1. *Cf.* GATS, art. X, ¶ 1 (requiring that any emergency safeguard measures be administered in a nondiscriminatory manner).

17. *Compare,* e.g., GATT, art. XX (excepting from GATT requirements measures undertaken for morals, life or health, precious metals, compliance with certain regulatory laws, products of prison labor, national treasures or patrimony, conservation, certain commodity agreements, world-price adjustment, and short-supply materials) *with* GATS, art. XIV (excepting from GATS requirements measures undertaken for morals

judging special exception for essential security interests of member states, similar to the special security exception contained in the GATT.[18] Presumably, this exception would shield U.S. international economic sanctions measures from the requirements and strictures of the GATS.[19]

Second, the current financial crisis that began in 2008[20] has discouraged progress in liberalizing the rules governing trade in services. There is growing resistance by some WTO members to any further liberalization of services markets.[21] Supporters of the WTO services negotiations have argued that this response is inappropriate, because the financial crisis apparently resulted from lax regulatory standards rather than liberalization of financial services markets.[22]

§ 9.11   Entry Rules

Rules for entry into the international banking market are complicated by the fact that entry is controlled by two entirely independent jurisdictions, the home country of the entrant and intended host country. Hence, successful entry requires coordination between the regulatory requirements of both home and host. Sections 9.129.13 will focus on applicable U.S. rules when the United States is the intended host country and when the United States is the home country of the bank seeking entry into a non-U.S. market.

Available methods for entry vary. The general menu of options is illustrated in Figure 9–2, *infra*. However, specific options may or may not be available from one jurisdiction to the next, depending upon local rules.

or public order, life or health, compliance with certain regulatory laws, and taxation).

18. *Compare* GATT, art. XXI (providing exceptions from GATT obligations with respect to any measure undertaken that a member "considers necessary for the protection of its essential security interests") *with* GATS, art. XIV *bis*, ¶ 1 (providing exceptions from GATS obligations with respect to any measure undertaken that a member "considers necessary for the protection of its essential security interests"). *But cf.* GATS, art. XIV *bis*, ¶ 2 (requiring reporting of certain excepted measures and of their termination to WTO Council for Trade in Services).

19. *Cf. Panel Report on Nicaraguan Complaint*, GATT Activities 1986 58–59 (1987) (noting that GATT panel examining complaint by Nicaragua concerning U.S. trade sanctions not authorized to examine U.S. invocation of GATT, art. XXI).

20. On the financial crisis, see 1 Michael P. Malloy, Banking Law and Regulation § 1.4 (1994 & Cum. Supp.).

21. *See* Daniel Pruzin, *Officials, Experts Divided on Impact Of Financial Crisis on WTO Services Talks*, BNA Banking Daily (Oct. 8, 2008), *available at* http://pubs.bna.com/ (discussing likely linkage between crisis and WTO services negotiations).

22. *Id.*

Figure 9–2
Methods of Entry: Menu of Options

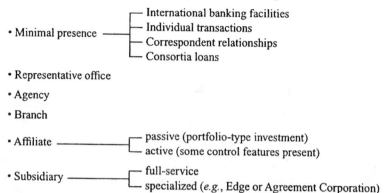

• Minimal presence
  ┌ International banking facilities
  ├ Individual transactions
  ├ Correspondent relationships
  └ Consortia loans

• Representative office

• Agency

• Branch

• Affiliate
  ┌ passive (portfolio-type investment)
  └ active (some control features present)

• Subsidiary
  ┌ full-service
  └ specialized (*e.g.*, Edge or Agreement Corporation)

These menu choices reflect varying degrees of intervention into the host-country market. Correspondent banking relationships are similar to domestic correspondent bank relationships, involving virtually no direct contact with the target market. Representative offices typically have significantly limited powers; they cannot take deposits, make loans, accept drafts, or transfer funds.

International deposit facilities are essentially book entry facilities within a bank and are functionally similar to a foreign branch, except that they are located within the bank's home office.[1] For example, in U.S. practice, these facilities are allowed to take time deposits and to grant loans to non-U.S. citizens. Reserve requirements are waived for facility deposits.[2] In many states they may be exempted from state and local income taxes.

Alternatively, a bank may establish a locally licensed agency, which operates in the same manner as a branch bank, except it cannot accept deposits from the general public. In contrast, a locally licensed branch offers a full range of banking services.[3] It is not separately chartered, and the home office may be liable for its obligations.[4]

---

§ 9.11

1. These facilities, known as international banking facilities ("IBF") in U.S. practice, are available under the Fed's Regulation K. *See* 12 C.F.R. § 211.8 (authorizing IBFs).

2. 12 C.F.R. § 204.8.

3. The establishment and operation of these branches are governed by the Fed's Regulation K, 12 C.F.R. pt. 211. In October 2001, the Fed extensively amended subparts A, B, and C of Regulation K, 12 C.F.R. §§ 211.1–211.34. 66 Fed. Reg. 54,346 (2001) (codified at 12 C.F.R. pts. 211, 265), *corrected*, 66 Fed. Reg. 58,655 (2001).

4. *See, e.g., Vishipco Line v. Chase Manhattan Bank*, 660 F.2d 854 (2d Cir. 1981), *cert. denied*, 459 U.S. 976, 103 S.Ct. 313 (1982) (so holding); *Garcia v. Chase Manhattan Bank, N.A.*, 735 F.2d

An affiliate bank may represent a passive portfolio-type investment, in which control is not exercised by the outside parent banking enterprise. It may be controlled by local or by other foreign banks. On the other hand, an active affiliate, or consortium bank, may operate as a joint venture, separately incorporated and owned by multiple banks, usually from different countries, often with no majority-controlling shareholder.

Finally, a bank may seek to enter a host-country market through the establishment of a separately chartered subsidiary. In U.S. practice, the possibility also exists for creating a specialized subsidiary limited to international and foreign business. This would be either an Edge Act corporation, chartered under federal law,[5] or an Agreement corporation, chartered under state law but subject to an agreement with the Fed to limit its activities to those of an Edge Act corporation.[6] In either event, the subsidiary would be limited to deposits related to international and foreign transactions. It could also make international-related loans, confirm letters of credit, create bankers acceptances, maintain foreign exchange markets, and act as a collection or disbursement agent.

In contrast, a full-service subsidiary operates as a separate, locally incorporated bank owned or controlled by parent banking enterprise. In either case, the banking enterprise that serves as the parent of the subsidiary bank is generally not subject to liability for subsidiary's obligations.[7]

§ 9.12   Entry into the U.S. Market

The range of options available to foreign banks for entry into the U.S. banking market is essentially the same as that illustrated in Figure 9–2, *supra*. However, at least since the passage of the International Banking Act ("IBA") in 1978, the range of options is somewhat broader, since the dual banking system within the United States makes available many duplicate (federal/state) alterna-

645 (2d Cir.1984) (so holding; citing, *inter alia, Vishipco Line*). *But cf. Perez v. Chase Manhattan*, 61 N.Y.2d 460, 463 N.E.2d 5, 474 N.Y.S.2d 689 (Ct.App. 1984) (liability of foreign branch discharged). *See generally* Heininger, *Liability of U.S. Banks for Deposits Placed in Their Foreign Branches*, 11 Law. & Pol. Intl. Bus. 903 (1979) (discussing foreign branch liability). Other jurisdictions may treat a foreign branch as distinct from its home office for purposes of liability. *Cf. X AG and others v. A bank*, 2 All Eng. L. Rep. 464 (1983) (treating foreign branch as legally distinct from home office); *Libyan Arab Foreign Bank v. Bankers Trust Company*, Queen's Bench, Commercial Court (2 September 1987) (same; citing, *inter alia, X AG*).

5.   12 U.S.C.A. § 613 *et seq.*

6.   *See, e.g.,* 12 C.F.R. § 211.4.

7.   *See, e.g.,* AMERICAN LAW INSTITUTE, RESTATEMENT OF FOREIGN RELATIONS LAW OF THE UNITED STATES (3D) § 414 (noting subsidiary may be subject to home-country supervision, though generally distinct for purposes of private liability). *But cf. S.E.C. v. Banca Della Svizzera Italiana*, 92 F.R.D. 111 (S.D.N.Y.1981) (claiming jurisdiction over foreign parent of U.S. subsidiary bank).

tives. Since the 1970s, foreign banks have increasingly taken advantage of these options. In part, efficient access to U.S. dollar markets may explain some of this growth in interest. Figure 9–1, *supra*, illustrates which regulators are authorized to approve which methods of entry.

Federal policy with respect to branching by non-U.S. banks has become a controversial issue in recent years. The IBA as originally enacted was intended to implement a policy of "national treatment" for foreign banks seeking entry into the U.S. market.[1] However, following the BCCI scandal,[2] the IBA was amended in several significant respects by the Federal Deposit Insurance Corporation Improvements Act ("FDICIA").[3] Among the effects of FDICIA were the following.

FDICIA significantly altered the rules governing the establishment and operation of federal branches and agencies[4] of foreign-based banks. Under FDICIA, the Comptroller is required, in considering any application for approval of an initial federal branch or agency, to include any condition imposed by the Fed as a condition for the approval of the application.[5] The Comptroller is also required to coordinate examinations of such branches and agencies with examinations conducted by the Fed, to the extent possible, to participate in any simultaneous examinations of U.S. operations of foreign banks requested by the Fed.[6] Furthermore, in considering any application to establish an additional federal branch or agency of a foreign-based bank, the Comptroller is required to provide the Fed with notice and opportunity for comment on the application.[7] The Fed's supervisory authority was substantially expanded,[8] and

§ 9.12

1. *See Conference of State Bank Supervisors v. Conover,* 715 F.2d 604 (D.C.Cir.1983), *cert. denied,* 466 U.S. 927, 104 S.Ct. 1708 (1984) (discussing national treatment under IBA).

2. *See* R. K. BHALA, FOREIGN BANK REGULATION AFTER BCCI (1994) (discussing BCCI scandal and its effect on U.S. regulation of international banking). *See also* Note, *Putting the Super Back in the Supervision of International Banking, Post–BCCI,* 60 Fordham L. Rev. S467 (Survey Issue 1992) (discussing effects of FDICIA on U.S. regulation).

3. Pub. L. No. 102–242, 105 Stat. 2236 (December 19, 1991) (codified at scattered sections of 12 U.S.C.A.) ("FDICIA").

4. The Gramm–Leach–Bliley Act, Pub. L. No. 106–102, Nov. 12, 1999, 113 Stat. 1338 (1999) (codified at scattered

sections of 12, 15, 16, 18 U.S.C.A.) ("GLBA"), allows a federal or state *agency* of a foreign bank to upgrade to a *branch* with the approval of the appropriate licensing authority (the Comptroller or the state regulator, respectively) and the Fed. GLBA, § 732 (codified at 12 U.S.C.A. § 3103(a)(7)).

5. 12 U.S.C.A. § 3102(a)(2).

6. *Id.* § 3102(b).

7. *Id.* § 3102(h)(2).

8. The Fed implemented its authority to supervise U.S. branches and agencies of foreign banks in regulations published in 1996. 12 C.F.R. 211.30 (establishing criteria for evaluation of U.S. operations of foreign banks not subject to consolidated supervision). For examples of recent branching decisions by the Fed under this authority, see *ICICI Bank Limited, Mumbai, India, Order Approving Establishment of a*

special examination fees were imposed for examinations of U.S. based operations of non-U.S. banks.[9]

The FDICIA also restricted retail deposit-taking by foreign banks. To accept or maintain deposit accounts with balances of less than $100,000, foreign banks are required to establish one or more U.S. banking subsidiaries for that purpose, and to obtain federal deposit insurance for any such subsidiary.[10] However, if the foreign bank had a U.S. branch that was an insured branch prior to FDICIA, the branch was permitted to continue to accept or maintain retail deposits.[11]

The increased burdens placed upon U.S. operations of foreign banks by the FDICIA provoked criticism.[12] These burdens have also exacerbated the uncertainty over the question whether U.S. banking regulation was sufficiently reciprocal to allow entry by U.S. banks into the European Union's Community-wide banking market.

It was against the statutory background of the FDICIA that the Interstate Banking and Branching Efficiency Act of 1994 ("IBBEA")[13] undertook to amend the IBA. Two objectives may be discerned in the amendments: dealing with the practical implications of the 1991 amendments to the IBA,[14] and readjusting the IBA in light of the changes in interstate banking and branching instituted by the IBBEA itself.[15]

The IBBEA amended the IBA rules governing interstate operations of foreign banks.[16] In general, it subjects the establishment of interstate operations of a federal branch or agency of a foreign bank to the same rules that would apply if the foreign bank were a

---

Branch, available at *http://www.federalreserve.gov/newsevents/press/orders/orders20071019a1.pdf;* China Merchants Bank Co., Ltd., Shenzhen, People's Republic of China: Order Approving Establishment of a Branch *(Nov. 8, 2007),* available at *http://www.federalreserve.gov/newsevents/press/orders/orders2007 1108a1.pdf;* China Construction Bank Corporation Beijing, People's Republic of China: Order Approving Establishment of a Branch *(Dec. 8, 2008),* available at *http://www.federalreserve.gov/ newsevents/press/orders/orders20081208 a1.pdf.*

9. 12 U.S.C.A. § 3105(c)(1)(D) (1994).

10. 12 U.S.C.A. § 3104(d)(1). Thus, for any foreign-based bank interested in the U.S. retail deposit market, this provision requires the bank's U.S. operations to be conducted through a subsidiary.

11. *Id.* § 3104(d)(2).

12. *See, e.g.,* Cynthia C. Lichtenstein, *U.S. Restructuring Legislation: Revising the International Banking Act of 1978, For the Worse?*, 60 Fordham L. Rev. S37 (Annual Survey Issue 1992).

13. Pub. L. No. 103–328, 108 Stat. 2338 (Sept. 29, 1994) (codified at scattered sections of 12 U.S.C.A.) ("IBBEA").

14. *See, e.g.,* IBBEA, § 115 (codified at 12 U.S.C.A. § 3105 note) (moratorium on examination fees under § 3105(c)(1)(D)).

15. *See, e.g.,* IBBEA, § 104(a) (codified at 12 U.S.C.A. 3103(a)(1)) (subjecting U.S. interstate branching and agency operations of foreign banks to rules of 12 U.S.C.A. §§ 36(g), 1831u).

16. For a discussion of the pre-IBBEA rules under IBA for interstate operations of foreign banks, see *Conference of State Bank Supervisors, supra.*

national bank seeking to branch interstate.[17] Similarly, the IBBEA subjects the establishment of interstate operations of a state-licensed branch or agency of a foreign bank to the same rules that would apply if the foreign bank were a state bank seeking to branch interstate.[18] These rules are generally preemptive and exclusive.[19]

Operation of any interstate branch or agency of a foreign bank is subject to the same IBBEA rules governing domestic branches of national and state banks resulting from interstate merger transactions.[20] However, an additional, potentially controversial requirement may apply to foreign banks. The 1991 FDICIA required foreign banks entering the U.S. retail deposit market to operate through a separately chartered U.S. subsidiary, rather than a direct branch.[21] The IBBEA extends this requirement, under certain specified circumstances, to interstate operations of any foreign bank. If the Fed or the Comptroller finds that, in light of differing regulatory or accounting standards in a foreign bank's home country, adherence by the bank to applicable U.S. capital requirements could only be verified if the foreign bank's U.S. banking activities were carried out in a separate U.S. subsidiary, the agencies[22] have

17. IBBEA, § 104(a) (codified at 12 U.S.C.A. § 3103(a) (1)). On the criteria for determining approval of interstate operations of a foreign bank's federal branch or agency, see 12 U.S.C.A. 3103(a)(3)(A)–(C).

18. 12 U.S.C.A. § 3103(a)(2). On the criteria for determining approval of interstate operations of a foreign bank's state branch or agency, see *id.* § 3103(a)(3)(A)–(C).

19. *See id.* § 3103(a)(5), which provides:

Except as provided in this section, a foreign bank may not, directly or indirectly, acquire, establish, or operate a branch or agency in any State other than the home State of such bank. *But see id.* § 3103(a)(7)(A)–(B) (providing additional authority for interstate operations of foreign banks where a host state expressly permits the operations, and the branch deposit operations are limited to international-or foreign-related deposits). On the definition of "home State" for these purposes, see *id.* § 3103(a)(9). On the rules for determining the home state of a foreign bank for purposes of the interstate branch and agency rules of the IBBEA, see *id.* § 3103(c)(1)(2).

20. *Id.* § 3103(a)(4). In addition, a U.S. branch or agency of a foreign bank

is not permitted to manage, through a managed or controlled office located outside the United States, any type of activity not permitted to be managed by a domestic bank through a branch or subsidiary located outside the United States. *Id.* § 3105(k)(1). This prohibition is effective 180 days after the enactment of IBBEA. IBBEA, § 107(e)(2) (codified at 12 U.S.C.A. § 3105 Note).

21. 12 U.S.C.A. § 3103(a)(6). However, the IBBEA clarifies the impact of the new rules in the following respects. A foreign bank that has a U.S. bank subsidiary is still eligible to establish a direct federal or state branch or agency, in accordance with the IBBEA rules. *Id.* § 3103(d)(1). Similarly, a U.S. bank that is a subsidiary of a foreign bank with a direct federal or state branch or agency is itself still eligible to establish a federal or state branch or agency, in accordance with the IBBEA rules. *Id.* § 3103(d)(2).

22. If the foreign bank intended to carry out interstate branching or agency activities under a federal license, both the Fed and the Comptroller would have the authority to make the finding. *Id.* § 3103(a)(6). If the foreign bank intended to carry out interstate branching or agency activities under a state license, the Fed alone would have the authority to make the finding. *Id.*

the authority to require that the foreign bank (or the company controlling the foreign bank) establish a U.S. subsidiary to carry out the interstate operations.[23] This provision potentially moves the United States further away from the original policy of national treatment for foreign bank operations in the United States that underlies the IBA.[24] Since most members of the European Union participate in the BIS capital adequacy guidelines, the degree of potential confrontation with our European allies in this regard may be minimized. In addition, IBBEA grandfathers foreign bank operations in place on the day before the enactment of the IBBEA.[25] Nevertheless, depending upon the U.S. agency practice that emerges under this provision, the United States banking market may become significantly less transparent to foreign banks.[26]

One salutary effect of the act was its moratorium on the examination fee provisions included in the IBA by the FDICIA amendments.[27] During a three-year period beginning July 25, 1994, the examination fee provisions of the FDICIA did not apply to examinations of U.S. branches, agencies or affiliates of foreign

---

23. *Id.*

24. This movement away from the policy of national treatment is underscored by the IBBEA provisions requiring the agencies to pursue the objective of

> affording equal competitive opportunities to foreign and United States banking organizations in their United States operations [and] ensur[ing] that foreign banking organizations do not receive an unfair competitive advantage over United States banking organizations.

Id. § 3104(a) (directive to Comptroller and FDIC under IBA as amended by IBBEA). *See also* IBBEA, § 107(b) (codified at 12 U.S.C.A. § 3104 Note) (requiring review of regulations by federal banking agencies and revision of regulations under § 3104 to equalize competitive opportunities for U.S. and foreign banks). The IBBEA also clarifies that domestic consumer protection laws apply to foreign banks with U.S. operations. 12 U.S.C.A. § 3106a(b) (1)(A), (2)(A).

25. IBBEA, § 104(b) (codified at 12 U.S.C.A. § 3103(b)).

26. Similar concern over regulatory barriers to entry arose in connection with the Fed's promulgation of interim rules with respect to treatment of for-

eign banking enterprises as financial holding companies (FHCs) under 12 U.S.C.A. § 1843(k). *See* 65 Fed. Reg. 3785 (2000) (codified at 12 C.F.R. pt. 225). In March 2000, the Fed amended the management criterion and certain provisions concerning election of FHC status applicable to foreign banking organizations. 65 Fed. Reg. 15,053 (2000) (codified at 12 C.F.R. pt. 225). *See* 12 C.F.R. §§ 225.81(c) (providing requirements for foreign banks that are or are owned by bank holding companies (BHCs) to elect FHC status); 225.90–225.92 (specifying requirements and procedures for foreign bank to be treated as FHC). On the regulation of FHCs, see *supra* §§ 6.3–6.5. Under current rules, a foreign banking enterprise will generally be considered "well managed," and thus in certain circumstances eligible for expedited treatment, if its combined operations in the United States have received at least a satisfactory composite rating at the most recent annual assessment. 12 C.F.R. §§ 225.2(s)(3). *See, e.g., id.* §§ 225.14(c)(2)(i) (providing expedited action for certain bank acquisitions by well-managed BHCs); 225.23(c)(2)(i) (expedited action for certain nonbanking proposals by well-managed BHCs).

27. *See* IBBEA, § 115 (codified at 12 U.S.C.A. §§ 3105 Note, 3107 Note).

banks,[28] or to examinations of U.S. representative offices of foreign banks.[29] Before the expiration of this three-year period, the IBA was amended to require that examination fees with respect to each branch or agency of a foreign bank be imposed "only to the same extent that fees are collected by the Board for examination of any State member bank."[30]

IBBEA imposes a continuing requirement on foreign banks with U.S. operations to meet community credit needs, after their initial entry by acquisition in the interstate market.[31] If a foreign bank acquires a U.S. bank or branch in a state in which the foreign bank does not maintain a branch, and the bank is a "regulated financial institution" under the CRA,[32] the CRA continues to apply to each branch of the foreign bank that results from the acquisition.[33]

§ 9.13   Entry into Non–U.S. Markets

Legal and regulatory constraints of both home-country and host-country policy may affect a bank's ability to enter a foreign market.[1] For convenience of discussion, this section focuses on the home-country requirements of the United States. As to host-country restrictions, patterns vary considerably, from relatively familiar chartering or licensing requirements in Group of Ten countries,[2] to virtual exclusion in many less developed countries.[3]

---

28.   IBBEA, § 115(a).

29.   IBBEA, § 115(b).

30.   Pub. L. No. 104–208, § 2214(a)(4), 110 Stat. 3009–411 (1996) (codified at 12 U.S.C.A. 3105(c)(1)(D)).

31.   12 U.S.C.A. § 3103(a)(8).

32.   *See id.* § 2902.

33.   *Id.* § 3103(a)(8)(A). This requirement does not apply to any resulting branch that is limited to international-or foreign-related deposits. *Id.* § 3103(a)(8)(B).

§ 9.13

1.   *See, e.g.,* Korsvik, *Legal and Regulatory Constraints Within Other Countries, in* W. H. BAUGHN & D. R. MANDICH, THE INTERNATIONAL BANKING HANDBOOK (1983) (discussing host-country restrictions on entry).

2.   The law of the European Union as it affects, among other things, bank regulation, is of considerable interest in this regard. *See generally* Lui, *A Banker's Guide to the European Community's*

1992 Program, 107 Banking L.J. 148 (1990). Certain recent EU developments may significantly restrict or modify entry of U.S. banks into the single integrated EU banking market. *See* Lee, *1992: Promise or Problems for non-EC Companies?,* Int'l Fin. L. Rev. (April 1988) (discussing integration of EU markets). Under the Second Banking Directive (1988), reciprocity of treatment of EU banks is the basis on which U.S. and other non-EU based banks are permitted to enter the single European market. *See* Note, *The Second Banking Directive,* Int'l Fin. L. Rev. 19 (April 1988) (discussing effects of directive). Banks that had not established or acquired a pre-Directive local subsidiary are required to obtain authorization from the relevant member state, but only after the Commission has determined that such bank's home country would grant reciprocal treatment to EU banks. *See* George Zavvos, *1992: One Market,* Int'l Fin. L. Rev. 7 (March 1988) (discussing Directive requirements).

3.   Korsvik, *supra.*

Entry by U.S. banks into foreign markets is authorized under the FRA subject to Fed approval.[4] For entry by national banks, the authority of the Comptroller of the Currency is limited to notice and filing requirements triggered by submission of an application to the Fed.[5] The Fed's entry approval requirements are contained in Regulation K.[6] Approval of the Fed is required to establish a foreign branch.[7] Separate requirements are applicable to the establishment of an Edge Act or Agreement corporation.[8] Since Agreement corporations are state-chartered, pertinent state law requirements must also be consulted.

Entry into a foreign banking market through the establishment or acquisition of a subsidiary or affiliate also requires approval of the investment by the Fed.[9] These requirements apply whether the "investor" in the subsidiary is a member bank, a bank holding company, or an Edge Act or Agreement corporation.[10]

The structure of the regulations would seem to suggest that the decision to enter a foreign market requires a choice of one of the possible methods of operation discussed in the regulations; namely, branch, Edge or Agreement corporation, affiliate, or subsidiary. In fact, there are alternative arrangements that a bank might make in structuring its entry into a foreign market. These arrangements might be particularly useful if the foreign jurisdiction prohibits or significantly restricts a method of entry favored by the bank. For example, if foreign jurisdiction *Nusquam* requires entry through a branch, but the U.S. bank is concerned about possible exposure of home office to the obligations of the Nusquami branch, the bank might create a second-tier subsidiary to branch into Nusquam. Figure 9–3 illustrates this alternative arrangement.

---

4. 12 U.S.C.A. §§ 601–619.

5. 12 C.F.R. Pt. 28.

6. *Id.* Pt. 211. In October 2001, the Fed extensively amended subparts A, B, and C of Regulation K, 12 C.F.R. §§ 211.1–211.34. 66 Fed. Reg. 54,346 (2001) (codified at 12 C.F.R. pts. 211, 265), *corrected*, 66 Fed. Reg. 58,655 (2001).

7. *Id.* § 211.3.

8. *Id.* § 211.5.

9. *Id.* § 211.8.

10. *See id.* § 211.2(*o*) (defining "investor" for these purposes).

Figure 9–3
Branch Entry through Second–Tier Subsidiary

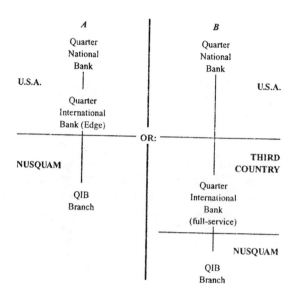

The *A* approach illustrated in Figure 9–3 would involve the incorporation of an Edge Act subsidiary of QNB, which in turn would branch into Nusquam. The creation of the Edge would require compliance with applicable provisions of the Comptroller's notice requirements[11] and of the Fed's Regulation K.[12] In addition, of course, compliance with Nusquami banking law would be required.

The *B* approach illustrated in Figure 9–3 is a variation on the first approach. It might recommend itself to QNB if the geographic area that includes Nusquam were one that QNB expected to exploit as a regional banking market. This investment by QNB in a foreign bank would be subject to applicable provisions of the Comptroller's notice requirements[13] and of the Fed's Regulation K,[14] and any applicable requirements or restrictions of Nusquami law and the laws of the third country involved.

Other further variations on the *B* approach can, of course, be imagined. QNB might create an Edge, QIB, which would in turn coordinate (and directly hold) the investment in the third-country subsidiary. This might recommend itself to QNB, depending on its management style, as a way to coordinate and consolidate its international activities, not only in Nusquam and the third country involved here, but also in other countries in the region as well, where the pattern of indirect ownership and control might repeat itself.

11. *Id.* § 28.3(a)(1)(ii).
12. *Id.* § 211.4(a).
13. *Id.* § 28.3(a)(1)(ii).
14. *Id.* § 211.5(a)–(c).

§ 9.14   International Activities

To the extent that international banking is banking, we may expect that international banking activities include the same range of traditional powers that we encounter in the domestic banking market. A number of features change, however, when a bank moves into the international market. First, there is the obvious fact that international transactions may raise transnational choice of law issues that do not exist in the domestic market. Second, there is the corresponding fact that these transactions may be subject to the constraints of both home-country and host-country regulation. Third, there may be certain activities that do not exist outside of international banking, broadly conceived, or are not as widely permitted in the domestic banking context.

There are certain activities that by their nature are an integral part of international banking. For U.S. banks, some of these activities are delimited by the U.S. regulatory framework that governs international banking. Essentially, this category of international activities is delineated by the Fed's Regulation K.[1] In addition to the core activities of banking (*i.e.*, lending and deposit-taking),[2] foreign branches of member banks, Edge Act and Agreement corporations and other bank subsidiaries are authorized by the Fed to engage in a range of activities in their host market. These activities include: (1) guarantees of third-party debt obligations;[3] (2) underwriting, distributing, and dealing in host-country government obligations and other permitted securities investments;[4] (3) credit extensions to bank officers;[5] (4) real estate loans;[6] (5) acting as an insurance agent or broker;[7] (6) participating in employee benefits programs;[8] (7) securities and commodities repurchase agreements;[9] (8) investing in subsidiaries;[10] and, (9) with Fed prior approval, engaging in other activities that the Fed determines are usual in connection with the transaction of a banking business in the jurisdiction where the branch transacts business.[11]

Though it is limited to international and foreign banking and financial services and investments, an Edge Act corporation may operate through branches within the United States.[12] Beyond core banking activities, an Edge is authorized by the Fed to engage in a

---

§ 9.14

1. 12 C.F.R. pt. 211. In October 2001, the Fed extensively amended subparts A, B, and C of Regulation K, 12 C.F.R. §§ 211.1–211.34. 66 Fed. Reg. 54,346 (2001) (codified at 12 C.F.R. pts. 211, 265), *corrected*, 66 Fed. Reg. 58,655 (2001).

2. 12 C.F.R. § 211.4(a).

3. *Id.* § 211.4(a)(1).

4. *Id.* § 211.4(a)(2)–(3).

5. *Id.* § 211.4(a)(4).

6. *Id.* § 211.4(a)(5).

7. *Id.* § 211.4(a)(6).

8. *Id.* § 211.4(a)(7).

9. *Id.* § 211.4(a)(8).

10. *Id.* § 211.4(a)(9).

11. *Id.* § 211.4(b).

12. *Id.* § 211.5(f).

range of other activities in its U.S. branches. These activities include: (1) activities incidental to international or foreign business;[13] (2) payments and collections in connections with international or foreign transactions;[14] (3) foreign exchange transactions;[15] (4) fiduciary and investment advisory activities;[16] (5) banking services for employees;[17] (6) with Fed prior approval, other U.S. activities that the Fed determines to be incidental to the international or foreign business of an Edge.[18]

Similarly, Agreement corporations are subject to restrictions on their activities within the United States. With prior Fed approval, a member bank or bank holding company is permitted to invest in a corporation that has entered into an agreement or undertaking with the Fed limiting itself to activities permissible for an Edge.[19]

Finally, member banks, bank holding companies, Edge Act and Agreement corporations are permitted to engage in activities outside the United States through investment in foreign subsidiaries and affiliates.[20] Beyond core banking activities,[21] these investors are authorized by the Fed to engage in a range of other activities through their foreign subsidiaries and affiliates.[22] These activities include: (1) financing;[23] (2) leasing real or personal property, or acting as agent, broker, or advisor in leasing real or personal property;[24] (3) fiduciary activities;[25] (4) underwriting credit life insurance and credit accident and health insurance;[26] (5) services for other direct or indirect operations of U.S. banking organizations, including representative functions, sale of long-term debt, name saving, holding assets acquired to prevent loss on debt previously contracted in good faith, and other activities permissible domestically for bank holding companies under the Bank Holding Company Act ("BHCA");[27] (6) holding the premises of a branch of an Edge or a member bank, or the premises of a direct or indirect subsidiary, or holding or leasing the residence of officer or employee of branch or subsidiary;[28] (7) investment, financial, or economic advisory services;[29] (8) general insurance agency and brokerage activities;[30] (9) data processing;[31] (10) organizing, sponsoring, and

13. *Id.* § 211.6(a)(1)–(3).

14. *Id.* § 211.6(a)(4).

15. *Id.* § 211.6(a)(5).

16. *Id.* § 211.6(a)(6).

17. *Id.* § 211.6(a)(7).

18. *Id.* § 211.6(b).

19. *Id.* § 211.5(g).

20. *Id.* § 211.8.

21. *Id.* § 211.10(a)(1).

22. For investment procedures, see *id.* § 211.9.

23. *Id.* § 211.10(a)(2).

24. *Id.* § 211.10(a)(3).

25. *Id.* § 211.10(a)(4).

26. *Id.* § 211.10(a)(5).

27. *Id.* § 211.10(a)(6). *See* 12 U.S.C.A. § 1843(a)(2)(A), (c)(1)(C) (BHCA provisions concerning bank servicing).

28. 12 C.F.R. § 211.10(a)(7).

29. *Id.* § 211.10(a)(8).

30. *Id.* § 211.10(a)(9).

managing mutual funds, if fund shares are not sold or distributed in United States or to U.S. residents, and the fund does not exercise managerial control over firms in which it invests;[32] (11) management consulting services;[33] (12) underwriting, distributing and dealing in debt securities outside the United States;[34] (13) underwriting, distributing, and dealing in equity securities outside the United States;[35] (14) dealing in equity securities outside the United States;[36] (15) operating a travel agency;[37] (16) insurance underwriting;[38] (17) acting as a futures commission merchant for financial instruments of the type, and on the exchanges, that the Fed has previously approved;[39] (18) acting as principal or agent in swap transactions, subject to limitations applicable to state member banks;[40] (19) BHCA "closely related" activities;[41] and, (20) with prior specific Fed approval, activities determined to be usual in connection with the transaction of the business of banking or other financial operations abroad, consistent with the Federal Reserve Act or the BHCA.[42]

In each of these sets of authorizations, the wild card is the "other activities" provision.[43] Since the authorizations focus on what activities are "usual" in connection with banking in a host market,[44] or on what is "incidental" to international and foreign banking,[45] they are highly contextual and must be examined country by country.

§ 9.15 Lending

One essential, traditional role of banking is as a source of funding, *i.e.*, as a commercial lender. Within the international banking context, then, one may expect this role also to be central. Whether international or domestic, certain considerations—like the creditworthiness of the borrower and the adequacy of the spread between cost of funds and rate of return—will be key considerations in the bank's decision to lend. But are there any consider-

---

31. *Id.* § 211.10(a)(10).

32. *Id.* § 211.10(a)(11).

33. *Id.* § 211.10(a)(12).

34. *Id.* § 211.10(a)(13).

35. *Id.* § 211.10(a)(14).

36. *Id.* § 211.10(a)(15).

37. *Id.* § 211.10(a)(16).

38. *Id.* § 211.10(a)(17).

39. *Id.* § 211.10(a)(18).

40. *Id.* § 211.10(a)(19). *See id.* pt. 208 (limitations applicable to state member banks).

41. *Id.* § 211.10(b). *See id.* § 225.28(b) (providing prior determina-

tions by Fed of closely related activities under BHCA).

42. *Id.* § 211.10(c).

43. *See, e.g.,* 12 C.F.R. §§ 211.4(b) (providing for other activities by foreign branches), 211.6(b) (providing for other U.S. activities by Edge corporation), 211.10(c) (providing for other Edge corporation offshore activities).

44. *Id.* §§ 211.4(b) (foreign branches), 211.10(c) (foreign Edge activities).

45. *Id.* § 211.6(b) (U.S. activities by Edge).

ations in the lending decision that are peculiar to *international lending?*

Lending is lending. To some extent, therefore, the considerations that go into the lending decision are the same, whether one is operating in the domestic or international market. However, certain considerations may be peculiar to international banking, or they may have a relatively greater emphasis in the international banking context. Some important features of international lending may be identified as follows. International lending usually involves "cross-national" or transborder risk, a risk to the success of the transaction related not necessarily to the creditworthiness of the borrower, but to the social, political, and economic environment in which the borrower or its project is placed. Components of transborder risk include (*i*) "country risk," taken in its broadest sense to include the complex of socio-political factors that affect success; (*ii*) "regulatory risk," the effect of differing regulatory features in the country of the borrower; and, (*iii*) "jurisdictional risk," the effect of performing and enforcing the lending agreement in a different legal jurisdiction (i.e., the borrower's) or, if the agreement is to be enforced in the lender's home jurisdiction, the indirect effect that the law of the borrower's jurisdiction may have on enforcement.[1] Where the borrower is a "foreign state"—a sovereign nation, a political subdivision, or an agency or instrumentality of a sovereign nation[2]—there may also be risks associated with the immunity from suit that may be available to defeat jurisdiction over the borrower.[3]

§ 9.15

1. *See, e.g. Callejo v. Bancomer, S.A.,* 764 F.2d 1101 (5th Cir. 1985) (requiring deference to legal effects of act of foreign state in regulating debt obligations of its banks) *But see. Allied Bank Int'l v. Banco Credito Agricola de Cartago,* 757 F.2d 516 (2d Cir. 1985), *cert. dismissed,* 473 U.S. 934, 106 S.Ct. 30 (holding that acts of foreign states did not affect debt owed to U.S. bank where debt was "located" in United States); *Blanchard & Co., Inc. v. Barrick Gold Corp.,* 2003 WL 22071173 (E.D.La. 2003), *reconsideration denied,* 2003 WL 22533641 (E.D.La. 2003) (holding no act of state defense where no "nexus" with the foreign state is shown); *Lloyds Bank PLC v. Republic of Ecuador,* 1998 WL 118170 (S.D.N.Y. 1998) (so holding with respect to application of pre-existing foreign law to debt located in United States); *Libra Bank Ltd. v. Banco Nacional de Costa Rica,* 570 F.Supp. 870 (S.D.N.Y. 1983) (similarly holding).

2. *See, e.g. Flatow v. Islamic Republic of Iran,* 308 F.3d 1065 (9th Cir. 2002), *cert. denied,* 538 U.S. 944, 123 S.Ct. 1632 (2003) (upholding presumption that bank wholly owned by state was still juridical entity separate from state and not subject to execution of judgment entered against state); *Allen v. Russian Federation,* 522 F.Supp.2d 167 (D.D.C. 2007) (finding oil and gas producing company not an "agency or instrumentality" of Russian Federation).

3. Foreign Sovereign Immunities Act, Pub. L. No. 94–583, Oct. 21, 1976, 90 Stat. 2891(1976) (codified at 28 U.S.C.A. §§ 1330, 1602–1611). *See, e.g., Croesus EMTR Master Fund L.P. v. Federative Republic of Brazil,* 212 F.Supp.2d 30 (D.D.C. 2002) (holding, in breach of contract action against state, FSIA commercial activity exception not triggered by state's purported promotion of bonds in U.S. bond market; commercial activity and direct effect exceptions not triggered by alleged omissions concerning value of bonds or by failure to pay interest and principal; dismissal on *forum non conve-*

Another important, and fairly obvious feature is exchange rate risk and other attendant problems connected with, for example, foreign currency lending.

These concerns are relevant whether the "bank" involved in international lending is a commercial bank, or an Edge or Agreement corporation. In addition, special rules apply to credit activities of Edges.[4] Edges may finance: contracts, projects, or activities performed substantially offshore;[5] importation into or exportation from the United States of goods (either directly or through brokers or other intermediaries);[6] domestic shipment or temporary storage of goods being imported or exported (or accumulated for export);[7] and, assembly or repackaging of goods imported or to be exported.[8]

Edges may also finance *domestic* production costs of goods and services for which export orders have been received or which are identifiable as being directly for export.[9] They may also assume or acquire participations in extensions of credit, or acquire obligations arising from other transactions, so long as the extensions or transactions are ones that an Edge corporation could have financed originally (including acquisitions of obligations of foreign governments).[10]

In addition, Edges may guarantee debts, or otherwise agree to make payments on the occurrence of "readily ascertainable events,"[11] if the guarantee or agreement specifies the Edges's maximum monetary liability thereunder and is related to an offshore or export-or import-related transaction.[12] Finally, Edges may provide credit and other banking services, for domestic and foreign purposes, to foreign governments and their agencies and instrumentalities, foreign persons, and other similar foreign entities.[13]

§ 9.16   Lending limits

National banks are subject to limitations on the amount of total loans and extensions of credit to any one borrower at any

---

niens grounds appropriate); *De Sanchez v. Banco Central de Nicaragua,* 770 F.2d 1385 (5th Cir. 1985) (recognizing sovereign immunity of central bank) *.. But see* Callejo v. Bancomer, S.A., 764 F.2d 1101 (5th Cir. 1985) ("commercial activity" exception to FSIA not available with respect to sale of certificates of deposit by Mexican bank later nationalized by Mexican Government).

4. 12 C.F.R. § 211.6(a)(3).

5. *Id.* § 211.6(a)(3)(i)(A).

6. *Id.* § 211.6(a)(3)(i)(B).

7. *Id.* § 211.6(a)(3)(i)(C).

8. *Id.* § 211.6(a)(3)(i)(D).

9. ID. § 211.6(a)(3)(ii).

10. ID. § 211.6(a)(3)(iii).

11. "Readily ascertainable events" include, but are not limited to, events such as nonpayment of taxes, rentals, customs duties, or cost of transport and loss or nonconformity of shipping documents. *Id.* § 211.6(a)(3)(iv).

12. *Id.* On offshore and export-or import-related transactions, see *supra* text and accompanying notes 2–6.

13. 12 C.F.R. § 211.6(a)(3)(v).

time, calculated as a percentage of unimpaired capital and surplus.[1] Lending to certain interrelated or commonly controlled groups of borrowers are aggregated for purposes of calculating lending limits.[2] In lending to foreign sovereigns, governmental entities, and other entities owned or controlled by the foreign government, the question may naturally arise whether all such loans should be treated as if they were loan to one "person" for purposes of lending limitations. Some guidance in this regard is offered by the Comptroller's regulations. In general (i.e., for domestic or private foreign borrowers), the basic rule is that loans or extensions of credit to one borrower should be attributed to another person, with each person deemed the borrower, when either the proceeds of a loan or extension of credit are to be used for the direct benefit of the other person, to the extent so used,[3] or a "common enterprise" is deemed to exist between the persons.[4]

However, in the case of loans to foreign governments, their agencies, and instrumentalities, the generally applicable rules are displaced by special aggregation rules.[5] Loans and extensions of credit to such borrowers are aggregated only if the loans or extensions of credit fail to meet both a "means test" and a "purpose test" at the time the loan or extension of credit is made.[6]

The means test requires that the borrower have resources or revenue of its own, sufficient to service its debt obligations.[7] If the government's support (excluding guarantees by a central government of the borrower's debt) exceeds the borrower's annual revenues from other sources, the Comptroller presumes that the borrower fails the means test.[8] The purpose test requires that the purpose of the loan or extension of credit be consistent with the purposes of the borrower's general business.[9]

The practical consequences of these tests is that, in certain circumstances, loans to interrelated governmental or governmentally controlled entities will not be aggregated, although the same loans to similarly interrelated private borrowers would have been

---

§ 9.16

1. 12 U.S.C.A. § 84(a)(1) (15 percent of capital and surplus); *id.* § 84(a)(2) (additional and separate 10 percent limit for loans and extensions of credit fully secured by readily marketable collateral). On exemptions from these lending limits, see *id.* § 84(c).

2. *See* 12 C.F.R. § 32.5 (Comptroller's combination rules under § 84).

3. *Id.* § 32.5(a)(1). For the meaning of "direct benefit" for these purposes, see *id.* § 32.5(b).

4. *Id.* § 32.5(a)(2). On the test for the existence of a "common enterprise" for these purposes, see *id.* § 32.5(c). Special rules for attribution apply to corporate groups, *id.* § 32.5(d), and to partnerships, joint ventures, and other unincorporated associations. *Id.* § 32.5(e).

5. *Id.* § 32.5(f).

6. *Id.* § 32.5(f)(1).

7. *Id.* § 32.5(f)(1)(i).

8. *Id.*

9. *Id.* § 32.5(f)(1)(ii).

combined as loans to one borrower for purposes of calculating lending limits. Consider the following hypothetical case.

Assume that Quarter National Bank has a general lending limit of $30 million dollars. It has lent $25 million to the Nusquami Port Authority, a governmental corporation controlled by statute by the Ministry of Development of the Republic of Nusquam. NusBank, a commercial bank 90 percent-owned by the Nusquami Ministry of Finance, applies for a $10 million loan from Quarter. NusBank is marginally profitable, and its external debt is guaranteed by investment guarantees provided by the Nusquami Central Bank. NusBank intends to loan the proceeds of the proposed loan to the Ministry of Development, as a project loan to complete renovations of the port facilities managed by the Nusquami Port Authority.

If the proposed loan were combined with the outstanding loan to the Nusquami Port Authority—as it most likely would be if these were private, domestic borrowers with equivalent interrelationships—the proposed loan would exceed Quarter's lending limit. However, under the special rules, the proposed loan probably meets both the means and purpose tests.[10] NusBank has resources or revenue of its own, sufficient to service its debt obligations, since the Central Bank guarantees are excluded from the means test. The purpose test is also met, because *lending*—even to another Quarter borrower—is obviously consistent with the purposes of NusBank's general business.

---

10. Of course, in order to demonstrate that the means and purpose tests are satisfied, Quarter must, at a minimum, retain in its files the following:

(i) A statement (accompanied by supporting documentation) describing the legal status and the degree of financial and operational autonomy of the borrowing entity;

(ii) Financial statements for the borrowing entity for a minimum of three years prior to the date the loan or extension of credit was made or for each year that the borrowing entity has been in existence, if less than three;

(iii) Financial statements for each year the loan or extension of credit is outstanding;

(iv) The bank's assessment of the borrower's means of servicing the loan or extension of credit, including specific reasons in support of that assessment. The assessment shall include an analysis of the borrower's financial history, its present and projected economic and financial performance, and the significance of any financial support provided to the borrower by third parties, including the borrower's central government; and

(v) A loan agreement or other written statement from the borrower which clearly describes the purpose of the loan or extension of credit. The written representation will ordinarily constitute sufficient evidence that the purpose test has been satisfied. However, when, at the time the funds are disbursed, the bank knows or has reason to know of other information suggesting that the borrower will use the proceeds in a manner inconsistent with the written representation, it may not, without further inquiry, accept the representation.

Id. § 32.5(f)(2)(i)(v).

Imagine this hypothetical case multiplied countless times. Given the potential concentrations of credit that the special rules invite, is it any surprise that U.S. international banks confronted a less-developed-country debt crisis in the 1980s?[11] Ironically, even if the outstanding official debt is later consolidated under a central obligor in a qualifying restructuring,[12] such debt will not be aggregated and attributed to the central obligor, so long as the previously outstanding loans and other extensions of credit qualified for separate lending limit treatment under the special rules.[13] However, when this restructuring rule applies, a national bank's loans and other extensions of credit to a foreign government, its agencies and instrumentalities—including the restructured debt—is limited in the aggregate to a total equal to 50 percent of the bank's capital and surplus.[14]

Lending limits clearly apply to lending occurring within the United States. In addition, the Federal Deposit Insurance Corporation Improvements Act ("FDICIA")[15] imposes on state-licensed branches and agencies the same limits on lending to a single borrower that apply to federally-licensed branches and agencies.[16] The Fed and the FDIC have each promulgated regulations implementing the FDICIA's limitations on the activities of state-licensed branches and agencies of non-U.S. banks.[17]

The Fed also has lending limit regulations that apply to Edges.[18] These set lending limits and capital requirements covering

---

11. For representative cases illustrating the difficulties of enforcing loan agreements involving official debt, see, e.g., *Libra Bank Ltd. v. Banco Nacional de Costa Rica*, 570 F.Supp. 870 (S.D.N.Y.1983); *Allied Bank Int'l v. Banco Credito Agricola de Cartago*, 757 F.2d 516 (2d Cir.1985), *cert. dismissed*, 473 U.S. 934, 106 S.Ct. 30; *A.I. Credit Corp. v. Government of Jamaica*, 666 F.Supp. 629 (S.D.N.Y.1987).

12. To qualify, the official debt must be restructured in a sovereign debt restructuring approved by the OCC, upon request by a bank for application of the non-combination rule. The factors used in making this determination include:

(A) Whether the restructuring involves a substantial portion of the total commercial bank loans outstanding to the foreign government, its agencies, and instrumentalities;

(B) Whether the restructuring involves a substantial number of the foreign country's external commercial bank creditors;

(C) Whether the restructuring and consolidation under a central obligor is being done primarily to facilitate external debt management; and

(D) Whether the restructuring includes features of debt or debt-service reduction.

Id. § 32.5(f)(3)(ii)(A)–(D).

13. *Id.* § 32.5(f)(3)(i).

14. *Id.* § 32.5(f)(3)(iii).

15. Pub. L. No. 102–242, 105 Stat. 2236 (December 19, 1991) (codified at scattered sections of 12 U.S.C.A.).

16. 12 U.S.C.A. 3105(h)(1).

17. 59 Fed. Reg. 55,026 (1994) (codified at 12 C.F.R. 211.29), *replaced by*, 66 Fed. Reg. 54,346 (2001) (codified at 12 C.F.R. § 211.28) (Fed rule); 59 Fed. Reg. 60,703 (1994) (codified at 12 C.F.R. § 346.101) (FDIC rule).

18. 12 C.F.R. § 211.12.

such activities as acceptances,[19] discussed in § 9.22, *infra*, as well as loans and extensions of credit to one person.[20]

§ 9.17   Lending Supervision

Lending, whether domestic or international, also raises concerns about its effects on the safety and soundness of the lending bank. Such concerns can be dealt with under the generally applicable enforcement provisions of federal banking law.[1] However, in the case of international loans, another statutory enactment, the International Lending Supervision Act of 1983 ("ILSA"),[2] specifically addresses such concerns, and others such as capital adequacy.[3]

§ 9.18   Deposits

Deposit-taking is also a core activity in international banking, particularly given the importance of Eurodollar transactions.[1] International-related deposits raise interesting policy issues concerning the applicability of regulatory regimes such as deposit reserves and deposit insurance. Deposit insurance (§§ 2.10, 5.11) and deposit reserve requirements (§§ 2.11, 5.12) are discussed elsewhere in this hornbook.

Essentially, two rules of thumb should be kept in mind. First, as to deposit reserve requirements, although foreign deposits of U.S. depository institutions can be subjected to reserve requirements,[2] deposits that are payable only outside the United States are currently not subjected to reserve requirements.[3] Deposit reserve requirements apply generally to any deposit payable within the United States, even if also payable elsewhere.[4] U.S. branch and

---

19. *Id.* § 211.12(a).

20. *Id.* § 211.12(b).

§ 9.17

1. *See, e.g.,* 12 U.S.C.A. § 1818(b) (administrative cease and desist order available to address unsafe and unsound practices).

2. Pub. L. No. 98–181, 97 Stat. 1153 (1983) (codified at 12 U.S.C.A. §§ 3901–3912).

3. *Compare, e.g.,* 12 U.S.C.A. § 1818(b) (general enforcement of safety and soundness) *with id.* §§ 3901–3904, 3907 (specific provisions for lending supervision, including imposition of administratively determined loan loss reserves, known as "allocated transfer risk reserves," or "ATRRs").

§ 9.18

1. On the legal implications of Eurodollar deposits, see, *e.g., Citibank, N.A.*

v. Wells Fargo Asia Limited, 495 U.S. 660, 662–663, 110 S.Ct. 2034, 2036–2037 (1990), *on remand, Wells Fargo Asia Limited v. Citibank, N.A.*, 936 F.2d 723 (2d Cir.1991).

2. *See, e.g.,* 12 C.F.R. §§ 211.3(d) (providing that member bank foreign branch deposits are susceptible to reserve requirements of Regulation D, 12 C.F.R. Pt. 204), 211.5(i) (providing that deposits of Edge and Agreement corporations are subject to Regulations D "in the same manner and to the same extent as if the Edge or Agreement corporation were a member bank").

3. *Id.* § 204.2(a).

4. *See id.* §§ 204.2(a)(1) (definition of "deposit"); 204.2(t) (definition of "payable only at an office located outside the United States"); 204.3(a) (maintenance of reserves).

agency deposits are generally subject to the deposit reserve requirements.[5] Inter-office deposits of branches, agencies and Edges are not considered "deposits" for purposes of the reserve requirements.[6] Deposits of international banking facilities are not "demand deposits" for purposes of the reserve requirements.[7]

Second, although foreign deposits of U.S. depository institutions may be covered by federal deposit insurance,[8] resolution of the problems of a failing U.S. depository institution cannot include payments to the benefit of foreign depositors.[9]

A further complication arises under the International Banking Act ("IBA"). Originally the IBA required deposit insurance for "retail deposits" of U.S. branches of non-U.S. banks (*i.e.*, "deposits of less than $100,000"), with some transitional treatment of state branches of such banks.[10] However, the Federal Deposit Insurance Corporation Improvements Act ("FDICIA")[11] added a provision that prospectively requires such retail deposit-taking to be done in separately chartered and FDIC-insured U.S. subsidiaries, rather than through branches.[12]

§ 9.19 Edge Act Corporations

Edge corporations are permitted to engage directly or indirectly in deposit-taking activities within the United States, to the extent that the activities are incidental to international or foreign business.[1] Ordinarily, the Fed considers the following U.S. deposit-taking activities to be "incidental" to international or foreign business: (1) deposits in the form of transaction accounts, savings, and time deposits (including issuing negotiable certificates of deposits) from foreign governments and their agencies and instrumentalities;[2] (2) deposits in the form of transaction accounts, savings, and time deposits (including issuing negotiable certificates of deposits) from foreign persons;[3] (3) deposits from U.S. persons, if the deposits are international-or foreign-related;[4] and, (4) liquid funds not currently employed in the Edge's international or foreign business, if

---

5. *See* 12 U.S.C.A. § 3105; 12 C.F.R. § 204.3(a)(1).

6. *See* 12 C.F.R. § 204.2(a)(2)(xii).

7. *See* *id.* §§ 204.2(b)(3)(iv), 204.8(a)(2).

8. *See, e.g.*, 12 U.S.C.A. § 3104 (requiring deposit insurance for retail deposits held by foreign branches and subsidiaries within United States).

9. *Id.* § 1831r(a).

10. 12 U.S.C.A. § 3104 (1978).

11. Pub. L. No. 102–242, 105 Stat. 2236 (December 19, 1991) (codified at scattered sections of 12 U.S.C.A.).

12. 12 U.S.C.A. § 3104(c).

§ 9.19

1. 12 C.F.R. § 211.6(a)(1).

2. *Id.* § 211.6(a)(1)(i).

3. *Id.*

4. 12 C.F.R. § 211.6(a)(1)(ii).

held or invested in the United States, in the form of cash or specified money market instruments.[5]

§ 9.20   Documentary Letters of Credit

The basic structure of a documentary letter of credit transaction in illustrated in Figure 9–4, *infra*. One could argue that a letter of credit ("L/C") is a peculiar form of secured lending. For the brief time that the bank has accepted the documents and paid the beneficiary's draft but has not yet been reimbursed by the account party, there is something not unlike a collateralized loan relationship between bank and account party. On the other hand, the letter of credit is also a payment transfer mechanism. The best approach, of course, may be simply to consider the letter of credit on its own terms.

FIGURE 9–4
Typical Documentary Letter of Credit

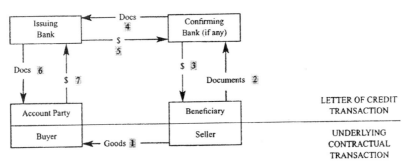

SELLER PERFORMS ➡ LETTER OF CREDIT TRIGGERED

1 Seller ships goods; obtains necessary documents from shipper
2 Seller submits docs and draft to C bank
3 C bank pays Seller on draft
4 C bank submits docs and draft to I bank
5 I bank reimburses C bank
6 I bank makes docs available to Buyer
7 Buyer reimburses I bank in exchange

The L/C is primarily governed by transactional rules, embodied in Article 5 of the Uniform Commercial Code,[1] and, for certain international L/Cs, the International Chamber of Commerce's Uniform Customs and Practices for Documentary Credits (UCP)[2] or

---

5. 12 C.F.R. § 211.5(j)(2).

§ 9.20

1. Uniform Commercial Code, art. 5 (1962, as amended 1990) or revised art. 5 (as amended 1995).

2. *See Bank of Cochin Ltd. v. Manufacturers Hanover Trust*, 612 F.Supp. 1533 (S.D.N.Y.1985), *aff'd*, 808 F.2d 209

(2d Cir.1986) (discussing UCP); *Blonder & Co., Inc. v. Citibank, N.A.*, 28 A.D.3d 180, 808 N.Y.S.2d 214 (N.Y. App. Div. 2006) (applying UCP). The UCP is a compilation of usages of trade for letters of credit. *Banca Del Sempione v. Provident Bank of Maryland*, 75 F.3d 951, 954 (4th Cir.1996). It consists of rules negotiated by the International Cham-

other applicable international rules.[3] There is, however, a regulatory dimension to these instruments.

For example, under a former interpretive provision of the Comptroller's regulations,[4] L/Cs were explicitly subject to regulatory considerations concerning sound banking practices. For these purposes, a bank would be required conspicuously to entitle or otherwise indicate that the instrument was an L/C;[5] to condition the L/C by a specified expiration date or definite stated term,[6] and to limit the bank's exposure under the L/C to a stated maximum amount.[7] The bank's liability was required to be limited to presentation of a specified draft or other documentation,[8] and the bank was prohibited from agreeing to undertake the determination of questions of fact or law in dispute between the account party and beneficiary of the L/C.[9] Finally, the bank was required to obtain its customer's unqualified obligation for reimbursement under the L/C.[10]

The Comptroller recently replaced this provision with another, more streamlined interpretation.[11] Under this new interpretation, the Comptroller would not permit a national bank to make its obligation to pay under the L/C to be dependent "upon nondocumentary conditions or resolution of questions of fact."[12] Presumably, a national bank would therefore still be prohibited from performing a physical inspection of goods that were the subject of the transaction for which the L/C was issued.[13]

National banks now have the general authority to issue, confirm or otherwise undertake to honor or purchase L/Cs and other

---

ber of Commerce (ICC) that typically are referenced in a letter of credit, thus becoming part of the terms. The UCP rules have been regularly updated since the ICC issued the first version in 1930. The L/C involved in *Bank of Cochin* was ostensibly governed by the UCP, pursuant to its own express terms. In U.S. commercial practice, the assumption is that the L/C transaction is governed by Article 5 of the UCC unless the parties agree to apply the UCP. A similar approach is apparently taken in English commercial law. *See* Robert Wight & Alan Ward, *The Liability of Banks in Documentary Credit Transactions under English Law*, [1998] J. Int'l Banking L. 387. The latest version of the UCP is the UCP 600, which became effective on July 1, 2007. James J. White & Robert S. Summers, Uniform Commercial Code, § 26–3(b) n.6 (5th ed.2008).

3. United Nations Commission on International Trade Law ("UNCI-

TRAL"), Convention on Independent Guarantees and Standby Letters of Credit (adopted by UNCITRAL 1995); Uniform Rules for Bank-to-Bank Reimbursements Under Documentary Credits (International Chamber of Commerce, Publication No. 525).

4. 12 C.F.R. § 7.7016 (1990).

5. *Id.* § 7.7016(a).

6. *Id.* § 7.7016(b).

7. *Id.* § 7.7016(c).

8. *Id.* § 7.7016(d).

9. *Id. See, e.g., Maurice O'Meara Co. v. National Park Bank of New York*, 239 N.Y. 386, 146 N.E. 636 (Ct.App.1925) (so holding under common law).

10. 12 C.F.R. § 7.7016(e) (1990).

11. 12 C.F.R. § 7.1016.

12. *Id.* § 7.1016(a).

13. *Cf. id.* § 7.1016(b)(1)(i).

independent undertakings within the scope of the applicable transactional laws or rules of practice recognized by law.[14] The bank's obligation to honor depends upon the presentation of specified documents and not upon nondocumentary conditions or resolution of questions of fact or law at issue between the account party and the beneficiary.[15] The new interpretation focuses primarily on the safety and soundness considerations involved in a bank's involvement in L/C transactions.[16]

§ 9.21 Standby Letters of Credit

The basic structure of a standby letter of credit transaction in illustrated in Figure 9–5, *infra*. Neither the Comptroller's regulations[1] nor the basic applicable law[2] differentiate between documentary letters of credit, issued to effect payment to a beneficiary-seller for goods under documents, and standby letters of credit, issued to compensate a beneficiary-buyer for the account party's failure to perform services under contract. This lack of distinction may not be surprising, since the power of national banks to issue standby letters of credit was originally justified on the basis of their essential equivalence to traditional documentary letters of credit.[3] Nevertheless, the respective operating assumptions of the two types of letters of credit are diametrically opposed.

14. *Id.* § 7.1016(a).

15. *Id.*

16. *Id.* § 7.1016(b).

§ 9.21

1. *See* 12 C.F.R. § 7.1016 (making no distinction between documentary and standby letters of credit).

2. *See, e.g., American Bell International, Inc. v. Islamic Republic of Iran,* 474 F.Supp. 420 (S.D.N.Y.1979) (applying traditional letter of credit analysis to standby letter of credit guaranteeing performance).

3. *See, e.g., Legality of Guaranty Letters of Credit,* [1974 Transfer Binder] Fed. Banking L. Rep. (CCH) ¶ 96,301 (July 1, 1974) (equating documentary and standby letters of credit).

FIGURE 9–5
Typical Standby Letter of Credit

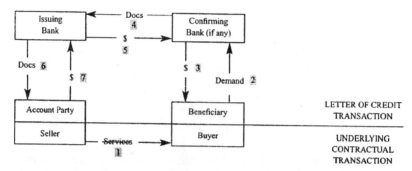

SELLER *FAILS* TO PERFORM ➡ LETTER OF CREDIT TRIGGERED

1. Seller allegedly breaches contract to provide services to Buyer
2. Buyer submits demand and draft to C bank
3. C bank pays Buyer on demand and draft
4. C bank submits demand and draft to I bank
5. I bank reimburses C bank
6. I bank notifies Seller of demand and payment
7. Seller reimburses I bank

In cases like *American Bell International*,[4] courts are essentially applying generally applicable principles (developed in the commercial L/C context) to instruments that, despite their name, are significantly different from traditional commercial L/Cs, and that are more like third-party guarantees. In this regard, consider the effect on a "fraud in the transaction" claim[5] involving a standby letter of credit. In the case of a documentary letter of credit,[6] the stringencies of the "fraud in the transaction" theory can be straightforwardly met by simple facts—have the goods been shipped, or do the boxes contain trash? Do these requirements work out satisfactorily when we are really arguing about the good faith of an undocumented demand under a standby letter of credit, rather than a documented demand?[7] At least in the case of the documented demand, we can assume that there are some goods floating around to secure the bank's risk.

Obviously, *American Bell International* rejects the suggestion that more refined rules should be applied in the case of standby letters of credit. The result is an outcome that, intuitively, seems to be contrary and unsatisfying, since the court assumed that an adequate remedy would exist for the account party in Iran, which

4. *Supra* note 2.

5. Uniform Commercial Code, § 5114(2).

6. *See, e.g., United Bank Ltd. v. Cambridge Sporting Goods Corp.*, 41 N.Y.2d 254, 360 N.E.2d 943, 392

N.Y.S.2d 265 (Ct.App.1976) (involving "fraud in the transaction" claim where mildewed goods had been shipped on a cancelled contract).

7. *Cf., e.g., Sava Gumarska in Kemijska Industria d.d. v. Advanced Polymer*

at the time was already exhibiting extreme hostility toward Americans and American firms. As the U.S.-Iran crisis of 1979 worsened, however, there were at least some indications that courts were beginning to consider the plight of account parties to standby letters of credit (and their issuing banks) in a more thoughtful fashion.[8]

Eventually, of course, the U.S. Government would intervene and freeze the standby letters of credit, so that potentially fraudulent demands could not be effected.[9] This development means that we lack any definitive judicial resolution of the problem of adapting rules that arose in the documentary letter of credit context to the standby letter of credit context.

§ 9.22   Bankers' Acceptances

A bankers' acceptance is a time draft or bill of exchange drawn on a bank by its customer, and "accepted" by the bank. Acceptance makes the draft an obligation of the accepting bank, much as certification of a check makes the check the bank's own obligation. Because the bank customer or the accepting bank may negotiate the accepted draft or bill in a secondary market in which the Fed itself participates and thus raise short-term funds, bankers' acceptances are useful and efficient devices in financing international sales of goods.

The typical acceptance transaction is illustrated in Figure 9–6, *infra.*

Sciences, Inc., 128 S.W.3d 304 (Tex.App. 2004) (holding no fraud in beneficiary's draw on L/C).

8. *See, e.g., Stromberg–Carlson Corp. v. Bank Melli Iran*, 467 F.Supp. 530 (S.D.N.Y.1979) (finding serious risk of fraudulent or nonauthentic demand suf-ficient showing for preliminary injunction against payment under standby letter).

9. *See* Michael P. Malloy, *The Iran Crisis: Law Under Pressure*, 1984 Wisc. Int'l L.J. 15 (1984) (discussing standby letter of credit problem).

FIGURE 9–6
Bankers' Acceptance: Typical Transaction

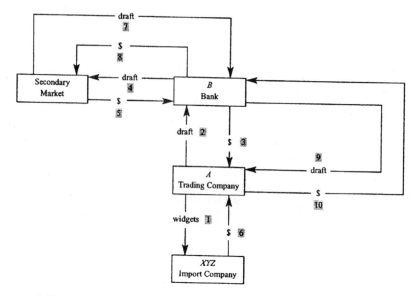

A Trading Company sells widgets to *XYZ* Import Company (1). To finance these sales, for which it normally receives payment in 180 days, *A* arranges with *B* Bank to accept its drafts. in a predetermined amount, at an agreed discount rate plus an acceptance commission. Pursuant to this arrangement, B accepts *A*'s drafts (2), and it credits *A*'s account (3) with an amount equal to the face amount of the drafts, minus the discount (in effect, the interest charged on the financing provided to *A*) and the commission. *B* may then hold the drafts to maturity, or it may rediscount them in the secondary market (4) in order to liquidate its position (5). When the drafts mature (which should be timed for some time shortly after *XYZ* pays *A* (6)), whoever holds them presents them to *B* for payment as the accepting bank (7). *B* will pay the drafts (8), and debit *A*'s account for the amount of the payment (9), *A* having deposited the proceeds of its sale into its account (10).

The key to this market as a financing device is its liquidity, and that depends in large part on the easy negotiability of drafts. Negotiability is enhanced if the acceptance is eligible for rediscount by Federal Reserve banks, consistent with the requirements of the FRA.[1] A member bank, or a federal or state branch or agency of a foreign bank may accept drafts drawn upon under the following conditions: (1) The draft must have no more than six months sight to run, exclusive of days of grace.[2] (2) It must "grow out of" an

§ 9.22   2. *Id.* § 372(a).
1. 12 U.S.C.A. § 372.

import or export transaction[3] or a transaction involving the domestic shipment of goods,[4] or it must be secured at the time of acceptance by a warehouse receipt or similar document of title, covering readily marketable staples.[5] (3) With certain exceptions,[6] the aggregate amount of acceptances for any institution at any one time must be no more than 150 percent of its paid-up and unimpaired capital stock and surplus (or its dollar equivalent, in the case of a U.S. branch or agency of a foreign bank);[7] however, aggregate acceptances "growing out of" domestic transactions is limited in the aggregate to an amount equal to 50 percent of the aggregate of all acceptances.[8] (4) Institutions are prohibited from accepting bills for any one person at any one time in an aggregate amount greater than ten percent of its paid-up and unimpaired capital stock and surplus, or its equivalent for a U.S. branch or agency of a foreign bank, unless the institution is secured either by attached documents or by some other actual security "growing out of" the same transaction as the acceptance.[9]

Generally, these rules apply to agreements to participate in acceptances as well as to acceptances themselves.[10] However, the limitations do not apply to that portion of one institution's acceptance that is covered by a participation agreement sold to another institution.[11]

Essentially, the FRA restrictions attempt to ensure that a bank's exposure in these transactions is relatively short-term and is linked to goods in commerce, the sale of which is likely to extinguish the obligation of the bank with little risk. The regulatory concerns relevant in this context are not unlike those seen in the letter of credit context. However, a bank's own discounted acceptance is treated as a loan for accounting purposes, and so regulatory policy with respect to lending is also relevant. For example, "ineligible" acceptances (those not qualifying under the FRA) would be included in the lending limit calculations.[12]

§ 9.23   Securities Activities

Securities activities of depository institutions are more fully treated elsewhere in this book. However, distribution of securities

---

3. *Id.* § 372(a)(i).

4. *Id.* § 372(a)(ii).

5. *Id.* § 372(a)(iii).

6. The Fed has the authority to permit an institution to accept bills in an aggregate amount not exceeding at any one time equal to 200 percent of its paid-up and unimpaired capital stock and surplus or (in the case of a U.S. branch or agency of a foreign bank) its dollar equivalent. *Id.* § 372(c).

7. *Id.* § 372(b).

8. *Id.* § 372(d).

9. *Id.* § 372(d).

10. *See, e.g., id.* § 372(b) (applying rules on ratio limit of bills to obligation for participation share therein).

11. *Id.* § 372(f).

12. 12 U.S.C.A. 84.

and the syndication and distribution of participations in loans are important and cognate activities of international banking. With the increasing internationalization of capital markets,[1] banks are compelled to sustain and broaden their participation in international capital markets if they are to maintain a share of their wholesale customer's business. Participation occurs both in the Eurobond market[2] and the Euroequity market.[3]

Domestically, U.S. depository institutions are not permitted to engage fully in the underwriting of securities.[4] However, to the extent that underwriting and related activities take place outside the U.S. domestic market, with no "bleed-back" of the underwritten securities into the U.S. market, depository institutions may be authorized to participate.

Typically, U.S. banking enterprises are authorized to participate in securities activities internationally, despite U.S. domestic restrictions, through the invocation of the wild card, or "other activities," provisions of the Fed's Regulation K.[5] In addition, under certain specified circumstances, a bank holding company may engage in debt-for-equity swap investments in firms engaged in activities outside of banking and financial services.[6] These swap invest-

§ 9.23

1. See, e.g., SECURITIES AND EXCHANGE COMMISSION, INTERNATIONALIZATION OF THE SECURITIES MARKETS: REPORT OF THE STAFF OF THE SECURITIES AND EXCHANGE COMMISSION TO THE SENATE COMMITTEE ON BANKING, HOUSING AND URBAN AFFAIRS AND THE HOUSE COMMITTEE ON ENERGY AND COMMERCE (27 JULY 1987) (discussing internationalized capital markets).

2. See id. at II–35–II–51 (discussing Eurobond markets, i.e., markets for bonds issued in one country or group of countries, but denominated in currency of another country).

3. See id. at II–51–II–62, III–43–III–53 (discussing Euroequity markets, i.e., markets for equity securities underwritten and distributed in one country or group of countries outside issuer's home country by syndicate of international securities firms and banks).

4. 12 U.S.C.A. §§ 24(Seventh), 378(a)(1).

5. See, e.g., 12 C.F.R. §§ 211.4(b) (providing for other activities by foreign branches), 211.6(b) (providing for other U.S. activities by Edge corporation), 211.10(c) (providing for other Edge corporation offshore activities). But see 12 U.S.C.A. § 604a, which provides in part:

Regulations issued by the Board of Governors of the Federal Reserve System ... may authorize such a foreign branch, subject to such conditions and requirements as such regulations may prescribe, to exercise such further powers as may be usual in connection with the transaction of the business of banking in the places where such foreign branch shall transact business. Such regulations shall not ..., except to such limited extent as the Board may deem to be necessary with respect to securities issued by any "foreign state" ... authorize a foreign branch to engage or participate, directly or indirectly, in the business of underwriting, selling, or distributing securities.

6. Id. § 211.8(g). Upon application, the Fed may permit a swap investment to be made through an insured bank subsidiary of a bank holding company, if the company demonstrates that such ownership is consistent with the purposes of the FRA. In granting its consent, the Fed may impose such conditions as it deems necessary or appropriate to prevent adverse effects, including prohibiting loans from the bank to the company in which the investment is made. Id. § 211.8(g)(2).

ments are subject to the following conditions. A bank holding company may make such investments only through the conversion of sovereign or private debt obligations of a country that has restructured its official debt,[7] either through direct exchange of the debt obligations for the investment or by a payment for the debt in local currency, the proceeds of which are used to purchase investments specified by Regulation K.[8] The specified investments are as follows: (1) Up to and including 100 percent of the shares of, or other ownership interests in, any foreign company located in an eligible country, if the shares are acquired from the government of the eligible country or from its agencies or instrumentalities;[9] or, (2) Up to and including 40 percent of the shares, including voting shares, of, or other ownership interests in, any other foreign company located in an eligible country subject to certain conditions.[10]

The company is required to divest the shares of, or other ownership interests in, any company acquired through a debt-for-equity swap[11] within ten years from the date of acquisition of the investment[12] or within two years from the date on which the company is permitted to repatriate in full the investment in the foreign company, whichever is longer.[13] However, in either case divestiture must occur within fifteen years of the date of the acquisition.[14] The bank holding company must report to the Fed on its plans for divesting the investment two years prior to the final date for divestiture.[15] In addition, all swap investments are subject to prompt divestiture,[16] if the acquired company engages in imper-

---

7. *See id.* § 211.2(e) (defining "eligible country" for these purposes).

8. *Id.* § 211.8(g)(1). The proceeds in local currency may include as part of the investment an additional cash investment not exceeding in the aggregate more than 10 percent of the fair value of the debt obligations being converted. *Id.*

9. *Id.* § 211.8(g)(1)(i).

10. The conditions are as follows:

(1) The company may invest in more than 25 percent of the voting shares if and only if another shareholder or control group of shareholders unaffiliated with the bank holding company holds a larger block of voting shares of the company.

(2) The company and its affiliates may not lend, or otherwise extend credit to, the foreign company in amounts greater than 50 percent of the total loans and extensions of credit to the foreign company.

(3) The company's representation on the board of directors or on man-

agement committees of the foreign company may be no more than proportional to its shareholding in the foreign company.

12 C.F.R. § 211.8(g)(1)(ii)(A)–(C).

11. *Id.* § 211.8(g)(3)(i). A bank holding company may retain such shares or ownership interests if the retention is otherwise permissible at the time required for divestiture. *Id.* § 211.8(g)(3)(ii)(B).

12. *Id.* § 211.8(g)(3)(i)(A). The Fed may extend such period if, in its judgment, such an extension would not be detrimental to the public interest. *Id.*

13. *Id.* § 211.8(g)(3)(i)(B).

14. *Id.* § 211.8(g)(3)(ii)(A).

15. *Id.* § 211.8(g)(3)(iii).

16. *See id.* § 211.8(e) (concerning divestiture requirements). The Fed may nevertheless authorize retention, upon application. *Id.* § 211.8(g)(3)(iv).

missible business within the United States that exceeds in the aggregate 10 percent of the company's consolidated assets or revenues calculated on an annual basis.[17]

§ 9.24 Foreign Exchange Transactions

National currencies serve three basic purposes. Domestically, they are legal tender for all debts and other obligations. They are also a measure of value of other property. Internationally, they are a medium of exchange for transactions and investment.[1] Consequently, in the international market they are a commodity. For an Italian importer, for example, the dollar (for example) is a commodity that the importer must purchase, directly or indirectly, to obtain what she really wants—goods for import denominated in dollars. Likewise, for the U.S. importer, the lira is a commodity that he must purchase, directly or indirectly, to obtain what he really wants—goods for import denominated in lira.

The multifaceted nature of foreign exchange raises some complicated issues for fiscal policy. If the lira, as a commodity, becomes *less* expensive (relative to the dollar), Italian exports ultimately become cheaper for the U.S. importer, but U.S. exports ultimately become more expensive for the Italian importer. The reverse is true, of course, if the lira becomes relatively more expensive in relation to the dollar.

Eventually, these effects will have an impact on the standard of living in Italy. (Consider for example Italian imports of oil and petroleum products, denominated in dollars.) In addition, if consumers and investors (particularly at the high end) believe that the lira is a poor measure of value (because, for example, it tends to decrease in value relative to other currencies), then they will prefer to store their net worth in dollars, or some other currency other than the lira. Complicating this situation will be the activities of "speculators" in currencies, who may sell short or buy long at a current price in international currency markets, depending upon whether they bet that the currency on the date their foreign exchange contract becomes due for "delivery" will be decreasing or

17. *Id.* § 211.8(g)(3)(iv). In any event, the acquired company may not engage in activities in the United States that consist of banking or financial operations, *per id.* § 211.23(f)(5)(iii)(B), or types of activities permitted by regulation or order under section 4(c)(8) of the Bank Holding Company Act, 12 U.S.C.A. § 1843(c)(8), except under regulations of the Fed, or with its prior approval. 12 C.F.R. § 211.8(g)(3)(iv).

§ 9.24

1. On the choice of law aspects of foreign exchange transactions, see *Indosuez International Finance B.V. v. National Reserve Bank*, 98 N.Y.2d 238, 746 N.Y.S.2d 631, 774 N.E.2d 696 (2002) (applying New York law to forward currency exchange transactions involving Russian bank and Netherands corporation, involving exchange pegged to value of U.S. dollar with payment to be made in U.S.dollars).

increasing in value, respectively.[2] Because currency markets are sensitive to these transactions, the result of this "artificial" demand may be to drive a currency's value further down or up.

The question for the student of international banking policy is: If the monetary authorities in Italy are worried about the effect of speculation on the stable value of the lira, what should they do about it? They could just say, "Speculation in the lira is prohibited," but with what result? Italian monetary authorities would confront the possibility of hidden transactions and difficult questions about whether or not a particular transaction is speculative. If this prohibition is aggressively pursued, possibly calling into question the legality of what are actually legitimate transactions, merchants will move away from lira-denominated goods.

In the alternative, the authorities could ask themselves, what does speculation look like on the books of the currency trader? At the end of a given trading day, it would have sold significantly more than it had bought, or *vice versa*. So, why not prohibit the symptoms of speculation, rather than speculation itself? This is basically the typical approach taken by foreign exchange regulations.[3] What result? Complicated off-shore transactions involving foreign jurisdictions with bank secrecy laws that prevent the authorities from examining the other end of transactions that appear to "square" the books of currency traders within Italy. This is a regulatory problem that confronts even sophisticated currency regulations.

In a sense, this situation illustrates a typical problem in international banking. With a host of national authorities each acting independently with respect to *international* transactions, how can national regulatory policy objectives be effectively realized? Of course, this dilemma is present not only in international bank regulatory policy, but in public international fiscal policy as well.[4]

The BIS addressed this problem in the 1983 Concordat.[5] The basic operating principle that it advanced to deal with this problem was one of cooperation and information flow between home-country and host-country regulators. In the view of the BIS Committee, it was particularly important for parent banks to establish internal monitoring systems to supervise overall foreign exchange exposure, and it was equally important for home-country authorities to moni-

---

2. *See, e.g.*, Carley, *Close Encounters*, Wall St. J., Sept. 4, 1982, at 1 (describing speculative currency trading of Citibank).

3. *See id.* (describing Italian foreign exchange restrictions).

4. On the implications for public international fiscal policy, see Michael P. Malloy, *Shifting Paradigms: Institution-*

al *Roles in a Changing World*, 62 Fordham L. Rev. 1911 (1994).

5. Bank for International Settlements, Committee on Banking Regulations and Supervisory Practices, Principles for the Supervision of Banks' Foreign Establishments (1983), *reprinted in* Michael P. Malloy, International Banking 79–83 (2d ed. 2005).

tor those systems. Host-country authorities should also monitor the foreign exchange exposure of foreign establishments in their territories.

The BIS Committee also approached the problem of supervising foreign exchange activities from a more technical perspective in revisions of its capital adequacy guidelines.[6] These cover such issues as increasing the capital charge for potential future counterparty exposure on exchange rate contracts, and recognition of the effects of bilateral netting arrangements in calculating the potential future exposure for exchange contracts.[7]

Ordinary contract law sometimes experiences difficulty in dealing with problems in the performance and enforcement of foreign exchange contracts. Parties to such transactions, whether one-time or on an on-going basis, often do business without a written contract, except for documentation generated during the execution of a specific transaction. For example, in *Interactive Intelligence, Inc. v. Keycorp*,[8] a commercial customer sued its bank and a former bank employee, claiming contractual and tort theories of liability arising out of foreign exchange (FX) currency transactions for which the customer was allegedly overcharged more than $2 million. The District Court granted defendants' summary judgment, and the customer appealed. The Seventh Circuit affirmed, holding that: (*i*) the customer was not a beneficiary of any employment contract or code between the employee and the bank; (*ii*) the employee owed no duty to the customer, as required for a negligence claim against the bank; (*iii*) the bank owed no fiduciary duty to the customer; and, (*iv*) the customer's alleged oral contract with the bank was too vague to be enforceable. As the Seventh Circuit noted,

> It is true that a bank may owe a customer a fiduciary duty if a confidential relationship exists between them. Paulson v. Centier Bank, 704 N.E.2d 482 (Ind.Ct.App.1998). But there is nothing confidential in the FX transaction. The uncontroverted evidence shows that Interactive's employees knew that exchange rates were available on the Internet and in the Wall Street Journal.In fact, on occasion, Interactive employees asked KeyBank about the reasons for the difference between published rates and the rates the bank was using. This is simply not a situation in which the bank was acting as a fiduciary.[9]

---

6. Bank for International Settlements, Committee on Banking Regulations and Supervisory Practices, Final Report for International Convergence of Capital Measurement and Capital Standards, *reprinted in* 1 Fed. Banking L. Rep. (CCH) ¶ 5403 (July 29, 1988). For full discussion of the guidelines and their successive revisions, see § 7.9, *supra.*

7. *See* § 7.9, *supra.*

8. 546 F.3d 897 (7th Cir. 2008).

9. 546 F.3d at 901.

§ 9.25   Resolution of Transborder Failures

National and international policy with respect to the resolution of transborder failures has stiffened over the past two decades, particularly in the case of the United States. The Federal Deposit Insurance Corporation Improvements Act ("FDICIA")[1] prohibits federal bank regulatory agencies from making, directly or indirectly, any payment or from providing any financial assistance in connection with any insured depository institution, if the payment would have the direct or indirect effect of satisfying any claim, in whole or in part, against the institution for its obligations on foreign deposits.[2] This prohibition excludes foreign depositors from direct or indirect benefit from a decision by U.S. regulators to place an institution in receivership and resolve its obligations. However, it does not apply to "open bank assistance" provided by the FDIC[3] to a troubled institution.[4] Thus, an institution—even if technically close to receivership—could be revived with open bank assistance, and foreign depositors are permitted to benefit from this process. Similarly, the prohibition does not apply to "discount window lending," Fed bank advances or other extensions of credit consistent with the Federal Reserve Act.[5]

FDICIA also gave the Fed direct authority over U.S. branches, agencies, and commercial lending subsidiaries of foreign-based banks.[6] The Fed has broad authority to examine U.S. branches, agencies and affiliates of foreign-based banks, whether state-or federally-approved.[7] Under specified circumstances, the Fed has the authority to order the closing of any state-licensed office of a foreign-based bank,[8] and to *recommend* to the Comptroller the termination of the license of any federally-licensed office of a foreign-based bank.[9] The Fed can also terminate the activities of any representative office.[10]

Finally, FDICIA broadened the penalties directly applicable to U.S. activities of foreign-based banks. It established authority for civil money penalties (administrative fines) to be assessed against any foreign bank, and any office or subsidiary of a foreign bank, that violates, and any individual who participates in a violation of, any provision of the International Banking Act ("IBA"), or any regulation prescribed or order issued under the act.[11] FDICIA also established criminal penalties for the knowing violation of any

§ 9.25

1. Pub. L. No. 102–242, 105 Stat. 2236 (December 19, 1991) (codified at scattered sections of 12 U.S.C.A.).

2. 12 U.S.C.A. § 1831r(a).

3. *Id*. § 1823(c).

4. *Id*. § 1831r(b).

5. *Id*. § 1831r(c).

6. *Id*. § 3105(d)(1), (g).

7. *Id*. § 3105(b)(1).

8. *Id*. § 3105(e)(1)–(4), (g).

9. *Id*. § 3105(e)(5).

10. *Id*. § 3107(b).

11. *Id*. § 3110.

provision of the IBA or any regulation or order issued by a federal banking agency under the act, with the intent to deceive, to gain financially, or to cause financial gain or loss to any person.[12]

On the positive side, FDICIA explicitly authorizes disclosure of supervisory information by federal bank regulatory agencies to foreign bank regulatory or supervisory authorities.[13] This is consistent with the objective identified by the BIS Committee to improve the supervision of transborder banking enterprises.[14] With respect to such supervision, the BIS Concordat establishes a two-fold classification system for dealing with problems of troubled or failing international banks. This system is illustrated in Figure 9–7, *infra*.

Figure 9–7
Supervision under the Concordat

Type of Establishment	Type of Problem	
	Solvency	Liquidity
Branch	primarily matter for home country authority	primary responsibility for host country authority
Subsidiary	joint responsibility of host and home	primary responsibility for host
Joint Venture	primary responsibility with country of incorporation	primary responsibility with country of incorporation

Thus, in deciding on the proper division of responsibility in a transborder problem, we must first ask what type of foreign bank presence are we dealing with. Second, we must ask what kind of problem is the banking enterprise are we actually facing—liquidity (*i.e.*, troubled condition), or insolvency (*i.e.*, failure).

Thus, if the subject enterprise is a joint venture, the host-country regulator is likely to be saddled with the primary responsibility, whether the problem is one of solvency or liquidity. However, if the enterprise is a subsidiary of, for example, a U.S. national bank, and if the host-country authorities determine that it is facing a solvency problem, resolution will be the joint responsibility of host-country and U.S. authorities. If on the other hand it is facing a liquidity problem, this will be the primary responsibility of the host-country authorities.

Of course, only a handful of national supervisors directly participated in the construction of the Concordat. Would it make a

---

12. *Id.* § 3111.

13. *Id.* § 3109(a).

14. *See* BANK FOR INTERNATIONAL SETTLEMENTS, COMMITTEE ON BANKING REGULATIONS AND SUPERVISORY PRACTICES, PRINCIPLES FOR THE SUPERVISION OF BANKS' FOREIGN ESTABLISHMENTS (1983), *reprinted in* MICHAEL P. MALLOY, INTERNATIONAL BANKING 79–83 (2d ed.2005).

difference if the host country involved was not a member of the BIS Committee? First, it should be noted that the Concordat is not, by its own terms, a binding international treaty or agreement. It is at best a statement of principles. Hence, it may be less important that the host country is not a member of the Committee, so long as it endorses the principles.

Second, the Concordat purports to set forth the optimal operating principles endorsed by the members of the Committee. Hence, at the very least the Concordat should be the argumentative focus of discussion between host- and home-country authorities.

Post–Concordat issuances of the BIS have refined the operating assumptions with respect to supervision of multinational banking enterprises.[15] Neither the April 1990 SUPPLEMENT nor the June 1992 MINIMUM STANDARDS affect the basic framework established by the Concordat. However, to the extent that these issuances result in better information flows between national regulators and better national controls over the entry of a multinational banking enterprise into the national market supervised by the regulator, presumably the supervision of multinational bank failures could be more efficiently anticipated and managed. In April 2002, the Basel Committee on Banking Supervision issued a report by its Task Force on Dealing with Weak Banks[16] that identified guidelines for financial sector supervisors and bank managers dealing with weak banks.[17] The report identifies six guiding principles: prompt responsive action; cost-efficiency in choosing a response; flexibility and administrative discretion in the deployment and timing of the response; consistency; avoidance of moral hazard; and, transparency and cooperation.

While the MINIMUM STANDARDS are not, on their own terms, binding on states, BIS participating states are expected to implement them, and other states are encouraged to do so. U.S. implementation has occurred primarily in connection with the enactment

---

15. BANK FOR INTERNATIONAL SETTLEMENTS, COMMITTEE ON BANKING REGULATION AND SUPERVISORY PRACTICES: SUPPLEMENT TO THE BASEL CONCORDAT ENSURING OF ADEQUATE INFORMATION FLOWS BETWEEN BANKING SUPERVISORY AUTHORITIES (APRIL 1990), *reprinted in* MALLOY, INTERNATIONAL BANKING, *supra*, at 84–87; BANK FOR INTERNATIONAL SETTLEMENTS, COMMITTEE ON BANKING REGULATION AND SUPERVISORY PRACTICES: REPORT ON MINIMUM STANDARDS FOR THE SUPERVISION OF INTERNATIONAL BANKING GROUPS AND THEIR CROSSBORDER ESTABLISHMENT (JUNE 1992), *reprinted in* MALLOY, INTERNATIONAL BANKING, *supra*, at 87–91.

16. *See* Daniel Pruzin *Basel Task Force Issues Guidelines on Dealing With Weak Banks Worldwide*, BNA Banking Daily, Apr. 9, 2002, at d8 (discussing report).

17. For these purposes, the term "weak bank" is defined as a bank the liquidity or solvency of which is or will be impaired absent significant improvement in its financial resources, risk profile, strategic business direction, risk management capabilities and/or quality of management. *Id.*

of FDICIA. The parallels between the MINIMUM STANDARDS and FDICIA provisions are illustrated in Figure 9–8, *infra*.

Figure 9–8

Parallels between BIS MINIMUM STANDARDS and FDICIA

MINIMUM STANDARD	FDICIA	SUBJECT MATTER
1. All international banking groups and international banks should be supervised by a home-country authority that capably performs consolidated supervision	12 U.S.C.A. § 3105(d)(2)(a)	comprehensive supervision of applicant for U.S. branch on consolidated basis by home state required
2. The creation of cross-border banking establishment should receive the prior consent of both host-country supervisory authority and bank's and, if different, banking group's home-country supervisory authority	3105(d)(3)(A)	consent of home state to establishment of U.S. branch required
3. Supervisory authorities should possess right to gather information from cross-border banking establishments of banks or banking groups for which they are the home-country supervisor	3105(d)(3)(B) 3105(d)(3)(C)	foreign bank must furnish information needed to assess application adequacy of foreign bank's assurances that it will make available information on its operations and activities (and those of its affiliates) deemed necessary to determine and enforce compliance with IBA, BHCA, and other applicable Federal law made condition of approval of application
4. If host-country authority determines that any one of the foregoing minimum standards is not met to its satisfaction, that authority could impose restrictive measures necessary to satisfy its prudential concerns consistent with the minimum standards, including prohibition of creation of banking establishments	3105(e)(1)(A)	termination of U.S. office of foreign bank when foreign bank is not subject to comprehensive supervision on consolidated basis by home state authorities

§ 9.26 International Responses to the 2008 Financial Crisis

The U.S. subprime mortgage crisis that emerged in 2008[1] has also had devastating effects internationally. By late October 2008,

---

§ 9.26

1. On the U.S. subprime mortgage

crisis, see 2 MICHAEL P. MALLOY, BANKING LAW AND REGULATION § 4A.2.5 (1994 &

the Bank of England sounded the alarm in its semi-annual *Financial Stability Report*, estimating that total losses to banks, insurance companies, and pension funds in Europe and the United States as a result of the financial crisis could reach $2.8 trillion.[2] The Bank acknowledged "the need for a fundamental rethink internationally of appropriate safeguards against systemic risk, including through the development of macroprudential policies to dampen the financial cycle."[3] Increasing capital and liquidity requirements for individual institutions was not a sufficient response to a systemic problem, and the Bank has argued for "a fundamental overhaul of the regulatory safeguards used to mitigate systemic risk within the financial system."[4] Enhanced safeguards were needed to address "problems within the banking system [that] were deep seated, rooted in structural weaknesses in banks' balance sheets that had developed during the boom years."[5] These weaknesses included (i) inflated aggregate balance sheets, (ii) expansion into complex securities whose underlying value, credit quality and liquidity were uncertain, (iii) liability structures that relied excessively on the sustained availability of wholesale funding and short maturities; (*iv*) capital levels that were relatively inadequate in light of underlying balance sheet risks; and, (*v*) underappreciated but significant financial interconnections among firms operating transnationally.[6]

In October 2008, EU finance ministers agreed to raise the minimum standard for bank account guarantees to €50,000 (about $67,500).[7] In addition, in an effort to create a more coordinated response to the financial crisis among EU member states, in October 2008 EU finance ministers adopted a range of principles dealing with liquidity, accounting, and recapitalization issues.[8] These principles include: (*i*) a commitment that regulatory intervention should be timely and support temporary; (*ii*) an intervening govern-

Cum. Supp.).

2. See Bank of England Financial Stability Report 11 (Oct. 2008), *available at* http://www.bankofengland.co.uk/publications/fsr/2008/fsrfull0810.pdf. See also Ali Qassim, New Countercyclical Tools Needed Against Systemic Risk, Bank of England Says, BNA Int'l Bus. & Fin. Daily (Oct. 29, 2008), *available at* http://pubs.bna.com/ (discussing Bank of England report).

3. Financial Stability Report at 4. Fed Chairman Bernanke has also endorsed, if in somewhat vaguer terms, "macroprudential oversight" to maintain lending practices across financial services the system, as opposed to prudential supervision of specific troubled

institutions. *See* http://www.federalreserve.gov/newsevents/speech/bernanke20080822a.htm.

4. Financial Stability Report at 51.

5. *Id.* at 8.

6. *Id.*

7. Joe Kirwin, EU Ministers Raise Bank Guarantee Threshold, Adopt Guide to Crisis Response, BNA Int'l Bus. & Fin. Daily (Oct. 8, 2008), available at http://pubs.bna.com/ip/bna/ibd.nsf/eh/A0B7E7J6H0. Then current EU law requires member states to guarantee bank accounts to a maximum of €20,000 ($27,000). Id.

8. Joe Kirwin, EU Ministers, *supra*.

ment should be watchful of taxpayers interests, and existing share-holders should bear the due consequences of the intervention; (*iii*) an intervening government should be empowered to bring about a change of management; (*iv*) management should not retain undue benefits and governments should have the power to intervene when it comes to remuneration; (*v*) the legitimate interest of competitors should be protected, especially with regard to state aid rules; and, (*vi*) negative indirect or "spill-over" effects with respect to other EU member states should be avoided. There is a peculiar oscillation in the responses emanating from the EU. At the EU level, there is a determined push towards increased global supervision in financial services markets, while at the member-state level, the individual member states are repudiating legislative proposals to establish enhanced regional supervision in the insurance[9] and banking sectors.[10] The result was a "shared approach" in which the 27 EU member states agreed in mid-December to a $256 billion economic stimulus response that set parameters for individual member states to increase domestic spending and reduce taxes, with EU-wide measures covering the automotive industry, broadband Internet penetration, and road and rail infrastructure.[11]

In January 2009, Angel Gurría, OECD secretary general, argued that—if not the entire EU—at least the 16 countries of the Euro Zone needed a single EU-wide supervisor or central agency with authority to supervise the financial sector in order to help avoid a future episode of financial crisis.[12] Yet in March 2009, the Competition Commissioner Neelie Kroes suggested that responding to the financial crisis remained primarily an individual nation-state responsibility.[13]

9. Joe Kirwin, EU Finance Ministers Reject Enhanced Supervision in Insurance, Banking Sectors (Dec. 3, 2008) (reporting that EU member state agreement to new insurance regulatory regime conditioned on omission of EU-wide insurance supervision), available at http://news.bna.com.

10. Joe Kirwin, Despite G–20 Stance, EU Members Resist EU–Wide Supervision of Insurance, Banking, BNA Banking Daily (Nov. 24, 2008), available at http://news.bna.com. But see Joe Kirwin, EU, U.S. Should Work to Forge Joint Economic Recovery Package, Barroso Says, BNA Int'l Bus. & Fin. Daily (Dec. 10, 2008), available at http://news.bna.com (reporting that France and United Kingdom had embraced commission plan for EU-wide stimulus package, with Germany still dissenting).

11. Joe Kirwin, EU Leaders Back $256 Billion Package of Economic Stimulus, BNA Int'l Bus. & Fin. Daily (Dec. 15, 2008), available at http://news.bna.com.

12. Rick Mitchell, *Euro Area Needs Single Authority To Supervise Finance Sector, OECD Says*, BNA Int'l Bus. & Fin. Daily (Jan. 15, 2009), available at http://www.bna. The secretary-general's comments were made in connection with the release of the latest OECD economic survey for the Euro Zone. For further information on the survey, see http://www.oecd.org/document/49/0,3343,en_2649_34569_41985521_1_1_1_1,00.html.

13. *EU Commissioner Urges Banking Sector To Shoulder Responsibility for Credit Crisis*, BNA Int'l Bus. & Fin. Daily (Mar. 17, 2009), available at http://www.bna.com.

By the end of October 2008, the European Commission had already approved bank rescue plans to stabilize financial markets in Denmark, France, Germany, Ireland, the Netherlands, Portugal, Sweden, and the United Kingdom.[14] By mid-November, approval

14. Sweden, Portugal Latest Nations to Receive EC Approval of Financial Rescue Plans, BNA Int'l Bus. & Fin. Daily (Oct. 31, 2008), available at http://news.bna.com; Bengt Ljung, Rescue Plans for French, Dutch Banks Approved by EC, Spain, Italy Plans Up Next BNA Banking Daily (Nov. 3, 2008), available at http://news.bna.com. In June 2009, the European Commission approved a € 4 billion ($5.6 billion) emergency recapitalization of Anglo Irish Bank by the Irish Government. *EC Supports Ireland's Emergency Recap Of 'Systemically Important' Anglo Irish Bank*, BNA BANKING DAILY, June 29, 2009, available at http://www.bna.com. In February 2010, the European Commission approved a $9.3 billion capital injection by the Dutch Government to finance the separation of ABN Amro from its parent company. *EC Approves More Bailout Funding For Dutch Banks Fortis, ABN AMRO*, BNA BANKING DAILY, Feb. 9, 2010, available at http://www. bna.com. In light of relaxed state-aid guidelines put forward in early December, the European Commission approved on December 23, 2008, changes submitted by the U.K. government to alter its bank guarantee and recapitalization plan, in order to stimulate more lending by financially sound banks. Joe Kirwin, *European Commission Gives Green Light To Amended British Bank Bailout Program*, BNA INT'L BUS. & FIN. DAILY (Dec. 24, 2008), available at http://news. bna.com. In April 2009 the EU Competition Commissioner authorized a six-month extension of UK bank credit guarantee and recapitalization provisions, in light of continued "severe stress" in global and British financial services markets. Joe Kirwin, *EU Gives Approval for Extension Of British Banking Bailout Plan*, BNA INT'L BUS. & FIN. DAILY (Apr. 16, 2009), available at http://www.bna.com/corp/index.html. On April 21, 2009, the Commission approved a UK plan to stabilize the British market for mortgage-backed securities and to revitalize the UK housing market by offering $72.5 billion in government guarantees to banks providing loans to homeowners. Joe Kirwin, *EU Approves British Government Plan To Guarantee Mortgage Backed Securities*, BNA INT'L BUS. & FIN. DAILY (Apr. 22, 2009), available at http://www.bna.com. In October 2009, the Commission approved a continuation of the UK plan until year-end 2009. Bengt Ljung, *EC Extends U.K. Bank Credit Guarantee, Recap Scheme as Meeting EU State–Aid Limitations*, BNA BANKING DAILY, 2009, available at http://www.bna.com. EU member state subsidies almost tripled in 2008 in an effort to stem the critical drop in economic growth. *EU Governments' Subsidies Nearly Triple In 2008 as Result of Economic Crisis*, BNA BANKING DAILY, Dec. 8, 2009, available at http://www.bna.com. For the text of the European Commission report, see http://ec.europa.eu/competition/state _ aid/studies _ reports/2009 _ autumn _ en.pdf.

Commission review is necessary because of treaty restrictions on state aid limiting member state ability to grant aid or other incentives or supports under certain specified circumstances. See Consolidated Version of the Treaty Establishing the European Community art. 87, Mar. 25, 1997, 2002 O.J. (C 325) 33 ("[A]id granted by a Member State . . . in any form whatsoever which distorts or threatens to distort competition . . . shall, in so far as it affects trade between Member States, be incompatible with the common market...."). See also art. 88, formerly Article 93 (providing for review of state aids provided by member states to determine compatibility with single market). So, for example, the Competition Commissioner has already questioned the $22 billion paid by the Dutch government in nationalizing Dutch operations of Fortis Bank and its subsidiary ABN AMRO, since the recapitalization of the bank did not comply with November 2008 Commission rules with respect to EU members' overall bank rescue plans. European Commission Raises Doubts About Dutch Government Bank Bailout, BNA Int'l Bus. & Fin. Daily (Apr. 9, 2009), available at http://www.bna.com. The question is whether the Fortis Bank Nederland rescue aid was "limited to the minimum necessary and did not create undue dis-

was extended to Finland and Italy.[15] In late December, approval of a financial aid for Spanish commercial banks was also approved.[16] In February 2009, the European Commission approved a $17 billion Danish government plan to bail out banks, the second such plan in the past four months, and a French government plan to provide low-interest loans for businesses that manufacture products considered beneficial to the environment.[17]

For the first time since the financial crisis emerged, in May 2009, the European Commission authorized a unique rescue plan by the German government to nationalize Hypo Real Estate Holding AG, the largest German bank specializing in real estate lending.[18] By May 29, 2009, the Commission had authorized a fourth major bank bailout in Germany, a package for NHSH Nordbanken, a state-owned regional bank facing insolvency, consisting of $4.17 billion worth of recapitalization and $13.9 billion in "risk shield" loan.[19] The risk shield is designed to protect a broad asset portfolio

tortions of competition liable to cause problems for banks in other member states." *Id.* However, responding to pressure from EU member states, in early December 2008 the European Commission agreed to issue more flexible, expeditious rules for review of member state bank bailout plans. Joe Kirwin, European Commission Bends to EU States, Will Ease Controls on Bank Bailout Proposals, BNA Banking Daily (Dec. 3, 2008), available at http://news.bna. com. The new state aid guidelines for banks, published on December 8, 2008, differentiated between "distressed" financial institutions compared to "sound" ones and imposed "safeguards" ensuring that a bank receiving state funds would use the resources to make loans rather than simply improving its capital position or acquiring other financial institutions. Joe Kirwin, EC Outlines New Guidelines for Aid By States to Banks in Need of Bailout, BNA Int'l Bus. & Fin. Daily (Dec. 9, 2008), available at http://news.bna.com. This is in striking contrast with the disingenuous approach of the U.S. Treasury Department, which has essentially allowed large firms to dictate their own terms of use, to the detriment of the retail market. *See* 3 MICHAEL P. MALLOY, BANKING LAW AND REGULATION § 11.4.1 (1994 & Cum. Supp.) (discussing U.S. approach to crisis). However, the strain of maintaining the balance between necessary bank rescue measures and the transparency of the single European market is beginning to show. To prevent distor-

tions to the single market, EU member states insisted in December 2009 that there was a need for broad-based, coordinated exit strategy once the unwinding of rescue measures begins. Joe Kirwin, *EU Leaders Call for Coordinated Effort To Unwind State Aid, Consolidate Finances*, BNA BANKING DAILY, Dec. 14, 2009, available at http://www.bna.com.

15. Joe Kirwin, *EC Quickly Gives Green Light to Plans To Rescue Italian, Finnish, Dutch Banks*, BNA INT'L BUS. & FIN. DAILY (Nov. 17, 2008), available at http://news.bna.com; Joe Kirwin, *Italian Bank Recapitalization Plan Approved by European Commission*, BNA INT'L BUS. & FIN. DAILY (Dec. 29, 2008), available at http://news.bna.com.

16. Joe Kirwin, *European Regulator Approves Spain's Plan To Provide Guarantees to Commercial Banks*, BNA INT'L BUS. & FIN. DAILY (Dec. 29, 2008), available at http://news.bna.com.

17. Joe Kirwin, *EU OK's New Danish Bank–Bailout Plan, French Government Loans for Green Goods*, BNA Int'l Bus. & Fin. Daily (Feb. 5, 2009), available at http://www.bna.com.

18. Joe Kirwin, *European Commission OKs German Plan For First Bank Nationalization Since 1930s*, BNA INT'L BUS. & FIN. DAILY (May 18, 2009), available at http://www.bna.com.

19. Joe Kirwin, *EU Commission Clears Fourth Bailout Providing $18 Billion for State–Owned Bank*, BNA INT'L

worth approximately $200 billion focused primarily in the shipping, transportation and renewable energy sector.[20] The aid package was valid for three months.[21]

It was expected that most if not all of the 27 EU member states would seek approval of bank rescue plans, although some of these may only be pursued as a precaution.[22] As of the end of Q1 2009, EU member states had issued more than $4 trillion in the form of guarantees, risk shields, and recapitalization measures in favor of financial services firms in the 27 EU member states.[23] Nevertheless, on May 18, 2009, the EU approved an increase in its fund for non-Euro Zone member states from $33.7 billion to $67.5, in light of new economic data indicating that economies such as Estonia, Latvia, Lithuania, Hungary, Romania, and Slovakia had experienced severe economic contraction in Q1 2009.[24] In the period of November 2008 to May 2009 the European Commission had already approved 54 different bailout plans either for individual banks or for the overall banking industry of an applicant member state, and was beginning to face potentially controversial decisions on which plans should be given six-month extensions.[25] In May 2009, EU finance ministers requested that the EU Committee of European Banking Supervisors conduct stress tests on European banking enterprises subject to EU oversight,[26] similar to the exercise that has just been completed in the United States.[27] The Committee stressed, however, that unlike the U.S. stress tests, the results of the EU stress tests of banks to be completed by September 2009 would be kept strictly confidential.[28]

Thus, transactional efforts and traditional government intervention remained the typical response to the crisis. For example, in mid-September, the European Central Bank made an extra €30 billion in overnight funds available to Euro Zone banks, in an effort

Bus. & Fin. Daily (June 1, 2009), available at http://www.bna.com.

20. Id.

21. Id.

22. *Sweden, Portugal, supra.*

23. Joe Kirwin, *EU Member States Have Authorized $4 Trillion to Bail Out Financial Sector*, BNA Int'l Bus. & Fin. Daily (Apr.10, 2009), available at http://www.bna.com/corp/index.html.

24. Joe Kirwin, *EU Ups Bailout Fund While Eastern, Central European Economies Deteriorate*, BNA Int'l Bus. & Fin. Daily (May 19, 2009), available at http://www.bna.com/corp.

25. Joe Kirwin, *EC Faces Delicate Task as Bank Bailouts Need Approval*

for Six–Month Renewals, BNA Int'l Bus. & Fin. Daily (May 22, 2009), available at http://www.bna.com/corp/index.html. For a list of all state aid cases approved by the Commission since October 2008 or pending, see http://europa.eu/rapid/pressReleasesAction.do?reference=MEMO/09/246&format=HTML&aged=0&language=EN&guiLanguage=en.

26. *EU to Conduct Bank Stress Tests Amid Member State Questions Over Utility*, BNA Int'l Bus. & Fin. Daily (May 14, 2009), available at http://www.bna.com.

27. For discussion of the U.S. stress tests, see § 8.2, *supra*, text and accompanying Figure 8–1.

28. *EU to Conduct Bank Stress Tests, supra.*

to calm money markets and reassure lenders.[29] However, this total amount was only about one-third of the aggregate amount being requested by banks in the zone.[30] In late October 2008, European Commission proposed to double the EU crisis fund for troubled member states, to €25 billion, to assist them in providing economic recovery supports.[31] In June 2009 the European Commission granted temporary six-month approval to state aid in the form of recapitalization and impaired asset relief measures to Landesbank Baden–Wütemberg in Germany and KBC financial group in Belgium.[32] In August 2009 the European Commission approved a $9.9 billion bailout for the German bank IKB, but it rejected a German Government restructuring plan for the bank.[33] Commission skepticism of German Government rescue efforts has steadily increased.[34] In November 2009 the European Commission approved restructuring plans that include significant divestitures for three large EU-based banks, the Belgian bank KBC, British bank Lloyds HBOS, and the Dutch bank ING.[35] At the same time, the Commission

29. ECB Pumps 30 Billion Euros in Cash Into Banks in Wake of Lehman Failure, BNA Banking Daily (Sept. 16, 2008), available at http://news.bna.com.

30. *Id.*

31. Bengt Ljung, EC Moves to Double EU Crisis Fund; Almunia Urges Rate Cuts, Stimulus Spending, BNA Int'l Bus. & Fin. Daily (Oct. 30, 2008), available at http://news.bna.com. See also Joe Kirwin, EC to Announce Major Economic Stimulus Plan to Include Infrastructure, Green Tech, BNA Int'l Bus. & Fin. Daily (Nov. 26, 2008), available at http://news.bna.com (reporting on EU proposal for major economic stimulus package).

32. Bengt Ljung, *EC Approves State Assistance To Two European Banks for Six Months*, BNA Banking Daily, July 1, 2009, available at http://www.bna.com.

33. Joe Kirwin, *EU Approves Third Bailout of German Bank, But Rejects German Plans for Restructuring*, BNA Banking Daily, Aug. 18, 2009, available at http://www.bna.com.

34. By October 2009, the European Commission had initiated an investigation of the EU compatibility of a German Government plan to provide approximately $4.5 billion in recapitalization and $15 billion in guarantees to HSH Nordbanken, the fifth largest Landesbank in Germany. Joe Kirwin, *European Commission Launches Probe Of State Aid Given Leading German Bank*, BNA Banking Daily, 2009, available at http://www.bna.com. In particular, the Commission was concerned whether the rescue plan violated Commission guidelines for responding to "toxic assets" without unnecessarily distorting the EU single market. For the text of the restructuring guidelines, see http://ec.europa.eu/competition/state_aid/legislation/restructuring_paper_en.pdf. *See also* Joe Kirwin, *EC Clears More German Aid for WestLB, But Move to Probe Legality Raises Tensions*, BNA Banking Daily, Dec. 23, 2009, available at http://www.bna.com (reporting on political tension between European Commission and German Government over continuing banking crisis in Germany).

35. Joe Kirwin, *European Commission Clears Restructuring For Three Big Banks; 28 More to Be Decided*, BNA Banking Daily, Nov. 19, 2009, available at http://www.bna.com. In accordance with a European Commission initiative to force "too-big-to-fail" banks to restructure in exchange for financial assistance, ING had agreed in October 2009 to divest its insurance and investment management divisions, as well as its U.S.-based internet banking division. Joe Kirwin, *Under EC Pressure, Ailing Dutch Bank ING Will Divest Insurance Division, Two Others*, BNA Banking Daily, Oct. 27, 2009, available at http://www.bna.com.

announced that 28 other financial institutions would be required to submit to a restructuring as a condition for significant infusions over the past year.[36] In January 2010, the European Commission approved a $140 billion Spanish Government bank recapitalization plan, to support the solvency of hundreds of banks struggling with the collapse of the EU real estate market and construction industry.[37]

In May 2009 the European Commission outlined a plan calling for a new European Systemic Risks Council (ESRC) and new agencies to replace a series of committees that currently deal with cross-border banking, insurance and financial services prudential issues.[38] To avoid a repeat of the financial crisis, the Commission plan calls for the ESRC to keep a continuous gauge on macroeconomics in the EU and to issue warnings when potential problems such as under capitalized banks or real estate bubbles threaten economic foundations.[39]

Also in May 2009, the European Parliament voted overwhelmingly in favor of amendments to the EU Capital Requirements Directive that establish a new "college of supervisors" to oversee approximately 44 banks with cross-border operations, strengthen banking supervision and prevent future financial meltdowns.[40] It also establishes a controversial five-percent retention rule requiring any banking institution selling securitized products, such as those backed by real estate loans, to retain a portion of ownership.[41] It also limits large exposures of banks to a single client, including interbank lending, to 25 percent of own funds to any client or group of clients.[42]

In December 2009 EU finance ministers approved a new EU-wide banking and financial services supervision structure designed to prevent future financial crises, with a sovereignty concession demanded by the UK.[43] The structure includes a "macro-prudential" European Systemic Risk Board and a "micro-prudential" cluster of three new agencies to supervise cross-border activities in

36. *Id.*

37. Joe Kirwin, *EC Approves Spain's Proposal For $140 Billion Bank Bailout*, BNA BANKING DAILY, Jan. 29, 2009, available at http://www.bna.com.

38. Joe Kirwin, *EC to Outline Plan for New Council To Monitor Banking, Financial Services*, BNA BANKING DAILY, May 26, 2009, available at http://www.bna.com.

39. Id.

40. Joe Kirwin, *EU Parliament OKs Plan to Tighten Supervision of Cross–Border Banking*, BNA BANKING DAILY,

May 7, 2009, available at http://www.bna.com.

41. *Id.*

42. *Id.* The 25 percent limit may be exceeded only for exposures between credit institutions and then only up to €150 million (approximately $200 million). *Id.*

43. Joe Kirwin, *EU Finance Ministers Reach Compromise On Bank Supervision, but Parliament Objects*, BNA BANKING DAILY, Dec. 3, 2009, available at http://www.bna.com.

the banking, financial services, insurance and pension sectors.[44] These sectoral agencies would not have the authority to require a member state to rescue a particular financial institution with its headquarters in the member state.[45] However, it is unclear whether the European Parliament, where there is considerable sentiment for a single EU banking and finance supervisory authority with broad powers, will approve the structure as compromised.[46]

The crisis continued to mutate. In December 2009 the Austrian Government was forced to nationalize Hypo Alpe–Adria, one of the leading Austrian banks in order to prevent a collapse due to bad loans made to companies in Eastern Europe and the debt-ridden balance sheet of its owner, German regional bank BayernLB.[47] The Austrian Government took over the shares for a token amount of $1.46.[48] As a result Munich-based BayernLB, the second largest state-owned bank in Germany, was forced to write off more than $3 billion in losses stemming from its purchase of Hypo Alpe–Adria. The Austrian Government also agreed to put inject approximately $1 billion into Hypo Alpe–Adria.[49]

The situation in Asia was also critical. Three leading Asian economies, Japan,[50] China, and Korea, reached an agreement in October 2008 to monitor financial institutions and to strengthen financial disclosures and risk management.[51] The three states are planning a macro economy and financial stability workshop, which might ultimately lead to the establishment of an "Asian Financial Stability Forum," a regional version of an International Monetary Fund facility.[52] The forum is intended to analyze current economy

44. *Id.*

45. *Id.*

46. *Id.*

47. Joe Kirwin, *European Banking Crisis Erupts Again; Austria Forced to Nationalize Leading Bank*, BNA BANKING DAILY, Dec. 15, 2009, available at http://www.bna.com.

48. *Id.*

49. *Id.* The European Commission gave temporary approval to the rescue plan because of the systemic role that Hypo Alpe–Adria plays both in Austria and in other southeastern European countries. *See EC Gives Temporary OK to Nationalized Bank In Austria, But Asks New Restructuring Plans*, BNA BANKING DAILY, Dec. 24, 2009, available at http://www.bna.com (reporting on rescue). The Commission also indicated that it was extending its in-depth investigation of state aid not only to cover the

rescue but also BayernLB, which had already received almost $40 billion in bailout funds through capital injections and risk guarantees from the German Government. *Id.*

50. According to the Japanese Financial Services Agency, as of second quarter 2008, Japanese depository institutions had experienced losses of ¥895 billion from securities tied to subprime loans, an increase of 5 percent over first quarter 2008. Toshio Aritake, *Japanese Banks' Subprime Securities Losses Rise 5 Percent to $8 Billion in Latest Quarter*, BNA BANKING DAILY (Sept. 8, 2008), *available at* http://news.bna.com.

51. Toshio Aritake, *Japan, China, Korea Reach Agreement For Meeting to Monitor Financial Institutions*, BNA BANKING DAILY (Oct. 23, 2008), *available at* http://news.bna.com (reporting on financial stability agreement).

52. *Id.*

conditions, regional capital and financial markets and financial services systems, and related concerns.[53]

In late October 2008, the Bank of Japan announced that it would begin lending unlimited amounts of U.S. dollars for one month to Japanese financial institutions within the value of collateral that they tender to the central bank, at a fixed rate of 2.11 percent, in an effort to spur lending.[54] This was followed by the Bank of Japan's injection of significant amounts into the Japanese banking system in an ultimately unsuccessful effort to ameliorate the wave of selling of U.S. dollars.[55] Within the week a second economic stimulus package followed, totaling ¥26.9 trillion yen in tax cuts, spending, regulatory relief, monetary policy measures, and public-private cooperation.[56] Likewise, in November 2009, the Chinese Government initiated a 4 trillion yuan (approximately $587 billion), two-year economic stimulus package to keep the Chinese economy on a positive growth track.[57] Indeed, the World Bank is predicting a 7.5 percent GNP growth for China in 2009, with over half of projected growth linked to government spending.[58]

Still, a coordinated response by states affected by the crisis has been slow to emerge. One obvious vehicle for coordination would seem to be the G–20, the informal consultative group of the twenty largest industrialized democracies. However, efforts to mobilize the G–20 have been fitful at best. The president lobbied other G–20 leaders to adopt a financial activity tax (FAT), or "bank tax" as part of the coordinated response to the financial crisis.[59] Ironically, while the FAT made its way into the conference version of U.S. regulatory reform legislation, it was abruptly dropped from the final version of the bill in the face of opposition from swing votes in the Senate (e.g., Senator Brown of Massachusetts, a key Republican

---

53. *Id.*

54. Japanese Central Bank to Lend Unlimited Amount of U.S. Dollars to Banks, BNA Int'l Bus. & Fin. Daily (Oct. 22, 2008), available at http://news.bna. com. .

55. Toshio Aritake, BOJ Injects Liquidity; ASEAN Plus 3 Agree to Expand Chanmai Initiative, BNA Int'l Bus. & Fin. Daily (Oct. 27, 2008), available at http://news.bna.com.

56. Toshio Aritake, Japan's 26.9 Trillion Yen Stimulus Package For Global Crisis Much Larger Than Planned, BNA Int'l Bus. & Fin. Daily (Oct. 31, 2008), available at http://news.bna.com.

57. Kathleen E. McLaughlin, China Unveils Substantial Stimulus Plan; Will Spend $586 Billion Over Two Years, BNA Int'l Bus. & Fin. Daily (November 12, 2008), available at http://news.bna. com.

58. Kathleen E. McLaughlin, World Bank Labels China's Stimulus Plan Critical to Sustain Economy's Growth Track, BNA Int'l Bus. & Fin. Daily (Nov. 26, 2008), available at http://news. bna.com.

59. Aaron Lorenzo, *Obama Letter Urges G–20 Leaders To Tackle Bank Tax at Toronto Summit*, BNA BANKING DAILY (June 21, 2010), available at http:// www.bna.com. For the text of the president's letter to G–20 leaders, see http:// www.whitehouse.gov/the-press-office/ letter-president-g–20–leaders   (visited June 22, 2010).

vote in favor of the previous Senate version of the bill) who were opposed to the FAT.

The Dodd–Frank Wall Street Reform and Consumer Protection Act (Dodd–Frant Act),[60] the U.S. statutory response to the financial crisis enacted in July 2010, contains some modest yet realistic provisions to encourage greater international interaction in fashioning coordinated responses to future crises. Dodd–Frank Act § 175,[61] for example, seeks to encourage international policy coordination by authorizing the president to "coordinate ... similar policies as those found in United States law relating to limiting the scope, nature, size, scale, concentration, and interconnectedness of financial companies, in order to protect financial stability and the global economy."[62] There is little guidance and no clear mandate here, but the language does at least establish a direction for future developments.

The Dodd–Frank Act gives a similar directive to the new Financial Stability Oversight Council,[63] to "consult with the financial regulatory entities and other appropriate organizations of foreign governments or international organizations on matters relating to systemic risk to the international financial system."[64] Consultation is likely to be a soft process with no particular end-state presupposed. Further, it is not clear what this directive adds as a practical matter. Did congressional sponsors honestly believe that the Council and other regulatory bodies would not "consult" in the absence of such language? Proof to the contrary exists in the longstanding practice of the Fed, the Treasury Department, and other federal financial regulators to consult and coordinate with their opposite numbers in other states on an irregular but continuing basis, in formalized settings like the Basel Committee, the G–20 and others, and in more ad hoc setting as well.

Nevertheless, one might argue that, when the provision tells the Council that it "shall regularly consult," that mandate adds something meaningful to past informal practice. Similarly, Dodd–Frank Act § 175 also requires the Fed and the Secretary of the Treasury to "consult with their foreign counterparts and through appropriate multilateral organizations to encourage comprehensive and robust prudential supervision and regulation for all highly

---

60. Pub. L. No. 111–203, 124 Stat. 1376 (2010) (codified at scattered sections of 2, 5, 7, 11, 12, 15, 18, 20, 22, 26, 28, 31, 42, 44 U.S.C.A.) (DFA). For discussion of the changes effected by the DFA, see 1 Michael P. Malloy, Banking Law and Regulation § 1.4.11 (1994 & Cum. Supp.).

61. DFA § 175, 124 Stat. at 1442 (codified at 12 U.S.C.A. § 5373).

62. 12 U.S.C.A. § 5373(a).

63. See id. §§ 5322–5323 (establishing Council and its mandate).

64. Id. § 5373(b).

leveraged and interconnected financial companies."[65] At this stage, t is hard to ascertain whether this mandate will have any appreciable impact on policy.

Potentially, a more important implication of the Dodd–Frank Act may be the mandate requiring the Commodities Futures Trading Commission (CFTC), the SEC and other agencies to make specific harmonization efforts toward the establishment of "consistent international standards with respect to the regulation (including fees) of swaps, security-based swaps, swap entities, and security-based swap entities."[66] Significantly, the provision specifically authorizes federal agencies to conclude agreements for "such information-sharing arrangements as may be deemed to be necessary or appropriate in the public interest or for the protection of investors, swap counterparties, and security-based swap counterparties."[67] Furthermore, the CFTC is required to "consult and coordinate" with non-U.S. regulators in establishing "consistent international standards with respect to the regulation of contracts of sale of a commodity for future delivery and options on such contracts."[68] The CFTC is also authorized to conclude agreements "as may be deemed necessary or appropriate in the public interest" to protect users of commodity futures contracts.[69]

§ 9.27 Foreign Bank Secrecy

With this section, we begin to focus on what might be called conflicts between extraneous public policy and international banking regulation. By "extraneous" we mean public policy not directly related to the policy values and objectives of banking regulation. Obviously, given the multinational character of banking regulation and the transborder nature of banking itself, conflicts of law and public policy are always a possibility in international banking. By and large, however, we expect to find a relatively high degree of agreement from system to system, at least in principle, over the basic policy values and objectives of banking regulation: maintenance of a safe and sound banking system, maintenance of the public confidence in the system, and the like.

Other public policy concerns and objectives may intersect with, and possibly conflict with, the objectives of banking regulation, however conceived. For example, there is often an obvious conflict between bank secrecy laws and generally applicable criminal and civil enforcement procedures.[1] Frustration may occur in either

---

65. *Id.* § 5373(c).

66. DFA § 752(a) (codified at 15 U.S.C.A. § 8325(a)).

67. *Id.*

68. 15 U.S.C.A. § 8325(b).

69. *Id.*

§ 9.27

1. Bank secrecy laws are not only a feature of havens for money-laundering and insider trading offenses; they are

direction. If bank secrecy is vindicated, legitimate policy interests in the investigation and enforcement of criminal and civil wrongs are frustrated. On the other hand, if the enforcement policy interests are vindicated, this may result in the frustration of legitimate policy values favoring confidentiality between a bank and its customers. Again, the conflict can often be serious and unresolvable.

Bank secrecy is viewed as a fundamental personal right under Swiss law,[2] the classic source of bank secrecy rules, and it is protected by criminal penalties in Swiss codes.[3] In contrast, under U.S. law, there is no constitutional right to the privacy of bank records of your transactions,[4] although there are limited notice procedures now available as a matter of statute.[5] Naturally, a high degree of secrecy protection leads to the serious possibility of the abuse of bank secrecy in the service of criminal activity. Accordingly, some limits exist even under Swiss law.[6] There is in fact a growing tendency of Swiss authorities to apply and enforce bank secrecy rules in a more restrained fashion, in order to protect significant public policy interest in the avoidance of securities manipulation, fraud and asset conversion, and undesirable activities of foreign states.[7]

Easing of Swiss bank secrecy practices, particularly through such devices as government-to-government or government-to-industry memoranda of understanding on investigative procedures and mutual cooperation treaties, may moderate possible conflicts when Swiss banks are involved. However, the practical effect has been to move transactions to other bank secrecy havens.[8] In that regard, it

also extremely attractive to depositors seeking to avoid or evade tax consequences in their home jurisdictions. *See, e.g.,* Nash, *Germans in Tax Revolt Embrace Luxembourg,* N.Y. Times, Nov. 25, 1994, at D7 (discussing ways in which bank secrecy laws benefit Luxembourg, as depositors from Germany seek to avoid 1993 German withholding tax on interest income of residents).

2. *See* Honegger, *Demystification of the Swiss Banking Secrecy and Illumination of the United States Swiss Memorandum of Understanding,* 9 N.C. J. Int'l L. & Com. Reg. 1 (1983) (discussing fundamental policy bases for Swiss bank secrecy rules).

3. *See* Swiss Banking Law of 1934, art. 47(b) (providing fines and/or imprisonment for willful violation of bank secrecy; fines for negligent violation); Swiss Penal Code, art. 273 (providing imprisonment and fines for eliciting or disclosing business secrets).

4. *See United States v. Miller,* 425 U.S. 435, 96 S.Ct. 1619 (1976) (so holding). *See also Walker v. S.W.I.F.T. SCRL,* 491 F.Supp.2d 781 (N.D.Ill. 2007) (discussing *Miller*).

5. Right to Financial Privacy Act, 12 U.S.C.A. §§ 3401–3420, 3422.

6. *See* Honegger, *supra* (discussing limits, including contractual understandings between depositor and Swiss bank, and statutory and regulatory limits mandating disclosure to Swiss authorities and courts).

7. *See* Hirsch, *"Dirty Money" and Swiss Banking Regulations,* 8 J. Comp. Bus. & Cap. Market L. 373 (1986) (describing the emergence of "new duties" under Swiss banking law).

8. *See, e.g., In re Grand Jury Proceedings,* 532 F.2d 404 (5th Cir.1976), *cert. denied sub nom. Field v. United States,* 429 U.S. 940, 97 S.Ct. 354 (involving Cayman Islands bank secrecy laws).

is important to keep in mind that significant individual variations exist as one moves among the bank secrecy laws of different jurisdictions, and it is dangerous to generalize in this area. The Greek bank secrecy provision, as discussed in *First National Bank of Chicago*,[9] seems very harsh in terms of its penalties, but it seems to be relatively narrow in terms of the scope of possible parties affected by it. In contrast, the Bahamanian bank secrecy provision, considered in *In re Grand Jury Proceedings (Bank of Nova Scotia)*,[10] seems much broader in scope, expressly including even outside advisers. The Swiss bank secrecy provision, considered in *Banca Della Svizzera Italiana*,[11] seems to take the middle ground.

A claim of bank secrecy under the laws of one state triggers a policy conflict only if the information subject to the claim is itself relevant to another state's fundamental policies.[12] Where fundamental U.S. policies are involved, U.S. courts have tended to be intolerant of claims of bank secrecy.[13] U.S. courts have traditionally reached these results in reliance on the policy-balancing test of Section 40 of the *Foreign Relations Restatement (2d)*,[14] starting with

9. *United States v. First Nat'l Bank of Chicago*, 699 F.2d 341 (7th Cir.1983).

10. *See, e.g., In re Grand Jury Proceedings*, 691 F.2d 1384 (11th Cir.1982), cert. denied sub nom. *Bank of Nova Scotia v. United States*, 462 U.S. 1119, 103 S.Ct. 3086 (1983).

11. *Securities and Exch. Comm'n v. Banca Della Svizzera Italiana*, 92 F.R.D. 111 (S.D.N.Y.1981).

12. *See, e.g., Trade Dev. Bank v. Continental Ins. Co.*, 469 F.2d 35 (2d Cir.1972) (finding account information not relevant to bank's claim under fidelity bond).

13. *See, e.g., In re Grand Jury Proceedings*, 691 F.2d 1384 (rejecting bank secrecy claim in tax and narcotics investigation); *In re Grand Jury Proceedings*, 532 F.2d 404 (rejecting bank secrecy claim in tax evasion case); *Strauss v. Credit Lyonnais, S.A.*, 249 F.R.D. 429 (E.D.N.Y. 2008) (rejecting bank secrecy claim in terrorist attack case); *Banca Della Svizzera Italiana, supra* (rejecting bank secrecy claim in securities fraud investigation). *But cf. First Nat'l Bank of Chicago, supra* (upholding bank secrecy claim in tax assessment case, where criminal penalties in secrecy jurisdiction were disproportionately severe).

14. American Law Institute, *Restatement (2d) of the Foreign Relations Law of the United States* § 40, provides:

Where two states have jurisdiction to prescribe and enforce rules of law and the rules they may prescribe require inconsistent conduct upon the part of a person, each state is required by international law to consider, in good faith, moderating the exercise of its enforcement jurisdiction, in light of such factors as

(a) vital national interests of each of the states,

(b) the extent and the nature of the hardship that inconsistent enforcement actions would impose upon the person,

(c) the extent to which the required conduct is to take place in the territory of the other state,

(d) the nationality of the person, and

(e) the extent to which enforcement by action of either state can reasonably be expected to achieve compliance with the rule prescribed by that state.

For cases applying § 40 as the basis for decision, *see, e.g., In re Grand Jury Proceedings; First Nat'l Bank of Chicago, supra*. The Southern District of New York favors an application of 40 that emphasizes 40(a)–(b), almost to the exclusion of the other specified factors. *See, e.g., Banca Della Svizzera Italiana, supra*.

the assumption that the conflicting states both have the right to apply their rules.

Section 40 has had a significant influence in shaping this area of policy conflict in the U.S. courts. However, they have not necessarily adopted § 40 uncritically. The provisions of § 40 on their own terms, for example, do not give greater emphasis to any one of the factors identified in deciding whether to exercise jurisdiction in the face of inconsistent law of another jurisdiction. Yet Judge Pollack in *Banca Della Svizzera Italiana* appears to give primary emphasis to § 40(a) and (b), while lumping § 40(c)–(e) together with little real attention. On the other hand, in the inverse case where analysis of the § 40(a)–(b) factors do not appear to counsel application of U.S. law in the face of conflict—Judge Fairchild in *First National Bank of Chicago* analyzes the remaining § 40 factors carefully. If the approaches of Judge Pollack and Judge Fairchild are reconcilable, this would mean that as interpreted and applied by the courts, there is a bias in favor of applying U.S. law in the face of conflicting foreign law.

However, Section 403 of the *Restatement (3d)*,[15] which seems rigged against U.S. enforcement in its balancing test,[16] starts with a

---

15. American Law Institute, *Restatement (3d) of the Foreign Relations Law of the United States*, § 403, provides:

(1) Even when one of the bases for jurisdiction ... is present, a state may not exercise jurisdiction to prescribe law with respect to a person or activity having connections with another state when the exercise of such jurisdiction is unreasonable.

(2) Whether the exercise of jurisdiction over a person or activity is unreasonable is determined by evaluating all relevant factors, including, where appropriate:

(a) the link of the activity to the territory of the regulating state ...;

(b) the connections ... between the regulating state and the person principally responsible for the activity to be regulated, or between that state and those whom the regulation is designed to protect ...;

(c) the character of the activity to be regulated, the importance of the regulation to the regulating state, the extent to which other states regulate such activities, and the degree to which the desirability of such regulation is generally accepted;

(d) the existence of justified expectations that might be protected or hurt by the regulation;

(e) the importance of the regulation to the international, political, legal or economic system;

(f) the extent to which the regulation is consistent with the traditions of the international system;

(g) the extent to which another state may have an interest in regulating the activity; and

(h) the likelihood of conflict with regulation by another state.

(3) When it would not be unreasonable for each of two states to exercise jurisdiction over a person or activity, but the prescriptions by the two states are in conflict, each state has an obligation to evaluate its own as well as the other state's interest in exercising jurisdiction, in light of all the relevant factors ...; a state should defer to the other state if that state's interest is clearly greater.

16. *Cf.* David B. Massey, Note, *How the American Law Institute Influences Customary Law: The Reasonableness Requirement of the Restatement of Foreign Relations Law*, 22 Yale J. Int'l L. 419,

different assumption—that a state lacks jurisdiction to prescribe or enforce if exercising jurisdiction would be unreasonable. Section 403 has been adopted by U.S. courts,[17] but it is sometimes characterized by them as simply an extension or revision of 40.[18]

The provisions of the *Restatement (3d)* dealing with jurisdictional conflicts were hotly debated over an extended period of time both within and outside the American Law Institute. The compromise text that eventually became § 403 may not significantly change results in bank secrecy cases.[19] As a practical matter, however, there are some areas of congruence between the two sections. Figure 9–9, *infra*, offers some assistance in considering the differences between the two sections.

Figure 9–9
Comparison: § 40 and § 403

Restatement (2d) § 40	*Restatement (3d) § 403*
"is required . . . to consider, in good faith, moderating the exercise of its enforcement jurisdiction" under such factors as:	(1) ". . . state may not exercise . . . jurisdiction . . . when the exercise . . . is unreasonable."
	(2) "unreasonable" depends on:
(c) within	(a) within or affecting the regulating state
(d) nationality of person [(a) vital national interest?] [(a)]	(b) state's connection with person regulated or protected (c) character of activity, importance to each state, desirability generally accepted
[(b) hardship of inconsistent rules?]	(d) justified expectation protected or hurt by regulation in question

437 (1997) (arguing that § 403 did not accurately reflect customary law when published).

17. *See, e.g., Timberlane Lumber Co. v. Bank of Am.*, 749 F.2d 1378 (9th Cir.1984) (adopting seven-factor analysis based on § 403(2)); *Trugman–Nash, Inc. v. New Zealand Dairy Bd.*, 954 F.Supp. 733, 737 (S.D.N.Y.1997) (*citing Timberlane*). *See generally* Massey, *supra*, at 437–439 (surveying U.S. court citation of § 403); Louise Ellen Teitz, *et al.*, *International Litigation*, 31 Int'l Law. 317, 331–334 (1997) (discussing cases).

18. *See, e.g., Filetech S.A.R.L. v. France Telecom*, 978 F.Supp. 464, 477 (S.D.N.Y.1997), *vacated*, 157 F.3d 922

(2d Cir.1998) (referring to "direct line of succession" between § 40 and § 403 cases); *United States v. Nippon Paper Indus. Co.*, 109 F.3d 1, 7 (1st Cir.1997) (noting § 403 "merely reaffirms"); *In re Grand Jury Proceedings*, 40 F.3d 959, 965 (9th Cir.1994), *cert. denied sub nom. Marsoner v. United States*, 515 U.S. 1132, 115 S.Ct. 2558 (noting § 40 as "revised and . . . encompassed within" § 403). *Cf. In re Grand Jury Proceedings*, 709 F.Supp. 192, 195 (C.D.Cal. 1989) (invoking § 40).

19. *See, e.g., Filetech S.A.R.L., supra* (applying § 403(2)); *In re Grand Jury Proceedings*, 40 F.3d 959 (applying § 403).

Restatement (2d) § 40	Restatement (3d) § 403
	(e) importance of regulation to international political, legal, or economic system (f) regulation consistent with traditions of international system
(a) vital national interest [(e) reasonable expectation of compliance?]	(g) another state's interest in regulating (h) likelihood of conflict with other states

The provisions of Part D of the 1990 Supplement to the BIS Concordat[20] deal with domestic bank secrecy laws that may impede transnational regulation and supervision of banking. The BIS Supplement is not binding, but to the extent its principles are followed, it has the effect of moderating the effect of bank secrecy laws. However, this effect is specialized to the concerns of bank regulators with respect to the availability of information for supervisory purposes. Thus, the BIS Supplement might not alter the outcome in policy conflicts involving the enforcement of nonbanking regulations.

In addition, the provisions of the 1992 BIS Minimum Standards[21] were intended to ensure adequate supervision of transnational banking enterprises through effective coordination among national supervisors, and would also affect the application of bank secrecy laws. The Minimum Standards are "expected" to be implemented by BIS participants, and other states are encouraged to implement them as well. To the extent the standards are implemented, however, their effect is specialized primarily to the concerns of bank regulators considering an application for entry into the domestic banking market. Thus, as with the Concordat Supplement, the standards might not alter the outcome in policy conflicts involving nonbanking regulatory enforcement.

§ 9.28 International Sanctions and Banking

The imposition of international economic sanctions is a traditional, if specialized, technique of foreign affairs, particularly in

---

20. BANK FOR INTERNATIONAL SETTLEMENTS, COMMITTEE ON BANKING REGULATION AND SUPERVISORY PRACTICES: SUPPLEMENT TO THE BASEL CONCORDAT ENSURING OF ADEQUATE INFORMATION FLOWS BETWEEN BANKING SUPERVISORY AUTHORITIES (APRIL 1990), *reprinted in* MALLOY, INTERNATIONAL BANKING, *supra*, at 84–87.

21. BANK FOR INTERNATIONAL SETTLEMENTS, COMMITTEE ON BANKING REGULATION AND SUPERVISORY PRACTICES: REPORT ON MINIMUM STANDARDS FOR THE SUPERVISION OF INTERNATIONAL BANKING GROUPS AND THEIR CROSS-BORDER ESTABLISHMENT (JUNE 1992), *reprinted in* MALLOY, INTERNATIONAL BANKING, SUPRA, at 87–91.

U.S. practice.[1] Depending upon the form of the sanction, the interests of banks involved in international banking activities may be significantly affected.[2] Given the extensive nature of some of the economic sanctions programs administered by the U.S. Department of the Treasury ("Treasury") in particular,[3] the precise effect on those interests may manifest itself in unexpected ways.

§ 9.29   U.S. Statutory Sources of Authority for Economic Sanctions

The statutory authorities described in this section support a range of sanctions programs that affect banks involved in international banking activities. There are many other sanctions-related statutory provisions, but these provide the typical authority for sanctions significantly affecting banks involved in international banking activities.[1]

Section 5(b) of the Trading With the Enemy Act ("TWEA")[2] provides in pertinent part:

> During the time of war [or during any other period of national emergency declared by the President,[3]] the President may, through any agency that he may designate, or otherwise, and under such rules and regulations as he may prescribe, by means of instructions, license, or otherwise . . .
>
> (B) investigate, regulate, direct and compel, nullify, void, prevent or prohibit, any acquisition, holding, withholding, use,

---

§ 9.28

1. *See, e.g.,* Michael P. Malloy, *Memorandum to the Select Committee on Economic Affairs of the House of Lords of the United Kingdom on the Impact of International Economic Sanctions* (30 Sept. 2006), *reprinted in* II SELECT COMMITTEE ON ECONOMIC AFFAIRS, U.K. HOUSE OF LORDS, THE IMPACT OF ECONOMIC SANCTIONS 158 (2007) (discussing trends in and effects of international economic sanctions); Michael P. Malloy, *Remarks* in *Are the U.S. Treasury's Assets Control Regulations a Fair and Effective Tool of U.S. Foreign Policy? The Case of Cuba,* 1985 Proc. Am. Soc. Int'l L. 169, 188 (identifying varied policy purposes of economic sanctions).

2. For example, in the U.S. "blocking" of assets of the Government of Iran in 1979, it is estimated that approximately $12 billion worth of assets were immobilized (*see* Michael P. Malloy, *The Iran Crisis: Law Under Pressure,* 1984 Wisc. Int'l. L.J. 15, 34) of which some $2.2 billion represented U.S. domestic bank branch deposits, and some $5.5 billion represented deposits and interest in foreign-situs branches of U.S. banks.

Id. at 85–88. The aftermath of the Iran crisis generated over 400 claims by banks before the Iran–United States Claims Tribunal. *See id.* at 91 & n.453.

3. *See, e.g.,* Figure 9–10, *infra* (detailing variety of sanctions programs affecting banking).

§ 9.29

1. For a broader discussion of the effects of international economic sanctions, see MICHAEL P. MALLOY, UNITED STATES ECONOMIC SANCTIONS: THEORY AND PRACTICE (Kluwer Law International, 2001).

2. 50 U.S.C.A. app. § 5(b).

3. This language was deleted by Pub. L. No. 95–223, § 101(a), 91 Stat. 1625, 1625 (1977) (amending 50 U.S.C.A. app. 5(b) on a prospective basis only). For purposes of then current exercise of emergency powers under Section 5(b) of the TWEA, the bracketed language was not deleted. *See generally Regan v. Wald,* 468 U.S. 222, 104 S.Ct. 3026 (1984), *reh'g denied,* 469 U.S. 912, 105 S.Ct. 285 (1984) (discussing effect of TWEA savings clause).

transfer, withdrawal, transportation, importation or exportation of, or dealing in, or exercising any right, power or privilege
with respect to, or transactions involving, any property in
which any foreign country or a national thereof has any interest, by any person, or with respect to any property, subject to
the jurisdiction of the United States.[4]

The specific TWEA programs pertinent to the present discussion
are: (1) the Foreign Assets Control Regulations ("FACRs"),[5] which
currently impose sanctions on North Korea and nationals thereof;[6]
and, (2) the Cuban Assets Control Regulations ("CACRs"),[7] which
were originally promulgated in 1963 and currently impose sanctions on Cuba and its nationals. The TWEA authority for the
CACRs is augmented by the Cuban Liberty and Democratic Solidar-
ity Act of 1996 ("CLDSA")[8] and the International Emergency
Eocnomic Powers Act (IEEPA).[9]

Section 5 of the United Nations Participation Act of 1945
("UNPA")[10] is also a statutory source of economic sanctions authority. It authorizes the President to apply economic and other sanctions against a target country or national thereof in accordance
with any mandatory decision by the U.N. Security Council under
Article 41 of the U.N. Charter.[11] The UNPA has been invoked by
the President many times in recent years, but its most famous
invocation is probably still its use in the initial U.S. response to the
Iraqi invasion of Kuwait in 1990.[12] Other current uses are highlighted in Figure 9–10, infra.

4. 50 U.S.C.A. app. § 5(b)(1)(B).

5. 31 C.F.R. Pt. 500.

6. *Id.* § 500.201(d) schedule.

7. *Id.* Pt. 515.

8. Pub. L. No. 104–114, 109 Stat.
826 (Mar. 12, 1996) (codified at scattered Sections of 22 U.S.C.A.). *See* 22
U.S.C.A. § 6033(c) (CLDSA; requiring
executive branch enforcement of extant
CACRs); 22 U.S.C.A. § 6064 (subjecting
presidential termination of Cuban embargo to requirements of CLDSA).

9. Pub. L. No. 95–223, tit. II, 91
Stat. 1626 (1977) (codified at 50
U.S.C.A. §§ 1701–1706). For discussion
of IEEPA, see text and accompanying
notes 13–15, *infra*.

10. 22 U.S.C.A. § 287c.

11. Article 41 provides in pertinent
part:

The Security Council may decide
what measures not involving the use
of armed force are to be employed to
give effect to its decisions, and it may

call upon the Members of the United
Nations to apply such measures.
These may include complete or partial
interruption of economic relations and
of rail, sea, air, postal, telegraphic,
radio, and other means of communication, and the severance of diplomatic
relations.

U.N. Charter, art. 41. Members of
the United Nations are required to
fulfill in good faith obligations, such
as those implicit in article 41, assumed by them under the Charter.
U.N. Charter, art. 2, ¶ 2. *See also* U.N.
Charter, art. 25, which provides that:
"[t]he Members of the United Nations
agree to accept and carry out the decisions of the Security Council in accordance with the present Charter."

12. Ex. Order No. 12,724, 55 Fed.
Reg. 33,089 (1990) (prohibiting transactions with Iraq under UNPA and IEE-
PA); Ex. Order No. 12,725, 55 Fed. Reg.
33,091 (1990) (prohibiting transactions
with Iraq-occupied Kuwait); Ex. Order

The IEEPA[13] gives the President broad authority over financial transactions and property in which any foreign country or national has any interest, provided that the President first declares the requisite national emergency.[14] The IEEPA essentially recodifies, for peacetime emergency use, the range of powers available to the President under Section 5(b) of the TWEA. The two statutory authorities differ in that the IEEPA does not contain the following TWEA powers still available to the President during time of war: (1) the power to "vest" (*i.e.*, expropriate) property in which foreign states or their nationals have an interest; (2) the power to regulate purely domestic transactions; (3) the power to regulate gold or silver coin or bullion; and, (4) the power to seize records.[15]

The major effect of these authorities has been the blocking[16] of property, typically bank deposits and other bank-issued instruments and guarantees, subject to the jurisdiction of the United States.[17] "Blocking" of assets simply means that no transaction of any kind involving the affected assets can occur without a Treasury license.

No. 12,817, 57 Fed. Reg. 48,433 (1992) (ordering transfer and consolidation of blocked assets representing proceeds of sale of Iraqi petroleum or petroleum products, *per* U.N. Security Council Resolution No. 778).

13. Pub. L. No. 95–223, tit. II, 91 Stat. 1626 (1977) (codified at 50 U.S.C.A. §§ 1701–1706).

14. *Dames & Moore v. Regan*, 453 U.S. 654, 671–673, 101 S.Ct. 2972, 2982–2983 (1981). *See Charles T. Main Int'l v. Khuzestan Water & Power Auth.*, 651 F.2d 800, 807 (1st Cir.1981) (noting that "language of IEEPA is sweeping and broad"); *American Int'l Group v. Islamic Republic of Iran*, 657 F.2d 430, 439 (D.C.Cir.1981).

15. In addition, the IEEPA contained new restrictions on certain other substantive powers that were otherwise available to the President under TWEA. Thus, under the new authority, the President does not have power to: (1) regulate or prohibit personal communications not involving the transfer of anything of value; (2) regulate uncompensated transfers of articles for humanitarian aid, unless he determines that transfers of this type would either (a) seriously impair his ability to deal with the emergency situation; (b) respond to coercion against the potential donor or recipient; or (c) endanger U.S. armed forces. 50 U.S.C.A. § 1702(b). *See*

generally Veterans Peace Convoy, Inc. v. Schultz [sic], 722 F.Supp. 1425 (S.D.Tex. 1988) (interpreting humanitarian aid exception to include donation of trucks).

16. The term "blocking" (or "freezing") of assets is not itself a term of art within the regulations, but refers metaphorically to the legal effect of the prohibitions of § 500.201 on property (or persons) affected thereby. *Cf., e.g.,* 31 C.F.R. § 500.319, defining "blocked account" to mean:

> an account in which any designated national has an interest, with respect to which account payments, transfers or withdrawals o[r] other dealings may not be made of effected except pursuant to an authorization or license authorizing such action. The term "blocked account" shall not be seemed to include accounts of unblocked nationals.

Blocked assets are generally required to be held in interest-bearing accounts. *See id.* § 500.205.

17. Blocking of liquid assets historically has been one of the major effects to the imposition of Treasury controls under Section 5(b) of the TWEA. *See* U.S. DEPARTMENT OF THE TREASURY, 1970 CENSUS OF BLOCKED CHINESE ASSETS; U.S. DEPARTMENT OF THE TREASURY, CENSUS OF FOREIGN OWNED ASSETS IN THE UNITED STATES (1945).

Because of the expansive way in which they have been defined in implementing sanctions regulations, certain terms are essential to the sweeping application of blocking provisions. Such terms as "transfer," "property," and "interest" have been interpreted by the courts to be broad enough to prohibit virtually any direct or indirect transaction involving anything of value when there exists even the most attenuated interest of a designated country or national thereof in the property.[18] For example, in *Welch v. Kennedy*,[19] a case involving both financial and export restrictions, the D.C. District Court held that an attempted donative transfer of funds in favor of Vietnam (blocked at the time under the Foreign Assets Control Regulations (FACRs)[20]) was prohibited under the regulations. The court reached this holding despite the fact that the donee, Vietnam, had no "interest" in the intended but frustrated gift in any legal or equitable sense under traditional property law.

In *Welch*, an American Quaker applied for a license to donate funds to the Canadian Friends Service Committee to be used to purchase medical supplies that were to be sent to Vietnam for the relief of noncombatants. In addressing the question whether Vietnam had an "interest" under the regulations in this donative transfer, the court stated:

> Plaintiff argues that the words "property" and "interest" must be taken as evidencing a congressional intent to regulate only commercial transactions and not donations to international relief organizations. Such an interpretation would be inconsistent with the broad purpose of the [TWEA], which was to give the President full power to conduct economic warfare against belligerent nations in time of war or national emergency.[21]

The provisions of traditional sanctions programs like the FACRs also typically contain a particularly effective enforcement device with respect to banking transactions. On the effective date of the regulations with respect to any of the designated countries to which they have applied from time to time, all transactions, including those in progress, are prohibited unless otherwise licensed by Treasury. Any transfer after the effective date in violation of the regulations is "null and void and shall not be the basis for the assertion or recognition of any interest in or right, remedy, power or privilege with respect to" property blocked under the regulations.[22] The regulations also contain a presumption against the

---

18. *See., e.g., Behring Int'l Inc. v. Miller*, 504 F.Supp. 552, 556–557 & n. 8 (D.N.J.1980).

19. 319 F.Supp. 945 (D.D.C.1970).

20. 31 C.F.R. § 500.201(d) (1970).

21. *Welch*, 319 F.Supp. at 946–47 (citations omitted).

22. 31 C.F.R. § 500.203(a). Essentially the same rule of invalidity applies to any unlicensed attachment, judgment, decree, lien, execution, garnishment, or other judicial process entered or effected with respect to property in which a blocked country or national thereof has

asserted validity of putative "pre-effective date" transfers when the fact of the asserted transfer cannot be corroborated by independent evidence. In this regard, 500.203(b) states:

> No transfer before the "effective date" shall be the basis for the assertion or recognition of any right, remedy, power, or privilege with respect to, or interest in, any property in which a designated national has or has had an interest since the "effective date" unless the person with whom such property is held or maintained had written notice of the transfer or by any written evidence had recognized such transfer prior to such "effective date."[23]

Thus, if a North Korean national entered into a contract for services with a foreign subsidiary of a U.S. national, with payment by means of an irrevocable letter of credit issued by a foreign bank and confirmed by First Credulity, a U.S. domestic bank, a purported transfer to the U.S. national from First Credulity would constitute a transaction involving property (*i.e.*, the letter of credit) in which a foreign national (*i.e.*, the account party) would have an interest.[24] Hence, once the FACRs became effective, any payment in accordance with the letter of credit would be null and void, and First Credulity would be required to establish a blocked account in the name of the North Korean national. It should be noted that the existence of ongoing contractual relationships and commitments would not be a basis in and of itself for Treasury licensing of any particular transfer or transaction after the effective date of the regulations.[25]

Sanctions programs like the FACRs do contain a limited safe harbor for unlicensed transactions or transfers rendered null and void by Section 500.203. Transactions or transfers otherwise rendered null and void are not deemed so, only as to any person with whom the property in question had been held or maintained, when the person establishes the following: (1) that the transaction or transfer did not represent a willful violation by that person; (2) that the person "did not have reasonable cause to know or suspect, in view of all the facts and circumstances known or available to such person,"[26] that the transaction or transfer was in fact unlicensed and prohibited;[27] and, (3) that, promptly upon discovery of the

any interest. *See id.* § 500.203(e). *Cf. id.* § 500.504 (providing limited license for judicial proceedings with respect to blocked property).

23. *Id.* § 500.203(b).

24. *See id.* § 500.406. Of course, transfer in the reverse direction (request or authorization from bank or other person within the United States to a person outside the United States to make payment or transfer to blocked person) would also be prohibited by Section 500.201 *See id.* § 500.409.

25. *See id.* § 500.203(b).

26. *Id.* § 500.203(d)(2).

27. *Id.* If under the circumstances, a license or authorization was purported to have covered the transaction or trans-

pertinent facts,[28] the person filed with Treasury a report setting forth the full circumstances with respect to the transaction or transfer.[29]

§ 9.30 Impact of Sanctions on International Banking

Figure 9–10, *infra*, illustrates the overall impact of economic sanctions on banks involved in international banking activities across a range of sanctions programs. Further complicating the situation for banks is the existence of the investment prohibitions in various sanctions imposed on states like Iran. Furthermore, it is becoming commonplace for sanctions programs to include specific prohibitions against provision of financial support or services to sanctions targets, and in some cases prohibitions of financing of prohibited activities.

Figure 9–10
Economic Sanctions: Impact on Banking

Target	Date(s) Imposed	Authority	Intended Impact on Banks
Balkans, Western	June 26, 2001, May 28, 2003	• International Emergency Economic Powers Act (50 U.S.C.A. §§ 1701–1706) (IEEPA) • UN Security Council Res. No. 1244 (June 10, 1999)	Blocks assets, including bank assets, of designated persons who engaged in, assisted, sponsored, or supported extremist violence in the Republic of Macedonia and elsewhere in the Western Balkans region, or obstructed implementation of the Dayton Accords in Bosnia or the U.N. Security Council Resolution in Kosovo, or provided material financial assistance to such actions
Belarus, members of Government of	June 16, 2006	IEEPA	Blocks assets, including bank assets, of certain members of the Govern-

fer in question, it must be established that the person did not have reasonable cause to know or suspect "that such license or authorization had been obtained by misrepresentation or the withholding of material facts or was otherwise fraudulently obtained." *Id.*

28. For these purposes, the "pertinent facts" are:

(i) Such transfer was in violation of the provisions of [31 C.F.R. ch. V] or any regulation, ruling, instruction, license or other direction or authorization thereunder, or

(ii) Such transfer was not licensed or authorized by the Secretary of the Treasury, or

(iii) If a license did purport to cover the transfer, such license had been obtained by misrepresentation or the withholding of material facts or was otherwise fraudulently obtained.

Id. § 500.203(d)(3)(i)–(iii).

29. *Id.* § 500.203(d)(1)–(3). Filing of the report pursuant to the third requirement does not in itself represent compliance or evidence of compliance with the first two requirements of the safe harbor. *Id.* § 500.203 (d)(3).

Target	Date(s) Imposed	Authority	Intended Impact on Banks
			ment of Belarus, and other persons undermining democratic processes or institutions in Belarus
Burma (Myanmar)	July 28, 2003, Oct 18, 2007, Apr 30, 2008, July 29, 2008	• Burmese Freedom and Democracy Act of 2003 (Public Law 108–61, As amended, 50 U.S.C.A. § 1701 note) • Foreign Operations, Export Financing, and Related Programs Appropriations Act, 1997 (Public Law 104–208) • IEEPA	Blocks senior Burmese government officials, persons involved in human rights abuses or facilitating corruption, or providing financial support for any blocked persons, or persons owned, controlled, or acting on behalf of any blocked person, or a spouse or dependent child of any blocked person
Colombia, narcotics traffickers centered in	Oct 21, 1995	IEEPA	Blocks assets, including bank assets, of and prohibits transactions with significant narcotics traffickers centered in Colombia Blocks anyone providing financial support or services to such persons
Congo, Democratic Republic of the, persons contributing to conflict in	Oct 27, 2006	• IEEPA • UNPA	Blocks property of certain persons contributing to conflict in the Congo Blocks anyone providing financial support or services to such persons
Côte d'Ivoire	Feb 7, 2006	• IEEPA • UN Participation Act of 1945 (22 U.S.C.A. § 287c) (UNPA)	Blocks assets, including bank assets, of specified persons
Cuba	July 8, 1963, Mar 1, 1996, Feb 26, 2004	• Cuban Liberty and Democratic Solidarity Act of 1996 • IEEPA • Trading With the Enemy Act (50 U.S.C.A. App. § 5(b) (1963 emergency) (TWEA)	Blocks assets, including bank assets, of Cuba and any national thereof Prohibits transactions with Cuba or any national thereof
Iran: Comprehensive Sanctions	July 1, 2010, Sep 28, 2010	• Comprehensive Iran Sanctions, Accountability, and Divestment Act of 2010 • IEEPA • Iran Sanctions Act of 1996 (Pub. L. 104–172, 50 U.S.C.A. 1701 note)	Prohibits opening of new branches, subsidiaries, or representative offices of Iranian banks Prohibits Iranian banks from establishing or maintaining correspondent relationships with banks within the U.S. jurisdiction Prevents provision of financial services, if they could contribute to Iran's proliferation-sensitive nuclear activities or development of nuclear weapon delivery systems Strengthens existing sanctions under Iran Sanctions Act Sanctions foreign financial institutions that facilitate Iran's proliferation-related activities or support for terrorism or that do significant business with Iran's Islamic Revolutionary

Target	Date(s) Imposed	Authority	Intended Impact on Banks
			Guard Corps or certain other blocked persons Blocks property of persons involved with serious human rights abuses by Government of Iran
Iran: Hostage crisis	Nov 14, 1979	IEEPA	Blocked assets, including bank accounts, of Government of Iran, its agencies and instrumentalities during the hostage crisis Currently continues to support the claims settlement process
Iran: National security threat	Mar 15, 1995, May 6, 1995, Aug 19, 1997	• IEEPA • International Security and Development Co-operation Act of 1985	Prohibits financing of development of petroleum resources located in Iran, financing of goods, technology, or services of Iranian origin
Iraq	Aug 28, 2003, July 29, 2004, July 17, 2007	• IEEPA • UNPA	Initially blocked assets of former Iraqi regime, its senior officials, and their family members Currently blocks assets of persons involved in violence against Iraq or U.S. forces there, or providing financial support or services for those involved in such violence
Korea, North	Dec 17, 1950, June 26, 2008, Aug 30, 2010	• IEEPA • TWEA • UNPA	Blocks assets of North Korea and nationals thereof Blocks any person engaged in money laundering, counterfeiting of goods or currency, bulk cash smuggling, narcotics trafficking, or other illicit economic activity that involves or supports the Government of North Korea or any senior official thereof
Lebanon, persons interfering with sovereignty of	July 1, 2007	IEEPA	Blocks assets of persons undermining the sovereignty of Lebanon or its democratic processes and institutions Blocks anyone providing financial support or services for such persons
Liberia, former regime of Charles Taylor in	July 22, 2004	• IEEPA • UNPA	Blocks assets of former regime members, related persons, and anyone providing financial support to or services for such persons
Myanmar (see Burma, supra)			
Somalia, conflict in	Apr 12, 2010	• IEEPA • UNPA	Blocks assets of certain persons contributing to conflict in Somalia Blocks anyone providing financial support to or services for such persons
Sudan (Darfur conflict)	Nov 3, 1997, Apr 26, 2006,	• Darfur Peace and Accountability Act of	Blocks property of certain persons connected with the

Target	Date(s) Imposed	Authority	Intended Impact on Banks
	Oct 13, 2006	2006 (Public Law 109–344) • IEEPA • UNPA	conflict
Syria	May 11, 2004, Apr 25, 2006, Feb 13, 2008	• IEEPA • Syria Accountability and Lebanese Sovereignty Restoration Act of 2003 • UNPA	Blocks assets of persons involved in terrorist acts in Lebanon implicating Syria Blocks anyone providing financial support or services for such acts Blocks assets of persons who have secured improper advantage as a result of public corruption by senior officials within the Government of Syria
Terrorism, Global	Sep 23, 2001. July 2, 2002	• IEEPA • UNPA	Blocks assets of and prohibits transactions with the Taliban or persons who commit, threaten to commit, or support terrorism Blocks anyone providing financial support or services for such persons
Terrorist Organizations, Foreign	Oct 8, 1997	Antiterrorism and Effective Death Penalty Act of 1996	Requires U.S. financial institutions to block financial transactions involving assets in their possession or control of foreign organizations proposed for designation
Terrorists	Sep 14, 2001	IEEPA	Blocks assets of terrorists and persons facilitating, including banks
Terrorists threatening to disrupt the Middle East peace	Jan 23, 1995, Aug 20, 1998	IEEPA	Blocks assets of terrorists and persons facilitating, including banks
Traffickers, narcotics	July 5, 2000	Foreign Narcotics Kingpin Designation Act, Pub. L. No. 106–120, title VIII, 113 Stat. 1606, 1626–1636 (1999) (codified at 8 U.S.C.A. § 1182(a)(2)(C), 21 U.S.C.A. §§ 1901-1908)	Blocks assets of significant foreign narcotics traffickers or of designated foreign persons providing financial support for or to international narcotics trafficking activities
Weapons of mass destruction	Nov 14, 1994, July 28, 1998, June 28, 2005	• Arms Export Control Act (22 U.S.C.A. 2751) • IEEPA	Blocks assets, including bank assets, of persons engaging in, or attempting to engage in, activities or transactions that materially contribute to, or pose a risk of materially contributing to, the proliferation of weapons of mass destruction Blocks assets of any firm providing, or attempting to provide, financial support for, or services in support of, any such activity or transaction
Zimbabwe	Mar 6, 2003, Nov 22, 2005, July 25, 2008	IEEPA	Blocks assets, including bank assets, of senior officials of the Government of Zimbabwe, persons who are owned or controlled by the Government or an official thereof, or are under-

Target	Date(s) Imposed	Authority	Intended Impact on Banks
			mining democratic processes or institutions in Zimbabwe, have facilitated corruption, or have participated in human rights abuses, or providing financial support for, or services in support of, the Government of Zimbabwe, any senior official thereof, or any person blocked under these sanctions

The formidable array of economic sanctions administered by the United States is a daunting reality for any U.S. national subject to their reach. Particularly troublesome for a bank involved in international activities is the possibility of having to defend the validity of any of these sanctions programs in a foreign forum. Until recently, there has not been any appreciable body of foreign case law directly challenging U.S. economic sanctions programs. Nevertheless, according to knowledgeable practitioners, U.S. banks today feel the need to take the effect of sanctions into account in their planning, even those not generally involved in international activities.

One particular problem faced by U.S. banks is the applicability of a blocking prohibition to dollar-denominated accounts held by a U.S. bank in the United States in the name of a foreign-situs bank or branch, which in turn holds a dollar-denominated account for a target country or nationals thereof. This is a serious concern for such broadly conceived economic sanctions programs as the FACRs and the Cuban Assets Control Regulations (CACRs),[1] broad economic sanctions against Cuba in particular, and would be so especially in the early stages of the implementation of such a program, when ongoing banking relationships are being disrupted.

It is obviously less of a concern for later programs, otherwise similar to the FACRs and CACRs, that have expressly licensed cover account situations out from under the blocking prohibition.[2] Furthermore, this is of virtually no concern for those later programs that are so limited in the scope of their prohibitions as to raise no issue in the first place concerning cover accounts, such as the UNITA/Angola arms embargo[3] or the arms embargo with respect to Rwanda.[4]

§ 9.30

1. 31 C.F.R. §§ 515.101 *et seq.*

2. *See., e.g.,* 31 C.F.R. § 535.901 (1980) (IACRs provision explicitly authorizing, by general license, transactions in cover accounts).

3. 31 C.F.R. pt. 590 (2000).

4. Ex. Order No. 12,918, 59 Fed. Reg. 28,203 (1994) (prohibiting certain transactions with respect to Rwanda).

From the point of view of the international banker, the potential application of blocking prohibitions to a cover account is perhaps one of the more grotesque effects of economic sanctions, working as it does a complete frustration of normal expectations in international transactions. For example, *Wholly Foreign Bank* maintains a dollar-denominated cover account with *A Bank* of New York City, in part to hedge dollar exposure from its own dollar-denominated accounts held for its own depositors. An office of *Wholly Foreign* in a third country issues dollar-denominated irrevocable letters of credit ("L/Cs") for *B* Company, a local depositor of *Wholly Foreign*, an importer of foreign goods. Neither *Wholly Foreign* nor *B* has any office or other business presence in the United States.

Based on certain information unavailable to *Wholly Foreign* or *B*, the Treasury Department determines that *B* is acting as a purchasing agent on behalf of a country blocked under a sanctions program like the FACRs. Treasury could argue that the cover account held by A in New York is blocked because *B* has an indirect—a *very* indirect—interest in the account. The natural result would be litigation initiated by *B* against the local office of *Wholly Foreign* demanding performance of its obligations in accordance with local law. One such case is *China Mutual Trading Co., Ltd. v. Banque Belge*,[5] a 1954 Hong Kong case involving facts similar to those described above, in which the court insisted upon the application of local law. The court's reaction, from the viewpoint of the ordinary expectations of the banking industry, is unremarkable:

> I consider that rights of the plaintiffs re those which ordinarily arise out of the relationship of banker and customer where the latter has made a deposit with the former....
>
> There is no privity of contract between the customer of the bank and that bank's correspondent elsewhere.... A debt is situated or localized where it is recoverable. A debt which arises out of the relationship of banker and customer is localized at the branch of the bank where the account is kept.[6]

This straightforward choice-of-law principle—looking to the place where the account is "kept"—prevailed over any suggestion of a cognizable interest on the part of the United States in the application of the economic sanctions. Thus, the court rejected one defense offered by Banque Belge, to the effect that:

> by paying the U.S. dollars, held by [Banque Belge] with their agents [the correspondent bank] in New York, into a blocked account already existing in the name of the plaintiffs with

---

5. 39 Hong Kong L. Rep. 144 (1954).   **6.** *Id.* at 151.

those agents, [Banque Belge had] discharged [its] obligations. I consider that this defence also fails on the ground that payment by a debtor into a blocked account without the consent of the creditor cannot be a good discharge of a debt.[7]

C Bank, a U.S. bank, agrees to provide short-term financing, possibly through bankers' acceptances, for the manufacture and sale of heavy trucks by a U.S. manufacturing company's foreign subsidiary *D* to a trading corporation *E*, incorporated under the local laws of *D*'s host country. None of the parties to this transaction are targets of any U.S. economic sanctions program. However, as the contract term proceeds, it is discovered that *E* intends to resell to the development agency of a country that is blocked under the U.S. regulations. D, being a person subject to U.S. jurisdiction,[8] is informed by Treasury, through its U.S. parent, that it is prohibited from proceeding with the sale and subsequent delivery of the goods.[9] The financing of this transaction might also constitute a prohibited "dealing in" the property subject to sanctions.[10]

What, then, is *C Bank* to do if *D* is subjected to direct supervision (almost in the nature of a temporary receivership) by its host country, so that the sales transaction with *E* will be completed? Presumably, this would not represent a willful violation for *C* or *D*, but the situation is obviously a precarious one.

This situation loosely follows the facts in the famous Freuhauf episode,[11] in which Freuhauf's French subsidiary was subjected to such supervision in connection with a sale of trucks ultimately destined for the Peoples' Republic of China, then blocked under the FACRs. Here again, local host country law prevailed, and reach of U.S. economic sanctions was curtailed. While the subsidiary may be viewed as not acting in a willful manner, and hence ultimately not sanctioned under the FACRs, a considerable amount of expense and uncertainty ensued before the final outcome.

F Bank of New York has had ongoing relationships with country *G*, which is beginning to experience some foreign policy difficulties with the United States. In particular, *F* maintains an interest-bearing time deposit, at its London branch, in the name of *H Bank*, a bank organized under the laws of *G* and owned or controlled by the Government of *G*. The account is denominated in dollars. In addition, some time after the opening of the London

---

7. *Id.* at 152.

8. *See* 31 C.F.R. § 500.329 ("person subject" defined as including foreign subsidiary of corporation organized under laws of any state of the United States).

9. *See id.* § 500.201(b)(1) (prohibition on transfers by any "person sub-

ject" of property in which target country has an interest).

10. *Id.*

11. *See* Craig, *Application of the Trading With the Enemy Act to Foreign Corporations Owned by Americans: Reflections on Freuhauf v. Massardy* 83 Harv. L. Rev. 579 (1970).

branch account, G established a demand deposit at F *Bank*'s New York headquarters, also denominated in dollars.

This second account was established only after considerable negotiation between F *Bank* and G, and it was ultimately agreed that amounts in the New York account above a specified "peg" amount would be "swept" into the London account as of a specified time each business day. (If the balance in the New York account fell below the peg as of a specified time each business day, funds would be transferred from the London account to make up the difference.)

On a particular day, the difficulties between G and the United States reach a crisis, and limited trade sanctions are imposed. By the following day, a considerable balance exists in the New York account, calling for a sweep of the account and a transfer to the London branch. However, during the morning of the second day, F *Bank*'s president is contacted by U.S. Government officials and prevailed upon to delay the requisite sweep. He does so, and at some time after the established time for the sweep, a second set of economic sanctions regulations is put into place, blocking G assets that are subject to U.S. jurisdiction. The intended effect of the regulations is to block not only the New York account, but also dollar-denominated accounts held by foreign branches of U.S. banks in the name of G and entities controlled by it.

On their own terms, the application of such regulations to accounts held by foreign-situs branches of U.S. banks are vulnerable to attack under local host country law.[12] However, the same choice-of-law principles that would counsel defeat of the sanctions as to foreign-situs blocked deposits ought to dictate vindication of the sanctions with respect to U.S.-situs assets. The complicating factor in our example is the gratuitous action of F *Bank*'s president in delaying a transfer of funds to the foreign-situs account.

In a case exhibiting features similar to our example, *Libyan Arab Foreign Bank v. Bankers Trust Company*,[13] a British court essentially found the U.S. bank liable for both the amount of the London branch account and the amount that should have been transferred from New York to the London branch prior to the imposition of the blocking of GOL assets. The reasoning is similar to that of the court in *China Mutual*, though perhaps more sophisticated in its analysis. The *Bankers Trust* court reached the conclu-

---

12. Such challenges were mounted by Iranian banks during the pendency of the blocking under the IACRs in London and elsewhere. *See* Edwards, *Extraterritorial Application of the U.S. Iranian Assets Control Regulations*, 75 Am. J. Int'l L. 870, 876 (1981). However, these challenges were largely mooted by an intervening settlement entered into by the United States and Iran in January 1981.

13. 1 Lloyd's Rep. 259 (1988).

sion that the law of the contract governing the overall relationship between the Libyan bank and the U.S. bank was split; English law still governed the London account. Essentially, the court viewed the London branch as distinct from its New York headquarters, and fully subject to English law. The court decisively vindicated the principle of the place were an account is "kept."

Chapter 10

BANK REGULATION AND
SOCIAL POLICY

Table of Sections

---

§ 10.1   Introduction

Throughout the preceding chapters of this hornbook, we have been considering the various implications of depository institutions regulatory policy. This policy is grounded on certain objectives. Primary among these policy objectives is the promotion of the safety and soundness of the depository institutions system[1] and, correspondingly, the maintenance of public confidence in that system.[2] Where these objectives are not realized in specific cases, an additional policy objective involves the resolution of troubled or failing institutions with the least risk to the deposit insurance funds,[3] and with preference given to the interests of depositors.[4] Related policy objectives include the encouragement of competitive-

---

§ 10.1

1. *See, e.g.,* 12 U.S.C.A. § 1818(b)(1) (identifying safety and soundness as an objective of regulatory enforcement).

2. *See generally* Michael P. Malloy, *Balancing Public Confidence and Confidentiality: Adjudication Practices and Procedures of the Federal Bank Regula-*

tory Agencies, 61 Temple L. Rev. 723 (1988) (discussing policy objective of maintenance of public confidence).

3. *See, e.g.,* 12 U.S.C.A. § 1823(c)(4)(A)(ii) (providing for least-cost assistance to troubled institution).

4. *Id.* § 1821(d)(11).

ness in the provision of depository institution services,[5] and the insulation of depository institution services from other, potentially more risky activities.[6]

There are, however, other public policy objectives applied to depository institutions that may be unrelated, or only indirectly related, to the core objectives of depository institutions regulatory policy. Some of these objectives may focus on the effects of the concentration of economic power and resources within the depository institutions industry, such as nondiscriminatory credit policy.[7] Other objectives may simply use the regulation of depository institutions as a convenient mechanism for achieving other, unrelated objectives, such as the attainment of foreign policy objectives.[8]

This chapter discusses the application of such policy objectives to depository institutions. This set of issues is examined through a discussion of selected areas of regulation whose policy objectives are extraneous to the public policies underlying depository institutions. The discussion begins with the issue of privacy of financial information, primarily an enforcement concern for targets of investigation. It then turns to two areas of social policy with significant implications for depository institutions: rules requiring significant community reinvestment by depository institutions, and rules prohibiting discrimination in the provision of credit. The chapter concludes with a survey of other extraneous regulatory concerns that are implemented in part through the regulation of depository institutions.

§ 10.2   Privacy of Financial Information

Under U.S. law, a bank customer has no constitutional right to privacy with respect to the bank records of the customer's transactions.[1] Counterbalancing this, in 1978 Congress enacted the Right

---

5. *See, e.g., id.* §§ 1828(c), *as* amended, Dodd–Frank Wall Street Reform and Consumer Protection Act (DFA), Pub. L. No. 111–203, §§ 604(f), 623(a), 124 Stat. 1376, 1602, 1634 (2010) (codified at 12 U.S.C.A. § 1828(c)(5), (c)(13)(A)) (prohibiting anticompetitive mergers); 1842, *as* amended, DFA § 604(d), 124 Stat. at 1601 (codified at 12 U.S.C.A. § 1842(c)(7)) (prohibiting anticompetitive holding company acquisitions of banks).

6. *See, e.g., id.* U.S.C.A. § 378 (separating banking from securities); 1843(a) (separating bank-related activities of holding companies from nonbanking activities).

7. *See, e.g.,* 15 U.S.C.A. § 1691(a)(1) (prohibiting discrimination in provision

of credit based upon race, color, religion, national origin, sex, marital status, or age).

8. *See, e.g.,* 50 U.S.C.A. §§ 1701 *et seq.* (authorizing imposition of economic sanctions in response to threats to U.S. national security, foreign policy, or economy).

§ 10.2

1. *United States v. Miller,* 425 U.S. 435, 96 S.Ct. 1619 (1976). *See Walker v. S.W.I.F.T. SCRL,* 491 F.Supp.2d 781 (N.D.Ill. 2007) (discussing *Miller*); *McDonough v. Widnall,* 891 F.Supp. 1439 (D.Colo.1995) (discussing *Miller* and subsequent enactment of legislation). *See also Rodriguez v. Federal Sav. &*

to Financial Privacy Act ("RFPA")[2] to regulate the disclosure of such records to the federal government in specified circumstances.[3] Of course, the protection afforded by the RFPA is susceptible to amendment and revision to a significantly greater extent than a constitutional privacy right would be, and it evinces a level of detail that limits its flexibility. It is nevertheless the only measure of privacy protection currently available to these records.

§ 10.3   Right to Financial Privacy Act

As a general rule, under the RFPA government authorities[1] are prohibited from obtaining access to information contained in financial records[2] of any customer[3] from a financial institution,[4] unless

---

Loan Ins. Corp., 712 F.Supp. 159 (N.D.Cal.1989) (rejecting customer's Fifth Amendment privilege, since customer had neither actual nor constructive possession of records). The appropriate scope of confidentiality accorded to bank records remains a subject of some controversy. *See generally* William C. Hefernan, *Property, Privacy, and the Fourth Amendment*, 60 Brook. L. Rev. 633 (1994); Paul B. Rasor, *Controlling Government Access to Personal Financial Records*, 25 Washburn L.J. 417 (1986); Dan L. Nicewander, *Financial Record Privacy—What are and What Should be Rights of Customer of Depository Institution*, 16 St. Mary's L.J. 601 (1985).

2. Pub. L. No. 95–630, tit. XI, §§ 1101–1121, 92 Stat. 3697 (1978), *as amended*, Pub. L. No. 101–73, §§ 744, 941, 103 Stat. 438, 496 (1989); Pub. L. No. 101–647, § 2596(c), 104 Stat. 4908 (1990) (codified at 12 U.S.C.A. §§ 3401–3422). For legislative history of the RFPA, see H.R. Rep. No. 95–1383, 1978 U.S. Code. Cong. & Admin. News 9273.

3. *See Young v. United States Dep't of Justice*, 882 F.2d 633 (2d Cir.1989), *cert. denied*, 493 U.S. 1072, 110 S.Ct. 1116 (1990) (discussing purpose of RFPA); *McDonough, supra* (discussing purpose in relation to prior decision in *Miller*); *In re Grand Jury Proceedings*, 636 F.2d 81 (5th Cir.1981) (emphasizing RFPA requirement of customer authorization); *In re Porras*, 191 B.R. 357 (Bkrtcy.W.D.Tex.1995) (discussing balance of competing interests in information); *United States v. First Nat'l Bank of Md.*, 866 F.Supp. 884 (D.Md.1994) (discussing same).

§ 10.3

1. For these purposes, the term "Government authority" is defined to mean "any agency or department of the United States, or any officer, employee, or agent thereof." 12 U.S.C.A. § 3401(3). Despite the breadth of this definition, the RFPA has been construed as inapplicable to federal courts and agencies deriving their authority from the courts. *Doe v. Board on Prof'l Responsibility of Dist. of Columbia Ct. of Appeals*, 717 F.2d 1424 (D.C.Cir.1983) (upholding issuance of subpoenas for financial records with respect to transactions in client funds). *Cf. Nichols v. Council on Judicial Complaints*, 615 P.2d 280 (Okla.1980) (noting that only federal agencies are affected by RFPA).

2. For these purposes, the term "financial record" is defined to mean the "original of, a copy of, or information known to have been derived from, any record held by a financial institution pertaining to a customer's relationship with the financial institution." 12 U.S.C.A. § 3401(2). *See, e.g., Waye v. First Citizen's Nat'l Bank*, 846 F.Supp. 310 (M.D.Pa.), *aff'd*, 31 F.3d 1175 (3d Cir.1994) (including canceled check in definition); *Neece v. Internal Revenue Serv.*, 922 F.2d 573 (10th Cir.1990) (mortgage and loan application records).

3. For these purposes, the term "customer" is defined to mean "any person or authorized representative of that person who utilized or is utilized any service of a financial institution, or for whom a financial institution is acting or has acted as a fiduciary, in relation to an account maintained in the person's name." 12 U.S.C.A. § 3401(5). "Custom-

the records are "reasonably described"[5] and meet one of the following requirements: (1) The customer authorized the disclosure;[6] (2) The records are disclosed pursuant to an administrative subpoena that meets applicable RFPA procedural requirements,[7] including

er" does not include a corporation. *See id*. § 3401(4) (defining "person" to mean an individual or partnership of no more than five individuals). *See also United States v. First Nat'l Bank of Md*., 866 F.Supp. 884 (D.Md.1994) (so holding); *Jobin v. Resolution Trust Corp*., 156 B.R. 834 (D.Colo.1993) (so holding); *Collins v. Commodity Futures Trading Comm'n*, 737 F.Supp. 1467 (N.D.Ill. 1990) (so holding); *United States v. Theron*, 116 F.R.D. 58 (D.Kan.1987) (so holding); *Pittsburgh Nat'l Bank v. United States*, 771 F.2d 73 (3d Cir.1985) (so holding); *Spa Flying Serv., Inc. v. United States*, 724 F.2d 95 (8th Cir.1984) (so holding). *Cf. Hunt v. Securities and Exch. Comm'n*, 520 F.Supp. 580 (N.D.Tex.1981) (holding that individual customer has right to complete subpoena, even though portions thereof concern request for corporate records not covered by RFPA). The scope of the term "customer" has generated considerable litigation. *See, e.g., In re Porras, supra* (excluding trust from meaning of "customer"); *United States v. Daccarett*, 6 F.3d 37 (2d Cir.1993), *cert. denied sub nom. Confecciones Zuny Ltda. v. United States*, 511 U.S. 1030, 114 S.Ct. 1538 (1994), and *cert. denied sub nom. Creaciones Viviana Ltda. v. United States*, 510 U.S. 1191, 114 S.Ct. 1294 (1994), and *cert. denied sub nom. Abuchaibe Hnos Ltda. v. United States*, 510 U.S. 1191, 114 S.Ct. 1294 (1994), and *cert. denied sub nom. Comercial Samora Ltda. v. United States*, 510 U.S. 1191, 114 S.Ct. 1294 (1994), and *cert. denied sub nom. Industrias Marathon Ltda. v. United States*, 510 U.S. 1191, 114 S.Ct. 1295 (1994), and *cert. denied sub nom. Manufacturera Del Atlantico Ltda. v. United States*, 510 U.S. 1192, 114 S.Ct. 1295 (1994), and *cert. denied sub nom. Organizacion JD Ltda. v. United States*, 510 U.S. 1191, 114 S.Ct. 1295 (1994) (construing claimants of funds held in custody pursuant to arrest warrants not "customers"); *Neece, supra* note 2 (construing loan applicant as "customer"); *Russell v. Department of Air Force*, 915 F.Supp. 1108 (D.Colo.1996) (construing Air Force to be "authorized representa-

tive" of military officer, not barred from access to officer's financial records); *In re Blunden*, 896 F.Supp. 996 (C.D.Cal. 1995) (construing loan applicant as "customer"); *Inspector Gen. v. Great Lakes Bancorp*, 825 F.Supp. 790 (E.D.Mich.1993) (excluding limited partnership with corporate general partner from meaning of "customer"); *Ridgeley v. Merchants State Bank*, 699 F.Supp. 100 (N.D. Tex. 1988) (excluding special interest nonprofit organization); *Donovan v. U.A. Local Plumbers & Pipe Trades Pension Fund*, 569 F.Supp. 1488 (N.D.Cal.1983) (construing individual trustees as "customers" as to pension fund transactions).

4. For these purposes the term "financial institution" is defined to mean:

> any office of a bank, savings bank, card issuer . . ., industrial loan company, trust company, savings association, building and loan, or homestead association (including cooperative banks), credit union, or consumer finance institution, located in any state or territory of the United States, the District of Columbia, Puerto Rico, Guam, American Samoa, or the Virgin Islands.

12 U.S.C.A. § 3401(1).

5. *Id*. § 3402. *See In re Blunden*, 896 F.Supp. 996 (C.D.Cal.1995) (discussing "reasonable specificity" requirement); *Dawar v. United States Dep't of Hous. and Urban Dev*., 820 F.Supp. 545 (D.Kan.1993) (discussing "reasonably described" requirement) *Ruggles v. Securities and Exch. Comm'n*, 567 F.Supp. 766 (S.D.Tex.1983) (finding sufficient specificity).

6. 12 U.S.C.A. § 3402(1). On customer authorization requirements, see *id*. § 3404. A financial institution cannot require a customer to sign such an authorization as a condition of doing business with the institution. *Id*. § 3404(b).

7. *Id*. § 3402(2). On the RFPA requirements for administrative subpoenas, see *id*. § 3405. *See Dawar, supra* (discussing requirements).

relevance "to a legitimate law enforcement inquiry"[8] and notice to the customer;[9] (3) The records are disclosed in response to a search warrant that meets RFPA procedural requirements;[10] (4) The records are disclosed in response to a judicial subpoena that meets RFPA procedural requirements;[11] or, (5) The records are disclosed in response to a formal written request that meets RFPA procedural requirements.[12]

The financial institution to which the subpoena, summons, or request for records is made has available whatever rights to challenge normally would apply to the subject of a subpoena or summons.[13] The customer's sole judicial remedy to prevent disclosure is an RFPA challenge to access.[14]

Within 10 days of service or 14 days of mailing of a subpoena, summons, or formal written request,[15] a customer may challenge

8. 12 U.S.C.A. § 3405(1). For these purposes the term law enforcement inquiry is defined to mean "a lawful investigation or official proceeding inquiring into a violation of, or failure to comply with, any criminal or civil statute or any regulation, rule, or order issued pursuant thereto." *Id.* § 3401(8). *See, e.g., Breakey v. Inspector Gen.*, 836 F.Supp. 422 (E.D.Mich.1993) (criticizing "official curiosity" as reason for subpoena); *United States v. Wilson*, 571 F.Supp. 1417 (S.D.N.Y.1983) (finding legitimate inquiry into transfers of funds from European banks); *Donovan, supra* (finding legitimate law enforcement inquiry); *McGloshen v. United States Dep't of Agric.*, 480 F.Supp. 247 (W.D.Ky.1979) (finding legitimate inquiry despite paucity of information in affidavit).

9. 12 U.S.C.A. § 3405(2). *See, e.g., Botero–Zea v. United States*, 915 F.Supp. 614 (S.D.N.Y.1996) (finding violation of RFPA for failure to provide prior notice); *Breakey, supra* (finding notice to meet RFPA requirements); *Pennington v. Donovan*, 574 F.Supp. 708 (S.D.Tex. 1983) (finding letter notification to customer sufficient); *Hunt, supra* (requiring complete subpoena to be disclosed to individual customer). This notice requirement does not apply to IRS notice to taxpayers. *FitzGerald v. United States*, 882 F.Supp. 959 (D.Idaho 1994).

10. 12 U.S.C.A. § 3402(3). On the RFPA requirements for search warrants, see *id.* § 3406. Notice of the search warrant to the customer may be delayed by court order. *Id.* §§ 3406(c), 3409. On the requirements for delay orders under § 3409, see *Botero–Zea, supra*; *Matter of*

Thirty–Nine Admin. Subpoenae, 754 F.Supp. 5 (D.Mass.1990).

11. 12 U.S.C.A. §§ 3402(4), 3407. *See, e.g., Waye, supra* (noting prior notice to customer required for administrative and judicial subpoenae, but forbidden for grand jury subpoenae); *In re Castiglione*, 587 F.Supp. 1210 (E.D.Cal. 1984) (concerning grand jury subpoenae). *But cf. United States v. A Residence Located at 218 Third St., New Glarus, Wis.*, 805 F.2d 256 (7th Cir. 1986) (rejecting *Castiglione's* narrow reading of grand jury procedure); *United States v. Kington*, 801 F.2d 733 (5th Cir.1986), *reh'g denied*, 806 F.2d 261, *cert. denied*, 481 U.S. 1014, 107 S.Ct. 1888 (1987).

12. 12 U.S.C.A. §§ 3402(5), 3408.

13. *Id.* § 3410(f).

14. *Id.* § 3410(e). *See id.* § 3416 (providing for jurisdiction in appropriate federal district court to enforce RFPA provisions). Agencies or departments may, however, be liable to the customer for civil penalties for obtaining or disclosing information in violation of the RFPA. *Id.* § 3417(a). Disciplinary action may be taken against federal agents or employees for willful or intentional violations. *Id.* § 3417(b). These provisions are the exclusive judicial remedies for violations of the RFPA. *Id.* § 3417(d). *But cf. id.* § 3418 (providing for injunctive relief to require compliance with RFPA).

15. Failure to follow the time requirements for a customer challenge is a

access to the records by filing a motion to quash a summons or subpoena or an application to enjoin the governmental authority from obtaining access.[16] If the court finds that the customer has complied with the filing requirements, it will then order the government authority to file a sworn response.[17] While the court usually will decide the matter on the basis of these filings, it may conduct additional proceedings as appropriate.[18]

In any event, the motion or application must be decided within seven calendar days of the government's response.[19] If the motion or application is denied, the court's decision is not a final order, and no interlocutory appeal is available under the explicit language of the RFPA.[20]

Even if government access to customer records is permissible under the RFPA, the act limits the ability of the government authority that has access to such records to transfer the records to other agencies and departments.[21] Records cannot be transferred unless the transferring authority certifies in writing that there exists "reason to believe that the records are relevant to a legitimate law enforcement inquiry within the jurisdiction of the receiving agency or department."[22] The transferring authority must mail a copy of the certification and a notice to the customer.[23] Exchanges of information between supervisory agencies,[24] transfer of records to defend against a customer action, and disclosure of information to duly authorized committees and subcommittees of the Congress are exempt from these requirements.[25]

jurisdictional defect. *Turner v. United States*, 881 F.Supp. 449 (D.Haw.1995).

16. 12 U.S.C.A. § 3410(a). *See Clark v. Inspector Gen.*, 944 F.Supp. 818 (D.Or.1996) (discussing requirement of service on government authority); *Donovan, supra* (discussing affidavit requirement); *Hancock v. Marshall*, 86 F.R.D. 209 (D.D.C.1980) (discussing affidavit requirement).

17. 12 U.S.C.A. § 3410(b). The government may request *in camera* consideration of its response. *Id. See, e.g., In re Blunden, supra* (upholding government access as relevant to legitimate law enforcement inquiry); *Rodriguez, supra* (upholding FSLIC subpoena); *Grafstrom v. Securities and Exch. Comm'n*, 532 F.Supp. 1023 (S.D.N.Y.1982) (finding SEC response sufficient to rebut customer challenge).

18. 12 U.S.C.A. § 3410(b).

19. *Id.* On the court's decision, see *id.* § 3410(c).

20. *Id.* § 3410(d).

21. *Id.* § 3412(a).

22. *Id.*

23. *Id.* § 3412(b). The notice may be delayed by court order in appropriate circumstances. *Id.* § 3412(c).

24. *See Adams v. Board of Governors*, 855 F.2d 1336 (8th Cir.1988) (upholding transfer of records from OCC to Fed).

25. 12 U.S.C.A. § 3412(d). Exchanges of financial records and other information among and between the five member agencies of the Federal Financial Institutions Examination Council ("FFIEC") (*i.e.*, OCC, Fed, FDIC, OTS, and NCUA) and the SEC are also exempt from these requirements. *Id.* § 3412(e). Transfer or disclosure of financial records to the Attorney General or to the Secretary of the Treasury are subject to separate procedures. *Id.* § 3412(f)(1)–(2).

In addition, there is a wide range of exceptions to the RFPA requirements. RFPA requirements do not apply to: (1) Financial records not identified to particular customers;[26] (2) Records disclosed to any supervisory agency or in connection with supervisory, regulatory, or monetary functions;[27] (3) Records disclosed in accordance with procedures authorized by federal tax law;[28] (4) Records disclosed pursuant to federal statute or rules promulgated thereunder;[29] (5) Records disclosed pursuant to Federal Rules of Civil or Criminal Procedure, "or comparable rules of other courts in connection with litigation to which the Government authority and the customer are parties;"[30] (6) Records disclosed under a subpoena issued by an administrative law judge;[31] (7) Records containing only customer name, address, account number, and type of account or as to an ascertainable group of customers, under specified circumstances;[32] (8) Records disclosed pursuant to a lawful proceeding, examination, or the like with respect to a financial institution, a legal entity, or with respect to government loan or guarantee programs;[33] (9) Records disclosed pursuant to grand jury subpoenae

26. *Id.* § 3413(a). *See, e.g., Donovan v. National Bank of Alaska,* 696 F.2d 678 (9th Cir.1983) (seeking information with respect to employee benefit plans).

27. 12 U.S.C.A. § 3413(b). *See, e.g., United States v. Davis,* 953 F.2d 1482 (10th Cir.1992), *cert. denied,* 504 U.S. 945, 112 S.Ct. 2286 (upholding exchange of information among Fed, FHLBB, and OCC); *Adams, supra* (upholding exchange under Change in Bank Control Act).

28. 12 U.S.C.A. § 3413(c). *See, e.g., Neece, supra* (criticizing access not in compliance with RFPA or tax law); *United States v. MacKay,* 608 F.2d 830 (10th Cir.1979) (applying summons authority of tax laws); *King v. United States,* 684 F.Supp. 1038 (D.Neb.1987) (same); *McTaggart v. United States,* 570 F.Supp. 547 (E.D.Mich.1983) (same); *United States v. Hill,* 537 F.Supp. 677 (N.D.Tex. 1982) (same).

29. 12 U.S.C.A. § 3413(d). *Cf. Coronado v. BankAtlantic Bancorp, Inc.,* 951 F.Supp. 1025 (S.D.Fla.1997) (upholding disclosure pursuant to Anti–Money Laundering Act).

30. 12 U.S.C.A. § 3413(e). For an interesting case applying this "government litigation" exception to military subpoenae issued in connection with a court martial of a soldier, see *Flowers v. First Hawaiian Bank,* 295 F.Supp.2d 1130 (D.Hawai'i 2003), *affirmed sub*

nom. Flowers v. U.S. Army, 25th Infantry Div., 179 Fed.App. 986 (9th Cir. 2006), *cert. denied,* 550 U.S. 933, 127 S.Ct. 2248 (2007).

31. 12 U.S.C.A. § 3413(f).

32. *Id.* § 3413(g). This exemption only applies to the RFPA notice requirements, customer challenges, and transfer of information to other agencies. *Id.* The records must involve either a particular financial transaction or class of transactions, *id.* § 3413(g)(1); *see In re Request for Assistance from Ministry of Legal Affairs of Trinidad and Tobago,* 648 F.Supp. 464 (S.D.Fla.1986), *aff'd,* 848 F.2d 1151 (11th Cir.1988), *cert. denied sub nom. Azar v. Minister of Legal Affairs of Trinidad and Tobago,* 488 U.S. 1005, 109 S.Ct. 784 (1989) (so holding), or transactions with a foreign country or subdivision thereof in the case of a government authority administering economic sanctions under applicable federal law. *Id.* § 3413(g)(2). In contrast, special procedures apply to disclosure of financial records in connection with either intelligence activities or Secret Service protective functions. *Id.* § 3414.

33. 12 U.S.C.A. § 3413(h). The confidentiality of customer records must still be maintained by the financial institution under § 3402, and the civil penalty and injunctive relief provisions of §§ 3417 and 3418 still apply to these records. *Id.* § 3413(h).

or judicial orders in connection with grand jury proceedings;[34] (10) Records disclosed pursuant to a General Accounting Office proceeding, investigation, or the like, directed at a government authority;[35] (11) Records disclosed as necessary for administration of federal old-age or retirement benefits programs;[36] (12) Records disclosed in connection with possible crimes by insiders against a financial institution;[37] (13) Records disclosed to employees or agents of the Federal Reserve Board ("Fed") or any Federal Reserve Bank in connection with extensions of credit to a financial institution or others;[38] (14) Records disclosed to the now defunct Resolution Trust Corporation or its employees or agents in connection with a financial institution conservatorship, receivership, or liquidation;[39] (15) Records disclosed to the Federal Housing Finance Agency or any Federal Home Loan Bank in connection with extensions of credit to a financial institution or others;[40] and, (16) Records disclosed as necessary for administration of federal veterans benefits programs.[41]

§ 10.4   Effect on Financial Institutions

While there can be considerable burdens for a depository institution that is the subject of a subpoena, summons, or request for customer records,[1] the RFPA does provide for reimbursement to a financial institution of reasonably necessary costs for assembling

---

34. *Id.* § 3413(i). *See generally In re 1980 U.S. Grand Jury Subpoena Duces Tecum*, 502 F.Supp. 576 (E.D.La.1980) (permitting access to customer records pursuant to grand jury subpoena); *In re Grand Jury Subpoena (Connecticut Sav. Bank)*, 481 F.Supp. 833 (D.Conn.1979) (permitting access to customer records notwithstanding Connecticut statute). The cost reimbursement provision of the RFPA, 12 U.S.C.A. § 3415, and specific provisions concerning grand jury proceedings, *id.* § 3420, still apply to these records. *Id.* § 3413(i). *But see McDonough, supra* (rejecting as impermissible under RFPA use of grand jury records in administrative proceeding). *But cf. Theron, supra* (permitting transfer of grand jury records to trustee in bankruptcy). On application of the specific RFPA provision with respect to grand jury proceedings, see *United States v. Jackson*, 11 F.3d 953 (10th Cir.1993) (permitting use of subpoenaed records to obtain search warrant prior to returning records to grand jury); *United States v. A Residence Located at 218 Third Street, New Glarus, Wis.*, 805 F.2d 256 (7th Cir.1986) (concerning presentation of records to grand jury, rejecting *In re*

Castiglione) *supra*; *United States v. Kington, supra* (same); *United States v. Mosko*, 654 F.Supp. 402 (D.Colo.1987), *aff'd sub nom. United States v. Pinelli*, 890 F.2d 1461 (10th Cir.1989), *cert. denied*, 495 U.S. 960, 110 S.Ct. 2568 (1990) (rejecting motion to suppress records on alleged improper presentation to grand jury).

35. 12 U.S.C.A. § 3413(j).

36. *Id.* § 3413(k).

37. *Id.* § 3413(*l*).

38. *Id.* § 3413(m).

39. *Id.* § 3413(n).

40. *Id.* § 3413(*o*).

41. *Id.* § 3413(p).

§ 10.4

1. Financial institutions have a statutory duty to comply with a request for customer records in accordance with the procedures and requirements of the RFPA. 12 U.S.C.A. § 3411. *See Waye v. First Citizen's Nat'l Bank*, 846 F.Supp. 310 (M.D.Pa.), *aff'd*, 31 F.3d 1175 (3d Cir.1994) (discussing RFPA duty); *Flowers, supra*.

or providing customer records.[2] The cost reimbursement provision does not apply to records with respect to the institution's perfection of a security interest, claims in bankruptcy, debt collection or application processing,[3] or to records with respect to the first eight exemptions discussed above.[4] Since the RFPA does not apply to records of corporate customers of a financial institution, the cost reimbursement provision has been held inapplicable to costs with respect to assembling and providing records of such customers.[5]

In general, there is no direct cause of action for damages under the RFPA for an institution's improper release of records.[6] However, financial institutions are directly subject to an RFPA requirement that they maintain the confidentiality of customer records absent a government inquiry that complies with the RFPA.[7] Financial institutions are prohibited from releasing such records until the government authority certifies in writing to the institution that it has complied with the applicable requirements of the RFPA.[8]

Nevertheless, this does not prohibit an institution from notifying an appropriate government agency that it has information that may be relevant to a possible violation of statute or regulation.[9] Nor is an institution prohibited from providing copies of financial rec-

---

2. 12 U.S.C.A. § 3415.

3. *Id.* § 3403(d).

4. 12 U.S.C.A. § 3415. In addition, where the financial institution is itself the target of a grand jury investigation, at least one court has held that the cost reimbursement provision does not apply to the target's costs in complying with a grand jury subpoena. *In re Grand Jury Proceedings*, 636 F.2d 81 (5th Cir.1981).

5. *Pittsburgh Nat'l Bank v. United States*, 771 F.2d 73 (3d Cir.1985).

6. *Neece v. Internal Revenue Serv.*, 922 F.2d 573 (10th Cir.1990).

7. 12 U.S.C.A. § 3403(a). Presumably, failure to comply with this duty of confidentiality would constitute a "violation of law" for purposes of federal administrative enforcement provisions. *See, e.g., id.* § 1818(b)(1) (providing for cease and desist orders for violation of law).

8. *Id.* § 3403(b).

9. *Id.* § 3403(c). The institution cannot be held liable, under U.S. or state law, for any such notification, or for failure to notify a customer of such notification. *Id. See, e.g., Miranda De Villalba v. Coutts & Co. (USA) Intern.*, 250 F.3d 1351 (11th Cir. 2001), cert. denied, 534 U.S. 953 (applying statutory defense to liability for disclosure of customer's identity and "nature" of suspected illegal activity to government); *Waye, supra* (reporting of check-kiting scheme); *Waye v. Commonwealth Bank*, 846 F.Supp. 321 (M.D.Pa.1994) (holding bank exempt from customer claim for negligence and bad faith, in light of § 3403(c)). *Cf. Stoutt v. Banco Popular De Puerto Rico*, 320 F.3d 26 (1st Cir. 2003) (applying implied good faith requirement for similar defense under anti-money laundering statute, 31 U.S.C.A. § 5813(g)(3); allowing bank's defense); *Nikrasch v. State*, 698 S.W.2d 443 (Tex.App.1985) (reporting information concerning lessee of safe deposit box to police). *But cf. Lopez v. First Union National Bank of Florida*, 129 F.3d 1186 (11th Cir. 1997), *rehearing and rehearing en banc denied sub nom., Coronado v. Bank Atlantic Bancorp, Inc.*, 141 F.3d 1191 (11th Cir. 1998), *appeal after remand*, 222 F.3d 1315 (11th Cir. 2000), *cert. denied*, 531 U.S. 1052, 121 S.Ct. 656 (discussing interplay of RFPA and Electronic Communications Privacy Act, 18 U.S.C.A. §§ 2510 et seq.); *Velasquez–Campuzano v. Marfa Nat'l Bank*, 896 F.Supp. 1415 (W.D.Tex.1995), *aff'd*, 91 F.3d 139 (5th Cir.1996) (suggesting that voluntary disclosure did not preempt liability under state law).

ords to a court or government authority "as an incident to perfecting a security interest, proving a claim in bankruptcy, or otherwise collecting a debt."[10] Likewise, an institution is not prohibited from providing any financial record necessary to a government authority "as an incident to processing an application for assistance to a customer in the form of a Government loan, loan guaranty, or loan insurance agreement, or as an incident to processing a default on, or administering, a Government guaranteed or insured loan."[11]

A word of caution is warranted. Financial institutions may be liable to the customer for statutorily specified *civil penalties* for "obtaining or disclosing financial records or information ... in violation of" the RFPA.[12] While rarely pursued successfully to date, the civil penalties can be potentially significant. They may consist of: (1) $100.00, without regard to the volume of records at issue;[13] (2) The customer's actual damages sustained as a result of the disclosure;[14] (3) Punitive damages determined by the court, if the violation was willful or intentional;[15] and, (4) Costs and reasonable attorneys' fees.[16]

A good faith defense is available. A financial institution, or any agent or employee, acting in good faith reliance on certification by a government authority of compliance with the RFPA,[17] or pursuant to the exception for reporting crimes against an institution by an insider,[18] is given a complete affirmative defense against a claim by the customer under the RFPA and any state constitution, law, or regulation.[19] These provisions are the exclusive judicial remedies for violations of the RFPA.[20]

§ 10.5 Effect on State Law

By its own terms, the RFPA does not apply to inquiries from state and local government agencies.[1] Uncertainty remains, howev-

10. 12 U.S.C.A. § 3403(d)(1). The debt may be owed to the institution, or in its capacity as a fiduciary. *Id.*

11. *Id.* § 3403(d)(2). *See, e.g., Bailey v. United States Dep't of Agric.,* 59 F.3d 141 (10th Cir.1995) (concerning food stamp program).

12. 12 U.S.C.A. § 3417(a).

13. *Id.* § 3417(a)(1). *See Duncan v. Belcher,* 813 F.2d 1335 (4th Cir.1987) (finding proof of actual damages unnecessary for recovery under RFPA).

14. 12 U.S.C.A. § 3417(a)(2). *See Neece, supra* (discussing proof of damages). *Cf. Duncan, supra* (finding proof of actual damages unnecessary).

15. 12 U.S.C.A. § 3417(a)(3).

16. *Id.* § 3417(a)(4). Fees and costs are available only in successful customer actions. *Id.*

17. *Per id.* § 3403(b).

18. *Per id.* § 3413(*l*).

19. *Id.* § 3417(c).

20. *Id.* § 3417(d).

§ 10.5

1. *United States v. Zimmerman,* 957 F.Supp. 94 (N.D.W.Va.1997); *Nichols v. Council on Judicial Complaints,* 615 P.2d 280 (Okla.1980); *Austin v. Old Nat'l Bank in Evansville,* 656 N.E.2d 886 (Ind.App.1995) (holding RFPA inapplicable to state agencies); *Matter of Grand Jury Applications for Court–Or-*

er, about the extent to which the RFPA overrides state law requirements and procedures.

Some courts have at least suggested that state law barring disclosure of financial records of a customer would be inapplicable in situations where the RFPA authorizes disclosure, though the courts routinely construe such state provisions as not creating conflict with federal law.[2] In addition, there is case law finding that contrary state law restricting or prohibiting access to customer records is preempted by the RFPA in certain instances.[3] Other courts have indicated that the RFPA does not have a broad preemptive effect.[4]

The better view is probably that the RFPA is only selectively preemptive of contrary state law, in fairly explicit terms. For example, it is clear from the text of the RFPA that any state constitution, law, or regulation that would prohibit an institution from notifying an appropriate federal government agency that it has information that may be relevant to a possible violation of statute or regulation is explicitly preempted by the RFPA.[5] Likewise, the good faith defense against customer claims for civil penalties expressly preempts contrary state law.[6] Thus, where the RFPA intends preemptive effect, it is quite explicit. Courts should therefore be hesitant to expand the scope of RFPA preemption beyond what the text appears to indicate is necessary.

§ 10.6 Nonpublic Personal Information under the GLBA

The expanded involvement of financial services firms in banking, securities and insurance under the Gramm–Leach–Bliley Act ("GLBA")[1] naturally raises concerns about the uses to which a financial services firm might put the nonpersonal financial information that it can aggregate from its various customer bases. In light of these privacy concerns, the GLBA requires the federal depository institutions regulators, the Secretary of the Treasury, the SEC and the FTC, after consultation with representatives of state insurance

dered Subpoenas and Nondisclosure Orders, 142 Misc.2d 241, 536 N.Y.S.2d 939 (N.Y.Sup.Ct.1988) (holding RFPA inapplicable to state court).

2. *See, e.g., United States v. Wilson*, 571 F.Supp. 1417 (S.D.N.Y.1983) (construing Texas Civ. St. art. 342–705).

3. *See, e.g., In re Grand Jury Subpoena (Connecticut Sav. Bank)*, 481 F.Supp. 833 (D.Conn.1979) (permitting access pursuant to federal grand jury subpoena without compliance with state law).

4. *See, e.g., Foxworth v. Trustmark Nat'l Bank*, 934 F.Supp. 218 (S.D.Miss. 1996) (taking selective approach to preemption issue).

5. 12 U.S.C.A. § 3403(c).

6. *Id.* § 3417(c).

§ 10.6

1. Pub. L. No. 106–102, Nov. 12, 1999, 113 Stat. 1338 (1999) (codified at scattered sections of 12, 15, 16, 18 U.S.C.A.).

authorities designated by the National Association of Insurance Commissioners ("NAIC"),[2] to establish comprehensive standards for ensuring the security and confidentiality of consumers' personal information maintained by financial institutions.[3] In May and June 2000, a number of agencies issued final rules in this regard.[4] All of these rules are "analogous set of regulations."[5]

The rules were challenged in *Individual Reference Services Group, Inc. v. Federal Trade Commission*,[6] on the grounds that the regulations exceeded the authority of the GLBA, that they were arbitrary and capricious, that they violated the plaintiff credit reporting agency's free speech, due process, and equal protection rights.[7] The Federal District Court for the District of Columbia rejected each of these claims.[8] The D.C. Circuit has also upheld the FTC's regulations, despite a challenge that the scope of the regulations was broader than authorized by the GLBA.[9]

The GLBA allows customers of financial institutions to opt out of having their personal financial information shared with nonaffiliated third parties, subject to certain exceptions.[10] It bars financial institutions from disclosing customer account numbers or similar forms of access codes to nonaffiliated third parties for telemarketing or other direct marketing purposes.[11] It mandates clear and conspicuous annual disclosure of a financial institution's policies and procedures for protecting customers' nonpublic personal infor-

---

2. On the role of the NAIC under the GLBA, see *supra* § 5.26.

3. GLBA, § 504 (codified at 15 U.S.C.A. § 6804).

4. On 18 May 2000, the NCUA issued final rules governing privacy of consumer financial information, effective as of 13 November 2000, although compliance is optional until 1 July 2001. 65 Fed. Reg. 31,722 (2000) (codified at 12 C.F.R. pts. 716, 741), *amended*, 65 Fed. Reg. 36,782 (2000) (codified at 12 C.F.R. pt. 716). Six days later, the FTC issued its rules, with the same effectiveness provisions. 65 Fed. Reg. 33,646 (2000) (codified at 16 C.F.R. pt. 313). On 1 June 2000, the OCC, Fed, FDIC and OTS finally issued their rules, with the same effectiveness provisions as the NCUA. 65 Fed. Reg. 35,162 (2000) (codified at 12 C.F.R. pts. 40, 216, 332, 573). On 29 June 2000, the SEC issued its final rule, with compliance required as of 1 July 2001. 65 Fed. Reg. 40,334 (2000) (codified at 17 C.F.R. pt. 248 (Regulation SBP)).

5. *Individual Reference Services Group, Inc. v. Federal Trade Commis-*

sion, 145 F.Supp.2d 6, 21 n. 10 (D.D.C. 2001), *aff'd*, 295 F.3d 42 (D.C.Cir.2002).

6. Note 5, *supra*.

7. *See Individual Reference Services Group, Inc.*, 145 F.Supp.2d at 31–38 (dicussing claims that rules exceeded authority of GLBA); *id.* at 26–31, 38–39 (discussing claims under Administrative Procedure Act); *id.* at 39–44 (discussing claim of violation of credit reporting agency's free speech rights); *id.* at 44–45 (discussing due process claim); *id.* at 46 (discussing equal protection claim).

8. *See id.* at 46.

9. *Trans Union LLC v. F.T.C.*, 295 F.3d 42 (D.C.Cir.2002) (upholding FTC's broad interpretation of "financial" to encompass any information that "is requested by a financial institution for the purpose of providing a financial product or service").

10. GLBA, § 502(a)–(b), (e) (codified at 15 U.S.C.A. § 6802(a)–(b), (e)).

11. *Id.*, § 502(c)–(d) (codified at 15 U.S.C.A. § 6802(c)–(d)).

mation.[12] Nothing in these provisions is to be construed to modify, limit, or supersede the operation of Fair Credit Reporting Act[13] ("FCRA").[14]

The privacy provisions do not supersede any state statutes, regulations, orders, or interpretations, except to the extent that such state provisions are inconsistent, and then only to the extent of the inconsistency.[15] A state provision is not considered inconsistent if the protection afforded by the state provision is greater than the protection provided under the privacy provisions, as determined by the Federal Trade Commission ("FTC") in consultation with the federal agency or authority involved.[16]

In addition, the GLBA prohibits any person from obtaining or attempting to obtain, or causing to be disclosed or attempting to cause to be disclosed, customer information of a financial institution through fraudulent or deceptive means.[17] Enforcement of the prohibition is placed in the FTC and the federal depository institutions regulators.[18] Knowing and intentional violations or attempts to violate the prohibition are criminal offenses punishable by fine

12. *Id.*, § 503 (codified at 15 U.S.C.A. § 6803).

13. 15 U.S.C.A. §§ 1681–1681u.

14. GLBA, § 506 (codified at 15 U.S.C.A. §§ 1681s, 6806). *See* 65 Fed. Reg. 63,120 (2000) (to be codified at 12 C.F.R. pts. 41, 222, 334, 571) (proposed OCC, FRS, FDIC, OTS FCRA rules); 65 Fed. Reg. 64,168 (2000) (to be codified at 12 C.F.R. pt. 706) (proposed NCUA FCRA rules); 65 Fed. Reg. 80,802 (2000) (to be codified at 16 C.F.R. pt. 600) (proposed FTC FCRA rule). The FCRA provides basic consumer protection at the federal level with respect to credit reporting. On the relatively limited purposes of the FCRA, see *Williams v. Equifax Credit Information Services*, 892 F.Supp. 951 (E.D.Mich.1995); *Wiggins v. District Cablevision, Inc.*, 853 F.Supp. 484 (D.D.C.1994); *In re TRW, Inc.*, 460 F.Supp. 1007 (E.D.Mich.1978); *Sizemore v. Bambi Leasing Corp.*, 360 F.Supp. 252 (N.D.Ga.1973). On private actions under the FCRA, see *Sheffer v. Experian Information Solutions, Inc.*, 249 F.Supp.2d 560 (E.D.Pa. 2003) (recognizing FCRA private right of action against card issuer furnishing credit information; upholding claim based on allegations that issuer failed to respond adequately to investigatory inquiries of credit reporting agencies after issuer mistakenly reported that consumer was deceased); *Lofton–Taylor v. Verizon Wireless*, 262 Fed.App. 999, 1002 (11th Cir. 2008), *rehearing and rehearing en banc denied*, 278 Fed.Appx. 1003 (11th Cir.), *cert. denied*, ___ U.S. ___, 129 S.Ct. 493 (holding vendor did not violate FCRA by sending consumer's check, returned to vendor by consumer's bank due to insufficient funds, to consumer reporting agency); *Beaudry v. TeleCheck Services, Inc.*, 579 F.3d 702 (6th Cir. 2009), *cert. denied*, ___ U.S. ___, 130 S.Ct. 2379 (2010) (holding consumer was not required to allege injury in form of consequential damages to state claim for willful violation of FCRA). *See generally* Jeffrey I. Langer & Andrew T. Semmelman, *Creditor List Screening Practices: Certain Implications under the Fair Credit Reporting Act and the Equal Credit Opportunity Act*, 43 Bus. Law. 1123 (1988); R. Glen Ayers, Jr., *Beyond Truth-in-Lending–Federal Regulation of Debt Collection*, 16 St. Mary's L.J. 329 (1985) (discussing implications of FCRA).

15. GLBA, § 507(a) (codified at 15 U.S.C.A. § 6807(a)).

16. *Id.*, § 507(b) (codified at 15 U.S.C.A. § 6807(b)).

17. *Id.*, § 521 (codified at 15 U.S.C.A. § 6821).

18. *Id.*, § 522 (codified at 15 U.S.C.A. § 6822).

or imprisonment for not more than 5 years, or both.[19] Where accompanied by violation of another U.S. law or where part of a pattern of any illegal activity involving more than $100,000 in a twelve-month period, such violations are subject to double the fine or imprisonment for not more than 10 years, or both.[20]

As with the privacy provisions, these prohibitions do not supersede any state statutes, regulations, orders, or interpretations, except to the extent that such state provisions are inconsistent, and then only to the extent of the inconsistency.[21] A state provision is not considered inconsistent if the protection afforded by the state provision is greater than the protection provided under the privacy provisions, as determined by the FTC in consultation with the federal agency or authority involved.[22]

§ 10.7 Community Reinvestment Rules

Few areas of depository institutions regulation have engendered the commentary and controversy that has accompanied the Community Reinvestment Act ("CRA").[1] One central feature has been the continuing debate over whether state and federal CRAs can effectively achieve their objectives. Empirical studies in the mid–1990s, focusing on the Texas market, suggested that CRA regulations had not increased the availability of banking services in low-income communities, and that the number of branches in low-income areas actually decreased in the period following the relevant regulatory changes.[2] Other commentators have tentatively argued that it remains to be seen whether the state and federal CRAs and related policies can offset the effects of current federal interstate banking and branching policy and the emerging industry consolida-

---

19. *Id.,* § 523(a) (codified at 15 U.S.C.A. § 6823(a)).

20. *Id.,* § 523(b) (codified at 15 U.S.C.A. § 6823(b)).

21. *Id.,* § 524(a) (codified at 15 U.S.C.A. § 6824(a)).

22. *Id.,* § 524(b) (codified at 15 U.S.C.A. § 6824(b)).

§ 10.7

1. Pub. L. No. 95–128, tit. VIII, 91 Stat. 1147 (1977) (codified at 12 U.S.C.A. §§ 2901–2907), *as amended,* Dodd–Frank Wall Street Reform and Consumer Protection Act (DFA) § 358(1)–(2), Pub. L. No. 111–203, 124 Stat. 1376, 1548 (2010) (codified at 12 U.S.C.A. §§ 2902, 2905). For legislative history of the CRA, see H.R. Rep. No. 95–128, 95th Cong., 1st Sess. (1977); H.R. Conf. Rep. No. 95–634, 95th Cong., 1st Sess. (1977), *reprinted in* 1977 U.S.

Code Cong. & Admin. News 2884. *See generally Symposium Issue,* 143 U. Pa. L. Rev. 1285–1593 (1995) (assorted articles on CRA); David Evan Cohen, *The Community Reinvestment Act—Asset or Liability?,* 75 Marquette L. Rev. 599 (1992); Michael E. Schrader, *Competition and Convenience: The Emerging Role of Community Reinvestment,* 67 Ind. L.J. 331 (1992).

2. Leonard Bierman, Donald R. Fraser, Javier Gimeno & Lucio Fuentelsaz, *Regulatory Change and the Availability of Banking Facilities in Low-Income Areas: A Texas Empirical Study,* 49 S.M.U. L. Rev. 1421 (1996). *See also* Leonard Bierman, Donald Fraser & Asghar Zardkoohi, *Community Reinvestment Act: A Preliminary Empirical Analysis,* 45 Hastings L.J. 383 (1994).

tion that has resulted from the interstate policy.[3] The regulatory apparatus has responded to these market changes with a heightened focus on reinvestment transactions and new data collection and reporting obligations,[4] increasing the CRA burden on insured institutions, but in the view of some commentators these developments are unlikely to satisfy advocates of CRA public policy.[5]

Nevertheless, revitalized by 1994 amendments intended to retool the act to deal with the increasingly interstate depository institutions market,[6] the CRA is undoubtedly here to stay. The discussion that follows will analyze the statutory provisions that implement the CRA public policy of encouraging depository institutions "to help meet the credit needs of the local communities in which they are chartered consistent with the safe and sound operation of such institutions."[7]

The Gramm–Leach–Bliley Act ("GLBA")[8] contains a general provision stating that nothing in the act is to be construed to repeal any provision of the CRA.[9] Nevertheless, some significant amendments to the CRA are included in the GLBA, and these will be noted as appropriate in the discussion that follows in the next section.

§ 10.8   Requirements and Procedures

The impetus of the CRA is explicitly based upon Congressional findings that embody the following loose syllogism:

Major Premise: In order to be chartered, and for other

3. Dwight Golann, Fred H. Miller, Alvin C. Harrell, *Introduction to the 1996 Annual Survey of Consumer Financial Services Law*, 51 Bus. Law. 825 (1996). *See generally* John H. Huffstutler, *Bank Holding Company Restructuring Alternatives Following the Enactment of the Riegle–Neal Interstate Banking and Branching Efficiency Act of 1994*, Practicing Law Institute, Corporate Law and Practice Course Handbook Series (Dec. 1996) (noting three layers of CRA review applicable to interstate banks, as well as state regulation); Mark D. Rollinger, *Interstate Banking and Branching Under the Riegle–Neal Act of 1994*, 33 Harv. J. on Legis. 183 (1996) (surveying potential effect of interstate banking legislation on banking industry).

4. *See* 12 C.F.R. §§ 25.42, 228.42, 345.42, 563e.42 (imposing data collection, reporting, and disclosure requirements).

5. David E. Teitelbaum & John M. Casanova, *Regulatory Reform or Ret-*

read? The New Community Reinvestment Act Regulations, 51 Bus. Law. 831 (1996). *Cf.* Charles R. Whitt, *Eleven Accuse NationsBank of Bias in Mortgages*, 8 Loy. Consumer L. Rep. 6 (1996) (noting lawsuit against interstate-expanding NationsBank Corp., alleging mortgage-lending discrimination).

6. Pub. L. No. 103–328 §§ 10, 108 Stat. 2364 (1994) (codified at 12 U.S.C.A. § 2906).

7. 12 U.S.C.A. § 2901(b). *See Hicks v. Resolution Trust Corp.*, 970 F.2d 378 (7th Cir.1992) (seeking to balance CRA obligations and safety and soundness and limiting effect of CRA accordingly).

8. Pub. L. No. 106–102, Nov. 12, 1999, 113 Stat. 1338 (1999) (codified at scattered sections of 12, 15, 16, 18 U.S.C.A.).

9. GLBA, § 714 (codified at 12 U.S.C.A. § 1811 note).

regulatory approvals, depository institutions[1] are required to demonstrate that their deposit facilities serve the convenience and needs of the community in which they are chartered to do business.[2]

Minor Premise: The convenience and needs of the community includes the need for credit services as well as deposit services.[3]

Conclusion: Therefore, depository institutions have a continuing and affirmative duty to help meet the credit needs of the local communities in which they are chartered.[4]

Taken in the abstract, there is nothing particularly remarkable about this conclusion. The CRA explicitly links itself to the traditional banking factor of "convenience and needs," which is routinely applied by regulators in deciding a wide variety of applications. However, on the basis of this rather vague and flexible concept, the CRA imposes some relatively specific and arguably inflexible expectations about serving the credit needs of low-income segments of an institution's local market. Furthermore, in an increasingly interstate market, determining what the "local" market of a given institution is can often be problematic.

The basic tools used to implement CRA policy are the assessment and evaluation. In examining an insured depository institution, the institution's appropriate federal financial supervisory agency[5] must assess its record of "meeting the credit needs of its

§ 10.8

1. The CRA actually uses the term "regulated financial institution" as its basic reference point. This term is defined to mean "an insured depository institution (as defined in [12 U.S.C.A. § 1813])." 12 U.S.C.A. § 2902(2).

2. *Id.* § 2901(a)(1).

3. *Id.* § 2901(a)(2).

4. *Id.* § 2901(a)(3).

5. For these purposes, the term "appropriate Federal financial supervisory agency" is defined as follows:

(1) the Office of the Comptroller of the Currency ("OCC"), with respect to national banks;

(2) the Federal Reserve Board ("Fed"), with respect to state-chartered member banks and bank holding companies;

(3) the Federal Deposit Insurance Corporation ("FDIC"), with respect to

insured state-chartered nonmember banks and savings banks; and

(4) the Office of Thrift Supervision ("OTS") with respect to insured savings associations and savings and loan holding companies, until July 21, 2011.

Id. § 2902(3)(A)–(D), *as amended*, DFA § 358(1), 124 Stat. 1376, 1548 (2010) (conforming amendment). Under DFA § 313 124 Stat. at 1523 (codified at 12 U.S.C.A. § 5413), the OTS and the position of the Director of the OTS are scheduled to be abolished, effective 90 days after the "transfer date," *id.* §§ 311(a), 313 (codified at 12 U.S.C.A. §§ 5411(a), 5413)—21 July 2011—on which date the functions and authority of the DOTS and the OTS are first transferred to the other federal regulators. *See id.* § 312(b) (codified at 12 U.S.C.A. § 5412(b)) (mandating transfer of functions). The OCC will be responsible for the supervision of federal savings associations. The Fed will be responsible for savings and loan holding companies.

entire community, including low- and moderate-income neighborhoods, consistent with the safe and sound operation of such institution."[6] The assessment is based upon a set of tests implemented in the agencies' CRA regulation. The data that is plugged into these tests is derived from a number of sources specified in the regulations.[7] In effect, these sources establish the context within which CRA performance is assessed and evaluated.

At the conclusion of a CRA examination, the agency is required to prepare a written evaluation of the examined institution's CRA record,[8] consisting of a public section and a confidential section.[9] The public section of the CRA written evaluation is required to include: (1) The agency's conclusions for each CRA factor assessed, as identified in its regulations;[10] (2) Discussion of facts and data supporting its conclusions;[11] and, (3) The examined institution's CRA rating, together with an explanation of the basis for the rating.[12]

The FDIC will be responsible for state-chartered savings associations.

6. *Id.* § 2903(a)(1). *See* Hicks v. Resolution Trust Corp., 970 F.2d 378 (7th Cir.1992) (balancing CRA requirements and safety and soundness, limiting effect of CRA accordingly). On application of the CRA requirements to financial holding companies, see 12 U.S.C.A. § 2903(c). In assessing an institution's record, the CRA discriminates between "majority-owned institutions" on the one hand, and "minority-" or "women-owned institutions" on the other. *Id.* § 2903(b). In assessing a majority-owned institution's record, the agency may consider the institution's capital investment in, and loan participation and other joint ventures with, minority- and women-owned financial institutions and low-income credit unions. *Id.* These activities may be considered only if they "help meet the credit needs of local communities in which such institutions and credit unions are chartered." *Id.* On operation of branch facilities by minorities and women, see *id.* § 2907.

7. 12 C.F.R. §§ 25.21(b) (OCC regulations) 228.21(b) (Fed regulations), 345.21(b) (FDIC regulations), 563e.21(b) (OTS regulations).

8. 12 U.S.C.A. § 2906(a)(1).

9. *Id.* § 2906(a)(2).

10. *Id.* § 2906(b)(1)(A)(i). *See, e.g.,* 12 C.F.R. §§ 25.21–25.24, 228.21–228.24, 345.21–345.24, 563e.21–563e.24 (lending, investment and service tests of

OCC, Fed, FDIC, and OTS, respectively). *See also id.* §§ 25.25, 228.25, 345.25, 563e.25 (community development test for a wholesale or limited purpose bank of OCC, Fed, FDIC and OTS, respectively); 25.26, 228.26, 345.26, 563e.26 (small bank performance standards of OCC, Fed, FDIC, and OTS, respectively). The conclusions must be presented separately for each metropolitan area in which the institution maintains a domestic branch office. 12 U.S.C.A. § 2906(b)(1)(B). For these purposes, "metropolitan area" is defined to mean:

> any primary metropolitan statistical area, metropolitan statistical area, or consolidated metropolitan statistical area, as defined by the Director of the Office of Management and Budget, with a population of 250,000 or more, and any other area designated as such by the appropriate Federal financial supervisory agency.

Id. § 2906(e)(2).

11. 12 U.S.C.A. § 2906(b)(1)(A)(ii). This discussion must be presented separately for each metropolitan area in which the institution maintains a domestic branch office. *Id.* § 2906(b)(1)(B).

12. 12 U.S.C.A. § 2906(b)(1)(A)(iii). The CRA requires the use of the following ratings:

> (1) Outstanding record of meeting community credit needs;
>
> (2) Satisfactory record of meeting community credit needs;

The confidential section of the written evaluation contains any references that identify customers, institution officers or employees, or any other person who has provided information to a state or federal supervisory agency in confidence.[13] It also contains any statements considered in the judgment of the agency to be too sensitive or speculative to disclose to the examined institution or to the public.[14]

The emergence of interstate banking and branching as a matter of federal depository institutions policy has complicated CRA assessment and evaluation. Special procedures now apply to the assessment and evaluation of a depository institution with interstate domestic branches.[15] For such institutions, the agency must prepare a written evaluation of the entire institution's CRA record of performance,[16] and a separate written evaluation for each state in which the institution maintains a domestic branch.[17] In addition, in situations in which the examined institution maintains domestic branches within one multistate metropolitan area, the agency is required to prepare a separate written evaluation of the institution's CRA record of performance within the metropolitan area.[18]

The agency is also required to take a depository institution's CRA record into account in its evaluation of any application by the institution for a "deposit facility."[19] The CRA definition of this

---

(3) Needs to improve record of meeting community credit needs; and

(4) Substantial noncompliance in meeting community credit needs.

Id. § 2906(b)(2)(A)–(D). *See, e.g.,* 12 C.F.R. §§ 25.28, 228.28, 345.28, 563e.28 (providing for assigned CRA ratings under OCC, Fed, FDIC, and OTS regulations, respectively). The ratings must be disclosed to the public. 12 U.S.C.A. § 2906(b)(2).

13. 12 U.S.C.A. § 2906(c)(1).

14. *Id.* § 2906(c)(2). The agency may disclose the confidential section, in whole or in part, to the examined institution if the agency determines that disclosure will promote CRA objectives. *Id.* § 2906(c)(3). However, such disclosure may not identify a person or organization that has provided information in confidence to a state or federal supervisory agency. *Id.*

15. For these purposes, the term "domestic branch" is defined to mean "any branch office or other facility of a regulated financial institution that accepts deposits, located in any State." *Id.* § 2906(e)(1).

16. *Id.* § 2906(d)(1)(A).

17. *Id.* § 2906(d)(1)(B). This state-by-state evaluation is specifically required to include information required by § 2906(b)(1)(A)–(B) separately for each metropolitan area in which the examined institution maintains a domestic branch office, and separately for the remainder of the non-metropolitan area of the state, if the institution maintains any domestic branch offices in the non-metropolitan area. *Id.* § 2906(d)(3)(A). *But cf. id.* § 2906(d)(2), discussed in following note (noting that state-by-state evaluation is to be adjusted where separate evaluation is done of multistate metropolitan area). The state-by-state evaluation must also describe how the agency performed the examination, including a list of the individual branches examined. *Id.* § 2906(d)(3)(B).

18. *Id.* § 2906(d)(2). If the agency prepares a multistate metropolitan area evaluation, the scope of the state-by-state evaluation, *per id.* § 2906(d)(1)(B), should be adjusted accordingly. *Id.* § 2906(d)(2).

19. *Id.* § 2903(a)(2). In evaluating an institution's record, the CRA discriminates between "majority-owned institutions" on the one hand, and "minority-"

term is the key to the act's potentially broad effect. The term "application for a deposit facility" is defined for these purposes to mean any application for: (1) A charter for a national bank or federal savings and loan association;[20] (2) Deposit insurance, in the case of a newly chartered state bank, savings bank, savings and loan association, or similar institution;[21] (3) The establishment of a domestic branch or other facility that can accept deposits;[22] (4) The relocation of a home or branch office;[23] (5) The merger, consolidation or purchase/assumption requiring approval under the Bank Merger Act ("BMA");[24] or, (6) The acquisition of shares in, or the assets of, a depository institution requiring approval under federal holding company law.[25]

The Gramm–Leach–Bliley Act ("GLBA")[26] amends the CRA to provide that election by a bank holding company ("BHC") to become a "financial holding company" ("FHC")[27] is not effective if the Federal Reserve Board finds that, as of the date of the election, not all of the subsidiary insured depository institutions of the company had received a "satisfactory" or better CRA rating at their most recent CRA examinations.[28] The GLBA also amends the Bank Holding Company Act ("BHCA")[29] to require the appropriate federal banking agency to prohibit an FHC (or a bank, through a financial subsidiary) from commencing any new activity, or acquiring any company, under section 4(k) or (n) of the BHCA,[30] or under the National Bank Act ("NBA")[31] or Federal Deposit Insurance

---

or "women-owned institutions" on the other. *Id.* § 2903(b). In evaluating a majority-owned institution's record, the agency may consider the institution's capital investment in, and loan participation and other joint ventures with, minority- and women-owned financial institutions and low-income credit unions. *Id.* These activities may be considered only if they "help meet the credit needs of local communities in which such institutions and credit unions are chartered." *Id.* On operation of branch facilities by minorities and women, see *id.* § 2907.

20. *Id.* § 2902(3)(A).

21. *Id.* § 2902(3)(B).

22. *Id.* § 2902(3)(C). *See, e.g., Corning Sav. & Loan Ass'n v. Fed. Home Loan Bank Bd.*, 571 F.Supp. 396 (E.D.Ark.1983), *aff'd*, 736 F.2d 479 (8th Cir.1984) (upholding FHLBB approval of branch application in light of CRA).

23. 12 U.S.C.A. § 2902(3)(D).

24. *Id.* § 2902(3)(E). On approval of mergers and similar acquisition transac-

tions under the Bank Merger Act, see *id.* § 1828(c).

25. *Id.* § 2902(3)(F). The text of this provision refers to 12 U.S.C.A. § 1842, the appropriate Bank Holding Company Act provision, but it also continues to refer to the repealed savings and loan holding company provision of 12 U.S.C.A. § 1730a(e) (1988), which has been replaced by 12 U.S.C.A. § 1467a.

26. Pub. L. No. 106–102, Nov. 12, 1999, 113 Stat. 1338 (1999) (codified at scattered sections of 12, 15, 16, 18 U.S.C.A.).

27. On the establishment and regulation of FHCs, see *supra* §§ 6.3–6.4.

28. GLBA, § 103(b) (codified at 12 U.S.C.A. § 2903).

29. 12 U.S.C.A. §§ 1841 *et seq.* On the regulation of BHCs under the BHCA, see *supra* §§ 4.3, 6.2–6.5.

30. 12 U.S.C.A. § 1843(k), (n).

31. *Id.* § 24a. On the establishment of a financial subsidiary of a national bank under this provision of the NBA, see *supra* § 5.25.

Act,[32] if the bank or any of its insured depository institution affiliates (or any insured depository institution affiliate of the FHC) fails to have at least a "satisfactory" CRA rating at the time of its last examination.[33] The prohibition ceases to apply once the bank and all of its insured depository institution affiliates (or all of the insured depository institutions controlled by the FHC) have restored their CRA performance rating to at least the "satisfactory" level.[34]

On the other hand, the GLBA amends the CRA to direct that regulated financial institutions with aggregate assets not exceeding $250 million are subject to routine CRA examinations (i) not more than once every 60 months, if the institution received a CRA rating of "outstanding" at its most recent examination; (ii) not more than once every 48 months, if the institution received a rating of "satisfactory" at its most recent examination; and, (iii) as deemed necessary by the appropriate federal banking agency, if the institution received a rating of less than "satisfactory" at its most recent examination.[35] However, an institution remains fully subject to CRA examination in connection with any application for a deposit facility.[36] In addition, the agencies may subject an institution to more frequent or less frequent examinations for reasonable cause.[37]

Obviously, if vigorously implemented[38] and administered by the agencies,[39] these CRA requirements may have a significant impact on an institution's credit and asset-management policies. Most commentators have not found that administration of the CRA has had any marked effect on the availability of credit to low- and moderate-income neighborhoods within institution's "local" community, however defined.[40] Effective or not, however, the CRA presents institutions with a significant supervisory challenge and a potentially substantial regulatory cost. Failure to take the CRA into

---

32. 12 U.S.C.A. § 1831w(a).

33. *Id.* § 1843(l)(2).

34. *See id.* (applying prohibition in relation to "most recent examination under the Community Reinvestment Act of 1977").

35. GLBA, § 712(a) (codified at 12 U.S.C.A. § 2908(a)).

36. *Id.*, § 712(b) (codified at 12 U.S.C.A. § 2908(b)).

37. *Id.*, § 712(c) (codified at 12 U.S.C.A. § 2908(c)).

38. *See id.* § 2905 (mandating promulgation of regulations), *as amended*, DFA § 358(2), 124 Stat. at 1548 (codi-

fied at 12 U.S.C.A. § 2905) (conforming amendment). The agencies have promulgated substantially identical CRA implementing regulations. 12 C.F.R. Pts. 25, 228, 345, 563e, (CRA regulations of OCC, Fed, FDIC, and OTS, respectively).

39. *See* 12 U.S.C.A. § 2904 (requiring annual report to Congress by agencies outlining CRA actions taken).

40. *See, e.g.,* Leonard Bierman, Donald R. Fraser, Javier Gimeno & Lucio Fuentelsaz, *Regulatory Change and the Availability of Banking Facilities in Low–Income Areas: A Texas Empirical Study,* 49 S.M.U. L. Rev. 1421 (1996) (discussing empirical findings).

account in formulating credit and asset-management policies can result in frustration in corporate planning.[41]

Institutions may take advantage of an alternative mechanism for CRA assessment and evaluation offered by the agencies' CRA regulations—the development and implementation of a CRA strategic plan.[42] With an approved plan[43] in effect and operating for at least one year,[44] an institution's CRA record is assessed under the criteria of the plan developed by the institution, rather than under the lending, investment, and service tests imposed by agency regulations.[45]

The plan may have a term of no more than five years, and any multi-year plan must include annual interim measurable goals under which the institution's appropriate agency will evaluate the bank's performance.[46] Institutions with more than one assessment area may prepare a single plan for all assessment areas, or one or more plans for one or more of assessment areas.[47] In addition, affiliated institutions may prepare a joint plan if the plan provides measurable goals for each institution.[48] Activities may be allocated among institutions at their option, provided that the same activities are not considered for more than one institution.[49]

The finalized plan must be submitted to the appropriate agency at least three months prior to its proposed effective date.[50] The institution must submit with the plan a description of its informal efforts to seek suggestions from members of the public, any written public comment received, and, if the plan was revised in light of comments received, the initial version plan released for public comment.[51] The agency applies the following criteria in evaluating the plan and deciding whether or not to approve it: (1) Extent and breadth of lending or lending-related activities, including distribution of loans among different geographies, businesses and farms of different sizes, and individuals of different income levels, extent of community development lending, and use of innovative or flexible lending practices to address credit needs; (2) Amount and innovativeness, complexity, and responsiveness of institution's qualified investments; and, (3) Availability and effectiveness of institution's

41. *See, e.g.,* 12 C.F.R. §§ 25.29, 228.29, 345.29, 563e.29 (effect of CRA performance on applications).

42. 12 C.F.R. §§ 25.27, 228.27, 345.27, 563e.27.

43. *See, e.g.,* 12 C.F.R. § 25.27(g) (OCC Regulations; providing for approval of CRA strategic plan).

44. *See, e.g., id.* § 25.27(a)(1)–(4).

45. *See, e.g., id.* § 25.27(a). Agency approval of a plan does not affect an

institution's obligation to report data as required by the regulations. *Id.* §§ 25.27(b), 25.42.

46. *See, e.g., id.* § 25.27(c)(1).

47. *See, e.g., id.* § 25.27(c)(2).

48. *See, e.g., id.* § 25.27(c)(3).

49. *Id.*

50. *See, e.g., id.* § 25.27(e).

51. *Id.*

systems for delivering retail services, and extent and innovativeness of institution's community development services.[52]

The approved plan may be amended during its term, subject to approval by the agency, on the grounds that there has been a material change in circumstances.[53] Development of an amendment to a previously approved strategic plan requires the same public participation procedures as development of an original plan.[54]

There are several advantages to the use of a CRA strategic plan that may be beneficial to an institution. First, and most important, development of strategic plan allows an institution to fine-tune the performance criteria and goals to its particular situation, rather than subject itself to generally applicable criteria and goals contained in the CRA regulations. Second, the development process, requiring public participation and comment, gives the institution an opportunity to solicit, identify, and resolve community concerns with respect to it CRA activities and services outside of the formal supervisory process. Third, the development of the plan allows the institution to take a more proactive and positive approach to its CRA responsibilities, which may have the beneficial effect of building a rapport with the local communities.

In practice, these interchanges between an institution and community groups seeking enhancement of CRA performance by the institution sometimes result in specific agreed undertakings by the institution with respect to its future performance. The GLBA now requires full disclosure of agreements entered into between insured depository institutions or their affiliates and nongovernmental entities or persons made pursuant to or in connection with the fulfillment of the CRA.[55] The GLBA does not confer any authority on the federal banking agencies to enforce the provisions of these agreements.[56] However, the federal banking agencies are required to issue regulations mandating procedures reasonably designed to ensure and monitor compliance with these requirements.[57]

§ 10.9   Equal Credit Opportunity Rules

Under the Equal Credit Opportunity Act ("ECOA"),[1] it is

52. *Id.* §§ 25.27(g)(3)(i)–(iii), 228.27(g)(3)(i)–(iii), 345.27(g)(3)(i)–(iii), 563e.27(g)(3)(i)–(iii).

53. *Id.* §§ 25.27(h), 228.27(h), 345.27(h), 563e.27(h).

54. *Id.* §§ 25.27(d), (h), 228.27(d), (h), 345.27(d), (h), 563e.27(d), (h).

55. GLBA, § 711 (codified at 12 U.S.C.A. § 1831y).

56. 12 U.S.C.A. § 1831y(g).

57. *Id.* § 1831y(h).

§ 10.9

1. Pub. L. No. 93–495, tit. V, 88 Stat. 1521 (1974), *as amended* (codified at 15 U.S.C.A. §§ 1691–1691f). For legislative history, see Sen. Rep. No. 93–902, 93d Cong., 2d Sess. (1974), H. Conf. Rep. No. 93–1429, 93d Cong., 2d Sess. (1974), *reprinted in,* 1974 U.S. Code Cong. & Admin. News 6119. *See Midkiff v. Adams*

unlawful for any creditor[2] to discriminate against any applicant[3] for credit,[4] with respect to any aspect of a credit transaction,[5] on the basis of race,[6] color, religion, national origin, sex or marital status,[7]

County Regional Water District, 409 F.3d 758 (6th Cir. 2005), *rehearing and rehearing en banc denied*, (discussing coverage of ECOA); *Brothers v. First Leasing*, 724 F.2d 789 (9th Cir.1984), *cert. denied*, 469 U.S. 832, 105 S.Ct. 121 (discussing purposes of ECOA); *Anderson v. United Fin. Co.*, 666 F.2d 1274 (9th Cir.1982) (same); *Haynie v. Veneman*, 272 F.Supp.2d 10 (D.D.C. 2003) (discussing scope of ECOA); *Riggs Nat'l Bank v. Linch*, 829 F.Supp. 163 (E.D.Va.1993), *aff'd*, 36 F.3d 370 (4th Cir.1994) (discussing spousal creditworthiness); *Diamond v. Union Bank and Trust of Bartlesville*, 776 F.Supp. 542 (N.D.Okla.1991) (discussing credit discrimination against married women). *See generally* Stephen M. Dane, *Eliminating the Labyrinth: Proposal to Simplify Federal Mortgage Lending Discrimination Laws*, 26 U. Mich. J. L. Reform 527 (1993) (discussing ECOA); Ann Fagan Ginger, *Enforcing the Hidden U.S. Equal Rights Law*, 20 Golden Gate U. L. Rev. 385 (1990) (same).

2. For these purposes, the term "creditor" is defined to mean "any person who regularly extends, renews, or continues credit; any person who regularly arranges for the extension, renewal, or continuation of credit; or any assignee of an original creditor who participates in the decision to extend, renew, or continue credit." 15 U.S.C.A. § 1691a(e). *See, e.g., American Bar Ass'n v. F.T.C.*, 671 F.Supp.2d 64 (D.D.C. 2009) (holding lawyers not "creditors" for purposes of ECOA); *In re Brazil*, 21 B.R. 333 (Bkrtcy.N.D.Ohio 1982) (finding utility, regularly providing gas to customers prior to payment, to be "creditor").

3. For these purposes, the term "applicant" is defined to mean "any person who applies to a creditor directly for an extension, renewal, or continuation of credit, or applies to a creditor indirectly by use of an existing credit plan for an amount exceeding a previously established credit limit." 15 U.S.C.A. § 1691a(b). *Cf. Cragin v. First Fed. Sav. and Loan Ass'n*, 498 F.Supp. 379 (D.Nev.1980) (finding oral request for credit not credit "application" for purposes of ECOA). On meaning of "appli-

cant" for purposes of ECOA, see *Midlantic Nat'l Bank v. Hansen*, 48 F.3d 693 (3d Cir.1995), *cert. dismissed*, 515 U.S. 1184, 116 S.Ct. 32 (discussing spouses as joint applicants); *Gorham–DiMaggio v. Countrywide Home Loans, Inc.*, 592 F.Supp.2d 283 (N.D.N.Y. 2008) (holding mortgagor not "applicant" protected by ECOA); *Federal Deposit Ins. Corp. v. Medmark, Inc.*, 897 F.Supp. 511 (D.Kan. 1995) (finding wife required to join husband in guaranty of corporate indebtedness "applicant" for ECOA purposes). *But cf. Delta Diversified, Inc. v. Citizens & S. Nat'l Bank*, 171 Ga.App. 625, 320 S.E.2d 767 (1984) *(contra)*; *Mercado Garcia v. Ponce Fed. Bank*, 779 F.Supp. 620 (D.P.R.1991), *aff'd*, 979 F.2d 890 (1st Cir.1992) (former bank employee/borrower not "applicant" under circumstances of special loan program).

4. For these purposes, the term "credit" is defined to mean "the right granted by a creditor to a debtor to defer payment of debt or to incur debts and defer its payment or to purchase property or services and defer payment therefor." 15 U.S.C.A. § 1691a(d). *See, e.g., Roberts v. Walmart Stores, Inc.*, 736 F.Supp. 1527 (E.D.Mo.1990) (finding tendered check in payment for goods not "credit" for purposes of ECOA); *Dunn v. American Express Co.*, 529 F.Supp. 633 (D.Colo.1982) (finding express teller card not "credit").

5. *See Garcia v. Johanns*, 444 F.3d 625 (D.C.Cir. 2006) (discussing meaning of "credit transaction"); *Love v. Johanns*, 439 F.3d 723 (D.C.Cir. 2006) (same); *Shaumyan v. Sidetex Co., Inc.*, 900 F.2d 16 (2d Cir.1990) (holding home improvement contract not "credit transaction" for purposes of ECOA); *Butler v. Capitol Fed. Sav.*, 904 F.Supp. 1230 (D.Kan.1995) (application to open savings account not "credit transaction").

6. *See, e.g., Cherry v. Amoco Oil Co.*, 481 F.Supp. 727 (N.D.Ga.1979) (addressing racial discrimination in credit transaction); *cf. Douglas County Nat'l Bank v. Pfeiff*, 809 P.2d 1100, 1104 (Colo.App. 1991) *(citing Cherry)*. *But cf. Higgins v. J.C. Penney, Inc.*, 630 F.Supp. 722 (E.D.Mo.1986) (declining to follow *Cher-*

or age.[8] Likewise, creditors are prohibited from discriminating on

ry analysis as to specificity requirements with respect to denial of credit).

7. *See, e.g., Silverman v. Eastrich Multiple Investor Fund, L.P.*, 51 F.3d 28 (3d Cir.1995) (permitting creditor to obtain signature of guarantor's spouse where guarantor not considered independently creditworthy); *Mayes v. Chrysler Credit Corp.*, 37 F.3d 9 (1st Cir.1994) (addressing sex discrimination in credit transaction); *Anderson, supra* (same); *Miller v. American Express Co.*, 688 F.2d 1235 (9th Cir.1982) (finding credit card company policy of automatic cancellation of surviving spouse's supplementary account upon death of basic card-holder discrimination on basis of marital status); *Haynes v. Bank of Wedowee*, 634 F.2d 266 (5th Cir.1981) (permitting creditor's consideration of husband's bankruptcy in accelerating loan to wife); *Carroll v. Exxon Co.*, 434 F.Supp. 557 (E.D.La.1977) (permitting inquiry concerning number of dependents).

However, for purposes of the ECOA it is not considered prohibited discrimination for a creditor to make an inquiry concerning marital status if the inquiry is for the purpose of ascertaining the creditor's rights and remedies applicable to a particular extension of credit, and not to discriminate in a determination of credit-worthiness. 15 U.S.C.A. § 1691(b)(1). *See id.* §§ 1691d(a) (providing for requests for signature of husband and wife for creation of valid lien, and the like); 1691d(b) (concerning state property laws affecting creditworthiness); 1691d(c) (concerning state laws prohibiting separate extension of consumer credit to husband and wife); 1691d(d) (permitting combination of credit accounts of husband and wife with same creditor to determine permissible finance charges or loan ceilings under federal and state laws). *See also United States v. ITT Consumer Fin. Corp.*, 816 F.2d 487 (9th Cir.1987) (concerning required signature of spouse in equal management community property state); *Evans v. Centralfed Mortgage Co.*, 815 F.2d 348 (5th Cir.1987) (permitting creditor to require spouse to sign deed of trust and be included as grantee on warranty deed); *In re Farris*, 194 B.R. 931 (Bkrtcy.E.D.Pa.1996) (finding debtor-spouse's signature necessary to encumber residence and provide creditor

with legal right to proceed against property in event of default under loan). *Cf. Markham v. Colonial Mortgage Serv. Co.*, 605 F.2d 566 (D.C.Cir.1979) (finding state laws attaching in the event of marriage no justification for creditor's refusal to aggregate incomes of unmarried joint applicants); *In re DiPietro*, 135 B.R. 773 (Bkrtcy.E.D.Pa.1992) (finding no ECOA violation in required wife's signature on term note as condition of creditworthiness); *Bank of Am. v. Hotel Rittenhouse Assocs.*, 595 F.Supp. 800 (E.D.Pa.1984) (permitting bank to obtain spouse's signature on joint credit application). *See generally* Richard J. Wirth & Jonathan B. Alter, *Spousal Defenses Based in Equal Credit Laws*, 99 Com. L.J. 93 (1994) (discussing ECOA).

8. 15 U.S.C.A. § 1691(a)(1). The prohibition with respect to age discrimination is modified by the proviso that the credit applicant must, of course, have the capacity to contract. *Id. Cf. Restatement (Second) of Contracts* § 14 (concerning capacity of infants to contract). Furthermore, for purposes of the ECOA, it is not considered prohibited discrimination for a creditor to make an inquiry of an applicant's age if the inquiry is for the purpose of determining the amount and probable continuance of income levels, credit history, or other pertinent elements of credit-worthiness, as provided in regulations promulgated by the Fed. 15 U.S.C.A. § 1691(b)(2). On the authority of the Fed to promulgate regulations under the ECOA, see *id.* § 1691b. *See also id.* §§ 1691d(g) (authorizing exemption from ECOA, by Fed regulation, of credit transactions covered by state law; failure to comply with state law deemed violation of ECOA); 1691e(e) (providing that good faith compliance with Fed rule, regulation, or interpretation, or interpretation or approval by duly authorized Fed official or employee shields creditor from ECOA liability). *See generally Miller, supra* (upholding Fed's rule-making authority).

In addition, a creditor may use an empirically derived credit system that considers age, if the system is "demonstrably and statistically sound," in accordance with Fed regulations, except that in the operation of such system the

the basis of the fact that all or part of a credit applicant's income derives from a public assistance program.[9] Finally, creditors are prohibited from discriminating against a credit applicant because the applicant has exercised in good faith any right under the ECOA or related laws.[10]

Certain programmatic activities do not constitute "discrimination" under the ECOA.[11] It is not an ECOA violation for a creditor to refuse to extend credit offered pursuant to any of the following types of programs: (1) A credit assistance program expressly authorized by law for an economically disadvantaged class of persons;[12] (2) A credit assistance program administered by a nonprofit organization for its members or for an economically disadvantaged class of persons;[13] or, (3) A special-purpose credit program offered by a profit-making organization to meet special social needs, provided the program meets standards prescribed in Fed regulations.[14] These exceptions are available if refusal to provide credit is required by, or made pursuant to, the requirements of such a program.[15]

The ECOA requires that a creditor notify an applicant of its action on the credit application within a specified period of time.[16]

---

age of an elderly applicant may not be assigned a negative factor or value. 15 U.S.C.A. § 1691(b)(3). However, a creditor may make an inquiry concerning or consider the age of an elderly applicant, if the age of the applicant is to be used by the creditor in the extension of credit in favor of such applicant. *Id.* § 1691(b)(4).

9. 15 U.S.C.A. § 1691(a)(2). For purposes of the ECOA, it is not considered prohibited discrimination for a creditor to make an inquiry of whether an applicant's income derives from any public assistance program if the inquiry is for the purpose of determining the amount and probable continuance of income levels, credit history, or other pertinent elements of credit-worthiness, as provided in regulations promulgated by the Fed. *Id.* § 1691(b)(2).

10. *Id.* § 1691(a)(3). *See, e.g., Bryson v. Bank of N.Y.*, 584 F.Supp. 1306 (S.D.N.Y.1984) (finding ECOA cause of action for bank's denial of credit because of applicant's inquiries under Truth-in-Lending Act); *Owens v. Magee Fin. Serv. of Bogalusa, Inc.*, 476 F.Supp. 758 (E.D.La.1979) (finding violation in creditor's requirement that applicant sign document settling and releasing claims).

11. 15 U.S.C.A. § 1691(c).

12. *Id.* § 1691(c)(1).

13. *Id.* § 1691(c)(2).

14. *Id.* § 1691(c)(3). *But see United States v. American Future Sys., Inc.*, 743 F.2d 169 (3d Cir.1984) (ECOA violation in designing and administering credit program discriminating on prohibited basis, not related to social need program sought to address).

15. 15 U.S.C.A. § 1691(c).

16. *Id.* § 1691(d)(1) (action on application is typically within 30 days of receipt of completed application). *See Jochum v. Pico Credit Corp. of Westbank, Inc.*, 730 F.2d 1041 (5th Cir.1984) (discussing notice requirement); *Williams v. Mid-Am. Fed. Sav. and Loan Ass'n*, 624 F.Supp. 160 (S.D.Ohio 1985) (same). On the running of the period of time for notification, see *Dufay v. Bank of Am.*, 94 F.3d 561 (9th Cir.1996); *Riggs Nat'l Bank v. Webster*, 832 F.Supp. 147 (D.Md. 1993); *Howard Oaks, Inc. v. Maryland Nat'l Bank*, 810 F.Supp. 674 (D.Md. 1993); *High v. McLean Fin. Corp.*, 659 F.Supp. 1561 (D.D.C.1987). ECOA notification is post-credit-decision only. *Cartwright v. American Sav. & Loan Ass'n*, 880 F.2d 912 (7th Cir.1989); *Vander Missen v. Kellogg–Citizens Nat'l Bank*, 481 F.Supp. 742 (E.D.Wis.1979).

Failure to notify may constitute an ECOA violation even in the absence of prohibited discrimination.[17] Where adverse action[18] is taken, the ECOA requires the creditor to provide a statutorily specified statement of reasons for the such action.[19] If an appraisal report was used in connection with the application for a loan to be secured by a lien on residential real property, upon written request of the applicant (within a reasonable time of the application) the creditor must promptly furnish the applicant with a copy of the appraisal.[20]

While the ECOA is implemented through regulations promulgated by the Fed,[21] it is enforced under the authority of a variety of

---

17. *Sayers v. General Motors Acceptance Corp.*, 522 F.Supp. 835 (W.D.Mo. 1981).

18. For these purposes, "adverse action" if defined to mean:

a denial or revocation of credit, a change in the terms of an existing credit arrangement, or a refusal to grant credit in substantially the amount or on substantially the terms requested. Such term does not include a refusal to extend additional credit under an existing credit arrangement where the applicant is delinquent or otherwise in default, or where such additional credit would exceed a previously established credit limit.

15 U.S.C.A. § 1691(d)(6). *See, e.g., O'Dowd v. South Cent. Bell*, 729 F.2d 347 (5th Cir.1984) (discussing meaning of "adverse action"); *Jochum, supra* (same).

19. 15 U.S.C.A. § 1691(d)(2). According to the ECOA, this obligation can be satisfied by:

(A) providing statements of reasons in writing as a matter of course to applicants against whom adverse action is taken; or

(B) giving written notification of adverse action which discloses (i) the applicant's right to a statement of reasons within thirty days after receipt by the creditor of a request made within sixty days after such notification, and (ii) the identity of the person or office from which such statement may be obtained. Such statement may be given orally if the written notification advises the applicant of his right to have the statement of reasons confirmed in writing on written request.

Id. § 1691(d)(2)(A)–(B). A statement of reasons meets these requirements only if it contains the specific reasons for the adverse action taken. *Id.* § 1691(d)(3). *See, e.g., Pierce v. Citibank (South Dakota), N.A.*, 843 F.Supp. 646 (D.Or.1994), *on reconsideration*, 856 F.Supp. 1451, *aff'd*, 92 F.3d 1193 (9th Cir.1996) (excusing inadvertent error in notification and statement); *Higgins v. J.C. Penney, Inc.*, 630 F.Supp. 722 (E.D.Mo.1986) (finding reasons given by creditor sufficient); *O'Dowd, supra* (discussing requirement of statement of reasons); *Fischl v. General Motors Acceptance Corp.*, 708 F.2d 143 (5th Cir.1983) (criticizing insufficiency of statement); *Cherry v. Amoco Oil*, 481 F.Supp. 727 (N.D.Ga.1979) (same); *Carroll v. Exxon Co.*, 434 F.Supp. 557 (E.D.La.1977) (finding violation in failure to provide sufficient statement of reasons).

If the creditor is requested by a third party to make a specific extension of credit directly or indirectly to an applicant, the notification and statement of reasons may be made directly by such creditor, or indirectly through the third party, provided in either case that the creditor's identity is disclosed. 15 U.S.C.A. § 1691(d)(4). These requirements may be satisfied by verbal statements or notifications in the case of any creditor who did not act on more than 150 applications during the calendar year preceding the calendar year in which the adverse action was taken, as determined under Fed regulations. *Id.* § 1691(d)(5).

20. 15 U.S.C.A. § 1691(e). The creditor may require the applicant to reimburse it for the cost of the appraisal. *Id.*

21. *See id.* 1691b (noting Fed authority). *Cf. id.* § 1691c(d) (authorizing regulations by other designated agencies

federal agencies, depending upon the creditor involved. Figure 10–1, *infra*, illustrates the division of enforcement authority under the ECOA.

Figure 10–1

ECOA: Division of Enforcement Authority[22]

Agency	Authority[23]	Scope
Office of the Comptroller of the Currency ("OCC")	12 U.S.C.A. § 1818	> national banks > Federal branches and Federal agencies of foreign banks[24]
Federal Reserve Board ("Fed")	12 U.S.C.A. § 1818	> state-chartered member banks > state-licensed, noninsured branches and agencies of foreign banks > commercial lending companies owned or controlled by foreign banks > foreign branches of U.S. banks > Edge Act and Agreement Corporations[24]
Federal Deposit Insurance Corporation ("FDIC")	12 U.S.C.A. § 1818	> insured state nonmember banks > insured state-licensed branches of foreign banks[24]
Office of Thrift Supervision ("OTS")	12 U.S.C.A. § 1818	> insured savings associations[24]
National Credit Union Administration ("NCUA")	12 U.S.C.A. §§ 1751 *et seq.*	> federal credit unions
Secretary of Transportation	49 U.S.C.A. subtit. IV 49 U.S.C.A. subtit. VII	> carriers subject to jurisdiction of Surface Transportation Board > air carriers and foreign air carriers subject to Part A
Secretary of Agriculture	7 U.S.C.A. §§ 181 *et seq.*	> except as provided in 7 U.S.C.A. §§ 226, 227, with respect to activities subject thereto
Farm Credit Administration	12 U.S.C.A. §§ 2001 *et seq.*	> federal land banks > federal land bank associations > federal intermediate credit banks > production credit associations
Securities and Exchange Com-	15 U.S.C.A. §§ 78a *et seq.*	> securities brokers and dealers

with respect to ECOA enforcement procedures).

22. Source: 15 U.S.C.A. § 1691c.

23. Violations of the ECOA are deemed to be violations of the identified authorities. *Id.* § 1691c(b), (c).

24. Under DFA § 313, 124 Stat. at 1523 (2010) (codified at 12 U.S.C.A. § 5413), the Office of Thrift Supervision (OTS) and the position of the Director of the OTS are scheduled to be abolished, effective 90 days after the "transfer date," *id.* §§ 311(a), 313 (codified at 12 U.S.C.A. §§ 5411(a), 5413)—21 July 2011—on which the functions and authority of the DOTS and the OTS were first transferred to the other federal regulators. *See id.* § 312(b) (codified at 12 U.S.C.A. § 5412(b)) (mandating transfer of functions). The OCC will be responsible for the supervision of federal savings associations. The Fed will be responsible for savings and loan holding companies. The FDIC will be responsible for state-chartered savings associations.

Agency	Authority[23]	Scope
mission ("SEC")		
Small Business Administration	15 U.S.C.A. §§ 661 et seq.	> small business investment companies
Federal Trade Commission ("FTC")	15 U.S.C.A. §§ 11 et seq.	> overall enforcement authority as to all other "creditors" under ECOA[25]

Agencies may also seek ECOA enforcement by request to the Attorney General for a civil action against a creditor.[26] The Attorney General is authorized to bring a civil action enforcing the ECOA whenever he or she has reason to believe that a creditor is engaged in a pattern or practice in violation of the ECOA.[27] The Attorney General may seek any relief deemed appropriate, including actual and punitive damages, as well as injunctive relief.[28]

As an alternative to referring the matter to the Attorney General, an agency authorized to enforce the ECOA may, under certain circumstances, notify the Department of Housing and Urban Development ("HUD") of violations.[29] Such notification is appropriate in situations in which the agency does not refer the matter to the Attorney General,[30] and: (1) The agency has reason to believe, as a result of a consumer complaint, a consumer compliance examination, or otherwise, that an ECOA violation has occurred;[31] and, (2) It has reason to believe that the alleged violation would also be a violation of the Fair Housing Act.[32]

Under these circumstances, the agency is required to notify the HUD Secretary of the violation.[33] The agency must also notify the applicant that the Secretary has been notified of the alleged violation and that remedies for the violation may be available under the Fair Housing Act.[34]

Any creditor that violates the requirements of the ECOA may also be liable to the aggrieved applicant[35] for any actual damages

25. See, e.g., United States v. Blake, 751 F.Supp. 951 (W.D.Okla.1990) (discussing ECOA two-year limitation and FTCA five-year limitation); United States v. Landmark Fin. Servs., Inc., 612 F.Supp. 623 (D.Md.1985) (upholding FTC authority under ECOA).

26. 15 U.S.C.A. § 1691e(g).

27. Id. § 1691e(h).

28. Id. Cf. United States v. Beneficial Corp., 492 F.Supp. 682 (D.N.J.1980), aff'd, 673 F.2d 1302 (3d Cir.1981) (finding Attorney General not authorized to seek money damages on behalf of nonparties).

29. 15 U.S.C.A. § 1691e(k).

30. Id. § 1691e(k)(3).

31. Id. § 1691e(k)(1).

32. Id. § 1691e(k)(2). See 42 U.S.C.A. §§ 3601 et seq. (Fair Housing Act).

33. 15 U.S.C.A. § 1691e(k).

34. Id. Cf. id. § 1691e(i):

No person aggrieved by a violation of [the ECOA] and by a violation of section 3605 of Title 42 shall recover under [the ECOA] and section 3612 of Title 42, if such violation is based on the same transaction.

35. See generally Integra Bank/Pittsburgh v. Freeman, 839 F.Supp. 326 (E.D.Pa.1993) (finding co-guarantor, whose wife was not required to sign,

sustained, either individually or as a member of a class.[36] In addition, a non-governmental creditor may be liable to the aggrieved applicant for punitive damages in an amount not greater than $10,000, in addition to any actual damages.[37] In determining

lacked standing to assert ECOA claim for creditor's alleged discrimination in requiring other guarantor's spouse to sign); *Riggs Nat'l Bank v. Linch*, 829 F.Supp. 163 (E.D.Va.1993), *aff'd*, 36 F.3d 370 (4th Cir.1994) (same); *Ford v. Citizens and S. Nat'l Bank*, 700 F.Supp. 1121 (N.D.Ga.1988) (finding person signing deed to secure promissory note could be aggrieved party with standing to bring ECOA action); *Morse v. Mutual Fed. Sav. & Loan Ass'n of Whitman*, 536 F.Supp. 1271 (D.Mass.1982) (finding wife signing as guarantor of husband's note not "aggrieved applicant" under regulations).

36. 15 U.S.C.A. § 1691e(a). *See Fischl, supra* (noting that actual damages under ECOA may include out-of-pocket monetary losses, injury to credit reputation and mental anguish, humiliation or embarrassment); *Anderson, supra* (same); *Shuman v. Standard Oil Co. of Cal.*, 453 F.Supp. 1150 (N.D.Cal.1978) (finding harm to reputation for creditworthiness compensable as actual damages); *Integra Bank/Pittsburgh, supra* (finding permissibly bound debtor may suffer ECOA-cognizable injury resulting from being impermissibly required to secure spouse's or other party's signature). *Cf.* 15 U.S.C.A. § 1691e(f) (concerning jurisdiction of courts in ECOA suits; two-year limitation for maintenance of action). *See Farrell v. Bank of New Hampshire–Portsmouth*, 929 F.2d 871 (1st Cir.1991) (discussing limitation of ECOA action); *Sony Elecs., Inc. v. Putnam*, 906 F.Supp. 228 (D.N.J.1995) (same); *Silverman v. Eastrich Multiple Investor Fund, L.P.*, 857 F.Supp. 447 (E.D.Pa.1994), *rev'd*, 51 F.3d 28 (3d Cir. 1995) (same); *Pierce v. Citibank (South Dakota), N.A.*, 856 F.Supp. 1451 (D.Or. 1994), *aff'd*, 92 F.3d 1193 (9th Cir.1996) (same); *Riggs Nat'l Bank of Washington, D.C. v. Webster*, 832 F.Supp. 147 (D.Md.1993) (same); *Stern v. Espirito Santo Bank of Fla.*, 791 F.Supp. 865 (S.D.Fla.1992) (same); *Blake, supra* (discussing ECOA two-year limitation and FTCA five-year limitation); *In re Remington*, 19 B.R. 718 (Bkrtcy.D.Colo.1982) (finding recoupment claim for alleged

ECOA violation not barred). *See generally Owens v. Magee Fin. Serv. of Bogalusa, Inc.*, 476 F.Supp. 758 (E.D.La.1979) (discussing jurisdiction).

An ECOA violation may also constitute a compulsory counterclaim in a collection action, and, if proven, it would entitle the debtor to recoupment of damages, as a setoff against amount owed under the loan. *CMF Va. Land, L.P. v. Brinson*, 806 F.Supp. 90 (E.D.Va.1992); *In re Remington, supra* this note.

No showing of specific intent to discriminate or statistical showing of adverse impact on a protected class is necessary to establish *prima facie* case of violation under the ECOA. *Miller, supra. But see Moore v. United States Dep't of Agric.*, 857 F.Supp. 507 (W.D.La.1994), *vacated*, 55 F.3d 991 (5th Cir.1995) (requiring showing that aggrieved party was member of protected class, and that party was denied credit though qualified); *Mercado Garcia v. Ponce Fed. Bank*, 779 F.Supp. 620 (D.P.R.1991), *aff'd*, 979 F.2d 890 (1st Cir.1992) (same); *Gross v. United States Small Bus. Admin.*, 669 F.Supp. 50 (N.D.N.Y. 1987), *aff'd*, 867 F.2d 1423 (2d Cir.1988) (same).

A jury trial is required in a damages action brought under the ECOA. *Vander Missen v. Kellogg–Citizens Nat'l Bank of Green Bay*, 83 F.R.D. 206 (E.D.Wis. 1979).

37. 15 U.S.C.A. § 1691e(b). However, in the case of an ECOA class action, the total punitive damages award may not exceed $500,000 or one percent of the net worth of the creditor, whichever is less. *Id. See Fischl, supra* (noting punitive damages may be awarded, regardless of proof of actual damages, where creditor's conduct is wanton, malicious, or oppressive, or creditor acted in reckless disregard of applicable law); *Anderson, supra* (same); *Ricci v. Key Bancshares of Me., Inc.*, 662 F.Supp. 1132 (D.Me.1987) (same); *Sayers v. General Motors Acceptance Corp.*, 522 F.Supp. 835 (W.D.Mo.1981) (concerning reckless disregard of legal duty owed to

the amount of punitive damages, the court is required to consider, among other relevant factors: (1) The amount of any actual damages; (2) The frequency and persistence of failures in ECOA compliance by the creditor; (3) The resources of the creditor; (4) The number of persons adversely affected; and, (5) The extent to which the creditor's failure of compliance was intentional.[38]

Equitable and declaratory relief is also available to an aggrieved applicant in the appropriate U.S. district court, or any other court of competent jurisdiction, "necessary to enforce the requirements imposed" under the ECOA.[39]

In any successful action for damages, punitive damages, or equitable or declaratory relief, the ECOA requires that costs of the action, together with reasonable attorneys' fees as determined by the court, are to be added to any damages awarded by the court.[40]

One innovation in the enforcement scheme under the ECOA is the provision for incentives for self-testing and self-correction by creditors.[41] A creditor may conduct, or authorize an independent third party to conduct, a self-test of any aspect of a credit transaction by a creditor, in order to determine the level and effectiveness of its ECOA compliance.[42] To maintain this self-test as privileged, the creditor must identify any possible ECOA violations and take appropriate corrective action to address any such possible violations.[43]

If a creditor meets these conditions,[44] any report or results of that self-test shall remain privileged,[45] and such results may not be obtained or used by any applicant, department, or agency in any proceeding or civil action in which one or more ECOA violations are alleged.[46] In addition, they may not be obtained or used in any examination or investigation relating to ECOA compliance.[47]

However, an applicant, department, or agency can obtain and use a report or the results of a self-test in a proceeding or civil action, or in an examination or investigation in a situation where:

plaintiff); *Vander Missen, supra* (discussing punitive damages); *Smith v. Lakeside Foods, Inc.*, 449 F.Supp. 171 (N.D.Ill.1978) (noting that, even in absence of actual damages, punitive damages may be available under ECOA).

38. 15 U.S.C.A. § 1691e(b).

39. *Id.* § 1691e(c). *See Smith, supra* (noting that, even in absence of actual damages, equitable relief may be available under ECOA). *Cf., e.g., Integra Bank/Pittsburgh, supra* (creditor violating ECOA not be permitted to look for payment to party who, but for violation, would not have incurred personal liability on underlying debt).

40. 15 U.S.C.A. § 1691e(d). *See Anderson, supra* (discussing attorneys' fees); *Markham, supra* (denying interim fee award); *Owens, supra* (discussing attorneys' fees).

41. 15 U.S.C.A. § 1691c–1.

42. *Id.* § 1691c–1(a)(1)(A).

43. *Id.* § 1691c–1(a)(1)(B).

44. *Cf. id.* § 1691c–1(c) (providing for adjudication challenging asserted privilege).

45. *Id.* § 1691c–1(a)(2)(A).

46. *Id.* § 1691c–1(a)(2)(B)(i).

47. *Id.* § 1691c–1(a)(2)(B)(ii).

(1) The creditor or any person with lawful access to the report or results voluntarily releases or discloses all, or any part of, the report or results to the applicant, department, agency, or the general public;[48] (2) The creditor or person with lawful access refers to or describes the report or results as a defense to charges of ECOA violations against the creditor to whom the self-test relates;[49] or, (3) The report or results are sought in conjunction with an adjudication or admission of an ECOA violation for the sole purpose of determining an appropriate penalty or remedy.[50]

§ 10.10   Consumer Protection

In the decade leading up to the collapse of the subprime mortgage market,[1] federal preemption principles were frequently applied against the application of state consumer protection law to federally regulated entities or their affiliates.[2] In January 2004, the Comptroller adopted regulations asserting broad preemptive authority based on his "visitorial" powers,[3] and under his substantive regulatory authority.[4] Likewise, in an October 2004 legal opinion,[5] the OTS Chief Counsel took the position that federal law preempted state restrictions on business agents of federal savings associations with respect to any agent with an exclusive relationship with an association, if the agent agrees to significant supervision by it and works to advance the association's deposit and lending activi-

---

48. *Id.* § 1691c–1(b)(1)(A)(i).

49. *Id.* § 1691c–1(b)(1)(A)(ii).

50. *Id.* § 1691c–1(b)(1)(B). On disclosures with respect to determination of a penalty or remedy, see *id.* § 1691c–1(b)(2).

§ 10.10

1. On the subprime mortgage collapse and the crisis that followed, see § 8.2, supra.

2. *See, e.g., Rules, Policies and Procedures for Corporate Activities*, 68 Fed. Reg. 6363 (2003) (to be codified at, *inter alia*, 12 C.F.R. § 7.400(a)(3)(i)–(ii), (b)) (interpretive provisions of OCC regulations with effect of strengthening preemption). The preemption initiative of the OCC generally invoked the exclusive "visitorial" powers of the federal regulator under U.S.C.A. § 484. On the Comptroller's exclusive visitorial authority over national banks and its relationship to the dual banking system, *see* 69 Fed. Reg. 1895, 1896–1900 (2004). *See generally Watters v. Wachovia Bank,*

N.A., 550 U.S. 1, 127 S.Ct. 1559 (2007) (holding OCC regulation limiting application of state law to national bank operating subsidiaries to same extent as applied to national banks themselves to be reasonable interpretation of NBA; concluding that state had no visitorial powers over such subsidiary); Martinez v. Wells Fargo Home Mortg., Inc., 598 F.3d 549 (9th Cir. 2010) (holding state unfair competition law preempted by OCC regulation of mortgage refinance fees).

3. 69 Fed. Reg. 1895 (2004) (codified at 12 C.F.R. § 7.4000(a)(3), (b)).

4. 69 Fed. Reg. 1904 (2004) (codified at 12 C.F.R. §§ 7.4007–7.4009, 34.3(a)–(c), 34.4) (identifying types of state laws preempted and types generally not preempted with respect to national bank lending, deposit-taking, and other operations; adopting supplemental anti-predatory lending standard for national bank lending activities).

5. P–2004–7, Oct. 25, 2004 (released Nov. 5, 2004), *available at* http://www.ots.treas.gov/docs/5/560404.pdf.

ties.[6] Thus, the battle lines were drawn for the Supreme Court's 5–3 decision in *Watters v. Wachovia Bank, N.A.*[7] in April 2007, upholding the application of the OCC preemption initiative.

In *Watters*, the Supreme Court held that the mortgage business of a national bank conducted by a non-banking operating subsidiary of the bank was subject to the exclusive (and preemptive) supervisory jurisdiction of the OCC, and not to the licensing, reporting, and visitorial authority of any state in which the subsidiary operated. Preemption of the state law regime was required because of the "unduly burdensome and duplicative"nature of the state regulation. This analysis was bolstered by the fact that federal statutory law barred national banks from being subject to any "visitorial powers" of the states except as authorized by federal law.[8] The fact that this ban referred only to national banks, not to *nonbanking* affiliates and subsidiaries, was not relevant in the majority's view.

The broadening invocation of preemption in the financial services context obviously created serious tension with respect to the effectiveness and equity of state financial services and consumer protection policies. To the extent that national banks and their operating subsidiaries were significant participants in a state's financial services market, application of a state's policy was rendered markedly less effective when federal preemption intervened. Furthermore, the application of the state policy to state-chartered institutions could, after federal preemption, be an inequitable competitive burden on those state institutions;[9] this competitive consequence invited elimination of the policy or flight by the state institutions to federal charters.[10]

In direct response to this source of tension, the Dodd–Frank Wall Street Reform and Consumer Protection Act[11] established a

---

6. For a discussion of the effects of current federal preemption policy on lending, *see* Dreher & Anstaett, Preemption Developments Impacting Interstate Lending by Federally Regulated Financial Institutions, 58 Consumer Fin. L.Q. Rep. 8 (2004).

7. 550 U.S. 1, 127 S.Ct. 1559 (2007).

8. 12 U.S.C.A. § 484(a).

9. There is also a potential problem with respect to the free movement of goods and services under Commerce Clause doctrine, which could further confine a state's financial services and consumer protection policies to firms chartered under its own laws, while insulating other state-chartered institutions, as well as federally chartered entities protected by preemption doctrine. *See, e.g.*, (S.D. Ind. 2009) (holding that

enforcement of Indiana Uniform Consumer Credit Code against Illinois consumer installment loan company, with respect to loan transactions occurring wholly within state of Illinois, violated dormant Commerce Clause).

10. *But see Cuomo v. Clearing House Association, L.L.C.*, ___ U.S. ___, 129 S.Ct. 2710 (2009) (holding that OCC regulation interpreting visitorial powers provision not reasonable interpretation, since it precluded state officials from using courts to enforce compliance by national banks with *non-preempted* state law).

11. Pub. L. No. 111–203, 124 Stat. 1376 (2010) (codified at scattered sections of 2, 5, 7, 11, 12, 15, 18, 20, 22, 26, 28, 31, 42, 44 U.S.C.A.) (DFA).

Consumer Financial Protection Bureau within the Fed to create and enforce effective consumer protection principles with respect to financial services at the federal level.[12] Title X of Dodd–Frank also appears to repudiate the broad preemptive effect of *Watters* and its progeny. The act insulates state consumer protection law from much of the preemptive effect that has otherwise frustrated state consumer protection policy.[13] However, Dodd–Frank does not represent a clean break with past preemption practices of the OCC and the OTS; rather, in certain respects it substantially preserves federal preemption of state regulation of financial services, but with important exceptions in the consumer protection area.[14]

§ 10.11   Other Regulatory Initiatives

Given the pervasiveness of the regulation of depository institutions, it should not be surprising that the regulatory system has often been harnessed to implement other extraneous policy objectives. The preceding sections have discussed some of the major regulatory initiatives in that regard, but it must be emphasized that federal law is replete with such unrelated uses of the depository institutions regulatory system. Figure 10–2, *infra*, illustrates a selective sample of these other regulatory initiatives.

Figure 10–2
Selected Statutory Provisions

Enactment	Citation	Policy Objective
Anti–Money Laundering Act	Pub. L. No. 102–550, tit. XV, 106 Stat. 4044 (1992) (codified at scattered sections of 12, 18, 31 U.S.C.A.)	Criminal investigation and enforcement
ATM Fee Reform Act of 1999	Pub. L. No. 106–102, §§ 701–705, 113 Stat. 1338, 1463–1465 (1999), (codified at 15 U.S.C.A. §§ 1601 note, 1693b(d)(3), 1693c(a)(10), 1693h(d))	Disclosure of nondepositor ATM user fees
Bank Secrecy Act	Pub. L. No. 91–508, tit. I, II, 84 Stat. 1114–1124 (1970), *as amended* (31 U.S.C.A. §§ 321, 5311–5314, 5316–5322)	Criminal investigation and enforcement

12. DFA §§ 1001–1067 (codified at 12 U.S.C.A. §§ 25b, 1465, 5481, 5491–5497, 5511–5519, 5531–5536, 5551–5587; 20 U.S.C.A. § 9702(c)(1), (d)). For an excellent survey of the history and current state of consumer protection law and policy in the United States, see Mark E. Budnitz, The Development of Consumer Protection Law, the Institutionalization of Consumerism, and Future Prospects and Perils, 26 Ga. St. U. L. Rev. 1147 2010 (arguing that consumer protection principles are embedded in U.S. law and policy, both in terms of individual litigation and likely state and federal legislative policy).

13. See DFA § 1044 (codified at 12 U.S.C.A. § 25b(b)) (establishing narrow grounds for federal preemption of state consumer protection laws).

14. See generally R. Christian Bruce, Dodd–Frank Act's Language on Preemption Forces Some Quick Decisions, Lawyers Say, BNA Banking Daily (July 23, 2010), available at http://www.bna.com (discussing implications for preemption).

Enactment	Citation	Policy Objective
Community Development Banking and Financial Institutions Act	Pub. L. No. 103–325, § 102, 108 Stat. 2163 (1994) (codified at scattered sections of 5, 12, 15, 18 U.S.C.A.)	Economic revitalization and community development
Consumer Credit Protection Act	Pub. L. No. 90–321, 82 Stat. 146 (1968), *as amended* (15 U.S.C.A. §§ 1601–1649, 1661–1667e, 1671–1681u, 1691–1693r; 18 U.S.C.A. §§ 891–896)	Consumer protection
Consumer Leasing Act	Pub. L. No. 94–240, 90 Stat. 257 (1976) (15 U.S.C.A. §§ 1667–1667e)	Consumer protection
Credit Card Fraud Act	Pub. L. No. 98–473, tit. II, ch. XVI, 98 Stat. 2183 (1984) (18 U.S.C.A. § 1029)	Consumer protection
Credit Repair Organizations Act	Pub. L. No. 104–208, § 2451, 110 Stat. 3009 (1996) (15 U.S.C.A. §§ 1679–1679j)	Consumer protection
Cuban Liberty and Democratic Solidarity Act (Helms–Burton)	Pub. L. No. 104–114, 110 Stat. 785 (1996) (U.S.C.A. §§ 1643*l*–1643m, 6021–6024, 6031–6046, 6061–6067, 6081–6085, 6091)	Foreign Affairs
Electronic Fund Transfer Act	Pub. L. No. 95–630, tit. XX, 92 Stat. 3728 (1978) (15 U.S.C.A. §§ 1693–1693r)	Consumer protection
Emergency Low Income Housing Preservation Act	Pub. L. No. 100–242, tit. II, 101 Stat. 1877 (1988), *as amended* (12 U.S.C.A. §§ 4101–4124, 4141–4147)	Housing policy
Fair Credit Billing Act	Pub. L. No. 93–495, tit. III, 88 Stat. 1511 (1974) (15 U.S.C.A. §§ 1666–1666i)	Consumer protection
Fair Credit Reporting Act	Pub. L. No. 91–508, § 601, 84 Stat. 1128 (1970) (15 U.S.C.A. §§ 1681–1681u)	Consumer protection
Fair Debt Collection Practices Act	Pub. L. No. 95–109, 91 Stat. 874 (1977) (15 U.S.C.A. §§ 1692–1692o)	Consumer protection
Home Equity Loan Consumer Protection Act	Pub. L. No. 100–709, 102 Stat. 4725 (1988) (15 U.S.C.A. §§ 1637a, 1665b, 1647)	Consumer protection
Home Mortgage Disclosure Act	Pub. L. No. 94–200, tit. III, 89 Stat. 1125 (1975) (12 U.S.C.A. §§ 2801–2810)	Consumer protection
International Emergency Economic Powers Act	Pub. L. No. 95–223, tit. II, 91 Stat. 1626 (1977), as amended (50 U.S.C.A. §§ 1701–1706)	Foreign affairs
Iran and Libya Sanctions Act (D'Amato Act)	Pub. L. No. 104–172, 110 Stat. 1541 (1996)	Foreign affairs
Money Laundering Control Act	Pub. L. No. 99–570, tit. I, 100 Stat. 3207 (1986) (18 U.S.C.A. §§ 981–982; 31 U.S.C.A. § 5324)	Criminal investigation and enforcement
Money Laundering Prosecution Act	Pub. L. No. 100–690, tit. VI, 102 Stat. 4354 (1988) (31 U.S.C.A. §§ 5325–5326)	Criminal investigation and enforcement
Money Laundering Suppression Act	Pub. L. No. 103–325, tit. IV, 108 Stat. 2243 (1994) (31 U.S.C.A. § 5330)	Criminal investigation and enforcement

Enactment	Citation	Policy Objective
National Consumer Cooperative Bank Act	Pub. L. No. 95–351, 92 Stat. 449 (1978), *as amended* (12 U.S.C.A. §§ 3001, 3011–3026, 3041–3051)	Consumer credit
Real Estate Settlement Procedures Act ("RESPA")	Pub. L. No. 93–533, 88 Stat. 1724 (1974) (12 U.S.C.A. §§ 2601–2610, 2614–2617)	Consumer protection
Removal of Regulatory Barriers to Affordable Housing Act	Pub. L. No. 102–550, tit. XII, 106 Stat. 3938 (1992) (42 U.S.C.A. §§ 12705a–12705d)	Housing policy
Trading With the Enemy Act § 5(b)	Act of Oct. 6, 1917, ch. 106, 40 Stat. 411 (1917), *as amended* (50 U.S.C.A. app. § 5(b))	Foreign affairs
Truth-in-Lending Act	Pub. L. No. 90–321, tit. I, 82 Stat. 146 (1968), *as amended* (15 U.S.C.A. §§ 1601–1608, 1610–1613, 1631–1635, 1637–1646, 1648–1649, 1661–1667f)	Consumer protection
Truth-in-Savings Act	Pub. L. No. 102–242, tit. II, 105 Stat. 2334 (1991) (12 U.S.C.A. §§ 4301–4313)	Consumer protection
United Nations Participation Act § 5	Pub. L. No. 264, 59 Stat. 619 (1945), *as amended* (22 U.S.C.A. § 287c)	Foreign affairs

Many of these initiatives concern consumer protection, and they may seem unavoidable in a regulatory system that countenances such significant concentration of economic power within one specialized industry.[1] Others, however, are more obviously extraneous to the depository institutions system; they simply take opportunistic advantage of the fact that these institutions are optimally placed to assist in the attainment of a particular policy objective.

For example, various initiatives apply specialized rules to money-transfer transactions of depository institutions, among other entities.[2] The objective here is primarily the identification of criminal activity by persons engaged in the laundering of proceeds of illicit activity, not the maintenance of safety and soundness in the banking system. Depository institutions simply represent a convenient vehicle for federal investigators to test for symptoms of illegal activity that generates significant funds in need of laundering. Nevertheless, compliance with such initiatives is extremely important for depository institutions. Regardless of the attenuated rela-

§ 10.11

1. See § 10.10, *supra* (discussing changes in consumer protection under DFA). *See also* 15 U.S.C.A. §§ 1601–1649, 1661–1667e, 1671–1681u, 1691–1693r; 18 U.S.C.A. §§ 891–896 (codifying Consumer Credit Protection Act).

2. *See, e.g.,* 31 U.S.C.A. §§ 321, 5311–5314, 5316–5322 (codifying Bank Secrecy Act); 18 U.S.C.A. §§ 981–982; 31 U.S.C.A. §§ 5324–5326, 5330 (prohibiting money laundering).

tionship between these extraneous rules and the objectives of depository institutions regulation, an institution is well advised to comply.

Another example of the attenuated relationship between depository institutions regulatory policy and extraneous policy objectives is afforded by various foreign policy provisions of federal law.[3] Under the broad authority granted by these provisions, depository institutions are often drafted into the service of U.S. economic warfare, regardless of the effect on the policy objectives of depository institution regulation.[4] Yet the mandatory nature of these foreign policy sanctions programs makes compliance unavoidable.

It should be clear from the preceding chapters that the regulation of depository institutions is an extremely complex undertaking. This undertaking is rendered all the more complicated by the intersection of so many varying, and often unrelated policy initiatives. Perhaps this situation is ultimately a testament to the extremely significant position that depository institutions occupy in contemporary society—what touches these institutions affects and is affected by a congeries of social, political, and economic aspects of our modern society.

---

3. *See, e.g.,* 22 U.S.C.A. § 287c (authorizing imposition of economic sanctions in compliance with U.N. Security Council resolutions); 50 U.S.C.A. §§ 1701 *et seq.* (authorizing imposition of economic sanctions in response to foreign threat to U.S. national security, foreign policy, or economy).

4. *See supra* § 9.30 (discussing effects of U.S. economic sanctions on depository institutions).

Table of Cases

D

N

Southeast Banking Corp. v. Adler, 1982 WL 1383 (S.D.Fla.1982)—§ **4.19, n. 11.**

Southwest Mississippi Bank v. Federal Deposit Ins. Corp., 499 F.Supp. 1 (S.D.Miss.1979)—§ **4.14, n. 42.**

Spa Flying Service, Inc. v. United States, 724 F.2d 95 (8th Cir.1984)—§ **10.3, n. 3.**

Speer v. Dossey, 177 Ky. 761, 198 S.W. 19 (Ky.1917)—§ **2.3, n. 15.**

Spiegel v. Ryan, 946 F.2d 1435 (9th Cir. 1991)—§ **8.7, n. 10.**

State v. _____ (see opposing party)

State Bank of Fargo v. Merchants Nat. Bank and Trust Co. of Fargo, 593 F.2d 341 (8th Cir.1979)—§ **3.5, n. 13; § 3.7, n. 5; § 3.8, n. 1.**

State Bank of Fargo v. Merchants Nat. Bank & Trust Co. of Fargo, 451 F.Supp. 775 (D.N.D.1978)—§ **3.5, n. 20.**

State ex rel. v. _____ (see opposing party and relator)

State of (see name of state)

Sterling Nat. Bank of Davie v. Camp, 431 F.2d 514 (5th Cir.1970)—§ **1.11, n. 134; § 2.3, n. 3.**

Stern v. Espirito Santo Bank of Florida, 791 F.Supp. 865 (S.D.Fla.1992)— § **10.9, n. 36.**

St. Louis County Nat. Bank v. Mercantile Trust Co. Nat. Ass'n, 548 F.2d 716 (8th Cir.1976)—§ **5.22, n. 5.**

Stoutt v. Banco Popular de Puerto Rico, 320 F.3d 26 (1st Cir.2003)—§ **10.4, n. 9.**

Strauss v. Credit Lyonnais, S.A., 249 F.R.D. 429 (E.D.N.Y.2008)—§ **9.27, n. 13.**

Stromberg–Carlson Corp. v. Bank Melli Iran, 467 F.Supp. 530 (S.D.N.Y. 1979)—§ **9.21, n. 8.**

Suburban Trust Co. v. National Bank of Westfield, 211 F.Supp. 694 (D.N.J. 1962)—§ **5.1, n. 7.**

Sunrise Securities Litigation, In re, 916 F.2d 874 (3rd Cir.1990)—§ **8.18, n. 1.**

Swanton v. State Guaranty Corp., 42 Del.Ch. 477, 215 A.2d 242 (Del.Ch. 1965)—§ **4.11, n. 33.**

Swerdloff v. Miami Nat. Bank, 584 F.2d 54 (5th Cir.1978)—§ **5.9, n. 2.**

Synovus Financial Corp. v. Board of Governors of Federal Reserve System, 952 F.2d 426, 293 U.S.App.D.C. 70 (D.C.Cir.1991)—§ **4.2, n. 2; § 4.3, n. 30.**

T

Talbot v. First Nat. Bank of Sioux City, 185 U.S. 172, 22 S.Ct. 612, 46 L.Ed. 857 (1902)—§ **5.10, n. 29.**

Taylor v. Anderson, 234 U.S. 74, 34 S.Ct. 724, 58 L.Ed. 1218 (1914)— § **5.10, n. 12.**

TeamBank, N.A. v. McClure, 279 F.3d 614 (8th Cir.2002)—§ **4.15, n. 6.**

Telematics Intern., Inc. v. NEMLC Leasing Corp., 967 F.2d 703 (1st Cir. 1992)—§ **8.18, n. 1.**

Texas & P. Ry. Co. v. Pottorff, 291 U.S. 245, 54 S.Ct. 416, 78 L.Ed. 777 (1934)—§ **5.1, n. 6; § 5.23, n. 4, 23.**

Texas State Bank v. United States, 423 F.3d 1370 (Fed.Cir.2005)—§ **1.6, n. 4; § 5.13, n. 8.**

Theron, United States v., 116 F.R.D. 58 (D.Kan.1987)—§ **10.3, n. 3.**

Third Nat. Bank in Nashville, United States v., 390 U.S. 171, 88 S.Ct. 882, 19 L.Ed.2d 1015 (1968)—§ **2.3, n. 19; § 4.14, n. 46.**

Third Nat Bank & Trust Co of Scranton v. McMahon, 17 F.Supp. 869 (M.D.Pa.1937)—§ **5.23, n. 23.**

Thirty–Nine Administrative Subpoenae, Matter of, 754 F.Supp. 5 (D.Mass. 1990)—§ **10.3, n. 10.**

Tiffany v. National Bank of Missouri, 85 U.S. 409, 21 L.Ed. 862 (1873)— § **5.10, n. 3.**

Tikkanen v. Citibank (South Dakota) N.A., 801 F.Supp. 270 (D.Minn. 1992)—§ **5.10, n. 7.**

Timberland Design Inc. v. Federal Deposit Ins. Corp., 745 F.Supp. 784 (D.Mass.1990)—§ **8.18, n. 3.**

Timberland Design, Inc. v. First Service Bank for Sav., 932 F.2d 46 (1st Cir. 1991)—§ **8.18, n. 11.**

Timberlane Lumber Co. v. Bank of America Nat. Trust and Sav. Ass'n, 749 F.2d 1378 (9th Cir.1984)— § **9.27, n. 17.**

Tose v. First Pennsylvania Bank, N.A., 648 F.2d 879 (3rd Cir.1981)—§ **5.9, n. 9.**

Trade Development Bank v. Continental Ins. Co., 469 F.2d 35 (2nd Cir. 1972)—§ **9.27, n. 12.**

Transohio Sav. Bank v. Director, Office of Thrift Supervision, 967 F.2d 598, 296 U.S.App.D.C. 231 (D.C.Cir. 1992)—§ **8.17, n. 40.**

Trans Union LLC v. F.T.C., 295 F.3d 42, 353 U.S.App.D.C. 42 (D.C.Cir. 2002)—§ **10.6, n. 9.**

Index

A

Acquisitions. See Holding company acquisitions; Mergers and acquisitions, **infra**

Adequately capitalized, meaning of, 5.16

Affiliate transactions
Dodd–Frank Wall Street Reform and Consumer Protection Act (DFA) and, 5.8
generally, 5.9

Agreement corporations. See Edge Act corporations

Antiterrorism, 9.29

ATMs, 3.5

B

Bank for International Settlements (BIS)
Basel I, 9.9
Basel IA, 9.9
Basel II, 9.9
"Basel III," 9.9
Basel Concordat, 9.8, 9.24, 9.25, 9.27
BIS Minimum Standards, 9.8, 9.25, 9.27
capital adequacy, 9.9
international regulation and, 9.6
regulatory environment and, 9.2
risk-weighted methodology, 9.9

Bank Holding Company Act (BHCA)
acquisition, 4.3
approval requirements, 4.3
bank service companies and, 5.25
closely related activities, 6.5
closely related exemption, 6.3
Community Reinvestment Act, 4.7
control transactions, 4.1
exclusive jurisdiction of Fed, 6.2

Bank Holding Company Act (BHCA) —Cont'd
exemptions, 6.3
financial holding companies, 6.1, 6.3, 6.5, 7.20
financial in nature, activities, 6.1, 6.3, 6.5, 7.20
generally, 4.3, 6.2
Gramm–Leach–Bliley Act and, 6.1, 6.3, 6.5
Home Owners' Loan Act, compared, 4.4, 4.9, 6.6
holding company acquisitions, 4.3
k4 activities, 6.5
market activities of depository institutions, 7.11
permissible activities, 6.5
prudential limitations (Glass–Steagall Act Section 20), 6.5
regulations, 6.4
restrictions of formation/expansion of bank holding companies, 4.3
source of strength doctrine, 4.3
structure of statute, 6.3

Bank Insurance Fund (now Deposit Insurance Fund (DIF)), 1.11, 2.10, 5.13

Bank Merger Act (BMA)
change in control transactions and, 4.18
Dodd–Frank Wall Street Reform and Consumer Protection Act (DFA) and, 4.14
mergers and consolidations, 4.2, 4.14
national bank transactions, 4.14

Bank secrecy laws, 9.27

Bank Service Company Act, 5.24

Bank service companies, 5.24

Bankers' acceptances, 9.22

Bankruptcy. See Failed institutions, **infra**

D

D'Oench, Duhme rule, 8.18

Defaulting institutions. See Failed institutions, **infra**

Deposit insurance
  Bank Insurance Fund (now Deposit Insurance Fund (DIF)), 1.11
  commercial banks, 2.10
  Economic Growth and Regulatory Paperwork Reduction Act, 2.10
  generally, 2.10, 5.13
  Savings Association Insurance Fund (now Deposit Insurance Fund (DIF)), 1.11

Deposit Insurance Fund (DIF)), 1.11, 2.10, 5.12

Deposit payoff
  insured, 8.13
  modified, 8.14

Depository institution, 1.10

Depository Institutions Deregulation and Monetary Control Act of 1980, 5.14

Depository Institutions Management Interlocks Act (DIMIA), 8.11

Deposits
  brokered, 5.15
  deposit insurance, 5.12
  interest rates, 5.14
  international banking, 9.18
  reserve requirements, 5.13
  tying arrangements, 5.16

DIF. See Deposit Insurance Fund, **supra**

DIMIA. See Depository Institutions Management Interlocks Act, **supra**

Disclosure requirements, securities, 7.4

Discount brokerage services, 3.6, 7.12

Division of enforcement authority, ECOA, 10.9

Documentary letters of credit, 5.20, 9.20

Dodd–Frank Wall Street Reform and Consumer Protection Act (DFA)
  affiliate transactions, 5.8
  Bank Merger Act and, 4.14
  Change in Bank Control Act and, 4.19
  Commodity Futures Trading Commission, 5.1, 7.1

Dodd–Frank Wall Street Reform and Consumer Protection Act (DFA) —Cont'd
  Consumer Financial Protection Bureau, 5.1
  Federal Deposit Insurance Corporation, increased powers of, 1.11, 4.14, 4.19, 8.6, 10.8, 10.9
  Federal Reserve System, increased powers of, 1.9, 1.11, 4.4, 6.6, 8.6, 10.8, 10.9
  financial instruments, securitization of, 5.1, 7.1
  Financial Stability Oversight Council
    international policy, 9.26
    systemically significant financial institutions and, 8.20
  hedge fund adviser, supervision of, 5.1, 7.1
  Home Owners' Loan Act and, 4.4
  insurance, regulation of, 5.27
  international policy, 9.26
  interstate branching, 3.10
  loans to directors, officers, and insiders, 5.5, 5.7
  mergers of savings associations, 4.13, 4.14
  mortgage lending standards, 5.1, 5.4
  Office of the Comptroller of the Currency, increased powers of, 1.9, 1.11, 2.5, 4.13, 4.14, 4.19, 8.6, 10.8, 10.9
  Office of Thrift Supervision, abolition of, 1.9, 1.11, 2.5, 4.4, 4.9, 4.13, 4.14, 4.19, 6.6, 7.3, 8.2, 8.6, 10.8, 10.9
  private equity fund adviser, supervision of, 5.1, 7.1
  Sarbanes–Oxley Act and, 7.8
  savings and loan holding companies, 4.4, 4.9, 6.6
  savings association
    federal chartering of, 2.5
    mergers of, 4.13, 4.14
  securities activities and, 7.1
  Securities and Exchange Commission
    hedge fund adviser, supervision of, 5.1, 7.1
    private equity fund adviser, supervision of, 5.1, 7.1
    swaps, securities-based, 5.1, 7.1
  securities trading, proprietary, 5.1, 7.1
  securitization of pools of financial instruments, 5.1, 5.4, 7.1
  subprime mortgage crisis and, 1.9, 5.4, 8.2
  swaps, regulation of, 5.1, 7.1
  systemically significant financial institutions and, 8.12, 8.20

E

ECOA. See Equal Credit Opportunity Act (ECOA), **infra**

Economic Growth and Regulatory Paperwork Reduction Act (EGRPRA)
ATMs, 3.5
branching, 3.5
deposit insurance, 2.10

Economic revitalization and community development, 10.11

Edge Act corporations
deposits, 9.19
establishment, 9.11, 9.13
Federal Reserve Act and, 9.1
lending, 9.15
U.S. activities authorized, 9.14

EGRPRA. See Economic Growth and Regulatory Paperwork Reduction Act, **supra**

Electronic banking, location of, 3.5

Emergency Economic Stabilization Act of 2008, 8.2
Emergency interstate acquisitions
generally, 8.21
target banks in danger of default, 8.23
target banks in default, 8.22
target savings associations, 8.24

Enforcement actions for troubled institutions
capital directives, 8.10
cease and desist orders, 8.7
civil money penalties, 8.9
other enforcement devices, 8.11
suspension/removal of management and affiliated persons, 8.8

Enforcement, ECOA, 10.9

Entry rules
chartering, 2.2–2.8
conversions
charter, 2.12–2.15
cross-industry conversion, 2.17
form, 2.16
generally, 2.12
generally, 2.1
international banking, 9.11–9.13
secondary entry restrictions, 2.9–2.11

Equal Credit Opportunity Act (ECOA), 10.9

European Union (EU), 9.2, 9.12

Examination function, 1.9

Exemptions, affiliate transactions, 5.9

F

FAC. See Federal Advisory Council, **infra**

FACRs. See Foreign Assets Control Regulations, **infra**

Failed institutions. See also Troubled institutions, **infra**
claims against directors/officers, 8.19
claims against third parties, 8.18
conservatorship, 8.17–8.19
deposit payoff
insured, 8.13
modified, 8.14
Emergency Economic Stabilization Act of 2008, 8.2
emergency interstate acquisitions
generally, 8.21
target banks in danger of default, 8.23
target banks in default, 8.22
target savings associations, 8.24
financial crisis (2008), international responses to, 9.26
general business bankruptcy, contrasted, 8.12
international responses to financial crisis (2008), 9.26
open-bank assistance, 8.16
purchase and assumption, 8.15
receivership, 8.17–8.19
systemically significant financial institutions, 8.12, 8.20
transborder failures, 9.25
Troubled Assets Relief Program (TARP), 8.2

FDIA. See Federal Deposit Insurance Act, **infra**

FDIC. See Federal Deposit Insurance Corporation, **infra**

FDICIA. See Federal Deposit Insurance Improvements Act, **infra**

Fed. See Federal Reserve System, **infra**

Federal Advisory Council (FAC), 1.11

Federal Credit Union Act, 2.7

Federal Deposit Insurance Act (FDIA)
chartering standards, 2.3
generally, 1.11

†

5